Framing the Domains of IT Management

Projecting the Future . . .
. . . Through the Past

(www.pinnaflex.com/framing)

Edited By
ROBERT W. ZMUD
Michael F. Price Chair of MIS
University of Oklahoma

Pinnaflex Education Resources, Inc.
www.pinnaflex.com

Production Editor: JaNoel Lowe
Production Specialist: Tammy Haskins
Cover Design: Vincent L. Iacobucci
Art: Vincent L. Iacobucci and Kevin Cox

This book was set in New Century Schoolbook. It was printed and bound by Malloy Lithographing, Inc., Ann Arbor, Michigan.

ISBN: 1-893673-06-5

Preface

The last 30 years represent the world's most explosive period of growth regarding both technological advance and knowledge accumulation. In no field of study is this more true than for the domain of information technology (IT). Today, IT has deeply penetrated the day-to-day lives of each of us as well as the institutions within which we work or otherwise receive goods and services. Increasingly, all organizations, regardless of whether they operate in a for-profit or nonprofit manner, and their environments are being transformed through IT-based innovation and their dependence on IT-enabled work processes.

The systematic study of IT management and use in organizations has likewise evolved in substantial ways over the last 30 years. The number of doctoral programs producing well-trained scholars across a variety of academic disciplines has significantly increased. The value of intellectual "cross-training," where multiple theoretical and methodological bases are applied, has gained increased recognition—especially over the last decade. IT phenomena have been recognized as being quite "messy" in that only a limited understanding of these phenomena is likely to be acquired when viewed through a narrow theoretical or methodological lens. Finally, the number of publication outlets (scholarly journals, business periodicals, books, research reports, and Web sites) for research on IT management and use has literally exploded over the last five years.

An incredible amount of material on the topic of IT management and use has been produced—and this volume of information only accelerates with time. For the IT researcher or professional attempting to "keep up" with the leading edge of this dynamic field, a number of difficult problems arise:

- How can I find out what is known about a particular topic?
- How can I filter out the really good material from the rest?
- What is the very best material?
- How should I be thinking about a topic?
- What is the next "hot zone" regarding a topic?

This book has attempted to address these questions, first by identifying a set of subjects that represent current, critical concerns of IT executives and second by identifying subject-area experts who are aware of both the best research done in a subject area and practitioners' perspectives regarding the subject area.

THE CONTENT OF THE BOOK

Each of the invited subject-area experts was given a topic area and asked to prepare a chapter that accomplished three goals. First, the authors were asked to place the topic area within today's emerging globally competitive economic milieu. As a result, readers should quickly understand the importance of the topic for today's—and more importantly, tomorrow's—organizations. Second, the authors were asked to provide a frame through which the best research completed to date on the topic was synthesized. As a result, readers are quickly brought "up to speed" in a topic area by being exposed to a rich conceptualization of what is currently known about the topic and about how it has been studied. Third, the authors were asked to apply their own insights to identify important and potentially fruitful future research directions regarding the topic. As a result, readers should themselves begin to understand how the topic area is most likely to evolve in the near term and how they might best prepare themselves to maintain an awareness of and potentially contribute to the accumulating body of knowledge regarding the topic. Finally, each author was asked to prepare his or her chapter in a manner as accessible as possible. Ideally, these chapters should both represent the very best thinking regarding a topic area and present this in a manner that would be easily understood and grasped by readers unfamiliar with either these prior works or the style and tone of scholarly research.

These resulting chapters have been divided into four sections. The first section, The Value-Adding Consequences of Information Technology, reminds the reader that IT is applied within organizations for one purpose only: to carry out or enable a value-adding purpose. The second section, Successfully Implementing Technologies and Technology-Based Solutions, sensitizes the reader to the fact that the successful implementation of an IT-based solution is an increasingly difficult task and that the majority of these difficulties arise when new technologies interact with humans and institutions. The third section, The Intertwining of Business Strategy and Information Technology, establishes within the reader an understanding of the dramatic and dynamic influences of IT on organizational strategic directions. Finally, the fourth section, Information Technology Management in an Information Age, addresses six IT management topic areas of important to today's IT-enabled organizations. The chapters within each of these sections are now briefly introduced.

THE VALUE-ADDING CONSEQUENCES OF INFORMATION TECHNOLOGY

Each of these first three chapters focuses on an subject that represents a fundamental means by which organizations have and will continue to create value through IT: decision making, knowledge management, and virtual teams. The enterprise of the twenty-first century is increasingly seen as being dependent on as well as creating value through the expertise and capabilities of its members as they interact with one another and with individuals from other organizations. An enterprise's success will largely follow its success in interconnecting its members with the sources (both human and archival) of knowledge required in an emerging situation and then empowering these human collectives with the information and tools allowing them to act quickly and smartly.

In Chapter 1, Peter Todd and Izak Benbasat examine the very core of any decision-aiding technology—the behavior of an individual user, working with a specific technology, on a specific task. Such a perspective enables the authors to explore how the use of IT influences the way people think about problems, their decision-making behavior, and, consequently, the outcomes of decision making in terms of effectiveness, efficiency, confidence, satisfaction, and related factors. More specifically, this chapter examines the roles that decision strategy (i.e., the pattern of steps applied in resolving a decision situation) and the cognitive cost-benefit paradigm (i.e., the effort versus accuracy trade-off that must explicitly or implicitly be made in any decision situation) might serve in enabling a richer understanding of the emerging role of IT in human decision making.

In Chapter 2, Maryam Alavi builds a strong case for the increasing attention given to knowledge management by many of today's best organizations. Knowledge (along with other intangible assets such as brands, innovativeness, and speed to market) have become as important, if not more important, than the traditional resources of capital, labor, and land. Here, the focus is on how knowledge management systems (i.e., IT applications directed toward enabling an organization's knowledge management capabilities) facilitate the generation, structuring, and use of both explicit (maintained in formal archives) and tacit (maintained in humans) knowledge. Particular attention is directed toward the identification of the key issues and challenges associated with the design and implementation of knowledge management systems.

In Chapter 3, Carol Saunders examines the growing use of virtual teams, that is, the staffing of initiatives by teams of individuals separated by geographic, temporal, and organizational boundaries. Virtual teams enable organizations to bring together the very best expertise available globally to collaborate in accomplishing critical projects as well as to coordinate and carry out on-going tasks. In addition to introducing the value and challenges of virtual teams, the chapter emphasizes the nature of the technical and managerial infrastructures required to sustain a virtual team from its formation through the accomplishment of its assigned purpose.

The final two chapters of this section adopt a completely different perspective than the first three chapters. Rather than examine specific domains within which IT is being applied, the authors of these two chapters more broadly assess the nature of the impacts of an organization's IT investments.

In Chapter 4, Daniel Robey and Marie-Claude Boudreau address one of the oldest, most interesting, and most important topics in the management of information technology: the organizational consequences of IT. In other words, how have (and will) IT applications changed the nature (structure and processes) of organizations as well as the roles and behaviors of organizational members? Despite a history of more than 40 years of sustained scholarly inquiry, IT's organizational impact has more often than not proven to be quite unpredictable. This chapter exploits this diversity to introduce new ways of thinking about how to study, explain, and anticipate such consequences.

In Chapter 5, Anitesh Barua and Tridas Mukhopadhyay examine an "enduring challenge" of all IT executives—justifying the value of IT investments. While much of the capital investment undertaken by organizations today has a sizable IT component, debate has only intensified as to whether or not the financial returns from these IT investments have been both positive and substantial. Most recently, the evidence from empirical studies indicates that the economic return from IT investment is indeed positive and significant. This chapter provides overviews of the debate regarding the "IT productivity paradox" and recent empirical findings that are beginning to resolve the "paradox." Then the authors advocate the very convincing notion that the economic impact of IT investments are best understood when viewed along with complementary actions—new business strategies, redesigned structures and processes, readjusted employee incentive programs, and so on—taken by organizations.

SUCCESSFULLY IMPLEMENTING TECHNOLOGIES AND TECHNOLOGY-BASED SOLUTIONS

It has become quite evident that the introduction of IT-based solutions into organizations is far more than a technical endeavor. As is discussed in Chapters 4 and 5, IT-based initiatives are undertaken to achieve intended organizational purposes (and, invariably, induce unintended effects in the process). Sometimes these effects prove to be minor, but in other cases they prove to be massive. Work roles are changed, jobs and departments are created and eliminated, and marketplace opportunities are exploited and lost. As a result, the implementation of an IT-based solution is perhaps best viewed as an orchestrated intervention into an organization's lifeblood.

The first two chapters in this section look at the implementation of IT-based solutions from a perspective of managing a technological innovation. Here, a *technological innovation* refers to a means of accomplishing work that is being considered for the first time—by an individual, by a group, or by an organization (actually, by an organization's senior executives). Decisions regarding the adoption and use of any technological innovation are surrounded by much uncertainty. What exactly does the technology do? Is it fully developed? Will it work as expected? Will it be easy to use? How will it change my job . . . or how our group behaves . . . or how the organization performs? A distinct benefit from applying a "technological innovation" lens is that scholars (across many disciplines) have been studying how to manage efforts to introduce technological innovations far longer than researchers have been studying the implementation of IT-based solutions.

In Chapter 6, Ritu Agarwal examines the decisions made by individuals as they decide whether to use available IT-based solutions and, if they decide to do so, the extent to which they will learn about and utilize the full functionality of an IT-based solution. Individual users of technologies exhibit a variety of behaviors toward these technologies: They may completely reject some or all of them; they may engage in sabotage or active resistance; they may accept a technology but only partially utilize its available functionality; or they may whole-heartedly embrace a technology. How and why do an organization's members make such decisions? The chapter offers robust explanations to such questions, explanations that encompass aspects of the individual, the technology being introduced, managerial actions, social influences, and situational influences.

In Chapter 7, Rob Fichman also applies a "technological innovation" lens but applies it to the adoption of IT-based solutions across organizations (e.g., early adopters versus laggards) and within an organization (widespread usage versus minimal usage). What is clear is that organizations differ substantially both in the extent to which they seek to introduce new technologies and their success in introducing these new technologies. This chapter explores what is known about why some organizations are more innovative than others, what is unique about IT-based innovations, why some IT-based innovation might be easier to introduce than others, and what organizations might do to increase their IT innovativeness.

In Chapter 8, Lorne Olfman and Proadpran Pitsatorn overview the growing body of research on training the intended users of new IT-based solutions. As brought out in Chapters 6 and 7, a considerable amount of uncertainty confronts anyone desiring or expected to use a new IT application. Specialized training on the technology and how it is intended to be applied in the workplace can significantly reduce this uncertainly. If the right type of training is delivered to the right person at the right time, the likelihood that the IT application will be used productively should dramatically increase. This chapter covers the many issues that must be addressed if effective user training is to occur: the nature of training strategies, approaches, methods, and tools; the nature of the users being trained; and the nature of the technology serving as the target for training.

The final two chapters in this section examine two especially "messy" IT-based solution contexts, that associated with business process reengineering and that associated with ERP implementation. These two IT-solution contexts share a number of common attributes: They involve large, complex projects; they are intended to produce radical, rather than incremental, consequences; they require substantial resources (financial and labor); and they most often reflect strategic business initiatives. But, if successful, the benefits of their organizational impact can be tremendous.

In Chapter 9, Varun Grover and Bill Kettinger provide a rich treatment of what has been learned from the efforts undertaken by many organizations during the 1990s in introducing business process change initiatives as a means to cut cycle time, enhance customer satisfaction, and improve business performance. Above all, it is recognized that process reengineering is much more than applying IT to streamline complicated work procedures. Process reengineering is first and foremost a multifaceted process of change involving organizational structures, management systems, human resource practices, and many other aspects of organizational life. The chapter presents and assesses a view of business process change that emphasizes the creation of an organizational culture supportive of change through learning, knowledge sharing, and internal and external partnering.

In Chapter 10, Lynne Markus and Cornelis Tanis discuss the more recent phenomena of ERP system implementation and introduce a straightforward but elegant framework for understanding ERP implementation success. ERP systems are prepackaged IT applications that provide for the nearly complete redesign of an organization's business processes, databases, and legacy information systems. The authors introduce a framework intended to be used both retrospectively (for tracing back and resolving problems in a current implementation effort) and prospectively (to identify potential problems in a planned implementation effort). This framework should enable readers to better understand how to improve the likelihood of success with either an ERP implementation or other large-scale IT-based initiatives.

THE INTERTWINING OF BUSINESS STRATEGY AND INFORMATION TECHNOLOGY

Chapters 9 and 10 illustrate quite dramatically the ways in which appropriately directed and managed IT-based initiatives can enhance an organization's performance. In the future, the most successful organizations are sure to be those whose strategists understand the potential for IT to dramatically alter the nature of competition and the nature of the industries in which competition occurs. The three chapters in this third section of the book examine the increasingly intimate, potent and dynamic relationship between IT and business strategy.

In Chapter 11, Jeff Sampler develops a vivid and compelling view of what many consider to be the most significant technological phenomena yet seen—the Internet. The Internet has already exerted and will continue to exert a tremendous influence on individuals, on organizations, and on society. Many of these impacts can be traced to the widespread, inexpensive, readily available "reach" of the Internet. However, the truly profound implications of the Internet are likely to arise in the areas of industry reconfiguration, business strategy, and the likely reemergence of the individual rather than the institution as the most powerful force in directing the nature of business competition and societal movements.

In Chapter 12, Al Segars and Jim Dean continue this exploration of the synergies between IT and business strategy by focusing on the industry dynamics through which new, disruptive business models emerge. Such radical IT-based change initiatives challenge organizations to reinvent themselves in terms of their philosophy (attitudes, assumptions, beliefs), strategic posture, receptivity toward knowledge sharing, managerial systems, and managerial and operational processes. After depicting why and how such radical change processes unfold, the chapter identifies the organizational capabilities that must be in place if such radical change propositions are to be successfully undertaken.

In Chapter 13, V. Sambamurthy pushes further the ideas introduced in Chapter 12 in proposing a new "logic" by which organizations are able to differentiate themselves from their competitors through IT—by emphasizing the role that IT can serve in generating new business models and otherwise enhancing strategic flexibility. The chapter articulates the strategic value of this new logic for IT differentiation and describes the linkages between business strategies, IT competencies, and firm performance.

INFORMATION TECHNOLOGY MANAGEMENT IN AN INFORMATION AGE

The three chapters of the preceding section of the book argue for the heightened importance of IT in determining an organization's strategic direction and suggest that this evolving role of IT has produced and will continue to produce changes in the role of an organization's IT function and how this function is managed. These last six chapters explore a set of issues likely to determine the nature of effective IT management over the next decade.

The first two chapters in this section focus on the acquisition and development of IT applications. Many changes have occurred over the last 30 years regarding the means by which IT applications are acquired, the manner they are built, and our understanding of how to manage such projects. Just as many changes, if not more, are expected to occur over the next decade.

In Chapter 14, Joey George provides a history of evolving practices regarding application acquisition and development as well as a snapshot of current trends and likely future directions. The chapter gives special attention to the options available for acquiring application software and the tools, techniques, and methods used to develop application software.

In Chapter 15, Laurie Kirsch describes more fully the emerging "computing paradigm" (i.e., the nature of today's and tomorrow's software applications) and explores the impact of this new paradigm on software project management. As described, project management encompasses both hard skills, such as estimating and scheduling tasks, and soft skills, which include motivating and managing team members. Particular attention is given to identifying aspects of this emerging computing paradigm, which is not accounted for or is addressed poorly with existing approaches to software project management.

The third and fourth chapters of this section focus on what are increasingly recognized as the critical assets of any IT organization: the IT professional staff and the IT infrastructure. Any organization failing to appropriately align these two IT assets with its long-term business direction is unlikely to be very successful.

In Chapter 16, Soon Ang and Sandy Slaughter direct their attention to perhaps the most critical asset for any organization desiring to successfully exploit IT—a highly skilled, adaptable IT staff. Recognizing the importance of anchoring any understanding of IT personnel within the context in which work is done, the chapter begins by describing those key aspects of an organization's internal and external environments that must be considered when examining IT personnel issues. Then this rich context is applied in addressing the organizational roles of IT professionals, staffing decisions, and how best to motivate and develop an organization's IT staff.

In Chapter 17, Peter Weill and Marianne Broadbent examine the increasing importance of an organization's IT infrastructure to a firm's capability to differentiate itself from its competitors. Here, IT infrastructure is defined as the base foundation of IT capability, delivered as reliable services shared throughout the firm and coordinated centrally, usually by the IT function. An organization's decision of just how much infrastructure capability should be put in place is shown to depend primarily on its strategic direction. The chapter also discusses how one might measure the extent of an organization's IT infrastructure and how one might determine the business value of IT infrastructure investments.

Finally, the last two chapters of the book focus on the behaviors of an organization's senior IT executives. An IT organization's senior management team must craft effective strategies and processes for dealing with a variety of stakeholders (vendors, consultants, the organization's senior executive team, and business managers throughout the organization) as well as for "taking care of the business of IT."

In Chapter 18, Mary Lacity and Leslie Willcocks investigate the nature of customer-supplier relationships associated with IT outsourcing arrangements. While IT outsourcing practices have matured considerably over the last decade, most organizations continue to struggle with how best to manage the myriad of vendor/partner relationships they have established. This chapter examines this complex and difficult issue first by identifying the stakeholders directly involved with IT outsourcing and the different types of customer-supplier relationships that might be established and then by exploring the interplay between these stakeholders and relationships through the six phases through which typical IT outsourcing arrangements proceed.

In Chapter 19, Jeanne Ross and David Feeny provide an overview of how the CIO role has transitioned from a time when the CIO serves as a functional head of the "computing department" with responsibility to "deliver on promises" through an era in which the CIO became a "strategic partner" to the other senior executives in the firm to today's role as a proactive business visionary with the charge to recognize the emerging capabilities of IT and to work with other senior executives in setting the organization's strategic agenda. Accordingly, the authors relate role changes to corresponding changes regarding the nature of IT, the attitudes of an organization's senior executives toward IT, and the characteristics of the principal vendors who deliver and service the technologies.

INTENDED READERSHIP

This book has been developed with three target audiences in mind.

One objective is to produce a volume that coalesces much of the burgeoning literature on IT management and provides direction for navigating through this body of research. Clearly, the intended audience here includes both new and established IT scholars. Thus, the book should find a home in research and personal libraries as well as being used across a variety of doctoral seminars.

A second objective is to connect each chapter to the world of practice. It is impossible to conduct research on IT management in isolation from the pragmatic experiences of those organizations striving to use the technology to improve their performance. The authors of these chapters were thus asked both to frame their material within the concerns of today's organizations and to use a style and tone in writing that would reflect a pragmatic as well as a scholarly perspective. The challenge for the authors became one of maintaining both the integrity of the scholarship to be communicated and an orientation that linked the ideas being communicated to the concerns of practice. The authors responded admirably in confronting this challenge, and I both congratulate and thank them for their achievement.

Given the book's style and tone, two other likely readerships thus emerge: students in master's-level courses and IT professionals. The book should meet the needs of many master's-level courses associated with MBA and MS programs. (It may also prove itself useful as a primary or secondary text for an advanced undergraduate IT management course.) The book also may prove to be a useful and accessible reference source for IT professionals desiring a "quick-but-rich" overview of what we currently know about and of how to think about IT management.

From the Editor

As explained in the Preface, the genesis of the book took root in the explosion over the last decade of interest and knowledge regarding the use of information technology (IT) by organizations and associated efforts to manage both the technology and its use. Keeping up with relevant scholarly and business literatures (journals, books, magazines, etc.) has itself become an industry, exemplified by firms such as Forrester Research, GartnerGroup, and IDS. Exactly what are today's (and tomorrow's) students, established scholars, or professionals supposed to do?

My objective in piecing together this volume was to provide, in a single source, a roadmap to the *past* as well as to the *future* of IT management. Knowledge of prior thinking about IT management is crucial because it sets the context for our current understanding; essentially, an effective synthesis of the past provides a meaningful mental frame with which to interpret what we currently are observing. Even more useful, especially for such a dynamic field as IT management, are views of what the future might hold. I sincerely hope this effort to build from the past to project into the future proves valuable to the information systems education as well as research and practice communities. I hope also that its value stands up well to the challenges of time—an almost impossible goal given today's ever-accelerating rate of technological change and the eroding sense of time associated with today's hypercompetitive business arenas.

Finally, I wish to thank a number of individuals for their contributions to this volume. First, I can express only endless gratitude to the authors of the book's chapters, each of whom produced material that exceeded my expectations while working in "Internet time." Second, I an indebted to Jim Sitlington, Pinnaflex's publisher, whose trust in my insights enabled this project to be undertaken and completed in full alignment with my initial vision. Third, I wish to graciously thank the production editor, JaNoel Lowe, whose editing and sense of design have dramatically improved the final product. Finally, I wish to thank my wife, Jo Anne, for giving me the time and space to undertake and complete this project.

Bob Zmud
Norman, Oklahoma

About the Authors

Ritu Agarwal (Ph.D., Syracuse University) is Associate Professor of Information Systems at the Robert H. Smith School of Business, University of Maryland, College Park. Her current research focuses on individual behavior toward new information technology and innovative structures for organizing IT activities in firms. Dr. Agarwal's research has been published in journals such as *MIS Quarterly, Information Systems Research, Decision Sciences,* and the *IEEE Transactions on Software Engineering* and *Engineering Management.*

Maryam Alavi (Ph.D., Ohio State University) is John M. and Lucy Cook Chair in Information Strategy at the Goizueta Business School at Emory University. Dr. Alavi's research focuses on technology-mediated learning, knowledge and group support systems, and application of information technology in business and managerial process design. Dr. Alavi serves or has served on the editorial boards of several information systems journals including *Information Systems Research, MIS Quarterly* (1987–1990), and *Journal of Management Information Systems.*

Soon Ang (Ph.D., University of Minnesota) chairs the Division of Strategy, Management and Organization at the Nanyang Business School in Singapore. She serves on editorial boards of *Information Systems Research, MIS Quarterly, Journal of Organizational Behavior,* and *Groups and Organization Management.* Dr. Ang's research areas are in IT Personnel, Outsourcing, and Cross-Cultural Competencies.

Anitesh Barua (Ph.D., Carnegie-Mellon University) is Assistant Professor of Information Systems at the University of Texas at Austin and Associate Director of the Center for Research on Electronic Commerce. His research on the business value of information technology has been published in leading information systems journals, including *Information Systems Research* and *MIS Quarterly.*

Izak Benbasat (Ph.D., University of Minnesota) is CANFOR Professor of Management Information Systems at the Faculty of Commerce and Business Administration, The University of British Columbia. His current research interests are in investigating the role of explanations in intelligent systems; measuring information systems competence in line managers and business competence in information systems professionals, and the impact of these competencies on the successful deployment of information technologies; evaluating human-computer interfaces; and comparing methods for conducting information systems research.

Marie-Claude Boudreau is a Ph.D. candidate in Computer Information Systems at Georgia State University. She has published in *Information Systems Research, The Academy of Management Executive*, and *Information Technology & People.*

Marianne Broadbent (Ph.D., University of Melbourne) is Vice-President, Head of Research—Executive Programs Worldwide of GartnerGroup. Dr. Broadbent was previously a professor in the Management of Information Systems at the Melbourne Business School, University of Melbourne. She is co-author of the book *Leveraging the New Infrastructure: How Market Leaders Capitalize on Information Technology* published by Harvard Business School Press in 1998.

James W. Dean (Ph.D., Carnegie Mellon University) is Professor in the Kenan Flagler Business School at the University of North Carolina at Chapel Hill. He is also the Associate Dean of the Master's of Business Administration program. Professor Dean teaches courses and conducts research in the areas of organizational transformation, performance improvement in organizations, and international management.

David Feeny is Vice-President of Templeton College, Oxford, and Director of the Oxford Institute of Information Management. Professor Feeny's own interests center on the connections between Strategy, Organization, and Information Management. His work has been published in the *Harvard Business Review, Sloan Management Review and McKinsey Quarterly.*

Robert G. Fichman (Ph.D., Massachusetts Institute of Technology) is Assistant Professor of Management at Boston College. His research on technology adoption and diffusion has been published in *Management Science, Information Systems Research,* and *Sloan Management Review.*

Joey F. George (Ph.D., University of California at Irvine) is Professor of Information Systems and Thomas L. Williams Jr. Eminent Scholar in IS at Florida State University. His research interests focus on the use of information systems in the workplace, including computer-based monitoring, group support systems, and deception in computer-mediated communication.

Varun Grover (Ph.D., University of Pittsburgh) is Professor of Information Systems, Distinguished Researcher, and Business Partnership Foundation Fellow at The Darla Moore School of Business, University of South Carolina. He recently coedited two special issues of the *Journal of MIS* on the topic of business process change. Dr. Grover's most recent book is *Process Think: Winning Perspectives for Business Change in the Information Age,* Idea Group Publishing.

William J. Kettinger (Ph.D., University of South Carolina) is Associate Professor and Director of the Center of Information Management and Technology Research at The Darla Moore School of Business of the University of South Carolina. His research focuses on strategic information management. Dr. Kettinger is currently completing a three-year study sponsored by IMD and Andersen Consulting exploring senior managers' perceptions of corporate effectiveness in the use of information and its relationship to business performance.

Laurie J. Kirsch (Ph.D., University of Minnesota) is Associate Professor at the Katz Graduate School of Business at the University of Pittsburgh. She conducts research on IS project management, the deployment of global IT solutions, and the impact of information technology on organizational processes.

Mary Cecelia Lacity (Ph.D., University of Houston) is Associate Professor of MIS at the University of Missouri–St. Louis and Research Affiliate at Templeton College, Oxford University. She has written four books on the topic of information systems outsourcing, and her articles have appeared in the *Harvard Business Review, Sloan Management Review,* and *MIS Quarterly,* among other journals.

M. Lynne Markus (Ph.D., Case Western Reserve University) is Professor of Management and Information Science at the Peter F. Drucker Graduate School of Management, Claremont Graduate University. Her research on enterprise systems integration has been funded by The Advanced Practices Council of SIM International, the Financial Executives Research Foundation, and Baan Institute.

Tridas Mukhopadhyay (Ph.D., University of Michigan) is Professor of Industrial Administration (Information Systems) at Carnegie Mellon University. He is also the Director of the Masters of Science in Electronic Commerce program at CMU. His research interests include electronic commerce, Internet use at home, business value of information technology, business-to-business commerce, and software development productivity. Dr. Mukhopadhyay's primary area of interest is in the economics of information technology.

Lorne Olfman (Ph.D., Indiana University) is Dean of the School of Information Science at Claremont Graduate University. He began doing research in the field of end-user training during his days as a doctoral student.

Proadpran Pitsatorn is a Ph.D. candidate at the School of Information Science, Claremont Graduate University. She also serves as a faculty member at the Department of Computer Engineering, Faculty of Engineering, Chulalongkorn University, Bangkok, Thailand. Her research interests include software training, end-user training, object-oriented technology, and software engineering and methodology.

Daniel Robey (D.B.A., Kent State University) is Professor in the Departments of Computer Information Systems and Management at Georgia State University. Professor Robey is currently Senior Editor of *MIS Quarterly* and Associate Editor for *Accounting, Management and Information Technologies* and *Information Systems Research*.

Jeanne W. Ross (Ph.D., University of Wisconsin, Milwaukee) is Principal Research Scientist at Massachusetts Institute of Technology's Center for Information Systems Research where she lectures, conducts research, and directs executive education courses on IT management practices. Her research focuses on the interdependence of business processes and IT infrastructure and on IT-driven organizational change.

V. Sambamurthy (Ph.D., University of Minnesota) is Associate Professor of Decision and Information Technologies at the Robert H. Smith School of Business of the University of Maryland, College Park. His current research interests are focused on understanding how business firms can leverage value from information technologies in contemporary digital economies. Dr. Sambamurthy's research has been funded through grants from the Financial Executives Research Foundation and SIM's Advanced Practices Council. He is currently on the editorial boards of *MIS Quarterly, Information Systems Research,* and *Management Science*.

Jeffrey L. Sampler (Ph.D., University of Pittsburgh) is Associate Professor of Information Management and Strategy at the London Business School. His research interests include electronic commerce, the management of information as a strategic resource, and developing information-based strategies. Dr. Sampler's work has appeared or is forthcoming in such journals as *Accounting, Management, and Information Technology, Journal of Management Studies, Journal of Management Information Systems, MIS Quarterly, Sloan Management Review,* and *Strategic Management Journal*.

Carol Stoak Saunders (Ph.D., University of Houston) is W.P. Wood Professor of Management Information Systems at the University of Oklahoma. Her current research interests include interorganizational linkages and virtual teams. She is Associate Editor of *Decision Sciences* and *Information Resources Management Journal* and the General Conference Chair of *ICIS 1999.*

Albert H. Segars (Ph.D., University of South Carolina) is Associate Professor in the Kenan Flagler Business School at the University of North Carolina at Chapel Hill. He is also the Director of eUNC, the University's institute for research in next generation commerce and technologies. Dr. Segars teaches courses and conducts research in the areas of eCommerce, supply chain management, and strategic IT management.

Sandra A. Slaughter (Ph.D., University of Minnesota) is Assistant Professor at Carnegie Mellon University in the Graduate School of Industrial Administration. Her research focuses on productivity and quality improvement in the development and maintenance of information systems and on effective management of information technology professionals. Dr. Slaughter has published articles in *Information Systems Research, IEEE Transactions on Software Engineering, Management Science,* and *Communications of the ACM.*

Cornelis Tanis is responsible for the European operations of Key Performance International. KPI, headquarted in Henderson, Nevada, is an international consulting firm specializing in professional development, change management, OD&D, and systems implementations management. Prior to joining KPI, he was a consultant and research program manager for a leading ERP vendor.

Peter Todd (Ph.D., University of British Columbia) is Professor of Information Systems, Director of the Information Systems Research Center, and Associate Dean for Academic Affairs and Research in the College of Business Administration at the University of Houston. Prior his appointment at UH, he was Professor of Management Information Systems at Queen's University in Kingston, Ontario, where he also served as Director of Research and Ph.D. Programs.

Peter Weill (Ph.D., New York University) is Foundation Chair of Management (Information Systems) and Director of the Center for the Management of Information Technology at the Melbourne Business School, University of Melbourne. His research and advising activities center around the business value of information technology (IT) in organizations. Dr. Weill has been an associate editor for both *MIS Quarterly* and *Information Systems Research* and is co-program chair for *ICIS 2000* in Australia.

Leslie Willcocks (Ph.D., University of Cambridge) is Fellow in the Oxford Institute of Information Management, Templeton College, University of Oxford, Professor in Management at Erasmus Universiteit, Professorial Associate at the University of Melbourne, and Editor-in-Chief of the *Journal of Information Technology.* He is coauthor of 14 books and 130 plus refereed papers, mainly on information management, evaluation, and sourcing issues.

Robert W. Zmud (Ph.D., University of Arizona) is Professor and Michael F. Price Chair in MIS at the Michael F. Price College of Business, University of Oklahoma. He is past Editor-in-Chief of *MIS Quarterly,* past Senior Editor with *Organization Science,* and a current or past editorial board member for numerous information systems journals.

Contents

The Impact of Information Technology on Decision Making: A Cognitive Perspective

Peter Todd and Izak Benbasat

The study of management information systems (MIS) broadly deals with understanding the design, implementation, management, and use of information technologies (IT) in organizations. The systems that support management in its key role of decision making represent a major component of MIS. From simple spreadsheets and reports to decision support systems, data warehousing, data mining, knowledge management, and expert systems, a wide range of technologies intended to support and assist decision makers in organizations has evolved over the last three decades. In order to design and implement these decision support technologies more effectively, it is important to understand how they influence the process and outcomes of managerial decision making. Such a goal is of considerable importance as organizations not only commit more resources to the use of such technologies but also increasingly rely on these technologies to make critical and costly decisions about new business directions.

The influence of IT on decision making is so profound that it has, in many cases, become transparent. Systems that support decision making permeate the organizational value chain and have become so common that they are not even viewed as separate decision-making systems. On the inbound side of the value chain, just-in-time inventory management systems have been entrenched as a normal part of an organization's automated transaction processing. In manufacturing, sophisticated cost and materials management systems are critical to the operation of a business.

Marketing and sales rely on research data and analytical tools to set price, establish promotional strategies, and make determinations about new product offerings. Sales force automation systems provide increased automation and decision-making intelligence to the field sales force. Logistics and yield management systems help many organizations to put their products into the marketplace in a way that maximizes return. These technologies have become so tightly entwined with the business that the influence of IT on decision making is, in many ways, synonymous with the impact of IT on the success or failure of the organization as a whole.[1]

Recent technological developments such as the Internet have strengthened and extended this relationship. Today IT supports decisions not only taken within the organization but also made about organizations. External stakeholders are increasingly bringing decision technologies to bear on their interactions with organizations. Beyond acquirers and investors, customers are interacting with organizations through IT, using, for example, on-line banking and investing services and managing traditional supplier and customer relationships. Beyond this, customers increasingly utilize decision-making technologies that are made available as part of the customer interface. Financial services firms include portfolio analysis tools as part of their services. Airline and travel services include tools to compute and compare ticket prices and evaluate products such as frequent flyer programs. Computer vendors include configuration tools for customers as an aid to product purchase. In these ways, decision support is becoming embedded in many on-line product and service offerings, and the increase of such uses seems inevitable.[2]

Understanding how IT impacts these decision processes in wide-ranging contexts is critical and will become increasingly so as a larger and larger proportion of our economy is driven by and through the Internet and other computer-based devices. The sheer scope of the proliferation of different types of IT support at different organizational levels and its intra- and interorganizational dimensions make it difficult to cover the topic of the impact of IT on decision making in a comprehensive fashion in one short chapter.[3] However, at the core of most decision-aiding technology is the behavior of an individual user working with a specific technology on a specific task. Thus, we focus on this relationship between the individual decision maker, task, and technology as a basis from which to understand the broader implications of the impact of IT on decision making. This approach allows us to understand how the use of IT influences the way people think about problems, their decision-making behavior, and, consequently, the outcomes of decision making in terms of effectiveness, efficiency, confidence, satisfaction, and related factors. It is important to understand the role of the individual user in this fashion in order to develop understanding of technology impacts in more complex situations. These include the use of group support systems, so-called organizational decision support systems, and embedded decision-making systems, all of which ultimately are still dependent on the behavior of the individual user.

EMERGENCE OF DECISION SUPPORT SYSTEMS AS A FIELD OF STUDY

Research in IT support for decision making has a long history. In the 1960s, work by Herbert Simon, Allan Newell, and their colleagues (Newell & Simon, 1972; Simon, 1957) laid much of the foundation on which research in the area of decision support is still based today. In particular, their work established a behavioral perspective on the relationship between information technology and decision making. About the same time, the development of management science and operations research laid down the mathematical framework that is still at the core of many decision support technologies in use today.

These streams of work were brought together under the rubric of decision support systems (DSS) in the mid to late 1970s. Influential works by Michael Scott Morton (Scott Morton, 1971), Peter Keen (Keen & Scott Morton, 1978), John Bennett (Bennett, 1983), and others helped to shape conceptual thinking that, in various ways, integrated notions of behavioral decision making and cognitive science with ideas from mathematical modeling and operations research. This led to the concept of DSS as it is still broadly conceived and implemented today: *systems that are designed to aid or assist decision makers in dealing with semistructured or ill-structured decision problems.*[4]

These important conceptual frames were complemented by early empirical work that began to explore the relationship between managerial decision making and information technology. Perhaps most notable among these works was a stream of research from the University of Minnesota that became known as the Minnesota experiments (Dickson, Senn, & Chervany, 1977). These are important not so much for their outcomes as for the way they focused on factors related to decision makers, decision tasks, and decision-aiding technologies. This approach continues to influence how research in the area of decision making and IT is carried out today, almost 30 years after the original studies.

At the individual level, the emphasis is on the way that managerial work may be enhanced or altered using IT that supports, automates, or replaces individual cognitive processes. Consistent with their mathematical and behavioral roots, various schools of thought exist about how such support should be provided. These range from the automation of processes that provide normative decision support (a management science approach) to strategies that guide and direct decision makers (a behavioral decision-making approach) and to those that merely support a user's desired behaviors (a nondirected approach) (Silver, 1990, 1991). These alternatives place differing emphasis on the degree of control the decision maker has over the selection of strategies in problem solving. In all three instances, the commonly accepted goal of providing decision support is to improve the effectiveness of the decision maker and the quality of decisions that the decision maker makes. Empirical reviews of the research that examines this premise are included in Benbasat, DeSanctis, and Nault (1993), and Sharda, Barr, and McDonnel (1988).

Eom (1996) catalogs 944 articles written between 1971 and 1993 that examined various aspects of decision support, including empirical studies that tested the relationship between DSS and decision performance. Despite this large base of research, these relationships are still not well understood (Benbasat, DeSanctis, & Nault, 1993; Eierman, Niederman, & Adams, 1995; Sharda, Barr, & McDonnell, 1988). The reasons for this are unclear but may be due, in part, to the inadequate and inconsistent application of methods to study this relationship (Sharda, Barr, & McDonnell, 1988). One of the difficulties is that there is an extensive set of DSS capabilities that might be tested, across a multitude of task settings, with a wide variety of performance measures. In addition, the equivocal relationships may result from a failure to adequately account for the mediating influence of the decision processes that occur when a DSS is used (Jarvenpaa, 1989; Silver, 1991; Todd &

Benbasat, 1987, 1991; Vessey, 1991). Failure to explicitly articulate and integrate these processes into comprehensive theoretical models has also been identified as an important stumbling block to the advance of knowledge in DSS (Eierman, Niederman, & Adams, 1995). In the next section, we present a comprehensive model of the impact of decision support technologies on decision-making outcomes that provides a basis by which to study these issues.

A MODEL OF THE IMPACT OF IT ON INDIVIDUAL DECISION MAKING

Broadly speaking, decision making can be divided into two major activities: problem finding and problem solving. Problem finding emphasizes uncovering an underlying problem or issue to be dealt with as distinct from the symptoms associated with the problem. This involves information gathering or intelligence as well as diagnostic evaluation aimed at problem identification. Problem identification is fuzzy, difficult, and not traditionally viewed as being amenable to technology support in any systematic fashion. Furthermore, it has often been demonstrated that problem frames can significantly influence how a problem is identified and the subsequent solutions that a decision maker will generate (Kahneman, Slovic, & Tversky, 1982).

Problem solving, in contrast to problem identification, has long been the focus of IT–supported decision-making research. The emphasis in problem solving is on the design, evaluation, and choice of alternative solutions to a specified problem. For a DSS, this involves the use of various modeling and analytical tools that are designed to assist in or support problem solving. These modeling tools help to structure potential solutions for a given task. Support tools are often defined based on an understanding of the underlying demands of the task.

To understand how a decision maker will approach the decision-making task, and, as a consequence, what the impact of decision support technologies will be, it is necessary to articulate some assumptions about motivations underlying decision maker behavior. The core assumption in most decision research is that decision makers will behave in a rational way within the decision context and their own processing capabilities and limitations (Newell & Simon, 1972). That is, a decision maker is motivated to behave rationally in trying to arrive at the best possible decision but must do so within his or her own limited cognitive capabilities, the demands of the task, and external environmental constraints. This has been described as "bounded rationality" (Simon, 1957).

Decision support systems are typically designed to augment the capabilities of decision makers and thus to extend their bounds of rationality. This is expected, in turn, to lead to better decisions. This implies that the use of a DSS will be focused on finding a high-quality solution. Indeed, this assumption has been the major motivation behind the development of decision support technologies. The idea is that by extending the capability of the decision maker to process information, better decisions will result. This results in a DSS–decision quality that can be represented as in Figure 1.1.

While the view represented in Figure 1.1 is entirely consistent with the perspective of a rational decision maker motivated to make high-quality decisions, it is

FIGURE 1.1
The Traditional
DDS–Decision
Performance
Relationship

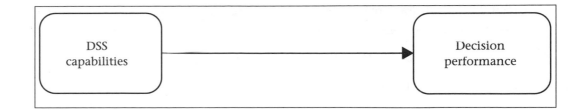

limited in terms of its practical application. It implicitly suggests a direct relationship between the use of decision support systems and decision quality that is robust across types of DSS, tasks, users, and work environments. However, such a model lacks explanatory power, as evidenced by the number of studies testing this relationship that have found largely equivocal results (Benbasat, DeSanctis, & Nault, 1993; Eierman, Niederman, & Adams, 1995; Sharda, Barr, & MacDonnell, 1988). The limited applicability of this model suggests that it is important to understand what other factors mediate and moderate the relationship between DSS capabilities and decision performance.

Critical among these factors has been the notion of task technology fit (Goodhue, 1995), that is, the idea that the impact of decision support tools for a particular task can be understood only by examining the way in which the technology supports the steps, or strategies, that are needed to complete the task.[5] This has been an important notion in the development of decision support research and suggests one critical factor, namely task, which moderates the relationship of DSS usage to decision performance. This leads to a refined model of the relationship between decision support and decision quality that is depicted in Figure 1.2.

To further clarify the role of various moderating and mediating variables that influence the link between IT for decision support, decision maker capabilities, and decision task to decision quality, we will use the model in Figure 1.3. It provides an overview of the key constructs that determine the impact of information technology on decision outcomes, adding decision maker capabilities and the key mediating processes related to decision strategy, effort, and accuracy to the model in Figure 1.2.

In the following sections, we describe each of the key constructs in the model and their relationships.

FIGURE 1.2   The Task-
Technology Fit
Perspective

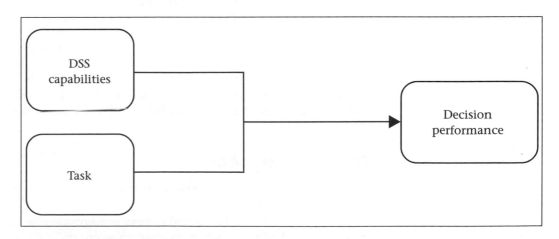

FIGURE 1.3   Factors Influencing the Impact of IT Support on Decision Performance

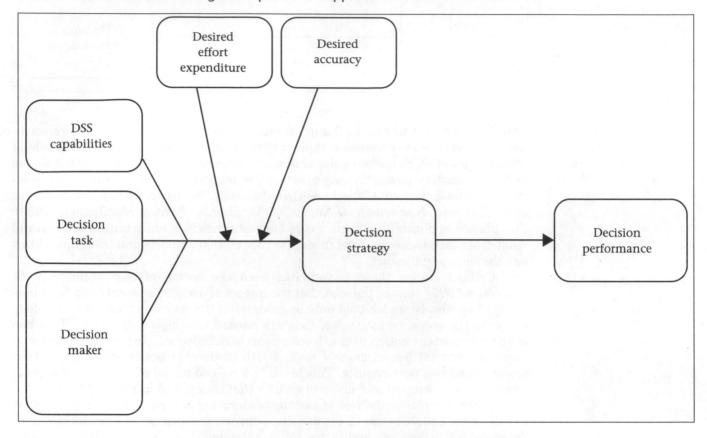

DECISION SUPPORT SYSTEM CAPABILITIES

Different labels have been used over the years to characterize the types of IT–based support for decision making. They include management information systems, decision support systems, group support systems, expert and expert support systems, and executive information systems. These names refer to different degrees of IT support for decision makers at different organizational levels and in support of different tasks, although what is common to all is that they facilitate access to computational aids, databases, knowledge and expertise sources, modeling tools, and means of communicating with other decision makers. Zachary (1988) offers a detailed taxonomy that encompasses the types of support that can be offered. This taxonomy categorizes decision support techniques as (1) process models, (2) choice models, (3) information control techniques, (4) analysis and reasoning methods, and (5) representational aids.

THE DECISION MAKER

All decision makers share a set of core cognitive capabilities that DSS are utilized to enhance. They include

- Being a relatively slow serial information processor.
- Having extremely limited short-term memory.

- Having apparently infinite long-term memory capacity but highly fallible retrieval of information from that memory.

Considering these basic capabilities of the decision maker is critical to the development of effective decision support systems.[6]

In addition to the shared characteristics among decision makers, individual differences between decision makers may help to distinguish among the types of DSS an individual user is likely to benefit from. During the earlier phases of DSS research in the late 1970s, decision maker characteristics, especially a particular characteristic labeled *decision* or *cognitive style* (Benbasat & Taylor, 1982), were investigated in many empirical studies of decision support systems. The rationale of taking into account such individual characteristics was similar to that of considering task characteristics; that is, the expectation that certain types of decision makers would prefer and/or perform better with particular types of decision support. However, the investigation of decision maker characteristics became less common after a critique by Huber (1983), who stressed both the equivocal findings of the research and the difficulty of implementing alternative designs based on individual differences in organizational settings. Together, these factors were thought to severely limit the value of research on individual differences in the context of DSS design.

To fully understand this critique, however, it is important to contrast the study of individual preferences versus individual differences in cognitive capability. While differences in preferences may not have strong influence on DSS user performance, differences in cognitive abilities may. For example, those who have difficulty in integrating the different components of a problem in order to understand it in a holistic fashion would benefit from modeling tools that facilitate such integration (Benbasat & Dexter, 1982). Thus, to further research in this area, what is important is to articulate precisely how and why a particular individual difference factor might influence the way a DSS is used and then to study that hypothesized impact.

As an example, the role of individual differences was investigated in the context of expert or knowledge-based systems (Dhaliwal & Benbasat, 1996; Gregor & Benbasat, 1999; Nah, Mao, & Benbasat, 1999). It was observed that the types of support and explanations requested differed between users who were experts and novices in the problem domain. Such differences are due to the different types of internal problem representations and processing strategies that are employed by those with different levels of domain expertise.

Another context in which the role of the decision maker has been taken into account is in the area of information representation and decision support. The fit notion discussed in the previous section has been extended by Vessey (1991) to incorporate the decision maker's internal representation of the problem. Vessey and Galletta (1991) suggest that the task and technology fit is based on the cognitive demands of the problem and its relationship to the support system combined with the internal problem representation employed by the decision maker. They argue that for performance to be enhanced, users must develop an appropriate mental model for the effective completion of the task (Vessey & Galletta, 1991).

DECISION TASK

Beyond the decision maker's capabilities, it is also important to consider the impact of DSS usage in the context of the decision task. The importance of task or decision type (e.g., structured vs. unstructured problems) to information systems design has been discussed in the literature since the 1970s (Gorry & Scott Morton, 1971). It has been commonly accepted since the 1980s that the nature of the decision task and the type of decision support provided jointly influence decision performance (Benbasat, Dexter, & Todd, 1986; Jarvenpaa, 1989). The greater this alignment between decision support and task, the more likely the DSS will lead to a higher-quality decision outcome (i.e., the influence of a DSS on performance is contingent upon the degree to which the capabilities provided by the system match the requirements of the task). For example, Benbasat and Dexter (1985) found that the advantage of utilizing a graphical representation was directly related to the fact that it showed the slopes that corresponded to the marginal returns associated with investing in different marketing territories; this information was needed to reach the best solution. While a tabular report contained the data to derive the marginal returns, the cost of applying the better strategy was lower with a graphical report.

Unfortunately, there are no commonly accepted task taxonomies to facilitate the design of IT–based support. In our view, rather than focusing on macrolevel task characteristics such as degree of structure or generic task types, it is preferable for the designer to understand the specific decision task, the decision strategies that are applicable to solve it, and the kind of IT support that will make the implementation of those strategies easier.

One way to achieve this type of understanding is to engage in a process of task decomposition that reduces a task to an elementary set of information processes (EIP). An EIP is a low-level cognitive operation such as reading a value, comparing two values, or storing a result in long-term memory. EIPs have been used to model a variety of decision processes or strategies (see, for example, Chase, 1978; Johnson & Payne, 1985; Johnson, Payne, & Bettman, 1988). A strategy is a set of processes that are used by the decision maker to achieve his or her goal. Identifying the EIPs included in a strategy helps the decision maker to understand the level of effort involved and the type of support that may be appropriate for a given strategy. As an example, in Table 1.1 we show a set of EIPs associated with common preferential choice tasks.

These EIPs form the basic building blocks for various decision strategies that may be used in making a choice from among a set of alternatives. For example, a commonly suggested normative strategy for making a choice is the additive compensatory (AC) strategy. Using the AC strategy, a decision maker evaluates one alternative at a time along all its relevant attributes. Each attribute is assigned a

TABLE 1.1   EIPs for Preferential Choice Tasks

Elementary Process	Brief Description
Read	Reading the value of a single item of information from a display.
Move	Shifting attention to a particular item of information.
Retrieve	Accessing an item of information from memory.
Store	Placing a value into long-term memory for subsequent use.
Add	Summing two values from a display.
Multiply	Multiplying two values from a display.
Difference	Subtracting two values from a display.
Compare	Make a logical comparison ($>$, $\leq$, $=$) between two values in a display.

weight, with larger weights indicating higher value or importance. For a particular alternative, the decision maker reads the first attribute value. The attribute value is then combined with its weight. This process is repeated for each attribute of the alternative. A score for each alternative is determined by summing the products of the attribute values and weights. Once these computations are completed for each alternative, the one with the highest weighted score is chosen.

This process can be specified as a series of elementary information processes. The sequence of EIPs needed for each attribute would involve these steps: *move* to the specific attribute value, *read* the attribute value, *retrieve* attribute weight from long-term memory, *multiply* attribute value and weight, *yield* a weighted attribute score, *retrieve* the current alternative score, *add* the weighted attribute score to the current alternative score, and *store* the updated alternative score. To completely evaluate *one* alternative, this process of seven operators is repeated r times for each attribute in the choice set. These $7*r$ processes must be completed c times, where c equals the number of alternatives in the choice set. The result of this set of operations is a score for a specific alternative. This score is then compared to the score of the current best alternative. This requires the decision maker to *retrieve* the score of the current best alternative, *compare* the current best alternative score to the score of the new alternative, and *store* (a pointer to) the alternative with the higher score, and *store* the new best alternative score. This series of four processes is repeated $(c - 1)$ times as each alternative is considered. Thus, the total processing for AC is $7*(r*c) + 4*(c - 1)$.

Using such computations along with the specification of EIPs for a set of strategies allows us to compare levels of effort and identify *generic support tools*. For example, the AC strategy can be supported by tools that allow for the specification of weights (as an aid to long-term memory storage and retrieval), a tool that allows the weights to be multiplied by the attribute values (a multiplication function), and a tool that facilitates the summing of the weighted attribute values (an addition function). These three tools can replace the processing steps associated with the AC strategy, with three system functions (further details of this type of analysis are found in Todd & Benbasat 1994a, 1994b, 2000). To better understand the nature of this process, we need to look more closely at the role of decision strategy in DSS usage.

DECISION STRATEGY

DSS capabilities, decision task, and decision maker capabilities should be considered together in order to understand how they jointly influence decision-making performance. However, for most decision tasks, there are typically many alternative strategies, or combinations of processing steps, that can be used to solve a problem (Simon, 1957). As noted earlier, we often describe these strategies in terms of EIPs. Each alternative strategy imposes on the decision maker different requirements in terms of time, effort, and resources needed to implement the strategy and make a decision. This implies that the mediating role of decision strategy needs to be examined in order to understand the impact of decision support technologies on outcomes such as decision performance.

The model in Figure 1.3 suggests that task and DSS capabilities jointly influence the decision strategy employed and that this strategy, in turn, will influence decision performance. In other words, the way a DSS is used by the decision maker to handle a specific task will influence decision performance; for example, if the support system guides the decision maker to apply a more accurate strategy, the decision outcome will be better. Therefore, it is important to understand the mechanisms that influence the way in which a decision maker selects a particular strategy for a given task within the context of the set of decision support tools available.

Silver (1990) suggests such a mechanism that emphasizes the role of the designer. The design of a DSS restricts the decision maker to certain decision processes that are embedded into the system. Within this restricted design space, designers may guide users, both directly and indirectly, toward certain types of decision strategies. They could use restriction and guidance to direct users toward a normative decision approach or to prevent them from employing undesirable strategies (Silver, 1988). However, if a variety of strategies for a particular task is supported, how does the decision maker determine which to employ?

As noted in Figure 1.1, implicit in the DSS literature is the somewhat simplistic notion that the decision maker will choose a strategy that leads to the best performance, indicating a rational or normative approach to the problem. However, this view is not supported by empirical evidence. Other factors also come into play. In particular, as indicated in Figure 1.3, the choice will also be influenced by the manner in which the decision maker looks at the constraints of the decision situation as it relates to effort expenditure. Put another way, the impact of a DSS on decision performance will be moderated by how the individual trades off the effort required to perform the task versus the desired level of accuracy to be obtained. Together these factors lead to a more complete model of the DSS–performance relationship by taking into account the influence of perceived effort and accuracy on strategy selection.

INFLUENCE OF PERCEIVED EFFORT AND ACCURACY

Trade-offs between effort and accuracy have been demonstrated to lead to strategy adaptation in a variety of studies; Payne, Bettman, & Johnson (1993) provide a comprehensive literature review of the cost-benefit framework of cognition and associated empirical work. According to this framework, the joint objectives of a decision maker are to maximize accuracy (or decision quality) and minimize effort. Because these objectives often conflict, trade-offs are made between the two. Overall, the *empirical* (Russo & Dosher, 1983; Christensen-Szalanski, 1980; Bettman, Johnson, & Payne, 1990; Bettman & Kakkar, 1977; Johnson, Payne & Bettman, 1988), *simulation* (Thorngate, 1980; Johnson & Payne, 1985; Payne, Bettman, & Johnson, 1990), and *conceptual* (Beach & Mitchell, 1978; Shugan, 1979; March, 1978; Jungerman, 1985; Einhorn & Hogarth, 1978; Kleinmuntz & Schkade, 1993) literatures indicate that *effort* is the more important factor influencing strategy selection.

This emphasis on effort extends to strategy selection in the context of IT support for decision making where decision-making effort plays a *moderating* role in the proposed relationship between a DSS, strategy selection, and decision performance for a given task. Earlier, we discussed how a DSS could reduce the cost of implementing particular decision strategies by automating one or more of the EIPs that are needed to implement a strategy. If a DSS provides support features in such a way as to make a more accurate strategy at least *as easy* to employ as a simpler, but less accurate, heuristic, it may induce the use of that more accurate strategy and as a consequence improve decision performance. Otherwise, a DSS may influence decision-making efficiency only by allowing the same strategy to be executed with less effort. This occurs because decision makers appear to use decision support in such a way as to minimize their overall level of effort expenditure (Todd & Benbasat, 1991, 1992, 1993, 1994a, 1994b, 1999, 2000).

In summary, the cost-benefit or the effort-accuracy notions imply the following for decision outcomes. The quality of decision outcomes is a function of the accuracy of the strategies supported by the DSS. By *support*, we mean that the DSS reduces the cognitive effort required to implement a given strategy. If there is only one strategy supported, the decision maker will follow that strategy if he or she perceives that the cognitive cost of doing so is lower than pursuing a nonsupported strategy. If multiple strategies are supported, the selection will be guided by the relative level of effort needed to implement the various strategies given the nature of the support tools provided. The quality of the decision made will then depend on the effectiveness of the particular strategy chosen in the context of the task.

SUPPORT FOR THE PROPOSED MODEL

There is strong empirical support for the key role effort plays in how a DSS is appropriated and how it ultimately influences strategy. This was observed in a series of studies that investigated DSS containing different features to support elimination-based heuristics or additive normative strategies for preferential choice problems of different sizes and complexity (Todd & Benbasat, 1991, 1992, 1993, 1994a, 1994b, 1999, 2000). Even when incentive mechanisms that encouraged the utilization of more effortful strategies were provided, the lowest-cost strategies (as determined by the DSS features provided) were still utilized (Todd & Benbasat, 1999).

Cost considerations were also found to be influential in other studies. Gregor and Benbasat (1999), in their review of the literature on knowledge-based system explanation use, have observed that explanations that require less effort to access and assimilate were used more and were more effective with respect to performance and learning. Mao and Benbasat (1999) found that when multiple types of explanations were available, those that could be accessed more easily, through hypertext type links, were more likely to be used and led to better learning. Similarly, in studying information acquisition, Jarvenpaa (1989) observed that the way that decision makers acquired data from a given display was explained by the desire to minimize effort, regardless of the demands of the task (i.e., the strategy needed to follow for a good solution).

IMPLICATIONS FOR DSS DESIGN

The ultimate goal of the information systems designer is to provide an IT–based support system that will improve the quality of the decision maker's performance.[7] Improving quality typically necessitates a *change* from the current strategies, either toward the better execution of an existing decision strategy (i.e., working harder) or toward a better decision strategy (i.e., working smarter). How best to create such changes in order to achieve both effectiveness and efficiency has been an issue of much discussion in the DSS literature (Silver, 1990). The designer needs to understand how a particular DSS, with the tools and features it contains, can influence decision strategy in a particular decision setting. The perspective we have described in this chapter shows how task, decision maker capabilities, and decision support capabilities come together and are moderated by effort and accuracy considerations to influence strategy selection and ultimately decision quality. Designers can use this perspective to guide the behavior of decision makers.

Guidance by the designer, if properly applied, should lead to improvement in decision-making effectiveness and efficiency. How can such guidance be provided? The answer we offer is that this can be done principally by manipulating effort (i.e., by making available, and/or restricting, certain DSS features in order to alter the costs associated with alternative problem solving strategies). The engineering of effort as a conscious part of DSS design is central to the notion of guiding the decision maker toward the objective of "working smarter."

As Silver (1988) notes, restrictiveness and guidance are closely related since a designer can influence the behavior of the user by either means. It appears that the effect of DSS in terms of their influence on decision quality cannot be understood without taking into account the way the DSS influences the effort required to use alternative strategies. Decision makers appear to use the DSS in such a way to maintain a low overall level of effort expenditure and will employ a particular strategy if the decision aid makes it easier to apply relative to competing alternative strategies. Thus, by attending to the relationship between DSS and decision-making effort, it becomes possible for the DSS designer to influence the way in which information is processed.

It is possible to induce more normatively oriented strategies when the *effort* relationships are changed sufficiently in favor of those strategies. A key question is *how low* the effort balance needs to be tipped in order to facilitate a strategy shift. Based on our studies, it appears that the influence of the decision aid will be most pronounced when it makes use of a desired strategy *very low* in terms of effort relative to alternative strategies. Furthermore, this result was consistent even in the face of relatively high incentives to perform well. Thus, the manipulation of effort provides a powerful lever for DSS designers to apply for guiding the use of decision strategies, a guidance strategy that can overcome commonly observed effects of task on strategy (Payne, Bettman, & Johnson, 1993). This points the way toward an engineering approach for DSS design that may be invariant across a variety of task characteristics. The cognitive engineering perspective that we have provided in the context of our "decision support–decision strategy–decision performance" model provides a basis from which to build IT support for decision making. It does this by balancing effort and accuracy trade-offs in such a way to guide decision makers toward more normative decision strategies and better decision outcomes.

DIRECTIONS FOR RESEARCH

There are several directions in which research examining the role of IT and decision making can be extended to advance and refine the model that we have presented in this chapter.

While "decision maker capabilities" are part of the model shown in Figure 1.3, the research to date has focused primarily on issues of effort and ignored how effort and the capabilities of the individual decision maker interact. Furthermore, while studies have measured effort, they have not considered *explicitly* how decision makers consider accuracy and how decision makers determine the way in which certain strategies would lead to better outcomes. Similarly, individual difference factors have received only limited attention in recent literature. More sophisticated methodological approaches and theoretical and methodological advances all make this a ripe area for additional study. In particular, the investigation of factors that can be explicitly tied to decision performance criteria is important. Key advances in this type of study require the explicit analysis of task and individual difference factors that lead to the specification of influences on information processing that can be developed into design prescriptions.

Decision outcomes have not been well integrated into the nomological net proposed here. Many studies link decision support and outcomes directly, ignoring the importance of the mediating effects of strategy and effort. This results in equivocal results. Other studies examine the mediators but consider outcomes in only a limited fashion, assuming that the selection and application of a good strategy leads to a good outcome. Thus, few studies have examined the complete set of linkages from decision aid through decision process to decision-making effectiveness. True tests of the model advanced here will need to incorporate all these elements.

Studies to date have examined the relationship in the model in the context of a narrow range of choice and information acquisition tasks supported by very specific decision support tools and information presentations. This focuses on only a limited range of the task continuum. It would be interesting to deal with basic processes in the context of different tasks while varying levels of complexity and other task-related attributes. This will help to identify the boundaries of the model in Figure 1.3.

Taking the notion of task further, there is also a need to translate some of these concepts into broader, more realistic, field-based settings. Decision support technologies are now being embedded in a wide range of applications being deployed on the Internet. These technologies have potentially profound impacts on the nature of commerce and selling.[8] The effects that we observe in experimental settings need to be studied more broadly in this environment. Environmental factors such as information load, interruptions, and technological limitations need to be examined to help understand the boundaries of the model and how well it translates into more realistic environments.

CONCLUDING REMARKS

We end, much as we began, with the desire to understand the continuously changing and emerging role of IT in decision making. The study of IT impacts on decision making has followed a path from the simplistic belief that a support tool would necessarily enhance decision quality to a more complex one providing a deeper understanding of the interrelationship of task, decision-aiding technology, and decision maker capability and their joint impact on decision performance. The recent emphasis in DSS research on decision strategy as an important mediating factor and the introduction of the cognitive cost-benefit paradigm have brought some important theoretical anchors to this field of study.

Much has been learned about the important relationships between these factors, but the learning has been isolated within a relatively narrow paradigm. It has also focused on information presentation and evaluation in the context of the limited range of tasks. Nonetheless, it has afforded us insights into system design and suggests practical guidelines for making decision support tools more useful and usable. As the reach of these support technologies is extended, there is a need to broaden work in this area across tasks and technologies and to push at environmental factors that will test the bounds of our basic model. In doing this, it is important that we begin to broaden our perspective on decision making with technology.

Our current theoretical and empirical paradigms most often treat decision making with IT as a narrow, focused, and discrete event. We need to move to considering decision making with IT as a continuous process, in which IT is a component of the process[9]—a process that involves mixtures of technology, individual thought, and group consultation, a process that includes problem identification and information gathering in addition to information processing. The interesting questions and insights may well lie beyond these underexplored boundaries. We believe that the wide body of evidence that has been accumulated supporting the core components of this model suggests that it is a good foundation from which to launch these new research directions.

ENDNOTES

1. Developing organizational knowledge is covered in the Alavi chapter.
2. The implications of Internet for business strategy are outlined in the Sampler chapter.
3. Related issues dealing with groups, teams, and organizational level effects are covered in the chapters by Alavi, Saunders, Robey and Boudreau, Baru and Mukhopadhyay, Graves and Kettinger, and Markus and Tanis.
4. The issue of the acceptance and use of these systems is discussed in the Agarwal chapter.
5. See also the chapters by Agarwal and Fichman for discussions of related issues.
6. The chapter by Offman and Pitsatorn on end-user training also builds on the importance of cognitive capabilities.
7. Alternative perspectives on software development are provided in the chapters by George and by Kirsch.
8. See the Sampler chapter on the internet and strategy.
9. See the chapters by Alavi and by Saunders on organizational knowledge and virtual teams.

Chapter 2

Managing Organizational Knowledge

Maryam Alavi

Knowledge and knowledge management (KM) are not new phenomena. As described in Polanyi's (1962, 1967) works summarizing the history of knowledge and epistemology, debate regarding knowledge and knowing, an urge to discover the "truth" has occupied the minds of Western philosophers over the past several centuries. Similarly, businesses have been engaged in the creation, accumulation, and application of knowledge for hundreds of years (Hansen, Nohria, & Tierney, 1999). According to Penrose (1959), accumulation of knowledge is "built in" the very nature of firms. Recently, however, there has been a surge in interest and emphasis on organizational knowledge and knowledge management among both scholars and practitioners. Conferences, workshops, books, articles, and other publications on the topic abound. A recent search on the term *knowledge management* on the World Wide Web by the author resulted in 465,920 hits. Many large firms are busy hiring chief knowledge officers and developing knowledge management systems.

In this chapter, I first discuss the importance of organizational knowledge and knowledge management in today's business. Second, a working definition, a classification of knowledge, and an analysis of organizations as knowledge management systems are presented. Next, knowledge management systems (KMS) are defined and categorized. Finally, a discussion of the key benefits, challenges, and the key research issues of KM and KMS is presented.

IMPORTANCE OF KNOWLEDGE MANAGEMENT TO BUSINESS

The foundation of industrialized economy is shifting from natural resources to intellectual (or intangible) assets (Hansen, Nohria, & Tierney, 1999; Davis & Meyer, 1998). With this shift, knowledge and other related intangible assets (e.g., innovation, brands, and speed to market) are viewed as factors of production that may be even more important than traditional resources of capital, labor, and land (Davis & Meyer, 1998). Furthermore, at the dawn of the new millennium and beyond, several forces in the developed economies, singularly and in combination, are fueling the need for explicit and large-scale strategies and systems for managing organizational knowledge. These forces consist of volatility of competitive business environment, globalization, and emergence of knowledge-intensive products and services.

Changes in the business and competitive environment in and of itself are not new. After all, it has been said that change is the only constant. However, the *rate* of change in today's economy is greatly accelerated, making it a major force to contend with.[1] The increased rate of change quickly erodes the competitive advantage of firms and market positions. Under these conditions, organizations' ability to learn and acquire knowledge quickly is believed to be the only source of sustainable competitive advantage (Winter, 1995; Dierick & Cool, 1989; Lippman & Rumelt, 1982). Prusak (1997, p. 11) defines a business firm that thrives in the current and future economic environment as one that "knows how to do new things well and quickly." Thus, a firm's ability to create, store, and apply knowledge in keeping up with rapid change is a critical success factor in its survival and growth.

Globalization of the economy and markets is another major force in the current business environment with significant implications for organizational knowledge management. Globalization gives customers a wide choice of goods and a services, leading to pricing pressures, the need for production efficiency, and product/service innovations. These conditions in turn increase knowledge management requirements of firms in global markets. Effective and efficient knowledge management is required in order to capitalize on previous learning and avoid reinventing the wheel and duplicating effort, and to enable firms to act with agility and speed in responding to global competitiveness.

The trend toward knowledge-intensive products and services is another driver of the need for improved organizational knowledge management and KMS. Development and delivery of services, by definition, are based on intangibles and know-how. Increasingly, however, manufacturing firms are trying to differentiate their products by offering "smart" features. Examples include elevators that can automatically perform preventive maintenance and automobiles that can sense, learn, and adjust to the driving habits of their operators (Davis & Meyer, 1998). According to Quinn (1992), intangibles that add value to firms' products are all knowledge-based including customization, innovative design, and superior technical know-how. Bundling knowledge in the composition, production, and delivery of goods and services requires effective knowledge management, similar to the way that tangible assets (e.g., capital and raw materials) are managed for production and delivery of goods and services.

The dynamics of the new economic era characterized by rapid rate of change, globalization, and knowledge-intensive products and services make knowledge management vital to organizations. Judging from the growing popularity of the topic in academic and professional press, and the level of intellectual and financial resources invested in it, knowledge management seems to be viewed as a critical aspect of effective organizations and competitive strategy in the new millennium.

DEFINITIONS: KNOWLEDGE AND KNOWLEDGE TYPES

For the purposes of this chapter, I have adopted the following working definition of knowledge based on the work of Huber (1991) and Nonaka (1994). Knowledge is justified personal belief that increases an entity's potential for effective action. In this definition, an entity may consist of one or more individuals (a group or an organization). Furthermore, according to this definition, availability of knowledge may not necessarily lead to effective action but only to an increase in the potential for effective action. For example, consider that only a portion of all individuals who know and believe in the health benefits of regular exercise follow a regular exercise regime. This definition further suggests that knowledge is initiated in individuals (or groups). As such, it implies a distinction between information and knowledge. Knowledge is the information that has been processed in the mind of individuals through a process of deliberation, learning, and thought. Information is the raw material for the creation of knowledge and may reside in a variety of sources (documents, computer files, or software) and in a variety of forms (printed or spoken words, digitized bits, or drawings). Some authors have defined *information* as data that has been given structure. *Data* is in turn defined to refer to symbolic representations. Having made these distinctions, it is important to note that a hierarchical relationship between data, information, and knowledge is not implied here. Symbols considered data by one individual may constitute information for another while being considered knowledge by a third individual. Consider a book on the topic of financial accounting written in English. This book represents only symbols (i.e., data) to someone who does not speak English. To an English-speaking individual who is interested in the topic (i.e., a potential reader), the book (structured in the form of chapters, sections, subsections, definitions, and a coherent content) represents information. And finally, the book's content represents the articulated knowledge of the author on the topic of financial accounting.

Having discussed a working definition of knowledge, I next describe some of the common knowledge taxonomies. Discussion of knowledge taxonomies is important because different types of knowledge have different knowledge management implications and require different models of knowledge management systems (KMS) as described later in the chapter.

A frequently cited taxonomy of knowledge is developed by Nonaka (1994) based on Polanyi's (1962, 1967) discussion of tacit and explicit dimensions of knowledge. Nonaka (1994) has identified two types of knowledge: tacit and explicit. Tacit knowledge is defined as knowledge that is unarticulated, is rooted in action and experience, and is situated in context. Examples of tacit knowledge include the knowledge of an expert golf player and the improvisation skills of a jazz player (Zack, 1999). Explicit knowledge refers to knowledge that is articulated in some symbolic form (spoken or written words, mathematical or chemical formulas).

It is important to note that the tacit and explicit knowledge categories are mutually constituted, not mutually exclusive (Tsoukas, 1996). That is, although tacit knowledge is the necessary component of all knowledge (Grant, 1996), it can be converted to an explicit form of knowledge through linguistic expressions (Polanyi, 1975; Moss, 1995). And explicit knowledge is always grounded on a tacit component (Polanyi, 1975).

FIGURE 2.1   A Classification of Organizational Knowledge

	Individual	Social
Explicit	Conscious	Objectified
Implicit	Automatic	Collective

Source: Spender, 1996, p. 54.

An important implication of the tacit-explicit knowledge taxonomy is the degree of ease of knowledge transfer (i.e., knowledge sharing in organizational settings). In general, the higher the degree of tacitness of knowledge, the more difficult its transfer (referred to as *sticky knowledge*). Explicit knowledge, on the other hand, is relatively easy to transfer and share (referred to as *leaky knowledge*). Thus, there are two factors that should be considered in determining the degree to which tacit knowledge is to be converted to explicit knowledge. These factors are (1) cost of the conversion and (2) the trade-offs between the organizational need to share and transfer knowledge versus the need for protection of significant knowledge items.

Another classification by Spender (1992, 1996) expands on Nonaka's knowledge types by categorizing knowledge along two dimensions: explicit-implicit and individual-social, leading to identification of four knowledge types (see Figure 2.1).

In Spender's classification, conscious knowledge refers to explicit knowledge of an individual (for example, knowing the spelling of words or syntax of a computer programming language). Automatic knowledge refers to an individual's implicit (i.e., tacit) subconscious skills (e.g., riding a bicycle). Objectified knowledge refers to the explicit and codified knowledge of a social system (e.g., the policy manual of an organization). And finally, collective knowledge refers to the tacit knowledge that is originated and held in a social system (e.g., culture of a firm).

In summary, the knowledge taxonomies described here demonstrate that knowledge is not a monolithic concept (Alavi & Leidner, 1999a) and that a variety of knowledge types coexists in organizations. The goal of an effective knowledge management strategy should be enhancing the creation, transfer, and utilization of all types of organizational knowledge. The KM implications of various knowledge types are discussed throughout the rest of the chapter.

ORGANIZATIONS AS KNOWLEDGE SYSTEMS

Recognition of the multidimensionality of organizational knowledge is the foundation of the knowledge-based view of the firm (Zack, 1998b). According to this view, firms exist because it is difficult to generate, transfer, and apply all the required types of knowledge via markets. Firms then are created as systems for generating, transferring, and applying the knowledge required for development and delivery of products and/or services. The resource-based view of the firm postulates that a firm's profitability is not only a function of its market and competitive position but also a function of its internal capabilities and know-how (i.e., its knowledge) in combining its resources to deliver products and services and to enhance organizational performance.[2] Thus, organizations operate based on the capabilities and knowledge that they generate through an ongoing process of absorbing information from internal and external sources, converting it to knowledge (primarily through the cognitive capabilities of their employees), and acting upon that knowledge. Organizations as knowledge systems may be analyzed in terms of three sets of knowledge activities focused on generation, codification, and utilization of knowledge (Davenport & Prusak, 1997; Pentland, 1995).

KNOWLEDGE GENERATION

Although knowledge generation is an ongoing organizational process, in general, it is the least systematic of organizational knowledge management activities (Davenport & Prusak, 1997). According to Spender's typology of knowledge described earlier, knowledge can originate and reside in individuals or groups of individuals (i.e., a social system). According to several authors, the interplay between the individual and social knowledge is an important aspect of organizational knowledge creation, amplification, and transfer. For example, Brown and Duguid (1998) state that knowledge is readily generated when people work together in the tightly knit groups known as "communities of practice." Coherent and synergistic organizational knowledge is generated through collaboration, interactions, and relations among individuals. The social genesis of organizational knowledge generation is the foundation of the network model of knowledge management systems.

Considering the importance of knowledge generation, some organizations allocate dedicated resources to this activity. Examples include research staff positions and R&D departments that are established for the primary purpose of creating "new" organizational knowledge. In some cases, new organizational knowledge may be obtained through acquiring and grafting on external knowledge sources (e.g., hiring new organizational members who posses the desired know-how). In some cases, acquiring external knowledge sources may occur on a large-scale basis and involve the acquisition of one organization by another (Huber, 1991). An example is IBM's acquisition of the Lotus Institute in 1993 in order to obtain the collaborative software (groupware) expertise and knowledge possessed by the Lotus Institute.

KNOWLEDGE CODIFICATION

Remembering what an organization has learned and reusing its relevant knowledge (generated internally or acquired externally) is an important aspect of effective knowledge management. Like individuals, organizations may lose track of their knowledge and forget. Thus, organizations codify their knowledge in order to preserve and reuse it. Since organizations are continuously engaged in the process of knowledge generation and application, it would be futile to attempt to codify and store all organizational knowledge. Thus, knowledge codification involves three primary considerations (Prusak & Davenport, 1997):

1. Determining the knowledge domain and content to be codified.
2. Identifying the source of the required knowledge, specifying the mechanisms and media for its collections, and determining the timing and frequency of its codification and updates.
3. Specifying methods and tools for access and retrieval of the codified knowledge.

The approach to codification of knowledge depends on its type. Using Spender's knowledge classification of Figure 1, at the individual level, it may be argued that implicit knowledge is mostly codified and stored in the individual's memory. Explicit knowledge, on the other hand, may be codified and stored in the individual memory as well as in external memory (e.g., documents and computer files). At the organizational level, implicit knowledge is codified and stored in collective memory that includes but extends beyond individuals' memory to include shared tacit knowledge and interpretations resulting from social interactions. Examples of tacit organizational memory include organizational culture, structure, and processes (Walsh & Ungson, 1991). Explicit knowledge of social systems is typically codified and stored in files and documents (manual or computerized). Most organizational KMS initiatives focus on application of information technologies for the capture, storage, and retrieval of explicit organizational knowledge. This approach to knowledge management is referred to as the *repository model of KMS*.

KNOWLEDGE UTILIZATION

Knowledge generation and codification do not necessarily lead to improved performance and business value. Knowledge creates value in use (Fahey & Prusak, 1998), that is, when it is applied by organizations to create capabilities and to take effective action. Thus, support and enhancement of knowledge utilization in organizations should be a major focus of a firm's KM initiatives.

Organizations are distributed knowledge systems in that they do not have an all-encompassing mind and a central memory. Since knowledge is generated and codified throughout the organization, a key challenge in the application of organizational knowledge is transferring it from the source where it is generated or resides to where it is needed and is used. Knowledge transfer in organizations may be challenging due to a number of factors, including the type of knowledge, the reward system, and an inability to locate and access the required knowledge.

The knowledge type (tacit or explicit) impacts the rate of its transfer as well as the choice of the transfer mechanisms. In general, given the situated and unarticulated nature of tacit knowledge, the rate of its transfer is slower than the rate of transfer of explicit knowledge. Furthermore, tacit knowledge is best transferred through collaboration, shared experience, and rich interpersonal interactions over time (e.g., a mentoring relationship). Explicit knowledge, on the other hand, may be effectively transferred through "leaner" interactions and communication channels (e.g., discussion databases or e-mail).

The organizational reward system can also influence knowledge transfer activities. For example, the reward systems that give recognition and status to individual expertise may encourage knowledge hoarding and discourage knowledge sharing. Knowledge transfer in large organizations is particularly challenging. In these organizations, geographic, time, and relational distance (absence or infrequent communication and interactions) between the knowledgeable individuals and those who seek knowledge may impede locating and accessing the required knowledge. In general, knowledge transfer between those who need to know and the knowledge sources (other individuals, or knowledge repositories, for example) is not frictionless. In recognition of these potential barriers, many KM initiatives focus on the development of specific mechanisms for supporting knowledge transfer activities. An example is the development and publication of a knowledge directory (or a knowledge map) that identifies the source, content, and location of organizational knowledge.

Effective transfer of knowledge from its source to its intended recipient is only the first step toward effective organizational knowledge utilization. Knowledge transfer does not necessarily lead to its absorption and use by the recipient. Learning literature provides us with some important insights into the cognitive processes underlying knowledge absorption (i.e., learning) and its applications to problem solving and decision making by individuals.[3] For example, work in the area of knowledge structures has demonstrated that in most cases, cognitive processes (problem solving and decision making) of individuals in organizational settings are enacted with little attention and through invoking preexisting knowledge and cognitive "routines" (Gioia & Pool, 1984). This approach leads to a reduction in cognitive load and is therefore an effective strategy in dealing with individual cognitive limitations. On the other hand, it creates a barrier to the search, absorption, and use of knowledge in organizations.

Thus, conditions that lead to the creation of "demand pull" for knowledge at the individual level need to be explored and specified in order to promote search for, absorption, and active use of knowledge by individuals. Individuals' limited cognitive capacity in terms of attention, information processing, and memory constitutes a bottleneck in organizational knowledge absorption and use. Failing to explicitly consider cognitive processes and their limitation may result in increasing the cognitive processing load of already overburdened knowledge workers and lead to their frustration (Cross, 1997).

SUMMARY

In this section, drawing on the knowledge-based theory of the firm and viewing organizations as knowledge systems, I discussed three sets of organizational activities focused on knowledge generation, codification, and utilization. One of the important implications of this view is that knowledge management consists of a dynamic and continuous set of on-going activities and practices embedded in individuals, as well as in social and organizational structures. At any point in time, and in any part of a given organization, individuals and groups may be engaged in several different knowledge management activities. Knowledge management is not an occasional, discrete, independent, organizational occurrence.

KNOWLEDGE MANAGEMENT SYSTEMS: AN OVERVIEW AND SUGGESTIONS FOR RESEARCH

In this chapter, I define the term *knowledge management system* to refer to an IT–based system developed to support and enhance the primary organizational knowledge management processes of knowledge generation, knowledge codification, and knowledge transfer. Two underlying models for KMS have been identified: (1) the repository model and (2) the network model (Alavi & Leidner, 1999b; Fahey & Prusak, 1998; Hansen, Nohria, & Tierney, 1999). The repository model aims at codification of knowledge (i.e., creation and maintenance of stocks of explicit knowledge). The network model aims at using the power of information and communication technologies to support the flow of knowledge in organizational settings and among networks of individuals. Primary characteristics of each of the two KMS models and specific examples are described next.

THE REPOSITORY MODEL OF KMS

The repository model views knowledge as an object that can be collected, stored, organized, and disseminated. As such, these systems focus on managing explicit knowledge and primarily focus on the creation and storage/retrieval aspects of organizational knowledge management. Information management technologies in the form of relational database and document management systems play a dominant role in the development of these types of KMS. Corporate intranets present the most prevalent technical infrastructure for development and management of knowledge repositories. This is because intranets provide an ideal environment for multimedia publication of knowledge across multiple types of computer hardware and software, and for easy retrieval and display of interrelated knowledge items through hypertext links. According to a recent survey, development of knowledge repositories is a prevalent form of KM initiatives in organizations (Ruggles, 1998). Most repositories contain knowledge from both internal and external sources. Examples of external knowledge consist of competitive intelligence, industry trends, customer knowledge, and professional and trade journal publications. Examples of internal knowledge include contents of internal reports, document templates, memos, methodologies and manuals, product and marketing knowledge, and internal best practices. The consulting firm of Ernst & Young, for example, has made significant investments in codification of the firm's internal knowledge and development of large knowledge repositories. The 250 individuals at the Ernst & Young Center for Business Knowledge manage and maintain these knowledge repositories (Hansen, Nohria, & Tierney, 1999). According to these authors, the staff at the Center for Business Knowledge work with and help consultants to locate and access the required repository content. In addition to this central group, staff members throughout the various Ernst & Young practice areas are responsible for collecting, organizing, and storing practice-specific knowledge.

Creation of knowledge repositories for capture and sharing of internal best practices is becoming a popular form of KMS in most organizations. These repositories are created through internal benchmarking processes. For example, most consulting firms (e.g., Andersen Consulting, KPMG Peat Marwick, McKinsey, and Ernst & Young) have developed best-practice repositories to be used by their consultants to bring the knowledge of the firm to bear on client projects and issues.

Critical success factors in the creation and deployment of best-practice repositories include the allocation of organizational resources and the establishment of mechanisms for identifying, selecting, capturing, storing, and retrieving the best practices. Different approaches and mechanisms for allocation of organizational resources for this purpose may be undertaken. For example, at Chevron, a large integrated energy and chemicals company, best-practice teams have been established as permanent components of the organizational structure. These teams are given a charter to establish best-practice criteria, create best-practice knowledge repositories, and promote and support the use of these repositories throughout the organization. The best-practice teams consist of professionals and managers with similar responsibilities in different plants and divisions and are led by functional area experts. The team members meet and communicate on a regular basis to support the development, operation, and maintenance of best-practice repositories. Furthermore, these teams ensure easy, fast, and firmwide access to the repository content through the use of advanced information and telecommunication tools.

THE NETWORK MODEL OF KMS

The network model of KMS does not attempt to codify and extract knowledge from the individual who possesses it. In this KMS model, knowledge remains with the individual who has developed and possesses it and is transferred mainly through person-to-person contacts. This is in contrast to the repository model of KMS that involves person-to-repository and repository-to-person modes of knowledge transfer. Thus, the network model of KMS is predicated on providing access to knowledge that resides within individuals through establishing direct links among people rather than aiming at extracting and codifying the knowledge of individuals and capturing it in electronic knowledge repositories. As such, the network model of KMS primarily supports organizational knowledge management processes that involve social interactions and direct communication and contact among individuals. As mentioned before, this type of KMS is based on the premise that knowledge generation and knowledge application are fundamentally social processes that occur most efficiently though direct interactions among members of communities of practice (i.e., people who search for solutions to similar problems).

The network model of KMS varies in its technological orientation. Some systems rely on intranet tools and specialized forms of knowledge repositories to capture, organize, and disseminate the sources of knowledge and expertise in organizations. These specialized knowledge repositories, referred to as corporate *"yellow pages"*, *knowledge directories*, or *knowledge maps,* contain pointers to the knowledge source (i.e., people), not the knowledge itself. For example, Hoffman-LaRoche, a pharmaceutical company, has developed a knowledge map of its drug approval process. For each step of the process, a yellow pages of relevant people organized according to their knowledge of the key issues is developed (Ruggles, 1998). Use of the yellow pages during the drug approval process to locate and tap into the required knowledge has greatly expedited the process and has reduced the rework and repeat of process activities. Corporate yellow pages and knowledge maps are very useful in locating tacit knowledge and expertise embedded in the minds of knowledge workers. Once the source of knowledge is identified, it can be transferred from the source to the knowledge seeker through direct face-to-face and/or technology-enabled virtual interactions. Nevertheless, major organizational challenges remain in the creation and use of knowledge maps. The challenges include determining the level of know-how of organizational members, determining whom to include in corporate yellow pages, keeping the yellow pages current, and motivating the individuals with the required knowledge to spend the time and effort to share their knowledge with those who need that knowledge. Research aimed at addressing these and other related issues is needed to guide development of effective KMS.

Another interesting example of a network model of KMS, provided by Davenport and Prusak (1997), is British Petroleum's Virtual Teamwork Program. The objective of this program was to build a network of people, not to develop stocks of codified knowledge. The program employed an array of hardware and software tools including desktop videoconferencing, groupware, multimedia e-mail, and shared whiteboards to develop a KMS that enabled an ad hoc creation of rich communication networks among people. Once when the operations on a North Sea mobile drilling ship came to a halt due to equipment failure, the Virtual Team KMS was used to quickly diagnose and efficiently solve the problem. Through the use of a satellite link, an ad hoc communication network between the engineers on the ship and drilling equipment engineers in Aberdeen in eastern Scotland was established. The engineers in Aberdeen, through visual examination of the broken equipment (through the video link) and discussion with the ship engineers, were able to diagnose the problem and lead the ship engineers through the necessary repairs in a few short hours. Diagnosing the problem and fixing the broken part without the Virtual Team KMS would have taken longer at a cost of $150,000 for each day of delay.

SUMMARY

In this section, for the purpose of discussion, I have made a distinction between two types of KMS: the repository model of KMS and the network model of KMS. The repository model involves the specification, collection, and storage of organizational knowledge, using database and other forms of information storage and retrieval technologies. The network model of KMS attempts to identify the sources of the required knowledge and facilitate the flow of knowledge between the knowledge source and the knowledge seekers through the provision of effective and ubiquitous communication technologies. In practice, however, it is important to note that in most organizational settings, both types of KMS are needed and coexist.

In the following two sections, I will identify a set of issues and challenges that are associated with the design and implementation of effective KMS in organizational settings. These issues potentially identify some useful areas of investigation for KMS researchers.

ISSUES IN KMS DESIGN

Managing knowledge of the firm is advocated in the literature; however, it is not clear what specific knowledge (i.e., content, domain, type, and scope of knowledge) needs to or should be managed in the firm. Thus, a useful line of inquiry would be identification of factors that influence the knowledge management requirements of the firm and the development of effective and efficient methodologies for determining these requirements.

Another useful line of inquiry into KMS design would be the investigation of the relationship between the required knowledge attributes and the KMS type (repository or the network type). For example, it may be hypothesized that for well-defined and recurring knowledge requirements, the extraction and codification of knowledge (i.e., the repository model of KMS) may lead to an efficiency of operations and a preservation of organizational know-how. On the other hand, it may be hypothesized that the network model of KMS may be more effective under certain conditions including (1) those involving novel and/or nonrecurrent knowledge for which knowledge requirements cannot be prespecified and anticipated in advance or (2) conditions in which extraction and codification of knowledge are costly and time consuming. These and other hypotheses that attempt to map out the relationships between knowledge attributes and KMS types need to be empirically tested.

Research focusing on the relative effectiveness of different IT tools for support of various organizational knowledge activities (knowledge generation, knowledge codification, and knowledge utilization) would also be very important to establishing guidelines for the KMS design. For example, through application of modern communication and information technologies (e.g., groupware), a KMS can support knowledge generation by facilitating social interactions, discussion, and collaboration among the organizational members. KMS, in this role, can expedite knowledge generation by augmenting face-to-face modes of interaction by providing a "field" or space for organizational members to exchange ideas and perspectives more frequently and by establishing dialogs and discussions that, according to Nonaka (1994), are the primary means of knowledge development in organizations. This is particularly important and useful to large geographically dispersed organizations with infrequent face-to-face interactions among members. One useful line of KMS research would be the investigation of the relative effectiveness of various IT tools in support of the knowledge generation process. For example, an interesting research topic may be the investigation of the relative effectiveness of synchronous and asynchronous communication tools in support of various social interactions for knowledge generation.

As mentioned previously, organizational knowledge codification may occur through a variety of mechanisms. Files and documents constitute a significant component of codified organizational knowledge. Considering the enormous information processing, storage, and retrieval capacity of modern computers, KMS can play a significant role in support of knowledge codification and access in organizations. For example, technological capabilities such as data warehousing and data mining can greatly enhance the scope, depth, and accessibility of codified organizational knowledge. These assertions need to be substantiated through systemic and empirically based research.

Finally, KMS can be designed to enhance the organizational knowledge utilization activity. I described knowledge transfer as a significant component of knowledge utilization in organizational settings. In this author's view, another productive line of KMS research is the investigation of the role and scope of KMS's impact on the knowledge transfer within the firm. For example, KMS, by drawing on the high speed and flexible communication technologies, can greatly enhance the intra- and interorganization knowledge flows. Organizational knowledge flow (i.e., knowledge exchanges among individuals) typically occurs among immediate co-workers who are in regular and direct contact, which may in turn limit the sources of knowledge available to individuals (Alavi & Leidner, 1999b). Thus, it may be hypothesized that KMS, by drawing on flexible communication technologies (high-speed intranets, far-flung wide-area networks, and wireless technologies), can greatly expand the reach of individuals to various knowledge sources and increase the speed and scope of knowledge transfer among the individuals. An empirical test of this and related hypotheses in various organizational contexts may be a worthwhile research endeavor.

To summarize, research needs to be conducted to determine how knowledge management systems may be designed to create an infrastructure and environment for strengthening and accelerating organizational knowledge management activities. Research in this area needs to investigate the role of KMS features in actualizing, supporting, augmenting, and reinforcing these activities at a deep level through enhancing their underlying dynamics, scope, timing, and overall synergy. While some authors have downplayed the importance of KMS to knowledge management initiatives (e.g., Gill, 1995; Pentland, 1995; Malhotra, 1996), others (e.g., Alavi & Leidner, 1999b) contend that large-scale organizational knowledge management will be undermined without the appropriate application of information technology. Overall, a significant research contribution will be to establish and carve out the role and effectiveness of KMS in relation to the organizational knowledge management processes of knowledge generation, codification, and utilization.

ISSUES IN THE KMS IMPLEMENTATION

Implementation is an extensively researched area in the IS field. KMS may be viewed as a specific type of information system. Thus, it may be argued that the IS implementation research findings can be generalized to the KMS implementation area, diminishing the need for new implementation studies. Regardless of the merit of this argument, in my opinion, two areas of KMS implementation can benefit from new research: (1) establishing and measuring the benefits of KMS and (2) addressing the specific cultural and organizational challenges of KMS.

There is little evidence in the literature of firms systematically evaluating the benefits and outcomes of their KMS and KM initiatives (Alavi & Leidner, 1999a). Some studies suggest that knowledge management enables firms to improve the quality of customer solutions, establish consistent solutions to the same types of problems, increase first-call resolution to customer problems, reduce field service calls, and become more customer oriented (Davenport & Klahr, 1998). Some case studies have identified some specific benefits that were realized from KMS implementations (O'Dell & Grayson, 1998). Overall, two observations can be made regarding the KMS benefits: (1) benefits of KMS result from the use of the knowledge, not the KMS per se, and (2) benefits may be manifested in a variety of forms, thus requiring a variety of measurements and metrics. These two observations in turn lead to two suggestions for conducting KMS implementation research. The first is that the research on the benefits of KMS should focus on the organizational consequence/outcome of knowledge use, not on the KMS performance (e.g., the size of the knowledge repositories or the number of user queries to the repositories). This further suggests that research in this area needs to aim at the development of methodologies that establish the cause/effect relationship between specific knowledge management initiatives and organizational outcomes and consequences.

The second research suggestion is that since KMS benefits are context dependent, approximate, subjective, and varied, a multitude of approaches to measuring KMS benefits needs to be developed. The benefits of KMS cannot be measured in consistent, fixed, and objective ways, and a search for a single and universally applicable knowledge metric and measurement approach may turn out to be futile. Research on estimating or measuring benefits of KMS is needed, but it will not be easy, and a sustained effort will be required to effectively address and resolve the two key issues discussed here.

Another useful area of KMS implementation research would be to focus on alleviating the specific barriers to the KMS deployment in organizations. The KM and KMS research literatures have identified a cluster of cultural, behavioral, structural, and strategic factors that directly impact the success of KMS initiatives in organizations (see Alavi & Leidner, 1999a; Leonard & Sensiper, 1998; O'Dell & Grayson, 1998; and Teece, 1998). O'Dell and Grayson (1998), for example, identify several cultural factors as potential barriers to organizational KM and deployment of KMS. These factors consist of valuing and rewarding individual "experts" and stars and promoting a collaborative rather than a competitive organizational climate. They also identify a lack of individual motivation to contribute, share, or use knowledge as barriers to organizational knowledge transfer (e.g., not contributing to electronic knowledge repositories or not using best-practices repositories due to the not-invented-here syndrome). Another factor identified by these researchers is the lack of contact, relationships, and common perspectives among people who do not work side by side. This is exacerbated by organizational structures that promote "silo" behavior, that is, organizational units (departments, divisions, or functions) that exclusively focus on optimizing their own rewards and outcomes and spend little or no effort in overcoming time and space barriers to share knowledge across the organization. Similarly, Davenport and Prusak (1997) have identified several organizational and cultural inhibitors to knowledge management. These inhibitors, referred to as "frictions" by the authors, consist of organizational distrust, lack of common language and perspectives among different parts of organizations, intolerance for mistakes or the need for help, and insufficient time and resources for knowledge management processes. It is interesting to note that the key KMS challenges identified by both researchers and practitioners tend to be cultural and behavioral, not technical in nature. Thus, successful deployment of KMS in organizations requires not only technological tools and capabilities but also cultural and behavioral interventions for the creation of a knowledge-friendly organizational climate. A useful area for KMS implementation research would be research aiming at the identification of these organizational interventions. For example, the effectiveness of strategies such as establishing organizational norms that promote and value knowledge sharing, allocating organizational resources (time and space) for employees to become engaged in knowledge management activities, and adopting an incentive system that promotes and rewards knowledge creation and knowledge-sharing behavior needs to be investigated.

KMS benefits will be realized by those organizations that are not only technologically but also culturally adept. It is important that organizations make the long-term investment to align the cultural and behavioral elements for knowledge management. Thus, an organizational imperative to develop a contingency theory of KMS will be needed for addressing cultural and behavioral issues of KMS implementation (Alavi & Leidner, 1999b).

SUMMARY AND CONCLUDING REMARKS

The chapter started with a discussion of the importance of knowledge management and knowledge management systems in today's business. A definition of knowledge and an overview of knowledge types followed this discussion. Next, based on the knowledge-based theory of the firm, organizational knowledge management activities that centered on the generation, codification, and application of knowledge were described. In general, KMS supports organizational knowledge management in two fundamental ways: (1) by enhancing the organization, storage, and accessibility of explicit knowledge (the repository model of KMS) and (2) by identifying the individuals who possess the required knowledge and facilitating contact and communication between the source of knowledge and the knowledge seeker (the network model of KMS).

The issues associated with KM and KMS discussed in the chapter may be summarized in two major categories.

1. *Issues associated with the role of various forms of KMS in the support of organizational knowledge processes and activities.* While conceptual literature on organizational knowledge and knowledge management activities abounds, empirical and systematic investigations of the form and outcomes of these activities seem to be scant. Similarly, the existing body of work on KMS consists primarily of general and conceptual principles of KMS and case descriptions of such systems in organizations. Research-based guidelines for the design of KMS are needed. Several research areas that in the author's judgement can contribute to this area were identified in the chapter.

2. *A myriad of organizational, cultural, and behavioral issues that surround KMS implementation.* For example, developing effective metrics for measuring the benefits of knowledge management and KMS is a key factor for the long-term success and growth of KMS. Knowledge management systems are multifaceted. That is, effective deployment of KMS involves more that just technology and encompasses broad cultural and organizational challenges. Research-based strategies for profound cultural and organizational renovations associated with KMS implementation need to be developed.

The technology push (i.e., the availability of cost-effective and powerful communication and computer technologies) combined with the volatility of business and competition, globalization, and knowledge-intensive products and services will increase reliance on KMS. These systems will receive considerable attention from both scholars and practitioners in the foreseeable future. It is my hope that the ideas and discussions set forth in this chapter will serve as a step toward the development of a body of work to guide both KMS researchers and practitioners.

ENDNOTES

1. For example, for a discussion of the rapidly changing business environments brought on by the Internet, see the chapter on Internet and strategy by Sampler.
2. For example, for a discussion of the linkages between IT capabilities and firm performance, see the chapter on business strategy in hypercompetitive environments by Sambamurthy.
3. See the chapter on decision making by Todd and Benbasat for an in-depth discussion of cognitive and informational aspects of decision making (defined in terms of problem finding and problem solving).

Chapter 3

Virtual Teams: Piecing Together the Puzzle

Carol Stoak Saunders

"Virtual team is an oxymoron. . . . The idea violates my intellectual underpinnings of how teams work properly," explains Peopleware's *author Tom DeMarco. "They're never going to be a team, and the cost [in productivity] of separation is huge."* (Melymuka, 1997, p. 70)

How true is this? Virtual teams, or groups of people who use technology to transcend spatial, temporal, and organizational boundaries, may be considered to be counterintuitive, difficult to design, costly and complex to implement, and messy to manage. Yet they clearly are proliferating in today's work environment. The U.S. Department of Transportation estimates that at least 8.4 million U.S. workers are currently members of dispersed teams and predicts that there will be over 30 million virtual teams by the year 2000 (see Horvath & Tobin, 1999). The increasing popularity of virtual teams is rooted in several factors (Townsend, DeMarie, & Hendrickson, 1998). First, as knowledge to solve problems expands beyond what any single individual could be expected to know, organizations rely increasingly upon virtual teams to accomplish organizational goals. Second, because telecommunication technologies now provide greater bandwidths at increased economic value, they promote the use of networks linking individuals, internal and external, to the organization. Third, technology in the form of group support systems, groupware, and organizational decision assists virtual teams in collaborating and making decisions.

Virtual teams allow individuals in locations around the world to interact with one another to solve organizational and interorganizational problems. As organizations undertake global efforts either within or across organizational boundaries, the ability to perform asynchronously helps bridge barriers normally associated with different time zones. For example, Tandem Services Corporation has a virtual team of software developers that capitalizes on having team members in different time zones (Boudreau, Loch, Robey, & Straub, 1998). The London team members initially code the project. Each evening, their code is transmitted to the U.S. team for testing. After testing, U.S. members forward the code to Tokyo where Japanese members debug the code. The London team members start their next day with the debugged code and another cycle is initiated. Thus, increased team member productivity and reduced cycle time are benefits of using this approach with global virtual teams. But even within the same city or locale, telecommuting can benefit from virtual teams. And virtual teams composed of contract labor and colocated permanent employees can provide expertise missing in an organization and can help an organization cope with work demand uncertainty.

Virtual teams represent a relatively new phenomenon, and we still have much to learn about them before we can fully reap their potential benefits. The opening quote highlights some problems in managing virtual teams effectively. As organizations struggle to make effective use of virtual teams in decision making, managers are asking questions such as

- Why use virtual teams?
- What type of infrastructure is needed for effective virtual teams?
- How should virtual teams be managed?
- What are the indicators of effective virtual teams?

To answer these questions, I will work on a virtual jigsaw puzzle. Just as one does when putting a puzzle together, I will sort pieces of findings from different streams of research. However, instead of sorting by color and straight edges, I will use various theoretical frameworks. The findings on group support systems yield puzzle pieces about group decision-making process and performance. Because much of this research is based upon findings from lab studies involving student participants, there are missing pieces about distributed groups. The literature on traditional groups, computer-mediated groups, and distributed teams offers assistance here. The fledgling theoretical base being developed in the telecommuting, global information systems, and outsourcing literatures promises some additional pieces.

To present the limited findings on virtual teams, I first define a virtual team and then use a framework based on the virtual team's life cycle. The framework traces the life of virtual teams from their inception through their launch and the performance of their assigned project, to the delivery of their product or service. Within each of these four stages, I highlight current findings and related research that better inform our understanding of virtual teams. This framework is particularly useful in understanding not only the structure and processes of virtual teams but also how their interaction impacts the team's performance. The discussion of each stage of the life cycle concludes with research issues.

At the end of the chapter, I do not promise a complete understanding of virtual teams. The analogy of the jigsaw puzzle does not completely hold because some pieces do not fit well or are missing. In the process of piecing together this puzzle, I will sift through the literature and throw out some pieces that belong to other puzzles. Many pieces may fit neatly together. Others may appear to fit but are actually incompatible. My challenge (and yours) is to find the pieces that fit, create a meaningful pattern, and identify the missing pieces.

WHAT IS A VIRTUAL TEAM?

Townsend et al. (1998, p.18) define *virtual team* as "geographically and/or organizationally dispersed co-workers that are assembled using a combination of telecommunications and information technologies to accomplish an organizational task." This includes teams whose members seldom meet face to face yet are able to work together on cross-functional activities, undertake special projects, and deliver results to customers (Lipnak & Stamps, 1994). While the teams may require only a single meeting to accomplish the task, it is likely that virtual teams meet a series of times, either at the same time or at temporally distributed times. Thus, virtual teams may be temporally and/or spatially independent.

Can a team be virtual if some of its members meet face to face on a regular basis but others are pure telecommuters? While this might not be the standard view of a virtual team, such teams do exist and raise critical issues relevant to understanding the application and effectiveness of virtual teams even if only one team member is a telecommuter in the virtual mode. Thus, in a virtual team one or more members may be geographically or organizationally dispersed from the other team members. Furthermore, as outsourcing continues to become more popular, virtual teams may have one or more members who are temporary employees of the organization. Finally, the teams may have distinct, relatively permanent membership, or they may be very fluid as they evolve to respond to changing task requirements and as members leave and are replaced by new members.

WHAT ARE THE STAGES IN THE LIFE OF A VIRTUAL TEAM?

The framework I use for understanding virtual teams is displayed in Figure 3.1. It is based on a life cycle consisting of four stages: Startup, Launch, Performance, and Delivery.

STARTUP (WHY USE VIRTUAL TEAMS?)

During startup, the situation is assessed and information is gathered either by future team members or management after they notice anomalies in their environment.

FIGURE 3.1   Virtual Team Framework

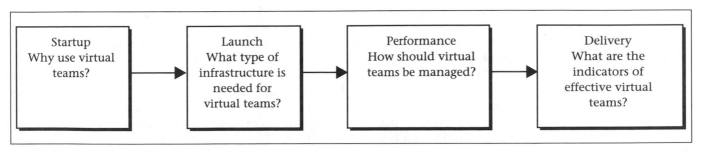

Team startup may result from one or more general factors promoting the use of virtual teams:

- *Interorganizational alliances.* Interorganizational alliances, either temporary or permanent, arise as organizations seek to capitalize on synergies created by combining their core competencies and to reap the benefits of larger economies of scale (Townsend et al., 1998). Other interorganizational alliances may result from corporate marriages such as British Petroleum and Amoco, Mobil and Exxon, and Daimler-Benz and Chrysler (Lipnack & Stamps, 1999).
- *Globalization.* Organizations are extending their activities around the world. Trade agreements such as GATT and NAFTA have promoted international trade. As organizations expand to thrive in the global marketplace, they increasingly find that desired team members are located around the world.[1]
- *Outsourcing.* Outsourcing allows companies to focus on core competencies by hiring workers to perform tasks that the organization chooses not to do or cannot do because its employees do not have the requisite skills. However, the high demand for IT skills often requires the company providing the outsourcing to hire contractors or rely on employees formerly employed by the company that is outsourcing.[2] Workers performing outsourced tasks are often teamed with permanent employees of the organization. These teams are virtual to the extent that members extend beyond the boundaries of the firm and sometimes beyond geographic boundaries.
- *Recognition of new forms of work relationships.* Workers' expectations are changing regarding their participation in the work environment. They often seek more flexibility in their work to respond to such personal needs as dealing with aging parents, children, and long commutes. Alternative work arrangements such as job sharing and telecommuting provide this flexibility and are increasingly used by organizations to entice and retain valued workers. Telecommuters are the impetus for forming virtual teams of telecommuters and their less-mobile co-workers.

While these general factors are the impetus for creating virtual teams, there are also more immediate triggers. A virtual team may acquire projects for the same reasons that they are acquired by other types of groups: A member proposes it; an outside agent, such as a boss, assigns it; or the project is an ordinary group activity (McGrath, 1991).

Research Issues Related to the Startup Stage

As is common with any new phenomenon, much of the early writing on virtual teams focused on why they should be used. As they proliferate, the reasons for using them are multiplying. As organizations grasp more and more reasons for adopting virtual teams, the research focus shifts to issues related to how they can be used more effectively, not whether they should be used. Furthermore, project inception for virtual teams is not problematic because virtual teams are typically assembled for specific reasons. Hence, future research on virtual teams appears to be most promising for issues related to the stages beyond startup.

One possible exception is the issue of risk. For all their benefits, there are countermanding challenges that may limit the effectiveness of virtual teams. Coordination and management costs may outweigh the benefits realized from their use for some projects. Future research should explore the types of risks associated with starting and using virtual teams.

LAUNCH (WHAT TYPE OF INFRASTRUCTURE IS NEEDED FOR EFFECTIVE VIRTUAL TEAMS?)

The launch is the turbulent period when the infrastructure for the group's work is laid. This infrastructure is based on three principles: purpose, people, and links (Lipnack & Stamps, 1999).

Purpose

Purpose provides direction to the team. It is broadly defined here to include the team's mission and goals and addresses three major functions: *production, member support,* and *group well-being* (McGrath, 1991). A clear purpose is critical to the virtual team because it serves as the team's most salient glue. In many cases, there is no hierarchy, chain of command, or rules and regulations to cement the team. A clear and agreed-upon purpose may challenge team members by giving them a heightened sense of urgency toward goal accomplishment (Locke, Shaw, Saari, & Latham, 1981), helping them form a group identity (Brandon & Pratt, 1999), and setting expectations of the team's performance for others outside the team (Duarte & Snyder, 1999).

In a recent study of global virtual teams, successful teams were characterized by high levels of trust and internalized clear mutual goals (Jarvenpaa, Knoll, & Leidner, 1998). These successful virtual teams discussed their teams' goals more than did the less successful teams. In contrast, the members of less successful teams did not always exhibit knowledge of the goals. Thus, it is crucial at the Launch Stage to ensure that everyone shares a common view of the work to be performed (Jarvenpaa et al., 1998; Lipnak & Stamps, 1994).

Research on more traditional groups helps clarify Launch Stage activities. It suggests that this stage not only involves a choice of goals and members but also typically involves an implicit selection of an initial performance strategy (McGrath, 1991). Studies of traditional groups have shown that this initial strategy is often ill formed and must often be altered because of poor task performance (e.g., Hackman, Brousseau, & Wiess, 1977; Gersick, 1988, 1989).

People

Team members, of course, are a basic element of virtual teams. Members may be selected to represent multiple points of view or to ensure mastery of skills or knowledge. They may also be selected from different time zones or shifts so that the team can be productive over more than one work period (Pape, 1997). Or they may be selected from different countries to achieve a desired level of cultural diversity.

The team's purpose can guide the selection of members to the extent that the purpose helps highlight knowledge, skills, and abilities (KSAs) that are required to accomplish the team's goals. Stevens and Campion (1994) highlighted five areas of KSAs that teams need to perform successfully: conflict resolution, collaborative problem solving, communication, goal setting and performance management, and planning and task coordination. However, Duarte and Snyder (1999) suggest a set of team member competencies that differs for virtual teams: project management, networking, use of technology, self-management, boundary management, and interpersonal awareness.

In addition to identifying KSAs, other challenges confront team formation:

- *Appropriate size.* Pape (1997) notes that "more is not better." He says that the ideal virtual team size is three to seven members. Research on group size (e.g., see Klimoski & Jones, 1995) indicates that the appropriate group size may vary, depending on factors such as task or purpose. If, for instance, the team's purpose is to develop a solution that will have buy-in by offices in 12 different global locations, it may be appropriate to have representatives from each of these locations on the team. Of course, as the size of the group increases, the communication links increase even faster. For n workers on a project, there are $(n^2 - n)/2$ possible communication links (Brooks, 1975, p. 78). It thus becomes more difficult for each individual to contribute meaningfully as size increases.

- *Interdependence vs. independence.* Lipnack and Stamps (1999, 4–5) suggest that virtual team members "must know how to be 'me,' while simultaneously holding on to being 'we.'" That is, virtual team members must work cooperatively to accomplish team goals. Yet because they are often separated by space and/or time, they must also be self-reliant and able to work autonomously. Research indicates that this is especially true for teams with telecommuters (e.g., Belanger & Collins, 1998; Nilles, 1994; Ramsower, 1985). Candidates for telecommuting jobs frequently are selected on the basis of their self-control. Even then managers are often unwilling to turn to telecommuting because they perceive that they have less control over their subordinates (Kavan & Saunders, 1998; Fritz, Narashimhan, & Rhee, 1998).

- *Motivation.* If group membership is voluntary, there must by definition be motivation for the members to undertake group activities. If membership is not voluntary, necessary participation, loyalty, and commitment may be absent. Commitment can be especially problematic in virtual teams with outsourced members because these members may hold little, if any, allegiance to the company whose work they are performing. However, Pearce (1993) and Galup, Saunders, Nelson, and Cerveny (1997) observed that the commitment or involvement of contract laborers was not significantly different from that of traditional workers.

- *Evaluation and compensation systems.* Good evaluation and compensation systems enhance motivation and encourage task- and group-related behaviors. New evaluation systems may be needed to assess both individual contribution to the team and the nature of team performance as a whole. Virtual teams may make greater use of peer-based evaluation systems, especially if managers have little contact with team members (Furst, Blackburn, & Rosen, 1999). Rewards should be based on the evaluation of both individual and team contributions. Orlikowski (1992) found that individual rewards inhibited implementing a groupware product that was based on cooperative behavior. A complication may be that differing cultural values and behavioral norms may hinder the effectiveness of companywide evaluation and compensation systems (Townsend et al., 1998; Furst et al., 1999; Duarte & Snyder, 1999). But when companywide compensation systems are absent, it is more difficult to manage team members working under different compensation structures and cultural values (Duarte & Snyder, 1999).

- *The down side of different time zones/shifts.* As noted earlier, selecting members from different time zones or shifts may lead to greater productivity. Unfortunately, having members in different time zones also can create delays. For example, if a team member in Europe is waiting on the work of a colleague in the United States, the delay will be exacerbated compared to when both colleagues are working in Europe. And normal working hours for one may be midnight for another. Thus, different time zones or shifts necessitate greater coordination.

• *Overcommitted team members.* Typically, virtual team members are selected for their competence and knowledge in an area. Consequently, they may be asked to serve on a number of teams. Because team members are dispersed, it may not be readily apparent that a person has been placed on too many teams and is overcommitted (Melymuka, 1997; Lipnack & Stamps, 1994).

Links

Links are the internal ties or infrastructure that give shape to the team. They are the team's skeleton around which communications flow and processes take place. Virtual teams require three major types of links: technical, structural, and normative. During the Launch Stage, these three types of links are established to facilitate group communications and activities. At least initially, these links are passive. Over time, the infrastructure is modified by group processes and repeated interactions of group members. This interaction process and the consequent structural and normative evolutions will be discussed more fully in the Performance Stage.

Technical Links   *Technical links* refer to technologies for communication, coordination, and collaboration. They include telephones, faxes, and digital technologies such as e-mail, desktop videoconferencing systems, virtual private networks, and Web-centric systems including intranets and extranets. Other linking tools include groupware and collaborative software. The choice of these technologies is based upon a number of factors, including the nature of the work, the physical location of team members, the availability of technological training and support, organizational and functional cultures, the symbolic meaning conveyed by use of the media, and member preferences.

Technical Link Selection—Startup Factor   The selection and use of technologies may depend on startup factors. The following are examples:

• *Interorganizational alliance.* Virtual teams created from interorganizational alliances cross organizational boundaries. They rely more on technology and less on hierarchical structures for communications. Extranets and collaborative software allow team members in different organizations to more easily overcome communication barriers. Interorganizational systems provide members with information available from their coupling of transactions between organizations (Boudreau et al., 1998). Rich media, including periodic face-to-face meetings and desktop videoconferencing, may clear up misunderstandings and ambiguities arising from differences in organizational cultures.

• *Globalization.* Global teams rely heavily on technology to bridge distance and time. Language translation software speeds information transfer when team members are from different countries. The Internet and intranets promote relatively cheap and timely communication and information sharing across global boundaries (Boudreau et al., 1998). They give employees access to newsletters, human resources information, calendars, product inventories, recruiting data, and electronic mail that is secured against outside surveillance. Like teams created from intraorganizational alliances, collaborative software that integrates electronic messaging with group scheduling, meeting support, group writing, and other applications helps the group generate information-based outputs. Differences in national culture require multiple communication channels (Lipnack & Stamps, 1994) with at least some rich media to resolve ambiguities. National cultures also impact the way in which technology is used by a team (Duarte & Snyder, 1999). For instance, team members from highly collective, group-oriented cultures may prefer face-to-face interactions, while those from cultures with a greater tendency to avoid uncertainty may prefer technology that produces permanent records of discussions and decisions.[3]

• *Outsourcing.* Virtual teams with outsourced employees as part of a team with permanent workers may require less reliance on technical links. The assignment of the outsourced work is typically communicated in a straightforward manner through leaner media. On the other hand, the coordination work involved in establishing and maintaining work processes where an outsourcing firm assumes some of a firm's processes (e.g., order taking, stocking, shipping) would likely require richer media to achieve the required level of "embeddedness."

• *Recognition of new forms of work relationships.* Some virtual teams, most notably teams with telecommuters, are created to respond to employee expectations. Telecommuters usually rely heavily on computer and communication technology to stay in touch with their managers and co-workers. Telecommuters can retrieve internal information from intranets and communicate with customers and suppliers via extranets. Fritz et al. (1998) found that undirected electronic communication, such as project-tracking tools and electronic bulletin boards, helped increase the satisfaction of telecommuters because it allowed them to keep in touch with co-workers and monitor work-related events.

Technical Link Selection—Compatible Tools   The selection and use of technologies may also depend upon the extent to which the same tools are available across team members. Compatible technology should be made available to the team members, and they should receive the training necessary to effectively use the tools. It is not always easy to spot incompatible tools. For example, Melymuka (1997) relates the case of a team that discovered that the Japanese version of a major application was different when the members tried unsuccessfully to open a file sent from Japan.

Technical Link Selection—Media Choice   Daft and Lengel's (1984) media richness model is a prominent model of media choice that may be used to understand the establishment of technical links in virtual teams. *Media richness* relates to the amount and variety of information flowing through specific communication media. Four criteria define media richness: speed of feedback, variety of communication channels employed, personalness of source, and richness of language. The model suggests that rich media convey more cues and that individuals select media whose richness is most appropriate for resolving the ambiguities with which they are faced. The model was revised to include e-mail and reflect additional selection criteria of geographical separation of communication partners, time pressures, and the unavailability of critical mass of communication partners in computer-based networks. In their review of a sizable body of media richness research, Fulk and Boyd (1991) conclude that the results are more supportive of applications of the media richness model to (1) traditional rather than new media and (2) communication activities rather than whole tasks.

The model suggests that lean media such as fax and e-mail are appropriate for tasks that are low in ambiguity, but richer media, such as face-to-face meetings and videoconferencing, are needed for communications that have ambiguities and subtleties of meaning. For example, Verifone suggests that virtual teams use fax, e-mail, and application sharing over their network for disseminating information, but use conference calls and videoconferencing for decision-making tasks (Pape, 1997).

Duarte and Snyder (1999), using media richness and social presence, describe at length the usefulness of 10 synchronous and asynchronous technologies in performing four tasks based on McGrath's (1984, 1991) task circumplex: generating ideas and plans, problems with answers, problems without answers, and negotiating technical or interpersonal conflicts. Their analysis is commendable in that it acknowledges different activities in these tasks and shows the fit of each technology with task activities.

Structural Links   In addition to the technical infrastructure for communication, teams must develop an internal structure. The team must be organized, and member and leader roles must be defined. Thus, the structural link defines the role network and the way group members interact with each other. These links are closely associated with what McGrath (1991) calls the well-being function: dealing with the development and maintenance of the group. As we will see in the next section, these roles may be altered by group activities and interaction patterns. But even in the state of flux and evolution, the structure of relationships helps channel the team's activities.

In a virtual team's Launch Stage, work is specified and tasks divided among members. At the heart of the virtual team are core members who work regularly on the project. In addition, the virtual team may include extended members, such as consultants, who provide support and advice, and ancillary members who review and approve the team's work and deliverables (Kiser, 1999; Duarte & Snyder, 1999). It is important that virtual team members not only know what their individual work is and how it can help accomplish the team's purpose but also what tasks the other team members are assigned (Coutu, 1998). Throughout the life of the project, these tasks may change and the roles of the members may evolve. But even as roles evolve, the shared understanding about roles sustains the interaction of members who cannot see one another working (Duarte & Snyder, 1999).

An important role to consider is that of the virtual team's leader(s). While research support is limited, it appears that the most successful virtual teams are characterized by rotating leadership (Lipnack & Stamps, 1994; Jarvenpaa et al., 1998). Members filled leadership positions as a need arose that demanded their level of expertise (Jarvenpaa et al., 1998). Raymond Smith (1994, 13), CEO of Bell Atlantic, also describes leadership on "ever-shifting, cross disciplinary teams" as "determined by who's most expert on the matter—not the corporate hierarchy."

In contrast to advocates of rotating virtual team leaders, Duarte and Snyder (1999) imply a constant leader throughout the life of the virtual teams. They prescribe competencies and behaviors for virtual team leaders. The inconsistency may be explained by looking at the type of task assigned to the virtual team. Duarte and Snyder (1999) suggest that the seven types of virtual teams may be distinguished by the extent to which the team has clear boundaries, distinct membership, and ongoing work. Teams with less distinct boundaries, diffuse or fluid membership, or ad hoc assignments may require rotating leadership to a greater extent than other virtual teams.

Unlike the other researchers, Duarte and Snyder may be focusing solely on the administrative role of virtual team leaders. This role may be a fairly stable role. Other leadership roles, such as that of technical leader, may also exist. These may be less stable and require rotating leadership.[4]

Normative Links   To augment technical and internal structural links, normative links reflect the nature of relationships among group members. They address group norms and the ways in which individuals are embedded within the group. Group norms are informal rules of conduct that groups develop to standardize the behavior of their members. Norms help assimilate outsourced workers into virtual teams and increase the productivity of workers who cannot see one another. Thus, they are critical for member support.

In the Launch Stage, team norms should be established concerning telephone, e-mail, and videoconferencing etiquette (e.g., warning group members when they would be out of town, guidelines for returning phone calls), meeting attendance and scheduling, work to be performed (Kiser, 1999; Duarte & Snyder, 1999), punctuality, and constructive feedback (Furst et al., 1999). These norms, especially in global teams, must honor different ways of doing business (Duarte & Snyder, 1999).

The degree of embeddedness of virtual team members affects the team's normative infrastructure. Team members can be described as *embedded* when the team's and the organization's structure and processes support and nurture their activities. Startup factors may be impacted by member embeddedness. For example, in teams with outsourced members, the work may be structured to reduce interdependencies and avoid strongly embedded links for the outsourced group members (Galup et al., 1997). Permanent team members work with the more ambiguous aspects of the assigned projects because of their embeddedness in organizational networks. They are more familiar with the organization and are better able to communicate with other organizational members.

Launch Stage Activities While the emphasis in the Launch Stage is on building the team's infrastructure, popular press writings on virtual teams proscribe formative stage activities of the team:

• *Determine the team's duration.* Purpose largely determines how long the team will exist. The duration can vary from very short term to long term. The virtual team, such as a process-improvement team, may even be established on a relatively permanent basis (Pape, 1997).

• *Conduct a team-orientation session.* A best practice for virtual teams is an initial face-to-face meeting that is attended by all members (Duarte & Snyder, 1999). If a face-to-face meeting is not possible, a relatively rich medium such as audio or videoconferencing should be used to orient the team to its task.

• *Introduce the team members.* Before starting on the work at hand, team members should introduce themselves, provide some personal background (Coutu, 1998), and indicate other projects on which they are working (Kiser, 1999). Duarte and Snyder (1999) recommend using Web pages to provide the information about each member: contact information; name of time zone; time zone differences in hours; work hours; availability on evenings, weekends, and holidays in the team member's country; and hardware and software tools and applications that the team member can access and use.

• *Training.* Virtual teams need training in a variety of areas. The most obvious area is training on new technologies. McGrath, Arrow, Gruenfeld, Hollingshead, and O'Connor (1993) found that the newness of a technology for a group rather than the newness of the group itself created the most burden for groups. Other training is needed in addition to technology training (Kiser, 1999). For example, global teams need training on diversity. And telecommuting research has found that telecommuting programs are most successful when managers and telecommuters know about the policies and characteristics of new telecommuting programs (Nilles, 1994). Training on how to work together in virtual teams may also be critical.

Research Issues Related to the Launch Stage   In contrast to the Startup Stage, the Launch Stage suggests a number of fruitful avenues for research. Two are related to the manner of structuring and choice of means. Based on the previous discussion, a number of questions emerge. See Table 3.1 for a summary of intriguing

TABLE 3.1   Important Research Issues Related to Launch Stage

Major Questions	Related Research	Comments/Caveats
Manner of Structuring		
Purpose • What initial performance strategies are most likely to be associated with effective virtual teams? • What is the most effective way for establishing agreement on and commitment to virtual team's purpose?	McGrath, 1991 Zigurs & Buckland, 1998 Locke, Shaw, Saari, & Latham, 1981	Certain task types may be more amenable to virtual environments. Establishing commitment to the team's purpose, as well as a team identity, will probably differ in colocated and virtual teams.
People • How do you go about selecting, recruiting, and training members for virtual teams? • How large should the team be? • What team member KSAs are necessary for effective virtual team performance? • How must organizational performance evaluation and compensation systems change to support virtual teams? • How do cultural differences affect the way virtual team members perform their tasks?	Hackman, 1983 Hackman & Morris, 1972 Kelly & Thibaut, 1978 McGrath, 1984 Davis, 1969 Stevens & Campion, 1994 Duarte & Snyder, 1999*	Much of colocated group research is guided by an analytic paradigm that presumes causal relations without adequately considering physical, temporal, or social context. Empirical foundation of group research is based on a limited range of types of small ad hoc groups under controlled experimental conditions that do not adequately represent naturally occurring groups. Is old theory appropriate for studying new phenomena?
Links • What norms should be developed for the effective functioning of virtual teams? • How do virtual teams distribute their tasks among the members? • Will differences in national or organizational culture affect the acceptance of norms in virtual teams? • What activities will be necessary to successfully implement virtual teams?	Hackman & Morris, 1972 Kelly & Thibaut, 1978 Davis, 1969 Jarvenpaa et al., 1998* Duarte & Snyder, 1999*	As noted above, group theory based on research to date has its limitations
Choice of Means • Which technology is most appropriate for which tasks? • What levels of technology support are needed for virtual team tasks? • How do organizational, functional, and national cultural differences affect the choice of technology?	Research on Group Support Systems and Computer-Mediated Communications: Daft & Lengel, 1984 Fulk & Boyd, 1991 Duarte & Snyder, 1999*	In this stage, choice means do not reflect the fact that use of media may be altered by the virtual team when it begins performing the tasks they are assigned to accomplish.

*Reference directly focuses on virtual teams.

questions, some research that may prove helpful in answering these questions, and caveats and comments about applying the research.

PERFORMANCE (HOW SHOULD VIRTUAL TEAMS BE MANAGED?)

In the Performance Stage, virtual team members work together to solve problems and achieve team objectives. While many factors impact the effective performance of virtual teams, this section focuses on those factors distinguishing virtual teams from more traditional ones. In particular, how do virtual teams use the technology, and how do members actually perform their tasks? Because rotating leadership appears to be a characteristic of many virtual teams studied to date, the managerial roles are specifically addressed. In essence, this section elaborates on how the infrastructure (technical, structural, and normative links) impacts performance. Whereas the Launch Stage focuses on structures, the Performance Stage focuses on processes. This section addresses changes that processes effect on team structures. It concludes with suggested research questions.

Use of Technology

Findings from Group Support Systems (GSS) and computer-mediated communications studies inform our understanding of performance in virtual teams. In their extensive review of the effect of task type on performance of GSS groups, Hollingshead and McGrath (1995) found that computer-supported groups tended to have more equal participation, achieve greater consensus, generate more solutions, create more conflict, and require more time to perform their assigned tasks than did face-to-face groups. They also found that computer-mediated communication technologies are more appropriate for certain problem-solving tasks than others. They found that GSS groups performed better, worse, and about the same as face-to-face groups across different task types. (See Table 3.2 for a summary of the findings reported by Hollingshead and McGrath [1995]). While a number of other researchers suggest the moderating role of task on group performance, only a few studies—e.g., Easton, George, Nunamaker, & Pendergast (1990); Finholt, Sproull, and Kiesler (1990); Hiltz, Johnson, & Turoff (1991); Hollingshead, McGrath, & O'-Connor (1993); McLeod & Liker (1992); Saunders & Miranda (1998); Straus & Mc-Grath (1994)—have attempted to study the differences in decision quality across two types of tasks.

Zigurs and Buckland (1998) offer a task-technology fit framework to help explain differences in findings about the effect of task type on decision quality. They suggest that GSS technology offers three types of support: (1) communication support from such features as simultaneous input, anonymity, public group display, and input feedback; (2) process structuring support from such features as agenda setting, agenda enforcement, facilitation, and a complete record of group interaction; and (3) information processing support, which derives from its ability to facilitate gathering, aggregating, evaluating, and structuring information. (These types of support are similar to the levels of support defined by DeSanctis and Gallupe [1987].) According to Zigurs and Buckland (1998), different types of tasks require different types of support, and GSS helps improve the quality of the decision when the type of support they offer matches the needs of the task. For instance, idea-generating

TABLE 3.2   Findings of Studies About Performance of GSS Compared to Face-to-Face Across Task Types

Outcome	More	No Difference	Less
Equality of participation (14)	10	4	
Satisfaction with process (13)	4	3	6
Satisfaction with outcomes (3)	1		2
Degree of consensus (6)	6		
Number of solutions (14)	13	1	
Level of conflict (3)	3		
Outcome	**Shorter**	**No Difference**	**Longer**
Task completion time (14)		1	13
Type of Task (Total Studies)	**Better Performance**	**No Difference**	**Worse Performance**
Idea generation (8)	4	4	
Intellective (8)	1	2	5
Decision making (7)	2	1	4
Negotiation (2)			2

Source: Adapted from Hollingshead and McGrath, 1995.

or brainstorming tasks require high levels of communication support only. On the other hand, many decision tasks characterized by multiple possible solutions but limited approaches to solution require high levels of process-structuring and information-processing support. Zigurs and Buckland (1998), as well as Lim and Benbasat (1995), note that most of the GSS research has involved GSS technology that provides primarily communication support. To date, information-processing support with GSS has been very limited.

What do these findings and the model tell us about how virtual teams will use the technology? The Zigurs and Buckland model and research on computer-mediated communication suggest that technology has features that are designed to promote various aspects of decision making, depending on task type. However, insights about the match between tasks and technology features provide only a partial answer for managers seeking to learn how to effectively harness the technology for their teams.

For the most part, the tasks used in these studies are not similar to those performed by virtual teams. The study tasks are relatively simple tasks suitable for lab experiments performed by students. Furthermore, GSS and computer-supported technologies seem best suited for brainstorming but are not at all suitable for conducting negotiations. Tasks used in these studies clearly do not reflect the complexity of tasks typically found in the business environment. Virtual teams are more likely to be asked to perform multiple tasks that are intertwined over time. That is, the team may be charged with generating solutions and then evaluating them to select the best one. The technology to support the team's work must respond to the various task components. At times, the communication component is especially critical. At other times, the team needs analytical tools and models to help it evaluate alternatives. Teams focused on knowledge work may need communication and collaborative tools to gather information and share it with group members. Teams may also need more support in the form of models and tools to perform analyses.

Appropriating the Technology

The Zigurs and Buckland model suggests how virtual teams can use various features of a technological tool, GSS, to solve problem-solving tasks. But what if virtual teams do not use the technology as it is intended to be used? DeSanctis and Poole (1994) propose adaptive structuration theory (AST), which suggests that a group may intentionally or unintentionally change the structural features of GSS as it uses them. The structural features of GSS or other advanced information technologies may be appropriated by a group in a consistent way that is reproduced in a similar form over time. The features of the technology, along with the task, the organizational environment, and the team's normative and structural links, act as opportunities and constraints in which appropriation occurs. AST suggests that advanced information technologies trigger adaptive structurational processes that over time lead to changes in rules and resources that organizations use in social interaction. Group members can either use the structural features as intended, use them in ways that are not intended, use only some of the features provided by the technology, use the technology in a fashion that is allowed by the team's or the organization's structure, or modify the team's or organization's structure in a way that allows the group to appropriate the technology in an agreed-upon manner.

During the Launch Stage, teams may establish norms about how the technology should be used to link the members and facilitate interactions among them. Over time, the technology may be adapted to better meet the team's needs. Team members may expand perceived channel capabilities as they learn how to better communicate with their teammates on certain topics or in certain contexts (Carlson and Zmud, 1999). Over time, normative and structural links may be refined by patterns of interactions.

The Social Construction of Meaning

AST helps us understand how virtual teams appropriate the technology provided in the technical links. It does not address how the groups use the technology in deriving meaning from information. Media richness theory and many other theories of media choice tend to focus on the objective attributes of media and information. However, Lee (1994) proposes that the perspective of information as an "objective" element in a social setting is constricting and suggests that meaning requires a subjective social interpretation. That is, meaning is constructed not individually but through social interactions. Markus (1994) also notes the importance of social construction in understanding media use. She suggests that social definitions about how a technology should be used tend to converge over time when social units interact or participate in a common culture.

Much of the work of virtual teams may involve sharing and exchanging information (Duarte & Snyder, 1999). This is often accomplished using electronic media, yet electronic media may actually inhibit information sharing. A number of researchers (i.e., Hightower & Sayeed, 1996; McLeod, 1997; Hollingshead, 1996) found that computer-supported groups were less efficient in their exchange of information than groups not using the technology. Relational links among team members was found to significantly contribute to the effectiveness of information exchange in virtual teams (Warkentin, Sayeed, & Hightower, 1997). A possible reason for these findings is that the computer-supported groups were constrained by the technology and unable to construct social meanings for the information. An implication would then be that virtual teams periodically need to schedule face-to-face meetings.

This implication must be taken with a grain of salt. Many information-sharing studies have been North American based. Other cultures may be willing to share information to a greater or lesser extent (Duarte & Snyder, 1999).

Structural Links—Managerial Roles

During the Performance Stage, the team structure that was laid out in the Launch Stage may change as the group performs its tasks. AST suggests that the manner in which the group uses its communication technology may affect and be affected by normative and structural links. One important structural link is managerial roles.

Jarvenpaa et al. (1998) found that the most successful global virtual teams were the ones with rotating leaders. Rotating leadership also may be characteristic of interorganizational teams. Because the members come from multiple organizations in these teams, it may be difficult to assign management roles based upon any one existing hierarchy. Since no preexisting hierarchy is available in some virtual organizations, the team may be empowered to select and change leadership to better respond to environmental events (Klimoski and Jones, 1998).

On the other hand, virtual teams rooted in more traditional organizational structures, such as virtual teams composed of telecommuters, may not experience rotating leaders. The managers may remain stable over the life of these virtual teams. In such programs, managers work with telecommuters to identify goals, provide timely feedback on their performance, and ensure an adequate level of support for telecommuters.

One motivation for adopting GSS and computer-mediated communications is that they help equalize participation and reduce status differences (e.g., Hiltz, Johnson, & Turoff, 1986; George, Easton, Nunamaker, & Northcraft, 1990; Siegel, Dubrovsky, Kiesler, & McGuire, 1986; Straus & McGrath, 1995; Zigurs, Poole, & DeSanctis, 1988). This may promote changing managerial roles as suggested by rotating leadership. Yet managerial roles may still persist in group environments supported by technology. First, there may be multiple status contexts within the group. Saunders, Robey, and Vaverek (1994) found that in a computer-conferencing group engaged in a master's of health administration program, the hierarchy of the teacher and students was supplanted over time by the hierarchy of doctor, nurse, and health administrator from which the program's students had migrated. Second, total anonymity within virtual teams is unlikely. Thus, multiple status differentials may exist and persist (Weisband, Schneider, & Connolly, 1995). Third, certain types of task may be more susceptible to status differentials. A stream of GSS work (e.g., Clapper, McLean, & Watson, 1991; Huang, Raman, & Wei, 1993; Tan, Raman, & Wei, 1994; Tan, Wei, & Watson, 1993; Tan, Wei, Watson, Clapper, & McLean, 1998) found that status effects were more pronounced in judgmental tasks characterized by differences in the values and preferences of group members than in intellective tasks where one right answer existed. Tan et al. (1998) further found that the impact of computer-mediated communications on majority influence was more pronounced in national cultures characterized by individualism.

Structural Links—Communication Roles

Important structural links in addition to status or leadership roles are communication roles. Over time, a structure may evolve due to patterns of communications. In theory, this structure may remain less stable in virtual teams than in more traditional teams that are protected by a formal chain of command. However, recent studies have found that patterns of communication may be fairly stable in virtual teams over time (Ajuha, Galletta, & Carley, 1998). In virtual teams, members may define their own information, providing or receiving roles by choosing the manner in which they use media to perform their tasks. The information about providing or receiving roles can be considered communication roles and can affect individual performance in virtual groups (Ajuha et al., 1998).

Other Structural Issues

In teams with rotating leaders, members' roles change as they assume leadership and then yield to other members. Members' roles evolve in other ways over time. In successful global virtual teams, the roles of individual team members emerged after individuals took the initiative to produce something on their own (Jarvenpaa et al., 1998). The temporary nature of many virtual teams encourages flexible, yet not totally independent, role arrangements.

Furthermore, virtual teams, unlike many traditional teams and nearly all teams that inhabit our experiments, are dynamic. Members come and go. This creates the need to constantly alter both the team's internal structure, as well as its normative links.

Normative Links

Research on networks offers insights about the normative links of virtual teams, including the benefits of both strong and weak ties. For example, Galup et al. (1997) suggest that virtual teams with outsourced workers are characterized by weak links to the extent that the outsourced workers do not have time to become embedded within organizational structures. They are not familiar with organizational meanings and symbols that have developed over time. Their more permanent counterparts on the virtual teams who are familiar with these meanings and symbols interacted with other organizational members in systems analysis and design and information systems projects where trust and associated strong ties were needed. On the other hand, weak ties made it possible for outsourced workers to transfer knowledge into the organization that has been gained through work in other organizations.

In addition to embedded ties, trust is an important aspect of normative links. While trust is important to any type of team, it is particularly important in preventing geographical distance from leading to psychological distance in a virtual team (Snow, Snell, & Davison, 1996). Trust is pivotal in most virtual teams because distance renders other forms of social control, such as direct supervision or similarity in backgrounds, inoperable. Since virtual teams, especially global virtual teams, tend to be relatively transitory, they are not based on the trust associated with embedded relationships in social networks. Instead, a "swift trust" is created to link the members in relationships that would benefit from networks typically characterized by strong ties.

Jarvenpaa et al. (1998) found that swift trust developed in the more successful virtual teams that they studied. *Swift trust* is a form of depersonalized action that allows team members to act as if trust were present from the start of the project. It enables members to take action and deal with the uncertainty, ambiguity, and vulnerablilty that arises while working on complex interdependent tasks with strangers. Rotating leaders, defining roles, and clearly establishing the team's purpose help provide the illusion of reduced vulnerability (Meyerson, Weick, & Kramer, 1996).

Virtual Teams and Time

The infrastructure is laid during the Launch Stage, but it evolves during the Performance Stage. While studies about virtual teams are cited, most citations are from research on more traditional teams. Understanding differences between virtual and traditional, face-to-face teams in the treatment of time may help to further integrate the pieces of past research.

Meyerson et al. (1996) argue that temporary teams rarely exhibit dysfunctional group dynamics, such as dealing with jealousy and hurt feelings, because they do not have enough time to do so. They must concentrate on the primary task, the production function. Jarvenpaa et al. (1998) found that the most successful virtual teams in their study used their time well and had few purely social exchanges.

Past research does not tend to consider the decision-making processes of groups over time. McGrath's (1984, 1991) TIP (time, interaction, performance) model and Walther's (1992, 1995) SIP (social information processing) theory are exceptions. Other exceptions are the work of Tan et al. and Saunders and Miranda. Tan et al. (1993) discuss possible effects of status influence on stages of decision making. Saunders and Miranda (1998) explore the impact of information access on decision making across judgmental and intellective tasks. They found that the patterns of information access differed for these two types of tasks. Groups making judgmental decisions accessed significantly more external information in the selection phase of decision making than did groups solving intellective tasks. GSS groups accessed significantly more information than traditional face-to-face groups, and when compared to the traditional groups, most of the DSS groups' information accesses were later in the decision-making process.

One promising research stream for virtual teams characterized by a limited life span, such as command-and-control and some production and professional decision-making teams, is Gersick's (1988, 1989) punctuated equilibrium model. This model suggests that the processes of a team may change shortly after the midpoint as teams structure themselves to meet group deadlines. Teams that start fast and develop solid plans may use the transition as a time to pause, analyze their work, actively debate, and make improvements. Teams that start more slowly, disagree more often, and engage in power struggles may pull together and focus on execution after they reach the midpoint (Duarte & Snyder, 1999). Citurs and Yoo (1999) found that after the project midpoint was reached, e-mail messages of virtual team members in an executive development program became more efficient as team members increasingly referred implicitly to knowledge and expertise held by other team members. In his study of computer-supported groups, Chidambaram (1996) found that while transitions occurred at the groups' midpoint, the stability before and after the midpoint that Gersick had predicted was not apparent.

Gersick's research (1988) found that group members cast the tone for their group in their first few message exchanges. This has clear implications for scheduling group activities in projects with specific deadlines. It also suggests that there may be a rotation of leadership as the team transitions from the first half into the second half of the project. Furthermore, the initial face-to-face meetings recommended by many for virtual groups may be especially important in helping them overcome the inertia associated with the group's first phase (Furst et al., 1999) and in helping them get to know one another (Duarte & Snyder, 1999).

Research Issues Related to the Performance Stage

To answer questions about how to manage virtual teams, this section has revealed a number of areas of potential study. The Zigurs and Buckland (1998; also see Duarte & Snyder, 1999) task-technology fit model may help determine the appropriate levels of information-processing, communication, and process-structuring support that is required for tasks assigned to virtual teams. But since the technology may not be used as managers may have intended when they established the technical infrastructure, research based on AST and the social construction of meaning may provide answers to questions such as those listed in Table 3.3.

TABLE 3.3   Important Research Issues Related to Performance Stage

Major Questions	Related Research	Comments/Caveats
Technical Links		
• What can be done to reduce the constraining effects of electronic communication media? • How can interactions among team members be structured to facilitate the social construction of meaning? • How can information sharing among group members be improved? • Can tasks be aggregated to improve the work flow in virtual teams? • Can the timing of team activities improve the performance of virtual teams? • Are certain technologies used more effectively at various points in the team's life cycle?	Hollingshead & McGrath, 1995 Zigurs & Buckland, 1998 DeSanctis & Poole, 1994 Duarte & Snyder, 1999*	Tasks in research are relatively simple rather than the complex tasks found in business environments. Most research was performed by student samples in ad hoc teams. In these teams, the membership was stable—quite dissimilar from the dynamic membership found in many virtual teams. Most information-sharing research has been performed in North America using hidden profile tasks.
Structural Links		
• Under which conditions should leadership be rotated in virtual teams? • How can virtual teams more successfully integrate new members?	Jarvenpaa et al., 1998* Duarte & Snyder, 1999*	In evaluating the impact of rotating leadership, the characteristics of the virtual team should be considered, as should the possibility of multiple leader roles.
Normative Links		
• How can teams that are formed on a very temporary basis create and sustain needed levels of trust? • How do norms develop in virtual teams? • How can norms be effectively reinforced or sanctioned in virtual teams?	Galup et al., 1997 Jarvenpaa et al., 1998* Meyerson, Weick, & Kramer, 1996 Gersick, 1988, 1989	

*Reference directly focuses on virtual teams.

DELIVERY (WHAT ARE THE INDICATORS OF EFFECTIVE VIRTUAL TEAMS?)

Perhaps the most quoted model of team development is Tuckman's (1965) forming, storming, norming, performing, and adjourning. The Delivery Stage is akin to Tuckman's adjourning. During this stage, the team's purpose is realized to some extent, and its defined end point is reached. The team's adjournment requires and deserves its own ritual in which the team's accomplishments are celebrated and the transition to new projects is begun (Duarte & Snyder, 1999). The transition should include the team leader's contacting local managers to express gratitude for each team member's participation in the virtual project. The work of virtual team members often goes unrecognized because their efforts are often neither included in formal evaluations of their performance nor directly observed by their managers or local co-workers. Team leaders can help ensure that the efforts of the team members are adequately recognized. They can also help the members find their next assignment. Ironically, rotating leaders may be the least likely to follow through on these adjournment activities with interorganizational and global teams—the teams that most need such member recognition.

According to McGrath (1991), group effort can result in production, member-support, and group well-being functions. Because virtual teams tend to form for specific reasons, production is likely to be their focal function. However, because of their relative uniqueness, virtual teams are probably heavily dependent upon the member-support and group well-being functions to cement the team relationships, facilitate the accomplishment of the team's assigned tasks, and strengthen the networks of relationships among the members that enable them to work together in the future. That is, well-being or member-support outcomes of one virtual team project may serve as the antecedents, or cornerstones, for future virtual team projects.

Production Function

The team's products or services must meet standards of quality, quantity, and timeliness of those who receive, review, and/or use them (Hackman, 1983). Much GSS research has dealt only with the production function of circumplex tasks (McGrath, 1991). Future research on virtual teams must assess quality, quantity, and timeliness on a full range of tasks.

Well-Being Function

The well-being function describes "activities that have to do with development and maintenance of the group as a system" (McGrath, 1991, 156). It reflects relations among group members. Critical outcomes related to this function include learning and conflict resolution.

Learning   "Learning" in virtual teams can benefit the organization in three ways: (1) over time, team members can learn to work more efficiently with one another; (2) virtual teams allow their members to expand their social networks within the organization; and (3) the work methods of the team can become part of the organization's knowledge repository or "organizational memory" (Furst et al., 1999). The team's history and progress should be documented, stored, possibly in distributed databases, and exchanged. For instance, at NORTEL, project folders that contain information about requirements, testing, schedules, costs, and customer reactions are maintained by team members (Duarte & Snyder, 1999). The "organizational memory" can be especially helpful in teams with fluid membership by quickly bringing new members up to speed, as well as assisting future teams in performing similar tasks.

When a group is embedded in the organization, strong ties may help spread the learning as new groups are formed from members of the network. However, weak ties may also promote organizational learning. An example is outsourcing expertise that is not available within the organization. The outsourced workers can help train organizational members in skills and knowledge acquired in other organizations.

Conflict Resolution   Conflict resolution may be critical to all three functions in subsequent virtual teams. It applies to the member-support function to the extent that a group can more successfully develop and thrive if it is relatively free of dysfunctional conflict at its startup. Table 3.2 suggests that the results of past studies about the level of conflict surfacing in GSS groups indicate that conflict tends to be greater than in traditional face-to-face groups. Over time, however, the ability of GSS groups to manage conflict may improve (Miranda, 1991). Similarly, virtual teams relying heavily upon computer-mediated communications may experience initial conflict as differences in opinions and values surface and as the medium constrains its resolution. Strategies learned previously in other virtual teams may be applied to successfully resolving conflict. Furthermore, when team members renew their working relationships in new virtual teams, an environment free of dysfunctional conflict from previous interactions can help promote trust and lead to the development of more effective initial strategies.

Member-Support Function

The member-support function describes "activities that have to do with the ways in which the individual is embedded within the group as a system" (McGrath, 1991, 156–157). It reflects relations between individual members and the group. Member-support outcomes addressed earlier in this chapter include member satisfaction with group processes and outcomes, trust, and norms.

Member Satisfaction   Satisfaction is a desirable outcome at the individual member level that may also have positive organizational consequences. As noted in Table 3.2, findings about the positive impacts of computer-mediated and GSS groups on satisfaction in the studies reviewed by Hollingshead and McGrath (1995) are mixed. This pattern can also be found in subsequent studies. Many of these studies use ad hoc groups over short periods of time. Walther's SIP theory suggests that satisfaction of group members using computer-mediated communications will increase and become similar to that found in face-to-face groups. This relationship was supported in the research of Chidambaram (1996).

Trust   Swift trust may be necessary in virtual teams in which members have only a short time to complete the team's task. Once a team member has demonstrated competence, integrity, and concern for other team members, the other members may develop trust in him or her (Duarte & Snyder, 1999). While the development of trust has important implications for the Performance Stage, it also may be an outcome in the Delivery Stage. Trust realized during the Delivery Stage of a project can carry over to future virtual teams with overlapping memberships.

Norms   The development of norms may be expedited in virtual teams. However, a number of challenges may inhibit norm development: Virtual team members may not be able to observe those behaviors used to establish informal rules or norms (Finholt & Sproull, 1990), or team behaviors acceptable in one culture may not be viewed as such in another culture (Furst et al., 1999). Once a team develops norms, team members may carry them over to future virtual teams. Norms may facilitate the team's work and ease the entry of new members into future virtual teams.

Research Issues Related to the Delivery Stage

Factors in the Launch and Performance Stages probably affect outcomes in the Delivery Stage. The infrastructure that is established in the Launch Stage and that evolves during the Performance Stage may impact the efficient and effective performance of the team. A number of questions emerge (see Table 3.4).

In future research, it will be important to assess the value added by virtual teams. In so doing, it may be easier to measure the specific products and services

TABLE 3.4   Important Research Issues Related to Delivery Stage

Major Questions	Related Research	Comments/Caveats
Production Function		
• To what extent does task/ technology fit lead to improved outcome quality? • Do heightened levels of trust result in improved outcome quality? • How do team members' KSAs impact the quality and quantity of the team's products?	Stevens & Campion, 1994 Zigurs & Buckland, 1998 Duarte & Snyder, 1999*	Outcomes in this and the other functions are probably impacted by factors in the preceding stages. Future research needs to be expanded beyond McGrath's task circumplex.
Well-Being Function		
• Do heightened levels of trust result in improved team member satisfaction? • How can learning be transferred most effectively to future teams? • Is task completion as satisfying in virtual environments as in more traditional ones? • How must organizational performance evaluation and compensation systems change to support virtual teams? • How do cultural differences affect the way virtual team members perform their tasks?	Jarvenpaa et al., 1998* Meyerson, et al., 1996 Duarte & Snyder, 1999* Furst et al., 1999*	The value added by virtual teams must be assessed across the outcomes of the production, well-being, and member-support functions.
Member-Support Function		
• How can norms impact the performance of future virtual teams? • How do norms affect the productivity of virtual teams?	Furst et al., 1999*	Valid and reliable measurements of outcomes of the member-support function of virtual teams are limited.

*Reference directly focuses on virtual teams.

produced by the teams than to assess the by-products related to member-support and well-being functions.

Furst et al. (1999) also question whether task completion will be as satisfying and fulfilling in the virtual environment as in more traditional ones. Organizations need to deal with virtual team successes and failures. Furst et al. (1999, 6) wonder "how do you dump Gatorade on virtual team leaders/members in virtual environments? . . . Throw a sympathetic arm around a virtual team member's shoulder after a virtual team's failure?"

CONCLUSION

To date, much of the literature on virtual teams is prescriptive in nature. Most of these prescriptions have not been drawn from a theoretical base, and little empirical work has been performed to test their validity. This may be because the virtual team phenomenon is new or because managers and academicians do not yet appreciate that working on virtual teams may require approaches different from those used with more traditional teams (Furst et al., 1999).

Many previous writings on virtual teams have focused on reasons for their adoption and applications for which they have been used. Most prescriptions have focused on one dimension and fail to recognize the intertwined issues related to leadership, technology, member selection, and so forth. To my knowledge, no work has yet assessed the risks in using virtual teams, nor is there a theoretically supported framework for identifying those environments that promote and inhibit effective virtual teams.

My analysis of the puzzle pieces leads me to believe that the work on virtual teams is like an old jigsaw puzzle from the attic. Most puzzle pieces from group research probably belong in the box. Yet there are enough differences between virtual and traditional teams that some of the pieces with findings from traditional groups really belong in the box of another puzzle. And a number of missing pieces need to be found to fill in the portions of the puzzle about virtual team leadership, culture, and task-technology fit. This chapter seeks to lay out the available puzzle pieces for you. In the process, it suggests some areas in which virtual teams may differ from more traditional ones, provides a framework to explore what we know about virtual teams, and suggests strategies for filling the gaps.

ENDNOTES

1. The chapter by George on software development discusses five reasons for the use of global teams.
2. See the chapter by Lacity and Willcocks on outsourcing for a discussion of outsourcing vendors needing to hire subcontractors. This chapter also notes that most customer IT employees agree to transfer to the outsourcing vendor.
3. The chapter by Ang and Slaughter on IT personnel discusses the challenges of managing global diversity in global software teams.
4. The chapter by Ang and Slaughter on IT personnel notes that project leaders may assume roles previously performed by subordinates when their subordinates are transplanted to outsourcing vendor companies. The managers may need to learn to manage their previous subordinates as vendors.

Organizational Consequences of Information Technology: Dealing with Diversity in Empirical Research

Daniel Robey and Marie-Claude Boudreau

This chapter addresses one of the oldest, most interesting, and most important topics in the management of information technology (IT): its organizational consequences. It is an old topic because it has been present since the 1950s, when IT was first applied commercially to the management of organizations. Like many information systems (IS) research areas, serious academic inquiry into the organizational consequences of IT was stimulated by practitioner concerns expressed well in advance of IS's establishment as an academic discipline. Leavitt and Whisler's (1958) *Harvard Business Review* article is usually cited as the origination point of inquiry. As IS research became established in the 1980s, IT's organizational impact was identified as a primary subfield (Culnan, 1986). Today, speculations and research about IT's impacts on organizations continue to fill the pages of both practitioner and academic publications.

The study of IT's organizational consequences is both interesting and important. Much of its interest stems from the steady introduction of new IT with new capabilities.[1] Like so many topics in IS, interest is renewed as technologies change. Research findings from a few years earlier often lack relevance because IT changes so fast. Nonetheless, good academic research produces durable lessons that may not depend on particular technologies. Drawing ideas from past research and applying them to emerging technologies is risky unless such research is based on theories that remain relevant across broad classes of technologies. This chapter focuses on the fundamental theoretical choices that can be used to guide research on the organizational consequences of IT. Research on IT's organizational consequences continues to be important because organizations have clearly become dependent upon IT. Effective IT applications may enable radical and innovative organizational designs that carry the potential for enormous economic and social advantage. The potential of IT to transform organizations rather than to simply automate or improve their business processes underlies the continuing value of studying IT and its organizational consequences at multiple levels of social analysis (i.e., individuals, groups, and organizations) (Klein, Dansereau, & Hall, 1994).

Traditional thinking about IT's organizational consequences has conformed to the framework illustrated in Figure 4.1. On the left-hand side of the figure are the variables or factors presumed to cause changes in organizations. The most significant of these is IT, but it is rare that researchers claim IT to be the only variable accounting for organizational changes. Rather, numerous other factors such as managerial goals, organizational size, and environmental demands are frequently mentioned. Together, these factors interact to produce consequences in the organization. For example, research may attempt to show how competitive environments increase pressures on managers, who then adopt IT to make their organizations more effective. While IT is partly responsible for organizational changes such as downsizing or reengineering of business processes, managers and competitive pressures are factors that help to explain why IT was employed to produce change.

On the right-hand side of Figure 4.1, organizational consequences at several levels of analysis are listed. At the level of the individual, changes include the scope of peoples' jobs, the amount of decision latitude they enjoy, and the location of their work. For example, some workers may become "telecommuters" by using IT from their homes to connect with co-workers, customers, and databases. At the group level, IT may affect the communication practices of workers, the incentives to which team members are subject, and the degree of spatial dispersion among group members. For example, "virtual teams" that include workers from widely dispersed locations may be formed.[2] Organizational structures may also be affected by IT, which is often associated with a flattening of hierarchy and radical reengineering of core business processes. Finally, at the interorganizational level of analysis, IT may be associated with the formation of "seamless" alliances and partnerships with other organizations in a firm's supply and distribution chains, including customers.[3]

FIGURE 4.1 Traditional Framework for Research on the Organizational Consequences of IT

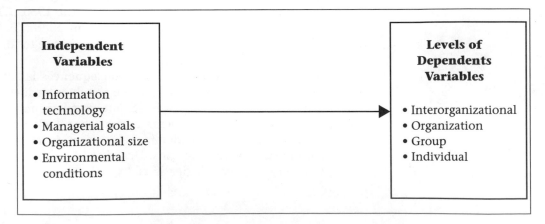

The groups of independent variables on the left and dependent variables on the right are meant to be representative rather than exhaustive. Each independent variable may also include a large number of specific characteristics, which may have different influences or effects on the organizational outcomes. This is especially true of IT, which has proven notoriously difficult to conceptualize as a variable for research purposes. The dependent variables in the framework are likewise multidimensional.

Research studies on the organizational consequences of IT do not always follow the logic spelled out in this framework, but the causal relationships described by the model have guided a large amount of empirical work over the past 40 years. Significant theoretical work has also conformed to the basic logic of Figure 4.1. For example, Huber (1990) presented a theory of the impacts of advanced IT on organizational design, intelligence, and decision making in which IT plays the clear role of independent variable. The theory spells out a number of intervening variables between IT and organizational change, but the basic logic agrees with a causal relationship between IT as independent variable and organizational change as dependent variable.

DIVERSITY OF EMPIRICAL FINDINGS

With such a long-established tradition and consensus of thinking, one might expect that a consistent body of findings about IT's organizational impacts would have accumulated over the years. This is definitely not the case. Research studies in which theoretical expectations were confirmed represent only one class of research outcome, and it is hardly the most common. More frequently, IT's impacts on organizations are unpredictable and often resist even post hoc explanation. In this section, we describe the diversity of findings. In addition to the case of impacts occurring as predicted, we consider a variety of cases in which IT has had unexpected consequences. In some cases, it is the implementation of IT per se that produces problems. In other cases, although the technology is successfully implemented, the expected organizational consequences are absent. In yet other cases, IT is resisted or adapted to uses other than those for which it was designed. The literature also reveals contradictory organizational consequences of IT across and within studies. Each of these categories is discussed in following sections along with references to studies representative of the class. Although the categories are not necessarily mutually exclusive, they help to demonstrate the diversity of research outcomes in this topic area and motivate our proposal for a revised framework that may guide future inquiry on this topic.

IT HAS EXPECTED ORGANIZATIONAL CONSEQUENCES

IT has indeed sometimes been reported as being not only successfully implemented but also associated with organizational outcomes that researchers anticipate. For instance, in their study of 91 users of executive information systems in 22 organizations, Leidner and Elam (1995, 659) "found support for the propositions put forth by Huber (1990) that the use of decision support technologies can lead to improved organizational intelligence and decision making outcomes." They also extended Huber's theory by proposing two new constructs: greater analysis in decision making and enhanced user mental models. Robey (1974, 1976) also supported hypotheses that were drawn from a theory of task design pertaining to the effect of computers on decision tasks. The degree of satisfaction in manual and computer-supported decision tasks differed in accordance with the predictions of the theory. In sum, the literature on IT and organizational change does reveal accounts of studies in which expected outcomes actually occurred. That is, business is conducted more efficiently, users are more productive, business units are more flexible, organizational members are more satisfied, and so on. One might expect studies with predicted outcomes to be a more frequent occurrence, but the studies cited in the following categories show that unexpected research results occur frequently.

IT IS NOT SUCCESSFULLY IMPLEMENTED

One reason why IT may not produce expected consequences is that it is not successfully implemented. Therefore, IT is unavailable to the organization and logically cannot produce organizational outcomes. Although this category may seem trivial and irrelevant, researchers have shown that IT implementation projects frequently go astray. In 1995, U.S. companies canceled 31% of their new IT projects before completion, for an estimated combined cost of $81 billion (Ewusi-Mensah, 1997; Johnson, 1995). An example of such debacle was documented by Drummond (1996) in her account of the events leading up to the collapse of the Taurus project, an expensive long-term project designed to replace antiquated settlement procedures on the London Stock Exchange. Myers (1994) discussed a comparable disaster in his interpretive account of the abandonment of a centralized payroll system in the New Zealand Education Department in 1989.[4]

Even when IT projects are completed and IT is installed, organizational members may resist using the system. For instance, the implementation of the French Railways' computerized reservation system, described by Mitev (1996), was vigorously opposed by trade unions, employees, and customers. Thus, even when a technological implementation is successful, the use of a system may not necessarily follow, thereby jeopardizing the chance to observe expected organizational consequences. Studies of failed and incomplete implementation are rarely mentioned when discussing the organizational impacts of IT, but they can be considered as instances of unexpected impacts.

THE ORGANIZATIONAL CONSEQUENCES OF IT ARE ABSENT OR OPPOSITE TO PREDICTIONS

Some studies have revealed that the expected organizational consequences of IT were noticeably absent, even though IT was successfully implemented and used. For example, Bjørn-Andersen, Eason, and Robey (1986) expected structural changes to result from the implementation of IT in eight organizations. However, they found such changes in only three of the eight organizations. Likewise, Franz, Robey, and Koeblitz (1986) found insignificant effects of a system implemented to support a hospital's nursing stations. Vandenbosch and Ginzberg (1996–97) reported no increase in collaboration after implementation of Lotus Notes, an IT application designed to increase collaboration. Studies that report insignificant effects of IT are often rejected from academic journals because their results do not confirm hypothesized relationships, so it is difficult to estimate how many such studies have been conducted. When adequate care goes into the design of research and the analysis of its results, insignificant effects of IT should be accepted as divergent from the expectations of conventional theory.

In some cases, the hypothesized organizational consequences of IT are found to be insignificant, and the opposite outcomes are instead supported. In Klatzky's (1970) study on the decentralization of decision making, for example, automation was found to have a strong positive effect on decentralization, whereas size had a weak negative effect. Such relationships were exactly the opposite ones that the author expected. Likewise, Blau, Falbe, McKinley, and Tracy (1976, 32) found a negative association between computing and span of control, which contradicted the prediction that "computer use will reduce subordinate-supervisor ratios throughout the administrative hierarchy." More often than the case with insignificant results, opposite findings stimulate radical revision of theory.

IT IS REINVENTED

IT is reinvented when it is used in a way other than intended. Users may have appropriated IT to serve goals of their own rather than those of the organization. For example, Kraut, Dumais, and Koch (1989) studied the implementation of a computerized record system in which one of the organizational goals was to increase efficiency by removing opportunities for social interaction. Ironically, although workers were relatively more isolated than before, they ingeniously created a clandestine note-passing process because no electronic messaging feature had been intended. By leaving notes in a field of the database record intended for customer comments, users communicated with each other through their use of the system instead of talking to each other face-to-face. By reinventing the customer database to become an electronic mail system, these users enacted unexpected organizational consequences of IT. Another example is Markus' (1994a) study of electronic mail use, in which organizational members compulsively stored and organized messages to produce a trail of documentation to justify their decisions. Although the use of e-mail did increase productivity by supporting rich communication (see Markus, 1994b), ironically it also slowed the speed of communication.

Studies of reinvention pose a serious challenge to the straightforward thinking embodied in the framework in Figure 4.1. Because users exercise their own subtle control over the use of IT, they may alter the presumed logical relationship between IT and organizational outcomes. In essence, they control what happens after IT is implemented, potentially reversing managerial objectives that guided its design and implementation.

THE ORGANIZATIONAL CONSEQUENCES OF IT ARE INCONSISTENT ACROSS STUDIES

Reviews of the literature chronicle the inconsistent organizational consequences of IT across studies (Ang & Pavri, 1994; Attewell & Rule, 1984; Baskerville & Smithson, 1995; Fulk & DeSanctis, 1995; Robey, 1977; Robey & Boudreau, 1999). While conventional thinking expects widespread transformations of organizations at multiple levels, the emergence of new organizational forms has not been consistently documented in the research literature. Fulk and DeSanctis (1995) characterized the rate of progression by most organizations toward new forms as gradual, although dramatic changes have been celebrated in some and no changes have occurred in others. Indeed, inconsistent findings seem more characteristic of the research than central tendencies or clear trends. Over the years, researchers have associated IT with polarized outcomes: empowered employees (Attewell & Rule, 1984) and oppressed employees (Nelson, 1990; Whisler, 1970); extended hierarchy (Blau et al., 1976) and reduced hierarchy (Crowston, Malone, & Lin, 1987); rigidity (Whisler, 1970) and flexibility (Foster & Flynn, 1984); and increases in staff and radical downsizing (Brynjolfsson, Malone, Gurbaxani, & Kambil, 1994; Pinsonneault & Kraemer, 1997). Thus, it appears that hardly any of the organizational outcomes identified in Figure 4.1 have been consistently associated with the implementation of IT. The search for orderly relationships between IT and organizational change remains elusive (Fulk & DeSanctis, 1995).

THE ORGANIZATIONAL CONSEQUENCES OF THE SAME IT DIFFER IN COMPARABLE SETTINGS

Some studies reveal diverse organizational consequences from the implementation of the same IT application in comparable settings. For example, Barley's (1986) study of computerized tomography showed different effects on social roles in two hospitals; Robey and Sahay (1996) found distinctly different organizational consequences from the implementation of the same geographic information system in two organizations; and Orlikowski (1993) showed that CASE tools produced different degrees of change in adopting organizations. Studies of communication technologies have also shown how identical technologies are appropriated differently by different groups (DeSanctis & Poole, 1994), organizations (Zack & McKenney, 1995), and cultures (Carlson, Kahn, & Rowe, 1999). Clearly, the divergent outcomes in these studies cannot logically be attributed to IT characteristics, which are common across the different settings. Rather, outcomes diverge because IT is implemented in different social contexts and through different social processes.

THE ORGANIZATIONAL CONSEQUENCES OF IT DIFFER WITHIN ORGANIZATIONS

Finally, studies may reveal contradictory consequences of a single IT implemented in a single organization. For example, Burkhardt and Brass (1990) found that the introduction of an information system affected the distribution of power among users, making some more central in their networks and therefore more influential than others. While these results are not surprising, they are contrary to the common expectation that IT equalizes social power by distributing information more widely. Not only may IT affect different groups in different ways but also groups may manifest divergent interpretations of the same IT, depending on their organizational vantage points. For example, Orlikowski and Gash (1994) observed divergent interpretations of Lotus Notes among managers and technologists in a single firm. Karsten (1995) reported similar divergence in the understanding and the use of the same technology in a different firm. In Larsen and Myers' (1997) case study, the implementation of an enterprise resource planning (ERP) package revealed different outcomes when diverse organizational groups were taken into account. When the analysis focused on consultants, the ERP project was viewed as being successful. However, when the analysis focused on users, the ERP implementation was viewed as unsatisfactory. Differences in the social meanings ascribed to IT may clearly affect the way that IT is implemented and used, in turn affecting IT's organizational consequences (Sahay & Robey, 1996).

Studies of IT implemented in a single organization also reveal logical contradictions such as paradoxes, double binds, and ironies (Robey & Boudreau, 1999). For example, Star and Ruhleder (1996) studied a community of scientists who were provided an electronic infrastructure to support their communication with remote laboratories. Scientists experienced a double bind because the electronic infrastructure was useful for communication between labs, but it threatened the preservation of credit for making scientific discoveries. The system produced a disincentive for scientists to use it for sharing preliminary results, which were withheld pending publication in prestigious journals and newsletters. Orlikowski (1991) also detected irony in the use of CASE tools by systems consultants, whose actions were more restricted in their own use of IT while creating purportedly innovative solutions for their clients. Other recent studies (Bjørn-Andersen & Turner, 1998; Dickson, DeSanctis, Poole, & Jackson, 1997; Manning, 1996; Wilson, 1996) have reported similar contradictions.

DEALING WITH DIVERSITY

How can scholars of IT make sense of the diverse outcomes of research on the organizational consequences of IT? Although our classification scheme may appear to some as an indictment of IS research for producing total confusion, diverse findings characterize many fields within the social sciences. The traditional approach to resolving inconsistencies both among and within research studies is to critique the research methodologies used and to recommend improvements. We briefly describe this approach here, but our primary purpose is to recommend the use of different theoretical tools for guiding research on IT's organizational consequences. Ideally, scholars should combine their pursuit of interesting new theoretical approaches with rigor in the conduct of their research.

One of the most common conventional prescriptions for resolving inconsistencies in any research is to include additional "contingency" variables. For example, Pinsonneault and Kraemer (1997) resolved contradictory past research on the effects of IT on the size of middle management by including the degree of centralization as the contingency variable. They found that IT was associated with reduced middle management size in centralized organizations, whereas middle management size increased in decentralized organizations. Reviewers often identify overlooked contingency variables by sorting available research into groups with similar findings and by searching for potential (but unmeasured) similarities among the research sites or samples (Attewell & Rule, 1984; Nelson, 1990; Robey, 1977). This strategy potentially resolves future inconsistencies by including neglected variables and interaction effects that may account for greater variance in observed impacts of IT.

A second strategy to improve the methodological component of research is to rule out studies that use flawed research methods. Several articles in the IS literature have addressed methodological issues such as research design (Fulk & DeSanctis, 1995; Jarvenpaa, Dickson, & DeSanctis, 1985), construct measurement (Straub, 1989), and statistical power (Baroudi & Orlikowski, 1989). These articles have assessed research practices across the whole spectrum of IS research, and their recommendations also apply to research on the organizational consequences of IT. The hope is that a collection of unflawed studies will manifest greater consistency, thereby producing findings of general value about the organizational consequences of IT.

A third strategy is to conduct better reviews on substantive research questions and specific technologies. This approach rests on the belief that consistent findings may be discernible if sufficient care is taken to catalog and review studies that have addressed the same issue. IS research has depended primarily upon narrative reviews in which the author sometimes advocates a favored theoretical solution as the key to resolving conflicting findings. One means for overcoming editorial slants in narrative reviews is to conduct formal meta-analyses (Alavi & Joachimsthaler, 1992; Schaubroeck & Muralidhar, 1991). However, relatively few meta-analyses have been conducted in IS research because an insufficient number of comparable studies have addressed any single research question or focused on the same technology. Because the IT applications being studied constantly change, it is difficult to generate enough studies whose results can be treated as input data to a meta-analysis.

Making sense of the unexpected consequences of IT through methodological refinement may be quite helpful, but it is not the only avenue available to researchers. Indeed, methodological improvements offer no guarantee that diversity will be reduced and that convergence will increase. Unanticipated consequences have been observed even when a sound methodological approach was used. In the following section, we offer a revised framework for pursuing research on the organizational consequences of IT. The framework incorporates three approaches for rethinking the theoretical link between IT and organizations: the use of process theory, the employment of different theoretical logic, and the adoption of a multilevel perspective.

A REVISED FRAMEWORK: NEW THEORETICAL PERSPECTIVES

Figure 4.2 radically revises the framework offered earlier in this chapter by replacing the causal relationships between independent and dependent variables with a process model that includes a variety of explanations for change and multiple levels of analysis. This section explains how these revisions may serve as a more productive guide to research on IT's organizational consequences.

FIGURE 4.2   Revised Framework

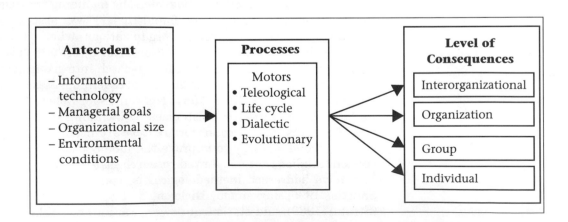

PROCESS THEORY

Studies about organizational change have typically concentrated on two questions: *What* are the antecedents and consequences of changes? *How* does organizational change emerge, develop, grow, or terminate over time (Van de Ven & Huber, 1990)? The first question is the primary focus of traditional "variance" theories (Markus & Robey, 1988) about the organizational consequences of IT. Figure 4.1 represents a conventional variance approach that seeks to associate IT as an independent variable with the dependent variable of organizational "impacts." Conversely, the second question posed by Van de Ven and Huber focuses on the antecedents and complex social processes through which IT produces organizational consequences. Such "process" theory allows one to understand better what actually happens between the antecedents and consequences of change, that is, how change occurs. A process approach to research differs from, but may complement, a variance approach (Mohr, 1982; Sabherwal & Robey, 1995). Process theories can be "valuable aids in understanding issues pertaining to designing and implementing information systems, assessing their impacts, and anticipating and managing the processes of change associated with them" (Kaplan, 1991, 593).

Sabherwal and Robey (1993) distinguished three broad groups of process research. First, some process models broadly characterize processes by defining their essential nature. For example, one model of implementation might be considered top down in contrast to another model that might be considered bottom up. Without describing specific events or stages of change, such models provide little more than labels that capture complex processes. Second, process research may use models that specify a series of a priori stages or phases. For example, the system development life cycle (SDLC) is a model that portrays system building as a sequence of stages such as the following: feasibility study, requirements determination, analysis and design, development, implementation, and maintenance. Such a model typically portrays only one possible progression of stages through which all instances of a process are expected to pass. Because the prescription of a single path is often hard to justify, many stage models map to generic sequences of activities that many processes can fit.[5]

The third group of process research identified by Sabherwal and Robey (1993) emphasizes the value of empirically examining sequences of events that occur over a phenomenon's history. More specifically, under this type of process research, the focus of the researcher must be on sequencing incidents and activities that lead to a particular outcome of interest. As a result, a process theory of this type should consist of statements that explain how and why a process unfolds over time (Van de Ven, 1992). This approach has shown to be very suitable for studying organizational change, particularly when information systems and technologies are involved (e.g., Markus & Robey, 1988; Kaplan, 1991). As exemplified in Robey and Newman's (1996) research, this type of process research allows one to account for both successful and unsuccessful organizational changes.

Process research may be conducted by using longitudinal research methods wherein data are collected as events occur or by using archival data sources (Orlikowski & Yates, 1994). In the case of large samples, the effects of logically opposed variables may be examined across time using econometric models (Brynjolfsson et al., 1994) or by conducting event-sequence analysis to detect recurring sequences of events that predict outcomes of interest in a large sample (Sabherwal & Robey, 1993). Process research techniques support theoretical reasoning used to explain change, and their relevance to research on the organizational consequences of IT has been demonstrated in several studies (e.g., Orlikowski, 1996; Orlikowski, Yates, Okamura, & Fiyimoto, 1995; Sahay & Robey, 1996). The process approach is thus an important component of the revised research framework.

ALTERNATIVE THEORETICAL LOGIC

The original framework in Figure 4.1 suggests a predominant deterministic logic that portrays IT as an agent capable of transforming organizations directly. Such logic has been frequently criticized as inadequate to describe the organizational consequences of IT (DeSanctis & Poole, 1994; Hirschheim, 1985; Kling, 1980; Markus & Robey, 1988; Mowshowitz, 1981; Orlikowski & Robey, 1991; Walsham, 1993). These authors have argued for a more complex relationship between IT and organizations, including concepts such as emergent and reciprocal causality. These critiques call for an alternative to deterministic logic that may guide empirical research more effectively and account more accurately for the diversity of empirical findings in the field. Van de Ven and Poole (1995) identified four alternative logics embedded within process theories about organizational change. They called these logics of change "motors" to denote their theoretical role as mechanisms driving change. The four motors are life cycle, teleology, evolution, and dialectics. Each of these four motors represents fundamentally different ways to explain how change unfolds.

A *life cycle* motor adopts the metaphor of organic growth to explain the development of an entity from its initiation to its termination. According to this theory of change, "the developing entity has within it an underlying form, logic, program, or code that regulates the process of change and moves the entity from a given point of departure toward a subsequent end that is prefigured in the present state" (Van de Ven & Poole, 1995, 515). An example of a life cycle theory applied to the field of IS is Nolan's stage model (Gibson & Nolan, 1974; Nolan, 1979), which pertains to the development of an IS department based on a progression through specific stages.

A *teleological* motor relies on the philosophical doctrine that a goal guides the change of an entity. This approach to change assumes that an organizational entity is purposeful and adaptive; that is, it "constructs an envisioned end state, takes action to reach it, and monitors the progress" (Van de Ven & Poole, 1995, 516). In IS research, a teleological theory has been applied to the implementation of information systems in health care (Paré & Elam, 1997).

An *evolutionary* motor of change refers to "cumulative changes in structural forms of populations of entities, [which occur] through a continuous cycle of variation, selection, and retention" (Van de Ven & Poole, 1995, 518). Whereas variation refers to the creation of novel entities, selection occurs through the competition of these entities for scarce resources, and retention involves forces that perpetuate the entities' existence. Within the IS field, an evolutionary perspective has been used to explain the differential impact of IT across industries (Segars & Grover, 1995).

Finally, in the *dialectic* motor of change, emphasis is on a "pluralistic world of colliding events, forces, or contradictory values that compete with each other, for domination or control" (Van de Ven & Poole, 1995, 517). From a dialectic perspective, the interplay between two or more opposing entities produces organizational change and eventually leads to the emergence of a new organizational form. Dialectical reasoning was the conceptual basis for Robey and Boudreau's (1999) explanation of the organizational consequences of IT. They argued that dialectical "logic of opposition" may explain a wider range of organizational outcomes.

Each of these alternative logics has the potential to explain divergent organizational outcomes of IT. The deterministic logic, represented by the variance framework in Figure 4.1, seems better equipped to account for orderly relationships among variables. Given the wide range of organizational antecedents, processes, and consequences surrounding the implementation of IT, researchers are advised to consider alternative logics to explain how change occurs (Boudreau & Robey, in press).

A MULTILEVEL PERSPECTIVE

As the framework in Figure 4.1 suggests, organizational change is usually viewed at a specific level of analysis. In most cases, organizational researchers prefer to adopt one level at a time. Nevertheless, considering multiple levels simultaneously may offer particular advantages. Although such a multilevel perspective is more complex and difficult to use (Barley, 1990), it may prove to be more useful in research on IT and organizational change because it does not oversimplify organizational phenomena (Klein et al., 1994; Markus & Robey, 1988; Rousseau, 1985).

The interplay of multiple levels of analysis has been the interest of both practitioners and researchers. Among the practitioners, Rashford and Coghlan (1994) have proposed an approach to understand the dynamic interrelationships between four organizational levels: the individual level, the team or group level, the interdepartmental level, and the organizational level. The four levels are interconnected so that each level may affect each of the others. Rashford and Coghlan's analysis of concepts such as their "domino effect" demonstrates little appreciation for the complexity of multilevel theories, but it does reveal an appreciation for interactions among individuals, teams, departments, and organizations as interrelated units of analysis.

The academic research community has developed useful guidelines for studying organizational change at multiple, interrelated levels of analysis. Building on Rousseau's seminal (1985) work, Klein et al. (1994) clarified many of the issues related to organizational research at multiple levels of analysis. More specifically, they explored different types of multilevel models, shedding light on how organizational change at different levels of analysis may be considered together. In the field of IS, Orlikowski (1993) used a multilevel perspective by showing how the antecedents, processes, and consequences of CASE tool adoption and use were influenced by three levels of institutional context: environmental, organizational, and IS context. Her analysis explains the diversity of outcomes between two organizations adopting comparable CASE tools. Outside the field of IS, a multilevel perspective was employed in Fox-Wolfgramm, Boal, and Hunt's (1998) study of the interplay between institutional, organizational, and strategic levels in the banking industry. Also illustrative of a multilevel approach is Bacharach, Bamberger, and Sonnenstuhl's (1996) study of the interplay between the institutional, the managerial, and the technical levels affected by the implementation of employee assistance programs for flight attendants in the U.S. airline industry.

Organizational changes associated with the implementation of IT are unlikely to be experienced at only one specific organizational level. Rather, multiple organizational levels will presumably be affected, and, therefore, the revised framework extends the notion of impacts occurring *at* multiple organizational levels to include the idea that the interaction *between* organizational levels should be investigated carefully. For example, the standardization of an organization's core work processes may result from the implementation of IT that enforces a particular work flow and order to the performance of the process. Correspondingly, this effect at the organizational level may restrict the latitude of authority granted to individual workers. Of course, such cross level effects should not be presumed to be deterministic. IT systems used to support core processes may also empower teams of workers rather than restrict their actions. In sum, the adoption of a multilevel perspective to study the organizational consequences of IT promises greater analytical power because the interactions between the levels of analysis are taken into account.

SUMMARY

This chapter has taken a critical look at the organizational consequences of IT. The relationship between IT and organizational form has historically been assumed to be one in which IT is one of several causal variables affecting organizations and their structure. However, empirical findings spread over decades of research have not produced convincing evidence supporting a simple causal model. We have reviewed the various ways in which empirical findings exhibit diversity, both between and within studies. In some instances, the presumed causal relations investigated by researchers have been supported, but in many more cases they have not. We have used this diversity to stimulate thinking about new directions for research on the organizational consequences of IT. In contrast to the prevailing variance approach to research in the area, we advocate a process approach in which social consequences are conceived as outcomes from a sequence of events that occur over time. We also advocate the application of alternative theoretical logic when thinking about organizational change. Rather than thinking of IT-related change as the result of simple deterministic forces, alternative logical arguments invoking life cycle, evolutionary, teleological, or dialectic processes could be used. Finally, we advocate analyses that recognize and span multiple levels of social analysis. Given that the organizational consequences of IT have produced such a great diversity of findings over the years, we believe that a greater variety of theoretical perspectives may provide more insights into this ever popular and important subject area.

ENDNOTES

1. Among the predominant technologies to surface in the 1990s were Enterprise Resource Planning (ERP) systems, which are analyzed in Markus and Tanis' chapter in this volume; the Internet, which is discussed in Sampler's chapter; and knowledge management systems, which are described by Alavi.
2. Virtual teams are described more completely in Saunders' chapter in this volume.
3. We acknowledge that IT's impacts are not limited to individual, group, organizational, and interorganizational levels. IT may have even broader impacts on society. For an example of societal impacts of Internet technology, see Sampler's chapter in this volume.

4. In their chapter in this volume, Markus and Tanis discuss another example of IT not successfully implemented: the case of Fox-Meyer Drug, where the ERP implementation turned out to be a total fiasco.

5. The framework proposed in Markus and Tanis' chapter in this volume, for example, describes the ERP process in a way that does not preclude a variety of potential activities within the stages of their model. The training process model described in Olfman and Pitsatorn's chapter in this volume is an example of an even more generic process framework.

Chapter 5

Information Technology and Business Performance: Past, Present, and Future

Anitesh Barua and Tridas Mukhopadhyay

From the early days of information technology (IT) deployment in commercial organizations, researchers and professionals have struggled with the problem of measuring the bottom-line contribution of IT investments. The challenge of measuring the economic impacts of IT lies in the indirect ways and processes through which IT applications create value in organizations. If an IT application could work in isolation from factors such as business strategies, processes, and incentive systems, it would be relatively straightforward to measure the changes and benefits brought about by the technology. In fact, this is one of the key reasons that IT is not comparable to traditional capital assets. In comparing IT investments to non-IT capital assets, Banker, Kauffman, and Mahmood (1993, p. 2) suggest, "The focus [of IT assessment] shifts from measuring hard and quantitative dollar benefits that will appear on the firm's income statement to measuring indirect, diffuse qualitative and contingent impacts that are very difficult to quantify well." Furthermore, an IT application can be used by an individual, team, department, entire organization, or multiple organizations in the case of an interorganizational system. Since objectives and incentives may vary across users within an organization, aggregating benefits of IT at the individual or team level to represent the total organizational benefit may become an exercise in futility.

While the unit of analysis varies, most academic studies focus on the organizational level for measuring IT contribution. Even though the impact of IT on the performance of the national economy is of great interest to the government and policy makers, such research belongs more in the domain of macroeconomics than that of management information systems (MIS). Our focus in this chapter is on measuring the ex post impacts of IT investments at the firm or business unit level, because they lend themselves to quantitative and statistical modeling and subsequent generalization of results.

The apparent lack of a positive contribution from IT investments has been discussed extensively in the literature (e.g., Kauffman & Weill, 1989; Attewell, 1991; Panko, 1991; Wilson, 1993; Brynjolfsson, 1993; Barua, Kriebel, & Mukhopadhyay, 1995). Many arguments have been made to explain the paucity of evidence in a majority of business value studies. For example, Baily and Gordon (1988) and Gordon (1989) note difficulties in measuring quality-adjusted output in traditional productivity studies. Brynjolfsson (1993) notes that IT investments may not pay off immediately after investment and that the time periods covered by productivity studies may not be sufficiently long to capture the delayed creation of value. Brynjolfsson (1993) also suggests that in a competitive business sector, firms may be compelled to pass on technology-related benefits to consumers and that productivity studies may fail to detect this redistribution effect. Barua and Lee (1997) have also hypothesized and empirically tested the conjecture that input measurement and modeling limitations may have also been responsible for lackluster results in the literature.

Despite a decade of relentless pursuit from the information systems and economics research communities, the economic impacts of IT continue to pose major challenges regarding theoretical foundation, measurement, and data issues. After a string of research showing insignificant or even negative returns from IT investments, a few recent studies have found a positive linkage between IT and economic performance (e.g., Brynjolfsson & Hitt, 1993, 1996; Lichtenberg, 1995; Dewan & Min, 1997). In a recent interview (Lohr, 1999), Nobel Laureate economist Robert Solow, who had once expressed his skepticism regarding the contribution of IT to productivity, has taken a more positive stance: "My beliefs are shifting on this subject . . . the story always was that it took a long time for people to use information technology and truly become more efficient. The story sounds a lot more convincing today than it did a year or two ago."

While the emergence of positive estimates in the literature is encouraging news for managers who make IT investment decisions, has the "IT productivity paradox"—or in a broader sense, the "IT business value paradox"—been solved? As discussed in this chapter, there are many unresolved issues involving underlying theories, methodology, and data. Specifically, a positive contribution does not tell us whether we are grossly over- or underestimating IT impacts. From a management standpoint, merely knowing that the overall contribution is positive is not enough: It is something that chief information officers (CIO) already know from intuition and daily experience in dealing with technology. Indeed, the magnitude of the contribution is more important than the sign in guiding corporate IT spending. Furthermore, we must ask how much confidence can be put in the estimates reported by current studies to make them a basis for future investment decisions.

This chapter begins with a historical perspective on information economics research linking the quality of information attributes to individual decision settings and outcomes (e.g., Barua, Kriebel, & Mukhopadhyay, 1989; Mukhopadhyay & Cooper, 1992a, 1992b). While the focus on individual decision makers in these studies makes it difficult to aggregate outcomes and benefits of information quality due to potential divergence of individual and organizational objectives, this stream of research offers valuable insights for assessing the contributions of a specific technology or application (e.g., electronic data interchange—EDI) in a given decision setting.

In parallel to the information economics studies, another stream of research focused on the association between IT budgets and firm performance metrics such as return on assets and market share. These studies and related methodological refinements are collectively referred to as "process-oriented" approaches. A more theoretically grounded approach to assessing IT contribution involves the deployment of a microeconomic production function. While production economics is highly restrictive in its ability to handle competition, product quality, and diversity, the chapter argues that the IS literature has focused only on the form of the production function and for the most part has ignored issues involving input selection and behavioral assumptions. Furthermore, the chapter notes some critical problems associated with IT deflators and how the choice of a deflator can have dramatic impact on productivity estimates.

The most recent literature on the business value of IT advocates the notion of complementarity between IT and other factors, including business strategies, processes, and incentives, as a key determinant of business performance. IT business value research is coming to terms with the notion that without a consideration of such complementarities, it may not be possible to assess the real magnitude of IT impacts. At the same time, the corporate IT landscape is changing rapidly due to the dramatic proliferation of the Internet and Internet-based technologies (e.g., standards and applications) in business. The important question facing researchers is whether the traditional approaches to measuring IT contribution will also work in the context of electronic commerce and electronic business. Furthermore, how does complementarity among IT, processes, strategies, and channel relationships determine business performance in this new era? The chapter surveys these latest developments and concludes with the development of a complementarity-based process model of IT value creation. The balance of the chapter is organized as follows. The next section discusses the literature focusing on the value of information in various decision contexts using the information economics approach. The third section is devoted to the measurement of IT impact on business performance. This section is divided into various subsections, each dealing with a specific aspect of measurement and methodology. The first subsection discusses early research on IT contribution; the next subsection concentrates on business value and production economics approaches to IT impacts measurement. The subsections on IT Dollars or Characteristics? and IT Without a Context? raise some issues regarding methodologies used in assessing IT contribution. The section on Where Do We Go from Here? provides directions for future research in IT business value in the areas of complementarity and electronic business. The fifth section, Managing IT Based on Business Value, combines findings from the academic literature into a prescriptive business value model for IT managers. Concluding remarks are provided in the final section.

INFORMATION ECONOMICS AND THE VALUE OF INFORMATION

A literature that is concerned with the value of information attributes in different decision contexts dates back to the 1960s (e.g., Marschak, 1963, 1971; Marschak & Radner, 1972; Hilton, 1981; Moore & Whinston, 1986, 1987; Ahituv, 1989; Barua et al., 1989). It is based on the disciplines of information economics and decision theory. While not directly focused on the economic contribution of IT investments, information economics research considers changes in the attributes of information (which may result from investments in IT applications) and their impact on the payoff(s) to decision maker(s) using the information. Mukhopadhyay (1993) notes that "the mechanism for determining IT value involves comparing the business value of IT-assisted decisions with unassisted decisions." The basic information economics framework involves a payoff function that depends on the state(s) of the world and the action(s) taken by a decision maker. In the early studies, information was characterized by the "fineness" of the state space partition induced by the information (Marschak & Radner, 1972). A "finer" partition of the state space indicates more detailed information, whereas a "coarser" partition represents less detailed information. Unfortunately, information economics primarily deals with the role of information in partitioning the state space, which is also known as an "information structure." The key difference between an information structure and an information system is that while an information structure is completely characterized by its fineness, an information system requires multiple attributes to describe its information outputs (Barua et al., 1989).

Barua et al. (1989) discussed the need to augment the notion of an information structure to include multiple attributes of information quality. They defined a set of "intrinsic" (context-independent) and "extrinsic" (context-dependent) attributes of information quality and how they affected a decision maker's payoff. This broadening of scope helps bring information economics-based research closer to information systems and enables the analysis of trade-offs and interdependencies between different attributes in a given decision setting.

In their seminal work on team theory, Marschak and Radner (1972) extended the applicability of the single decision maker framework to a set of decision makers who share a common objective function. They demonstrate how optimal rules of communication can be designed based on information needs of various decision makers in the organization. Using the principles of team theory, Barua and Whinston (1991) analyzed a procurement and production setting with two "interdependent" decision makers and analyzed their overall information requirements.

In a variation of the information economics approach, Mukhopadhyay and Cooper (1992a, 1992b) used a two-stage approach to examine the effect of information on decision accuracy, which in turn affects the payoff function. They used microeconomic production functions to model each stage of this approach and illustrated it in structured and high-volume decision-making contexts (e.g., inventory control).

While the information economics approach is theoretically sound and rigorous, the unit of analysis (individual or team decisions) makes it difficult to obtain meaningful and insightful results in a broader organizational context. For instance, by the very definition of a team, the divergence in objectives of the members of an organization and possibilities of moral hazard are precluded. Also, these studies generally do not relate characteristics of information to any cost function, thereby ruling out traditional cost benefit analysis with implications for how much to invest in information quality. However, as demonstrated by the studies of Mukhopadhyay and Cooper (1992a, 1992b) and Barua and Whinston (1991), the information economics approach can be useful in assessing the benefits of IT applications in well-defined contexts and decision settings. Furthermore, as pointed out by Mukhopadhyay (1993), attempts should be made to link specific applications (e.g., electronic data interchange) to the resulting information attributes, which will strengthen the tenuous ties between technology issues and information economics.

MEASURING IT IMPACT ON BUSINESS PERFORMANCE

THE EARLY YEARS

In the early 1980s, a stream of research focused on assessing the contribution of IT investments to performance metrics such as return on investment (ROI) and market share. Cron and Sobol, Strassman, and Bender did some of the earliest MIS studies in this area. Cron and Sobol (1983) investigated the relationship between the number and type of computer applications and firm performance in the pharmaceutical wholesale business. They found that the most profitable firms used the technology sparingly but for many purposes. Strassman (1985) studied the linkage between IT budgets and a performance metric he called "return on management" in the manufacturing sector and found a bimodal pattern rather than a direct relationship. Bender's (1986) investigation of the insurance business did not reveal a direct association between IT and performance. Like Strassman, Bender also found a bimodal relationship between IT and firm performance.

In a study of the life insurance business, Harris and Katz (1989, 1991) found some encouraging results in that higher performance was related to higher spending on IT. Weill (1990, 1992) examined IT investments in the valve-manufacturing business and found no overall relationship between IT investment and performance. However, he established a relationship between transactional IT capital and return on assets after accounting for the type of the system (transactional, informational, and strategic). There were several other MIS studies on measuring IT returns during the 1983–1990 period (e.g., Turner, 1988; Oman & Ayers, 1988; Krafcik, 1988; Pentland, 1989; Venkatraman & Zaheer, 1990) that did not find any significant relationship between IT and performance. For a detailed review of these and related studies, see McKeen and Smith (1993) and Wilson (1993).

Economics-based studies also pointed to disappointing results regarding IT productivity. Making a distinction between information and production workers, Roach (1987) estimated that labor productivity for information workers had either declined or had not kept up with corresponding increases for production workers. Along similar lines, Baily and Chakrabarti (1988) found a lack of productivity gains from IT and attributed the lackluster finding to several potential reasons including misallocation of resources, misstated output, and the role of IT in distributing a fixed amount of output within an industry. One of the most influential investigations of IT productivity was conducted by Loveman (1988). The data in Loveman's study were collected by the Strategic Planning Institute from 60 large strategic business units (SBUs) belonging to Fortune 500 organizations and included variables such as IT capital, non-IT capital, labor, and inventory during the 1978–1984 time period. Loveman's analysis revealed that the contribution of the IT capital input was slightly negative, prompting him to conclude that the non-IT factors of production would be preferred to IT for additional investments.

Based on the disappointing observation that there was no correlation between IT investments and productivity, Roach (1988, 1989) coined the term "IT productivity paradox," while Solow (1987) lamented, "You can see the computer age everywhere but in the productivity statistics." The IT productivity paradox quickly became a significant challenge for both MIS researchers and economists for the next decade, while Solow's remark became "the favorite punch line of the economic naysayers" (Lohr, 1999). The gloomy outlook and skepticism regarding IT productivity continued into the 1990s, as Morrison and Berndt (1990), Berndt and Morrison (1991), and Roach (1991) reported disappointing returns from IT investments. Using microeconomic production theory, Alpar and Kim (1990) found a more encouraging result that a 10% increase in IT spending led to 1.9% reduction in total costs. One of the early microeconomics-based studies that stand apart from the rest is that of Bresnahan (1986). Bresnahan assumed that due to competitive pressure in the unregulated parts of the financial service sector, firms act as agents on behalf of consumers. His estimates suggest that consumer surplus was five to six times larger than IT investments during the 1958–1972 period. Using Bresnahan's approach, Brynjolfsson (1996) later found sizable consumer surplus in more recent data. On the whole, however, the balance remained overwhelmingly tipped in favor of the "no productivity gains" school of thought.

PROCESS OR PRODUCTION ECONOMICS ORIENTATION?

In the 1990s, two streams of research on measuring the economic and performance contributions of IT have progressed concurrently and independently. One is based on production economics; the other focuses on building "process-oriented" models of IT value creation. Being disenchanted with the lackluster results from microeconomic production theory-based studies, MIS researchers started considering alternative approaches to assessing IT contribution. Crowston and Treacy (1986), Kauffman and Kriebel (1988a, 1988b) and Mukhopadhyay and Cooper (1992a, 1992b) argued that the enterprise-level impacts of IT can be measured only through a "web of intermediate level contributions" and called for more detailed investigation of how IT actually creates impacts close to the level of implementation. This line of research has been broadly classified as "process-oriented" approach due to its focus on the process of IT impacts creation, as exemplified by Barua et al. (1995).

Process-Oriented Studies

Although varied in their research approaches, process-oriented studies are generally not guided strictly by economic theory and develop models showing hypothesized relationships between IT and other input factors to performance measures at various levels of aggregation. Often multidimensional in terms of the output side, these studies attempt to analyze the impact of IT and other factors through a web of relationships between variables of interest. This multidimensional approach is close to the notion of business value of IT, which, unlike the productivity studies, has many facets including efficiency and quality. To the best of our knowledge, the earliest operationalization of the business value approach was due to Kauffman and Kriebel (1988a, 1988b, 1991). They defined the concept of "business value linkages" and applied it to a variety of IT applications including treasury management (Kauffman & Kriebel, 1988b) and point-of-sale technologies (Kauffman, Kriebel, & Zajonc, 1989). Using a process orientation in modeling the role of IT in the financial services sector, Banker and Kauffman (1988) showed positive strategic impacts of ATM network characteristics.

A distinct but related approach developed by Barua et al. (1995) involves the identification of "intermediate" level performance measures, which are similar to critical success factors (Rockart, 1979), establishing the impact of IT and other inputs on these intermediate measures and relating the intermediate measures to financial performance. A strong positive impact on the intermediate variables constitutes a "strategic necessity" in the sense that a firm or business unit must achieve high levels of intermediate performance to stay competitive; however, the linkage between intermediate and higher-level performance measures could depend on many external factors including competitive response and general economic conditions. Using the same data as in Loveman's study, Barua et al. (1995) identified intermediate variables such as capacity utilization, inventory turnover, relative prices, and product quality, which were strong predictors of two high-level measures: return on assets and market share. Various IT variables were shown to have a strong positive impact on the intermediate measures. In contrasting their approach with the prevailing practice of relating total IT investment to an aggregate performance measure, Barua et al. (1995) note: "Our study was motivated by the lack of a process-oriented model to trace IT contributions through low/intermediate impact variables to the higher level performance variables. . . . Unlike the production function approach . . . our two-stage model enables us to open up the 'black box' of IT usage, and detect and measure IT impacts where they occur."

Rogawoski and Adams (1998) argue that "the value information systems can add to organizational activities is strongly related to organizational operational characteristics." In essence, they suggest analyzing IT impacts creation at a deeper level than the operationalization of Barua et al. (1995) by incorporating organizational characteristics. This generalized approach of assessing the financial value of investing in IT through a chain of intermediate-level impacts has been applied and extended in subsequent research by Mukhopadhyay and associates (e.g., Mukhopadhyay, Rajiv, & Srinivasan, 1997; Mukhopadhyay, Lerch, & Mangal, 1997; Mukhopadhyay & Mangal, 1997; Davamanirajan, Mukhopadhyay, & Kriebel, 2000).

Mukhopadhyay, Rajiv, and Srinivasan (1997) examined the production and quality frontiers simultaneously for the mail-sorting process at the U.S. Postal Service. They used a set of productivity factors to model the differences in the quality of the output and inputs. They found that both output and quality of mail sorting significantly improve with higher use of automation in place of older technologies. In addition, IT improves quality, which in turn improves process output. They also report that productivity factors exert considerable influence on performance. For example, while absenteeism tends to retard productivity due to its disruptive consequences, a higher fraction of bar-coded mail enhances productivity.

In a later study, Mukhopadhyay, Lerch, and Mangal (1997) examined the impact of the toll collection system at the Pennsylvania Turnpike. Their results show that IT may have two types of impact. First, it can directly affect the time to process a transaction. Second, it can indirectly affect the role of a productivity factor. For example, we found that the unfavorable effect of employee turnover on labor productivity diminished with the introduction of the new system because it reduced the learning time for replacement workers (Mukhopadhyay & Mangal, 1997).

In a more recent work, Davamanirajan et al. (2000) have developed a two-stage approach to assess the impact of system designs on process performance and firm profitability. First, they study how IT can improve process performance by assessing the impact of system characteristics. Second, they examine whether improved process performance translates into higher firm profitability. In trade services, they found that a high level of electronic integration with customers is more fruitful than integration with internal funds transfer systems. In addition, this approach can pinpoint whether productivity or quality is the major driver of the economic performance of a process. In the trade services area, reducing the average time to issue a letter of credit seems to be more important in improving profit margin than increasing the number of transactions per employee.

Isolating a process for IT value measurement has its advantages and disadvantages. On the positive side, it does not involve the aggregation across a large number of processes, and it allows us to trace the effect of IT on specific processes and tasks. On the negative side, it does not work well for interdependent processes, and the results from one process do not generalize to other processes.

Two important studies that should also be classified as process oriented are Dos Santos, Peffers, and Mauer (1993) and Bharadwaj, Bharadwaj, and Konsynski (1999). Dos Santos et al. (1993) study the impact of IT investment announcements on the market value of a firm using the event study approach. Bharadwaj et al. (1999) show a significant relationship between IT investments and Tobin's q, a "financial market-based measure of firm performance."

Production Economics–Based Measurement

Continuing the tradition of production economics–based assessment, Brynjolfsson and Hitt (1993, 1996) and Lichtenberg (1993) independently used a common data set involving investments in computer capital from International Data Corporation and found significant productivity gains from IT. The estimates of the output elasticity of computer capital range from 0.01 to 0.04 (Brynjolfsson & Hitt, 1993, 1996) and are as high as 0.1 in Lichtenberg's study. This radical departure from the usual lackluster results made these studies a turning point in the history of IT productivity assessment. Brynjolfsson and Hitt (1993, p. 47) remarked: "Because the models we applied were essentially the same as those that have been previously used to assess the contribution of IT and other factors of production, we attribute the different results to the recency and larger size of our data set." Attributing a positive contribution to recent data would imply the true lack of IT contribution in earlier years. But Brynjolfsson (1993, p. 67) himself suggested that "a shortfall of evidence is not necessarily a shortfall" of IT productivity. The negative results from Loveman's study prompted Barua and Lee (1997) to argue that even earlier IT applications such as materials requirement planning (MRP) system should lead to tangible benefits such as lead time reduction, reduced material waste, reduced emergency orders and out-of-stock conditions, and increased inventory turnover. In other words, contrary to the implications of Brynjolfsson and Hitt's remark, IT applications from the late 1970s and 1980s should have led to significant productivity gains. Barua and Lee (1997) investigated the issue by using the same data as Loveman within a production economics framework. They found that the IT contribution was indeed significantly positive and that IT contributed more to the revenue product than either labor or non-IT capital.

Why did Loveman (1988) and Barua and Lee (1997) find strikingly different results from the same data? In replicating Loveman's results, Lee and Barua (1999) found that the negative contribution of the IT input is attributable primarily to the IT deflator. Loveman used the quality-adjusted computer price index of the Bureau of Economic Analysis (BEA) to deflate IT capital for different years. This choice implicitly assumes that IT capital consists only of computers. However, the definition of IT used in the management productivity and information technology (MPIT) data collection process corresponds to the information processing and related equipment (IPRE) category specified by BEA. Computers and peripheral equipment is one of the subcategories within IPRE (see Barua & Lee, 1997, for details). Other subcategories within IPRE include (1) office, computing, and accounting, (2) communications equipment, (3) instruments, science, and engineering, and (4) photocopy and related equipment. As expected, the IPRE deflators are substantially different from those of the computer and peripheral equipment subcategory. Given that the data definition corresponds to IPRE, it would be appropriate to use IPRE deflators rather than a computer price index or the computers and peripheral equipment deflator. In fact, using a computer price index under the assumption of all IT capital as consisting of computers resulted in overdeflation in Loveman's study (Barua & Lee, 1997). It is important to note that the data in Brynjolfsson and Hitt's (1993, 1996) and Lichtenberg's (1995) studies involved pure computer capital, thereby making it appropriate to use a computer price index as a deflator.

Given the preceding discussion, it appears that not all applications of the production economics framework are executed in the same way. Let us consider the production economics approach itself in some detail to obtain some more methodological insights. IT productivity studies relying on production economics as their theoretical foundation hypothesize that IT investment is an input to a firm's production function and that the firm's output is created by combining inputs according to a specific functional form. For instance, the Cobb-Douglas production function is the most commonly chosen form (e.g., Loveman, 1988; Brynjolfsson & Hitt, 1996; Barua & Lee, 1997; Lee & Barua, 1999; Mukhopadhyay et al., 1997), although it has some restrictions such as perfect substitution among inputs. More general forms, such as the translog production function, have also been deployed.

In addition to the specification of a production function, production economics proceeds further to specify how firms choose their input levels based on unit and output prices based on the behavioral assumptions of profit maximization or cost minimization. Interestingly enough, with the exception of Barua and Lee (1997), Lee and Barua (1999), and Menon, Lee, and Eldenburg (2000), the MIS literature using the production economics approach has largely ignored the very theoretical foundation involving the firm's choice of levels of input factors. As noted by Barua and Lee (1997, p. 149), "Unless the behavior of the firms in setting inputs, outputs and prices (where applicable) is explicitly modeled, we are not utilizing the theoretical premise of the production economics framework. In other words, apart from some assumptions about possible substitution between the various inputs, no 'theory' stands behind the estimation of a single production function."

How serious is this problem? It is well known in econometrics (e.g., see Christensen & Greene, 1976; Schmidt & Lovell, 1979) that consistent estimates can be obtained only when the inputs are exogenous. However, as shown empirically by Barua and Lee (1997) and Menon et al. (2000), the inputs to the production function are endogenous. This is not an unexpected finding. After all, IT budgets are determined by management based on many factors. For instance, IT prices decline rapidly, providing an incentive to firms to invest more in IT and to use less of other inputs. Furthermore, as noted by Menon et al. (2000), firms or business units in a given year face different input prices due to a variety of potential reasons (e.g., mix of IT capital, volume discounts, financing arrangements). In fact, varying input prices is an econometric prerequisite for statistical identification of an estimation process. Barua and Lee (1997) demonstrate how the assumptions of exogeneity and endogeneity of inputs lead to very different elasticity estimates.

This discussion makes it evident why it is important for multiple studies to use a common data set. It is possible that very different and even contradictory conclusions will emerge from the same data, thereby challenging previously held beliefs and assumptions and opening up an academic debate on the methodologies and models concerned. For instance, based on the studies of Loveman (1988) and Weill (1992) in the manufacturing sector, Markus and Soh (1993, p. 377) suggest, "It does seem more likely that positive effects from total IT spending, if any, would occur in firms in information-intensive industries than in manufacturing." While the service sector possibly stands to gain more than the manufacturing sector from IT applications, the latter can benefit significantly from IT-enabled supply chain and production management. Furthermore, one can argue that conventional productivity studies will not be able to capture appropriate outputs in information-intensive sectors and are more likely to account satisfactorily for basic productivity gains in the manufacturing sector. The business units in the data used by Loveman (1988) and Barua and Lee (1997) belong to large successful organizations that are likely to take advantage of IT innovations in their business. Indeed, the "shortfall of evidence" can now be attributed to the assumption of computers making up 100% of IT capital.

Stochastic Production Frontier Approaches

A straightforward application of the production economics framework is helpful in assessing the productivity contribution of IT and other factors of production. However, it does not let the researcher measure various efficiencies associated with the production process. More specifically, technical, allocative, and scale efficiencies indicate how well management chooses production inputs. For example, there is ample anecdotal evidence that IT applications such as CAD/CAM have increased the efficiency of production processes (see Barua & Lee, 1997, for a review). This issue can be systematically investigated through technical efficiency. Allocative efficiency measures how well management chooses levels of various inputs. For instance, given the rapid decline in IT prices, a firm with high allocative efficiency will use more of IT and less of other inputs. Note that this relates to the notion of endogeneity of inputs described earlier. Scale inefficiency can result from misjudging market demand or not being able to adjust the level of operation. IT can help firms to understand their markets better and to coordinate with trading partners to achieve an optimal scale of operation (Lee & Barua, 1999). While data envelopment analysis (DEA) can measure these efficiencies, given the widespread acceptance of the production economics approach within the economics of the IS community, it is desirable to combine efficiency and productivity measurements within a single framework.

Production economics research has addressed this need through the development of a stochastic production frontier method (e.g., see Kumbhakar, 1987; Kumbhakar, Biswas, & Bailey, 1989). It involves modifying a Cobb-Douglas specification into a production frontier and introducing three types of efficiencies described earlier. Lee and Barua (1999) have applied this integrated framework to the MPIT data and have found all three types of inefficiencies related to IT. For instance, the IT capital input was underutilized while the non-IT capital input was overutilized, indicating the presence of allocative inefficiency. Further analysis showed that increasing the IT intensity (IT's share of total inputs to production) reduced both technical and scale inefficiencies. The overall implication is that in an "optimal" sense, the business units in the data set should have invested more in IT applications. Happily enough, IT's relative share increased steadily over the time period covered by the data, indicating that the strategic business units (SBUs) became increasingly efficient in all three areas. Of course, this is a learning effect that one would expect from Fortune 500 organizations. In sharp contrast to the belief that the SBUs in the sample would have done better to invest the marginal dollar on other inputs to production, Lee and Barua's (1999) results indicate that the marginal IT dollar had threefold efficiency-related benefits. Menon et al. (2000) have also used the stochastic production frontier approach to assess the productivity and efficiency of IT investments in the health care sector.

Limitations of Production Economics–Based Approaches

In spite of its theoretical rigor, the production function–based approach does not have the explanatory power to pinpoint where and how IT impacts are created and where management action may be needed to increase the payoff from IT investments (Barua et al., 1995). The aggregate level of analysis in the production function approach makes it difficult to distinguish between different types of IT investments and their impacts on specific areas of business. Apart from the level of analysis, other measurement difficulties are associated with the production economics approach. These include the inability to handle quality and speed of service (Brynjolfsson, 1993; Hitt & Brynjolfsson, 1998) and to account for output in the service sector (Gordon, 1987).

Despite many weaknesses, some enhancements to the basic production economics framework are both possible and desirable. For instance, the price of output is generally assumed to be exogenously specified. Yet, as Kreps (1990) noted, in many settings the price may depend on the quantity of output produced. This feature can be easily incorporated in the standard production economics framework involving optimization. Note that without optimization, it is not meaningful to treat the price as endogenous to the model. Future research based on the production function approach should consider the characteristics of the markets in which the firms or business units in the data set operate and attempt to model the production process in more realistic ways through appropriate enhancements of the basic framework.

IT DOLLARS OR CHARACTERISTICS?

In a perfect world, where every IT dollar is invested with 100& efficiency and where management knows exactly what the technology investment outcomes are, the level of IT investment may be considered as a suitable input into a production function or business value model. But as Barua (1998) noted,

> the reality of IT investments is clouded by numerous uncertainties. As a result, the transformation of IT investment dollars into capabilities that users within the organization or external entities such as customers and business partners can appreciate is far from deterministic. So you can't assume that more IT dollars necessarily mean higher customer satisfaction, faster inventory turnover, or shorter time to market.

Weill (1992) has addressed this issue by introducing a construct called *IT conversion effectiveness* to measure the transformation of IT dollars into application features or characteristics. Markus and Soh (1993) have also used the conversion effectiveness construct in their business value study and found some empirical support for its inclusion in the model. Unfortunately, with the exception of Weill (1992) and Markus and Soh (1993), this important issue has not garnered much attention in the business value literature.

Weill's approach can potentially help bridge a gap between the information economics studies focusing on characteristics of information and IT investment-oriented production economics and business value studies. The major difficulty is that IT contribution measurement studies have often relied on secondary data, which typically do not include variables related to management practice or information characteristics such as the availability of timely information and the accuracy and compatibility of enterprisewide databases.

The use of a stochastic production frontier can also partly bridge the gap between IT dollars and characteristics. The technical inefficiency parameter in a stochastic frontier formulation varies across firms, allowing for the possibility of different firms using different amounts of the same input to produce a given output level, ceteris paribus.

IT WITHOUT A CONTEXT?

One potential limitation of most of the preceding studies is that they considered IT in the abstract in terms of the levels of investment. Given that there are many types of IT application areas (e.g., manufacturing, logistics, sales, and marketing), using the total IT investment figure may not be particularly useful in obtaining an accurate estimate of IT impacts. An alternative approach, therefore, will be to study the application of a technology in different contexts and to derive more meaningful results. One case in point is the series of EDI studies performed by researchers at Carnegie Mellon University.

By allowing computer-to-computer data exchange between trading partners, EDI facilitates electronic integration between manufacturers and their suppliers. In the first study, Kekre and Mukhopadhyay (1992) examine the effect of electronic integration between a large steel manufacturer and its (downstream) outside processors that perform coating, painting, stamping, and other value-added activities on steel products before they reach customers. They analyze how EDI can improve information attributes such as accuracy and timeliness and thus lead to higher performance by outside processors. They are able to quantify the additional benefits of electronic transactions in comparison to manual transactions. In the second study, Srinivasan, Kekre, & Mukhopadhyay (1994) examine the benefits of increasing vertical information integration between a large manufacturer and its (upstream) suppliers using EDI technology in a just-in-time (JIT) environment. Their results suggest that higher information integration through production schedule–sharing and integrated EDI systems can substantially reduce shipment discrepancy by suppliers.

Finally, Mukhopadhyay (1993) developed a model to assess the dollar impact of EDI based on information economics. Later, Mukhopadhyay, Kekre, & Kalathur (1995) applied this model to Chrysler assembly centers. After controlling for variations in mix, volume, parts complexity, model and engineering changes, and the use of various transportation modes, they found that operating costs can be reduced significantly if JIT practices are designed to exploit the improved information available due to EDI. Including the savings from electronic document preparation and transmission, the total benefits of EDI per vehicle amount to over $100. This research is the only attempt to date to establish the dollar value of EDI based on a longitudinal data set.

Because of its specificity and proximity to the point of technology implementation, this approach is likely to provide more accurate estimates of IT benefits than considering aggregate investment figures. Even though the aggregate-level production economics studies may show a positive overall contribution, context-specific studies can be more precise and help generate management insights and normative implications. However, the results of such studies cannot be generalized to other IT uses.

WHERE DO WE GO FROM HERE?

After a decade of research, both IT productivity and business value studies have established that the economic impact of IT is indeed positive and significant relative to other inputs such as labor and non-IT capital used by organizations. In fact, studies by Brynjolfsson and Hitt (1993, 1996), Lichtenberg (1993), and Barua and Lee (1997) have shown that the contribution of IT has been the highest of any other factor of production. With the productivity paradox dispelled as a myth of the past, we need to consider refinements to existing approaches to measuring the contribution of IT to business performance. These and similar advances will help address questions such as the following: Is it possible that in spite of the positive numbers we may still be grossly underestimating the returns from IT? Can we empirically distinguish between firms that make identical investments in IT but that may obtain very different returns from such investments? What are some key factors that might have been ignored in production function and business value studies? What additional information can these factors provide about the role and contribution of IT investments? Barua, Lee, and Whinston (1996), Hitt and Brynjolfsson (1997), Brynjolfsson et al. (1997), and Brynjolfsson and Hitt (1998) have focused on complementarity theory and its applications to provide a deeper understanding of the interactions between IT and other organizational factors and how such interactions determine the contribution of IT to business performance.

A COMPLEMENTARITY THEORETIC
PERSPECTIVE ON IT AND BUSINESS VALUE

Studies in both production economics and business value streams have ignored the synergy between IT and other related factors such as the levels of fit with business strategies, employee empowerment, and team orientation of business processes. In developing a formal theory of reengineering changes, Barua, Lee, and Whinston (1996) note that firms often undertake changes in IT applications without changing related or "complementary" factors such as business processes and incentive systems. Since the payoff from IT depends on the processes within which they are used and the incentives of people to use new systems, isolated investments in changing IT applications are unlikely to be productive.

The complementarity between IT and other factors is not limited to reengineering changes and applies to the entire domain of organizational design. Two activities or factors are complementary if the benefit of doing more of one increases by doing more of the other (Milgrom & Roberts, 1990). In other words, ". . . the central thesis [of complementarity] involves the combination of factors, objects, processes, people and technologies that have a value synergy among themselves" (Barua & Whinston, 1998, p. 46). As identified by Barua et al. (1996), Brynjolfsson, Renshaw, and Van Alstyne (1997), and Barua and Whinston (1998), IT inputs are a component in organizational design, and investments in IT must be complemented by investments in appropriate business strategies, processes, incentives, and control systems. If a firm does not invest in the implementation of complementary changes, the true payoff is likely to be limited. However, even if the firm makes complementary investments, the total return from the investment will not show up in measurement studies that consider input factors in isolation. Perhaps more importantly, unless this complementarity or synergy between IT and non-IT factors is considered in IT business value models, it will not be possible to capture performance differences arising from the fact that some organizations may recognize and act on such complementarities better than others.

A small but emerging body of empirical research is beginning to address the IT productivity contribution assessment problem within the complementarity framework. For instance, Hitt and Brynjolfsson (1997) and Brynjolfsson and Hitt (1998) have conducted the first empirical studies on complementarities between IT and "organizational architecture" (decision rights, workforce skills and education, and incentive systems). They found that higher levels of IT usage are associated with higher levels of decentralized decision rights and investments in human capital. Brynjolfsson and Hitt (1998) also conclude that "organizational practices are important determinants of IT productivity, and vice versa."

Grenci, Barua, and Whinston (1998) developed and tested a complementarity-based theory and business value model of the impact of technology-enabled customization in the financial service sector. Their model is based on the premise that the business strategy of customizing financial services such as mortgage loan processing is complementary with the sales process characterized by the number of alternatives generated and the speed of handling. Furthermore, the efficiency of the sales process is hypothesized to be complementary with the available decision support and task modularity. The results of the study involving mortgage loan processing support the hypotheses that the competitive benefit of a customization strategy is contingent upon the sales process and that the selling of a customized product is enabled by the level of decision support and task modularity.

Ignoring complementarities in business value measurement implies that the impact of IT could be seriously underestimated. Furthermore, it will have rich explanatory power to show why some companies may invest in sophisticated systems and yet fail due to lack of synergy with strategy-, process-, and incentive-related factors. Of course, the difficulty lies in collecting data on organizational factors. Generally, studies with large data sets rely on secondary sources for information on IT and other investments as well as performance measures. Since complementarity involves organizational factors, primary data collection becomes essential in order to test interactions between IT and organizational variables and their impact on the business performance.

The empirical research on complementarities is emerging along the two familiar paths of production economics (e.g., Hitt & Brynjolfsson, 1997; Brynjolfsson & Hitt, 1998) and business value (e.g., Grenci et al., 1999). Figure 5.1 shows a generalized business value model with complementary relationships based on Barua et al. (1995) and Barua and Whinston (1998). The basic tenet of business value complementarity (BVC) suggests that IT investments should be first related to intermediate performance measures such as time to market, customer service response time, and extent of product mass customization rather than to high-level measures such as profitability. The impact of these intermediate factors on high-level measures is likely to be positive, but the strength of the relationship depends on external factors as depicted in Figure 5.1. For example, if each player in a business sector has an equally fast customer response time, investing in IT to marginally increase response time may not be desirable from a cost-benefit standpoint. However, staying below the norm is likely to have a strong negative impact on the bottom line. An attempt to relate IT directly to profitability or shareholder value will miss these critical details.

The focal theme of BVC is the complementarity that potentially exists at each level in the model. At the lowest level, IT-related factors are complementary with business strategies, processes, and incentives. A theoretical result derived by Barua et al. (1996) suggests that even when each level exhibits complementarity in a multilevel business value model, the top level is not necessarily complementary in the lowest-level design variables. If the intermediate-level performance measures are "strongly" complementary in the design variables, then the overall complementarity in the business value model is ensured. Empirical testing of the strength of complementary relationships is likely to be an important and productive area for IT business value research.

FIGURE 5.1 A Generalized Business Value Complementarity Model

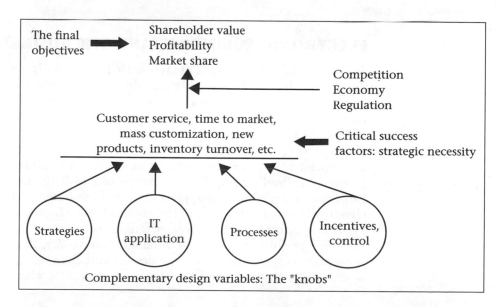

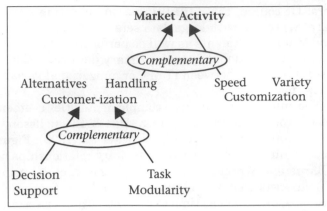

Source: Grenci et al., 1999.

The BVC model in Figure 5.1 is similar to the one developed and tested by Barua et al. (1995), with the difference that the intermediate-level factors are recognized as complementary in the lowest-level design variables. The final performance variables are also hypothesized to be complementary in the levels of intermediate variables. Furthermore, the model presented in Figure 5.1 recognizes the role of strategies, processes, and incentives in the creation of value from IT investments, while Barua et al.'s business value model focused only on IT and non-IT investments.

Grenci et al.'s (1999) BVC model in the context of mortgage loan processing is shown in Figure 5.2. The "customer-ization" construct (an intermediate level) is hypothesized to be complementary in the levels of decision support and task modularity. Furthermore, market activity (defined as dollar volume of mortgage loans as a percentage of dollar volume of deposits), the final performance measure, is also complementary in the intermediate performance measures of customization and customer-ization.

Table 5.1 shows different areas of research within the domain of IT contribution measurement, lists representative studies, and summarizes important findings.

ELECTRONIC COMMERCE AND THE BUSINESS VALUE OF IT

To this point, IT business value research has implicitly assumed that positive IT impacts exist but that they have remained elusive due to measurement limitations. The dramatic proliferation of the Internet in the business world since 1995 necessitates a reexamination of this assumption. The Internet and its related technologies and applications are widely available to organizations across the globe. Prior to the Internet revolution, organizations often invested in vendor- or technology-specific applications that were not open or ubiquitous in nature. By contrast, the Internet provides a "level playing field" in terms of a globally accessible network infrastructure, open standards, and applications that are based on the universal Web browser. Given this equalizing effect of the Internet, does investing more in IT lead to better financial performance in electronic commerce?

For traditional bricks-and-mortar companies, the existing technology infrastructure as well as business processes and channel relationships will determine how rapidly and successfully they can switch to electronic business. But what

TABLE 5.1 Key Areas, Representative Studies, and Findings in IT Value Assessment Research

Area of Research	Representative Studies	Main Findings
Information economics–based studies	Marschak (1963, 1971), Marschak and Radner (1972), Hilton (1981), Moore and Whinston (1986, 1987), Ahituv (1989), Barua et al. (1989), Mukhopadhyay (1993)	Operationalization of information attributes, tradeoffs, impacts on payoff, and outcomes in individual and team decision making
Early IT impacts studies	Cron & Sobol (1983), Strassman (1985), Bender (1986), Turner (1988), Oman and Ayers (1988), Krafcik (1988)	Generally IT investments are not related to business performance
Microeconomics (production economics) studies that did not find positive impacts	Roach (1987), Baily and Chakrabarti (1988), Loveman (1988), Morrison and Berndt (1990), Berndt and Morrison (1991)	IT investments are not related to productivity
Microeconomics studies that found positive impacts of IT	Bresnahan (1986), Alpar and Kim (1990), Brynjolfsson and Hitt (1993, 1996), Lichtenberg (1993), Brynjolfsson (1996), Dewan and Min (1997), Barua and Lee (1997), Lee and Barua (1999), Mukhopadhyay, Rajiv, and Srinivasan (1997)	IT contributes significantly to various measures of productivity and cost efficiency
Business value studies	Kauffman and Kriebel (1988a, b), Banker and Kauffman (1988), Weill (1992), Dos Santos et al. (1993), Barua et al. (1995), Mukhopadhyay, Lerch, and Mangal (1997), Rogawoski and Adams (1998), Bharadwaj et al. (1999)	IT impacts are created at levels close to implementation; impacts can also be isolated for specific IT applications; IT contributes to a firm's market value
Studies involving complementarity between IT and non-IT factors	Barua et al. (1996), Hitt and Brynjolfsson (1997), Brynjolfsson et al. (1997), Brynjolfsson and Hitt (1998), Grenci et al. (1999)	IT is shown to be complementary with processes, decision authority, and people characteristics

about organizations that are based completely on the Internet? Since their very existence is attributable to the Internet, do higher investments in IT lead to increased productivity for the so-called dot com companies? Barua, Fang, and Whinston (1999) investigate this issue through an empirical analysis of IT productivity in "digital" and "physical" "dot coms." Digital dot coms are Internet-based companies such as Yahoo, E-Bay, and America Online whose products and services are digital in nature and are delivered directly over the Internet. By contrast, the physical dot coms sell physical products (e.g., books, CDs, toys) that are shipped to consumers. Barua et al. hypothesize that IT investments contribute more to various output measures (e.g., revenue, revenue per employee, gross margin, and gross margin per employee) for digital dot coms than for physical dot coms. They argue that the level of digitization of business processes is much higher in digital products companies than in Internet-based companies selling physical goods. While the Internet and electronic commerce applications are equally accessible to both types of companies, electronic retailers (e-tailers) often build warehouses, handle inventory, and are subject to many of the physical constraints of bricks-and-mortar companies. By contrast, due to the very nature of their business, most of the business processes and delivery mechanisms of digital dot coms are implemented online. Furthermore, the ability of a digital dot com to differentiate itself from its competitors directly depends on being able to translate innovative business strategies into online capabilities. Barua et al.'s analysis of 160 publicly traded digital and physical dot coms shows that IT capital (computer hardware, software, and networking equipment) contributed significantly to each of the metrics for the digital dot coms. However, the corresponding contributions for physical dot coms were uniformly insignificant.

These results raise important issues and questions that deserve close attention in future research. The adoption of the Internet as an integral part of business provides an unprecedented opportunity for researchers to examine how the nature of IT contribution may depend on other factors such as business models, processes, and channel relationships. Some issues that merit research attention are listed here:

• As bricks-and-mortar organizations move to a "clicks-and-mortar" status, they will face organizational and technological hurdles as well as opportunities. The transition will take a considerable amount of time, and it is widely anticipated that there will be both winners and losers in the new Internet economy. When do existing IT infrastructure, business models, and processes help an organization create value in the new electronic economy? When do they become impediments?

• What is the contribution of IT and complementary factors such as business processes and channel relationships to the productivity and business value of bricks-and-mortar, clicks-and-mortar, and dot com organizations? Hypotheses regarding the impacts of IT in the new economy must not be unqualified like their counterparts in the industrial era studies. This new stream of research needs to be further linked to the valuation of publicly traded organizations.

• What are the different ways in which the Internet orientation of a firm creates business value? For instance, manufacturers may not sell certain products directly over the Internet. Yet they may get closer to the end user of their products through online interactions, obtain customer knowledge (which helps create new products), and reduce the bargaining power of retailers and other channel partners.

It should be noted that the discussion of complementarity between IT and other factors in the previous section applies fully in the context of electronic commerce and electronic business. For instance, the intellectual premise behind the results obtained by Barua et al. (1999) is that investing more in IT will pay off when there is an increase in the level of digitization of processes and online implementation of business strategies. As mentioned earlier, a conceptualization of IT impacts in the world of electronic commerce must involve complementary non-IT factors. Since Internet-related IT is widely available to most organizations, investing in IT alone cannot be sufficient to guarantee superior performance.

MANAGING IT BASED ON BUSINESS VALUE: A PRESCRIPTIVE APPROACH

To this point, we have focused exclusively on the academic literature on IT investments and business performance. What have we learned from scores of empirical studies that can be of value to business and IT managers? Both business value- and productivity-oriented studies have shown positive returns from IT investments. Regardless of its academic value, a positive sign on the IT contribution coefficient is not surprising for IT managers. As mentioned in the introduction, business managers have most likely known about IT benefits from intuition and day-to-day business operations. The more important issue is the magnitude of contribution, which can provide guidance regarding optimal investment levels. Until we can improve measures of output as well as deflators for IT inputs and are able to capture market characteristics in which business units operate, there is ample reason to question the accuracy of IT contribution estimates. More importantly, the "black-box" nature of the production function approach makes it difficult to draw meaningful implications and prescriptions for managers. Due to its detailed and multifaceted nature, the business value approach seems better suited for both ex ante and ex post assessment of IT contribution.

The three-tier business value complementarity model in Figure 5.1 provides a basis for management decisions regarding IT and complementary factors. Conceptually, the lowest layer can be considered as a set of "knobs" that can be set at different levels. That is, management can choose to invest different levels of resources in each of the four circles depicted in Figure 5.1. It is critical to recognize and analyze the synergies between IT and non-IT factors and to "turn" these knobs in tandem so that changes in IT are in tune with business strategies and are accompanied by complementary changes in processes and incentives. Many organizations make isolated investment decisions. For example, a business unit may redesign its customer service processes but continue to rely on fragmented information repositories with incompatible data definitions and formats. Another may decentralize decision authority but not ensure seamless flow of information between the decentralized units and headquarters, or it might invest in an elaborate information structure with an eye toward information sharing without introducing incentives that will encourage employees to share information. These isolated changes fail to meet the objectives of improving customer service, supporting new business strategies, and enhancing communication. Barua and Whinston (1998) provide a set of guidelines for management in identifying and acting upon complementary choices.

At the second level are intermediate performance measures that may be different across business sectors or even across firms within a given sector. At the highest level are overall performance measures such as shareholder value and profitability. These relationships should be estimated from industrywide data or determined qualitatively by guiding senior management through various scenarios (Barua & Whinston, 1998). Management should also consider the correspondence between IT characteristics and the dollar amount of IT investment, as discussed in the section on IT Dollars and Characteristics? It is also important to revisit the business value model frequently to analyze whether managerial action is needed on the basis of changes in the business environment. Managers must pay special attention to the external factors that are often the drivers of change. For example, new technologies bring new opportunities while changes may become necessary in response to competitive pressures. When changes are made at the lowest level in the business value model, management must ensure that the synergies between the knobs and the intermediate measures are restored.

Every senior manager knows that the opportunity cost of not investing in IT is high. However, organizations remain uncertain regarding the magnitude of benefits such as increasing profitability or shareholder value from IT investments. The BVC perspective enables management to assess the joint contribution of IT and other investments and to capture that elusive value.

CONCLUSION

After much frustration, confusion, and skepticism, the MIS research community has finally succeeded in establishing a positive linkage between IT investments and business performance. Furthermore, some recent studies have also pinpointed measurement-related shortcomings in the literature that may have been responsible for negative or insignificant IT contribution estimates. Also encouraging is the fact that the role of IT is being recognized at the economywide level. For instance, a recently released study by the U.S. Department of Commerce (Henry et al., 1999) indicates that even though the investment in IT during the 1995–1998 period is about 8% of the gross domestic product, it accounts for over a third of the real productivity growth in the U.S. economy during the same period.

These encouraging facts and findings do not signal the end of the IT contribution measurement research. Rather, they should serve to inspire IT scholars to embrace more challenging research questions involving output quality and input complementarity. Furthermore, although much of the existing literature has considered IT without its application context, new IT productivity and business value issues are bound to arise for specific types of applications. Electronic commerce is the exemplar domain for which the same issues and problems that have plagued IT productivity and business value research will most likely be reincarnated. As bricks-and-mortar organizations rush to invest in network infrastructure, applications, processes, and people to create their presence on the Internet, IT and business managers will be challenged to assess the payoff from such large resource commitments. The possibility of lower prices due to increased competition on the Internet and the availability of real-time online information is sure to raise the question of business value.

Given the widespread availability of Internet-compatible networking technologies and applications software, it is not the technology that is likely to make a difference today. Rather, firms that can recognize and act on complementarities between business strategies, processes, and incentives are likely to succeed in the new digital economy. Studies on business value of IT should move their focus away from isolated investments in IT applications to the interrelated nature of IT, business, and organizational factors.

Chapter 6

Individual Acceptance of Information Technologies

Ritu Agarwal

In today's increasingly global, digital, and networked economy, corporate spending and organizational dependence on information technology (IT) are mushrooming at unprecedented rates. In 1999, the IT budget of a single U.S. company, Federal Express, has been reported to be $1.4 billion (King, 1999). When spending on information technologies by other firms is added to this figure and the scope is extended to firms across the globe, it is clear that IT represents a substantial investment for organizations of all varieties. This technology is being utilized to support diverse strategic and operational objectives ranging from enabling competitive strategy, as in the case of Amazon.com and Dell Computers, to performing routine operational tasks. In this context of ubiquitous and pervasive use of IT, it is not surprising that all knowledge workers in today's economy need to utilize IT as an integral component of accomplishing organizational work.

Acquiring IT to support business needs is clearly a crucial prerequisite to exploiting the potential of IT. Unfortunately acquiring appropriate IT is a necessary but not a sufficient condition for utilizing it effectively.[1] Organizations (i.e., leaders and managers) make primary adoption decisions, yet it is individuals within the firm who are the ultimate users and consumers of IT. Thus, it is evident that true business value from any information technology would derive only through appropriate use by its target user group. In other words, systems that are not utilized will not deliver the returns anticipated by managers. Evidence suggests that individual users can exhibit a variety of different behaviors when confronted with a new information technology: They may completely reject it and engage in sabotage or active resistance, they may only partially utilize its functionality, or they may wholeheartedly embrace the technology and the opportunities it offers. Obviously, each behavior has some consequential outcomes—both negative and positive—for managers.

What causes individuals to exhibit these different behaviors? How can managers design appropriate implementation tactics and interventions that will alleviate problems associated with the rejection of information technologies? These and related questions have been the subject of considerable academic research over the past several decades. Their importance has been elevated because of the recognition that as technologies become more malleable and flexible, greater potential exists for users to discover new and innovative ways of exploiting them. Indeed, competitive advantage may accrue only through these nonimitable ways of utilizing technologies that are discovered within the firm by its knowledge workers at the confluence of business and technical knowledge. Such discovery and "learning," however, will occur only if the technology is accepted as an integral part of a work process and if users are appropriately motivated to expend effort in exploration. Thus, the problem of individual acceptance of information technology is a crucial one for those responsible for implementing technologies as well as those responsible for demonstrating the business value of an IT.

The purpose of this chapter is to provide an overview of existing research in individual acceptance of information technologies. In particular, the chapter summarizes what we know about this phenomenon and points out areas in which future research is warranted.

UNDERSTANDING INDIVIDUAL ACCEPTANCE

The issue of individual acceptance of IT has been researched from multiple theoretical perspectives using a wide range of constructs and definitions. Figure 6.1 presents a broad synthesis of existing theorizing about this phenomenon. The key dependent variable examined in the research literature is individual acceptance of information technology, which, as will be seen later, has been conceptualized and measured in several different ways. For instance, one definition of acceptance treats it as the act of adopting the information technology, that is, the initial decision to use it or not. Other

FIGURE 6.1 The Phenomenon of Individual Acceptance of IT

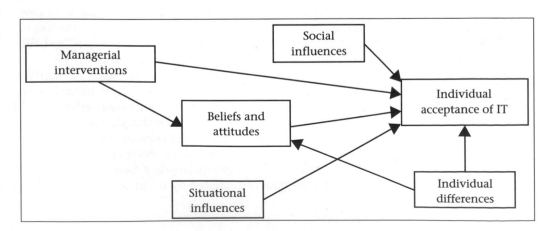

work adopts a richer and more complex definition of acceptance, approaching it as a construct that can span several meanings. Although not directly shown but implied in this theoretical frame is a relationship between individual acceptance of an IT and significant individual-level outcomes such as improved work performance, enhanced productivity, and user satisfaction. These outcomes are the first-order effects in a causal chain in which second-order effects such as enhanced competitiveness and profitability would eventually be manifested at the firm level. This chapter does not directly address such first- and second-order consequences of acceptance but confines the discussion to an examination of the antecedents of individual acceptance of IT.

Acceptance behavior is posited to be influenced by a variety of factors, including individual differences, social influences, beliefs and attitudes, situational influences, and managerial interventions. Managerial interventions and individual differences, in turn, are hypothesized to have an effect on beliefs and attitudes. The following discussion begins with an overview of the major theoretical paradigms that form the basis for the derivation of the overall frame. Subsequent sections elaborate on each construct and relationship in greater detail.

MAJOR THEORETICAL PARADIGMS

A majority of the conceptualizations of IT acceptance have drawn on robust theories from social psychology, notably the theory of reasoned action (TRA), the theory of planned behavior (TPB), diffusion of innovations (DOI) theory, and social cognitive theory (SCT). TRA and TPB were formulated as generalized explanations of a broad range of individual behaviors, including the use of information technology. In the TRA and the TPB, the dependent variable of interest is an overt and observable manifestation of the focal behavior in question. Both theories posit that such behavior is influenced by an individual's intentions to perform the behavior; that is, a person's performance of an actual behavior is preceded by the formation of a behavioral intention to engage in the activity. Intention, in turn, is determined by the individual's attitude toward the behavior and the subjective norm. Subjective norms capture an individual's assessment of the extent that referent others would desire the performance or nonperformance of the focal behavior, while attitude captures a general affective response toward the behavior. In contrast to TRA, the TPB introduces another construct, perceived behavioral control, as a predictor of intentions as well as actual behavior. Perceived behavioral control reflects an individual's perceptions that there exist personal and situational impediments to the performance of the behavior, that is, "the presence or absence of requisite resources and opportunities" (Ajzen & Madden, 1986, 457). Attitude in both theories is influenced by an expectancy formulation of beliefs about the consequences of performing the behavior weighted by an individual's evaluation of each consequence. Similarly, subjective norms are operationalized as a multiplicative construct in which the extent to which a referent other believes an individual should perform the behavior is weighted by the degree to which the individual wishes to comply with the source of normative influence. Ajzen and Madden (1986) propose an identical measurement approach to the construct of perceived behavioral control in the TPB: the extent to which an individual perceives she has the necessary resources to perform the behavior (i.e., the control beliefs) are weighted by the perceived importance of that resource to successful performance of the behavior. An example of a control belief in the usage of an IT such as the Internet might be "I have easy access to a high-speed connection to the Internet" with a corresponding perceived facilitation of "a high-speed connection is important to using the Internet."

A meta-analysis of 87 empirical studies that tested TRA provided strong overall evidence for the predictive power of the model, even in studies in which the initial boundary conditions identified for TRA were violated (Sheppard, Hartwick, & Warshaw, 1988). In addition to the substantial body of empirical support that this theory has garnered in other domains such as marketing and sociology, TRA has been empirically tested and has found support in the context of the acceptance of information technologies (Taylor & Todd, 1995a; Davis, Bagozzi, & Warshaw, 1989). Drawing upon the theoretical foundations of TRA, Davis (1989) proposed that the theory be specifically modified for the domain of IT in the form of a now widely accepted conceptualization of IT acceptance: the technology acceptance model (TAM). In the TAM as in the TRA, attitudes predict intentions, and intentions predict behavior. Unlike TRA, TAM does not include a subjective norm component as a determinant of intentions because of its uncertain theoretical and psychometric status (Davis et al., 1989). Subjective norms can create theoretical and empirical problems because it is difficult to distinguish the direct effects of norms on intentions from indirect effects via attitude (Fishbein & Ajzen, 1975). A second point of departure between the TAM and TRA is that unlike the expectancy formulation of beliefs utilized in TRA, TAM posits that only two beliefs—perceived usefulness and perceived ease of use—predict an individual's attitude toward using an IT. In addition to its indirect effect on intentions via attitude, perceived usefulness is also expected to exhibit a direct effect on usage intentions.

Recent work in technology acceptance has focused on empirical comparisons of extant theories to establish their explanatory and predictive power. Three significant studies in this context are those by Davis et al. (1989), Mathieson (1991), and Taylor and Todd (1995a; 1995b). Davis et al. (1989) compared TAM with TRA in a study involving the use of a word processing program by MBA students. Surveys operationalizing TAM and TRA constructs were administered at two time intervals: immediately following a one-hour introduction to the software and 14 weeks later. TRA accounted for 32% of the variance at time 1 and 26% of the variance at time 2. TAM, on the other hand, explained a larger proportion of the variance in intentions during those same time periods (0.47 and 0.51, respectively). Mathieson (1991) compared the TAM and the TPB with student subjects using a spreadsheet program as the target IT. Empirical results suggested that while TAM and TPB both exhibited considerable predictive power for intentions, TAM was able to predict attitude better than the TPB. Based on these findings, Mathieson concluded by noting that while TAM might be easier to use because of its parsimonious structure, TPB is richer in that it provided greater insight into the factors that influence an individual's behavior toward an IT.

In a replication of the Davis (1989) study, Adams, Nelson, and Todd (1992) tested the ability of TAM to predict individual use of voice mail, e-mail, and other software packages and found that while usefulness had a significant effect on system usage, ease of use was relatively less salient in determining use. Finally, the model comparison studies have been recently extended by Taylor and Todd (1995a). Arguing for the value of decomposed belief structures that can potentially be applied to a variety of research settings, Taylor and Todd described a decomposed theory of planned behavior (DTPB) and compared its explanatory and predictive performance to that of both TAM and TPB. DTPB decomposes the attitudinal, normative, and control beliefs from TPB into multidimensional belief constructs that are generalizable across situations and not specialized to each context. Normative beliefs, for example, were decomposed into relevant referent groups that would likely exhibit divergence of opinion and have a significant impact on an individual's decision to use an information system. Upon comparing the models, the researchers found that DTPB provided increased explanatory power for intentions as compared with TPB, although it is considerably less parsimonious than the TAM. The study also pointed out that because of its unidimensional belief constructs, DTPB provides greater diagnostic value, provides greater insight into the factors that influence IT usage, and suggests beliefs that can be targeted by designers or managers interested in influencing system use (Taylor & Todd, 1995a).

Rogers' (1983, 1995) theory of the diffusion of innovations has informed a considerable body of IT acceptance research (e.g., Brancheau & Wetherbe, 1990; Agarwal & Prasad, 1997). This theory, constructed through a meta-analysis of a variety of innovations in diverse contexts, may be characterized as a rich and complex information-centric view of innovation acceptance. The essence of this theory suggests that innovation adoption is a process of uncertainty reduction. Individuals gather and synthesize information about a new IT from the social system within which they are situated. This information processing results in the formation of beliefs about using the IT. Beliefs cause individuals to accept or reject the artifact; that is, beliefs are the drivers of the decision to adopt. Empirical tests of Rogers' conceptualization in the domain of IT have largely supported the major prediction of the theory (Brancheau & Wetherbe, 1990).

A final theoretical frame—social cognitive theory (SCT)—has been utilized recently by IT researchers not specifically to predict acceptance behaviors but to provide additional insights into the determinants of acceptance behaviors. Social cognitive theory is an outcome of over two decades of research by Bandura and his colleagues (see Bandura, 1997, for a recent review). The essence of SCT rests in the notion of triadic reciprocity, in which individual behavior is posited to be an outcome of a complex set of interactions between individual characteristics and environmental and situational factors: Behaviors, individual differences, and situational contingencies mutually influence and affect each other. Although the theory is rich and complex, particular aspects of it have been utilized to inform IS research, specifically the effect of the individual characteristic of self-efficacy on technology acceptance outcomes. Compeau and Higgins (1995a) posited and found support for positive effects of computer self-efficacy on computer usage, affect, and outcome expectations related to performance, a construct conceptually equivalent to perceived usefulness. In another study examining the role of computer self-efficacy in the context of computer training, Compeau and Higgins (1995b) empirically established the influence of self-efficacy on performance as well as personal outcome expectations.

It is important to note that all of these theories explicitly or implicitly apply to behaviors that are under the volitional control of individuals. Although the TPB acknowledges the presence of facilitating or inhibiting conditions, these are situational impediments rather than managerial fiat. Obviously, one way to induce technology usage is to simply mandate the use of the IT. Agarwal and Prasad (1997) suggested that while mandating technology use can provide the impetus to overcome initial inertia associated with a new behavior, such effects may not be sustainable over time. Moreover, given some evidence that mandating technology use against the explicit will of an individual may result in negative consequences (e.g.,

Ram & Jung, 1991), it would be desirable for managers to promote voluntary acceptance of information technologies.

In summary, it is evident from this brief review that researchers have drawn on theories from several reference disciplines in order to better understand the phenomenon of technology acceptance. While it is difficult to unequivocally identify one paradigm as dominant, it is clear that several themes recur across paradigms. One common theme is the notion of beliefs being critical antecedents to acceptance outcomes. Such beliefs have been variously labeled *perceptions, innovation characteristics,* and *outcome expectations.* A second recurrent construct is the affective belief construct (i.e., an individual's attitude toward the use of the IT). Finally, all of these theories accord salience to aspects of the individual as well as the social and environmental context within which technology acceptance behavior is likely to be exhibited.

ALTERNATE CONCEPTUALIZATIONS OF ACCEPTANCE

In general, while individual acceptance is the broad outcome that technology acceptance models and theories attempt to explain, this criterion construct has been operationalized by prior research in a variety of ways. Clearly, one simple view of IT acceptance is that for someone to commit to a technology, she must be willing to engage in use behaviors. Some models such as the TAM and TRA utilize intentions as a dependent variable, based on the supposition that intentions to use are predictors of future usage behavior. Recent extensions to TAM (Davis, 1993) also utilize current usage as a dependent variable. Innovation diffusion research, on the other hand, postulates that *many* different outcomes are of interest in technology adoption, including the initial decision to use the system and the continued or sustained use of the innovation. According to the DOI perspective, potential users make decisions to adopt or reject an innovation based on the beliefs they form about the innovation. If this decision favors adoption, overt behavior change as manifested in the use of the innovation results (Hage & Aiken, 1970; Rogers, 1983; Zaltman, Duncan, & Holbeck, 1973). The initial use of an artifact, however, may not always be sufficient to fully derive the benefits desired from the system. Users still need to institutionalize the innovation as part of regular work behaviors; this type of usage has been variously referred to as *confirmation* (Rogers, 1983), *routinization* (Hage & Aiken, 1970; Saga & Zmud, 1994), and *continued-sustained implementation* (Zaltman et al., 1973). Innovation diffusion research thus specifically recognizes that institutionalization of a behavior is different from, and perhaps more important than, its initial manifestation. Users may be persuaded to use a new system early in the implementation process, but the benefits from system usage may never be derived in the absence of continued, sustained usage.

Cooper and Zmud (1990), building upon Rogers' (1983) stage model and that described by Kwon and Zmud (1987), proposed a six-stage model of the IT implementation process that includes the stages of initiation, adoption, adaptation, acceptance, routinization, and infusion. A strength of this model is that similar to research grounded in the diffusion of innovations paradigm, it explicitly recognizes the existence of a variety of postadoption behaviors beyond the initial decision to adopt or reject the IT. Although their unit of analysis was the organization, Cooper and Zmud noted that the stage model is applicable to individual-level phenomena; thus, individual use of IT might also be viewed as progressing through the six stages.

Extending the work of Cooper and Zmud (1990), Saga and Zmud (1994) drew extensively on prior theoretical and empirical research and developed more detailed conceptual and operational definitions of constructs for each of the three stages represented by acceptance, routinization, and infusion. The constructs commonly utilized in the dominant technology acceptance models (i.e., attitudes toward use, intentions to use, and frequency of use) were categorized by Saga and Zmud as indicators of the acceptance stage. Measures of routinization included administrative infrastructure development, use perceived as "normal," and standardized use. Each of these constructs taps into the notion that in the stage of routinization, the IT is perceived as being a part of "business as usual" (Ritti & Silver, 1986; Yin, 1981). The final stage of implementation, infusion, reflects the extent to which an IT is embedded within the work processes of the individual and the broader organization in which the individual is situated. Saga and Zmud proposed that infusion be operationalized in three alternative ways: extended use, where an individual utilizes more of a technology's features to perform a more comprehensive set of tasks; integrative use, reflecting the use of an IT to forge or reinforce linkages among diverse organizational tasks; and emergent use, or using the technology to perform tasks that were not previously acknowledged as being amenable to technology support.

As the preceding discussion indicates, there is agreement among researchers that system usage represents a key behavior of interest in studying technology acceptance. Such usage may manifest itself in many different forms, ranging from a surface-level utilization of the IT to a more deeply ingrained behavior where value-added use of the IT is exhibited. Recent work has pointed to an additional outcome of interest in technology acceptance behavior (viz., intentions to explore an IT and find new ways of exploiting it). Arguing that users are an appropriate source for deriving the maximal value from today's malleable ITs through the generation of new ideas for technology use, Nambisan, Agarwal, Tanniru (1999) describe a construct labeled "intentions to explore." This construct is intended to span the conceptual domain of discovery and learning: Intentions to explore a technology measure a user's willingness and purpose to find new ways of applying an IT to work tasks. The construct is similar in spirit to Saga and Zmud's notion of emergent use. Nambisan et al. (1999) present an operational definition of intentions to explore together with a measurement scale.

From the array of definitions presented, it is evident that "individual acceptance of an IT" spans a broad range of constructs and definitions. Which outcome is particularly appropriate for future research? This decision needs to be made by researchers based on three key factors: (1) the stage of technology implementation that is the focus of inquiry, (2) managerial and pragmatic considerations regarding system use, and (3) the nature of the technology being examined. Research focused on the early stages of an emergent technology might utilize intent as a dependent variable, acknowledging that current use may not adequately represent future behavior patterns. Similarly, in the case of "simple" technologies that can be appropriated in a limited number of ways, an outcome that taps into extent of use might be sufficient. In contrast, for a complex technology with a potential multiplicity of uses (Tornatzky, Eveland, & Fleischer, 1990), a richer outcome such as emergent use or intentions to explore would be of greater value. Arguably, the ultimate end-state for any information technology should be infusion, where the technology is being utilized to its maximal value.

BELIEFS AND ATTITUDES

For conceptual clarity, Figure 6.1 encapsulates beliefs and attitudes as a single construct influencing technology acceptance behaviors. The supposition that beliefs and attitudes are proximal antecedents of technology acceptance finds considerable support in the attitude-behavior models from the social psychology literature. Indeed, beliefs recur as an important construct in each of the major theoretical paradigms that have been utilized to understand acceptance behaviors. Beliefs are an individual's cognitive evaluation of the consequences of a particular behavior (i.e., the use or acceptance of an information technology artifact) while attitudes reflect an affective response to the behavior in question (i.e., a generalized liking or dis-liking for the behavior). Two major views of beliefs and attitudes are prevalent in the research literature. In the disaggregated or tripartite view (Lutz, 1976), attitudes are composed of beliefs, affect, and conation. Beliefs are as defined; affect connotes emotional engagement with the concept; and conation represents the action taken in response to beliefs and affect. The key idea underlying the tripartite view is that each of the three components is an integral aspect of attitudes. The contrasting unidimensional view conceptualizes beliefs, attitudes, and behaviors as three separate constructs that are causally related. In both perspectives, the three components are posited to be consistent with each other: Positive beliefs about a concept such as using an IT are likely to coexist with positive affect and subsequent manifestation of the corresponding behavior of using the IT. A majority of the research in IT acceptance has adopted the unidimensional view of attitudes, treating beliefs, attitudes, and behaviors as distinct and separable constructs.

Although the relationship between beliefs and attitudes constitutes a central core in several theories, there is divergence in how this research approaches the identification of relevant beliefs. In the theory of reasoned action, the identification and measurement of relevant beliefs is a two-step process. Salient beliefs about the behavior in question have to be elicited first from target users for each specific context to which the theory is applied. Then the strength of each of these beliefs about the behavior is assessed and is weighted multiplicatively by the value assigned by the subject to that attribute of the behavior. Some researchers (Bagozzi, 1984; Schmidt, 1973) have criticized such an expectancy formulation of beliefs. Utilizing a general set of behavioral beliefs that apply across a range of technologies and other innovations would help circumvent the criticisms of these writers. Furthermore, if these beliefs were considered to be generally desirable, it would be unnecessary for respondents to evaluate their desirability and therefore unnecessary to use this evaluation to weight the beliefs, thus avoiding a multiplicative measure. Finally, an examination of disaggregated beliefs allows the researcher to specifically isolate the effects of each belief on attitude and to examine the effects of other external variables on the formation of beliefs. The TAM (Davis, 1989; Davis et al., 1989) is based on such an approach. While it derives its general structure and core constructs from TRA, TAM uses two general, unweighted beliefs—usefulness and ease of use—instead of eliciting beliefs for each specific technology and context.

Other research has proposed several alternate conceptualizations of the belief set salient to technology use behavior and has attempted to identify more comprehensive sets of beliefs or attributes of an innovation that influence user acceptance.[2] For example, Rogers (1983), through a synthesis of several previous studies examining adoption behaviors, identified several attributes of an innovation that are key influences on acceptance behavior. These characteristics include relative advantage, complexity, compatibility, trialability, and observability. In the domain of information technology, drawing on and refining the work of Rogers and others in the diffusion of innovations, Moore and Benbasat (1991) expanded the relevant innovation characteristics set and developed an instrument to measure the perceived characteristics of using an innovation.

According to Moore and Benbasat (1991), seven constructs compose the primary user perceptions that can help explain information technology (and other innovations) usage. *Relative advantage* captures the extent to which a potential adopter views the innovation as offering an advantage over previous ways of performing the same task. A second construct, *ease of use,* recurs in several studies as a significant predictor of adoption behavior (Adams et al., 1992; Davis et al., 1989). In addition to ease of use and relative advantage, Moore and Benbasat (1991) identify five other perceived characteristics of innovations and empirically demonstrate their effects on adoption behavior: compatibility, image, result demonstrability, visibility, and trialability. Moore and Benbasat use Rogers' (1983) notion of *compatibility* being "the degree to which an innovation is perceived as being consistent with the existing values, needs, and past experiences of potential adopters" (p. 195). The *image* construct, subsumed by Rogers as part of relative advantage, was shown by Moore and Benbasat to be an independent predictor of usage. Image captures the perception that using an innovation will contribute to enhancing the social status of a potential adopter. The characteristic of observability identified by Rogers was segregated by Moore and Benbasat as consisting of two separate constructs: *result demonstrability*—"the tangibility of the results of using an innovation" (p. 203)—and *visibility*—the extent to which potential adopters see the innovation as being visible in the adoption context. Finally, *trialability* measures the extent to which potential adopters perceive that they have an opportunity to experiment with the innovation prior to committing to its usage.

In summary, there is considerable support in the research literature for the importance of beliefs in technology acceptance behavior. Such beliefs have been utilized to explain system usage (Adams et al., 1992; Davis, 1993; Moore & Benbasat, 1991; Wynekoop, Sean, & Conger, 1992) as well as usage intentions (Davis et al., 1989; Mathieson, 1991; Szajna, 1996; Thompson, Higgins, & Howell, 1991). However, while the work of Moore and Benbasat (1991) suggests that several beliefs may drive individual usage behaviors, a very limited number of studies have examined such a comprehensive belief set. Indeed, other research points to the fact that there may be a more parsimonious set of beliefs that is salient to technology usage. For example, Agarwal and Prasad (1997) found that a smaller set of beliefs predicted current usage behavior as well as future use intentions. Similarly, the technology acceptance model that has garnered considerable empirical support posits that only beliefs about usefulness and ease of use predict technology acceptance. A meta-analysis performed by Tornatzky and Klein (1982), which reviewed much of the same literature as Moore and Benbasat (1991), suggested that only three beliefs—relative advantage, complexity, and compatibility—are consistently related to innovation adoption. In a field study examining pre- and postadoption beliefs related to the Windows operating system, Karahanna, Straub, and Chervany (1999) found that while preadoption attitudes were based on a multifaceted belief structure that included beliefs about usefulness, ease of use, result demonstrability, visibility, and trialability, postadoption attitude was based solely on instrumentality beliefs of usefulness and image beliefs.

The notion that there may be a more complex set of interactions among the beliefs salient to technology acceptance has been articulated in some recent work. Based on their empirical results, Agarwal and Prasad (1997) speculated that certain beliefs, specifically, result demonstrability and relative advantage, may need to operate in tandem with each other. In a study examining the acceptance of an expert systems application, Agarwal and Prasad (1998b) observed that individual adopters may utilize a linear and sequential approach to the consideration of the attributes of a technological innovation. Thus, whereas there is agreement that beliefs constitute an important antecedent of individual acceptance of IT, more work remains to be done in two areas: isolating a parsimonious set of beliefs that is consistently related to different operationalizations of technology acceptance outcomes and identifying causal pathways that might exist among different beliefs.

Although there is general agreement in the existing literature that beliefs determine attitude and that attitude affects intentions, there is still some discord about the role of attitudes in the overall relationship between beliefs and intentions. In the theory of reasoned action, attitude is conceived of as fully mediating the effect of beliefs on intentions. Such mediation is also posited in the theory of planned behavior. In contrast, the technology acceptance model (Davis et al., 1989) recognizes direct effects of beliefs on intentions in addition to the indirect effects through attitude. Although by and large empirical findings support these mediation effects, some recent research questions the full mediation of beliefs by attitude (e.g., Davis et al., 1989; Davis, 1993). Given the equivocal nature of prior findings related to mediation, there is a need for additional research examining the precise role of the attitude construct in technology acceptance. This issue of full versus partial mediation has important pragmatic implications because attitude plays a more critical role in the former case, and it could be argued then that the beliefs selected do not matter in and of themselves, provided other methods of directly influencing attitude can be devised. Researchers who retain the attitude construct in their theoretical models are encouraged to be particularly sensitive to its operationalization. As recommended consistently in the literature (e.g., Ajzen & Fishbein, 1980), the measurement of attitude should be focused directly and specifically on feelings about the focal behavior as opposed to the object associated with the behavior. In other words, attitudes as related to using an IT should be measured rather than attitudes that represent liking or disliking the technology itself.

INDIVIDUAL DIFFERENCES AND TECHNOLOGY ACCEPTANCE

The term *individual differences* can be interpreted most generally to connote dissimilarities among people including differences in perceptions and behaviors, traits and personality characteristics, and variables that connote differences attributable to circumstances such as education and experience. The notion that individual differences can play a crucial role in the implementation of any technological innovation recurs in a wide variety of research streams, including information systems, production, and marketing (e.g., Harrison & Rainer, 1992; Majchrzak & Cotton, 1988; Zinkhan, Joachimsthaler, & Kinnear, 1987).[3] Numerous individual difference variables have been studied including cognitive style (Benbasat & Taylor, 1978), gender, age, experience, and personality (Harrison & Rainer, 1992; Taylor & Todd, 1995b; Thompson, Higgins, & Howell, 1994), and motivation (DeSanctis, 1982).

Most of the major theories in technology acceptance discussed in this chapter recognize the importance of individual differences, although there is divergence in where the theory situates this construct within the overall nomological network of relationships. For instance, in theories grounded in social psychology, such as TRA, TPB, and TAM, individual differences are posited to influence attitudes, intentions, and behaviors only via the mediating construct of beliefs. In contrast, DOI theory postulates that there are systematic differences among early and late adopters of an innovation in the three major areas of socioeconomic status, personality traits, and communication behaviors (Rogers, 1995). Thus, Figure 6.1 depicts two pathways through which individual differences influence technology acceptance: an indirect effect through beliefs and a direct effect.

What is the set of individual differences that is germane to technology acceptance outcomes? One of the earliest and most comprehensive treatments of individual differences in IT usage was offered by Zmud (1979). Reviewing and synthesizing the research literature on IT implementation and use, Zmud developed a conceptual model explicating two causal pathways through which individual differences influence IT implementation success: cognitive and attitudinal. In essence, this theorizing is conceptually similar to the basic structure underlying theories from social psychology: The effects of external factors such as individual differences are mediated by beliefs (the cognitive pathway) and attitudes (the attitudinal pathway). Zmud further notes that individual differences can be categorized into three classes: (1) cognitive style, (2) personality, and (3) demographic/situational variables. *Cognitive style* represents the mode of functioning shown by an individual in his or her perceptual and thinking behavior. *Personality* refers to the cognitive and affective structures maintained by individuals to facilitate adjustments to events, people, and situations encountered. Personality variables believed to strongly influence IS usage include locus of control, dogmatism, ambiguity tolerance, extroversion/introversion, need for achievement, risk-taking propensity, evaluative defensiveness, and anxiety level. Finally, *demographic/situational variables* refer to a broad spectrum of personal characteristics including intellectual abilities, domain-specific knowledge, sex, age, experience, education, professional orientation, and organizational level.

While a wide range of individual differences has been examined in prior research, there is some empirical support for the mediation of their effects through the intervening construct of beliefs (Agarwal & Prasad, 1999). In addition to these mediated effects, however, recent studies have identified two important individual differences that have strong theoretical underpinnings and appear to exhibit consistent relationships to important technology acceptance outcomes—the constructs of self-efficacy and personal innovativeness.

Emerging from a rich theoretical background in social learning and social cognition, *self-efficacy* refers to individuals' beliefs about their ability and motivation to perform specific tasks (Bandura, 1977, 1986). This belief has been shown to be an important predictor of effort expended toward task completion, intrinsic motivation and involvement in the task, and task performance across a variety of different activity domains (Ellen, Bearden, & Sharma, 1991; Martocchio, 1994). In the domain of information technology in particular, studies of the effects of self-efficacy collectively point to its crucial role in determining individual behavior toward and performance using information technologies (Compeau & Higgins, 1995a, 1995b; Gist, Schwoerer, & Rosen, 1989). Surveying conceptual and empirical work related to the concept of self-efficacy, Marakas, Yi, and Johnson (1998) drew a distinction between general computer self-efficacy and task-specific self-efficacy.

General computer self-efficacy is defined (p. 129) as "an individual's judgment of efficacy across multiple computer application domains," whereas task-specific computer self-efficacy is defined as perceptions of ability to perform *specific* computer-related tasks in the domain of general computing. Marakas et al. made a compelling argument for a conceptual and operational distinction between these two constructs and recommended that researchers carefully identify the level of specificity at which self-efficacy is theorized to operate in a specific empirical context.

The second individual characteristic likely to exhibit consistent relationships to technology acceptance outcomes is personal innovativeness in the domain of information technology (PIIT). Drawing on research in marketing and the diffusion of innovations, Agarwal and Prasad (1998a) offered a conceptual and operational definition of PIIT. Noting that extant conceptualizations of personal innovativeness are limited because either they utilize "time of adoption" measures that do not support prediction or they use global operationalizations of innovativeness that have low predictive power, Agarwal and Prasad developed a domain-specific conceptualization for predicting information technology use. PIIT is defined (p. 206) as "the willingness of an individual to try out any new information technology." Empirical results suggest that PIIT moderates the relationship between beliefs and intentions. The authors conclude by noting that PIIT might well serve the role of a control variable in individual-level studies related to the phenomenon of technology acceptance.

In summary, the importance of individual differences as a significant theoretical construct in technology acceptance is indisputable. What is not clear, however, is the extent to which individual differences matter in work settings because of the limited managerial control that can be exercised over such differences. Agarwal and Prasad (1999) suggest that individual differences can be utilized to construct a profile of individuals more receptive to new technologies. The profile can then serve a key role in recruitment and selection. However, acknowledging the mediating influence of beliefs and the reality that managers often cannot pick and choose individuals to become users of IT, Agarwal and Prasad also suggest that technology acceptance can be facilitated by utilizing other interventions that directly affect beliefs, such as training and developing a learning culture. Thus, it might be fruitful for future studies to utilize key individual difference variables such as self-efficacy and PIIT as controls rather than as predictors. Parceling out the variance explained by these differences would permit clearer insight into the effects of other managerially controllable constructs on technology acceptance.

SOCIAL INFLUENCES

The salience of normative influences on technology acceptance behaviors has been acknowledged in a variety of IS research. Arguing that utilitarian and rational explanations of technology use do not pay sufficient attention to influences emanating from the social environment in which a potential user is situated, this stream of research posits that organizational members develop perceptions of a new technology in the context of complex and highly influential social systems (e.g., Kraut et al., 1998). Thus, the attitudes and beliefs of others in groups to which an individual belongs help shape technology usage behavior through overt communication or more subtle forms of suggestion. Social interactions are instrumental in generating shared meaning and mutual understanding in an organization and thereby provide an important basis for subsequent patterns of behavior. Acknowledging the importance of such influences, dominant technology acceptance theories such as TRA and TPB include the construct of subjective norms as a key antecedent of behavioral intentions to use an IT. These norms represent the perceived social pressure to engage in a specific behavior.[4]

The importance of social influence on individual behaviors in general has a long-standing tradition in organizational research. It was emphasized nearly four decades ago by Burns and Stalker (1961, p. 118) in their seminal work on innovation: "In working organizations decisions are made either in the presence of others or with the knowledge that they will have to be implemented, or understood, or approved by others. The set of considerations called into relevance on any decision-making occasion has therefore to be one shared with others or acceptable to them." More recently, social construction theory postulates that interactions with social agents control technology in organizations and that attitudes toward and uses of technologies converge in social systems. Walsh and Ungson (1991, p. 60) describe organizations as "a network of intersubjectively shared meanings that are sustained through the development and use of a common language and everyday social interaction." Thus, individual behavior in organizations is contingent on the conduct of significant others regardless of whether they are present or not (Weick, 1995).

Fulk (1993) argues that two predominant social processes can explain coordinated patterns of meanings and behaviors toward technology within social groupings. The first of these processes is grounded in social learning theory (Bandura, 1997), which predicts the emergence of coordinated behaviors and meanings through several behavioral modeling processes. Behavioral modeling is conceptualized as being considerably more complex than the simple imitation of observed behavior; it involves significant cognitive processing that can generate structures of shared meanings among individuals involved in the social learning process.

The second social process is social information processing. Social information from peers can influence the attitudes and behavior of individuals and can take the form of (1) overt statements that are assimilated, (2) interpretations of events, (3) communications that increase the saliency of events, and (4) declaration of standards for judging the appropriateness of particular behaviors in the workplace. Social information processing produces a similar pattern of media attitudes and use behavior within groups and different patterns of behavior across groups (Fulk, 1993).

Social influence has been found to emanate from a variety of sources that are generally context dependent. For example, depending on the specific population being studied, individuals may experience social pressure from friends, co-workers, and supervisors. In addition to such context-dependent sources, studies have also examined the role played by an influential individual—the technology champion (Orlikowski et al., 1995; Beath, 1991)—and have found that new technologies are more likely to be successfully implemented when they are actively promoted and endorsed by an influential individual. The level of the source of influence may also be important in determining use. Co-worker behavior has been found to be more influential than supervisor behavior in determining technology use (Schmitz & Fulk, 1991), suggesting that the closer a referent source of influence is to the potential user of a technology, the more salient the influence.

Empirical results related to the role of social influence in technology acceptance have been mixed. Researchers have found that the effects of social influence vary with the volitional versus nonvolitional nature of technology use, with the specific acceptance outcome being examined, and with the nature of the adopter population. For example, using the TRA as the underlying theoretical framework, Hartwick and Barki (1994) found that normative influences were more salient to users in mandated-use situations in a longitudinal field study of information systems development projects. In contrast, voluntary usage was predicted more strongly by the attitudinal component. Moreover, the influence of subjective norms varied with the stage of the systems development life cycle. Prior to system initiation, subjective norms exhibited considerably more influence on intentions than did attitudes. These relative effects were reversed after the systems had been completed, when presumably users had better information and were able to develop well-formed beliefs about the system. Other studies (Karahanna & Straub, 1999) reported results in which normative influences were found to be more salient in intentions to adopt, and attitudes dominated as a predictor of continued use intentions. Thus, while social pressure might induce new users to exhibit initial adoption behavior, the influence of such norms might attenuate over time (Agarwal & Prasad, 1997). In contrast, Carlson and Zmud (1999) found that perceived socialinfluence exhibited its greatest effects in the latter stages of a longitudinal study examining perceptions of media channel richness. Finally, studies that utilized predominantly student populations such as those by Mathiseon (1991) and Davis et al. (1989) found that subjective norms were nonsignificant in explaining behavioral intentions. Given these equivocal results, there is clearly a need for additional research that clarifies the precise role of social pressure in technology acceptance and isolates the contingencies under which such norms are likely to be more salient.

SITUATIONAL INFLUENCES

Situational influences refer to the idiosyncratic combination of person and situation that can influence technology acceptance. In comparison to the other predictors of technology acceptance shown in Figure 6.1, considerably less attention has been paid to situational influences in the dominant technology acceptance theories. One could argue that this lack of attention is not surprising, given that situational influences are not separate constructs in and of themselves but embody complex combinations of managerial interventions, individual differences, and social influences. Nevertheless, it is fruitful to examine the set of situational influences that has found support in prior work in technology acceptance.

One broad operationalization of the concept of situational influences may be found in the perceived behavioral control construct in the theory of planned behavior. Ajzen (1991, p. 183) argues that "the resources and opportunities available to a person must to some extent dictate the likelihood of behavioral achievement." Independent of an individual's affective response to a specific behavior, personal and situational impediments may interfere with the successful performance of the behavior. Consider, for example, the case of an information technology such as a spreadsheet program. An individual may clearly perceive the instrumental outcomes associated with using this technology and may also experience social pressure to engage in usage behavior. She may simultaneously believe that she does not have the requisite skills to use a technology or that she has been inadequately trained. Or it may be the case that there are constraints on technology access that inhibit the development of behavioral intentions. In the theory of planned behavior, such situational impediments are idiosyncratic to particular behaviors and thus must be elicited each time the theory is applied.

A second conceptualization of situational influences is the notion of task-technology fit, recently described and operationalized by Goodhue and Thompson (1995) and Goodhue (1998). Task-technology fit (TTF) is defined as the "correspondence between task requirements, individual abilities, and the functionality of the technology" (Goodhue and Thompson, 218). Thus, TTF is a complex multidimensional construct whose antecedents include a set of interactions among task, technology, and the individual. Goodhue reports the development and validation of an instrument to measure user perceptions of this construct that contains 12 distinct dimensions including the right data, accuracy, compatibility, locatability, systems reliability, currency, and training. In their theoretical development, Goodhue and Thompson argue that the impact of TTF on technology utilization is manifested via the intervening construct of beliefs about using the system. Empirical testing performed on a subset of this model that included a direct link from TTF to system utilization provided weak support for the theorized link.

Drawing on aptitude-treatment interactions widely discussed in the training literature, Agarwal, Prasad, and Zanino (1996) posited that situational variables would moderate the effects of training on the development of user perceptions. The situational variables examined by them were categorized into two classes: task-related variables and tool-related variables. Specific variables studied in each class were the availability of meaningful work to perform using the target IT in the former, the availability of the system prior to training, and the elapsed time since a user had access to the system in the latter category. Although data collected from more than 200 users of an IT innovation support the hypothesized moderating effects of individual difference variables, similar effects were not observed for the situational variables.

As alluded to earlier, one problem with the conceptualization of situational influences is the potential for confound with the other constructs shown in Figure 6.1. For instance, self-efficacy, which is often an element of perceived behavioral control (Ajzen, 1991; Taylor & Todd, 1995a), could well be categorized as an individual difference variable. Several dimensions of TTF have considerable overlap with beliefs and managerial interventions. Thus, while there is theoretical and empirical support for the inclusion of constructs generally categorized as situational influences on technology acceptance, it is not equally clear whether the construct should be retained as distinct in the conceptual frame of Figure 6.1 or its constituent variables might more appropriately be subsumed in other constructs. This is certainly an issue that merits further research.

MANAGERIAL INTERVENTIONS

Managerial interventions or institutional factors are specific management actions and policies that are posited to influence technology acceptance outcomes through two mechanisms: a direct effect and an indirect effect mediated by beliefs and attitudes. Institutional factors have long been thought to have an impact on the behavior of employees in organizations. Early researchers focused on technical (e.g., size, resources, knowledge) aspects of the organizational environment in attempts to explain behavior (Scott, 1995). Institutional theorists added cultural and social aspects of the environment to increase understanding and explanatory power. Indeed, numerous manifestations of institutional factors have been studied, including, but not limited to, user training (Fuerst & Cheney, 1982; Leonard-Barton & Deschamps, 1988; Raymond, 1988; Sanders & Courtney, 1985), knowledge management (Pennings & Harianto, 1992; Boynton, Zmud, & Jacobs, 1994), and organizational support (Delone, 1988; Leonard-Barton & Deschamps, 1988; Monge, Cozzens, & Contractor, 1992).

One institutional factor that has received consistent attention in the literature as an important influence on technology adoption in organizations is managerial commitment and support. Citing several other scholars, Zmud (1984) points out that the importance of the attitudes of an organization's "power elite" to the successful implementation of an innovation has been demonstrated in the literature. Innovation requires the reallocation of scarce organizational resources, and without the active support of management such reallocations are unlikely to occur. Managerial commitment may be demonstrated in a variety of ways: through the provision of appropriate messages, through the encouragement of technology use "by example," or through assurances regarding the availability of resources.

Several studies have empirically demonstrated a significant relationship between management support and different conceptualizations of technology acceptance. For example, in a field study involving 124 organizations and 378 DSS users, Sanders and Courtney (1985) reaffirm that the level of top management support is an important correlate of DSS success. A study of the perceptions of 47 software development managers found that innovation success is positively related to the existence of favorable management attitudes toward the innovation (Zmud, 1984). In describing a study of the implementation of structured system development in a large corporation, Leonard-Barton (1987) suggests that managers can speed the diffusion of innovations within organizations by building on positive influences and countering negative ones.

Management support of innovations, however, might not be so effective if it is not demonstrated at an appropriate level in the organizational hierarchy. Leonard-Barton (1987) observes that the effects of organizational influence on technology use are mediated by the supervisor. Top management decisions must filter down to employees through the organizational hierarchy. Since their immediate supervisor usually conducts employees' performance evaluations, organizational directives routed through the supervisor can have profound impacts on technology acceptance. The author found that use of an organizational innovation by employees was strongly related to their perception of the supervisor's preference.

Although the evidence pointing to the significance of management support in explaining IT use is compelling, empirical results suggest that such effects are likely to be context dependent. For example, one notable study found that management influence was more important for technical innovations than administrative ones (Zmud, 1984). Another found that managerial support was significant only for individuals who reported little interest in experimenting with the technology in question (Leonard-Barton & Deschamps, 1988).

A second managerial intervention that has been theorized to influence technology acceptance outcomes is the provision of appropriate training.[5] Training serves to reduce uncertainty about new technology by providing information about the features of the technology. Assuming that the system possesses some "objective" value for potential adopters, greater learning about its features should amplify perceptions in a positive direction. Prior research has suggested that an important outcome of training is the development of user motivation to engage in use behaviors (Bostrom, Olfman, & Sein, 1988). Indeed, Bostrom, Olfman, and Sein (1990) observe that TAM provides a good conceptualization for the outcomes of user training processes. Empirical results obtained in work related to information technology acceptance support this positive influence of training on usefulness and ease of use beliefs (Igbaria, Gamers, & Davis, 1995; Agarwal et al., 1996; Davis & Bostrom, 1993).

Finally, the manner in which managers orchestrate key organizational processes such as the systems development activity can have an effect on user acceptance. Hartwick and Barki (1994) and Barki and Hartwick (1989, 1994) investigated the influence of user participation and user involvement in the design of technological artifacts on information system success. In testing a model based on TRA that treated participation and involvement as external factors, Hartwick and Barki's (1994) results showed that participation significantly influenced postimplementation involvement and attitude toward the system. The influence of user participation on system use was mediated by involvement and attitude toward the system. Hartwick and Barki's results clearly underscore the importance of management initiatives in structuring system development activities so that users are actively engaged in the process.

In sum, as indicated by the work discussed, deliberate managerial action can have a profound impact on individual acceptance of information technology. Managers can provide overt support through appropriate communication, they can ensure adequate resource availability through the provision of training and other means of support, and they can structure systems development efforts to guarantee close interaction between technology providers and technology users. A final managerial intervention that has been identified in prior research as efficacious in encouraging greater technology use is the development of a work culture that is conducive to learning and experimentation (Scott & Bruce, 1994). Variously labeled the perceived climate for innovation, an "organic" culture, and a continuous learning culture, this construct taps into individuals' cognitive interpretations of the organizational climate in which they are situated. To the extent that this climate encourages experimentation, is supportive of failure, and provides incentives for technology use (e.g., Zmud, 1982; Scott & Bruce, 1994), technology users are more likely to exhibit higher levels of system utilization. Thus, it is clearly important for managers to focus attention on constructing such a climate.

RESEARCHING TECHNOLOGY ACCEPTANCE

The theoretical development and empirical findings reviewed in this chapter collectively point to a rich and robust stream of literature that has helped us better understand the phenomenon of individual acceptance of information technologies. While these studies have been successful in providing keen insights into the determinants of individual behavior, several areas for fruitful research remain.

One unanswered question that merits further study is the overall theoretical lens through which we should view the phenomenon of technology acceptance. Each of the multitude of theories utilized in prior work, while useful in providing diverse perspectives, approaches the problem with a specific theoretical stance. Which one of these theories should be used to guide management action? There is a pressing need for additional studies that help practitioners make sense of these diverse theoretical perspectives and provide explanations based on models that are parsimonious and powerful at the same time.

Technology acceptance outcomes need to be extended to more formally include the notions of adaptation, reinvention, and learning. Given the richness of today's information technologies in terms of features and functionalities, greater value would be derived from novel ways of technology use and application. Saga and Zmud's (1994) conceptualization of infusion and Nambisan et al.'s (1999) construct of intentions to explore provide a first step toward clear theoretical and operational definition of value-added technology acceptance outcomes. More work is needed to further clarify these dependent variables and to develop valid and reliable measures.

The review of prior research in this chapter reveals that, with a very limited number of exceptions, a majority of the studies in technology acceptance have employed cross-sectional research designs. Although such studies are operationally easier to conduct, they do not support truly causal inferences. In future research, more longitudinal studies should be conducted to closely examine the causal structure of the overall frame espoused in Figure 6.1. The frame is a comprehensive, albeit simplified, snapshot factor view of a phenomenon that is intrinsically processual in nature. Moreover, the paths shown in Figure 6.1 may need modification. For instance, some research suggests that individual differences moderate the effects of other antecedents on technology acceptance (Leonard-Barton & Deschamps, 1988; Agarwal et al., 1996). It might also be the case that situational influences have an effect on the formation of beliefs and attitudes. Furthermore, it is not clear whether all the antecedents shown in Figure 6.1 remain salient at all stages of the technology acceptance process. For example, social influences have been found to be important in early adoption decisions but less so in routinization or infusion stages. Similarly, attitudes dominate as predictors in later stages but are less important in initial stages because users have not had the opportunity to develop them. Longitudinal research designs will provide insight into these and other important questions.

Extant conceptualizations of beliefs and attitudes are in need of extension to move beyond purely instrumental aspects and include the "fun" aspects of IT usage. Some recent literature has started examining concepts related to playfulness (Webster & Martocchio, 1992), flow (Webster, Trevina, & Ryan, 1993), cognitive absorption (Agarwal et al., 1997), enjoyment (Davis, Bagozzi, & Warshaw, 1992), and engagement (Webster & Ho, 1997). Collectively, these concepts suggest that IT acceptance usage can be promoted by focusing on nonwork-related outcomes. A more in-depth understanding of the effects of such constructs on technology acceptance would be invaluable in helping managers appropriately position and target new technologies to potential users.

A final area for future research lies in the examination of a wider variety of situational influences and managerial interventions. Research in other domains has shown that the perceived climate for innovation is an important antecedent of innovative behaviors. To the extent that managers wish to promote new uses of technology (the notions of exploration and reinvention), such climates would be important to develop. What are the specific features that constitute such climates? What managerial interventions will promote the creation of such a climate? In recent work, Nonaka and Takeuchi (1995) describe a theory of organizational knowledge creation. A key tenet of this theory is that knowledge creation can be facilitated through organizational design actions in the form of structural mechanisms. For example, Nonaka and Takeuchi observe that cross-functional new product development teams promote knowledge creation and innovation. Nambisan et al. (1999) used Nonaka and Takeuchi's conceptualization to study the effects of a variety of organizational mechanisms on dependent variables typically associated with technology acceptance. Their findings suggest that organizational mechanisms, which are a product of deliberate managerial action, can be highly instrumental in promoting technology use. Researchers may wish to study the effects of a wider variety of mechanisms on technology acceptance behaviors.

SUMMARY

This chapter has provided an overview of the various theoretical lenses through which prior research has approached the problem of individual acceptance of information technologies. Specifically, five dominant theoretical paradigms—the theory of reasoned action, the theory of planned behavior, the technology acceptance model, social cognitive theory, and the diffusion of innovations theory—were reviewed. Although considerable diversity exists in constructs and relationships included in each theoretical paradigm, a few recurrent themes are evident. Individual beliefs about and attitudes toward the use of an information technology persist as important constructs in each of these theories.

Drawing on the dominant theoretical paradigms, an overall frame was utilized to examine key antecedents of technology acceptance outcomes. First, given that the criterion variable (viz., technology acceptance) has been operationalized by prior research in a variety of ways, alternate conceptualizations of this construct, including current usage, future use intentions, acceptance, routinization, and infusion, were presented. In the overall frame, determinants of technology acceptance outcomes included beliefs and attitudes, situational influences, individual differences, social influences, and managerial interventions. A synthesis of prior research led to the specification of causal paths among these constructs, of which a focal point was the mediating role of beliefs and attitudes. Each construct in the overall frame was discussed in detail, including a summary of empirical evidence supporting the relationship of this construct to others in the organizing frame. Overall, extant research suggests that the major antecedents of technology acceptance can influence these behaviors directly as well as via influence that is mediated by beliefs and attitudes.

The chapter concluded by identifying areas in which future research is warranted. Despite a rich body of literature on this topic, considerable work remains to be done. In particular, as societal experience with computing technology continues to grow, the relevance of certain constructs included in existing theoretical models may need to be revisited. Thus, the important question for the future might well not be how we influence individuals to use information technology but how we promote and facilitate value-added technology use.

ENDNOTES

1. See the chapter by Roby and Boudreau for an expanded discussion of the consequences of poorly implemented IT.
2. See the chapter by Fichman for additional discussion on innovation attributes.
3. See the chapter by Todd and Benbasat for a discussion of individual differences in IT–supported decision-making activities.
4. See the chapter by Fichman for additional discussion on social influences in technology adoption behaviors.
5. See the chapter by Olfman and Pitsatorn for a detailed discussion of alternative training approaches and their outcomes.

Chapter 7

The Diffusion and Assimilation of Information Technology Innovations

Robert G. Fichman

The task of deciding when and how to innovate is not an easy one. Consider the following managerial quandaries:

- A CIO has joined a firm that lags in the adoption of emerging information technologies. He wonders just how innovative should this firm be going forward and what can be done to position it to be more willing and able to assume the challenge of early adoption.
- A VP of marketing of a firm that generally leads in IT innovation must decide whether to endorse the immediate adoption of a particular innovation with major implications for marketing strategy. She wonders whether her firm's needs in this area and its "readiness" to adopt are sufficient to justify taking the lead with this specific innovation. If so, how should the assimilation process be managed?
- A product manager must design a deployment strategy for an innovative software development tool. He wonders how fast this technology can diffuse. What kinds of organizations should be targeted for early adoption? What kinds of barriers will early adopters face? What can be done to promote adoption among these organizations and to sustain diffusion across the much larger market of later adopters?

These types of questions—which motivate the bulk of research on the *diffusion* and *assimilation* of IT innovations—have become increasing commonplace. (*Diffusion* is the process by which a technology spreads across a population of organizations; *assimilation* refers to the process within organizations stretching from initial awareness of the innovation to potentially formal adoption and full-scale deployment.) The last quarter of the twentieth century is often called the *information age,* although perhaps it would be equally appropriate to look on this time as the *innovation age.* With the invention of the microprocessor in 1971, an era of accelerating innovation was launched and continues to this day. Not only has the pace of innovation increased in the general business environment, but also it appears that the ability to innovate has begun to eclipse more traditional contributors to organizational competitiveness (Hamel, 1998). Some have argued that innovation will be *the* key determinant of competitiveness over the next decade (Afuah, 1998). Furthermore, as an increasing number of industries move to "winner-take-all" dynamics, the stakes for successful innovation have become high indeed (Frank & Cook, 1995; Shapiro & Varian, 1998).

Organizations that persistently ignore new technologies risk a slide into uncompetitiveness, yet being on the leading edge brings its own perils. The processes of diffusion and assimilation rarely unfold in a smooth and predictable fashion (Attewell, 1992; Fichman and Kemerer, 1999; Moore, 1992; Swanson & Ramiller, 1997). Chew, Leonard-Barton, and Bohn (1991) report that from 50 to 75% of advanced manufacturing implementations experience some kind of a failure. It has been reported that a similar percentage of business process reengineering projects do not meet key objectives (Brynjolfsson, Renshaw, & Van Alstyne, 1997).[1] From AI (Gill, 1995) to CASE (Fichman & Kemerer, 1999) to ISDN (Lai, Guynes, & Bordoloi, 1993), it is not difficult to find examples of very promising technologies that failed to diffuse as expected.

Thus, the study of IT diffusion and assimilation represents a key area of investigation in the IT field. In this chapter, I present a broad overview of basic concepts, theories, and research findings in this area. I begin with a general discussion of the role of theory and related issues. I then present a framework that classifies key constructs and their effects on diffusion and assimilation. Finally I describe several emerging streams of research in the field and suggest directions for future research.

FUNDAMENTAL ISSUES IN THE STUDY OF IT DIFFUSION AND ASSIMILATION

THE ROLE OF THEORY

The study of innovation diffusion has a long history as a multidisciplinary field (Rogers, 1995) with contributions from sociologists, communication researchers, economists, organizational researchers, IT researchers, and many others. While there is much diversity across these traditions, they are unified by their concern with three basic research questions:

RQ 1:　What determines the rate, pattern, and extent of diffusion of an innovation across a population of potential adopters?

RQ 2: What determines the general propensity of an organization to adopt and assimilate innovations over time?

RQ 3: What determines the propensity of an organization to adopt and assimilate a *particular* innovation?

Nevertheless, no single theory of innovation exists, nor does it seem likely that one will emerge. The closest the field has come to producing such a theory is Rogers' classical model of diffusion (Rogers, 1995) (see Table 7.1). However, while this model has quite rightly had a profound role in shaping the basic concepts, terminology, and scope of the field, it does not—nor does it aim to—apply equally well to all kinds of innovations in all adoption contexts.

The classical model was synthesized from a body of research that focused primarily on *simpler* innovations being adopted *autonomously* by *individuals*. It applies less well to more *complex* technologies, to technologies for which adoption decisions are *linked* in some important way, and to technologies adopted in and by *organizations* (Attewell, 1992; Eveland & Tornatzky, 1990; Fichman, 1992; Kelly & Kranzberg, 1978; Rogers, 1991).

This brings us to a key point regarding the role of theory in innovation research. The absence of a general theory of innovation suggests that researchers should develop theories of the middle range—that is, theories tailored to specific

TABLE 7.1   Components of the Classical Diffusion Model

Component	Definitions/Generalizations
Definition of diffusion	The process involving the communication of an innovation through certain channels over time among the members of a social system.
Typical diffusion pattern	Process starts slowly among pioneering adopters, reaches "takeoff" as a growing community of adopters is established and the effects of peer influence arise, and levels off as the population of potential adopters becomes exhausted, thus leading to an "S-shaped" cumulative adoption curve.
Innovation characteristics	Innovations possess certain characteristics (relative advantage, compatibility, complexity, trialability, observability), which, as perceived by adopters, determine the ultimate rate and pattern of adoption.
Adopter characteristics	Some potential adopters are more prone to innovate than others are and can be identified as such by their personal characteristics (education, age, job tenure, etc.). Adopters can be classified according to when they adopt relative to others (innovators, early majority, etc.).
Adoption decision stages	The adoption decision unfolds as a series of stages flowing from knowledge of the innovation through persuasion, decision, implementation, and confirmation. Adopters are predisposed toward different kinds of influence (e.g., mass market communication versus word of mouth) at different stages.
Opinion leaders and change agents	The actions of certain individuals (opinion leaders and change agents) can accelerate adoption, especially when potential adopters view such individuals as being similar to themselves.

TABLE 7.2 Example Middle Range Theories of Diffusion

Researcher	Context Innovations	Context Adopters	Main Areas of Contrast with Classical Model
Markus, 1987	Communication technologies	Organizations	Inclusion of "critical mass" effects (e.g., the importance highly resourced individuals in gaining critical mass); identification of distinctive "all-or-nothing" diffusion pattern
Attewell, 1992	Complex organizational technologies	Organizations	Inclusion of influences arising from institutions for lowering knowledge barriers (e.g., consulting firms, adoption as a service, technology simplification, special buyer-supplier relationships)
Swanson, 1994	Information technologies	Organizations and IT units	Inclusion of IS unit characteristics (e.g., size, diversity, age of applications portfolio, professional orientation); classification of IT innovation types; postulates differential effects of the same variables depending on IT innovation type

classes of technologies and/or to particular adoption contexts. Table 7.2 provides some examples of these types of models. Some variables and relationships generalize more broadly than others. Therefore, I take two complementary approaches in presenting prior research in this area. In the next section, I present a framework structured around more generalizable variables and relationships. Then, in the following section, I focus on distinctive characteristics of different classes of IT innovations and examine the implications of these characteristics for the study of diffusion and assimilation.

STYLES OF RESEARCH

Most innovation studies conform to one of two general styles of research: *adopter* studies and *diffusion modeling* studies. Adopter studies are primarily interested in understanding differences in adopter "innovativeness." The typical approach is to survey organizations in some population of interest to capture data about (1) the characteristics of those organizations[2] and their adoption contexts and (2) the timing and/or extent of adoption of one or more innovations. The resulting data set is then used to construct a variance model positing effects of organizational and contextual variables on innovativeness. Adopter studies are usually designed to address the latter two research questions listed (i.e., what determines organizational innovativeness both in general [RQ 2] and with respect to particular technologies [RQ 3]?). However, they can also provide insights into the first question (see, for example, Gatignon & Robertson, 1989).

Diffusion modeling studies are primarily concerned with the first research question (i.e., what determines the rate, pattern, and extent of technology diffusion; Mahajan, Mueller, & Bass, 1990; Mahajan & Peterson, 1985; Parker, 1994). The typical approach here is to gather data on the timing of adoptions in some population and then to fit a time series of observed cumulative adoptions to some functional form, such as the logistic distribution (Brancheau & Wetherbe, 1990). Some studies seek to infer support for alternative theories of diffusion based on the observed pattern of adoption for a particular innovation (Gurbaxani, 1990; Gurbaxani & Mendelson, 1990; Hu, Saunders, & Gebelt, 1997; Venkatraman, Loh, & Koh, 1994).

Others compare multiple innovations, seeking to explain why some innovations diffuse more rapidly and widely than others (Mansfield, 1993). Still others have a more applied focus and seek to make predictions about the future course of innovation for a technology (Rai, Ravichandran, & Samaddar, 1998). Diffusion modeling studies represent a tiny fraction of IT innovation research to date. As a result, the main focus of this chapter will be on issues pertinent to adopter studies.

MEASURING INNOVATIVENESS

Both styles of research—adopter studies and diffusion-modeling studies—turn on the question of what it means for an organization to be "innovative" with respect to emerging technologies (Downs & Mohr, 1976; Fichman, 1999; Massetti & Zmud, 1996; Tornatzky & Klein, 1982; Zmud & Apple, 1992). The traditional notion centers on the timing of the formal adoption event, with *adoption* usually defined as physical acquisition or purchase of the innovation (Rogers, 1995). Under this view, organizations that adopt relatively early are more innovative than those that adopt later or not at all.

If organizations always rapidly implement the innovations they adopt, then adoption timing would serve well as the universal definition of innovativeness. However, postadoption behaviors can vary considerably across organizations. In fact, some research suggests that thorough and rapid implementation is the exception rather than the rule for many technologies (Fichman & Kemerer, 1999; Howard & Rai, 1993; Liker, Fleisher, & Arnsdorf, 1992). Furthermore, early adoption of one innovation does not necessarily ensure a systematic pattern of early adoption (Downs & Mohr, 1976). Due to these limitations, several other measures have been developed, including aggregated adoption, assimilation stage achieved, and extent of implementation (see Table 7.3).

The degree to which alternative measures all tap into a more general notion of innovativeness or, alternatively, capture distinct notions of innovativeness that require distinct models and explanatory variables has been the subject of debate. Some compelling arguments have been developed for reasons that different measures of innovativeness should be kept distinct (Downs & Mohr, 1976; Tornatzky & Klein, 1982). Yet more recent empirical studies cast some doubt on these arguments and suggest there may be considerable overlap and consistency in results across these measures (Damanpour, 1991; Fichman, 1999; Zmud & Apple, 1992). While there is not yet a definitive answer to this important question, researchers undertaking work in this area should be acquainted with these issues before selecting an innovativeness measure.

In addition, researchers should consider some key methodological issues. For example, the most rigorous studies now use survival analysis techniques when adoption timing is the outcome variable (Grover, Fielder, & Teng, 1997; Pennings & Harianto, 1992b; Russo, 1991; Singer & Willett, 1991). Studies employing the assimilation stage must take care to confront the issue of "differently directed effects" (i.e., variables that promote progress through early assimilation stages but inhibit progress through later stages or vice versa; see the section on Organizations and Adoption Environments). Studies using extent of implementation must consider how to account for nonadopters (i.e., whether to assign them some arbitrary score for innovativeness or to exclude them from the analysis). The latter can introduce problems resulting from range restriction in study variables (Hoffman, 1995) because analysis is confined only to those organizations innovative enough to have *already adopted*.

TABLE 7.3 Measure Adopter Innovativeness

Measure	Conceptual Definition	Example Operationalizations
Earliness of adoption	Relative earliness of adoption among population of potential adopters	Five-item categorical scale (Rogers, 1995) Adoption/nonadoption (Gatignon & Robertson, 1989) Elapsed time since adoption (Grover et al., 1997)
Aggregated adoption	Frequency or incidence of innovation adoption	Number of software process innovations adopted (Zmud, 1982) Number of telecommunication innovations adopted (Grover & Goslar, 1993)
Internal diffusion	The extent of use of an innovation across people, projects, tasks, or organizational units	Number of microcomputers per employee (Bretschneider & Wittmer, 1993) Percentage of stores using scanners (Zmud & Apple, 1992) Percentage of electronic switches (Cool et al., 1997) Volume and breadth of EDI use (Massetti & Zmud, 1996)
Infusion	The extent to which an innovation's features are used in a complete and sophisticated way	Infusion of supermarket scanners (Zmud & Apple, 1992) Infusion of MRP (Cooper & Zmud, 1990) CASE features used (Howard & Rai, 1993) Depth of EDI use (Massetti & Zmud, 1996)
Routinization	The extent to which an innovation has become a stable and regular part of organizational procedures and behavior	Routinization of government innovations (Yin, 1979) Routinization of supermarket scanners (Zmud & Apple, 1992)
Assimilation	The extent of assimilation of an innovation (where assimilation extends from initial awareness to full institutionalization)	Guttman scale for health care innovations (Meyer & Goes, 1988) Guttman scale for software process innovations (Fichman & Kemerer, 1997a)

FACTORS AFFECTING THE DIFFUSION AND ASSIMILATION OF IT INNOVATIONS

In this section, I classify factors affecting innovation diffusion and assimilation into broad categories and comment on key conceptual and methodological issues for each category. In selecting factors to highlight, my emphasis is on the most well-established and generalizable factors. As illustrated in Figure 7.1, these factors are grouped into three categories: (1) those pertaining to the technologies and their diffusion contexts; (2) those pertaining to organizations and their adoption contexts; and (3) those pertaining to the combination of technology and organization. These three categories map to the three basic research questions identified earlier as follows. The first category (technologies and their diffusion contexts) has the most direct impact on the rate and pattern of diffusion of a technology (RQ 1). The second category (organizations and their adoption environments) relates to the question of what determines the organizational propensity to adopt multiple innovations over time (RQ 2) and to adopt particular innovations (RQ 3). The final category (factors describing the intersection of organization and innovation) pertains only to RQ 3.

FIGURE 7.1   Factors Affecting IT Innovation Diffusion and Assimilation

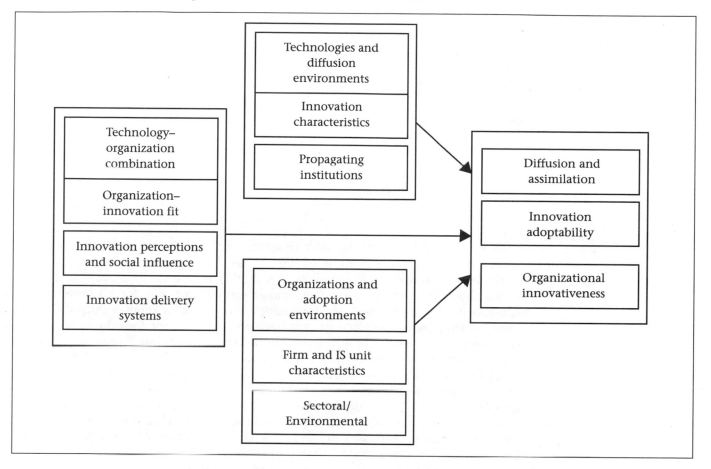

TECHNOLOGIES AND DIFFUSION ENVIRONMENTS
Innovation Characteristics

A central notion in the study of innovation is that technologies possess attributes or characteristics and that these characteristics have systematic effects on diffusion and assimilation. Rogers (1995) highlights five such characteristics, including *relative advantage, compatibility, complexity, trialability* and *observability* (see Table 7.4). Tornatzky and Klein (1982) provide a meta-analysis spanning Rogers' five characteristics and several others. In more recent work, Moore and Benbasat (1991) have developed an instrument to measure eight characteristics of information technologies. Other notable works in this area include Downs and Mohr's (1976) examination of conceptual and measurement issues related to innovation characteristics, Leonard-Barton's (1988a) explication of characteristics related specifically to technology implementation, and Ramiller's (1994) detailed review and assessment of the *compatibility* construct.

In general, innovations possessing favorable characteristics tend to be more attractive and easier to adopt and therefore tend to diffuse more rapidly than those

TABLE 7.4   Innovation Characteristics

Innovation Characteristics (Relation to Innovation)	Related Work
Classic innovation characteristics: Relative advantage (+), compatibility (+), complexity (–), trialability (+), observability (+)	Cooper and Zmud, 1990; Downs and Mohr, 1976; Meyer and Goes, 1988; Moore and Benbasat, 1991; Ramiller, 1994; Rogers, 1995; Tornatzky and Klein, 1982
Other Characteristics: Cost (–), communicability (+), divisibility (+), profitability (+), social approval (+), voluntariness (+/–), image (+), usefulness (+), ease of use (+), result demonstrability (+), visibility (+)	Downs and Mohr, 1976; Leonard-Barton, 1988; Moore and Benbasat, 1991; Tornatzky and Klein, 1982

with less favorable characteristics (Rogers, 1995). While this basic proposition is rather simple, the actual study of innovation characteristics presents challenges. Consider the statement "technology X is highly complex." This could be taken to mean the technology is objectively and invariably complex for all organizations. Alternatively, it could mean the technology is complex for some organizations (e.g., because they lack associated knowledge and skill) but not for others. In the first case, complexity counts as a *primary* characteristic of an innovation; in the second case, it counts as a *secondary* characteristic (Downs & Mohr, 1976). Values for primary characteristics have been assessed based on logical inferences about the innovation in question (e.g., Attewell, 1992; Fichman & Kemerer, 1993) or by relying on expert judgments (e.g., (Meyer & Goes, 1988). Values for secondary characteristics can be inferred from objective features of the organization (e.g., Cooper & Zmud, 1990) and can be captured by soliciting the perceptions of key informants (e.g. Premkumar, Ramamurthy, & Nilakanta, 1994)).

Some researchers view *primary* and *secondary* as mutually exclusive categories and argue that few (or possibly no) characteristics qualify as primary (Downs & Mohr, 1976; Tornatzky & Klein, 1982). This is an unsatisfying result because it leaves no way to conceptualize characteristics at the level of a technology. Perhaps a more useful approach would be to soften the distinction between primary and secondary and to recognize that many innovation characteristics can have facets of *both*. So we could take complexity, when viewed as a primary characteristic, to mean that a technology is likely to be perceived and/or experienced as complex by most organizations in a population relative to other common technologies confronting that population. In fact, it appears that Rogers implicitly embraces this soft-primary view by arguing that it is how the members of a population *collectively perceive* the characteristics of an innovation that determine its rate of adoption in that population (Rogers, 1995, chap. 5). This does not preclude complexity from being treated as a secondary characteristic in another (or even the same) study by measuring the characteristic in relation to particular adopters.

Propagating Institutions

Although some technologies initially emerge as more complex, expensive, and incompatible than others, these initial characteristics can be moderated by the actions

TABLE 7.5   Propagating Institutions and the Diffusion Environment

Factors	Related Work
Propagating institutions: Promotion (+), advertising (+), pricing (+/−), technology standardization (+), technology simplification (+), technology sponsorship (+), subsidies (+), reputation (+), industry competitiveness (+)	Attewell, 1992; Eveland and Tornatzky, 1990; Gatignon and Robertson, 1989; Katz and Shapiro, 1986; King et al., 1994; Mahajan et al., 1990; Mahajan and Peterson, 1985; Reddy, Aram, and Lynn, 1991; Robertson and Gatignon, 1986; Swanson and Ramiller, 1997

of institutions seeking to *propagate* those innovations (Eveland & Tornatzky, 1990; King et al., 1994; Reddy, Aram, & Lynn, 1991; Robertson & Gatignon, 1986; Swanson & Ramiller, 1997). These institutions—which include R&D laboratories, government agencies, technology vendors, consulting firms, and user groups—help to determine the level of resources applied to the task of communicating, promoting, and enhancing a technology and therefore can have a great deal of impact on the rate of technology diffusion (see Table 7.5).

Early work in this area examined the effect of *communication channels* on diffusion and found that adopters tend to respond to mass media channels during the knowledge stage of innovation but place more emphasis on word of mouth during the decision stage (Rogers, 1995). In other work, researchers have gone beyond communication channels to consider other factors including the following:

- Characteristics of supplier organizations, including *reputation,* extent of *marketing support,* and extent of *R&D support* surrounding the innovations they introduce (Robertson & Gatignon, 1986).
- The degree to which propagating institutions actively promote adoption via *sponsorship* or outright *subsidies* (Katz & Shapiro, 1986; King et al., 1994; Rogers, 1991).
- The degree to which the technology is *standardized* (Attewell, 1992; King et al., 1994; Robertson & Gatignon, 1986).

The ideal way to study propagating institutions is to analyze several technologies over time, comparing the effects of these institutions on unfolding diffusion processes. However, researchers have apparently found this approach feasible for only the simplest and most readily available factors, such as *pricing* and *advertising* expenditures (Mahajan et al., 1990). As a result, most research relies on other approaches. Economists usually employ analytical modeling (Katz & Shapiro, 1986) or historical case studies (Cusumano, Mylonadis, & Rosenbloom, 1992). Organizational and IT researchers have also used historical cases (Attewell, 1992; Cats-Baril & Jelassi, 1994). A third approach is to infer the effects of supply-side factors overall based on whether earlier adopters of a particular innovation report being influenced by such factors (e.g., Gatignon & Robertson, 1989).

ORGANIZATIONS AND ADOPTION ENVIRONMENTS

A central tenet of diffusion research is that to understand why some organizations are more innovative than others, we must look to the characteristics of those organizations, their leaders, and the environment in which they operate. Most studies of organizational innovation have been performed with this general objective in mind, and the same has been true of IT innovation studies (Fichman, 1992; Prescott, 1995). In this section, I briefly survey this work.

Organization and Leader Characteristics

Scores of organizational characteristics have been identified that distinguish more innovative organizations from those less prone to innovate. Table 7.6 provides a summary of some of the most prominent of these factors organized into four categories: (1) organizational size and closely related structural variables, (2) other structural characterizations of organizations, (3) personal characteristics of leaders and the workforce as a whole, and (4) characteristics of the communication environment. (For a summary of rationales linking many of these variables to innovativeness, see Damanpour (1991). I address each of these four categories briefly in the following paragraphs.

   1. *Size and Related Characteristics.* Among organizational characteristics, larger *size* has been most consistently related to adopter innovativeness (Rogers, 1995, chap. 10). This is a bit surprising, since in other domains, such as new product introduction, there has been mixed evidence over whether large or small firms lead the way (Lind, Zmud, & Fischer, 1989). Perhaps the best explanation is that size serves as a proxy for other positively related variables such as *scale, wealth, specialization,* and *slack resources* (Tornatzky & Fleischer, 1990, p. 162).

   2. *Other Structural Characteristics.* Regarding other structural characteristics, it has been found that more "organic" organizations (i.e., those with lower *centralization, formalization,* and *vertical differentiation*) will be more likely to embrace new ideas and, hence, will be more likely to initiate and adopt innovations (Zaltman, Duncanj, & Nolbeck, 1973). Interestingly, some researchers have hypothesized that "organic" firms have more difficulty establishing the consensus and singularity of purpose required to successfully implement innovations that have been adopted, and thus should be less likely to sustain implementation (Downs & Mohr, 1976; Zaltman et al., 1973; Zmud, 1982). Or, in other words, these variables may have *differently directioned* effects, depending on the stage of assimilation. As it turns out, studies of IT innovation have not found much support for this hypothesis (Fichman & Kemerer, 1997a; Grover & Goslar, 1993; Nilakanta & Scamell, 1990; Zmud, 1982), and a recent meta-analysis of organization innovation has found that these variables have effects in the same direction throughout the assimilation process (Damanpour, 1991).

   3. *Personal Characteristics of Leaders and the Workforce.* Traditional models of innovation have identified many characteristics that predispose individuals to adopt innovations for personal use outside of the organizational context. Not surprisingly, it has been found that these types of characteristics, when associated with key decision makers or aggregated across the entire organization, also affect organizational innovation. Prominent examples of such characteristics include *education level, professionalism, number of technical specialists, managerial tenure,* and *receptivity toward change* (Damanpour, 1991).

   4. *Characteristics of the Communication Environment.* Traditional models of innovation also hold that diffusion is driven primarily by communication (i.e., that

TABLE 7.6   Organization and IS Unit Characteristics

Factors	Related Work
Size and related characteristics: Host organization size (+), IS unit size (+), scale (+), slack resources (+)	Bretschneider and Wittmer, 1993; Damanpour, 1991; Fichman and Kemerer, 1997a; Grover et al., 1997; Kimberley and Evanisko, 1981; Lind et al., 1989; Meyer and Goes, 1988; Swanson, 1994
Other structural characteristics: Centralization (–), formalization (–), specialization (+), vertical differentiation (–)	Damanpour, 1991; Grover and Goslar, 1993; Kimberley and Evanisko, 1981; Kwon and Zmud, 1987; Zmud, 1982
Personal characteristics of leaders and the workforce: Professionalism (+), education (+), technical expertise (+), technical specialists (+), managerial tenure (+), receptivity toward change (+)	Ball, Dambolena, & Hennessey, 1987; Damanpour, 1991; Fichman and Kemerer, 1997a; Grover et al., 1997; Kimberley and Evanisko, 1981; Swanson, 1994
Characteristics of the Communication environment: Information sources and communication channels (+)	Ball et al., 1987; Nilakanta and Scamell, 1990; Rai, 1995; Zmud, 1983; Zmud, Lind, and Young, 1990

when and how a prospective adopter first hears about an innovation has a major influence on adoption). Naturally, then, organizations that make larger investments in a wide array of information sources and communication channels (e.g., professional society memberships, periodical subscriptions, external seminars, internal advanced technology groups) should be more likely to lead in innovating (Nilakanta & Scamell, 1990).

Adoption Environment

Organizations do not exist in a vacuum but operate in an environment that provides opportunities and imposes constraints. Thus, we see that certain sectors, such as telecommunications and financial services, tend to lead in the adoption of IT innovations while others tend to lag. Innovation researchers have identified a number of environmental factors that can influence the general propensity of an organization to innovate, including industry *concentration, competitive pressure, profitability/wealth, R&D intensity, IT intensity,* and *rate of technical change* (Eveland & Tornatzky, 1990; Meyer & Goes, 1988; Robertson & Gatignon, 1986) (see Table 7.7). Although environmental factors have not been much used in studies of IT innovation, this appears to be changing with the recent interest in technologies such as EDI, for which environment factors are especially important.

TABLE 7.7   Characteristics of the Adoption Environment

Factors	Related Work
Adoption environment: Concentration/Competitiveness (+), competitive pressure (+), profitability/wealth (+), R&D intensity (+), IT intensity (+), rate of technical change (+)	Eveland and Tornatzky, 1990; Gatignon and Robertson, 1989; Iacovou et al., 1995; Loh and Venkatraman, 1992; Meyer and Goes, 1988; Premkumar et al., 1994; Robertson and Gatignon, 1986

THE TECHNOLOGY-ORGANIZATION COMBINATION

Many of the factors that affect innovation diffusion and assimilation are not characteristics of either innovations or organizations per se but describe a particular innovation-organization combination. For example, an innovation may be highly compatible for one organization but not for another. Likewise, an organization may have a strong champion for one innovation but not for another. Therefore, compatibility and champions are most appropriately viewed as describing the *combination* of innovation and organization rather than either one in isolation. In this section, I survey three categories of such factors: (1) organization-technology "fit," (2) innovation perceptions and social influence, and (3) the *delivery system* used by organization to deploy an innovation.[3]

Organization-Innovation Fit

Even though an organization may exhibit a generally high propensity to innovate over time, it may still lag in the adoption of innovations that do not fit well with its organizational needs, strategies, resources, or capabilities. Likewise, a generally less innovative organization may still choose to be an early adopter of innovation that constitutes a good fit. This suggests attention to organizational characteristics that capture the relative fit between innovation and organization (see Table 7.8). For example, *wealthy* organizations are particularly well positioned to adopt high-cost innovations (Downs & Mohr, 1976). High *absorptive capacity* in a domain increases the organizational capacity to assimilate innovations in that domain (Cohen & Levinthal, 1990). This, in turn, suggests that the primary antecedents of absorptive capacity—*related knowledge* and *diversity of knowledge*—will also predict innovativeness with respect to particular innovations (Fichman & Kemerer, 1997a). Cooper and Zmud (1990) have shown that high *compatibility* between organizational tasks and the innovation predict adoption of materials requirements planning (MRP).

Innovation Perceptions and Social Influence

How potential adopters perceive an innovation is a key determinant of adoption (Rogers, 1995; Tornatzky & Klein, 1982). Since innovation perceptions vary across potential adopters and across technologies, they represent a feature of the organization-innovation combination. Innovation perceptions can operate on two levels. When the focus is the formal organizational decision to adopt, it is the perceptions of leaders and key decision makers that matter. Most innovation studies have concentrated on this level and have studied the generic innovation characteristics from Rogers' classical model (see Table 7.9).

TABLE 7.8 Organization-Innovation Fit

Factors	Related Work
Organization-Innovation fit: Absorptive capacity (+), related knowledge (+), diversity of knowledge (+), Task-technology compatibility (+), wealth (+)	Boynton, et al., 1994; Cohen and Levinthal, 1990; Cooper and Zmud, 1990; Downs and Mohr, 1976; Fichman and Kemerer, 1997a; Swanson, 1994

Table 7.9   Innovation Perceptions

Factors	Related Work
Classic innovation characteristics: Relative advantage (+), compatibility (+), complexity (−), trialability (+), observability (+)	Brancheau and Wetherbe, 1990; Hoffer and Alexander, 1992; Lai, 1997; Moore and Benbasat, 1991; Premkumar et al., 1994; Ramiller, 1994; Rogers, 1995
Technology acceptance model: Usefulness (+), ease of use (+)	Davis, 1989; Davis et al., 1989; Gefen and Straub, 1997; Karahanna and Straub, 1999; Szajna, 1996

However, there is a second level to consider. Even after formal adoption, individuals within the organization often have broad discretion about whether and how to use an innovation (Leonard-Barton and Deschamps, 1988). Thus, a key element of the postformal adoption process for many innovations is the extent to which the technology is *accepted* among intended users, and this intraorganizational adoption process is largely driven by individual perceptions of an innovation (Kraut et al., 1998). While researchers in this stream have examined the influence of characteristics from Rogers' classical model (Brancheau & Wetherbe, 1990), the bulk of this work has focused on two constructs originally identified by Davis as part of his *technology acceptance model (TAM),* namely perceived *usefulness* and perceived *ease of use* (Davis, 1989; Davis, Bagozzi, & Warshaw, 1989).[4] (These two characteristics may be viewed as closely related to perceived *relative advantage* and perceived *complexity,* respectively.)

While few would doubt that innovation perceptions have a major influence on adoption, this naturally raises the question of just how these perceptions are formed. There are two main schools of thought here: the *rational/contingent* school and the *social learning* school (Kraut et al., 1998; Webster & Trevino, 1995). Adherents of the first school argue that potential adopters form perceptions primarily based on an assessment of the objective features of the technology as conditioned by their own particular needs and capabilities (or, in the case formal adoption decisions, by the organization's needs and capabilities). Adherents of the second school argue that technology perceptions are primarily socially constructed (Fulk, 1993) (i.e., they are driven by an individual's observation of *group norms* and *co-worker attitudes and behaviors* toward the innovation) (Webster & Trevino, 1995) (see Table 7.10). While earlier work casts the two perspectives as competing (Fulk, 1993), more recent work has argued for integrating them (Karahanna & Straub, 1999; Kraut et al., 1998; Webster & Trevino, 1995). This integrative perspective is consistent with Rogers' model, which holds that innovation perceptions are affected not only by objective features of the technology but also by the actions of *opinion leaders* and *change agents* (Leonard-Barton, 1985; Rogers, 1995, p. 330).

Table 7.10   Social Influence

Factors	Related Work
Group norms (+/−), co-worker attitudes and behaviors (+/−), opinion leaders (+/−), change agents (+/−)	Chin et al., 1997; DeSanctis and Poole,1994; Fulk, 1993; Karahanna and Straub, 1999; Kraut et al., 1998; Leonard-Barton, 1985; Sambamurthy and Chin, 1994; Webster and Trevino, 1995; Wheeler and Valacich, 1996

Table 7.11   Innovation Delivery System

Factors	Related Work
Delivery system—factors: Top management support (+), technology champion (+), training (+), links to propagating organizations (+)	Howell and Higgens, 1990; Lai, 1997; Leonard-Barton, 1988b; Premkumar et al., 1994; Raho et al., 1987; Rai and Bajwa, 1997; Robertson and Gatignon, 1986
Delivery system—process models: Fit of process model with technology and organization (+)	Brynjolfsson et al., 1997; Chew et al., 1991; Fichman and Moses, 1999; Gallivan et al., 1994; Markus and Keil, 1994; Orlikowski, 1993; Orlikowski and Hofman, 1997

Innovation Delivery System

The means by which the implementation process is supported and managed for a particular innovation is the *delivery system* for that innovation (Leonard-Barton, 1988b). Much research has been devoted to identifying the characteristics of effective delivery systems (See Table 7.11). Some of the more popular factors in this category include the degree of *top management support* and *technology championship* (Howell & Higgens, 1990; Rai & Bajwa, 1997) and level of *training* and other resources invested in organizational learning (Raho, Belahlau, & Fielder, 1987). Another element of the delivery system concerns the extent to which the facilitating mechanisms developed by propagating institutions (see the earlier section on Propagating Institutions) are actually sought out and employed by a given adopter. So, the positive effects of such factors as *standardization*, *subsidies*, and *consulting services* will be most beneficial for those organizations that actually give preference to standard technologies, take advantage of subsidies, employ consulting firms, and so forth (Robertson & Gatignon, 1986).

Yet another key part of the delivery system is the *process model* used to guide innovation implementation (Leonard-Barton, 1988b). Several prescriptive models of the implementation process have been developed, each intended to address a different challenge. Thus, we now have models to address challenges related to organizational learning (Chew et al., 1991), the need to coordinate a large number of interdependent implementation elements (Brynjolfsson et al., 1997), the need to deal with indeterminacy about what an organization can or should accomplish with the technology (Orlikowski & Hofman, 1997), the need to build "implementability" into technologies from the start (Markus & Keil, 1994), and the need to sustain implementation commitment and momentum (Fichman & Moses, 1999). Other research has considered more general properties of implementation processes, such as the radicalness of change processes, and sought outcomes and the pace of change (Gallivan, Hofman, & Orlikowski, 1994; Orlikowski, 1993).

DISTINCTIVE CHARACTERISTICS OF IT INNOVATIONS AND IMPLICATIONS

For many years, researchers examining the adoption of innovations in and by organizations relied on Rogers' classical model of diffusion—or on models with similar structure and explanatory variables—to guide the model-building process (Rogers,

FIGURE 7.2   Traditional Diffusion Models and Related Design Elements

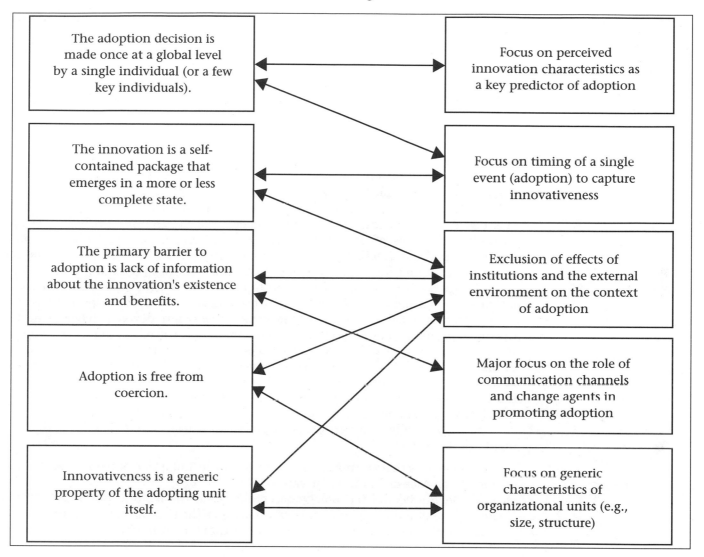

1995). However, along with the classical model comes a set of assumptions, often only implicit, about the nature of innovations and the typical circumstances surrounding their adoption (see Figure 7.2).

In some cases these types of assumptions hold—or at least do not introduce major problems—and traditional models can be expected to exhibit good explanatory power (Brancheau & Wetherbe, 1990). However, in other cases the assumptions do not hold, and so the burden falls on researchers to develop new models—or extensions to traditional models—that better reflect the nature of the innovations under study. This is just what many innovation researchers have done over the past decade or so. In this section, I identify several characteristics of IT innovations that are at odds with the implicit assumptions of traditional diffusion models and summarize the implications of these characteristics for research on the diffusion and assimilation of IT innovations.

TWO-PART ADOPTION DECISIONS

Many IT innovations involve a *two-part* adoption decision process inwhich a formal decision to make the innovation available to the organization as a whole is then followed by local decisions (by departments, work groups, projects, or individuals) about whether and how to actually use the innovation (Leonard-Barton, 1988b). Examples of innovations prone to two-part decision processes include software development tools (Fichman & Kemerer, 1999), work group support technologies (DeSanctis & Poole, 1994), and new communication technologies (Kraut et al., 1998).

For these kinds of technologies, the very notion of *adoption* deserves special scrutiny. Should we consider an organization to have "really" adopted when senior managers give the go-ahead? Or would it perhaps be better to wait until some threshold level of actual use is reached? Depending on which definition is used, a vastly different conclusion may be drawn about the rate of diffusion of some technologies (Fichman & Kemerer, 1999). Likewise, what it means to *use* these technologies deserves additional scrutiny. Technologies can be used *faithfully*, in keeping with the intentions of designers, or *ironically* (Chin, Gopal, & Salisbury, 1997; DeSanctis & Poole, 1994). Technologies can be used *richly*, in ways that expand the capacities of the medium, or they can be used *thinly* (Carlson & Zmud, 1999).

Two-part decision processes mean that the latter stages of technology assimilation—from formal adoption to full institutionalization—become especially worthy of focused study. This, in turn, suggests that researchers develop richer models of the intraorganizational processes of innovation. One good example is *adaptive structuration theory* (AST) (DeSanctis & Poole, 1994). As with models of innovation diffusion, AST posits that technologies have systematic features that influence the processes by which technologies are adopted and used. However, AST provides a more detailed view of the interplay between these features, the structures of adopting organizations, and the processes of technology appropriation.

More generally, two-part decision processes suggest the following design elements to researchers:

- Use measures that capture rich differences in postadoption outcomes (see earlier section on Measuring Innovativeness).
- Consider individual technology acceptance, and the factors that affect it, as a key element of the implementation process (see the earlier section on Innovation Perceptions and Social Influence and the chapter on individual acceptance by Agarwal).
- Focus attention on elements that have disproportionate influence on the latter stages of assimilation, such as factors associated with the delivery system and the process model supporting implementation (see the earlier section on the Innovation Delivery System).
- Develop richer models of the postformal adoption process (as just described).

In fact, the prevalence of two-part decisions among IT innovations perhaps explains why IT researchers have taken the lead in moving the innovation field forward along the lines outlined here.

KNOWLEDGE BARRIERS AND ORGANIZATIONAL LEARNING

Although all technologies require some measure of organizational learning to be adopted, some fall on the extreme end of the spectrum in the demands they place on adopters for associated knowledge and skills. Such technologies are said to be subject to *knowledge barriers* because the difficulty of acquiring the knowledge required to deploy them creates a barrier to diffusion (Attewell, 1992). Exemplars of IT innovations subject to knowledge barriers include technologies such as expert systems (Gill, 1995), CAD/CAM (Liker, Fleischer, & Arnsdorf, 1992), and CASE (Fichman & Kemerer, 1999).

Knowledge barriers have important implications for innovation diffusion and assimilation. At the macro diffusion level, they suggest that vendors and other supply-side institutions, rather than focusing primarily on communicating the existence of an innovation and its benefits (as per traditional models of diffusion), should turn their attention to developing mechanisms that actively lower knowledge barriers over time (Attewell, 1992). Examples of such mechanisms include these:

- Consulting and service firms that specialize in accumulating and disseminating technical know-how.
- Special buyer-supplier relationships that go beyond selling to include intensive training, technology sharing, and sponsorship of technology user groups.
- New services that permit indirect use of the innovation (e.g., via outsourcing).
- Technology standardization and simplification (Attewell, 1992).

At the micro level, organizations that are more able to bear the burden of organizational learning[5] should be more likely to appear on the vanguard of adoption and assimilation. Characteristics of such organizations include scale economies related to learning, pre-existing knowledge related to the focal innovation, and diversity in technical activities and knowledge (Attewell, 1992; Boynton, Zmud, & Jacobs, 1994; Cohen & Levinthal, 1990; Fichman & Kemerer, 1997a). This attention to organizational learning also suggests a detailed focus on individual learning and, in particular, how the *nature,* not just the *extent,* of prior experiences with a technology can affect technology perceptions, appropriation, and use (Carlson & Zmud, 1999).

Finally, knowledge barriers suggest that organizations must be prepared to invest in mechanisms to facilitate knowledge acquisition during the assimilation process. Such mechanisms include using intensive regimes of learning by doing on nonproduction systems (Fichman & Kemerer, 1997b), hiring mentors, a new type of consultancy that actively promotes organizational learning as part of its consulting mission (Fichman & Kemerer, 1997b), using prototyping and simulation (Chew et al., 1991), and participating in learning-related joint ventures (Kogut, 1988; Pennings & Harianto, 1992).

INCREASING RETURNS AND BANDWAGON EFFECTS

Telephones, e-mail, and communications technologies more generally are worth nothing to any one particular adopter unless others also adopt (Kraut et al., 1998; Markus, 1987). These technologies illustrate an extreme case of a more general characteristic of many information technologies, namely that the value of the technology to any particular adopter is determined largely by the size of the network of other adopters (Arthur, 1988; Farrell & Saloner, 1987; Katz & Shapiro, 1986; Schilling, 1998; Shapiro & Varian, 1998). Such technologies become more inherently attractive with each additional adoption and, hence, are said to possess *increasing returns* to adoption (Arthur, 1996). Exemplars include microprocessor chips (Arthur, 1996), packaged software (Brynjolfsson & Kemerer, 1997), and, as just mentioned, communications technologies.

The subjection of a technology to increasing returns sets the stage for a distinctive pattern of diffusion, one driven by positive feedback loops in adoption and associated "bandwagon" effects (Abrahamson & Rosenkopf, 1997; Arthur, 1996; Shapiro & Varian, 1998, chap. 7). Characteristics of this diffusion dynamic include the following:

- A tendency toward more dramatic diffusion outcomes, that is, rapid saturation when a self-reinforcing process takes hold or abandonment when it does not (Abrahamson & Rosenkopf, 1997; Markus, 1987; Shapiro & Varian, 1998).
- A tendency for a "critical mass" of adoptions to be required before the technology becomes attractive to a broad community of adopters (Markus, 1987; Rogers, 1991).
- A tendency for markets to be *tippy;* that is, once a particular instance of a technology gains the upper hand, it tends to go on to capture the market (Arthur, 1988; Kraut et al., 1998).
- A tendency for *excess inertia* to develop around an existing standard because of reluctance among users to leave a mature network and join an immature one (Farrell & Saloner, 1987).
- A tendency for a community to become *locked in* to widely adopted technology standards, even inferior ones such as the QWERTY keyboard (David, 1985; Schilling, 1998).

These diffusion patterns, in turn, have a number of implications for innovation researchers and managers. First, they suggest that the early part of the diffusion cycle is especially critical and that strong *sponsorship* or the use of outright *subsidies* for early adopters may be required for some technologies, particularly those facing a well-entrenched installed base, to reach "critical mass" (Katz & Shapiro, 1986; King et al., 1994; Rogers, 1991). It has even been suggested that the diffusion of such technologies falls into two separate "regimes," with the precritical mass regime being driven by different forces from the postcritical mass regime (Cool, Diericks, & Szulanski, 1997). Second, it suggests that the distribution of interests and/or resources in a potential adopter population can be particularly important; for example, a high degree of *heterogeneity* of interests can make it possible for some technologies to bootstrap to critical mass, even when the value of the innovation, in the absence of many adopters, is quite low for most candidate adopters (Granovetter & Soong, 1983; Huff & Munro, 1989; Markus, 1987; Oliver, Marwell, & Teixeira, 1985). Third, because the ultimate value of an innovation is so dynamic and uncertain, it suggests that *managerial expectations*—about the future course of an innovation, its complements, and its substitutes—will be especially influential in the minds of adopters (Rosenberg, 1976).

INCOMPLETE PRODUCTS/INFRASTRUCTURE DEPENDENCE

Many IT innovations—especially more radical breakthroughs—initially emerge as *incomplete products* in that they provide only partial solutions to the problems they aim to address or they are suitable only for very specialized applications, or both (Levitt, 1986; Moore, 1992; Rosenberg, 1994, p. 4). In extreme cases, an innovation simply can not be adopted prior to the diffusion of a some necessary supporting *infrastructure*[6] (e.g., ISDN telephony applications require that ISDN be supported by telecommunication service providers). Other IT innovations that emerged as incomplete products include RISC and document imaging systems (Moore, 1992).

To be attractive to a mass market, such technologies must be broadened and deepened into a *whole product* solution (Moore, 1992). For, example, for object-oriented (OO) programming[7] to be attractive to most potential users, it must be combined with development methodologies, modeling tools, and compatible databases (Fichman & Kemerer, 1997b). However, the primary means by which a technology is broadened and deepened is through self-reinforcing cycles of adoption and use (Fichman & Kemerer, 1999). This leads to a catch-22: To be accepted and used, a technology must become robust, but to become robust it must be accepted and used. To escape this catch-22, Moore has argued that suppliers must define a niche market narrow enough to enable the development of a whole product solution *in relation to that niche*. Then widespread adoption within that niche can provide the additional investment capital and market experience required to broaden the whole product solution to encompass nearby niches, and so on, until the technology has become attractive to the mass market.

Among adopters, incomplete products present especially high adoption risks. Since these technologies are also often subject to knowledge barriers, it can be difficult for managers to assess the full array of supporting components that compose a whole product solution (Fichman & Kemerer, 1997b). This suggests that to manage these risks, adopters should choose initial application areas based on the feasibility of assembling a whole product implementation *in relation to that area,* not just on the expected payoff from use in that area if the technology works as expected. Also, adopters can more explicitly acknowledge the risks involved through increased attention to expectation management (for example, by evaluating the adoption of such technologies not according to the logic of traditional cost-benefit analysis but according to the logic of real options (McGraith, 1997)).

LINKED ADOPTION DECISIONS

For most IT innovations, individual firms are free to adopt—or not adopt—based primarily on circumstances specific to their organizations. This is not to say that they can ignore what other firms might do in *aggregate,* since, as explained earlier, there are compelling reasons to go along with the crowd in adopting some technologies. However, for some IT innovations, the adoption decisions among two or more *particular* firms are tightly linked because the innovation changes the way they transact business. Exemplars include EDI, integrated supply-chain planning systems, extranets, and other interorganizational systems (Hart & Saunders, 1997).

When adoption decisions are linked in this way, the implications for models of innovation can be profound. To begin with, this linkage directs attention to the different *roles* firms may take within a network of firms transacting business (Iacovou, Benbasat, & Dexter, 1995; Premkumar et al., 1994). Some may become *initiators* in the network and actively promote adoption; others may prefer to be *followers,* with adoption being triggered by the actions of initiators. Linked adoption decisions also raise issues related to *power* (Hart & Saunders, 1997; Premkumar et al., 1994; Williams, 1994). In some cases, a powerful firm may encourage adoption using subsidies or other positive incentives (the "carrot" approach) or even compel adoption as a condition of doing business (the "stick" approach). As a result, different models of adoption may be required, depending on a firm's role and relative power in the network. In addition, since these types of systems create new dependencies and vulnerabilities among firms, *trust* emerges as a key explanatory variable (Hart & Saunders, 1997, 1998). Finally, since the initial decision to adopt may be triggered by different factors than subsequent decisions to expand the use of EDI, this suggests the use of multiple innovativeness measures, each with some potentially distinctive explanatory variables (Hart & Saunders, 1998; Massetti & Zmud, 1996).

FUTURE RESEARCH

Many promising avenues for future work are available to researchers interested in the diffusion and assimilation of IT innovations. In this section, I summarize a few of these research directions.

TESTS OF RECENT THEORETICAL WORK

The distinctive characteristics of IT innovations described here have motivated much of the recent theoretical work related to IT diffusion and assimilation. Recent tests of many of these ideas have been quite promising (see especially Attewell, 1992; Boynton et al., 1994; Cool et al., 1997; Fichman & Kemerer, 1997a; Hart & Saunders, 1997; Kraut et al., 1998; Pennings & Harianto, 1992) . However, the task of empirical confirmation has just begun. A vigorous stream of empirical research could be built around any one of these theoretical views.

In addition, since many IT innovations possess two or more of the distinctive characteristics described earlier and since there are theoretical overlaps among them, future research could work toward combining multiple theoretical streams into a more integrated view of IT innovation. In fact, some recent work seems to be heading in just this direction. Fichman and Kemerer (1999) use knowledge barriers and increasing returns to explain the distinctive patterns of diffusion exhibited by software process technology innovations. Abrahamson and Rosenkopf (1997) draw on ideas related to organizational learning, increasing returns, and managerial fashion to model bandwagon effects in social networks. Kraut et al. (1998) combine elements from traditional diffusion of innovation theory, increasing returns, and social influence to explain the intraorganizational diffusion (and nondiffusion) of competing video conferencing systems. Swanson and Ramiller (1997) combine ideas related to knowledge barriers, increasing returns, incomplete products, and managerial fashion into an institutional view of IT innovation.

GENERIC CHARACTERISTICS OF IT INNOVATIONS

The effects of generic innovation characteristics have provided a pillar of research on technology diffusion and assimilation. Yet only recently—with the stream of research on *technology acceptance* (Davis, 1989; Davis et al., 1989)—have researchers begun to seriously address the many conceptual and methodological difficulties (Tornatzky & Klein, 1982) with research in this area.[8] Future research could focus on incorporating the more rigorous elements of technology acceptance research into innovation field studies. This includes measuring innovation perceptions prior to adoption decisions and, in the case of organizational adoption, measuring the perceptions of informants who will actually be influential in the formal adoption decision process.

Also, it would be interesting to look beyond the perceptions of potential adopters when measuring innovation characteristics. As Figure 7.3 shows, there are two dichotomies in how innovation characteristics may be conceived: *primary* versus *secondary* (as discussed earlier) and *objective* versus *perceived*. Taken together, these two dichotomies result in four alternative approaches, only one of which (Quadrant I) has received much attention by innovation researchers.

Measures from Quadrant I capture how complex (compatible, etc.) a potential adopter perceives a technology to be relative to how other adopters perceive it. In studies employing this approach, respondents typically reply to agree/disagree Likert scales, such as those developed by Moore and Benbasat (1991). Quadrant II, by contrast, captures how inherently complex (compatible, etc.) a technology is for one adopter relative to how complex it is for other potential adopters. For example, Cooper and Zmud (1990) capture the relative complexity of MRP adoption by looking at the complexity of assemblies for manufactured parts within responding firms, the idea being that MRP adoption will be experienced as more complex by firms with more complex assemblies. Meyer and Goes (1988) capture the relative compatibility of medical innovations in part by measuring the presence of staff physicians for the associated specialties.

FIGURE 7.3   Innovation Characteristics

	Perceived	Objective
Primary (community level)	Captures how complex (compatible, etc.) a potential adopter population collectively perceives a technology to be in relation to other common technologies adopted by the population *Example:* None found III | IV	Captures how inherently complex (compatible, etc.) a technology is in relation to other common technologies adopted by a population *Example:* Meyer and Goes, 1988
	I | II	
Secondary (adopter level)	Captures how complex (compatible, etc.) a particular adopter perceives a technology to be relative to how other adopters perceive the technology *Example:* Most studies of IT innovation characteristics	Captures how inherently complex (compatible, etc.) a technology is for one adopter relative to how complex it is for other potential adopters *Example:* Cooper and Zmud, 1990

Technology perceptions are affected by many factors beyond features of the technology itself and its interaction with features of the adopting unit. These other factors include the characteristics of the perceiver and whether the prevailing social norms related to the technology are positive or negative (Kraut et al., 1998). Therefore, the values of characteristics in Quadrants I and II can differ markedly for the same technology (e.g., managers might perceive a technology as less complex than it actually turns out to be).

Quadrants III and IV map the concepts from Quadrants I and II to the community level, thus averaging away local differences. As result, Quadrants III and IV capture differences across *technologies,* whereas Quadrants I and II capture differences across *adopters.* Although no examples of Quadrant III measures could be found (thus suggesting a potential research opportunity), Meyer and Goes (1988) show how expert opinions can be used to capture measures in Quadrant IV.

While it makes sense that Quadrant I measures are most pertinent to understanding the timing of particular adoptions, for other kinds of questions (i.e., What determines the rate and pattern of diffusion? What determines the propensity to sustain assimilation of an innovation that has been adopted?), other approaches to incorporating innovation characteristics may be warranted. It might even be interesting to combine multiple approaches within the confines of the same study to address such questions as these: Which has the greater impact on adoption decisions, objective or perceived characteristics? On implementation outcomes? Does it ever happen that perceived characteristics *systematically* diverge from objective characteristics, either at the community or adopter level? When is this most likely to occur? What happens when it does?

MANAGERIAL FAD AND FASHION

The effects of increasing returns provide a normatively rational explanation for the bandwagon dynamics observed for many innovations. However, not all examples of bandwagons can be attributed to normatively rational forces. From the hula-hoop to Beanie Babies, there are many instances of *social bandwagons* driven by the forces of *fad* and *fashion.* In an interesting stream of research, it has been argued that managerial innovations can be driven by similar forces (Abrahamson, 1991, 1996; Abrahamson & Rosenkopf, 1997).

More specifically, this research posits that managers can feel pressure to keep up with current fashions in the domain of managerial innovations, and this pressure becomes an important determinant of adoption. Management-related institutions (consulting firms, university researchers, business "gurus") have an interest in creating fashion consciousness to increase demand for their innovative ideas and related services. And then, to the extent that adoption of new managerial ideas has become widespread, other forms of institutional pressure—from business partners, board of directors, and shareholders—can be brought to bear on perceived laggards. This pressure may result from a desire for the firm to look progressive, an assumption that if an idea is popular it must hold merit, or a desire to be assured of doing no worse than the competition (Abrahamson, 1996).

Although IT innovations do, of course, always have a technical component, they are also managerial innovations (Swanson & Ramiller, 1997), and so it would be surprising if managerial fashion played no role in the diffusion and assimilation of IT innovations. This suggests several interesting research questions. To what extent do the forces of fad and fashion apply to IT innovations? How can we discriminate the forces of fad and fashion from the lure of genuine economic benefits that arise from increasing returns? Are organizations less likely to sustain the assimilation of innovations for which initial adoption was driven primarily by fashion consciousness?

CONCLUSIONS

Successful innovation is a key contributor to organization success. However, what it means to innovate successfully and how to build organizations and processes that facilitate more effective innovation are complex issues. Organizations can err by adopting too few innovations (i.e., fewer than their needs and capabilities would suggest) or by adopting too many. They can err by adopting the wrong innovations that do not provide significant advantages given the organization's particular situation. They can err by adopting the right innovations but at the wrong time—so soon that the costs and risks of adoption exceed the likely payoff or so late that the competition has already gained a competitive advantage. They can err by adopting the right innovations at the right time but failing to implement them in a way that generates net benefits.

Fortunately, our understanding of the processes of innovation diffusion and assimilation has grown considerably since IT researchers first became interested in this area in the early 1980s. In this chapter I have endeavored to communicate the state of this knowledge. This chapter has summarized the major research questions, constructs, models, and empirical findings that constitute the field, yet there is much more good work to be done. As researchers have considered the many distinctive characteristics of IT innovations, there has been a corresponding effort to develop more sophisticated models that go beyond traditional approaches—to incorporate the effects of institutions, knowledge barriers, increasing returns, adaptive structuration, and social bandwagons, to name a few. A rich opportunity exists to confirm these promising streams and to synthesize them into more complex and realistic models of IT innovation diffusion and assimilation.

ENDNOTES

1. See the chapter on business process change by Grover and Kettinger.
2. While organizational characteristics can serve as important determinants of innovation adoption, it is also true that once adopted, new technologies can have major impacts on organizational characteristics; see the chapter on organizational consequences of IT by Robey and Boudreau.
3. See the chapter by Segars and Dean and the one on business process change by Grover and Kettinger for more on the subject of crafting effective delivery strategies for innovative systems and technologies.
4. See the chapter by Agarwal.
5. See the chapter by Alavi for more on the subject of organizational learning.
6. See the chapter by Weill and Broadbent.
7. See the chapter by George for descriptions of OO, CASE, component reuse, and other innovations in software process technology.
8. See the chapter by Agarwal.

Chapter 8

End-User Training Research: Status and Models for the Future

Lorne Olfman and Proadpran Pitsatorn

Businesses spend enormous sums of money on end-user training. With newer software architecture such as enterprise resource planning (ERP), it has been reported that 10 to 20% of the implementation cost was allocated to end-user training (Snell, 1997). The average (mean) organization devoted one-quarter of its total employee-training budget to teach the use of computers and computer systems (Anonymous, 1996). A simple research question is whether that money is spent wisely. It is important that organizations follow specific guidelines or strategies to implement their end-user training programs to gain maximum benefits. The strategies outline variables to consider, steps to follow, and methodologies to evaluate the results, given specific situations. This chapter recommends that researchers and practitioners consider end-user training strategies as a method for designing and assessing the value of end-user training efforts.

The chapter accomplishes its objective by summarizing previous research in the domain of end-user training through the lens of three key frameworks from the research on end-user training literature:

- "Framework for Research," Bostrom, Olfman, and Sein (1990).
- "Training Process Model," Compeau et al. (1995).
- "Learning/Training Strategy Model," Sein, Bostrom, and Olfman (1999).

For newcomers to the field, this chapter will serve as a primer on the scope of end-user training research. For researchers in the domain, the chapter summarizes past research and puts it in a context of where to go next. Finally, the gaps within the three frameworks are identified, and research areas for the future are suggested.

RESEARCH FRAME

End-user training research evolved from many fields in addition to information systems. Organizational behavior, psychology, education, and computer science all contribute to this field of study. Using these reference disciplines, a number of end-user training frameworks have been developed by researchers. These frameworks can be used to outline the extent of current research in end-user training and future directions for research and practice.

FRAMEWORK FOR RESEARCH ON END-USER TRAINING

Bostrom, Olfman, and Sein (1990) proposed a framework for research on end-user training that integrates cognitive psychology, educational psychology, information science, and computer science. This framework indicates that the target system, training method, and individual differences, individually and in combination, affect a user's mental model to produce training outcomes, which include learning performance and attitudes toward using the target system on the job.

PROCESS MODEL FOR TRAINING

Compeau et al. (1995) proposed a "process model for training." This framework highlights the key factors to consider in the management of end-user learning and training in order to provide for effective outcomes. Based on an early model of end-user training and learning (Sein, Bostrom, & Olfman, 1987) and more recent research in the field, the authors emphasize detailed activities within each phase of training, from the *initiation phase* to the *formal training and learning phase* to the *post-training phase*. The framework addresses important issues such as the transfer of learning to the workplace and computer-based approaches to learning and training.

LEARNING/TRAINING STRATEGY MODEL

By introducing this strategy model, Sein et al. (1999) demonstrated that to produce effective training outcomes, practitioners should shift their attention from "skilled-focused" training and move toward "conceptual" training. This is due to the ongoing rapid changes in technology and a typical shortage of skilled personnel. Today's client/server architectures, integrated processes, and integrated packages such as ERP systems lead to new requirements for effective training. Hence, the authors proposed a framework of knowledge levels that comprise a more complete range of knowledge outcomes, which can be used to develop a comprehensive training strategy.

RELATIONSHIP AMONG MODELS

The framework for research on end-user training was published with the goal of creating a systematic approach to the study of end-user training. The key element in this framework lies in detailing each factor that may influence training outcomes and the relationships between factors. However, another side of end-user training, that is, the details of the training process itself, also must be considered in doing research that will produce effective end-user training solutions. The process model training framework offered this aspect. It also addresses practitioners' concerns in terms of matching end-users' needs with types of training, evaluation of training, and post-training issues. Given that the first two models do not speak to how training strategies can be devised to match the key parameters defined by the first model and the processes outlined in the second model, the third framework, the learning/training strategy model, attempts to bridge that gap.

BOSTROM, OLFMAN, AND SEIN FRAMEWORK FOR RESEARCH

Many researchers have shown that individual differences or diversity among users, such as learning style, may affect users' learning about a new end-user computing (EUC) software package. Bostrom et al. (1990) proposed the framework shown in Figure 8.1 and showed how it could be used to conduct the study of end-user learning styles (as one example) in learning typical EUC tools. The framework integrates research from cognitive psychology, educational psychology, information systems, and computer science.

FIGURE 8.1   The Research Framework for End-User Training

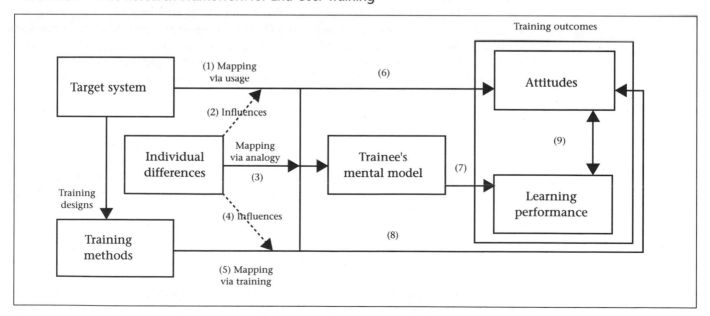

Each of the rectangles in Figure 8.1 represents a researchable set of variables. Each of the numbers in parentheses indicates linkages between the rectangles. For example, the dotted lines of relationships 2 and 4 indicate that individual differences interact with the target system and/or training method to influence training outcomes. The solid lines and associated relationships are direct influences.

Individual differences can directly influence the formation of mental models (relationship 3) or indirectly affect "mapping via training" (relationship 4) and "mapping via usage" processes (relationship 2). Individual difference variables define the cognitive aspects of human activities that are often referred to as "learning ability."

The target system, training method, and individual differences together influence a learner's mental model of the system. The mental model affects learning performance (relationship 7). Attitudes toward using the target system can be directly affected by the target system (relationship 6), training methods (relationship 8), or learning performance (relationship 9). Attitudes may also affect learning performance (relationship 9).

DEFINITION OF CONSTRUCTS

Constructs (variables) defined in this framework are explained in detail in Table 8.1. For each variable, a general definition and description are given followed by specific indicators of how the variable can be instantiated and a range of possible instantiations.

SUMMARY OF RELATED RESEARCH

Most IS research on end-user training focuses on individual differences, specifically on traits. Using the Bostrom et al. (1990) framework, this section categorizes previous research in terms of variables and their relationships specified in the previous section. However, attitudes and learning performance are combined as training outcomes because most of the research was conducted using both variables. Each subsection presented in Table 8.2 describes one or more studies that looked at a relationship among two or more variables. Almost all of the research studies were experimental in nature.

Most research on end-user training focuses on the relationships between training methods, individual differences, and mental models and how these are related to training outcomes. There are many components to the individual difference construct, including the difference between traits (long-lasting characteristics) and states (characteristics related to the current context); most research in end-user training has been related to traits.

Research associated with the constructs and relationships presented in the Bostrom et al. (1990) framework indicates that most of the relationships in the framework do affect training outcomes. However, there is a clear lack of research studying the relationship between target systems and training outcomes as well as the relationship between learning performance and attitudes.

TABLE 8.1 Definition of Constructs: Bostrom, Olfman, & Sein Framework for Research

Variables	General Definition	Types

Target system	A target system is the system on which a user is going to be trained. Users perceive the interface as the system. The fit between the target system and the task to be accomplished can prove to be an important facet of learning.	Types of target system include
		• Type of interface
		  Direct manipulation (icon based [graphic], menu based)
		  Command language
		• Type of system
		  Office productivity tool (word processor, spreadsheet, etc.)
		  ERP
		  Proprietary transaction system

Individual differences	Individual differences can influence the formation of mental models. Individual difference variables define the cognitive aspects of human activities (Bostrom et al., 1990). The cognitive process is at the heart of all such activities, including learning.	Individual differences may be categorized by: • Structures (sensory systems, time operations, semantic knowledge, etc.) • Strategies (learning problem solving and language processing) • Traits (learning style, cognitive style, personality variables, etc.) • States (emotion, feeling, motivation, etc.)
Mental model	A user's mental model is his/her representation of the system structure and function that provides explanatory and understanding power (Carroll, Olson, & Anderson, 1987). The target system, training method, and individual differences together influence a learner's mental model of the system.	A novice user can form a mental model of the system in three different ways: • Mapping via usage (formed by using the system and influenced by user characteristics) • Mapping via analogy (formed by drawing analogies from similar systems) • Mapping via training (formed by training and influenced by user characteristics)

Training method	The training method is the set of structures and activities that are designed to impart the required knowledge to the trainee. The training method is created by a curriculum developer and may be delivered through
	• Self-study (computer-based training, etc.)
	• Facilitation
	  Group workshop
	  Relevant task focus
	  Feature focus
	  One-on-one tutorial
		Training method components include
		• Training approach
		  Exploration orientation (inductive, trial and error, high learner control, incomplete learning materials, relevant task focus)
		  Instruction orientation (deductive, programmed, low learner control, complete materials, features focus)
		  Minimalist approach (design through analysis of user errors)
		  Behavioral modeling approach (show and tell with practice)
		  Tutorial (show and tell without practice)
		• Conceptual model
		  Analogical (utilizing an existing system as an exemplar)
		  Abstract (developing a definition of facets of the system)

Training outcome	Training outcomes are the results of the training process. These outcomes include the "correctness" of a subject's mental model of the system, attitude toward using the target system on the job, and learning performance, that is, the knowledge of the target system and its application to work problems.	Training outcomes may be measured through • Understanding (knowledge of commands and procedures, self-efficacy of system use) • Motivation to use (beliefs and attitudes toward the system)

TABLE 8.2 Summary of Related Research: Bostrom, Olfman, and Sein Framework for Research

Researchers	Summary
Target System → Training Outcome (relationships 1, 6)	
Davis and Bostrom (1993)	Direct manipulation interfaces led to better training outcomes than command-based interfaces. There was no difference in learning with an exploratory versus instruction-based manual, but this might have been due to the fact that the subjects were students and therefore used to the instruction-based approach.
Target System and Individual Differences → Training Outcome (relationships 1, 2, 6)	
Compeau and Higgins (1995)	Explored the impact of computer self-efficacy and behavior modeling across two packages: spreadsheet and word processor. Behavior modeling worked for spreadsheets but not for word processing.
Sein et al. (1993)	Showed the importance of visualization ability as an individual difference across a variety of software packages. The study showed that it is important to design training to reduce the gap caused by higher visualization ability.
Shayo and Olfman (2000)	Defined an outcome of training as the attitude toward learning similar software packages. The study showed that demonstrating more packages in training for databases led to higher levels of attitudes and better mental models.
Individual Differences → Mental Model (relationship 3)	
Lee, Kim, and Lee (1995)	Proposed an EUT-related causal model that showed empirical evidence for the following relationships: (1) Ability → (a) IS satisfaction, (b) IS acceptance, (c) Job satisfaction, (d) System utilization; (2) IS acceptance → (a) IS satisfaction, (b) Job satisfaction, (c) System utilization; (3) System utilization → (a) IS satisfaction, (b) Job satisfaction; (4) IS satisfaction → Job satisfaction.
Sein and Bostrom (1989)	Compared abstract versus concrete conceptual models and their effects on mental model formation. Abstract models lead to higher far transfer but are more difficult to understand. Abstract learners do better with abstract models, concrete learners with concrete models.
Webster and Martocchio (1993)	In training, task labeling as play is better than task labeling as work for younger employees. This was not true for older employees.
Training Method and Individual Differences → Training Outcome (relationships 4, 5, 8)	
Bohlen and Ferratt (1997)	Computer-based training is more effective than lecture-based training except for assimilators (persons with preferences for observation and abstraction), who showed no difference between methods.
Olfman and Bostrom (1991)	Applications-based (personally relevant) training did not produce better end-of-training outcomes than construct-based, but did produce more use six weeks after training.

TABLE 8.2   *(continued)*

Researchers	Summary
Individual Differences/Mental Model → Training Outcome (relationships 3, 7)	
Martocchio and Judge (1997)	A field study of 97 employees tested a model of the mediating influences of self-deception and task-specific self-efficacy in the relationship between conscientiousness and learning. Conscientiousness was positively related to self-efficacy, which was positively related to learning.
Martocchio and Webster (1992)	Cognitive playfulness (CP) is a factor in learning. Higher CP leads to higher test performance and more positive affective outcomes. Positive feedback may be a more effective external source of motivation for lower CP individuals.
Szajna and Mackay (1995)	In a training "situation" with undergraduates, it was found that computing aptitude and achievement are related to learning performance, whereas anxiety and experience are not.
Webster and Martocchio (1995)	Found some support for cognitive playfulness and software efficacy beliefs as affecting training outcomes.
Training Method → Training Outcome (relationships 5, 8)	
Bowman, Grupe, and Simkin (1995)	Compared classroom and computer-based training (CBT) instruction and basically found no differences, but this was for a computer class rather than a training situation.
Olfman and Mandviwalla (1998)	Training manuals with rich or sparse information did not produce different outcomes.
Gist, Schwoerer, and Rosen (1989)	A behavioral modeling approach relative to a tutorial approach yielded higher self-efficacy scores and computer mastery.
Olfman and Mandviwalla (1994)	Both procedural and conceptual training approaches generate similar outcomes—trainees tend to fill in what is not provided in one domain or the other.
Santhanam and Sein (1994)	The type of training provided, conceptual versus procedural, does not impact mental model formation.

THE COMPEAU, OLFMAN, SEIN, AND WEBSTER TRAINING PROCESS MODEL

To successfully conduct an end-user training program, it is essential to consider the factors that affect the organization even though it is costly to do so. A more relevant concern is that without proper preparation for an end-user training program, training could be far more costly in the future. Compeau et al. (1995) proposed, via the framework shown in Figure 8.2, that the complete process of end-user training starts from pretraining to get the right training program for the right end user and ends with post-training to ensure that the matching was and continues to be correct.

DEFINITION OF CONSTRUCTS

The framework presented in Figure 8.2 attempts to describe the key elements that make up the end-user training and learning process. The framework consists of

FIGURE 8.2 The Training and Learning Process Model

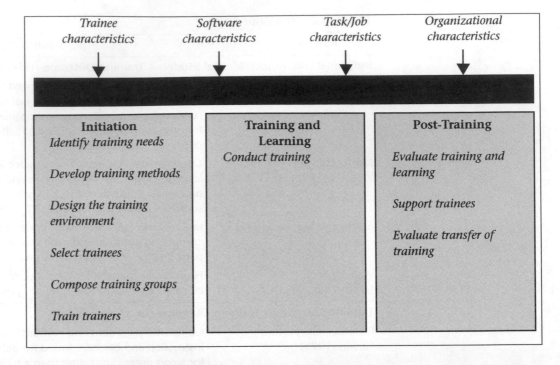

three phases: initiation, formal training and learning, and post-training. Trainee characteristics, the target system, the trainee's task and job, and organizational characteristics influence key decisions made at each phase of the process. Table 8.3 identifies each of the phases along with general definitions and key constructs.

TABLE 8.3 Definition of Constructs: Compeau, Olfman, Sein, and Webster Training Process Model

Phase/Construct	General Definition	Constructs and Issues
Initiation	Activities take place prior to the formal training phase. These activities range from developing training materials to forming training groups. The key purpose of initiation is to make sure that the training program is right for the trainees.	• Needs assessment methodology • Evaluation of training materials and methods • In-house/Outsource decision • Selection of trainers • Grouping of trainees
Formal training and learning	This phase focuses on the delivery of training. Various methods of training may be used including face-to-face, computer-based, video, or a combination of methods.	• Method of training delivery
Post-Training	After the actual training, many tasks need to be performed to ensure that the trainees maintain and improve their knowledge of and attitudes toward using the software. Moreover, it is essential to ensure that trainees are actually using the software.	• Evaluation of training and learning immediately after training • Long-term effects of training • Continuation of training • Transfer of knowledge
Moderating constructs	Trainee, software, task/job, and organizational characteristics.	These factors will influence decisions about training design and effectiveness.

SUMMARY OF RELATED RESEARCH

Table 8.4 shows selected research studies based on this framework grouped according to the phase(s) of training that were addressed by the cited research studies. It was found that most of the research conducted focused on a particular phase rather than across the three phases. What we learned from previous research is that good implementation of the initiation phase will lead to better training outcomes. However, a major issue, that of knowledge transfer, has not yet been extensively studied.

Table 8.4 Summary of Related Research: Compeau, Olfman, Sein, and Webster Training Process Model

Researchers	Summary
Initiation	
Ford, Ledbetter, and Roberts (1996)	Conducted a study to examine the effects of a training program designed to acquaint managers with DSS. The findings suggest it may be useful to use either amount of prior training or age as determinants of class membership. Further research is needed to relate specific training content and approaches to various trainee groups.
Nelson, Whitener, and Philcox (1995)	Determined that training is more effective when needs assessment includes consideration of the issues identified by a content-levels framework, when levels and training content are congruent and closely linked and when systems designers, project managers, and trainers are mutually responsible for effectiveness.
Shayo, Olfman, and Teitelroit (1999)	Address assessment of training needs through one-on-one meetings. It can enable development of specific exercises, help motivate the trainee, and point out potential pitfalls. A study was conducted with respect to learning a database query package but did not provide clear evidence of the effectiveness of this approach.
Initiation → Training	
Galletta et al. (1995)	Note that the same training method will be less successful when trainees are exposed to negative rather than positive word of mouth. The potential effects of negative word-of-mouth communications on training should be of concern.
Hayen, Cook, and Jecker (1990)	Suggest that end-user training involves three components: (1) conceptual perspective of a business problem, (2) conceptual perspective of software tools, and (3) task domain knowledge. Two types of end-user training appear to be evolving: (1) operating a software tool and (2) business problem solving. To expand their task domain, end users may need training in both areas.
Webster and Martocchio (1995)	Find that preview of training, especially "optimistic" ones, generate better outcomes.

(continued on the next page)

TABLE 8.4   *(continued)*

Researchers	Summary
Training	
Fitzgerald and Cater-Steel (1995)	Describe the development of a successful peer-training program. Success is based on maintaining a low budget to get started and a high rate of training. Trainers also provide post-training support.
Initiation → Training → Post-Training	
Olfman and Sein (1997)	Provide 10 lessons for trainees across the three phases of training. These lessons are based on findings from the research literature.
Kappelman and Guynes (1995)	Develop a partnership between end users and the IS department to develop organizational change. Success was measured in terms of motivation and morale. Providing users with an empowering experience in conjunction with training resulted in improving user attitudes. User participation in training contributes to IS success through understanding and/or motivation. Pretraining empowerment is one way to motivate trainees and increase training payoffs.
Post-Training	
Carroll and Rosson (1995)	By viewing training evaluation as continual information gathering, training evaluation coextends with the analysis, development, and deployment of training systems and requires a life cycle–oriented management process.
Kay and Thomas (1995)	Present a methodology for monitoring many computer users in their natural settings over the long term. It was difficult to determine user intentions from the data design.
Kraiger and Jung (1997)	Present a framework for linking training objectives to training evaluation criteria.

SEIN, BOSTROM, AND OLFMAN LEARNING/TRAINING STRATEGY MODEL

Sein, Bostrom, and Olfman (1999) posed a crucial question pertaining to training strategy: Given an IT tool on which a specific user type needs to be trained, what training approaches and methods should be used to attain the appropriate level(s) of knowledge? To answer the question, the authors proposed the training strategy framework shown in Figure 8.3, which was developed based on the learning and training research framework and training and learning life cycle.

The authors point out that traditional technology training is skills focused. Trainees typically learn to operate only their current tools and applications. This traditional approach may not be truly effective and is not appropriate for the newest software applications that are more complex and integrative. Snell (1997) found that the lack of successful implementation of new technologies often has been

FIGURE 8.3   Training Strategy Framework

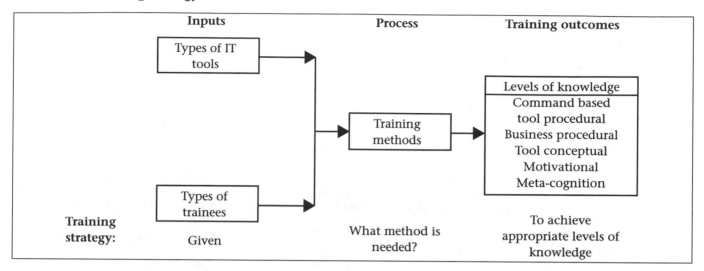

due to a lack of skilled personnel. The integrative enterprisewide architecture applications such as SAP require continuous learning and knowledge management.

The learning process for computer users must be rapid and continuous; it also requires a different level of focus in IT training practices. One of the aspects of a higher level of focus is that of conceptual training. The authors proposed a framework of knowledge levels, ranging from syntactical to meta-cognition, that compose a more complete range of knowledge outcomes for training the workforce of the future to develop an effective training strategy. *Training strategy* is defined as the selection of a training method appropriate to a specific type of trainee and a specific IT tool given specific knowledge outcomes. An effective strategy will match the appropriate method with the appropriate user for the appropriate tool.

DEFINITION OF CONSTRUCTS

Table 8.5 summarizes the definitions of constructs from the framework shown in Figure 8.3. This training strategy framework is based on a classification of trainees, specific training approaches for different classes of IT tools, and the level(s) of knowledge required for using the tools. The levels of knowledge acquired by the trainees define the output of the training process.

Different types of trainees may require different levels of knowledge about IT tools. For example, a trainee may be classified as a transactional, casual, or power user as proposed by SAP. However, Bostrom et al. (1990) believe that a classification of users must address end users' job features and functional levels as well. Therefore, business motivation and meta-cognition levels of knowledge should be incorporated into every type of training. It is important that types of trainees and training methods be matched according to levels of knowledge.

As per the Bostrom et al. (1990) framework, types of tools also play an important role. An interesting issue is how motivational knowledge affects different types of trainees' learning of IT tools. Another key issue is the type of training method to apply in each context. Numerous training methods are used in practice. A relatively new training

TABLE 8.5 Definition of Constructs: Sein, Bostrom, and Olfman Learning/Training Strategy Model

Construct	Description	Types
Types of IT tools	This refers to the importance of specifying how each category of tools requires specific content design. The use of IT tools may be mandatory or voluntary. Different types of users may use IT tools with different focus, too.	IT tools may be • Spreadsheet • Word processor • Integrative software application (e.g., ERP software) • Database • Programming languages
Types of trainees	The goal is to tailor the training approach and contents according to the trainee's characteristics, which include prior knowledge, demographics, cognitive abilities and preferences, and learning style.	SAP suggested types of trainees to be • Transactional (a user who will use the software to carry out specific transactions) • Casual (a user who will use the software to retrieve information) • Power user (a user who has strong knowledge of computing and can act as an interface between the project team and the user community)
Training methods	Training method is the approach to delivering training. The details are given in the framework for types of IT tools.	In addition to the definition of training method from the first framework, the following topics are proposed: • Competency-based experiential learning • Electronic performance support system (EPSS) • Benefits of on-the-job training • Utilization of low-cost, community college courses
Levels of knowledge	A six-level knowledge content hierarchy is proposed by integrating motivation and meta-cognition as key knowledge components.	Knowledge levels include • Command based (syntax and semantics) • Tool procedural (combining commands to do generic tasks) • Business procedural (application of tools procedures to a task) • Tool conceptual (the big picture of what to do with the tool) • Business motivational (what the tools can do for the trainee and the organization) • Meta-cognition (learning to learn)

approach called electronic performance support systems (EPSS), which combines learning with use in context, is being adopted by many organizations. However, little is known about the effects of this self-learning, and just-in-time approach to training.

SUMMARY OF RELATED RESEARCH

Since this model has been published recently, research based on its tenets has not yet been published.

GUIDE FOR FUTURE RESEARCH

The main focus for research in end-user training has been on how training methods interact with individual differences to influence training outcomes. Training outcomes are typically measured right after training. Very little research has addressed post-training outcomes. Nor has the end-user training literature focused on the relationship between types of software and types of training methods, types of software and individual differences, or a combination of each of these variables. Yet, as Bostrom et al. (1999) point out, the really important applied problem for organizations is to know who should get what kind of training when learning a specific type of software application.

Additionally, little research has been conducted on the relationship between the initiation phase of the training cycle, the delivery of training, and subsequent post-training efforts and outcomes. Experimental research makes it easy to isolate specific training treatments but makes it very difficult to explore the long-term consequences. Field experiments and case studies allow a more comprehensive analysis of the training life cycle but make it hard to trace consequences of training treatments. These difficulties to some extent explain the reasons that the end-user training literature is almost entirely based in experimental studies. Ideally, researchers should be able to develop meaningful training interventions, test them in the laboratory, and then analyze them in the field. However, another issue that arises, as with any aspect of IS, is the constant change caused by new software technologies. Experimentally testing the feasibility of a training method using a particular software application may prove difficult to retest in the field.

It behooves researchers in this domain to devise training solutions that are resilient to specific kinds of technologies. Moreover, the rapid changes in technologies demand much more research in the area of retraining. That is, it is important to devise methods to help users create mental models of various generic types of software applications that are very flexible so that they can easily update their knowledge base without having to revisit a full training curriculum.

Some possible research directions are listed in this section. These include areas that identify current trends and needs in end-user training that have not been developed as issues in the past. Furthermore, key research questions or issues are posed for each of the suggested areas.

RETRAINING (DELTA TRAINING OR INCREMENTAL TRAINING)

With today's modern technology, software is being built and implemented more rapidly than ever. Commercial software companies offer new versions of their product. Extra features introduced in the newest versions provide users with even further ease of use. Although organizations upgrade software for many reasons, it seems unreasonable that they do so if end users do not learn to apply these new features. Learning new features implies the need for training and, in most cases, retraining. An organization should have a retraining policy if it plays the upgrade game. Rapid changes affect not only organizations but also the trainers and the training providers. Trainers will have to devise new methods to accommodate the "retraining" of end users. No known academic research conducted in this area offers a framework to direct trainers in helping users build an incremental learning strategy. Sein et al. (1987) built their research framework around a continuous learning model. That is, they argued that a combination of the constructs of training method, target system, and individual differences leads to certain outcomes. As the trainee uses the system, however, these outcomes change the trainee's individual differences and mental model, so continuous learning takes place. However, when there are changes in the target system (i.e., upgrades), which type of training method will be most suitable to achieve training outcomes? The basic question is how to make the training effective and make the learner sustain the learned knowledge and be able to catch up with the new features of the new release with minimal cost and effort.

CULTURAL EFFECT (COMPUTER LANGUAGE, KEYBOARD FAMILIARITY, ETC.)

Basically, many cultures are well tuned to the high-tech mechanistic nature of computing. However, an important cultural barrier is the language. Since most of the major end-user software packages are developed in the United States, the bias for language requirements is English. To translate the material into a local language is not a solution since most of the technical terms and context find no equivalence in local dialect. Second, the rate of translation would be very slow and could not catch up with the rate of knowledge expansion in IT as new versions of software are released as often as every six months. While English is the universal medium of computing, how can IT training be delivered to a culture whose trainees are not using English in everyday life?

MASS IT TRAINING

Mass IT training refers to an organized training effort for large groups, say 1,000 people at a time. The students have diverse backgrounds and may not be familiar with IT or English. The traditional approach to training is not effective since (1) an instructor is not trained to handle this kind of training, (2) the courseware used is not structured for this type of student, and (3) no previous teaching model can be followed in this case. For example, this type of training is currently being carried out in Thailand. In an attempt to remedy unemployment problems of new graduates, the Thai government authorized the training of 20,000 new programmers, primarily in Visual Basic (300–500-hour course over a period of six months). It is therefore a challenge to learn the most effective means to deliver IT training for a large group in general and to train programmers in particular. Specific issues concern the methodology, the courseware design, the delivery, and the measurement.

One of the possibilities for understanding mass training is to extend the Compeau et al. (1995) framework to include a new phase between the initiation and the training and learning phases. The new phase as shown in Figure 8.4 is called "pre-training." This phase should not be embedded in the initiation phase since actual training, with objectives that differ from the main training phase, is carried out. This phase is important in mass training because it is necessary to prepare or "condition" the trainees and equalize the knowledge background so that effective training can be carried out at the main training phase. However, a more elaborate model is needed to study the learning behavior of the trainees who concentrate on a particular topic for an extended duration.

FIGURE 8.4 Extension of the Compreau et al. Framework for Mass Training

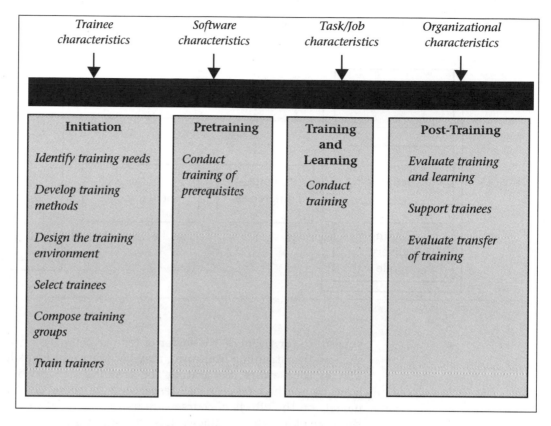

ELECTRONIC PERFORMANCE SUPPORT SYSTEMS

The EPSS training approach provides self-based, just-in-time training, and minimizes instructor-led training. Many organizations now implement this type of training to reduce cost. So far, very little academic research has looked at the effects of EPSS in organizations. A new framework is needed to accommodate EPSS into the end-user training scope. Several examples of research in this area are given here. Atlas et al. (1997) described animated demonstrations, which are on-screen playback of correct procedures, as training tools for software. Benko (1997) stated that EPSS are more complex and broadly based than training systems. Desmarais et al. (1997) argued that while the fundamental goals of an EPSS are to provide assistance in learning and performing tasks, it has been viewed by some as a knowledge management system.

COURSEWARE AND TRAINER COMPETENCY

Two crucial factors in end-user training have been classified into the construct category of training methods. Courseware, the technology for delivering training through media other than face-to-face training, is a growing part of the end-user training landscape. This is especially true because the World Wide Web enables more cost-effective delivery of training materials than ever before. Since courseware is essentially a

FIGURE 8.5 Extension of the Bostrom et al. Framework

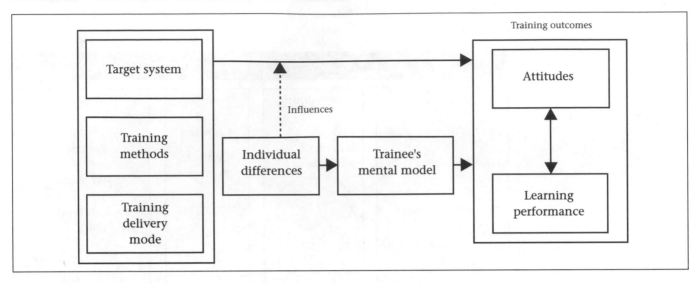

substitute for trainers, the factor of trainer competency, previously not addressed in the end-user training literature, may become an issue as it interacts with the utilization of courseware. Separating the training delivery mode from the construct of training method may enable researchers to more clearly formulate their research models on the effects of courseware as well as EPSS. A possible reformulation of the Bostrom et al. (1990) framework is shown in Figure 8.5.

END-USER TRAINING COST

In a real-world situation, many constraints affect the training outcome. One of the important constraints is the budget. Many practitioners have addressed the importance of the cost of end-user training. However, the three frameworks used to discuss previous end-user training research in this chapter do not address the issue directly. One of the possibilities is the extension of Compeau et al.'s (1995) framework as shown in Figure 8.6. Injecting cost factors into the training process model will allow researchers to formulate research questions such as given a budget, what is the optimal approach to allocate costs for each of the phases of the training process? To answer this question, research must be carried out to identify all the cost drivers associated with each phase of the framework. Also, an overall cost model must be constructed so that optimal budget allocation can be identified.

OPTIMAL TRAINING DURATION

In performing end-user training, it is assumed that the longer the period of training, the better will be the understanding and skill transfer result. If the period of training is too short, the user might not be able to perform at the desired level. This means that repeated training must be carried out to raise the performance level of

FIGURE 8.6   Extension of the Compeau et al. Framework of EUT Costing

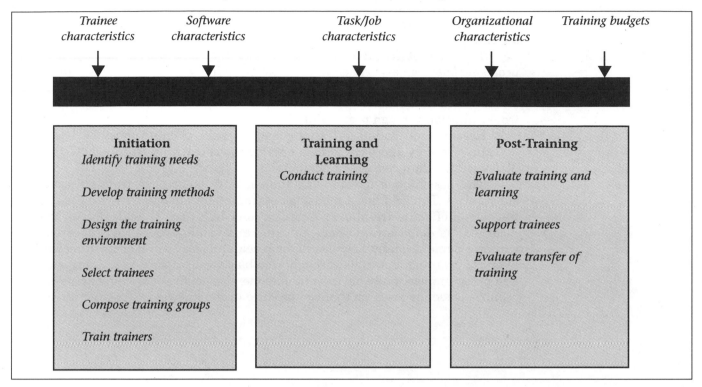

an end user. Hence, it can be reasoned that an optimal period exists that will produce training outcomes at a desired performance level. A detailed mathematical model could be constructed to study various parameters involved to determine the optimal period.

CONCLUSION

The three training models, namely, the framework for end-user training, the end-user training process model, and the learning/training strategy proposed by Bostrom et al. (1990), Compeau et al. (1995), and Sein et al. (1999), respectively, provide a foundation for conducting research in the general areas of end-user and IT staff training. The first framework points out variables and their relationships in evaluating effective end-user training programs. The second framework presents a wider picture that focuses on the sequence of training and procedures required. The last framework makes clear that designing end-user training requires a context-sensitive approach.

All three frameworks have been shown as valid either through empirical research or logical argument. We found that most of the existing research on end-user training has been conducted to determine how training methods interact with individual differences to influence training outcomes. However, much research is needed to determine the relationships of other variables in the Bostrom et al. (1990)

framework such as how the target system affects training outcomes. The more that can be learned about all of these relationships, the more likely it will be that practitioners can effectively design the most successful and appropriate training programs for end users.

The current research literature shows that the typical methodological approach is based on experimentation, most often in laboratory or classroom settings. We encourage researchers to attempt to study end-user training processes and strategies in field studies and to do so by following the training through all phases, from initiation through post-training.

Research on end-user training and IT skill training must be based on a learning strategy approach to help organizations catch up with technology and to deal with constant releases of new versions of software.

The possibilities for studying the software technology training process are substantial. The field has a robust set of frameworks to guide researchers, and the impacts of effective training on organizations are great. These frameworks can be modified, as demonstrated here, to explore new innovations and concerns in the training domain. Many new issues for research have been identified recently. Delivery of training materials through Web-based courseware, retraining end users and programmers, and analysis of the economic benefits of training are issues that require academic research that can produce useful knowledge for practitioners.

Business Process Change: A Reflective View of Theory, Practice, and Implications

Varun Grover and William J. Kettinger

There are many terms for the phenomenon that swept corporations in the early 1990s, as reflected in the use of words such as *business, process, redesign, innovation,* and, most commonly, *reengineering.* Early books on this topic became phenomenal best-sellers. Consultants repackaged old methodologies and printed glossy brochures and charged thousands for their "proprietary" solutions to "fundamental" business problems (Hammer, 1990). Surveys of senior executives indicated that by the mid-1990s, "reengineering" was the number one initiative taken by companies to achieve strategic goals. Academics, both cynics and proponents, jumped on the bandwagon, writing scholarly prose on why such a radical change is good or that they have seen it all before.

It is against this backdrop that business process change (BPC) initiatives played a dominant role throughout the 1990s as the preeminent managerial intervention to cut cycle time, enhance customer satisfaction, and improve business performance. From its beginnings in radical IT-driven reengineering of the late 1980s, to holistic change management efforts of the mid 1990s, to business process–based electronic commerce and ERP of the late 1990s, business process change has held the spotlight. Now as we enter the twenty-first century, some argue that BPC

Acknowledgments: Studies 1 and 3 in this chapter were partially funded by a grant from the Center for International Business Education and Research (CIBER) and the United States Department of Education. Study 2 was partially funded by a major IT company.

initiatives are dead. Critics contend that it has not shown itself worthy of the hefty resources spent on these projects, and, in fact, after more than 10 years of experience, we have learned very little concerning how to effectively change organizations by changing business processes.

An opposing school of thought argues that over the past 10 years we have learned a great deal concerning what works and what does not work in changing organizations via a business process perspective. These advocates of BPC state that it has integrated useful principles and techniques from other management disciplines and that BPC methods have been incrementally modified to improve their effectiveness. While these proponents believe that some factions of the BPC practitioner and research community followed evolutionary paths that did not bear fruit, over time a clear body of understanding concerning BPC has emerged. Furthermore, these researchers contend that a set of enduring management principles/lessons has emerged that can direct future scholarship and shape management practice well into the next century. This chapter presents this evolving steam of BPC research in a framework that should help guide practitioners and researchers. While we recognize the major contributions of scholars worldwide on this topic, to frame this discussion, we focus primarily on the outcome of three empirical studies conducted by faculty at the University of South Carolina over the past 10 years as a vehicle to offer insights on what we have learned and where we are headed.

A FRAMEWORK FOR PROCESS-BASED ORGANIZATIONAL CHANGE

Reengineering is difficult to evaluate without considering the business environment in which it was engendered. Born in recession, the global economy mandated greater operational efficiency and imposed tremendous pressures for cost reductions. These pressures to cut across different segments of the economy greatly impacted the operations of service and manufacturing firms. Unfortunately, many corporations responded by performing major workforce reductions under the aegis of reengineering. Such efforts were not strategically driven and often looked for an IT "silver bullet"; ultimately, many firms lost vital components of their human knowledge base needed to compete as information-based organizations. This early type of "downsizing/reengineering" compromised a firm's future competitiveness and was destined to fail. In fact, a large proportion of documented cases of unsuccessful "reengineering" projects represent this early "slash and burn" approach.

Since its original conception, however, various realities of accomplishing business process change and minimizing its pain have set in. Probably the most important lesson learned to date is the recognition that reengineering is really another form of organization change (Kettinger & Grover 1995; Grover, 1999). BPC takes place in the context of people and organizations, and any attempt at it without appropriate plans for organizational change greatly increase its risk of failure. In this regard, BPC follows a long stream of knowledge gained on how best to change human behaviors, energize and focus organizations, and introduce technology and work systems. Our research on this phenomenon over the past 10 years indicates that when stripped down to its core, reengineering is about *organizational change*. Hence, we now prefer to refer to this area as business process change.[1] Once researchers recognized this perspective and moved away from the quick-fix mentality, we have been able to apply well-established principles concerning orchestrating effective change from such fields as strategy, organizational behavior, social psychology, industrial engineering, and quality management disciplines.

The theoretical basis of BPC concerns the creation of an organizational environment that develops a culture supportive of change through learning, knowledge sharing (including IT enablement), and internal and external partnering. Implied in this statement is the vital role that the strategic leader plays in establishing strategic initiatives. Such a supportive environment facilitates the conduct of effective process and change management practices and leads to improvements in business processes and stakeholder benefits, both important in achieving measurable performance improvements (Kettinger & Grover, 1995). To help develop this strategic perspective, a framework of process-based change is presented in this chapter.

Because business processes cut horizontally across the organization, we can view BPC in an interrelated organizational subsystem context. This view suggests that we look at patterns of relationships between organizational subsystems affected by BPC. Past researchers identified the interrelated and mutually adjusting subsystems of organizational change as task, technology, people, and structure. Cumulatively adding to the theory of organizational change have been contributions on strategy, job design, organizational design, organizational dynamics, and decision making and modeling.

Process thinking originated with the quality movement. Its focus on the customer primarily emphasized minimizing variation of defects in manufactured products. Early quality literature tended to focus on modest incremental improvements over radical change. In 1980, Nadler and Tushman proposed an organizational change model that described strategy input to a transformation process of interrelated subsystems including task, people, and formal and informal organization, leading to organizational, group, and individual outputs. In the MIT90s framework, Scott-Morton (1991) extended his earlier model by enlarging the role of culture and recognizing the importance of both intra- and interorganizational network relationships; in addition, the knowledge-sharing capabilities of IT were identified as having the capacity to change business processes and, possibly, fundamentally redefine the scope of a business. Based on these past contributions, we propose a theoretical model of business process change that relates these sets of concepts and constructs.

Our overarching framework is presented as a temporal model for accomplishing organizational change[2] (see Figure 9.1). Elements of four broad phases of organizational process-based change are depicted: sources of organizational impetus leading to BPC, initiating process change, selecting change enablers, and managing change implementation. While the middle two phases correspond to specific actions in managing the process change, the first and the last phases represent the interface between the process change effort and the rest of the organization in terms of input/causes (impetus of change) and outcomes of a project (managing change implementation). These phases of organizational change will be discussed, and constructs that can be used to represent each phase will be described. After describing this framework from a conceptual perspective, we will explore its validity based on a program of research. Abbreviated presentation of results from three studies from this research program that are reported in the second half of the chapter provide strong and convincing empirical support to many key elements of the framework

FIGURE 9.1
Framework Process-Based Organizational Change

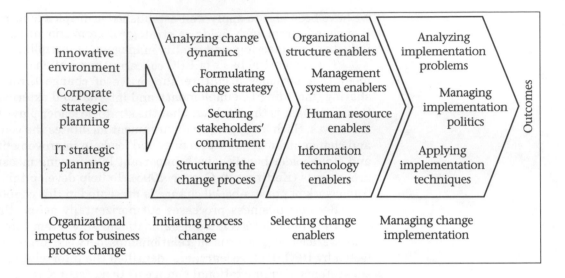

ORGANIZATIONAL IMPETUS FOR BUSINESS PROCESS CHANGE

Several sources facilitating the drive toward BPC are identified in Figure 9.1 and discussed here.

Innovative Environment and BPC Initiatives

Process change may be conceptualized as a form of organizational innovations (Lewin, 1951). While no empirical studies have been reported on patterns of BPC innovation, many reported reengineering cases corroborate central notions of successful organizational innovation: championship, management support, cross-functional collaboration, and the facilitating role of "structural overlay." (Grover, Teng, & Fiedler, 1993).

As revealed by a field study based on 20 reengineering projects (Hall, Rosenthal, & Wade, 1993), top management involvement and participation are critical to success. The depth and magnitude of organizational changes associated with reengineering often warrant the dedicated efforts of a high-level "venture group" to create and sustain an environment that is conducive to innovative changes. The role of a "BPC champion" has also been identified in mobilizing resources necessary to launch the initiative.

Corporate Strategic Planning and BPC Initiatives

While it is possible to identify candidate processes for reengineering intuitively and quickly, many organizations prefer a more systematic planning approach to ensure linkage between BPC and corporate strategy (Kettinger & Teng, 1998). This can be facilitated by an enterprise model involving the identification of all business processes to establish the basis for a long-term BPC program. In setting strategic direction to reengineering, performance measures for redesigned processes should be consistent with the firm's long-term strategic goals. Empirical studies conducted by Hall et al. (1993) indicate that greater performance improvements can be achieved by setting multiple performance measures that are linked to strategic objectives of the firm.

IT Strategic Planning and BPC Initiatives

While the deployment of IT is not always required for reengineering, it has been shown to be a powerful enabler (Teng, Grover, & Fiedler, 1994). Careful evaluation is needed to determine the "fit" between the desired IT enabler and the existing information resource architecture. A particularly important element of this architecture is data, since properly designed databases can support cross-functional applications, and the database structure can remain stable while applications undergo changes (Teng & Kettinger, 1995). At Continental Can, for example, a comprehensive information resource architecture was developed by examining the overall strategies and the various functions delivering products and services critical to the strategies. The interactions between these functions and their shared data were also examined, leading to the design of an enterprise model that provided the base for Continental Can's technology strategy that included an IT platform, database design, and an application development plan.

INITIATING PROCESS CHANGE

The conceptual and theoretical root of BPC may be traced to the sociotechnical systems approach, which views a work system as an open system consisting of two interacting subsystems: the technical and the social (Mumford, 1994). With this approach, we optimize the entire work system, not just the technical subsystems, emphasizing changes to human resources in light of altered tasks or processes. Building on theories of systems change and sociotechnical design, we identified critical elements for change planning and management for *initiating process change* in a BPC project. These elements include analyzing change dynamics, formulating change strategy, securing stakeholders' commitment, and structuring the change process.

Analyzing Change Dynamics

Because BPC often involves radical change, the level of resistance may be strong. In analyzing resistance to change, Markus (1983) suggests that a political perspective is appropriate when (1) organizational participants disagree about the nature of the problem that the proposed system is supposed to solve, (2) it is uncertain whether the system will solve the problem, and (3) the power bases involved are highly valued and in short supply. Because reengineering often involves complex sociotechnical changes with impacts on many stakeholders' power bases, analysis of the causes of resistance and political power dynamics are necessary to formulate specific change strategies and secure management commitment.

Formulating Change Strategy

Stoddard and Jarvenpaa (1995) discuss the distinction between evolutionary and revolutionary change strategy in process reengineering in terms of the sociotechnical perspective. Revolutionary change strategy calls for simultaneous change of both technical and social systems; evolutionary change may involve the choice of technical system first, social system first, or a gradual staged sociotechnical change (Liker, Roitman, & Roskies, 1987). If the forces of resistance are strong, the risk of revolutionary change increases. When an evolutionary strategy is adopted, change is adapted to the pace and capabilities of people, and frequent and open communication is considered essential.

Securing Stakeholders' Commitment

A stakeholder is anyone with a vested interest in the business process (Davenport, 1993). To succeed in the change program, commitment to change from all stakeholders must be secured. A number of approaches to securing commitment have been discussed in the literature. Davenport (1993) emphasized the importance of open and honest communication at all levels and throughout the initiative. Nutt's (1986) research points to direct intervention and persuasion as the most effective tactics to secure commitment. In intervention, change agents create rationales for action, compare the organization's performance with comparable organizations, establish new standards to judge performance, and develop descriptions of how current operations could be improved. Instead of letting consultants do all the convincing, project team members can "win over" employees who resist the change process by following various strategies of influence (Melone, 1995) in communicating the rationale and benefits of reengineering.

Structuring the Change Process

To help organize the BPC project, we need to bring some degree of control and structure to the otherwise chaotic process by recognizing certain stages, activities, and critical roles and tasks for the change endeavor (Kettinger, Teng, & Guha, 1997). In structuring the change process, one should recognize that BPC represents a continuum of approaches. While there is some commonality in how firms approach process change, individual projects will differ in the magnitude of planned change and the extent to which this change is supported. Varying project characteristics call for differing methodological choices and the emphasis of different techniques. For this reason, a formal BPC project planning perspective is needed to guide the assemblage of the "right" stages and activities to achieve success on a project-by-project basis.

SELECTING CHANGE ENABLERS

Successful BPC implementation can be facilitated by enablers related to organizational structure, management systems, human resource development, and information technology.

Organizational Structure Enablers

Research has shown that better performance may be attained through cross-functional reengineering rather than projects confined within a traditional function (Hall et al., 1993). To facilitate cross-functional cooperation, functional structure can be modified through structural enablers such as cross-functional teams, and process generalists. Another structural enabler for reengineering is the establishment of a case manager who has access to the latest status information on a given transaction and serves as the single contact point for customers. Case managers coordinate work performed by many functional specialists. Given proper safeguards against frauds, this may result in efficient "cross-functional" coordination. For example, at the financing service division within IBM, a single generalist performs credit checking, pricing, and other activities previously done by four different specialists in processing loan requests.

Management Systems Enablers

In redesigning a process, it is often necessary to change the basis of employees' work evaluation. In the context of functional specialization, employees are evaluated on narrow, internally oriented performance objectives (i.e., the small pieces of the work assigned to their department rather than the quality of the entire output). Successful BPC efforts, however, are based on external performance objectives such as customer satisfaction and overall quality. With the geographical spread of work teams and the redefinition of performance objectives, it becomes necessary to return decision-making power to the point where problems occur; this means giving employees decision-making power to act without waiting for "vertical" layers of approvals. For example, Chesebrough-Pond Inc.'s line workers can now routinely scan on-line information on sales and stock availability to adjust their production schedules.

Human Resource Enablers

Changes in training, appraisal, and compensation have been instituted in many firms with the implemention of BPC. Important human resource enablers for process reengineering include multiple skill development and rewarding team performance. At Motorola's Government Electronics group, for instance, peers and others above and below the employee evaluate his or her performance in a process. Reward is now based on team performance in addition to individual performance. Furthermore, companies such as GE have altered the basis of work compensation, with employees being paid on the basis of the skill they develop rather than merely on the individual work they perform.

Information Technology Enablers

Conceptually, an organization should be able to redesign business processes without modern IT. However, most successful BPC efforts would be difficult to consummate without enabling IT (Teng et al., 1994). Using IT, many firms have reconfigured their business processes from a highly serial pattern to a parallel pattern, permitting several functions to proceed independently. In the well-publicized Ford Motor Corp. case, for example, the old accounts payable process involved three functions: purchasing, inventory, and accounts payable, which participated in the process *serially* with many intermediate steps and a sequential flow of paper documents. With direct access to a shared database, the three functions now participate in the reengineered process in a parallel fashion. The application of imaging and Web-enabled technology help to break the serial pattern of work flow as different functional personnel access the same digitized document simultaneously. Increasingly, by combining both telecommunication and shareable computing resources, a shared environment for teamwork may be developed. Currently, a number of emerging technologies, including workflow software, intranets, groupware, customer and sales force automation, and ERP systems,[3] hold great promise in providing this shared environment for effective team.

MANAGING CHANGE IMPLEMENTATION

As amply demonstrated by the case studies conducted by Smith and Willcocks (1995), change implementation requires flexibility and a multidisciplinary perspective, paying attention to a myriad of human, social, cultural, and political issues while not allowing rigid BPC methodologies and technical issues to subvert human and organizational considerations. Several critical aspects of managing change implementation associated with BPC will be discussed here, including approaches to analyzing implementation problems, managing implementation politics, and applying implementation tactics.

Analyzing Implementation Problems

During the course of change implementation, the dynamics of change itself may change from time to time. New sources of resistance not anticipated in a project's beginning may emerge. It is necessary to periodically assess and analyze the forces that are favorable as well as unfavorable to the change efforts. To facilitate this assessment, many techniques can be used. For example, force field analysis developed by Miller (1987) provides a pictorial representation of a "tug of war," identifying negative forces that are "tugging" to the left of the center line in the direction of "catastrophe" and positive forces "tugging" to the right toward the ideal situation.

Managing Implementation Politics

The force field analysis just discussed primarily involves political forces. To strengthen, weaken, or add forces requires active management of implementation politics through subtle actions to affect people's perceptions and motivations. To strengthen a positive force, for example, the BPC team may attempt to communicate clear images of the future to organizational members and to increase the level and extent of participation. Adding a new positive force normally involves the mobilization of power in support of the planned change through negotiation and coalition building (Keen, 1981). Weakening a negative force, on the other hand, may require directing people's attention to the consequences of not carrying out change (Smith & Willcocks, 1995).

Applying Implementation Techniques

The field of organization development (OD) is concerned with planning and implementing change in organizations. A number of OD techniques may be applied in BPC implementation, especially as tools for the management of implementation politics. For example, the organization mirror technique developed by French and Bell (1978) can be used to ease the conflict between individuals and groups. The technique prescribes a set of activities in which one group gets feedback from a number of other groups about how it is perceived. This feedback would help to identify sources of the conflicts and develop possible solutions.

EMPIRICAL EVIDENCE FROM THE FIELD

We have developed a framework of process-based organizational change. We treat BPC as an organizational innovation and change phenomenon and focus our attention on the macro level strategic factors that are of significance to the long-term viability of the initiative in organizations. If the framework is valid, strategic guidelines for successfully implementing process change may be formulated. As researchers, however, we hesitate to offer these guidelines without first collecting empirical evidence from the field that supports key precepts of our framework. To accomplish this, we have conducted a program of research that examines the validity of the framework. In this chapter, we will report results of three field studies from this research program that address these aspects of the framework:

1. *Organizational Impetus for BPC.* In the first study, we focus on the beginning phase of our change framework to examine the impact of innovative environment and corporate and IT strategic planning on BPC initiatives and success.
2. *BPC Project Planning.* In this study, we focus on the next two phases of our change framework in determining whether a BPC archetype exists that permits contingent configuration of the most appropriate BPC project plan with suitable methodologies and techniques to meet unique strategic and organizational requirements.
3. *BPC Implementation Problems and Success.* How critical is the management of organizational change to BPC success? What is the extent of difficulty of change management and other BPC implementation problems? These are the types of questions probed in the third study to examine the severity of various BPC implementation problems (the fourth phase of our change framework) and how they are related to success.

Because a complete reporting of all three studies would be impossible within the space of this chapter, results of each study are presented in summary form. Interested readers may refer to more detailed coverage of the study results published separately; see Teng et al. (1998) for Study 1; Kettinger et al. (1997) for Study 2; and Grover et al. (1995) for Study 3.

SUMMARY OF STUDY 1: ORGANIZATIONAL IMPETUS FOR BPC

In this study, we seek to gather empirical evidence from the field to demonstrate the organizational impetus for BPC discussed in the first phase of our change framework. For example, will organic organizations with more decentralized decision making and greater collaboration across departments be more likely to initiate reengineering projects? Will more integration of IT strategic planning with corporate strategic planning generate more impetus to process reengineering?

RESEARCH MODEL: STUDY 1

We examine three sources of influence on BPC initiatives (independent variables): (1) the innovative capacity of the organization, (2) IS maturity, and (3) the strategy–IS interface, as all three influence the decision to reengineer and the perceived success of BPC (dependent variables).

Three variables gauge the innovative capacity of the organization. Integration and decentralization of decisions are related to the idea of organic organization. Because BPC often requires collaboration between departments, interdepartmental integration may provide a receptive environment for not only launching a reengineering project but also facilitating its implementation. However, the very success of BPC may induce a more decentralized structure since reengineering typically calls for empowering on-site personnel in the field (O'Hara & Watson, 1995). To compensate for the possible loss of innovative capacity in mechanistic organizations, a structural "organic overlay" may be superimposed on top of these organizations (Pierce & Deldecq, 1977). Unencumbered by the regular bureaucracies, such structural overlays typically take the form of a "venture group" dedicated to searching out and introducing innovative ideas (Zmud, 1982).

Three measures of IS maturity influence are included in this study to assess the impact of IT competence on BPC initiatives. Experience with mainframe computing would generally indicate IS maturity in terms of technical competence accumulated. It has been pointed out that client-server systems represent a departure from the traditional environment through its enabling role in facilitating the emerging management and organizational forms based on empowering on-site personnel and lateral collaborations, which are consistent with the principles of reengineering (O'Hara & Watson, 1995). Several researchers have studied the power and influence of the IS function in the organization (Lucas, 1984; Saunders & Scamell, 1986). In this study, we choose one decision area that is integral to IS responsibility—the selection of IS projects—and attempt to explore how the influence of IS in this decision may be related to reengineering project initiatives.

In our change framework, we stressed the alignment of IT strategies with overall corporate strategies as a main source of impetus for process reengineering. The variable representing strategy–IS interface is IS-business planning integration, which refers to the extent to which IS planning is aligned with and influences the overall strategic planning of the business (Premkumar & King, 1992).

RESEARCH METHODS AND RESULTS: STUDY 1

A survey of 313 IS executives (37% response rate) from companies with revenue more than $50 million employed an instrument with previously validated measures of our study constructs. Information on the *BPC decision* was obtained with a simple yes/no question: Have you attempted business process redesign in your organization? The approach for measuring reengineering success used in this study is the "perceived level of success" (DeLone & McLean, 1992). The measure for interdepartmental integration was adopted from Grover (1993). Centralization of decision making was assessed via a measure developed and validated by Ramamurthy (1990). Measurement of the existence of organic structural overlay is objectively accessed. The scale for IS-business planning integration was based on the work of Premkumar and King (1992). Of the 313 firms, 219 (70%) indicated that reengineering has been attempted in their companies. Seven relationships were examined, and the results are presented in Table 9.1.

TABLE 9.1 Study 1 Results—Organizational Impetus for BPR

Independent Variables	Mean (Overall) (N = 313)	Mean (BPR) (N= 219)	Mean (Non-BPR) (N = 94)	t-Test for BPR Decisions	Correlation with BPR Success
Innovative Capacity of the Organization					
1. Interdepartmental integration	4.94	5.11	4.55	***	0.2400***
2. Centralization of decisions	5.07	4.95	5.34	**	0.0252
3. Existence of organic structural overlay				***	n.s.
IS Maturity and Influence					
4. Experience in mainframe computing (years)	21.47	22.72	18.20	**	0.0918
5. Experience in client/server computing (years)	3.16	3.43	2.16	***	0.0547
6. IS department influence in IS project selection	3.89	3.73	4.27	**	–0.1598*
Strategy–IS Interface					
7. IS-business planning integration	5.12	5.32	4.67	***	0.2203***

Note: Maximum sample size (N) is indicated in the table. Actual N for the various cells varies slightly.

$*p < .05$ $**p < .01$ $***p < .001$

The first relationship is strong; the data showed a higher degree of interdepartmental integration for reengineering firms than nonreengineering firms ($p < .001$). Among reengineering firms, the extent of interdepartmental integration is significantly correlated to the perceived level of success ($r = .24$, $p < .001$). The second relationship is moderate because reengineering companies showed less tendency to centralize decisions than did nonreengineering firms ($p < .01$), but no relationship was detected for success. The result for relationship 3 is based on a chi-square table (not shown), which indicates that, with the organic structural overlay, organizations are more likely to attempt BPC than without the overlay ($p < 0.01$). Among BPC firms, however, no difference in perceived success was found between the two groups. For IS maturity and influence, we found that reengineering firms have more experience in mainframe and client/server computing than nonreengineering firms. Interestingly, for relationship 6, the data suggest that the extent of IS influence in IS project selection is higher among nonreengineering firms than among reengineering firms. This means that user influence, rather than IS influence, is higher among reengineering firms than nonreengineering firms. Furthermore, this user influence is also significantly associated with perceived reengineering success ($r = .1598$, $p < .05$). Finally, for the last relationship in Table 9.1, we found that IS-business strategic planning integration is significantly greater for reengineering firms than for nonreengineering firms ($p < .001$), and that it is significantly related to perceived success ($r = .2203$, $p < .001$).

DISCUSSION OF FINDINGS: STUDY 1

The results for the first two relationships suggest that the expanded capacity for innovation in organic organizations may be particularly helpful in reengineering projects initiatives. While decentralized decision making may facilitate the adoption of the reengineering concept, interdepartmental integration is important to both the decision and success. Thus, the likelihood of succeeding in reengineering, which typically involves the institutionalization of interfunctional cooperation and free flow of ideas, would increase for those organizations that have already been predisposed to this type of practice and culture. On the other hand, decentralized organizations that are low in interfunctional collaboration may have a better chance in undertaking the BPC initiative but may need extra efforts to break down the walls between functional departments to succeed.

The study results indicate that seven factors have facilitating influence on companies' decisions to initiate reengineering efforts: (1) interdepartmental integration (2) decentralization of decisions, (3) existence of organic structural overlay, (4) experience in mainframe computing, (5) experience in client/server computing, (6) IS-business planning integration, and (7) user influence in IS project selection. The following three factors, however, may facilitate both the reengineering decision as well as the eventual success: (1) interdepartmental integration, (2) user influence in IS project selection, and (3) IS-business planning integration.

As can be seen, all six factors are potential sources of facilitating influence on the reengineering decision. While factors related to IT competence, such as experience in mainframe and client/server computing, may facilitate the decision to reengineer, they are not critical in the eventual success. On the other hand, factors having significant relationships beyond the initial decision include variables pertaining to innovative capacity of the organization and strategy–IS interface. The only IS factor in this group—user influence in IS project selection—also relates to the organizational context of BPC.

These findings strongly suggest that technical IT competence as a critical enabler is necessary but never sufficient for reengineering success. Organization contextual conditions such as interdepartmental integration, user influence in IS decisions, and IS-business planning integration potentially have influence on reengineering implementation beyond the initial decisions. The pattern of results from Study 1, therefore, have provided very strong overall empirical support to arguments we made earlier regarding the conceptual change framework on the organizational impetus for process change.

SUMMARY OF STUDY 2: PROJECT PLANNING AND BPC METHODOLOGY SELECTION

In Study 2, we sought to gather empirical evidence from the field to demonstrate factors and guidelines related to the second two phases of our conceptual change framework: initiation of the change process and selecting change enablers. For example, how should project planners select the correct process to change? Is there a standard way to conduct a BPC project? How do you secure buy in and then structure a successful project?

RESEARCH METHODS AND RESULTS: STUDY 2

To examine these questions, the researchers conducted a study to determine whether a BPR project methodology archetype existed and, if so, under what conditions modifications to this archetype are made. The researchers participated in detailed case and field studies using semistructured interviews with BPR experts to gain a systematic understanding of BPR project methodologies. Twenty-five

BPR project methodologies practiced by leading reengineering consulting firms, such as Gemini Consulting, Ernst & Young, ISS, DMR Group, Andersen Consulting, Nolan & Norton Inc., CSC/Index, McKinsey Co., D. Appleton Co., Price Waterhouse, and Symmetrix, were examined. Table 9.2 highlights each step of the research methods used in deriving a BPR project archetype.

Based on the descriptions of the 25 BPR methodologies, a six-stage, 21-activity composite stage-activity (S-A) framework was derived. Each stage in this framework was subdivided into major activities. As depicted in Figure 9.2, a coding scheme is used where: Si = stage number i and Aj = activity j for stage i. It was found that although BPR methodologies vary based on philosophical differences, there is enough commonality among the practiced approaches to generally describe a prototypical BPR project effort. In a majority of cases (19 of 25), the original sequencing of stages within the methodologies before mapping is consistent with that of the BPR project S-A framework. Reliability testing and follow-up validation support this claim (see Table 9.2).

The S-A framework moves through six stages (see Table 9.3 for a brief description of each stage). The first stage, envision, involves rethinking the strategic direction of the business and identifying a vision for the future. It requires a high-level understanding of the business processes and their performance objectives. The output of this stage leads to the selection of the processes for reengineering. The second stage, initiate, includes project planning and setting the climate for change. The diagnose stage involves capturing existing process activities and determining existing problems. The redesign stage involves the recursive steps of creatively designing new process types that best link to strategic objectives. The reconstruct stage requires critical sociotechnical design to properly integrate the new process into the organization and entails people and technology process synthesis. Finally, the evaluate stage recognizes that even rejuvenated processes must be continually maintained and improved.

The key activities of the S-A framework correspond closely to the concepts outlined in the second and third phases of the conceptual BPC change framework as outlined in Figure 9.1. Surveyed methodologies tend to be strategy driven with top management interpretation of environmental and competitive factors. Most methodologies attempt to challenge existing assumptions concerning organizational systems. They generally recognized resistance to change and attempt to minimize this by assessing cultural readiness and using activities to establish project buy in. Methodologies generally focus on cross-functional and interorganizational processes. They take the customer view and leverage IT's coordination and processing capabilities. Methods included activities to empower individuals and teams and accommodate measurement of performance gains, particularly as they relate to customer satisfaction and profitability. In sum, the BPR project S-A framework portrays the essence of a BPR project as a set of coordinated efforts to modify various organizational subsystems through BPC. Practitioners may take the derived framework as a starting point in understanding "ingredients" descriptive of BPC and as a basis for evaluating alternative project approaches.

DISCUSSION OF FINDINGS: STUDY 2

The BPR project S-A framework provides project planners with a BPC methodological archetype. However, no two BPR projects are exactly alike. Due to the unique characteristics of the project and the amount of change sought as indicated in the

TABLE 9.2 Description of the Research Methodology for Study 2

To complete Study 2, the researchers conducted the following research steps:

Steps 1 & 2—Literature Review and Market Assessment: The researchers conducted a literature search on the state of the art in BPR project methods using secondary sources including scholarly and trade literature, on-line market intelligence services, and market research reports. This effort produced a list of initial sources of research data: (1) BPR market researchers and consultants, and (2) BPR tools and technology vendors. BPR practices were requested from these sources. When additional information was necessary, a request was made to conduct a follow-up interview.

Steps 3—Semistructured Interviews: Researchers selected key informants in each of the 25 major BPR consultancies identified in steps 1 and 2, usually one of the senior partners or someone having significant BPR project experience. The interviews began with open-ended questions regarding the respondents and his or her organization's view of reengineering. The interview progressed into details of their organization's offering to the BPR marketplace, which included methodologies practiced, activity sequences, and the use of advanced techniques and tools. To enhance the accuracy, interviews involved two researchers to allow one to conduct the interview and the other to probe and transcribe the information. Observations corroborated well between interviewees and with published sources. Interview notes were compiled to develop descriptions for each methodology's stages and activities.

Step 4—Establish Research Databases of BPR Methods: A research database was established containing descriptions of the 25 surveyed methodologies. The consulting firms included such firms as A.T Kearney, AT&T, Booz Allen & Hamilton, CSC Index, D. Appleton, Ernst & Young, EDS, Gateway, Hammer & Co., ISS, KBS Inc., McKinsey Co., Meritus, Nolan & Norton, Oxford Associates, Price Waterhouse, SRI, TI, and Wang.

Step 5—Discovering a Composite S-A Pattern Through Induction: Based on the inductive approach prescribed by research methodologists and the inductive research steps reported in prior IS studies, the researchers developed the following sequential steps to derive the potential Stage-Activity pattern from the database of 25 BPR methodologies. First each of the three researchers individually analyzed the commonalities and differences between the 25 methodologies in terms of stages and activities and identified a set of *distinct reengineering activities* included in each methodology. Next, as a group, the team identified a set of *core activities* through interpretation, discussion, reconciliation, and consensus voting. Standardized descriptions were developed for each of these activities. Then each researcher individually *sequenced* the core activities and divided them into *groups* perceived to logically constitute a stage based on temporal affinity and similarity in overall purpose. As a group, the researchers reached a consensus on the sequencing and grouping of activities. This assignment of stages to activities formed the baseline for further reliability and validity testing.

Step 6—Examining Reliability of the S-A Framework: Twelve judges participated in a Q-sort to assess the reliability of the S-A framework. Invited judges included IS professionals with BPR experience. For each of the 25 methodologies, subjects were instructed to indicate which of the six derived stages in the S-A framework best matches a particular stage in a consulting company's methodology in terms of the activities. Results of the Q-sort were analyzed following the guidelines for measuring reliability of qualitative data. The proportional reduction in loss (PRL) measurement technique, which is a direct extension of Cronbach's alpha for qualitative cases, was used. We found a very high proportion of interjudge agreement, with PRL levels exceeding 0.80 for 130 among a total of 134 stages sorted.

Step 7—Examine Validity of the BPR Framework in Three Case Sites: The researchers next attempted to ascertain additional validity of the composite stage-activity framework through field verification at three case study sites. The three firms—AT&T-GBCS, Comdisco Inc., and Bowater Inc.—had completed a comprehensive BPR project. In-depth field interviews were conducted in these companies. Results of these interviews indicated that the sequence of stages and activities at the three sites was closely aligned with those of the derived Stage-Activity framework. In fact, the mapping between the method and AT&T's BPR project had an almost 100% fit. Interestingly, Comdisco Inc. and Bowater Inc. had undertaken an initial unsuccessful BPR project with a preconceived solution centered around information technology (IT) and immediate redesign. However, these firms soon realized that their "radical IT solution" did not serve their business needs. To avoid failure, in both cases, the project teams reverted back to the envision stage, to develop a business vision and justification first. The fact that the project teams reverted back to the sequence of stages as laid out by the derived stage-activity sequence suggests additional validity of the framework.

For further information on Study 2's research methods, visit the MISQ Archivist at **http:// www.misq.org/archivist/appendices/article1.html,** which provides a detailed discussion and statistical results.

FIGURE 9.2 A Stage-Activity Framework for Business Process Reengineering

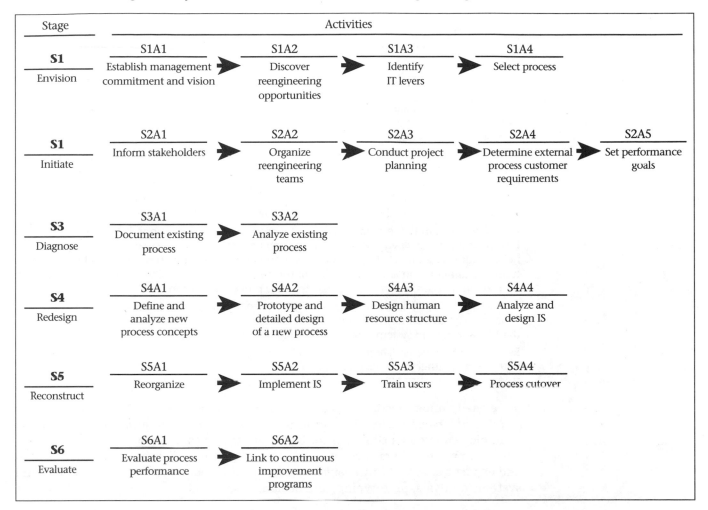

first phase (organizational impetus) of our conceptual change framework, the apportionment of effort dedicated to specific BPR project stages and activities should be adjusted to maximize effectiveness. Four contingent project characteristics were identified as most critical in BPR project planning: (1) project radicalness, (2) process structuredness, (3) customer focus, and (4) the potential for IT enablement (See Table 9.4). Most prominent among the four project characteristics, the degree of radicalness of change is crucial in customizing the S-A methodology framework. For instance, if radical reengineering strategy is adopted, the diagnose stage (S3) (see Figure 9.2), which involves documenting and analyzing the existing process (S3A1 and S3A2), requires less attention than activities such as designing the new process and the associated human resource architecture (S4A1 and S4A3). External customers have direct competitive significance to the firm, and processes interfacing with them warrant a more intensive *customer focus* (Ives & Mason, 1990). Therefore, those projects that directly involve external customers require increased emphasis on determining customer requirements.[4] *Process structuredness* is important in adjusting the project S-A framework since more structured processes can be

TABLE 9.3   Descriptions of Stages in Derived S-A Framework for BPR

The six stages can be categorized as containing the following activities:

Envision (S1). This stage typically involves a BPR project champion engendering the support of top management. A task force, including senior executives and individuals knowledgeable about a firm's processes, is authorized to target a business process for improvement based on a review of business strategy and IT opportunities in the hope of improving the firm's overall performance.

Initiate (S2). This stage encompasses the assignment of a reengineering project team, the setting of performance goals, project planning, and stakeholder/employee notification and "buy-in." This is frequently achieved by developing a business case for reengineering via benchmarking, identifying external customer needs, and cost-benefit analysis.

Diagnose (S3). This stage is classified as the documentation of the current process and sub-processes in terms of process attributes such as activities, resources, communication, roles, IT, and cost. In identifying process requirements and assigning customers value, root causes for problems surface and nonvalue-adding activities are identified.

Redesign (S4). In the redesign stage, a new process design is developed. This is accomplished by devising process design alternatives through brainstorming and creativity techniques. The new design should meet strategic objectives and fit with the human resource and IT architectures. Documentation and prototyping of the new process is typically conducted, and designs of new information systems to support the new process are completed.

Reconstruct (S5). This stage relies heavily on change management techniques to ensure smooth migration to new process responsibilities and human resource roles. During this stage, the IT platform and systems are implemented and the users go through training and transition.

Evaluate (S6). The last stage of a BPR methodology requires monitoring the new process to determine whether it met its goals and often involves linkage to a firm's total quality programs.

more easily understood, analyzed, modeled, and redesigned (Earl, 1994). The *extent of IT enablement* varies from project to project. Some projects require emerging technologies such as the Internet-based electronic commerce, imaging, work flow, and groupware; others involve adaptation of existing IT such as shared databases and expert systems. IT-intensive projects benefit from more time spent on formal IS systems analysis, prototyping, and design.

TABLE 9.4   Analyzing Change Dynamics and Structuring the Change Process

Project Characteristics	Project Contingencies	Project Emphases
All projects . . .	. . . require . . .	project management.
	. . . need . . .	problem solving and diagnosis.
The more customer focused . . .	. . . the more important is . . .	customer requirements analysis.
The more structured the process . . .	. . . the more useful is . . .	process capture and modeling.
	. . . the more feasible is . . .	process prototyping and simulation.
	. . . the more applicable is . . .	process measurement.
The more IT enables process change . . .	. . . the more relevant is . . .	IS systems analysis and design.
The more radical the project . . .	. . . the greater the reliance on . . .	business planning.
	. . . the higher the demand for . . .	creative thinking.
	. . . the more essential the . . .	organizational analysis & design.
	. . . the greater the criticality of . . .	change management.

Note: This table has been adapted from a table presented in *MIS Quarterly* by Kettinger, Teng, and Guha (1997).

In sum, findings from this study show that planning for BPC can be greatly facilitated by analyzing the change dynamics and then structuring a project using a customized stage-activity method.

SUMMARY OF STUDY 3: BPC IMPLEMENTATION PROBLEMS AND SUCCESS

As outlined in the third phases (managing change implementation) of our overarching change framework, an understanding of the impediments to process change and the use of appropriate tactics to minimize these impediments should increase the chances of implementation success. Drawing from the large body of literature on implementation within innovation, sociotechnical design, planning, and the management information systems fields, this study is focused on the following questions: (1) What are the problems related to implementation of business process change? (2) What is the relative severity of these problems? (3) How do these problems relate to the success of business process change?

RESEARCH METHODS AND RESULTS: STUDY 3

Following a review of past research of innovation and implementation, a grouping of recognized implementation problems was categorized within each of four themes: (1) management support, (2) technological competence, (3) change management, and (4) project preparation. Next a careful review of the popular literature was undertaken to identify specific problems experienced in actual BPC implementations. A combined problem set of past cited and BPC-specific implementation problems formed our derived implementation problem set. Further validation of the problems and their categorization was achieved through face-to-face interviews with managers who had participated in reengineering projects. Interviewees were given the initial version of the categorized problem list and problems were added, deleted, or modified during the interviews. Based on these field interviews, individual implementation problems were modified and new problems were added based on the interviewees' experience. These interviews alerted the researchers to an additional category of problems related to project management. Next, a Q-sort procedure was conducted to further validate the problem categorizations. This resulted in the project preparedness category being divided into project planning and process delineation. The final set of 64 problems used for field data collection are grouped into these six categories:

1. *Management support* problems consist of potential problems related to management's active understanding and support for reengineering.
2. *Technological competence* problems relate to the IT infrastructure[5] and expertise within the organization.
3. *Process delineation* problems are potential problems with identification of appropriate parameters (e.g., goals, scope, process owners, resources) for the process involved.
4. *Project planning* problems include potential problems with planning, setting up the team, and making other preparations for the reengineering project.

5. *Change management* problems focus on potential problems due to a failure to manage change from the old process to the new process.
6. *Project management* problems deal with the actual conduct of the project.

With a BPC project as the unit of analysis, the survey instrument was used to solicit the significance of each item in the problem set to the project identified. Respondents were asked to rate the extent to which they encountered each problem on a five-level scale where the extreme categories were represented from "not a problem" to "an extreme problem." Reengineering success was measured multidimensionally using two different perspectives: perceived level of success (Delone & McLean, 1992) and goal fulfillment (Hamilton & Chervany, 1981; Schriven, 1972).

Respondents were asked to answer one five-point scaled question about the perceived success level of their reengineering project. The goal fulfillment perspective measure is characterized as an objective compared to the subjective nature of perceived success. The study used five commonly emphasized goals: (1) cost reduction, (2) cycle-time reduction, (3) customer satisfaction level increase, (4) worker productivity increase, and (5) defects reduction (Davenport, 1993; Morris & Brandon, 1993). In the questionnaire, for each of these performance goals, respondents indicated the planned level of performance improvement (before reengineering) and the actual level of improvement achieved (after reengineering implementation). For the performance indicator, we compared the actual level of improvement to the planned level via the ratio of these two metrics.[6]

To help ensure validity, respondents must have actively participated in at least one reengineering project (Huber & Power, 1985). A total of 853 questionnaires was sent to members of the Planning Forum, the international business organization focusing on strategic management and planning. A total of 239 usable responses was returned, resulting in a final response rate of 29.2 percent. Of the 239 respondents, 105 (44%) had concluded at least one reengineering project and were able to respond to the entire instrument. To ensure homogeneity of problem sets, principal component analysis was performed on the items, and the final classification consisted of 49 items that fell into one of nine categories. Project planning problems were classified according to two factors related to strategic planning and tactical planning. Three items from change management problems loaded onto a factor that was interpreted as human resource problems. Finally, the project management problems split into two factors labeled project management problems and time frame problems. Table 9.5 lists the items in each category.

Severity of Implementation Problems

To assess the relative severity of the various BPC implementation problems, each potential problem received a "severity score" (i.e., the percentage of respondents who rated it as either a major problem or an extreme problem). Since our interest was in assessing whether each problem was pervasive and significant, a frequency measure was used as opposed to conventional averaging. The average severity score for each of the final nine problem categories follows:

- Change management (mean score = 21.9).
- Technological competence (mean score = 18.2).
- Strategic planning (mean score = 17.2).
- Time frame (mean score = 16.4).

TABLE 9.5 Items in Each Problem Category

Management Support Problems
- Lack of senior management leadership for reengineering efforts
- Lack of top management support in business reengineering efforts
- Top management's insufficient understanding about business reengineering
- Managers' failure to support the new values and beliefs demanded by the redesigned process
- Insufficient understanding about the goals of top management in relation to business reengineering
- Lack of BPR project champion

Technological Competence Problems
- Limited IS application portfolio
- Lack of expertise in IT in the organization
- Insufficient understanding about existing data, applications, and IT across the organization
- Lack of IS participation and assistance in the reengineering project
- Limited database infrastructure
- Failure to aggressively use IT enablers
- Limited telecommunication infrastructure

Process Delineation Problems
- Difficulty in establishing performance improvement goals for the redesigned process
- Failure to include process owners throughout the BR efforts
- Failure to identify process owners who are responsible for the entire business process
- Scope of the reengineered process was defined inappropriately
- Proposed changes to the process were too incremental, not radical enough
- Difficult to forecast human, financial, and other resource requirements

Strategic Planning Problems
- Lack of alignment between corporate planning and IT planning
- Lack of appropriate planning
- Identification of candidate process for reengineering not based on strategic planning
- Lack of strategic vision

Time Frame Problems
- The BR effort took too much time
- Uncertainty about BR project time frame
- Too much emphasis on analyzing the existing process
- Failure to effectively monitor progress of project according to the schedule

Tactical Planning Problems
- Failure to commit the required resources (financial, human resources, etc.) to BR efforts
- Difficulty in financially justifying benefits of BR
- Absence of appropriate training for BR team members
- Failure to understand customers' viewpoints in the BPR efforts
- Lack of external consultant support for BR efforts

Change Management Problems
- Failure to anticipate and plan for the organizational resistance to change
- Failure to consider politics of the business reengineering efforts
- Need for managing change not recognized
- Failure to communicate reasons for change to members of the organization
- Necessary changes in human resource policies for BR implementation not made
- Difficulty in gaining cross-functional cooperation
- Senior management's failure to commit to new values

Human Resource Problems
- Inadequate training for personnel affected by the redesigned process
- Not enough time to develop new skills for the redesigned process
- Absence of management systems (e.g., incentive, training system) to cultivate required values

Project Management Problems
- Poor communication between BR team members and other organizational members
- Difficulty in gaining control of reengineering efforts
- Lack of appropriate BR methodology
- Difficulty in modeling and simulating the proposed changes to the business process
- Failure to assess project performance in the early stage of BR efforts to provide feedback
- Difficulty in measuring reengineering project performance

- Management support (mean score = 15.6).
- Human resource (mean score = 14.5).
- Process delineation (mean score = 14.0).
- Project management (mean score = 11.7).
- Tactical planning (mean score = 10.3).

The results clearly indicate that change management problems are perceived as most severe in implementing process change. Problems such as the communication of the reengineering rationale to employees, the politics of reengineering efforts, and the commitment to new values, which have been suggested by reengineering experts and researchers (Stoddard & Jarvenpaa, 1995) as significant BPC issues, were among the change management problems identified in this study. This finding reveals and reaffirms the fundamental nature of reengineering, which typically entails multidimensional organizational changes involving roles/responsibilities, performance measures/incentives, shared values (culture), organizational structure, and skill requirements, in addition to information technology applications. These changes constitute the "depth" dimension of change required for process reengineering. The difficulty in managing these changes is further compounded by the "breadth" of reengineering projects that often involve processes that span different functional boundaries.

The sociotechnical nature of reengineering is vividly and "literally" demonstrated by the two most severe types of implementation problems: change management and technological competence. However, the order is of utmost significance here: social first and technology second. Information technology is an important enabler, but the reengineering project itself involves significant changes in areas such as roles and responsibilities, organizational structure, and shared values, and none of these changes can take place in an orderly fashion without careful planning and conscientious efforts to communicate with, educate, and motivate the affected employees.

Relating Reengineering Problem Severity and Project Success

To assess the relationship between various sources of implementation difficulties and reengineering success, the average score for each of the nine categories was correlated to the success measures. For overall success, the 5-point scale as described earlier was used. For the other five specific success measures, such as cost, cycle time, and defects reduction, we sought to capture the extent to which planned performance goals have been realized. This was represented by the ratio between the actual performance gain and planned performance gain. The results of the correlation analysis are shown in Table 9.6. As expected, all correlation coefficients are negative because more success should be associated with fewer problems. The nine problem categories are listed in descending order of the magnitude of their correlation with overall success. For specific performance goals, rankings of correlations are assigned only to those that are statistically significant. In an attempt to explore patterns, the correlations for each column in the table were split at the median, and the top five classified as H (high) as opposed to the bottom four, which were designated L (low).

As can be seen, coefficients in the overall success column are all significant. In fact, all but one are highly significant at $p < 0.01$. In addition, the magnitude of the

TABLE 9.6   Correlations between Problem Categories and Reengineering Success[†]

Problem Category	Overall Success (N = 95)	Cost Reduction (N = 49)	Cycle-Time Reduction (N = 55)	Customer Satisfaction Increase (N = 38)	Productivity Increase (N = 46)	Defects Reduction (N = 25)
Human resource	−0.51*** (1) (H)	−0.47*** (1) (H)	−0.30** (3) (H)	−0.40** (1) (H)	−0.43*** (2) (H)	−0.49** (2) (H)
Project management	−0.42*** (2) (H)	−0.35** (5) (H)	−0.33** (2) (H)	−0.36** (3) (H)	−0.33** (4) (H)	−0.48** (3) (H)
Management support	−0.36*** (3) (H)	−0.29** (8) (L)	−0.10 (L)	−0.25 (L)	−0.25* (7) (L)	−0.34* (9) (L)
Change management	−0.35*** (4) (H)	−0.43*** (3) (H)	−0.34** (1) (H)	−0.35** (4) (H)	−0.49*** (1) (H)	−0.39* (8) (L)
Tactical planning	−0.33*** (5) (H)	−0.37*** (4) (H)	−0.25* (5) (H)	−0.38** (2) (H)	−0.33** (4) (H)	−0.43* (7) (L)
Process delineation	−0.30*** (6) (L)	−0.44*** (2) (H)	−0.29** (4) (H)	−0.34** (5) (H)	−0.43*** (2) (H)	−0.45** (5) (H)
Strategic planning	−0.28*** (7) (L)	−0.32** (6) (L)	−0.18 (L)	−0.31* (6) (L)	−0.33** (4) (H)	−0.45** (5) (H)
Time frame	−0.27*** (8) (L)	−0.27* (9) (L)	−0.19 (L)	−0.20 (L)	−0.21 (L)	−0.47** (4) (H)
Technological competence	−0.19* (9) (L)	−0.30** (7) (L)	−0.12 (L)	−0.30* (7) (L)	−0.22 (L)	−0.51*** (1) (H)
Average correlation	−0.33	−0.36	−0.23	−0.32	−0.34	−0.45

[†]Overall success is based on a five-point scale. All other success measures are achieved/planned performance level ratios.

Numbers in parentheses following the coefficients are rankings for significant correlations based on magnitude.

For each column, the five highest correlations are classified H (high), the rest L (low). There are six Hs for the last two columns due to identical correlations.

*Significant at the 0.10 level. **Significant at the 0.05 level. ***Significant at the 0.01 level.

correlations is large, with six of the nine exceeding 0.30. While this is somewhat expected, the ranking pattern contains some interesting results and offers fresh insights. Human resource problems, which were originally categorized as part of the change management category, are very highly negatively correlated ($r = −0.51$) with perceived BPC success. While change management concerns the organizational context for change such as politics, communication, commitment, and resistance to change at the policy level, human resource problems focus on specific *tasks* pertaining to people within the project domain itself. These tasks include training personnel affected by the redesigned process, developing new skills needed by the new process, and setting up management systems to cultivate required values. This result suggests that to the extent that these critical human resource arrangements are not made in the actual conduct of the project, the success of the project may be in jeopardy. This finding once again demonstrates the overwhelming importance of managing organizational change and the social dimension of BPC initiatives. Failure to prepare the affected employees for the new "world order" of BPC and to cultivate new values that sustain the new order can lead to a detrimental outcome for the project.

The ranking of correlations for overall success contains some surprises. Technology competence, while being regarded as the second most severe type of problems, correlated the least with overall success. Note that the magnitude of the correlation ($r = −0.19$) is substantially lower than that for human resource problems ($r = −0.51$). Thus, reengineering project members may experience a great deal of difficulty in obtaining IT-related skills and infrastructure, but the lack of such problems will by no means guarantee project success. Apparently, taking good care of the required technology may be necessary but not at all sufficient for the eventual success of reengineering.

DISCUSSION OF FINDINGS: STUDY 3

To gain more insight into the study findings, we next made a broad examination of the overall patterns of results. To explore these patterns, both the severity of the problem and its relationship to success are included in Table 9.7. Because the research objective was to explore general patterns rather than to strive for precision in analysis, statistical measures were designated as either H (for the top five scores) or L (for the bottom four scores). This classifications scheme helps develop an overall portrayal of the various problem categories, as indicated in the last column of the table.

Change management stands out as the most severe source of difficulty in reengineering. It also has relatively high correlation (negative) with most success measures. The overall pattern is designated high severity-high correlation (HS-HC). This pattern clearly indicates that change management occupies the center stage in business process reengineering implementation. The daunting tasks in breaking the organizational status quo and introducing new practices, new values, and new structures must have been overwhelming for most reengineering team members, and our study results confirm this. The good news is that efforts devoted to solving these difficult change management problems should pay off in terms of reengineering project success. The warning message is equally striking, however—the inability to manage organizational change in reengineering will most likely lead to project failure!

For the other eight categories of implementation problems, we found either a high security-low correlation (HS-LC) pattern or a low severity-high correlation (LS-HC) pattern. In fact, with only a few exceptions, all four categories having higher severity (HS) are weakly correlated with the various success measures (LC). This HS-LC pattern suggests that implementation problems related to technological competence, strategic planning (of reengineering), project time frame, and management support are quite difficult to manage, but reducing these problems does not necessarily pave the way to success. In other words, addressing these vital problems is a necessary but not sufficient condition for reengineering success.

TABLE 9.7   Ranking Patterns of Severity and Problem–Success Correlations

Ranking of Problem Severity*		Correlation Between Problems and Reengineering Success[†]						
Problem Category	Average Severity Score	Overall Success	Cost Reduction	Cycle-Time Reduction	Customer Satisfaction Increase	Productivity Increase	Defects Reduction	Pattern of Severity vs. Correlation[‡]
Change management	H (21.9)	H	H	H	H	H	L	HS–HC
Technological competence	H (18.2)	L	L	L	L	L	H	HS–LC
Strategic planning	H (17.2)	L	L	L	L	H	H	HS–LC
Time frame	H (16.4)	L	L	L	L	L	H	HS–LC
Management support	H (15.6)	H	L	L	L	L	L	HS–LC
Human resource	L (14.8)	H	H	H	H	H	H	LS–HC
Process delineation	L (14.0)	L	H	H	H	H	H	LS–HC
Project management	L (11.7)	H	H	H	H	H	H	LS–HC
Tactical planning	L (10.3)	H	H	H	H	H	L	LS–HC

*A problem category with average severity score greater than 15 percent is classified H (high); otherwise it is classified L (low).

[†]For each success measure, the five highest correlations with problem categories are classified H (high); the rest are classified L (low). For productivity and defects, identical correlations result in six Hs.

[‡]HS = high severity; HC = high correlation; LS = low severity; LC = low correlation.

Interestingly, the opposite pattern (LS-HC) was found for the four categories having less severity (LS). These categories include human resource, process delineation, project management, and tactical project planning. These problems may not be major sources of difficulty during reengineering, but a tendency to neglect them will prove detrimental to project success. This is particularly evident in the fact that human resource problems can be mitigated by training personnel affected by the new process, developing new skills, and instituting new management systems to cultivate required values. Given other implementation problems, especially change management problems, reengineering team members may not always focus their attention on these problems. However, the redesigned process primarily depends on people, not machines, to operate. Poorly trained and undermotivated employees will inhibit success!

With the exception of change management, the overall macro patterns as discussed indicate the existence of two groups of implementation problems, one with the HS-LC pattern and one with the LS-HC pattern. The four categories included in the HS-LC group seem to relate more to the general project context and environment, whereas the second group (LS-HC) more directly involves the reengineering project itself. Problem categories in the first group include technological competence, strategic planning, time frame, and management support problems. These types of problems are often discussed in the context of MIS implementation and are not unique to reengineering (e.g., Ginzberg, 1981; Lucas, 1978). However, due to the breadth and depth of change required for reengineering, these problems will be potentially more difficult to manage and solve than in the traditional MIS project context.

On the other hand, reengineering team members may have unintentionally treated "lower-level" details of reengineering work lightly, perhaps a natural response after having handled the difficult organizational change and strategic planning problems. However, human resource, process delineation, project management, and tactical project planning efforts correspond directly to the core tasks of reengineering, and the consequence of neglecting these vital tasks will increase the likelihood of project failure. An inappropriately scoped process (process delineation) (Hall et al., 1993) and an inadequate BPC methodology (project management) (Kettinger et al., 1997) can seriously jeopardize the project. Human resource problems also correspond to the tactical dimension. While change management concerns the general *organizational context* for change at the *policy* level, human resource problems focus on the *specific tasks* pertaining to people, such as training and skill development within the project domain itself. When these tasks are done poorly, the new process will be staffed by underskilled and undermotivated employees. This would certainly lead to project failure even if the overall environment had been favorable with respect to management support, commitment to change, and required technological competence.

In general, Study 3 clearly demonstrated the central importance of change management in reengineering implementation, as discussed in the conceptual framework presented earlier. Not only was change management regarded as most challenging to undertake, but also it showed a critical relationship to project success. On the other hand, technological competence was viewed as difficult but had the least potential influence on project success. Thus, both social and technical components of reengineering initiatives have been recognized by the respondents as difficult, but the social elements are truly critical to reengineering success. While much conceptual discussion and numerous anecdotal accounts have been reported emphasizing the people and organizational aspects of reengineering, this is the first piece of empirical evidence based on a large sample showing a direct reflection of the sociotechnical characteristics of reengineering projects in the minds of those who have attempted it. This is a critical step in the development of the reengineering field because the confirmation of reengineering as essentially managing process and organizational change in a complex sociotechnical setting has profound implications for both researchers and practitioners. Change management is a complex, multifaceted process, and the steps and guidelines outlined in our framework for process and organizational change should help to lay the groundwork for further development in the field.

The study results have important implications for MIS professionals. Our findings suggest that technological competence is necessary but never sufficient for reengineering success. To succeed in reengineering, it is critical to master change management that demands sophisticated people and business skills. MIS professionals, being accustomed to more "structured" projects aimed at automation of existing procedures, may need reorientation and additional training for the "unstructured" project environment in reengineering (Markus & Robey, 1995).

IMPLICATIONS OF THE THREE STUDIES ON THE BPC CONCEPTUAL FRAMEWORK

Recent economic and competitive conditions have taken many organizations down the path of unprecedented process-based organizational change. To prepare for these changes, a conceptual framework is developed to depict elements of organizational change associated with process reengineering: sources of organizational impetus leading to reengineering initiatives, change initiation, selecting process change enablers, change implementation, and the various dimensions of possible organizational change resulting from redesigned business processes. In discussing these elements, we stress that process reengineering is much more than applying IT to streamline complicated procedures. It is first and foremost a multifaceted process of change involving organizational structure, management systems, human resource architecture, and many other aspects of organizational life.

The three empirical studies summarized provide results that strongly support the conceptual framework described in Figure 9.1. Results of the first study confirmed that organic organizations with greater interdepartmental integration, more decentralized decision making, and higher-strategy IS integration exhibit greater impetus toward process change initiatives. These integrated and decentralized decision-making structures provide a forum for holistic thinking and are further reinforced through the implementation of BPC initiatives, which emphasize empowerment and team-based structures for process ownership. The results also suggest that client/server architectures that epitomize the notion of user empowerment facilitate BPC efforts. Interestingly, control of IS applications for BPC initiators resides with user groups as opposed to the IS function. This is further testimony to two concurrent trends: the recognition of IS and IT as organizational resources and greater organizational rather than functional control of that resource. This is consistent with the broad organizational focus of BPC.

The true nature of BPC projects—social-technical design—was vividly demonstrated in both the second and the third studies. Empirical results of Study 2 indicate that comprehensive BPC project planning is vital to success. A BPC project planning archetype was derived that contained steps to ensure that each component of Phases 2 and 3 of our process-based organizational change framework was addressed. It was determined that analysis of the change dynamic of BPC projects lends support for the application of contingent BPC methodological solutions within an archetype of stages, activities, and proven techniques. By evaluating such contingent factors as the project radicalness desired, existing process structuredness, degree of customer focus sought, and the potential for IT enablement, BPC project planners can "stack the deck" in favor of project success.

Our third study's findings indicate that, among a number of reengineering implementation problems, change management was regarded as the most severe by project participants. We found that while both change management and project participants regarded technological competence problems as very difficult, the former was related much more strongly to reengineering success than the latter. Thus, evidence suggests that in implementing process change, social design is paramount and technical matters are secondary. Therefore, reengineering implementation must be treated and managed as large-scale organizational change. Here, organizational and human resource approaches are critical.[7] These include empowering workers, establishing autonomous work teams, and creating new, more process-oriented organizational structures and cultures.

FUTURE DIRECTIONS

With strong empirical support, the process-based change framework for process reengineering presented in this chapter should prove helpful in providing a high-level perspective for guiding the planning and implementation of BPC initiatives. Indeed, recent trends in research and practice have shifted from a narrow "one-shot" redesign effort to an ongoing "process management" orientation that emphasizes the critical importance of human and organizational factors in not only the initial but also the continuing sustainable success of BPC.

What we have learned is that BPC initiatives involve multifaceted sociotechnical change, and efforts to understand this complex phenomenon are only beginning. The conceptual framework and empirical evidence presented in this chapter need to be refined and extended with further theoretical and empirical work. Theoretical work can draw from the rich literature on quality of work life and organizational learning to identify better antecedents and metrics for successful change. On the empirical side, five avenues of research can be persued:

1. *Studies of Contrasts.* The wide repertoire of major change initiatives that have been concluded can allow systematical inquiry into both successful and unsuccessful endeavors.[8] The high variance prevalent in contrasting outcomes can facilitate the identification of critical success factors across the various phases of the process-change framework.

2. *Contingency Studies.* The frameworks and perspectives presented here represent general trends that need to be refined through contingency-based research approaches. The directions of organizational changes stemming from BPC, for example, may be extended by examining how these patterns of change vary in speed and scope for various types of organizations and how different industries may involve different facilitating and inhibiting factors.

3. *Process Studies.* Studies that focus on the process for accomplishing change across all phases would provide an important dimension to this stream of work. The "process" of successful process change becomes subsumed in content-based studies such as the ones described in this chapter. More direct prescriptions can

be obtained by identifying process characteristics (e.g., participation level, flow of decision making, frequency of meetings, methods of organizational communication) and their success under different conditions.

4. *Interpretive Research.* Based on a different research epistemology, interpretive work does not predefine independent and dependent variables but is aimed at understanding the context of process change and how process change influences and is influenced by the context. This can facilitate the construction of rich knowledge in the area by focusing on the full complexity of human sense making as a process change situation emerges.

5. *Business Network Studies.* While the primary emphasis of our work has been on processes internal to the organization, a broader and arguably more important context to process change that transcends organizational boundaries has developed. Studies that focus on effectiveness of processes involving supply-chain integration, e-commerce–based customer service, outsourcing processes, and other buyer-supplier-infomediary relationships are extremely important for successful implementation of both virtual and physical processes in a networked environment.

Collectively, these studies can facilitate the construction of knowledge on the how, when, and why of process management, whether it involves radical, incremental, or continuous change or no change at all. The ultimate objective, of course, is to create a flexible and responsive information-age organization whose processes facilitate effective codification and transfer of organizational knowledge and stimulate the company's valuable human resource to be motivated, creative, and entrepreneurial.

ENDNOTES

1. However, since the studies described in this chapter used the term *reengineering,* we use *business process change* and *business process reengineering (BPR)* interchangeably throughout the text.
2. The framework is derived from a more detailed and earlier version presented in *OMEGA* (Teng, Grover, & Fiedler, 1996). It should be noted that the original framework presented in the *OMEGA* article included a fifth phase that examined the direction of organizational change subsequent to a BPC effort. While we still subscribe to the need for examining this fifth phase, given space limitations, we have focused in this chapter on research related to successful BPC project implementation.
3. See the chapter by Markus and Tanis for a comprehensive discussion of enterprise systems and organizational change.
4. See the chapter by Segars and Dean, which emphasizes IT-enabled change that transcends organizational boundaries.
5. See the chapter by Weill and Broadbent.
6. See the chapter by Barua and Mukhopadhyay for a discussion of process-oriented performance metrics.
7. See Cooper and Markus (1995) for a description of techniques for managing human change in a large company.
8. One study we conducted recently involves a set of reengineering cases having a range of outcomes, from highly successful to miserable failures (Guha et al., 1997).

Chapter 10

The Enterprise System Experience— From Adoption to Success

M. Lynne Markus and Cornelis Tanis

"[T]he notion that a company can and ought to have an expert (or a group of experts) create for it a single, completely integrated supersystem—an 'MIS'—to help it govern every aspect of its activity is absurd." (Dearden, 1972, p. 101)

For some 20 years after John Dearden wrote these words, history proved him right. Today, however, there is a booming market for software packages claiming to provide a total, integrated solution to companies' information-processing needs. Even companies that choose not to adopt such packages are pursuing aggressive strategies of systems integration by redeveloping custom software and adopting technologies such as data warehousing. Integrated enterprise systems deserve serious research attention because of their great potential for financial, technical, managerial, human, and strategic benefits, costs, and risks.

This chapter provides a theoretical framework for analyzing, both retrospectively and prospectively, the business value of enterprise systems. We first describe the historical context in which enterprise systems emerged. Next we identify the key characteristics of enterprise systems, discuss the reasons companies do and do not adopt them, and summarize arguments about why enterprise systems are an important topic for research. We then analyze enterprise systems in terms of the concept of success. We argue that the many facets of success create difficulties for

Acknowledgments: The authors gratefully acknowledge the support of other members of their research team: Sheryl Axline, Lars Bo Eriksen, and Dave Petrie. In addition, they wish to thank the following individuals for helpful input at various stages in this work: Carole Agres, Matt Alvarez, David Brown, Dorothy Cooney, Sabine Hirt, Debbie Mahan, Christina Soh, and Nancy Wendt.

both academics and practitioners and require a framework for understanding the "enterprise system experience." Essential elements of this framework include phases, starting conditions, goals, plans, and quality of execution. We conclude with suggestions for future research.

HISTORICAL CONTEXT OF ENTERPRISE SYSTEMS

Whether because the capacity of computers and programming languages was too small or organizations were content to manage themselves along narrow functional lines, the 1970s vision of a single integrated information system for the enterprise remained a mirage for the majority of computer-using organizations. Instead, organizations created "islands of automation" (McKenney & McFarlan, 1982). When companies identified a new application for IT, they programmed a discrete new information system. If the new system had something in common with existing systems, it was loosely interfaced (sometimes manually) rather than integrated tightly with these existing systems. As a result, combining information about sales or manufacturing with accounting data was difficult and error prone. Analyses could be performed easily only at a summary level; detailed transaction-level analysis required special ad hoc programming or manual record sifting. Multiple systems contained the same data elements; because duplicate data entry promoted errors and because systems varied in update schedules, the data in different systems often did not agree. Decision making was stymied. Corporate restructurings necessitated major reprogramming (or were abandoned as technologically infeasible[1]). The total organizational costs of maintaining this loose patchwork of redundant and overlapping systems grew, eclipsing the funds available for building new ones (Lientz & Swanson, 1980). In short, organizations finally began to experience the burden of *not* having pursued the dream of "one-company, one-system."

But the dream did not die among members of the information systems community. Throughout the 1980s and 1990s, software entrepreneurs in Germany, the Netherlands, the United States, and elsewhere were developing integrated software packages in which multiple functional applications shared a common database.[2] A single transaction such as a sales order could "flow through" the entire applications suite, automatically updating financial and inventory records without additional data entry and feeding various planning and decision support systems. As the vendors enhanced the functionality of their integrated packages, they claimed with some (but not total) truth that their products met all the information-processing needs of the companies that adopted them. These packages became known as enterprise resource planning (ERP) systems, and they include some that have developed out of the administrative (financial and human resources) side of the business (e.g., SAP and Peoplesoft), as well as some that grew from materials resource planning in manufacturing (e.g., Baan).

Software packages have always been more acceptable for smaller enterprises than for large ones for a variety of historical, technical, and economic reasons. Therefore, integrated packages made relatively little headway in the largest organizations until the mid-1990s, when vendors began to offer versions for the client/server architecture. For some time, companies had been aware that the client/server architecture afforded advantages relative to mainframe-based applications. The latter had much higher operating costs, and they did not support graphical user interfaces for business applications. Many companies tried redeveloping their core transaction systems for the client/server architecture, only to discover that the process was extremely expensive and highly failure prone; packages as an alternative to in-house (re)development started to become an appealing option, even in large companies. Packages got a huge boost as companies began to realize the full impact of the Year 2000 (Y2K) problem—and came to see packages as a solution. (Other reasons for ERP adoption are discussed later.) Suddenly, nearly everyone got on the ERP bandwagon.

By 1998 approximately 40% of companies with annual revenues of more than $1 billion had implemented ERP systems (Caldwell & Stein, 1998). ERP vendors began aggressively targeting smaller firms because they represent a much larger market. In aggregate, the ERP marketplace is huge. SAP Inc., the largest ERP system vendor, had 1997 revenues of $3.3 billion (Davenport, 1998). A research firm recently predicted that the ERP market would reach $66.6 billion by 2003 (AMR Research, 1999).[3] The ERP systems and services market has cooled somewhat at present because many companies have already implemented ERP in response to Y2K concerns. Nevertheless, interest in related enterprise systems such as sales force automation, supply chain integration, and product configuration remains strong.

Enterprise systems are clearly a phenomenon in the IT marketplace. Their potential significance for computer-using organizations cannot be overstated. They represent a nearly complete rearchitecting of an organization's portfolio of transactions-processing applications systems to achieve integration of business processes, systems, and information—along with corresponding changes in the supporting computing platform (hardware, software, databases, telecommunications). On a societal scale, the enterprise system phenomenon seems to be about a complete renewal of enterprise IT infrastructure.[4] The potential consequences—economic, technical, and social—of this development are indeed significant. Two small examples will illustrate this point. One ERP implementation enabled a 70% reduction in accounting personnel by eliminating duplicate data entry and many consolidation tasks (Larsen & Myers, 1997). And analysts have speculated that widespread adoption of the same ERP package by the firms in a single industry (an observed phenomenon for semiconductor manufacturers) might lead to the elimination of process innovation–based competitive advantage (Davenport, 1998).

Despite the potential benefits of widespread IT renewal, the process to date has been far from smooth. Some organizations have utterly failed in their attempts to install ERP systems (Bulkeley, 1996). Others have achieved some benefits despite decidedly rocky beginnings (Cole-Gomolski, 1998; Stedman, 1998a, 1998b, and 1998c; Stedman, 1999b). Many have failed to achieve the hoped-for financial returns on their ERP investment (KPMG, 1998; Stedman, 1999a).

Of course, companies have had similar difficulties with each new wave of information technology since the first mainframe systems (McKenney, Copeland, & Mason, 1995). It takes years at best to realize some envisioned IT-enabled changes in organizational processes and performance, and there are many ways to fail along the way.[5] So one wants to know how, if at all, the enterprise system *experience* is similar to, or different from, experiences with any other type of information technology, such as decision support groupware, and workflow. In the IS field, theory and empirical findings related to this question are highly dispersed. Similar concepts are discussed under different names, such as implementation and adoption. Conceptually related ideas have generated literatures with little overlap; for example, the research literature on IT impacts remains quite distinct from the literatures on system development methodologies and on the payoffs from IT investments. Because the enterprise system experience cuts across all of these "islands of ideation," it is time to take an integrated view. This chapter attempts an integration of the diverse bodies of knowledge bearing on the enterprise system phenomenon.

ENTERPRISE SYSTEMS

In this section, we identify the key characteristics of enterprise systems, list reasons companies do and do not adopt them, and summarize arguments about why enterprise systems are an important topic for research. Enterprise systems are commercial software packages that enable the integration of transactions-oriented data and business processes throughout an organization (and perhaps eventually throughout the entire interorganizational supply chain). In our definition, enterprise systems include ERP software and such related packages as advanced planning and scheduling, sales force automation, customer relationship management, and product configuration. Organizations that adopt enterprise systems have a wide range of options for implementation and ongoing operations, from do it yourself, through selective external assistance, to total outsourcing.

CHARACTERISTICS OF ENTERPRISE SYSTEMS

Enterprise systems have several characteristics, each with important implications for the organizations that adopt them.

- *Integration.* Enterprise systems promise "seamless integration of all the information flowing through a company—financial and accounting information, human resource information, supply chain information, and customer information" (Davenport, 1998, p. 121). However, it is extremely important to note that achieving this integration depends on "configuring" (setting up) the system in particular ways. Configuration in this context[6] means choosing which package modules to install and setting software parameters to represent, for example, the company's products, customers, accounts and the particular arrangement of business processes, such as centralized or decentralized warehousing and purchasing. An additional important part of the configuration task is capturing configuration decisions and their rationale. The quality of such documentation is essential to the organization's ability to make future changes efficiently and effectively.

    - It is possible, especially in large, complex organizations, to configure enterprise systems so that the benefits of integration are not achieved. For example, companies may purchase and install only the "financials" modules of an enterprise system, thus depriving themselves of the potential advantages of integrating accounting data with sales, manufacturing, and distribution data. Furthermore, an organization may allow each of its business units to adopt a different enterprise system or to configure the same enterprise system however they see fit, with the result that it is not possible to obtain integration benefits from common purchasing or better decision making.[7]

- *Packages.* Enterprise systems are commercial packages; that is, they are purchased or leased from software vendors rather than being developed in-house from scratch. This has two important implications for the organizations that adopt them.

- First, the IS life cycle is different.[8] Rather than designing a system to meet the organization's idiosyncratic ways of working, the adopters of an enterprise system often adjust the organization's ways of working to fit the package (because modifying packages has numerous negative consequences). Consequently, package adopters sometimes forgo or curtail the analysis of current information requirements and business processes that is a hallmark of the traditional IS life cycle. Furthermore, the process of configuring an enterprise system for an organization differs substantially from software programming. Programming involves creating new software functionality. Configuration involves adapting the generic functionality of a package to the needs of a particular organization (usually by setting parameters in tables). Configuration is often performed by teams of end-users with IS specialists working primarily on infrastructural issues.[9] In other words, enterprise package implementation obsoletes some of the IT skills commonly found in IT adopting organizations and requires the acquisition of new skills. In particular, enterprise systems put a premium on skills related to (1) mapping organizational requirements to the processes and terminology employed by the vendor and (2) making informed choices about the parameter setting.[10]

- Second, organizations that purchase an enterprise system enter into long-term relationships with software vendors. It is true that some organizations purchase an enterprise system with the idea that they will modify the packages to suit idiosyncratic needs. But doing so reduces their ability to benefit from vendors' continued development of the packages, and it may create dependency on outside contractors who specialize in enterprise software customizations. (Vendors generally do not undertake to support or maintain customers' modifications of their software.) Consequently, many organizations depend on the vendor for continued enhancement of the package (for example, redeveloping the software for future computing architectures). As a result, purchasers of an enterprise system may need to become active in user organizations, a mechanism by which software buyers collectively try to influence the vendor's plans for package maintenance and enhancement. Because of their dependence on vendors, organizations are vulnerable in the event that their chosen vendor goes out of business or lacks the resources for continued technical development. Furthermore, they are committing themselves to upgrading the software periodically if they hope to avoid major conversion headaches.[11]

- *Best Practices.* Because they are designed to fit the needs of many organizations, enterprise systems are built to support generic business processes that may differ quite substantially from the way any particular organization does business. By talking to many businesses and looking to academic theory (or to APICS)[12] about the best way to do accounting or manage a production floor, the vendors of enterprise systems have crafted what they claim to be "best practices."[13] Best practices represent a powerful reason to adopt enterprise systems without modifying them because few organizations claim to have redesigned all their business processes for cross-functional efficiency and effectiveness—which was the stated purpose of business process reengineering (Hammer, 1990). But to realize the advantages of the best practices embedded in enterprise systems, most adopting organizations must commit themselves to some degree of business process reengineering (Connolly, 1999).[14]

- There is great debate about the relative advantage of doing business process reengineering[15] before, during, or after enterprise system implementation. But there is general consensus that business process change adds considerably to the expense and risk of the implementation of enterprise systems. The principal reason is the difficulty of managing large-scale human and organizational change. For example, four business functions are involved in the early phases of aircraft design and manufacture: contract management, project accounting, project management, and estimating. In traditionally organized aerospace firms, these four functions may be performed by different organizational units with consequent recycling and layers of approval. Baan's software for aerospace and defense industries *requires* (by means of screen design and software processing logic) that all four functions be performed by an "integrated product team" comprising all four sets of skills. Enterprise systems have many such embedded business practices, the details of which may vary from vendor to vendor. Some organizations rebel against the inflexibility of these imposed business practices; even when organizational leadership accepts the need for change, the process of implementing enterprise systems can involve considerable change in organizational structure, job design, work sequencing, training, and so on.

- *Some Assembly Required.* At one level, the claim of enterprise systems to be "integrated" is wildly overstated. What is integrated is the *software,* not the computing *platform* on which it runs. Empirically, enterprise system–adopting companies have had great difficulty integrating their enterprise software with a package of hardware, operating systems, database management systems software, and telecommunications suited to their particular organizational size, structure, and geographic distribution.[16] And this is only one of the integration challenges associated with enterprise systems. Marketing claims aside, in today's state of the art, no single enterprise system meets all the information-processing needs of the majority of organizations.

- In many cases, enterprise system–adopting organizations will need to interface the package to the company's own proprietary "legacy" systems, for which the enterprise system does not provide an adequate replacement. The organizations may also need to acquire and interface the package to any number of "bolt-on" applications from third-party vendors for various tasks.[17] Sometimes the adopting organization may turn to a third party that has integrated the enterprise package around the special needs of a particular industry segment.[18] Finally, some organizations adopt a "best-of-breed" strategy in which they try to integrate several enterprise packages from different vendors, each designed to be the best fit in its class with the needs of the adopting organizations. Examples of companies that have adopted the best-of-breed approach are American Standard Companies (Bashein et al., 1997) and Starbucks (Aragon, 1997).

- *Evolving.* Finally, like all of IT, enterprise systems are rapidly changing. First, they are changing *architecturally.* In the 1980s enterprise systems were designed for the mainframe system architecture. Today, they are designed for client-server architectures. Some vendors have just released Web-enabled versions of the software; most vendors have object-oriented versions under development. Baan is pursuing a strategy of "componentization," consisting of an open backbone to which the offerings of other vendors can be connected. The *functionality* of enterprise systems is also evolving. Today, enterprise software vendors are releasing extensions to their core products[19] designed to handle "front office" (i.e., sales management), "supply chain" (i.e., advanced planning and scheduling), data warehousing, specialized vertical industry solutions, and other functions. Enhancements such as customer relationship management and electronic commerce are in the works. *Service arrangements* are also changing. Some services firms offer packaged implementation services; others (often called application service providers) are offering ongoing enterprise software functionality on an outsourced basis. Enterprise systems *terminology* will undoubtedly change, too; only time will tell whether the extensions continue to be identified as something different from enterprise systems or are eventually folded into the enterprise system rubric.

- However things are called, many people now regard enterprise systems (or enterprise integration achieved in other ways) as *the* organizational infrastructure that will support future value-generating applications, such as linking the organization's operations with those of suppliers and customers, leading to substantial reductions in duplicated activities *across* firms.

REASONS FOR ADOPTING ENTERPRISE SYSTEMS

Given the richness of enterprise systems in terms of functionality and potential benefits to adopting organizations, it should not be surprising that companies are adopting these systems for many different reasons[20] (Ross, 1999). Some companies have largely technical reasons for investing in enterprise systems. Examples are the desire to reduce mainframe system operating costs, the need to solve the Y2K and similar problems, the need for increased systems capacity to handle growth, or the need to solve the maintenance headaches associated with aging legacy systems. Other companies give largely business reasons for adopting enterprise systems. For example, the company may need but not have, due to limitations in its legacy systems, the ability to present "one face to the customer" or to know whether it has finished goods inventory or planned production capacity "available to promise" to the customer on a regional or global basis. Many companies have both technical and business reasons for adopting enterprise software.

Both small and large companies can benefit both technically and strategically from investments in enterprise systems. Generally, the needs and opportunities of small companies are a subset of those facing large companies. For example, in addition to problems stemming from unintegrated legacy applications, large companies (particularly those that have grown through acquisition or have had a highly decentralized IT management regime) may also have the headaches of maintaining many different systems of the same application type. In large companies, it is not unheard of to find, say, 42 different general ledger packages or 22 separate purchasing applications in use at the time of adopting an enterprise system. Boeing, for example, had 14 bill-of-material systems and 30 shop-floor control systems before the company adopted ERP (Schneider, 1999). (See Table 10.1 for a summary of reasons that companies give for adopting enterprise systems.)

TABLE 10.1   Reasons for Adopting Enterprise Systems

	Small Companies/ Simple Structures	Large Companies/ Complex Structures
Technical reasons	• Solve Y2K and similar problems • Integrate applications cross-functionally • Replace hard-to-maintain interfaces • Reduce software maintenance burden through outsourcing • Eliminate redundant data entry and concomitant errors and difficulty analyzing data • Improve IT architecture • Ease technology capacity constraints • Decrease computer operating costs	Most small/simple company reasons plus • Consolidate multiple different systems of the same type (e.g., general ledger packages)
Business reasons	• Accommodate business growth • Acquire multilanguage and multicurrency IT support • Improve informal and/or inefficient business processes • Clean up data and records through standardization • Reduce business operating and administrative expenses • Reduce inventory carrying costs and stockouts • Eliminate delays and errors in filling customers' orders for merged businesses	Most small/simple company reasons plus • Provide integrated IT support • Standardize different numbering, naming, and coding schemes • Standardize procedures across different locations • Present a single face to the customer • Acquire worldwide "available to promise" capability • Streamline financial consolidations • Improve companywide decision support

It is important to take into account these wide variations in motivation to adopt enterprise systems when attempting to assess or explain their impacts and downstream consequences. Some goals are much more ambitious than others; if companies are like people, those with more ambitious goals are likely to achieve more than companies with less ambitious goals, but they are less likely to realize their full aspirations, and they may encounter many more difficulties along the way. Furthermore, enterprise systems may be better suited to realizing some goals than others. For example, the largest companies may face technical capacity constraints that prevent full data integration. Clearly, what companies think they are about when they adopt enterprise systems must figure somehow in the ways they approach the enterprise system experience and in the outcomes they achieve.

REASONS FOR NOT ADOPTING ENTERPRISE SYSTEMS

Of course, not all organizations adopt enterprise systems, even when they have some or all of the listed motivations for adopting. Some who do adopt enterprise systems choose to use only certain modules, relying on legacy systems or new custom development for their remaining needs. And some who do adopt discontinue implementing or using these systems for a variety of reasons.[21]

One reason for nonadoption, partial adoption, or discontinuance is *lack of "feature-function fit"* between the company's needs and the packages available in the marketplace. "There are very few companies that don't have specialized processes dictated by their industry," according to one consultant (Slater, 1999). Many ERP system manufacturing modules were developed for discrete part manufacturing; these systems do not support some processes in process industries (e.g., food, paper), project industries (e.g., aerospace), or industries manufacturing goods with dimensionality, such as clothing and footwear. When organizational size and scale of operations are taken into account, there simply may be no commercially available package suitable for a particular organization.

More commonly, the organization may choose to adopt only certain parts of an enterprise system or may modify the system to improve feature-function fit. Consider examples of the implementation of SAP R/3 from Visio (a software company) (Koch, 1997). The first example concerns "deferred channel revenue." The article implies that Visio met this need with legacy code.

> Many software companies "dump" extra product with distributors at the close of a quarter so that they can pump up weak sales revenue totals. The downside of the strategy is that some of the extra software may flood back to the company in unsold returns. . . . To break the cycle, Visio tracks sales through to the retail outlets and compares the retail sales with the number of units shipped to distributors each month. If the retail stores sell less than Visio anticipated, Visio defers some of the revenues from the sales . . . ; if sales are up, it adds back some deferred revenues from previous months. . . . Unfortunately for Myrick and the Visio team, it's a complex and fairly unique way of handling revenues—two attributes that really annoy R/3. (Koch, 1997)

The second situation in which SAP R/3 did not meet Visio's needs concerns Visio's method of handling inventory.

> Visio outsources its manufacturing. . . . But R/3 doesn't let companies track something they don't own outright, and it doesn't recognize inventory that has no assigned value, like trial software, marketing handouts and other freebies. The consultants offer Visio two massively unpopular choices: Visio could assume ownership of the inventory throughout the manufacturing cycle, or it could send two invoices . . . [to customers]. . . . [The consultant] agrees to absorb the cost of fixing the inventory ownership process, ultimately conceding that sending two invoices to customers each month was unacceptable. (Koch, 1997)

The consultants apparently found a way to change the process with a bolt-on that did not require expensive and risky modification of the SAP code itself.

In addition to the lack of feature-function fit, a second major set of reasons for nonadoption, partial adoption, or discontinuance of enterprise systems concerns company growth, strategic flexibility, and decentralized decision-making style. Dell Computer Corp., for instance, planned full implementation of SAP R/3 but stopped after the HR module. The CIO claimed that the software would not be able to keep pace with Dell's extraordinary growth rate (Slater, 1999). Visio cited strategic flexibility as a reason for performing sales commission analysis outside of its enterprise system:

> "I wanted to retain the flexibility to change the commission structure when I needed to because it's such a critical process. It was my understanding that it might take awhile to do that within SAP and that once it was done, it wouldn't be so easy to change."

> Because the commission structure is so closely linked to the organizational structure of the sales groups, Buckley and Myrick decided to keep commissions analysis out of R/3. (Koch, 1997)

Companies that continually change their organizational structures and business models and particularly those that are not run "in a very top-down manner" may find enterprise systems unsuitable as a corporate solution (Bancroft, Seip, & Sprengel, 1997).[22] For example, at Kraft Foods Inc., a highly decentralized company that is gradually moving toward a "one-company" philosophy, enterprise systems were viewed as a culturally inappropriate strategy for systems integration (Bashein & Markus, 2000).

A third factor in the nonadoption of enterprise systems is the availability of alternatives for increasing the level of systems integration. Data warehousing, a bundle of technologies that integrates data from multiple source systems for query and analysis, provides what some describe as the "poor man's ERP." The usefulness of data warehousing as an integration strategy is limited by the quality of the source systems. Nevertheless, it can provide enormous relief for some organizations suffering from some of the technical problems shown in Table 10.1. Data warehousing was the integration strategy favored by Kraft Foods Inc. (Bashein & Markus, 2000).

Another alternative to enterprise systems involves rearchitecting in-house systems around a layer of middleware that isolates application systems from stores of "master data." When Dell abandoned SAP R/3 as its integration strategy, the company "designed a flexible middleware architecture to allow the company to add or subtract applications quickly and selected software from a variety of vendors . . . to handle finance and manufacturing functions" (Slater, 1999). Consultants say that rearchitecting systems with middleware is a viable alternative to enterprise systems when a company is basically satisfied with its software functionality and wants only to improve software integration and upgrade the user interface. This strategy is widely adopted in the financial services industries, where enterprise systems have made relatively few inroads (other than for administrative systems).

Discussions of reasons for not adopting enterprise systems usually conflate the issues just mentioned above with three other issues—cost, competitive advantage, and resistance to change. For example, Allied Waste recently announced plans to "pull the plug" on a $130 million computer system (Bailey, 1999). The reason given was that SAP was "too expensive and too complicated to operate." Yet it also seems clear that the software no longer fits the management style and structure of the company, as it presumably did at the time the decision to adopt SAP was made. Apparently, Allied Waste grew rapidly in the 1970s and 1980s when the firm was acquiring hundreds of trash haulers. When industry profits suffered, the company responded by cost cutting through centralized operations, a style of management well supported by SAP. Today, the company is moving toward much greater management decentralization. In this case, cost reasons, it seems, are tightly bound up with issues of management culture.

Some analysts have cited competitive advantage as a major reason for not implementing enterprise software (Davenport, 1998). Here, too, it is difficult to disentangle competitive advantage from explanations based in fit. If a company claims it will lose competitive advantage from adopting an enterprise system, it is also saying that it does things differently than the enterprise system does. The question here is whether lack of fit reflects an organization's "value-adding best practice" (albeit different from best practices in the software) or a costly inefficiency that the organization is culturally unwilling to give up. Not surprising, vendors are more likely to cite "resistance to change" (or "lack of top management commitment") than they are to cite "competitive advantage" or "lack of feature-function fit" as a major reason for nonadoption of enterprise systems. In practice, careful analysis is necessary to determine whether or not an enterprise system is a good solution in a particular situation—and what the scope of the implementation project should be.

RECAP—IMPORTANCE OF ENTERPRISE SYSTEMS

Enterprise systems are an important topic for IS research for several reasons.

1. *Financial Costs and Risks.* Installing an enterprise system is an expensive and risky venture. Large companies have been spending on the order of hundreds of millions of dollars to make the technical and business changes associated with enterprise systems. There have been several visible enterprise systems failures, and nonacademic studies have questioned the financial and business payoffs from enterprise system projects. Therefore, enterprise systems raise questions that have long been studied in the IS field under the following labels: the payoffs from investment in information technology,[23] IS project success and failure,[24] and IS implementation process and change management[25] (training,[26] user involvement, communication, etc.).

2. *Technical Issues.* Enterprise systems are technically challenging. Among the more important technical areas of research around enterprise systems are the "development" life cycle for enterprise system packages; software selection approaches; enterprise modeling and software configuration tools and techniques; "reference models" for particular industry segments, systems integration strategies, and systems and software architectures; and data quality, reporting, and decision support for enterprise systems.

3. *Managerial Issues.* Enterprise system projects are managerially challenging since they may involve parties from many different organizations and cut across the political structures of the organization. Furthermore, enterprise systems have important implications for how companies should organize and manage their information systems functions. Finally, enterprise systems raise interesting challenges in terms of personnel and skill acquisition and retention. Therefore, the following areas of research are invoked by enterprise systems: IT project management;[27] IT project sponsorship and user involvement; IS-business relationships, vendor management, structuring the IS function and IT management more generally, and IS personnel management.[28]

4. *IT Adoption, Use, and Impacts.* Enterprise systems have been widely adopted across organizations, and the adoption of these technologies may spread further. However, it is not yet known how widely these technologies have been *assimilated* (Fichman & Kemerer, 1997)[29] in organizations, for example, how extensively they are used within the organization, how faithfully they are used, and how effectively they are used. Furthermore, these systems have large potential impacts[30] at all levels of analysis: individual and societal (employment, occupational structure, skills required, and quality of work), work system (cooperation, business process efficiency), organizational (competitive advantage, business results), and interorganizational (impact on supply chain, industry structure). For example, at the individual level, enterprise systems may entail a substantial increase in the visibility of an individual's performance, leading to changes in the accountability and control regimes in the organization. In addition to the general topics of IT adoption, use, and impacts, enterprise systems are linked to research on business process reengineering, interorganizational information systems, and the strategic use of information technology.

5. *Integration.* Finally, enterprise systems suggest some unique questions not easily subsumable within existing bodies of information systems research. First, to what extent are enterprise systems bound up in a complete restructuring of organizations and industries around the capabilities of information technologies? Second, to what extent are we observing a structural change in the provision of IT services, from predominantly in-house to predominantly outsourced? What is the emerging role of the so-called system integrators (such as Andersen Consulting and IBM)? How should organizations manage a long-term IT development trajectory involving heavy dependence on external products and service companies? Third, what are the pros and cons of the enterprise systems approach vis-à-vis other strategies for achieving integration around information technology, such as rearchitecting systems around middleware and the object development paradigm or the looser integration strategy implied by data warehousing?

In short, the enterprise system phenomenon has strong conceptual links with just about every major area of information systems research. In addition, the phenomenon suggests the potential value of entirely new research directions.

The enterprise system phenomenon is so all-encompassing for organizations and their key business partners that it virtually demands a framework by which to understand it as a whole. As suggested, many bodies of literature and, hence, many theories are relevant to understanding important *pieces* of the enterprise system phenomenon, but what is lacking is an overarching framework within which many specific questions can be asked and their answers integrated. Our purpose in the remainder of this chapter is to propose such a framework. The framework is designed around the perspective of an enterprise system–adopting organization.[31] That is, the framework is designed to shed light on the questions facing the executive leadership of an organization considering whether, why, and how to participate in the enterprise system experience and what to do at various points in the process.

FRAMING THE ANALYSIS OF ENTERPRISE SYSTEM SUCCESS

This section sets up the description of our framework. We first address the questions the framework is designed to answer: What is success with enterprise systems? Why does success not always occur? What can be done to improve the chances of success? In other words, success is the key outcome of interest in our framework. In academic terms, it is our dependent variable.[32] More specifically, we define the success outcome as a multidimensional concept, a dynamic concept, and a relative one (to the concept of "optimal success," representing the best an organization can hope to achieve with enterprise systems). Next, we briefly review several broad categories of theoretical perspectives that purport to explain how and why enterprise systems success occurs. Of three categories of theories, we choose the "emergent process" type and, in particular, a specific theory of the business value of information technology as the basis for our framework. In the following section, we develop the framework more fully.

THE IMPORTANT OUTCOME:
SUCCESS WITH ENTERPRISE SYSTEMS

> KPMG Management Consulting's recent report *Profit-Focused Software Package Implementation* showed some worrying results. Eighty-nine per cent of respondent companies claimed that their projects were successful, but only a quarter had actually obtained and quantified all the planned benefits. (KPMG, 1998)

To us, this quotation illustrates a fundamental gap in both practical and academic thinking about information systems—lack of consensus and clarity about the meaning of "success" where information systems are concerned. People rarely define terms such as success and failure; when they do, they invite endless complaints. For instance, one article in the trade press criticized a nonacademic study of enterprise system success for defining a project as a failure if project goals changed within a year (Ferranti, 1998).[33] Furthermore, people legitimately use a number of different definitions of success. As the KPMG quotation suggests, one can define success in terms of the implementation *project* (did the company succeed in getting the system up and running within some reasonable budget and schedule?) or in terms of *business results* (did the company succeed in realizing its business goals for the project?). The same ambiguity is clear in academic writing on the topics of information systems success and/or effectiveness. For example, one of the few academic studies of an enterprise system experience to date shows that success can look very different when examined at different points in time, on different dimensions, or from different points of view (Larsen & Myers, 1997).[34]

Our purpose is not to argue that one definition of success is inherently superior to another. Instead, we are claiming, first, that the key questions about enterprise systems *from the perspective of an adopting organization's executive leadership* are questions about success, for example: Will our investment pay off? Did our investment pay off? How should we go about implementing enterprise systems to achieve our goals? What can we do to increase the chances for success and avoid the risk of failure? Second, we are claiming that *no one measure* of enterprise system success is sufficient for all the concerns an organization's executives might have about the enterprise system experience. Instead, enterprise systems–adopting organizations require a "balanced scorecard" of success metrics addressing different dimensions (financial, technical, human) at different points in time. Based on our observations of enterprise systems projects, we argue that a minimum set of success metrics includes the following:

• *Project Metrics.* Performance of the enterprise system *project team* against planned schedule, budget, and functional scope. These are the classic performance measures applied to project managers.

• *Early Operational Metrics.* How *business operations* perform in the period after the system becomes operational until "normal operation" is achieved. Specifically, these metrics include some normally used to track the business as well as some unique to enterprise systems. Examples include labor costs, time required to fill an order, customer calls unanswered, partial orders filled, orders shipped with errors, inventory levels, and so on. Although the "shakedown phase" of an information systems project is transitional by definition, it is critically important for the implementing organization for several reasons, some of which have been well documented by others (Tyre & Orlikowski, 1994). When the business performs very poorly during the shakedown phase, the organization may lose business, sometimes permanently, when the organization has yet to experience any major benefits to offset the large up-front investment. Exceedingly poor performance can lead to internal or external pressures to disinstall the system and in extreme cases can tip the organization into bankruptcy, as happened to Fox-Meyer Drug (Bulkeley, 1996). Consequently, organizations should include early operational performance in their definition of enterprise system success and should aggressively manage to minimize early operational problems and to resolve them quickly.

• *Longer-Term Business Results.* How the *organization* performs at various times after normal business operation has been achieved. Examples of relevant metrics include return on investment, achievement of qualitative goals such as "one face to the customer," better management decision making attributable to higher-quality data, continuous improvement of business metrics after operations return to normal, maintenance of internal enterprise system competence (among both IT specialists and end users), ease of upgrading to later versions of the enterprise system software, and so on.[35]

The foregoing discussion makes it clear that the success (or failure) of enterprise systems is not a monolithic concept. Rather, it is multidimensional and relative. It is relative, first, to the time at which it is assessed. For example, in our conversations with executives and integrators, we identified some companies with disastrous project and shakedown metrics but high levels of subsequent business benefits from enterprise systems. Conversely, we found companies with acceptable project and shakedown metrics that could not identify business benefits from installing the system. Similarly, an enterprise system that gives competitive advantage today may not do so tomorrow when competitors catch up and having such a system becomes a cost of doing business (McKenney et al., 1995).

Second, success is often judged relative to the organization's unique goals for the system. Two organizations with identical improvements in inventory carrying costs can be judged successful in different ways if the one's goals were to replace its legacy systems (more successful than expected) and the other's were to achieve an increase in market share (less successful than expected). At the same time, the company's goals, taken alone, make a poor standard against which to judge success. First, the company's goals may be insufficiently ambitious if they are compared to the inherent capabilities of enterprise systems and how well the organization needs to perform given its competitive position. For example, a company that is losing market share because it cannot promise delivery on a global basis would be "leaving money on the table" if it adopted an enterprise system solely to solve the Y2K problem and implemented it so that available-to-promise capability was not possible.[36] For another example, highly decentralized businesses may achieve less than is theoretically possible with enterprise systems if they configure the software so that each product business unit presents its own separate face to the customer. Conversely, the success of a company that achieved more with an enterprise system than it expected at the outset should be judged against a higher standard of performance than its unambitious goals. It might better be judged against the average business benefits realized by similar firms in its industry.

To accommodate the multidimensionality and relativity of enterprise system success from the adopting organization's perspective, we define a standard of *optimal success,* which refers to the best outcomes the organization *could* achieve with enterprise systems, given its business situation, measured against a portfolio of project, early operational, and longer-term business results metrics. Optimal success can be *far more or less* than the organization's goals for an enterprise system. Furthermore, optimal success can be *dynamic;* what is possible for an organization to achieve may *change over time* as business conditions change. What we want the framework to help us predict or explain is an organization's *actual achievement* of an *enterprise system's success* (a scorecard of measures, assessed relative to optimal success—the best possible outcome). Looking ahead to the framework itself, we hope to show how and why an organization's decisions or actions at one point in time (e.g., during the "project") can result in optimal (or less than optimal) outcomes subsequently (e.g., during "shakedown").

We realize that organizations do not usually set out to achieve optimal success with information technologies; good enough is usually good enough. We also realize that optimal success is a theoretical abstraction that may be neither achievable in practice nor measurable in empirical research. Nevertheless, we believe the concept is theoretically useful because it "factors in" unintended positive and negative consequences of enterprise system adoption and organizational realities that are not fully reflected in the organization's enterprise system goals.

THEORETICAL PERSPECTIVES ON ENTERPRISE SYSTEM SUCCESS

Having defined the outcome of interest, we need a theory to explain it. An accepted classification scheme (Markus & Robey, 1988, derived from Kling, 1980, and Pfeffer, 1982) parses academic theories of IT-related outcomes into rational actor, external control, and emergent process theories. Rational actor theories emphasize the great, but bounded, ability of organizations and decision makers to realize their goals. An example of such a theory is the technology acceptance model (Davis, Bagozzi, & Warshaw, 1989),[37] which includes the factors that enter into an individual's choice of technology for particular tasks when faced with alternatives. On the plus side, rational actor theories highlight peoples' motivations and the actions they take to achieve their goals. Therefore, these theories tend to be very appealing to practitioners. A drawback of rational actor theories is that they downplay influential forces beyond the decision maker's control; furthermore, these theories accept managers' goals as givens without questioning their suitability relative to external constraints.

The second type of theory—external control theory—emphasizes the inexorable environmental forces, such as the trajectory of technological development or competitive industry forces. Academics employ external control theories when they claim that information technology alters industry structure or changes decision-making processes in an organization. A strength of external control theories is their explicit acknowledgment that organizations and people have less than perfect ability to make their goals a reality; on the downside, they minimize the ability of exceptional people and companies to change our world.

The third type of theory—emergent process—emphasizes the often unpredictable interactions between people in organizations and the environment. Emergent process theories assume that people try to achieve goals but acknowledge that the outcomes are often different from those intended—sometimes better and sometimes worse. External forces sometimes make a mockery of peoples' goals and actions, but sometimes the forces line up to favor the most unlikely goals. A prominent example of an emergent process theory in the IS field is structuration theory (De-Sanctis & Poole, 1994; Orlikowski & Robey, 1991). A strength of emergent process theories is that they account for mutual influences between the organization and its environment. Weaknesses include their greater explanatory than predictive power and the prominent role they assign to chance: Decision makers prefer prescriptive models that favor skill more than luck and that promise successful outcomes to those who follow the rules.

For a theory to be useful to practitioners, it must address their goals and "motivated behavior" (actions they can and do take with the intent to achieve their goals).[38] For a theory to fit the facts (not all companies are successful with enterprise systems, and not all the blame can be laid to their goals or actions), it must also address relevant factors that lie outside peoples' direct control. (For example, did the vendor actually deliver on the promise to release required functionality on a specified date? Is the software sufficiently bug free to support reliable operations?) Because emergent process theories combine goals and actions with external forces and chance, we chose this theoretical structure for modeling the enterprise system experience.

More specifically, we build our framework on a particular emergent process theory designed by Soh and Markus (1995) to explain how information technology creates (or fails to create) business value.[39] This theory contributes three key points to an understanding of the success of enterprise systems. First, it argues that the necessary conditions for a successful outcome (in their model, high-quality information technology "assets") are not always sufficient for success. Occasionally, an IT investment on track for success is derailed by an external event (e.g., competitors' responses) or changing external conditions (e.g., recession). Chance and randomness can play an important role in the outcomes achieved.

Second, the Soh and Markus (1995) framework describes the "IT investment to business value" process as a series of three linked models that correspond to the phases of a typical IT investment, roughly speaking, system development, implementation, and ongoing operation. (See Figure 10.1.) The outcomes of one phase became starting conditions for the next. Thus, decisions and actions in a phase may increase or decrease the potential for success ("optimal success") subsequently. Furthermore, because each phase generally involves different groups of people, the framework directs attention to communication difficulties that accompany "the handoffs" from one phase to the next.

Third, the Soh and Markus (1995) framework explains the outcomes of each phase as resulting from interactions between external conditions and the activities that characterize the phase. This means that both uncontrollable events and choiceful human actions can influence outcomes. At the same time, events and actions may be unsynchronized, and delayed effects may result in unresolved problems (or even opportunities) requiring action down the road. Thus, problems can accumulate, cascading toward a wildly unsuccessful outcome.

Two important changes are needed to adopt the Soh and Markus (1995) framework to the enterprise systems experience. First, the outcome variables need to be changed from business value (and other intermediate outcomes) to success as defined earlier. Second, the framework requires the addition of an initial phase that includes the important organizational decisions and actions before the project officially starts. In many organizations, executives, technical specialists, and consultants can spend considerable time (and money) making decisions about whether,

FIGURE 10.1   Soh and
Markus (1995) Model

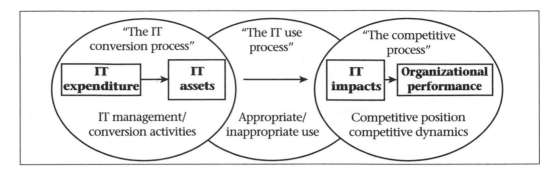

FIGURE 10.2
Enterprise System
Experience Cycle

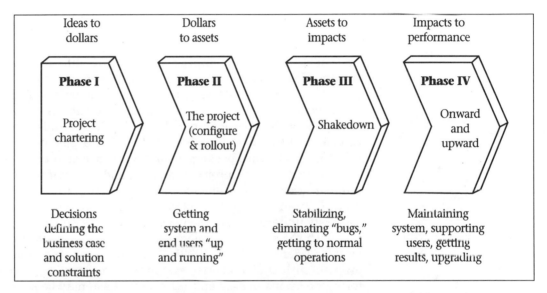

why, and how to undertake enterprise systems. For instance, any of the following
may occur before a project manager is named and a budget is approved: documenting
current business processes, analyzing the potential for improvement, comparing
processes with the "reference models" or "best practices" embedded in enterprise systems software, selecting software, deciding which software modules to implement in
what sequence, and deciding how to roll out the new functionality to various business units. Therefore, we identify a new first phase, which we call *chartering*. The remaining three phases in the enterprise system experience cycle (the *project phase,*
the *shakedown phase,* and the *onward and upward phase*) correspond loosely to the
three phases in the Soh and Markus model (see Figure 10.2).

In the next section, we describe our framework in greater depth.

THE DYNAMICS OF ENTERPRISE SYSTEM SUCCESS

An organization's experience with an enterprise system can be described as moving
through several phases, characterized by key players, typical activities, characteristic
problems, appropriate performance metrics, and a range of possible outcomes. Each
enterprise system experience is unique, and experiences may differ considerably,

depending, for example, on whether the adoption of the enterprise system is initiated by IS specialists or by businesspeople, involves external consultants or is done largely in-house, follows a process of strategic IT business planning or business process reengineering or does not follow such a process, and so forth.

Table 10.2 summarizes the four "ideal" phases of the enterprise system experience cycle,[40] and the phases are briefly described in the following section. It is important to note that organizations recycle through the phases when they undertake major upgrades and/or replacements of their enterprise systems.

THE PHASES DESCRIBED

The Chartering Phase

The chartering phase comprises decisions leading up to the funding of an enterprise system. Key players in this phase include vendors, consultants, company executives, and IT specialists, although the precise constellation of players may vary. (Sometimes vendors sell directly to company executives, with minimal IT involvement; other times the decisions are driven by IT specialists, with minimal executive involvement.) Key activities include building a business case for enterprise systems, selecting a software package (though this decision may be deferred until the project phase), identifying a project manager, and approving a budget and schedule. A large number of errors or problems can arise during this phase. The business case for investing in an enterprise system can be incomplete or faulty; the organization may seriously underestimate the need for business and organizational change in conjunction with the software implementation; objectives and metrics for the initiative may be left undefined (Ross, 1999). The outcome of this phase may be a decision not to proceed with the enterprise system or a decision to proceed. If the latter, the chartering decisions passed on to the next phase may be sound or unsound. An example of an unsound charter is a build-to-order company purchasing an ERP package designed for a make-to-stock business (Slater, 1999). Another example is the decision not to allocate sufficient resources for change management and training (Ross, 1999). A third is the decision of a decentralized company to require more standardization of business processes than is necessary to achieve business benefits (Davenport, 1998). Still another is the choice of a highly inexperienced project manager.

The Project Phase

The project phase comprises activities intended to get the system up and running in one or more organizational units. Key players include the project manager, project team members (often nontechnical members of various business units and functional areas), internal IT specialists, vendors, and consultants. Again, the constellation will vary, depending on the decision to do the project in-house, with outside assistance, or on an outsourced basis. Key activities include software configuration, system integration, testing, data conversion, training, and rollout. Again, a large number of errors and problems can occur. Project teams may be staffed with inadequate representation; teams may lack requisite knowledge and skills; teams may embark on extensive, unnecessary modifications; data cleanup, testing, or training may be inadequate. In addition, of course, the business conditions characterizing the chartering phase may have changed: The company may have fallen into financial

TABLE 10.2   The Enterprise System Experience Cycle by Phase

Phase Name, Description, and Key Actors	Typical Activities	Common Errors or Problems	Typical Performance Metrics	Possible Outcomes
Chartering ("ideas to dollars") • Decisions leading up to project approval and funding • Executives, selected IT specialists, enterprise systems vendor, and/or consultants (may be IT driven with low executive involvement or executive driven with low in-house IT involvement)	• Idea of adopting enterprise systems surfaced • Business case for investment developed (may be highly informal) • Definition of key performance indicators and process of measurement • Current state analysis (may be deferred or not done) • Selection of software, hardware platform, networking, database, implementation partner, project manager (may be partially or totally deferred to project phase) • Initial plans for how system will be rolled out, supported, and maintained, upgraded, etc. (may be deferred) • Communication to organization • Organizational changes and/or incentives related to enterprise system and/or organizational performance improvement, if any (may be deferred) • Decision to proceed, approval of project plan	• Overselling by software vendors and implementation consultants • Failure to link technology plan to business strategic plan • Unrealistic business case and project parameters • Key performance indicators not or poorly defined, including the measurement process and ownership of this • Selection of inappropriate software, hardware, integrator, and/or project manager; inadequate contracting with external parties • Inadequate contracting with vendors and consultants • Lack of long-term support and migration strategy • Failure to recognize need for business change; underestimating change management difficulty • Misunderstanding organizational requirements, particularly as related to need for data access and reporting	• Not usually formally measured • Possible metrics include quality of business case, fit with business strategy, relevance of key performance indicators, adequacy of schedule and budget, soundness of project parameters, and constraints	• Enterprise systems idea abandoned as unlikely to provide business benefits • Decision to proceed with a project with certain parameters (schedule, scope, and budget) • Business case for project is unsound, creating potential for problems later • Business case for project is sound

(continued on the next page)

TABLE 10.2 *(continued)*

Phase Name, Description, and Key Actors	Typical Activities	Common Errors or Problems	Typical Performance Metrics	Possible Outcomes
Project—Configuration, integration, and rollout ("dollars to assets") • Activities designed to get the system up and running in one or more organizational units • Project manager, project team members, and a variety of external technical and general management consulting resources, executives (in steering committee capacity), other organizational members (in consultative roles)	• Development of detailed project plan • Ongoing project management • Selection and assignment of project team members • Training of project team members and acquisition of supportive skills • Current and/or future business process modeling and reengineering, if any • Execution of change management plan, if any • Software configuration • Software customization, if any • System integration • Integration of software bolt-ons and/or legacy systems, if any • Data cleanup and conversion • Documentation • Testing, bug fixing, and rework • Executive and end-user training • Rollout and startup	• Staffing project subteams without appropriate cross-functional representation • Difficulty acquiring adequate knowledge and skill in software configuration (especially cross-module integration), integration of bolt-ons or legacy systems, and a variety of platform technologies • Poor-quality software, documentation, training materials • Inadequate knowledge on part of consultants and vendor personnel • Configuring software for multiple units on the basis of analyzing only one unit • Assuming that end-user training should be funded from operations budgets • Configuration errors that require rework if caught • Customizations that do not work • Failure to manage project scope, schedule, budget • Inadequate attention to data cleanup	• Project performance to schedule, scope, and budget	• Project terminated owing to overruns or intractable technical problems • Rollout of some operational enterprise system functionality to one or more organizational units • Functionality, operational performance, and organizational preparation are insufficient to address business needs • Functionality, operational performance, and organizational performance are sufficient to address business needs

TABLE 10.2 *(continued)*

Phase Name, Description, and Key Actors	Typical Activities	Common Errors or Problems	Typical Performance Metrics	Possible Outcomes
	• Inadequate attention to reporting • Short-cutting testing and/or training when schedule gets tight • Lack of technology transfer from external consultants • Vendor delivery and software performance problems • Lack of software ease of use • Turnover of project personnel			
Shakedown ("assets to impacts") • Period of time from "going live" until "normal operation" or "routine use" has been achieved • Operations managers, end users, remnants of the project team, IT support personnel, external technical support personnel	• Bug fixing and rework • System performance tuning • Adding hardware capacity • Problem resolution • Process and procedure changes • Retraining, additional training • Adding people to accommodate learning and shakedown needs	• Business disruption • Difficulty diagnosing and solving performance problems • Excessive dependence on "key users" (project team members) and/or IT specialists • Maintenance of old procedures or manual workarounds in lieu of learning the relevant system capabilities • Data input errors • Poor software ease of use • No growth of end-user skills after initial training • Underuse/nonuse of system • Failure to achieve normal operations ("system" never stabilizes)	• Relevant system performance measures such as downtime, response time, etc. • Short-term changes in key performance indicators such as customer calls missed, labor costs, order fulfillment cycle time and error rates, length of time required to complete financial close • Short-term impacts on customers and suppliers • Employee job quality/stress	• Project terminated owing to severe shakedown projects (e.g., disruption of business, poor technical performance, bugs and errors) • Normal operation with routine use of enterprise system is achieved • Impacts insufficient to address business needs • Impacts sufficient to address business needs

(continued on the next page)

TABLE 10.2 *(continued)*

Phase Name, Description, and Key Actors	Typical Activities	Common Errors or Problems	Typical Performance Metrics	Possible Outcomes
Onward and upward ("impacts to outcomes") • Routine operation of the business until such time as a new version of enterprise system is rolled out • Period during which business realizes business benefits from system, if any • Operations managers, end users, IT support personnel, executives	• Postimplementation investment audit (may not be done) • Continuous business improvement (may not be done) • Technology upgrading/migration (may not be done) • Additional end-user skill building (may not be done)	• Not assessing system-related outcomes on a routine basis • Enterprise system of today becomes legacy system of tomorrow (organizational unwillingness or inability to make technology upgrades) • No available documentation on configuration rationale • Turnover of knowledgeable personnel (IT and end user) • No organizational learning about IT projects, enterprise systems • Failure to manage to the intended results of the enterprise system	• Not usually formally measured • Possible indicators include continuous business performance improvement/learning metrics, end-user skill assessment, ease of upgrading/migration, shortening of project and shakedown phases over time, IT specialist competence measures	• Unwillingness or inability to improve business performance and/or migrate technically (e.g., extreme dissatisfaction with implementation process or outcomes, loss of technical or end-user competence) • Formal or informal assessment that investment has been unsuccessful (e.g., failure to achieve hoped-for business results, unexpected costs, or consequences) • Formal or informal assessment that project has achieved goals and/or unexpected benefits • Organization fails to improve its overall competitive position • Organization improves its overall competitive position

distress, it may have merged with another company, or it may have shifted business models. Some projects are terminated owing to cost or schedule overruns or severe technical problems. Others result in the rollout of the operational enterprise system functionality to one or more organizational units. If the latter, the enterprise system functionality, operational performance, and organizational preparation may be sufficient to fit the organization's goals and/or needs, or they may be insufficient for "success."

The Shakedown Phase

The shakedown phase is the organization's coming to grips with the enterprise system. The phase can be said to end when "normal operations" have been achieved (or the organization gives up, disinstalling the system). The project (or consulting) team may continue its involvement or may pass control to operational managers and end users and whatever technical support it can muster. Activities include bug fixing and rework, system performance tuning, retraining, and staffing up to handle temporary inefficiencies. To a large extent, this is the phase in which the errors of prior phases are felt—in the form of reduced productivity or business disruption—but new errors can arise in this phase too. For example, operational personnel may adopt workarounds to cope with early problems and then fail to abandon them when the problems are resolved. Similarly, the organization may come to rely excessively on knowledgeable project team members rather than building the enterprise system knowledge and skills in all relevant operational personnel. As mentioned, some enterprise systems are terminated during the shakedown phase, as in the case of Fox-Meyer Drug (Bulkeley, 1996). Alterntively, organizations may achieve (or declare) "normal operations." If the latter, the impacts attributable to the organization's use of the system may fit its goals or business needs, or they may fail to do so.

The Onward and Upward Phase

The onward and upward phase continues from normal operation until the system is replaced with an upgrade or a different system. It is during this phase that the organization is finally able to ascertain the benefits (if any) of its investment. Key players include operational managers, end users, and IT support personnel (internal or external). Vendor personnel and consultants may also be involved, particularly when deliberations about upgrades are concerned. Characteristic activities of this phase include continuous business improvement, additional user skill building, and postimplementation benefit assessment; however, these "typical" activities are often not performed. A common problem of the onward and upward phase is the loss of knowledgeable personnel who understand the rationales for prior configuration choices and how to improve the business processes through the use of the system. Several ultimate outcomes are possible: The organization may be unwilling to undertake further improvements or upgrades. The organization may decide that its investment has been unsuccessful in meeting goals or business needs. Or the organization may decide its experience has been a success. If the latter, the organization's competitive position may or may not have been improved as a result of its use of enterprise systems.

TOWARD A PROCESS THEORY OF ENTERPRISE SYSTEM SUCCESS

Each enterprise system experience runs a different course, but across the variations, regularities can be found.

- Many different things can go wrong in each phase of the enterprise system experience cycle. Furthermore, not all problems or errors are immediately detectable (and, hence, they are not all immediately correctable).
- There are several possible outcomes for each phase. One is an "optimal" outcome, for example, in the chartering phase, the decision to proceed with an enterprise system project that has a sound business case. A second outcome is a "termination" outcome, such as the decision not to proceed with the enterprise system because analysis revealed an unacceptable business case. A third outcome might be called "continuation with undetected and uncorrected problems" or "unresolved experience risk."[41] The subsequent phase inherits these unresolved risks.
- This third outcome is analogous to what sociotechnical systems theorists call a "variance" (Taylor, 1993). Variances in production processes are deviations from standards in the inputs to a production activity (e.g., raw material quality defects). Variances are not necessarily detected right away; if they cause problems, they may do so only much later in the production process after much money has been expended in working the raw material. Similarly, requirements definition errors in software development may not show up until the system is put into production. Unresolved variances in each phase of an enterprise system experience are passed on to the next phase, where they may or may not be detected and appropriately resolved (depending on probabilistic processes). So, for example, some variances in the chartering phase may remain uncorrected until they show up in the onward and upward phase as a lack of business benefits. In general, the cost of fixing problems increases with delays in recognizing and correcting variances.
- Generally speaking, different actors are involved in different phases of the enterprise system experience cycle. While there may be some continuity across phases (for example, oversight by an executive steering committee during the project phase), handoffs to a different group of people (with different specialties, experiences, and skills) increase the likelihood that variances passed on from earlier phases will not be caught and resolved until they create significant problems. For example, project teams rarely catch and correct significant errors (e.g., failure to match the project to business strategy) in the business case that forms their "charter."
- Of course, not all variances end up causing problems and requiring fixing or rework. Whether or not variances cause problems depends on probabilistic processes such as bad luck, changing business conditions, interactions with other variances, and so on. For example, a badly configured enterprise system requiring expensive rework may not be a problem if the organization's financial position remains sound. Furthermore, it is possible for external conditions and the organization's decisions and actions to interact in such a way that the outcome is better than it was at a prior point, increasing the standard of optimal success. For example, successful implementation of ERP software, while perhaps not providing immediate business value to the adopting organization, might nevertheless position that organization to take advantage of supply-chain integration, thus improving its competitive position relative to competitors.

Two brief examples illustrate how our framework works. The first example concerns Quantum Corp.'s implementation of the Oracle suite of enterprise software applications (Radosevich, 1997). Consultants generally advise against "big-bang" implementations (implementing all modules at once and/or implementing in all locations at once) because of the high potential for business disruption. During its chartering phase, Quantum's leadership determined that acquiring the capability instantly to commit inventory to customers on a worldwide basis (called available to promise, or ATP) was a strategic necessity.

> Because the ATP functionality touches on several areas, including sales processing, inventory and logistics, Quantum had to have the entire suite operating before attaining its key business goal. (Radosevich, 1997)

Quantum therefore decided to implement everywhere at once, but the leadership clearly understood the "bet-your-business" nature of this decision should the shakedown phase not go as well as planned. Therefore, during the project phase, the implementation team made extraordinary efforts in testing the system. Furthermore, when early testing revealed problems, the rollout date, scheduled for summer 1995, was postponed. The rollout finally began as a planned shutdown worldwide:

> At the stroke of midnight on April 26, 1999, every business system at Quantum Corp's offices across the globe went down. . . . The systems stayed down for a week. . . . On May 5, Quantum switched on the new system, and it has been running successfully ever since. (Radosevich, 1997)

In this example, the organization deliberately made a decision involving a high level of risk but took appropriate steps to ensure that the risks did not materialize into a disruption that might have threatened the existence of the organization.

Contrast this example with that of Fox-Meyer Drug (Bulkeley, 1996). When this SAP implementation was chartered, the CIO at least was aware that it was a "bet-your-business" proposition. Yet the $60 million project was approved at the same time that the company also embarked on a state-of-the art $18 million automated warehouse. During the project phase, bad luck intervened: Fox-Meyer Drug lost a large customer, accounting for 15% of its business. To increase revenues, the company aggressively bid on new business: It figured contract pricing on the assumption that the projected annual $40 million savings from the SAP project would be realized immediately on startup, and it decided to advance the SAP rollout by 90 days. That close to the end of the project, little was left to do other than training and testing. So project team members decided not to test modules that had not been customized (thus failing to detect configuration errors). Cutover to the new system resulted in disaster. Meanwhile, the automated warehouse also did not perform as planned. It was estimated that the company sustained an unrecoverable loss of $15 million from erroneous shipments. The company was forced into bankrupcy, and shareholders have since sued both the enterprise system vendor and the integration consultant for $500 million each.

In this example, the chartering decisions were moderately risky. When bad luck occurred during the project phase, the company's decisions had the effect of increasing rather than decreasing risk. When major problems finally materialized during shakedown, the organization did not have the time or the resources to overcome them.

FACTORS IN ENTERPRISE SYSTEM SUCCESS

One can abstract from such examples and the details of Table 10.2 a more general theory of success in the enterprise system experience. At any one moment in time (phase), an enterprise system–adopting organization faces a situation that involves conditions and events (some of them outside its direct control) with an ability to make plans and take actions (that is, goal-directed or "motivated" behavior). These elements of the situation are the factors in (influences on) the outcomes that become inputs at the next moment in time (phase). In the next section we briefly describe these success/failure factors.

Factors External to an Organization's Control

The organization adopting an enterprise system faces several *starting conditions* such as competitive position, industry, financial position, prior relevant experience, size, structure, and management systems that may predispose it to success or failure. While there are undoubtedly threshhold levels for some of these conditions, they generally can not be said to be necessary (or sufficient) for the success of the enterprise system, since organizations have been known to succeed or fail despite them. But these factors come into play in the enterprise system experience in two ways.

First, organizations' goals and plans for enterprise systems may or may not be realistic when viewed objectively in light of these conditions. Dell, for example, decided (after some experience) that an enterprise system was not sufficiently flexible for its rapid growth. For another example, an organization on the brink of bankruptcy may not have enough time and money to realize the benefits of an enterprise system. Starting conditions define the needs and opportunities of organizations relative to enterprise systems (whether or not organizations recognize them for what they are).

Second, starting conditions may not remain the same over the course of the enterprise system experience. After a company decides to customize the enterprise system software, the vendor delivers the needed functionality. After the company has configured the enterprise system for a particular way of doing business, the company merges or sells off a major line of business. Sometimes changes in conditions favor the organization's plans. But probably more often, changing business conditions derail plans. Successful organizations modify goals, plans, and execution to bring their behavior back into line with the environment.

Organization's Motivated Behavior

The organization's goal-directed enterprise system behavior can be defined in four categories: goals, plans, execution, and responses to unforeseen problems. First are the *goals* themselves. Some goals are more conducive to success than others, some are too unambitious to be motivating, and others are unrealistic in light of the objective characteristics of the enterprise system and the organization's starting conditions. Given the great complexity and expense of enterprise systems, for example, some analysts argue that only companies seeking to streamline business processes, to standardize data, or to standardize processes can achieve a positive return on their enterprise system investment (Connolly, 1999).

Plans are another factor in the equation. Plans (and policies) such as not to customize, to reengineer first (last, or not at all), and to phase the rollout are essential to keeping the project phase on track. Enterprise system integrators often claim to have "*the* methodology" that will guarantee success, but not all plans are created equal. The organization's plans for an enterprise system must be linked to its starting conditions and goals. Traditional organizations may need much more change management activity than those in the volatile high-tech sector. The need for a particular business capability may necessitate a risky big-bang rollout (Radosevich, 1997). For another example, the tier-one supplier to an automotive assembler should be much more concerned than a tier-two supplier about the potential negative impacts in lost business from plans that shortchange testing.

The best laid plans are worthless if they are not followed. Good *execution* is something that a consultant's methodology cannot guarantee. If configuration tasks exceed the schedule, cutting the time allotted to testing and training may not guarantee failure, but, given these choices, success will require more than a little luck.

No matter how well an organization executes plans well designed to meet its carefully thought-out goals, conditions may change and unforeseen problems may arise. Successful organizations successfully *resolve* problems by changing their goals, plans, and actions to get a favorable outcome.

Intermediate and Final Outcomes

Starting conditions, changes in conditions, goals, plans, and actions interact (Orlikowski, 1996). Resulting from these interactions are unresolved risks and problems (as well as opportunities, although avoiding failure is usually the primary concern). Unresolved risks and problems themselves interact with changing business conditions and the organization's actions in response to them. If the experience is not terminated, the interactions in one phase result in starting conditions for the next. In economic terms, the course of the enterprise system experience exhibits "path dependence." The final outcome may be very close to optimal success (itself a moving target) or suboptimal on one or more dimensions.

Graphically, the abstract theory described here is depicted in Figure 10.3 for a single phase (negative situation only). Table 10.3 summarizes the details of the process theory as it applies to the specific case of enterprise systems. Table 10.3 is organized according to the important dimensions of process models (Soh & Markus, 1995) by phase: outcome, necessary conditions, probabilistic processes, and recipe for success.

USES OF THE FRAMEWORK

This simple theory of the enterprise system experience has several benefits and uses. First, it is framed in terms that are meaningful to practitioners, but it avoids simplistic overemphasis on a single factor (such as methodology). Furthermore, it explicitly recognizes the role of factors outside the organization's direct control, thereby focusing attention on both planning and the resolution of unforeseen problems. Perhaps most important, it emphasizes the importance of goals—something that technical specialists in particular often take as givens. In view of their greater knowledge of system capabilities and limitations, technical specialists can increase the probability of success by (tactfully) challenging the organization's goals for the enterprise system and these goals' fit with business strategy and external conditions.

As noted by Silver and colleagues (Silver et al., 1995), the theory outlined here can be used both retrospectively and prospectively. Retrospectively, it is useful for

FIGURE 10.3 Factors in Suboptimal Success

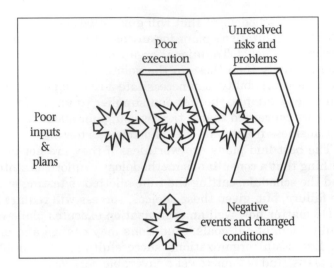

tracing back problems and suboptimal success at each phase to variances arising in earlier phases. For example, configuration errors (which disrupt business operations during shakedown) can result from chartering phase errors (selection of inappropriate goals, software, or partners) as well as from project phase problems (poor composition of project team, inadequate change management execution). Prospectively, the theory can be used to identify a large number of potential problems that should be addressed in basic and contingency plans. It can also help sensitize decision makers to the need to change plans and actions in light of common problems or changing business conditions.

DIRECTIONS FOR FUTURE RESEARCH

The theoretical framework outlined in this theory is too broad in scope for direct empirical testing. However, many lines of research follow directly from the framework, and the phenomenon raises some research themes and issues beyond the limits of the framework.

RESEARCH ON THE PROCESS THEORY

The basic structure of the framework is a sequence of phases, each with intermediate outcomes. The intermediate outcomes are argued to influence the final outcome, but not to determine it; in other words, events and actions taken at any point in the experience cycle may derail an experience that appears to be destined for success or may help a troubled experience get back on track. This general proposition lends itself to testing via multiple methods, including multiple case study and a survey approach. One wants to know the proportion of successes at each phase that are successful in the next and what kinds of actions and events are most likely to change the course of an experience. An important issue concerns the specific metrics of success. Which metrics in each phase have the greatest predictive and explanatory power?

The framework gives a special role to the decisions of the chartering phase. Since errors in chartering an enterprise system experience may not be caught and

TABLE 10.3 A Process Theory of Enterprise System Success

Phase	Successful Outcome	Necessary Conditions	Probabilistic Processes	Recipe for Success
Chartering ("ideas to dollars")	Decision to proceed with enterprise systems in a properly chartered project with a sound business case	• Executive participation • Sound assessment of business conditions and needs • Good understanding of enterprise systems' capabilities and limitations • Carefully constructed business case well communicated to relevant parties	• Managerial decision making ("garbage can" dynamics and politics) • Distribution of good information about environment and technology • Availability of people willing and able to challenge untested assumptions • Human communication gaps and acceptance of need to change • Volatility of business conditions	Success occurs when executives make sound decisions about investing in enterprise systems and bring the organization into alignment with these decisions
Project ("dollars to assets")	Rollout, within reasonable cost and schedule, of enterprise systems functionality that is operational and sufficient to address business needs to an organization prepared to accept it	• Expenditures • Participation by various organizational groups • Technical resources, methodologies, and expertise • Project, vendor, and stakeholder management • Organizational change management expertise • Knowledgeable and skilled IT specialists and project participants	• Quality of business plan resulting from earlier phase • Volatility of business conditions • Availability and quality of technical resources, methodologies, expertise • Execution of project plan • Stakeholder politics • Resolution of problems arising during project phase	Success occurs when 1. The project team faithfully executes a sound project plan and appropriately responds to technical and human challenges that arise during the project OR 2. The project team appropriately modifies the project plan to match changing business and organizational conditions
Shakeout ("assets to impacts")	Normal operations achieved within reasonable time frame and expense with impacts that are sufficient to meet business needs	• Trained users • Well-configured and integrated enterprise system • Redesigned business processes • Additional human, financial, and technical resources to cope with problems arising during shakeout	• Quality of assets resulting from earlier phases • Volatility of business conditions • Stakeholder politics • Execution of shakedown phase problem resolution activities	Success occurs when 1. The organization is well prepared to accept and use a system and related infrastructure of sufficient quality to meet business needs OR 2. Appropriate measures are taken to fix technical and organizational problems arising during shakedown quickly and effectively

(continued on the next page)

TABLE 10.3 *(continued)*

Phase	Successful Outcome	Necessary Conditions	Probabilistic Processes	Recipe for Success
Onward and upward ("impacts to outcomes")	Organization improves its competitive position as a result of enterprise system project and maintains its technological and business flexibility for future developments	• Managers committed to achieving business results (e.g., to use system-generated information to improve organizational performance) • Impacts attributable to use of high-quality enterprise system and infrastructure • System, technical infrastructure, business processes, and human resources sufficiently flexible to adapt to changing business conditions • Adequate resources devoted to maintaining and renewing system, technical infrastructure, and human competence	• Quality of assets resulting from earlier phases • Volatility of business conditions • Stakeholder politics • Execution of results management and maintenance/enhancement activities • Survival of software vendor	Success occurs when 1. Benefits from use of the system combine with favorable competitive conditions AND 2. The future evolution of the enterprise system and related infrastructure is well managed

corrected during the project phase, they are likely to prove expensive to correct later, if they are not outright irreversible. Empirical research is needed to address the chartering phase errors that are most likely, most consequential, and most difficult to detect. Why do these errors occur? What can be done to prevent or correct them?

Adopting organizations with many subunits face chartering and project complexities that single-location businesses do not. Many management theories assume that certain "configurations" of strategy or structural variables are better suited than others to the contingencies of particular environments. The same may be true of the strategies that companies develop to deal with enterprise systems, particularly in complex organizations with many subunits. One wants to know first of all whether there are relatively stable clusters of chartering decisions (e.g., big-bang rollout coupled with no local autonomy on software configuration). If they do exist, how do organizations decide which strategic configurations to adopt? Are these strategic configurations of decisions more successful in the enterprise system experience if they fit well with the various aspects of their environment such as industry type, organizational structure and business model, organizational culture, and the like?

An especially interesting part of the model is what happens after "normal operation" is achieved. When, how, and why does the organization decide to keep things as they are, making the enterprise system of today into the legacy system of tomorrow? When, how, and why do organizations upgrade? Is it better to upgrade frequently so as not to risk big conversions? Do organizations really perceive themselves to be locked in to a particular vendor? How does this influence their subsequent behavior?

Finally, an underlying theme in the framework is the role played by human knowledge and skill—and *gaps* in knowledge and skills—in enterprise system success. What are the relevant bodies of knowledge? How are they distributed externally (across vendors and consultants) and internally (across IT specialists, executives, and users)? Under what conditions are they transferred effectively? What are the barriers to effective knowledge transfer? How can organizations acquire and maintain the relevant expertise? These are just a few of the knowledge management questions posed by enterprise systems. One potentially significant knowledge issue concerns the loss of knowledge about enterprise system configuration (e.g., through poor documentation and personnel turnover). One system integrator told us he believed that it might be *more* costly to update a poorly documented enterprise system than a comparable legacy system because with the enterprise system, the requisite knowledge most likely lies outside the organization. This is an interesting testable hypothesis that gets at the heart of the advantages claimed for packages over in-house development.

BEYOND THE FRAMEWORK

In addition to the many questions raised by the framework itself, the phenomenon of enterprise systems raises interesting questions that go well beyond the framework.

• *Dependence on Vendors.* Because they are so all-encompassing, enterprise systems create a level of dependence on a single software vendor that far surpasses the dependence associated with prior technological regimes. Does this dependence have negative effects on organizations? How do the effects manifest themselves?

How do organizations cope? What are the costs of picking the "wrong" vendor (one that goes out of business or lacks the resources for continued product enhancement in the company's industry segment)?

• *Uniqueness.* To what extent do the enterprise system experience cycle and related process theory apply more generally to other types of information systems? What is truly unique and different about enterprise systems, as opposed, say, to software environments such as Lotus Notes or to homegrown applications?

• *Other Kinds of Integration.* Some organizations have eschewed enterprise systems for any number of reasons. Nevertheless, many of the motivations for enterprise systems remain, particularly in large, complex organizations. To what extent are these organizations pursuing alternatives to enterprise systems as a form of internal integration? (Alternatives might include summary-level integration via data warehousing, rearchitecting legacy systems with middleware, or redevelopment using the object paradigm.) What are the advantages and disadvantages of different integration approaches? What are the consequences of these alternative choices for organizational performance and future flexibility? In particular, are there observable negative consequences from the "tight coupling" entailed with enterprise systems?[42]

• *The "Extended Enterprise."* The enterprise system experience framework assumes that the organization is the most appropriate level of analysis. Increasingly, however, organizations are looking to extensions of enterprise systems to connect themselves more tightly with customers and suppliers in what is often called "supply-chain integration." Suppliers manage customers' inventory, and redundancies are eliminated across organizational lines instead of just within them. Software enables each party to access the other's data—perhaps it is more appropriate to speak of interorganizationally shared software and data resources. To what extent does the enterprise system experience framework apply to the interorganizational integration experience? Can the framework be extended, or is an entirely new framework needed? Finally, of course, what are the societal consequences of this trend, if it continues?

• *Other Kinds of Coordination.* Organizations for which supply-chain integration is not a valid option may still need interorganizational coordination that cannot be supplied by market mechanisms (King, 1999). What kinds of information technology–mediated mechanisms will industries such as health care use for coordination? How will the costs and benefits of "nonintegrated coordination" (King, 1999) differ from those of supply-chain integration and electronic markets?

• *Influences on Vendors.* How do enterprise system–adopting organizations influence the strategic development plans of enterprise system vendors? Which adopters are influential and how do they exert their influence? What are the other influences on vendors' behavior (e.g., shareholders, media, technology marketing research firms)?

CONCLUSION

Enterprise systems represent an important contemporary phenomenon in the organizational use of information technology. The most distinct differences between an enterprise system and other transaction-oriented systems are that the enterprise system is a package versus a system custom developed in-house (implying long-term dependence on a vendor) and that embedded in the enterprise system are normative business practices (requiring many adopting organizations to undertake some form of process reengineering). To date, collective experience with enterprise systems remains quite poorly codified; many organizations approach the phenomenon with little directly applicable knowledge and skill.

Whether or not enterprise systems will remain an enduring part of the organizational IT landscape clearly remains to be seen, but, because they have become such a large part of organizational IT infrastructure, they will continue to be a consequential phenomenon for some years to come. Enterprise systems affect nearly all aspects of organizational life, not only at the point of startup but also throughout their operational lives. Indeed, an organization's enterprise system affects its need and ability to upgrade or convert to more modern technologies. Consequently, we need a framework for understanding and analyzing these systems throughout an experience cycle that includes initial decision making, "development" and implementation, early use, and extended use. The framework outlined in this chapter is a first attempt at an integrated framework for understanding the systems intended to integrate organizations.

The key features of this framework include the following. First, it addresses both the motivated behavior of organizational actors, that is, the goals they are trying to achieve, and the factors outside their control, such as the performance of vendors and the reactions of customers and competitors. Second, the framework allows for both emergence—outcomes that are not deterministic but are influenced by both chance events and human actions—and dynamics—responses to problems and opportunities created by earlier decisions and actions. Third, the framework emphasizes the long-term nature of the enterprise system experience, including maintenance and future upgrades and conversions as major contributors to total costs and benefits. Fourth, the framework understands success as a multidimensional and relative concept and introduces the concept of optimal success to accommodate unintended consequences and external realities that are not fully represented in organizational goals. Fifth, as a process theory, the framework helps explain why organizations do not always achieve optimal success. Finally, the framework uses the concept of unresolved risk or variance to explain how errors can have consequences that show up long after the errors originally occurred. This explains why organizations often find it so hard to correct problems and to learn from their experiences with enterprise systems.

ENDNOTES

1. By the mid-1990s, it was common wisdom that business process reengineering in many companies had failed because of the difficulty and huge expense of reprogramming their core transaction processing systems to support the new processes.
2. See the chapter by George, this volume.
3. In the first draft of this chapter, we wrote: "The ERP total software licensing business is expected to grow to $20 billion by 2002 (Stein, 1998). And consulting firms have estimated that ERP consulting services will grow to $8 billion by the year 2002 (Stein, 1998)." David Brown, of Key Performance International, provided these interesting observations: "I noticed AMR Research released a new

report last week (5/18/99) projecting total ERP software revenues of $66.6 billion by 2003 (Enterprise Resource Planning Software Report, 1998–2003). I thought you might be interested in the large discrepancy between Stein's projections and AMR's. . . . Based on earlier studies by AMR, ERP consulting services range between 2 and 5 times ERP license revenues. AMR reported average ERP license revenues of $4,000 per seat (Baan or SAP) and ERP consulting fees of $8,000 (Baan) to $20,000 (SAP) per ERP seat. If AMR's report of ERP consulting fees is accurate, Stein's estimate of $8 billion in ERP consulting revenues supporting $20 billion in ERP license revenues is too low by a factor of 5 to 10" (Brown, 1999).

4. See the chapter by Weill and Broadbent, this volume.

5. See the chapter by Fichman, this volume.

6. The configuration of enterprise systems is not to be confused with (business) product configuration, a functionality supported by some ERP software extensions.

7. Davenport (1998) quite rightly points out that such lack of integration may be perfectly appropriate for some organizational structures and business models.

8. See the chapter by George, this volume.

9. In the language of SAP, installation work is divided into "applications" work (the province of end users) and "basis" work (the province of technical specialists).

10. For an example of some of the trade-offs involved and how they are resolved, see the case study of Microsoft's implementation of SAP R/3 financials (Bashein, Markus, & Finley, 1997).

11. Conversion may be unavoidable when the vendor redevelops the software for an entirely new computing architecture (e.g., mainframe to client/server, client/server to object oriented).

12. An industry association dedicated to issues related to production and inventory control.

13. When pushed, most analysts admit that there is no way to verify that their practices are really "best." Presumably, some organizations find ways to perform the process even better.

14. Conversely, the unwillingness to change how they do business requires many organizations to modify enterprise software.

15. See the chapter by Grover and Kettinger, this volume.

16. The difficulty stems in part from the lack of the relevant knowledge and skills, which are scarce and distributed across a variety of occupational specialties. Therefore, system integration often involves managing a sizable collection of technical experts from different fields and often from different organizations. New enterprise system developments such as Web-enabled software and outsourced implementation and operations are possible solutions to these problems.

17. To facilitate this integration, enterprise system vendors are now publishing the structure of their software, for example, SAP's business application programming interface (BAPI).

18. Most enterprise systems trace their roots to MRP II—a disciplined approach to managing discrete parts production. Many businesses differ substantially in form, structure, and business processes from discrete parts manufacturers, for example, process industries, service business such as repair operations, and manufacturers of products with "dimensionality" (e.g., clothing, footwear, telecommunications cables). (An inventory consisting of two 500 meter cables is *not* equivalent to one 1,000 meter cable.) Therefore, companies in particular

industry segments must buy a specialized version of the enterprise software created by either the vendor or by a third party. Otherwise, they face the need to modify the software at great cost and risk.

19. In some cases, these extensions are developed by the vendors. In other cases, the vendors have acquired third-party software firms to gain access to their products.
20. See the chapter by Fichman, this volume.
21. See the chapter by Fichman, this volume.
22. Even when enterprise systems are not adopted at a corporate level, they may be adopted by a corporation's individual business units.
23. See the chapter by Barua and Mukhopadhyay, this volume.
24. See the chapter by Kirsch, this volume.
25. See the chapter by Grover and Kettinger, this volume.
26. See the chapter by Olfman, this volume.
27. See the chapter by Kirsch, this volume.
28. See the chapter by Ang and Slaughter, this volume.
29. See the chapter by Fichman, this volume.
30. See the chapter by Robey and Boudreau, this volume.
31. In other words, our level of analysis is different from Alter's (1999).
32. See the chapter by Barua and Mukhopadhyay, this volume.
33. An argument in favor of the contested definition is that many enterprise systems projects are scaled back during installation, which usually means a failure to achieve the ambitious original goals. On the other hand, this definition would also count as failures projects that yielded unanticipated benefits.
34. This system and concomitant organizational changes succeeded in reducing accounting personnel by 70%, but morale plummeted, skilled people left the company, and the system was disinstalled when the company was acquired.
35. These metrics include business, human, and adaptability outcomes (Silver, Markus, & Beath, 1995).
36. Hirt (Hirt & Swanson, 1999) studied an organization in a declining industry with severe profit pressure that implemented SAP to reduce mainframe computer costs and solve the Y2K problem. Because the company had done some process redesign before implementing SAP, it did not do more reengineering when adopting SAP. Later, though, the company wondered whether more reengineering would have produced better gains.
37. See the chapter by Agarwal, this volume.
38. See the chapter by Robey and Boudreau, this volume.
39. See the chapters by Barua and Mukhopadhyay and by Robey and Boudreau, this volume.
40. This phase model differs from that proposed by Ross (1999).
41. We borrowed this term from Nidumolu (1995).
42. Perrow (1972) would argue that tight coupling increases the likelihood of various kinds of failures.

Chapter 11

The Internet Changes Everything (ICE) Age

Jeffrey L. Sampler

Unless you have been on a deserted island for the last few years, it has been impossible for you to miss the tidal wave of media attention to new technology innovations, such as the Internet. Actually, even on a deserted island, with wireless technology and global telephone networks, such as Iridium, you probably would have been aware of these changes. What is interesting is just how quickly an industry has developed, not only commercializing these new technologies but also reporting about them. For example, the companies on everyone's lips for the next hot investments are often Internet companies—Yahoo, Amazon.com, and eBay, to name but a few. Moreover, tracking new initial public offerings and their rises in first-day trading value has become almost a regular part of evening news coverage. The amazing valuations of these companies have in some cases made their founders billionaires. For example, Jeff Bezos of Amazon.com and Jerry Yang of Yahoo are now listed on the Forbes 400 annual list of the richest people in the United States. From nothing to billionaires in just a few years—rarely, if ever, have we witnessed such a meteoric wealth creation process.

Such wealth creation has created massive media attention, not only in tracking the creation of this new wealth but also in describing the business transformation process that created it, as well as the lessons to apply to other companies. New magazines have been established to chart this revolution: *Wired, Industry Standard,*

Business 2.0, Red Herring, and *Fast Company,* to name but a few. Similarly, the number of books exploring this topic has also skyrocketed. In many ways, it seems that history is repeating itself. In the last gold rush—the San Francisco gold rush of 1849—it was Levi Straus who made a fortune by selling supplies and blue jeans to prospectors. Similarly, the safe money of today may be held by those charting the revolution rather than diving into the turbulent competitive waters of digital competition.

For academics, as well as practitioners, one of the major problems with the Internet revolution is the speed with which it occurs and the scope of its impact. Much of the work to date in this area has been both useful and potentially dangerous. It is useful in that it highlights new trends or ideas, but it is dangerous in that the implications may not be clear because they may play out in a time frame longer than currently witnessed or across a broader arena. The analogy of the three blind men describing an elephant based on the part that each is feeling comes to mind. The generalizations they made based on their localized data were not accurate. Similarly, many of the situations described currently may not accurately reflect the broader phenomena underway in this transition to an information economy.

The purpose of this paper will be to take a small step toward correcting this problem. First, a summary of existing research describing implications of the Internet and information economy for individuals, organizations, and society will be provided. Finally, a model integrating these issues will be presented and guidelines for research in this domain will be suggested.

IMPLICATIONS OF THE INTERNET AND INFORMATION ECONOMY

The Internet and the arrival of the information economy have been among the most discussed phenomena of recent years. The impact of the Internet has broad and often overlapping implications. The following discussion will try to untangle these implications by exploring the impact of the Internet on organizations, individuals, and society.

ORGANIZATIONS

The impact of the Internet on organizations has already been profound, and undoubtedly this is just the beginning. When analyzing organizations to understand the impact of technology, it is important to understand that technological innovations lead to innovations in how firms are managed (Nelson, 1994) and that often there is a time lag between technological and managerial innovation (Brynjolfsson, 1993). Thus, while much current research has focused on questions about how the Internet is a more efficient tool or better optimizes current business models—for example by shifting from fixed to variable pricing or exploring the optimal number of suppliers because of reduced search costs (Bakos & Brynjolfsson, 1993; Barua, Ravindran, & Whinston, 1997)—there are also more far-reaching questions to ask, such as this: What will be the fundamental building blocks of organizations in the wired world? In the Internet economy, the more important question is not efficiency but relevance, and the competitive battles will be between business models (Hamel & Sampler, 1998). To that extent a brief overview of the evolution of thinking about strategy, industry boundary, and structure will be provided to facilitate the investigation into the inquiry about the nature of the future organization.

Strategy

In recent years, much of the theoretical strategy debate has been between competing schools of thought about the primary source of competitive advantage. The two main lenses of analysis in this debate have been the industrial organization (IO) economic view of strategy and the resource-based school.

The dominant perspective in the strategy discipline throughout much of the 1970s and early 1980s was the industrial organization economic perspective that is most associated with the work of Porter and others (Caves & Porter, 1977; Porter, 1980). Strategic planning in the IO school of strategy was concerned primarily with industry structure because this was considered to be the primary determinant of firm profitability. Thus, many of the strategic planning methods consisted of analyzing industry forces (Porter, 1980) to determine the attractiveness of an industry and how to influence the structure of the industry and, hence, profits.

However, over the last decade, much of the strategy literature has emphasized resources internal to the firm as the principal driver of firm profitability and strategic advantage (Wernerfelt, 1984; Barney, 1986, 1991; Prahalad & Hamel, 1990). Resources are said to confer competitive advantage to the extent that they must be difficult to create, buy, substitute, or imitate (Barney, 1991; Lippman & Rumelt, 1982; Peteraf, 1993). Moreover, recently much research in the resource school of strategic thinking has shifted from focusing on tangible assets as a source of advantage to intangible assets, which include knowledge (Winter, 1987); core competencies (Prahalad & Hamel, 1990); learning (Senge, 1990); and "invisible assets" such as brand image or corporate culture (Itami, 1987).

Competitive advantage from such resources comes not from their possession but, especially in the case of intangible resources, from the capability of firms that accumulate and utilize these resources to execute more complex strategies and thereby sustain competitive advantage over competing firms lacking such resources and skills (Barney, 1991; Hart & Banbury, 1994). Prahalad and Hamel (1990) summarize much of this thinking by noting that the logic underlying many of these ideas involves "the collective learning in the organization, especially with how to coordinate diverse production skills and integrate multiple streams of technology" (p. 82).

From both an academic and a practitioner viewpoint, the idea of strategy being based on intangible resources, especially core competencies, has received increasing attention. Indeed, it is difficult not to hear most companies discuss strategy in terms of their core competencies. This has occurred for several reasons. First, the rate of change has increased dramatically in terms of new product introduction and shifts in customer preferences. A static snapshot of a moving industry has not been an adequate means for formulating strategy in an increasingly dynamic environment (Bettis & Hitt, 1995). Second, traditional industry boundaries are blurring as many industries converge or overlap, especially in information technology–related industries (Bettis & Hitt, 1995; Hamel & Prahalad, 1994). Yet traditional IO strategic thinking is based on a stable industry, as are many strategic analysis tools, including competitor analysis, strategic groups, PIMS, and diversification typologies. Finally, the increasing rate of change has put pressure on firms to react more quickly because time is often seen as a source of competitive advantage (Stalk & Hout, 1990).

For our perspective, it is key to highlight that the dramatic changes in technology, particularly information technology, have caused industries to be less stable and increasingly have made industries difficult to define because of the blurring of industry boundaries due to technological convergence. These changes in strategy have resulted in a common theme arising in much of the current strategy debate, particularly for those focused on strategy in the Internet Age. The recurring mantra reflects variations of how to compete in unpredictable, chaotic times. Current thinking includes hypercompetition (D'Aveni, 1994), disruptive technologies (Christensen, 1997), strategy as revolution (Hamel, 1996), strategy as real options (Trigeorgis, 1996), competing on the edge (Brown & Eisenhardt, 1998), and surfing the edge of chaos (Pascale, 1999). The common theme seems to be how to reinvent the firm, expect the unexpected, and compete when the future is not forecastable.[1] The Internet has been a driving force in this destabalization. As a result, new paradigms, such as chaos theory and increasing returns, are emerging as part of the language of current strategic thinking.

Industry Boundary

As noted, for many years the dominant paradigm of strategy had its roots in (IO) economics and the structure-conduct-performance model (Mason, 1939; Bain, 1956). Empirical studies have noted such an industry effect, with between 17 and 20% of financial performance variance being explained by industry characteristics (Schmalansee, 1985; Wernerfelt & Montgomery, 1988; Rumelt, 1991; Powell, 1996; McGahan and Porter, 1997). However, this leaves much financial performance unexplained by industry effects. This, coupled with the arguments about the difficulties today in defining industry boundaries, has left many managers questioning the utility of such thinking and analysis. But are we throwing the baby out with the bathwater?

Recent research has suggested that redefining industry boundaries in terms of inputs (resources) rather than outputs (products) may lead to a potential way of reframing industry analysis. In particular, information may be the appropriate resource for redefining many industry boundaries (Sampler, 1998). The adoption of such a perspective requires a brief review about how scholars have viewed information.

One of the fundamental assumptions of neoclassical economists was that of perfect information, that is, information was available to all market participants at zero cost. Much of the early work done in the economics of information was to challenge this assumption by exploring the costs of attaining information, particularly with regard to the pricing and quality of information goods and the information asymmetries among market participants (Stigler, 1961; Arrow, 1962, 1971; Alchian, 1969; Rothschild, 1973; Spence, 1973). Arrow (1974) later examined the role of the uncertainty of information as a key failure of markets and one of the driving forces behind the formation of organizations.

Other scholars have studied the importance of information not from the perspective of market efficiency, as noted, but from seeking to understand the role of information in the production process, in particular as a source of wealth creation through discovery and innovation. For example, Bell (1981) noted that traditional economic theory in its analysis of production has been unable to account for technology, innovation, or entrepreneurship and suggested that information should now be acknowledged as a factor of production in its own right, given its importance in postindustrial society. It has also been argued that much economic growth is derived from the deployment of previously available information, not merely through the generation of new information and knowledge (Rosenberg, 1982).

Noticing the increasing importance of information in production in recent years has caused Hawken (1983, p.11) to assert that "the single most important trend to understand is the changing ratio between mass and information in goods and services." Others have referred to this trend as "mind over matter" (Gilder, 1989) and the "dematerialization of production," that is, the progressive reduction of energy content per unit of value created and the progressive increase in its information content (Davidse, 1983).

Such an increase in the importance of information in the production of goods and the creation of wealth has caused others to question the validity of existing measures for categorizing economic activity. For example, only 6% of IBM's employees worldwide are directly engaged in industrial manufacturing. However, IBM continues to be classified as an industrial in the SIC classification scheme (Quinn, 1992). Even more dramatically, the material costs of the silicon chip, one of the most important products in ushering in the Information Age, are approximately 1% of the total production costs (Gilder, 1989).

If we view information as a resource of the firm, then these advances in information technology have caused a dramatic increase in the supply of this resource and the ease with which this resource can be managed. Previously, as suggested by traditional economic thinking, information was viewed as a cost—an activity to support activities, such as sales (e.g., the necessary accounting and documentation to support the business). However, these new technologies represent a fundamental shift in the ability to capture, manipulate, store, and transfer information. With this change, information can now be viewed as a source of value creation, not a cost. For example, consider airline computer reservation systems, such as SABRE. These systems allow seat booking information to be used to support the transaction of booking seats and have created a new source of value by creating the basis by which airlines can create dynamic pricing for seats based on current and historical load factors (McKenney, 1995). This information revolutionized the airline industry and created a new metric by which to measure performance: revenue per seat. The value comes from the ability to capture and analyze information that before would have disappeared with the event or at best remain inaccessible, locked away in the minds of a few people.

Increasingly, information technology is allowing information to be separated from the transaction that generated the information. The stored information is then a resource that can be used as a competitive tool. The separation of this information asset from a transaction generating that information is increasingly causing the industry boundary to be redefined in terms of any firm that has access to the same critical information (Sampler, 1998). In summary, the rise of the importance of information coupled with improvements in IT to leverage this information has caused a fundamental shift in our understanding and conceptualization of the competitive landscape facing many firms.

Structure

Historically, much of the debate about the impact of IT on organizational structure has focused on the issue of centralization or decentralization of organizational control and decision making. Many studies support both sides of this argument (Leavitt & Whisler, 1958; Robey, 1981; Applegate, Cash, & Mills, 1988; Anshen, 1960; Blau et al., 1976).[2] Despite these and many other studies, this has been an unresolved debate because of the many other factors influencing the choice of organizational structure, such as environmental uncertainty, manufacturing technology, and organizational size (Woodward, 1965; Perrow, 1967, 1970; Child, 1973; Robey, 1977, 1981).

While much of this debate has focused on the *internal* flow of information and its corresponding effect on organizational structure, a more recent issue has been the impact of IT on the *external* flow of information. This became an issue as organizations developed systems that were not limited to the originating organizations but instead use IT to link with companies external to their organization, such as suppliers in their product value chain. Such interorganizational information systems (Johnston & Vitale, 1988) allow firms to radically alter current production and inventory practices based on the availability of real-time production and sales data. However, the enabling technology that allowed these systems was electronic data interchange (EDI), which required time to build a dedicated network, with both financial and manpower investments from participating organizations. However, the principles of EDI serve as a springboard for the open network of the Internet where companies can plug into an existing public infrastructure rather than building their own. Such an increase in the use of these public systems has caused an increase in debate about the rise and management of the virtual corporation (Venkatraman & Henderson, 1998).

The meteoric growth of the Internet and the rise of companies participating in e-commerce through the Internet are redefining the frequency and reach of interorganizational systems. The rise of vertical portals, such as Chemdex for suppliers and purchasers of chemicals, is shifting the basis of relationships, pricing, and power across the industry value chain. In addition to these specialized portals, we see the rise of global business superportals, such as Global Online, which claims to be the world's first international e-commerce portal. It boasts connections across 200 countries, 18 languages, 29 currencies, 81 auction sites, 36,000 trade and product forums, 250,000 URLs of merchant and service provider links, and 15 million global business information links. Clearly, the scale and complexity of such a network would not have been possible without the Internet as a platform for low-cost global connectivity.

In addition to the explosion of internetworked firms that the Internet has facilitated, there is an additional fundamental implication: The reach of each firm has been dramatically altered. In today's world, Internet start-up companies are global from birth (i.e., from their very first day of business). We are witnessing business history—a new type of company that is "born global," a birthright provided by the Internet. To further clarify the significance of this, it is important to realize that these firms achieve this with very few people, often less than one hundred. Never before has this been possible. Contrast this with the many studies of global corporations during the 1980s, such as the transnational corporation (Bartlett & Ghoshal, 1998). This and other works describe a similar process in which firms dominate one country and then roll out their operations and products to different parts of the world. These firms are enormous in resources and people, and the process of globalization takes years, if not decades. Today, because of the Internet, we see the rise of "de facto" global corporations. Such changes create many research opportunities to understand the implications of both business strategies and organizational structures necessary to manage firms that leverage technology to this extent.

INDIVIDUALS

Traditionally, much of the focus of the impact of IT on the individual has been around human-computer interaction and the characteristics of technology (e.g., usability) and individuals (e.g., age, education) that facilitated the adoption of technology.[3] The main benefits were increased organizational and individual productivity. However, compared to traditional IT, the Internet is having a much more fundamental impact on the individual, which is unfolding in several ways.

First, the Internet is fundamentally altering industry configurations and the balance of power among producers, intermediaries, and consumers. If this does not sound possible, a little tour through history might make you less skeptical. Are you old enough to remember Main Street—that humble row of shops operated by neighborly souls who knew your kids by name and catered to your every need? All that is gone now, replaced decades ago by lookalike shopping malls with Sears at one end, Penny at the other, and a row of specialty shops between. Then, when you weren't looking, those suburban malls started down the long road toward retail irrelevance. "Category killers" such as Toys R Us, Home Depot, and Staples slowly crushed many of the specialty retailers that once made the malls work. And Wal-Mart displaced Sears as the biggest U.S. retailer.

As the retailing model changed, the impact on producers was enormous. With each shift, the balance of power tilted toward the retailers, largely because of the use of mainframe computers, scanner data, and EDI. For the first time, the retailer knew more than the producer about what was being sold. The implications of this technology revolution, which also facilitated retail consolidation, were profound. Imagine the bargaining power of Wal-Mart when it orders a million television sets from Philips. In the grocery business, it doesn't matter whether you're Procter & Gamble or Unilever, you're still going to have to pay the big supermarkets for shelf space if you want to launch a new product. Mutual fund companies gave up a big chunk of their profits to be listed in Schwab's *OneSource* catalog of funds. The effects of retailing consolidation rippled back along the entire supply chain. Big producers gobbled up smaller competitors as it became nearly impossible for the number three or four seller in a product category to win shelf space.

The Internet's impact will be similarly far reaching and will cause a power shift away from producers and retailers toward consumers (Hamel & Sampler, 1998). Only this time, it will not be a ripple that slowly builds over time. Instead, it will be a tidal wave—because the Internet is going to empower consumers as nothing else ever has. Armed with perfect information and zero search costs, consumers are going to weed out mediocrity, hype, and inefficiency with a vengeance. Examples of this are already apparent in many industries. In the automobile industry, more than 20% of car buyers now shop on-line and have already decided what car they will buy and the price they will pay before setting foot in the dealer showroom. New infomediaries, such as Autobytel, which will aid consumers in shifting through these data, are already having a major impact. Autobytel is already responsible for more than \$550 million of automobile sales every month!

Behind each of these transitions, technology has played a critical role. In the early rise of the city-center stores, the design of multistory office buildings fitted with elevators allowed a greater concentration of foot traffic in a limited area than had ever been possible. The move to the suburbs was facilitated by the development of an extensive freeway system and the prevalence of affordable and reliable automobiles. Category-killer stores were enabled by the sophisticated use of information technology to control a very complex inventory and to order goods from suppliers using EDI to shrink the time needed to deliver the goods to the store.

As we begin to see the next major trend in retail, early signals of how it may unfold are already apparent. The critical technology trend is that consumers increasingly have sophisticated computers that are networked globally. Just as business has made extensive use of IT in the last generation of retail, IT is now shifting to the consumer. Currently, we see this in the form of the Internet, but in the future this may take many forms as low-cost access devices and satellite communication technology radically change the landscape of consumer technology. However, even today, the Internet is already beginning to radically alter the model of how goods are purchased. And the good news for consumers (and the potentially bad news for business/producers) is that the power has been moved to the consumer.

However, be very clear that the power shift to the consumer has occurred because of the primary group that technology impacts. In previous generations of technology, the main locus of technology impact was either in production or distribution, but now IT is aiding consumption. And the consumer is the beneficiary of this shift in the focus of IT. This power plays out not only in lower prices but also in potential bargaining power. For example, let us assume that I get bad customer service at a store. How many people can I tell? What does the large corporation have to fear from me, the individual consumer? However, what happens when each consumer has a global broadcast channel because of the Internet? The tables have turned, and the balance of power has been shifted. If you think this is not possible, ask Intel what happens when a math professor discovers an error in the math coprocessor of the Pentium II chip and posts this information on the Internet. Hundreds of millions of dollars were spent in correcting this error.

Moreover, because of the globally networked IT that is impacting the consumer, the consumer now has a very different role—that of technology innovator. In previous generations of IT, the individual was the recipient of technology innovations that played out at the corporate level, and his or her role was that of the adoptor of innovation. Increasingly, in the Internet world, individuals are the instigators or sources of innovation. Signs of this are everywhere, such as in on-line games, including Doom and Quake, where individuals add significant features to the game. However, two key trends are worth noting. First, individuals increasingly have a more sophisticated PC at home than at the office. Second, even though business-to-business Internet commerce will dominate business-to-consumer e-commerce many times over, we see most of the innovations in design and business models occurring at the consumer level. These ideas are then adopted in the business-to-business arena. Again, consumers are driving innovation, and large organizations are then adopting innovations from individuals—a total reversal of the innovation process that has been enabled by the Internet!

In addition to these economic benefits of the Internet, it also has career and social implications. For example, the trend of teleworking that has been enabled by advancements in IT may take a major shift forward as the Internet makes remote working more accessible and affordable. Such technological capabilities will enable individuals to participate in multiple organizations in often transitory or temporary roles, which has been suggested by advocates of virtual and knowledge-based work and such management gurus as Handy and Drucker.

What we have yet to understand, and a key issue for research, is the contradiction that greater connectivity through IT allows greater physical isolation or independence. The long-term implications of this on individuals are unclear but vital as we start to explore the nature of sustainable patterns of interaction between organizations and individuals.

In addition to greater flexibility in work practices that new technologies have enabled, there is also greater flexibility in terms of how individuals interact with others and society in general. Increasingly, because of the increased levels of connectivity among large groups of people that technology has enabled, we are beginning to see different forms of individuals interacting with society. Clearly, previous technologies, such as the telephone, have enabled connectivity, but the Internet is different in several dimensions. First, the Internet allows asynchronous as well as interactive communication. More important, the Internet has a memory or storage capability—information can be stored and accessed later by many people. Also, communication can be direct (i.e., one-to-one, or broadcast, one-to-many). These differences in communication and access enabled by the Internet allow individuals to effectively and efficiently participate in multiple interest groups or communities. Increasingly, these communities may represent transient interests as well as more sustainable or enduring interests. Individuals' ability to participate in several communities or societies simultaneously to differing extents is now possible because of the Internet (Turkle, 1997). Again, the implications of this are only beginning to be understood.

SOCIETY

The economic impact that technology has had on countries and society has been a much researched topic (e.g., Chandler, 1994; Rosenberg, 1982). However, what are the social impacts of technology, particularly IT, on society? Does the Internet have the potential to alter the reference group through which people shape their identity? Throughout history, society has been defined mainly through physical proximity because it was through this physical field of influence that most information was absorbed. However, with information-intensive technologies, such as the Internet, the main channel through which information is absorbed may start to shift from the physical to the virtual. Indeed, the potential impact of this has caused many to say that the Internet has lead to the "death of distance" (i.e., distance is no longer a major determinant in many economic and social situations).

However, with the advances in IT prior to the Internet, similar claims were being made, as the traditional nation-state border gave rise to regional economies (Ohmae, 1995) or even a borderless world (Ohmae, 1999). This economic blurring of society has only increased as the amount of trade among nations has increased. However, as we move more to an intangible economy, we increasingly will witness "phantom immigration." In other words, the visa or work permit system designed to limit the number of people from different countries entering another one will have little effect, especially with products such as software. Just think about how many people, particularly in offshore software havens such as Bangalore, India, and Shanghai, China, are effectively participating in the U.S. economy without ever setting foot inside its legal tax jurisdiction.

The economic and social implications of "phantom immigration" are enormous, but even at the most simple level, one must begin to question the ability of a country to tax in such a borderless world, where economic value is increasingly consumed within the legal tax jurisdiction but is actually purchased outside the legal physical boundaries of a country or state. Indeed, reports in England have suggested that e-commerce may reduce value-added tax revenue by up to 20%, or almost $16 billion per annum (*Financial Times,* 1999).

Such changes in the legal and tax jurisdiction of a nation-state may lead to upheaval in the current taxation systems. For example, as governments realize that more people are able to work or purchase goods outside their legal tax jurisdiction, will this lead to a decrease in personal income and sales taxes and a rise in real estate taxes? Increasingly, where you choose to live may be one of the few opportunities for a country to collect taxes. Also, enforcing product liability claims will become increasingly complicated when purchases again often occur outside the legal jurisdiction of a country.

In summary, technologies such as the Internet have caused the social, economic, and tax borders of a nation-state to shift. With these movements come massive opportunities in developing global economies, but the social implications are unclear as the ability of governments to pay for social goods or enforce product standards of people physically living within its borders comes into question. This coupled with many people identifying with virtual communities or societies, in addition to their physical community or society, suggests the potential for a fundamental reconstruction of social order (Fukuyama, 1999).

DISCUSSION AND CONCLUSIONS

Is the Internet really changing everything, or is this a case of much ado about nothing? In some cases, the Internet clearly extends existing organizational concepts such as when to go virtual (Chesbrough & Teece, 1996), the importance of knowledge management (Grant, 1996; Kogut & Zander, 1992; Nonaka, 1994), and the importance of flexibility in uncertain environments (Volberdra, 1996). The Internet extends these concepts because the range of activities and distance from which they can be performed are greatly increased.

However, the implications of the Internet in the areas of industry reconfiguration and strategy are more profound. The possibility that industry definition of relevant competitors may increasingly not be determined by product or services but by the possession of critical information is a reality for some industries already, such as retail financial services, and is becoming more relevant for others. In strategy, the ultimate goal is to define the new paradigm of competitive advantage in the Information Age—will it be tools from IO economics, resource-based views of the firm, knowledge management, some combination of all of these, or something entirely different? This will be one of the key contributions for academics to make in the coming years.

It is well understood that changes in technology lead to changes in management, but the Internet is different in that it is impacting not only organizations but also individuals and society as a whole. The other major difference is that because of the technological infrastructure on which the Internet is based, the individual is increasingly the focus of activity in terms of (1) being a source of innovation and (2) causing an overall economic power shift to the customer. This is something entirely new. No longer is technical innovation occurring at a societal or corporate level first; it first happens at the individual level. This transition is represented in Figure 11.1, the "centipede model" of Internet impact. This model attempts to capture two fundamental ideas: (1) individuals are increasingly the originator of innovation and at the center of activities in terms of power and (2) individuals are increasingly participating in multiple organizations and societies or communities.

This "centipede model" suggests three major issues for future research agendas in understanding the impact of the Internet. First, developing "individual-centric" models of industry power is necessary. Second, developing new innovation models is vital—ones in which the roles of the individual and corporation are often reversed (i.e., where the individual is the source of innovation, not the adoptor of innovation). Third, developing models that explore the impact of technology on individuals, organizations, and society in a parallel structure rather than serially will be necessary to understand the full impact of a technology that has a far greater potential impact in a much shorter time because of the level of infrastructure already in place. This infrastructure will be the springboard of new models of innovation, business, and society. Understanding the integrative complexity of these perspectives is vital as academics seek to interpret a world that seems to be increasingly unfolding before them in real time.

FIGURE 11.1
Centipede Model of
Internet Impact

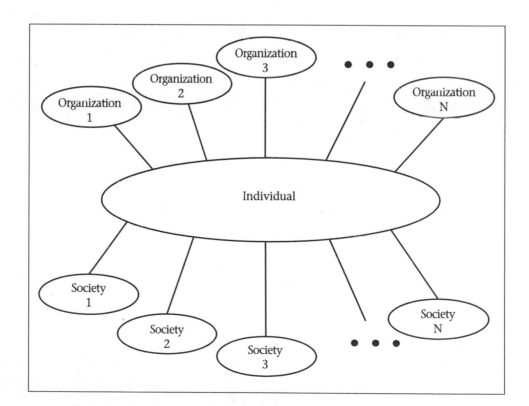

ENDNOTES

1. For a more in-depth treatment of this topic, please see the chapter by Sambamurthy.
2. Please see the chapter by Robey and Boudreau for a detailed discussion of this and related issues.
3. Please see the chapter by Agarwal for a more substantive treatment of this topic.

Managing the Nexus of Information Technology and Radical Change: An Organizational Capabilities Perspective

Albert H. Segars and James W. Dean

Advances in communications, processing, and storage technologies have made the global business environment a small and dynamic marketplace. Organizations continuously confront new markets and competition as well as increasingly complex customer expectations. To compete in this new environment, coalitions of business networks (suppliers, manufacturers, distributors, and customers) must coordinate their activities on a global scale. This requires most firms to comprehensively review the assumptions that underlie their processes, lines of authority, knowledge sharing, technologies, and mechanisms of economic exchange. In many instances, a nexus of innovative organizational design and information technology (IT) enables these new models of business. These transformations frequently represent stark departures from patterns and assumptions that have become part of the organizational fabric. Therefore, rather than an incremental change proposition, managers are increasingly faced with radical change propositions in the pursuit of competitive objectives.

The nexus of IT and innovative organizational design presents managers a multitude of new challenges. As developed in this chapter, the philosophical and methodological foundations of total quality management (TQM) and business process reengineering (BPR) provide a useful foundation for programs of process-based incremental change. However, radical change presents a larger array of organizational and competitive complexity that is not amenable to a particular approach or methodology. Instead, the proposition of radical change challenges the organization to reinvent itself in terms of philosophy (attitudes, assumptions, beliefs), strategy, economic exchange, knowledge sharing, and managerial systems, as well as process. We believe that a useful approach in addressing this challenge is the perspective of organizational capabilities. In short, our contention is that an organization must acquire unique abilities that allow it to understand and then successfully orchestrate radical IT-based change. In the sections that follow, radical change is framed as a discontinuity at both the industry and organizational levels. Our purpose is to develop a context for defining radical IT-based change and its potential impacts. We then develop a set of key organizational capabilities that are necessary for achieving radical change. The observations developed are based on an analysis of key literature as well as the experiences of managers actively involved in radical IT-based initiatives. Importantly, our objective is to stir debate and new avenues of research in this important area of IT management.

RADICAL IT-BASED CHANGE AS DISCONTINUITY WITHIN THE COMPETITIVE SPACE

Perhaps the most disruptive form of radical IT-based change is at the level of industry. Formal academic inquiry (Segars & Grover, 1998), as well as the popular press (Hamel & Sampler, 1995), has presented compelling evidence of the industry-changing nature of IT. In fact, the nature of industry change through IT can be so fast and so pervasive that many scholars and practitioners are beginning to question the very utility of "industry" as a definitional context for describing competitive space (Eisenhardt, 1989).

The unintended and/or unanticipated organizational and competitive consequences of radical IT-based change can spell catastrophe for those firms that fail to fully contemplate the potential interactions between industry structure and the capabilities of emerging technologies. Therefore, an important consideration in developing strategy for initiating or responding to radical change is the identification of industry dynamics that may be altered or completely reconfigured in the aftermath of IT deployment. A useful framework for identifying and analyzing key aspects of shifting competitive space is "strategic group dynamics." This perspective recognizes that firms within a competitive space compete for identical market segments with very different sets of resources and strategies (McGee & Thomas, 1986). Formally, a "strategic group" can be conceptualized as a set of firms within a competitive space that are highly symmetric along critical bases of competition. The mapping of strategic groups is a useful method for tracking radical changes in competitive structure as firms become similar to, or different from, each other over time. Moreover, the matching of market changes with strategic group evolution provides a means for predicting the nature of competition as well as explaining the past and potential influences of environmental, technological, and competitive events on industry structure.

THE NATURE OF RADICAL SHIFTS IN THE INDUSTRY DOMAIN

Figure 12.1 illustrates a general model of strategic group dynamics. As shown, this framework suggests that an innovation in strategy by some members of a strategic group can result in four different outcomes: *consolidation* (the merging of previously

FIGURE 12.1 Radical Shifts in Competitive Space

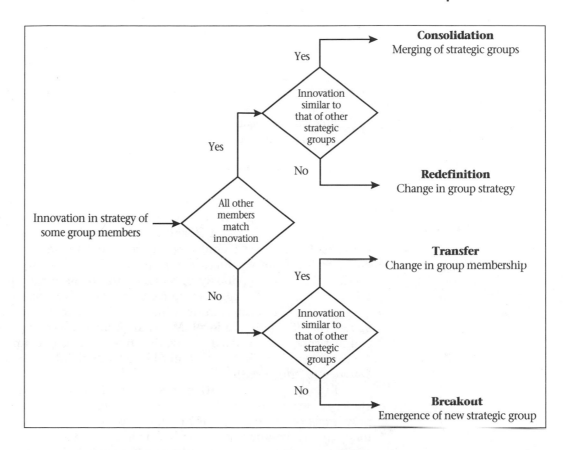

distinct strategic groups), *redefinition* (a change in group strategy), *transfer* (a change in group membership by one or more firms), and *breakout* (the emergence of a new strategic group). The ultimate outcome depends on (1) whether other group members match an initial change in strategy and (2) whether the revised strategy is similar to that of other strategic groups.

Group dynamics are initiated when organizations within a strategic group radically alter their strategy based on changing competitive or environmental conditions. If all other members of the group match the innovation in strategy, the outcome will be an overall shift in strategy or group redefinition. In essence, each participant within the group adopts the innovator's initiative, shifting the entire group to a different strategic base of competition. Depending upon context, this dynamic may be viewed as a loss of some asymmetric competitive advantage or the inability of the innovating firm to build in barriers of entry or switching costs. Such effects may be attributable to regulatory influences, stage of industry (or product) life cycle, or the acquired ability of industry competitors to duplicate unique structural or technological attributes. A potential scenario within the context of IT-based initiatives is the obligatory use of an innovation for continued competitive viability. In some instances, a redefined basis of competition can become unfavorable for the innovator if other members of the strategic group are able to compete more effectively in the new domain through superior or unique resources (Segars & Grover, 1996; Kettinger, Teng, & Guha, 1994; Vitale, 1986). Similarly, many IT-based change initiatives that are easily duplicated may become strategic necessities rather than sources of competitive advantage as other group participants quickly integrate the technology into the fabric of their business activity.

If an initial change in strategy parallels the strategy of another strategic group and if all other members of the initial group follow, then a reduction in the total number of strategic groups or consolidation occurs. If only a subset of firms within a strategic group adopts a strategic orientation that is parallel to that of another strategic group, membership shifts or transfer occurs. In both instances, emergent changes may reflect an intentional radical shift through development of improved technological or resource capabilities, acquired abilities through merger or acquisition, and/or expanded scope through market growth. From a rational perspective of competitive positioning, transfer or consolidation should occur in the most profitable strategic groups until a more profitable base of competition emerges.

Consistent with this notion, innovative use of IT may allow an organization or group of organizations to realize efficiencies in production and/or distribution that are similar to other, more profitable strategic groups. A widely cited example of this phenomenon is American Hospital Supply's (AHS) ASAP system (Short & Venkatraman, 1992). This technology allowed AHS to compete directly with Johnson & Johnson (J&J) for the lucrative medical and surgical supply market—a strategic direction that was previously untenable due to the large market presence and enormous resources of J&J. A more contemporary example of this phenomenon is the emergence of Amazon.com as a distributor of books, videos, and CDs in the retail space. At the wholesale level, Marshall Industries (marshall.com), as well as chemconnect.com, has utilized innovative business design and IT to become powerful channel members in the distribution of industrial products (El Sawy et al., 1999; Downes & Mui, 1998).

Finally, if an innovation in strategy does not parallel the strategy of another strategic group and if all other members of the innovator's group do not follow, a new basis of competition or breakout occurs. In this instance, the innovating firm forges a new competitive basis that is not viable and/or desirable for other members of the strategic group. Depending on the profitability and/or market strength of the emergent group as well as the sustainability of the new competitive position, this phenomenon may be evidence of competitive advantage. This competitive asymmetry is realized as firms acquire unique resources and skills as well as develop new and more lucrative bases of competition that are unattainable by other industry participants. If these bases are maintained through high entry barriers and/or high switching costs, then industry structure should remain relatively stable after breakout. However, if entry barriers are of short-term duration, then transfer and/or consolidation may follow breakout as individual organizations and/or entire groups migrate toward the more profitable basis of competition.

From the perspective of IT-based competitive positioning, benefits resulting from an innovative application of IT can be more readily defended if the system exploits unique resources of the innovating firm so that competitors cannot fully benefit from imitation. Differences in vertical integration, diversification, and resource quality may all be complementary resources that can be leveraged through innovative application of IT. Duplication or imitation of systems that exploit these unique structural attributes is difficult because such resources are developed over time and are not easily changed or acquired.

BASES OF RADICAL STRATEGIC POSITIONING THROUGH IT

Given a framework for describing the structure and dynamics of industries, an important consideration becomes the identification of competitive profiles that are enabled or influenced by the deployment of IT intended to create or respond to radical change. In other words, a basis for strategic grouping that captures the specific impact of IT in radically repositioning organizations within the competitive domain must be developed. Although the impacts of IT are varied, three major concepts seem to underlie comparative dynamics within the realm of IT-based competition. These bases are *efficiency, market power,* and *sustainability* (Bakos & Treacy, 1986).

Efficiency refers to the ability of participant firms to maximize outputs for a given set of inputs. Radical applications of IT may affect industrywide efficiency through economics of production—most likely through changes in economies of scale, scope, and specialization. IT can be used to reduce the basic transaction costs involved in the vertical flow of goods and services along a supply chain and/or to coordinate resources in similar or complementary activities in different supply chains. Evidence of these effects may be directly observed through comparison of production cost data (cost of goods sold, inventory turnover, employees to sales) among strategic groups. *Market power* refers to the ability of the firm to resolve competitive situations to its advantage. IT can affect this power (or competitive rivalry in general) by requiring substantial technological investment, changing the costs of entry, and/or altering the relation between fixed and variable costs. Measures related to the nature and changes in market power include scope characteristics such as market share, assets, and sales as well as measures of excess profits (or slack resources). The final characteristic, *sustainability,* refers to the ability of industry groups to preserve superior efficiencies, product characteristics, and/or economic returns over time (Feeny & Ives, 1990). IT may enhance or reduce sustainability, depending on the ability of competitors to copy the innovator's technology. This ability may be largely influenced by the existence and quality of strategic resources (resources that can be uniquely leveraged with IT) possessed by the innovator.

Together, these three bases of IT impact (efficiency, market power, sustainability) and four industry dynamics (consolidation, transfer, redefinition, breakout) form a lens for understanding how the nexus of IT and unique business design can radically alter the competitive space.[1] We believe it is of utmost importance to use frameworks such as this to build a common dialogue and systematic approach to assessing radical change. Once the organization identifies potential threats or exploitable opportunities within the competitive space, programs of radical change within the organization can be readily rationalized and then rallied around a common theme. Furthermore, the organization itself can be assessed for the required capabilities to meet emerging competitive challenges. In the next section, we develop a view of radical change as discontinuity within the organization and across the supply chain. Our objective is to cast the organization as a portfolio and trajectory of change propositions aligned with emerging changes in the competitive space.

RADICAL IT-BASED CHANGE AS DISCONTINUITY WITHIN THE ORGANIZATION AND ACROSS THE SUPPLY CHAIN

The notion of worldwide networks of interconnected computers that behave as a single entity has been until recently more science fiction than reality. But high-speed networks, client-server computing, and enterprise software have created an infrastructure capable of consolidating the islands of software, data, and hardware that characterize the platforms of most organizations. Users of information technology can now be presented the illusion of a single powerful computer rather than a collection of disparate machines. These revolutions in technology enable the enterprise to coordinate and reconcile formerly disparate operations and truly coordinate its worldwide activities. Furthermore, the scope of IT-based collaboration and coordination has expanded from the isolated organization to collections of organizations or the supply chain.

While this promise is attractive, the challenges facing organizations that embark on such transformations are daunting. Organizational operations as well as the operations of supply-chain partners are often designed on technological and competitive assumptions that are no longer valid. For example, many operations are designed to function optimally within a local geographic context. Structures and technology that are optimized for such federations are often suboptimal when incorporated as a part of a fully integrated entity. Contrary to expectations, the barriers that inhibit realization of integrated operations across supply chains are largely organizational and managerial rather than technical. Therefore, it is imperative for managers to understand and effectively manage the interactions created by emerging information technologies and new forms of competition. Because information technologies eliminate buffers in time, space, and inventory, operations become very tightly coupled, which, in turn, can stifle efforts to orchestrate organizational change (Dean & Snell, 1996). Therefore, many organizations may find themselves paralyzed in the aftermath of a radical shift in the competitive space. In essence, many of the organizational capabilities that were an advantage turn into a competitive disadvantage.

To understand how and when radical IT-based change should be orchestrated, it is useful to view the organization as a portfolio and trajectory of change propositions (Venkatraman, 1994). Figure 12.2 illustrates a model that captures seven change propositions (7CP) enabled by the nexus of IT and organizational design. Importantly, this model does not represent a linear progression of change activity within the firm. Rather, it represents a portfolio and trajectory of incremental and radical change propositions that confront many modern business enterprises. Organizations should balance investment across these change propositions with respect to prevailing shifts within the industry. In other words, the framework can be a useful perspective for correctly defining the nature and magnitude of a change effort. Often a program of process improvement is cast as radical change when in fact it is incremental change. It is also entirely possible that the change effort lacks a context or trajectory for its rationalization and reconciliation. Again, the 7CP model provides the context needed for legitimizing the change proposition. The model is also useful in recognizing how much change the organization is capable of successfully addressing. Viewing radical change as a trajectory provides a forecasting mechanism for developing and maintaining critical organizational capabilities. In the following sections, we further develop the definition of the 7CP framework.

As illustrated in Figure 12.2, two dimensions demarcate the definitional space of seven distinct change propositions. The vertical axis denotes the range of organizational/technological discontinuity introduced by the change proposition. Range of discontinuity is the degree of departure from known or experienced patterns of management and operations. In general two planes, radical and incremental, define this space. An incremental discontinuity is a migration, refinement, (re)design, or improvement in understood and institutionalized patterns of business. A radical discontinuity is a reinvention or fundamental shift away from understood and well-rationalized patterns of management and operations. The horizontal axis represents the reach of organizational/technological discontinuity introduced by the change propositions. Reach of organizational/technological discontinuity represents

FIGURE 12.2   Seven Organizational Change Propositions

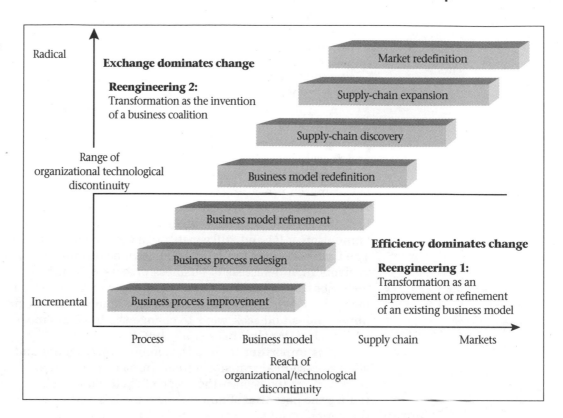

the span or scope of business processes and relationships that are encompassed by the change proposition. As shown, this level of discontinuity can occur within a process, a business model, a supply chain, or a product/service market.

Together, these dimensions provide a context for understanding seven critical change propositions that face many organizations. Three of these change propositions, a *business process improvement, business process redesign,* and *business model refinement,* are incremental in nature and will be discussed only briefly in this chapter.[2] The remaining four *(business model redefinition, supply-chain discovery, supply-chain expansion,* and *market redefinition)* are radical change propositions and represent a very new and challenging frontier to many forward-thinking managers. Rather than create another term or managerial buzzword for distinguishing these change propositions, we demarcate the incremental set of propositions as Reengineering 1 and the radical set as Reengineering 2 to denote the evolutionary nature of the change ideas and to differentiate between the level of change and, hence, the level of organizational commitment necessary to achieve success.

REENGINEERING 1: INCREMENTAL CHANGE PROPOSITIONS

The foundations for the sets of change propositions we term Reengineering 1 (R1) are the total quality movement and early research and methodologies within BPR. In general, early work in BPR suggested "changing the aircraft engines while the plane flies" or "obliterate rather than automate" (Hammer & Champy, 1993). While the radicalness of this idea was initially compelling, later work in the area suggested a more moderate approach and a more realistic set of expectations for reengineering efforts

(Davenport, 1994). In fact, many organizations and consulting firms now consider R1 to be a commodity with many well-established methodologies and techniques for its implementation. This is largely due to the recasting of R1 as a focused effort and the availability of proven techniques for process improvement from TQM (Kettinger, Teng, & Guha, 1997; Kettinger, Harkness, & Segars, 1997).

As illustrated in Figure 12.2, three change propositions constitute R1. The least radical of these change ideas is business process improvement. In this effort, a process or small set of business processes is primarily improved through monitoring and incremental change. The next proposition in terms of complexity is business process redesign. In these efforts, business process is either created or redesigned to better match prevailing competitive needs. The boundary of this effort is within the organization and is typically focused on a set of core processes that are considered high impact and critical to the functioning of the organization. Such efforts form the foundation of R1 and still constitute a large portion of organizational change efforts. The final component of R1 is business model refinement. Within this stage, the pervasiveness and success of business process redesign and business process improvement set the stage for refinement of the larger business model. Importantly, this is more than hyper-BPR. In this stage, organizations begin to adopt new operating philosophies and seek ways to change the business model to leverage the efforts of BPR and TQM (Harkness et al., 1997).

It is important to note that many practitioners and scholars may mistake R1 efforts as radical transformation. In fact, many organizations may mistakenly declare victory too soon if the scope of their change effort is anchored in R1. To fully realize the potential of new business models and IT, organizations must look beyond the boundary of their organization and into the network of suppliers, the suppliers of suppliers, the customers, and the customers of customers. Transformation in this context is radical in nature, yet it also builds on the principles and learnings of R1. Therefore, we term these types of change propositions R2 and describe them in the following section.

REENGINEERING 2: RADICAL CHANGE PROPOSITIONS

An important contextual property of literature and practice surrounding R1 is the assumption that narrow and stable collections of suppliers and customers are the optimal form of supply-chain design. The foundation for this belief is both operational and technological. From the operational viewpoint, a narrow space of customers and suppliers facilitates the mechanics of just-in-time (JIT) inventory. In essence, JIT principles can be easily implemented within a tightly integrated collection of firms with long histories of compatible transactions, operating philosophies, and market dynamics. In a best-case scenario, the supply chain realizes savings from reduced holding of inventory without sacrificing order-winning criteria such as product quality and time to delivery.

From a technological perspective, early assumptions surrounding business processes reflect very closed forms of network architectures. Proprietary and inflexible technologies that have evolved over a number of years within firms are assumed to be the most efficient means of establishing electronic ordering and billing across business enterprises. Such systems are often referred to as electronic data interchange (EDI) or interorganizational systems (IOS) (Grover, 1993). Because of these operational and technological assumptions, many business enterprises have adopted a silo approach to organizational design. Each distinct line of business (LOB) is organized as a self-sustaining collection of data, processes, knowledge, and business models. Such organization allows each LOB to develop a system of technologies and business processes that are well aligned with the customer and supplier bases prevalent within the competitive sector. In theory, the cost efficiencies of integrated production within an LOB greatly exceed any inefficiency that is generated by lack of integration in process and technology between LOBs.

Two closely related disruptions have altered the logic underlying traditional business models. Driven primarily by Y2K and productivity concerns, organizations have begun questioning the assumptions and costs underlying their IT infrastructure. Specifically, the openness of client-server technology and the emergence of enterprise software have the potential to favorably shift the cost structure of IT within many firms. To drive down the increasing costs of maintenance and applications development across LOBs, many organizations have attempted to reconcile infrastructure through common process, integrated data, and common software applications. Many of these same organizations are also utilizing Web technologies as an open "front-end" interface to customers as well as a "back-end" interface to suppliers. In essence, IT has become a catalyst for integrating and reconciling the operations within organizational silos. Achievement of such integration is now viewed as a more economical and maintainable model of IT infrastructure. Importantly, the development of these infrastructures is more easily accomplished in organizations without long histories of IT use or deeply imbedded business processes. Therefore, the initiative of a dynamic within the competitive space becomes easier for the less-established organization—a reversal of traditional business thinking.

A second disruption driving new organizational models is customer expectation. Increasingly, customers are demanding that suppliers exhibit "one face" in the procurement of products and services, even if the product is delivered by several LOBs. For example, a network solution may consist of routers from one LOB, a wireless network from another LOB, and a PBX switch from still another LOB. Rather than engage the customer with several processes and transactions for completing the sale, the supplying firm must give the customer a single entry point as well as the information necessary for developing the product specifications, cost, and delivery date. Obviously, such a proposition demands that organizations integrate data, expertise, process, and technology across LOBs and throughout the supply chain. As illustrated in Figure 12.3, this new business model is termed the "networked enterprise" and is the hallmark of R2 change propositions. In short, such a model represents a radical change for the business enterprise because underlying assumptions of competition, technology, and organizational design are dramatically shifted.

Business model refinement is the most radical change idea of R1 propositions. Such efforts are focused within a particular LOB and still support the traditional model of organization around production efficiencies and narrow supply chain channels. In contrast, business model redefinition attempts to integrate data, process, IT, and expertise across the organization's LOBs. Most commonly, these efforts are recognizable as ERP or knowledge management projects. In both instances, the overriding objective is to introduce efficiencies in operation through a common model of business crafted through common process and integrated IT. While the advantages of such efforts are clearly recognizable, the actual problems in implementation have been legendary. Such change is often viewed as a direct threat to "proven" business models within LOBs. In some instances, these LOBs have ongoing R1 projects and view

FIGURE 12.3
Reengineering 2:
Building the Networked
Enterprise

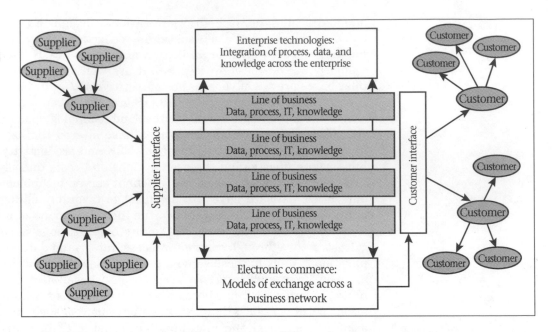

another round of reengineering as frivolous. This creates an interesting dynamic of using one reengineering effort to resist another! In other instances, disagreements over the best process for accomplishing a common task across LOBs force implementers to forge technology support of two rival models, thereby driving up cost. Clearly, this change proposition can cause many organizations to engage in a tug of war between overcustomization of the IT infrastructure, which in turn drives up development costs, and undercustomization of the IT infrastructure, which in turn dilutes effective processes. However, successful redefinition of the business model can lead to a common process and IT infrastructure for common business activity across LOBs as well as unique process models within each LOB that are effectively leveraged with IT.

As illustrated in Figure 12.3, the network enterprise model also recognizes the need for expanding the change idea of business model redefinition into the larger business network of the supply chain. The technological driver of this change proposition is the open architecture of World Wide Web (W3) technology. Developing effective mechanisms for this exchange involves development of front- and back-end interfaces that can readily exchange and process information within and between organizations. While such systems have typically been the domain of complex EDI systems, "open" W3 technology allows the organization to simplify development efforts and provide customers with the capability to access and manipulate data deep in the corporate archives. Transferring the change idea imbedded in the business model redefinition into the business models of suppliers and customers is the change proposition of supply-chain discovery.

Similar to business model redefinition, expansion of integrated activity into the supply chain is complex due to the diversity of processes and IT that characterize most business coalitions. Typically, the organization responds to this complexity by embarking on a program of supply-chain discovery. Suppliers and customers that are most closely aligned with the organization in terms of IT and process are integrated into a supply-chain coalition that attempts to realize efficiencies in production and cost through coordinated activity. Interestingly, such a coalition is very similar to the

R1 change proposition of business model refinement. However, in this instance, the silos of data, process, IT, and expertise are removed (or at least reconciled) across LOBs, facilitating vertical coordination across the enterprise (as illustrated in Figure 12.3) and horizontal coordination across a very narrow supply chain. Typically, such projects are recognizable as an "extranet" that links an organization with other business partners through W3 technology.

Again, many complexities can inhibit the progress of supply-chain discovery. Process complexities such as contract formulation, accounting systems, and conflicting business models can quickly escalate the cost and time required to successfully integrate business activity. On a global basis, culture-based differences in data collection, operating philosophy, and process development can also inhibit supply-chain discovery. In many instances, the initiating organization discovers that the network of potential business partners is far less sophisticated in terms of process development and IT infrastructure. This is a potentially dangerous set of circumstances because the efficiency of the supply chain can be "bottlenecked" by a single partner or set of partners who are not well versed in R1 philosophy but want to be a key component of the R2 effort. In such instances, the initiating organization may find it necessary to invest resources to help the coalition reach a stable level of process and IT infrastructure capability. Again, this state of affairs may necessitate a rather narrow set of partners for sophisticated transactions implying a more hierarchically oriented sourcing structure (Malone, Yates, & Benjamin, 1987). However, many organizations are now looking to expand the supply chain and create more market-oriented or "virtual" forms of sourcing and selling arrangements. Such change efforts are very radical in nature and are characteristic of the change proposition we term supply-chain expansion.

Supply-chain expansion recognizes the inherent value in market-based transactions. Rather than center the supply chain on product, this organizational form centers the supply chain on information and expertise (knowledge) about product and service offerings. Rather than constrain the coalition to a narrow set of members, the organization attempts to become virtual—sourcing products and services from the marketplace of potential vendors (Venkatraman & Henderson, 1998). In many respects, this change proposition seeks to create a "plug-and-play" capability across the supply chain. By searching for price data across the domain of suppliers or participating in online auctions, the organization seeks to expand the frontier of options with respect to buying and selling products/services. On the supply end of the operation, such a proposition radically changes the needed skills and processes that surround the procurement function. Procurement managers must carefully balance quality and reliability of suppliers with cost. On the customer end of the operation, the firm's sales and production managers must carefully consider cost and scheduling considerations before bidding on new contracts. In the case of an auction-based selling proposition, integration of process and data across the enterprise are critical in developing a proposal that is realistic and profitable. In an environment of electronic procurement, the time span of these decisions continues to be shortened and the range of potential bidders continues to be larger.

Perhaps the best definition of the supply chain expansion proposition is offered by Venkatraman and Henderson (1998, p. 34). These authors describe virtual organizing as

> a strategic approach that is singularly focused on creating, nurturing, and deploying key intellectual and knowledge assets while sourcing tangible, physical assets in a complex world.

Similar to the arguments of this chapter, these authors depart from the incremental notions of R1 that are based in the economics of the Industrial Age and suggest that new technological and business assumptions have created the possibility for entirely new forms of commerce and organizational design. Somewhat differently from these authors, we do not place IT solely at the center of these efforts. Instead, we view the nexus of IT and creative organizational design as the driver and centerpiece for R2. As noted by a senior executive of a firm undergoing these changes, a technology story is often woven for R2 types of initiatives—particularly supply-chain expansion. In such a story, IT is viewed as the target that the business should be driven toward. In other words, the parameters and capabilities of IT form the foundation for a new business model. All too often, such stories spell disaster when unique capabilities as well as designed advantages of the business cannot be accommodated by IT. Another perspective is a process story in which IT is driven toward a model of business. However, as noted earlier, customizations in the IT implementation drive up cost and development time, thereby hampering the objectives and efficacy of the supply-chain coalition and, more importantly, limiting the potential to create a market structure. Clearly, some middle ground or emergent perspective is needed to balance the extremes of these stories. Therefore, while IT is certainly a key component of the virtual organization, it can become an inhibitor without creative process design and a clear vision for the trajectory and outcomes of the change proposition.

The final change proposition of the 7CP framework is market redefinition. In this stage, the organization along with its virtual network of partners attempts to redefine the very nature of markets in terms of customer expectations, product/service offerings, logistics, and underlying economics. Consistent with the dynamics illustrated in Figure 12.1, the organization attempts to create disruption within the competitive space through a shift in strategic orientation. As noted earlier, IT-based competition offers enormous opportunity and presents incredible risk to modern enterprises. Once an industry king, Microsoft is now seeing the assumptions and price economics of its marketplace in operating systems being changed by the Linux "open-source" model of software development (Raymond, 1999). The leader of this effort, Redhat.com, has adopted a model of software development that follows two revolutionary principles: (1) release early and often and (2) delegate everything you can. This model creates a process of software development that resembles a bazaar of different agendas and approaches that seemingly form a coherent and stable system. Rather than focus on a manufacturing-based philosophy of creating software, Redhat focuses its efforts on being a source of expertise and knowledge about operating software. In essence, it gives away the operating system software and sells its expertise and knowledge. While such a business model can be readily supported by the process and IT infrastructure of Redhat, this proposition presents an enormous change proposition to Microsoft and other software houses.

Together, the change propositions outlined in the framework of Figure 12.2 provide a trajectory for organizations seeking to understand how their change efforts are aligned with changes in competitive positioning illustrated in Figure 12.1. Any of the described shifts in competitive space can be a stimulus for examining programs of change within the organization. The potential consolidation of strategic groups may be a precursor for lower profit margins, suggesting that the organization shift its efforts from R1 to R2. An entire strategic group may find that it needs to redefine its competitive space through R2 efforts. For pioneers, R2 efforts may facilitate the transfer from one strategic group to another or a complete breakout to a new competitive space. Importantly, the frameworks illustrate the diversity of change efforts possible within the organization and provide a better context for understanding the evolving nature of reengineering and radical change efforts across markets and within the organization. We believe that to meet the challenges of IT-based transformation, organizations must develop key capabilities. We also believe that distinct managerial roles are required to successfully manage radical change. In the next section, we outline the nature of these capabilities and roles as a framework for helping IT and general managers navigate the complex nexus of IT and radical change.

ORGANIZATIONAL CAPABILITIES AND ROLES FOR MANAGING RADICAL IT-BASED CHANGE

A key part of managing radical change is determining whether the organization has the energy or capability for the change effort. Assessing organizational readiness is as important as determining the technological feasibility of the change proposition (Leonard, 1998; Benjamin & Levinson, 1993). Table 12.1 outlines key organizational capabilities and managerial roles that are associated with successful orchestration of IT-based radical change. Many of these capabilities appear in various forms in both popular and academic literature (Markus & Benjamin, 1996, 1997); we have also observed these capabilities "firsthand" within organizations that are

TABLE 12.1   Key Organizational Capabilities and Managerial Roles for Managing IT-Based Radical Change

Organizational Capability	Managerial Role	Failure Outcome	Mid-Ground Outcome	Success Outcome
Discovery	Explorer	All signals of impending discontinuities are ignored.	Signals of discontinuity send the organization into a state of alert.	Signals of discontinuity are detected early and an appropriate response is formulated.
Resolve	Gatekeeper	Decisions and direction are slow due to internal conflicts—based in fantasy.	Decisions and direction are slow due to external complexities.	Decisions and direction are timely and accurate—based in fact.
Resources	Advocate	Critical resources to address effort are lacking.	Resources to address effort are limited.	Resources are readily available for response.
Articulation and communication	Facilitator	Commitment and understanding are lacking. No vision or theme for the change effort is communicated.	Vision and theme lag the effort. Effort precedes the articulation of the objective.	Forces are mobilized for common good across organizational boundaries.
Assessment	Scorekeeper	Metrics and performance standards are not developed. Decision making is not guided by objectivity.	Metrics and performance standards are reconciled for some but not all "key" dimensions of effort.	Metrics and performance standards are an integrated part of the change effort and guide decision making.
Learning	Teacher	No learning occurs. The organization repeats mistakes.	Learning occurs but the dissemination is spotty.	Lessons are applied to future incidents.

successful in addressing the challenges of the 7CP illustrated in Figure 12.2. Our framework attempts to unify these concepts along with associated managerial roles as a means of assessing organizational and managerial predisposition for successful transformation.

DISCOVERY

Traditionally, managers and academics have attributed great importance to scanning the environment for key information and trends. However, many organizations scan diligently but are still caught completely unaware of dramatic changes in their competitive space. Clearly, the ability to read the "competitive tea leaves" is important and is something more than merely collecting and disseminating information. In the organizations that most effectively manage radical change, the capability of discovery is a noticeable characteristic. Discovery is a proactive process of analysis (investigation and breakdown of events, information, trends, and other forms of intelligence), synthesis (integrating and reconciling information and intelligence), and thesis (developing assertions and hypotheses) with respect to information and trends that impact the organization's competitive domain. Effective organizations are able to rapidly reconcile a variety of competitive queues such as events, sector data, economic figures, and the industry grapevine to build a picture of how their competitive space is changing. This capability creates a mechanism for structuring a common dialogue about change and sharing this knowledge throughout the organization.

As shown in Table 12.1, organizations can vary in their outcomes with respect to discovery. In some organizations, impending discontinuities can be completely ignored. In many instances, this lack of awareness can be explained by a corporate "radar screen" that is simply too narrow. In other words, many organizations define their competitive domain in such narrow terms (or completely misdefine it) that any potential discontinuity is not registered. A classic example of these phenomena occurred when Microsoft initially failed to understand that Netscape's Web browser was a new form of operating system. In its early stages, the Web browser seemed to be a completely different technology than an operating system. However, as the Internet evolved into intra- and Internet, Microsoft's competitive space shifted drastically. As evidenced by Microsoft's reemergence in browser technology, the organizations best able to manage transformation know that the competitive radar screen must be robust and must be questioned constantly. Recently, IBM has undergone a rethinking of its competitive space by moving its core offerings to a service- rather than manufacturing-based framework. This shift has enormous competitive implications for Dell, Compaq, and other manufacturers of PCs and servers. As these and many other organizations have discovered, it becomes very difficult to build credibility for a change effort if management is constantly misreading or not accurately defining the competitive space.

Another potential problem in building a capability for discovery is a lack of effective knowledge transfer among managerial constituencies. However, it is important to note that discovery is more than good knowledge management. We have observed firms that are wonderful in transferring knowledge; however, if the knowledge domain is too narrow or if the effort is not a proactive process of unearthing competitive trends, then the outcomes are less than satisfactory. Typically, radical shifts in the industry send these organizations into a state of alert. While such an outcome is certainly better than complete ignorance of discontinuity, it complicates the transformation effort by compressing the time frame for garnering necessary direction and resources for orchestrating change. A natural outgrowth of this is a more complicated and costly effort to redirect the organization.

As noted in Table 12.1, organizations that exhibit strong capabilities of discovery are able to detect discontinuity early and quickly form an appropriate response. A distinct managerial role within these organizations is that of explorer. Rather than simply react to events or ponder reports, managers are challenged to explore how the competitive space is changing and how the company can successfully maneuver within the chaos. Managers must become inquisitive, instinctive, and yet objective in framing the competitive landscape. Mapping techniques similar to Figure 12.1 are a useful aid in such endeavors because they implicitly recognize that industry boundaries are blurring and that changes in competitive structure are dynamic. Furthermore, these techniques bring needed rationalization and reconciliation to strategic planners who seek to understand shifting competitive domains. The key to discovery is to build a consistent and common dialogue about change that can be used to uncover how IT and new business models are redefining or altering competition.

RESOLVE

In many organizations, resources and managerial attention may be focused simultaneously on TQM, BPR, and several other programs designed to improve performance. Related to Figure 12.2, the firm may be engaged in forms of R1 and R2 as it attempts to favorably position itself in the competitive space. An important key to a successful transformation effort is not to attend to each piece in isolation. Instead, the organization must connect and balance the pieces, understanding how changing one element changes the rest and how sequencing and pace affect the entire structure. We term this capability *resolve* and define it as the drive, determination, and resolution the organization builds for achieving the change objective through its decision making. In some organizations, lack of commitment for the change effort is readily evident in the passive and inconsistent decision making of managerial leaders. Those charged with making the change may become reluctant to implement a change agenda if they believe the organization will not embrace or "get behind" a change proposition.

Organizational resolve is created when managers set direction through timely and accurate decisions based on fact. These decisions create a form of credible communication within and between managerial constituencies that facilitate momentum and enthusiasm for radical change propositions. In many organizations, a lack of resolve is evidenced through a disinterest or lack of top-management support for IT-based change, the absence of a vision or focus for change projects, the lack of a managerial champion, or the lack of alignment between IT and strategy. In these instances, critical decision-making activity may be slow or nonexistent because of enormous internal conflicts. A natural outcome of this is a collection of change initiatives that have no common theme or direction. In one organization of our study, a CIO remarked that critical decisions are often encapsulated in a "hot-potato" e-mail that is passed throughout the managerial hierarchy. These decision points are rarely recognized and are not acted upon in a timely manner in this organization because managers have the ability to hide behind their stacks of e-mail messages. These delays in decision making and signaling of uncertainty to the organizational constituency have repeatedly hampered attempts to maneuver in a fast-moving industry.

A key managerial role in building organizational resolve is that of a gatekeeper. In successful organizations, managers embrace the idea that their decisions rather than their words define the direction, momentum, and, most importantly, the legitimacy of the change effort. To make a radical change effort credible and sustain critical momentum, managers must be willing to develop velocity in making decisions and create a common theme for the change initiatives within the organization. In the absence of these managerial interventions, the collection of change propositions can actually work against each other. In a company we have studied for the past few years, an R1-based change project for materials management within manufacturing was in direct conflict with an R2 project for customer ordering and billing that was underway in marketing and sales. In essence, the optimization of a manufacturing process within the organization suboptimized the larger process of selling across the supply chain. Clearly, organizational complexity and lack of resolve can create change propositions that are in direct conflict.

Along with velocity in decision making, the change effort must have a "face" in the form of a champion or senior management team who reconciles events and information associated with change and sets direction accordingly. As a gatekeeper, the manager or management team acts a clearinghouse of knowledge, policy, and decisions that is recognizable, accessible, and decisive. In several instances, a noticeable deterrent to orchestrating radical IT-based change is the lack of a "face" or recognizable managerial team charged with building the resolve necessary to sustain the program of transformation.

RESOURCES

Often organizations underestimate or simply do not appreciate the magnitude of resource commitment necessary for successful transformation. The key resources necessary for radical IT-based change are technological, financial, and intellectual. As many organizations have discovered, IT alone is not sufficient in creating a desired direction in strategy. In fact, many observers attribute the seemingly inverse association between IT spending and productivity to a lack of know-how in aligning IT with business opportunities and uncovering business opportunity enabled by IT. Garnering a base of expertise in designing and implementing IT that has a compelling business case is a critical resource in driving radical change. In some instances, this expertise is developed within the organization through training or executive development courses. In other instances, business partners provide the needed expertise. In most instances of successful transformation observed in our research, there is an underlying belief that driving radical change is a "contact sport" as well as a feat of IT engineering. As noted by one executive, "Without a good idea, IT is a collection of wires, circuits, and disks." People who can provide such ideas represent a key element of creating a resource capability necessary for successful competition.

Along with intellectual resources, organizations must amass adequate financial and technological assets to successfully address transformation challenges. From the perspective of technology, it is important for firms to develop architectures that ensure flexibility and adaptability. For many organizations, this translates into a move away from proprietary network and data storage architectures to open standards such as Web-based TCP/IP. As illustrated in Figure 12.2, R2 types of change propositions require the integration of technology across many partners in the supply chain. Therefore, the development of systems involves the coordination of IT specialists within and across organizational boundaries. Without an IT architecture that is adaptable, the organization can find itself isolated from potential partnerships and opportunities.

A final critical resource necessary for managing change is financial asset. Organizations must be willing to view IT-based organizational change as an investment in a new strategic direction rather than another system implementation. If the change effort is starved of financial resources in its early stages, the benefits of the change proposition are likely to be extremely limited, thereby undermining the credibility of such change efforts among members of the organization. The cost to restart a project that has been stalled by resource shortages is significant, and reinitiating the project is sometimes viewed as indecision about priorities and direction by management (in other words, a lack of resolve). Organizations must be willing to take a leap of faith in change efforts by investing the resources needed to get the initiative off the ground. Investing limited resources as a "seed" for a change proposition tends to starve the effort at its most critical stage. A key managerial role for creating the needed resource base is that of an advocate. Managers must promote the needed change proposition as well as solicit and defend the resources needed to support the initiative.

ARTICULATION AND COMMUNICATION

In many instances, the lack of communication is cited as a major inhibitor in transformation efforts. Ideally, established lines of communication facilitate information exchange about organizational direction and the role of IT in supporting new strategic initiatives. A somewhat surprising finding among companies we have examined is that high levels of corporate communication (as defined by these firms) do not always facilitate successful IT-based change. In fact, some firms that believe they communicate extraordinarily well point to this attribute as a potential inhibitor in their efforts to change, particularly if no clearly defined change message has been developed. A likely resolution of this paradox is to more clearly define the process of communication as a process of articulation (creating an embraceable dialogue about the change effort) and communication (disseminating the change message through the organization). Without this capability, change propositions will lack an identity or theme that is needed for creating a sense of urgency among organizational members and building legitimacy for the change idea. In organizations that are semisuccessful in building a vision, a significant portion of the change effort will precede the articulation of an objective. While not as bad as having no vision at all, transformations of this type are needlessly long and costly. In the best case, articulation and communication mobilize forces for the change effort across organizational boundaries.

As implied in the prior section, a fundamental task for managers is to create a strategy map with which organization members can readily identify. A broadly defined strategic initiative must be guided, clarified, and given concrete meaning. The development of a compelling vision builds commitment and a common goal. A key managerial role associated with this capability seems to be that of a facilitator. In general, such managers tend to focus their efforts on building awareness, quelling rumors, and forging relationships to facilitate the successful implementation of the change proposition. The overriding objective is to link or meld the identities of various subunits into the organization's emerging new identity. The view of the facilitator is that most resistance is normal and rational and can be effectively managed if understood. Effective facilitators believe that the single largest opportunity for moving a change effort forward is to understand sources of resistance and develop explicit contingency plans for its management.

ASSESSMENT

Measurement and accountability seem to be a hallmark of successful transformation efforts. Organizations with a history and capability for developing benchmarks and other performance criteria that are consistently reconciled with organizational performance can readily formulate contingency plans and direct resources to better orchestrate their change efforts. In the worst case, organizations fail to develop appropriate metrics for assessing change. A very common example of this phenomenon is the use of financial metrics to assess the progress and impact of change. Within a global manufacturer familiar to the author(s), all IT-related depreciation was accumulated in the budget of the IT department. When benchmarked against competitors, the corporate IT expenditure appeared 8% higher that the industry average, yet no discernible competitive advantage was evident through the seemingly heavy IT expenditures. Top management immediately cut IT spending by 20% while major transformation projects were underway in supply-chain management. After a tumultuous first quarter, it was discovered that most participants in the industry charged depreciation to the departments that were serviced by IT. When adjusted for this effect, the firm found that its IT budget was actually 6% below the industry average before the 20% cut in the IT budget. While such a mistake seems alarming, many organizations take a very similar and mistake-prone approach to assessing their change efforts. Financial metrics are impacted by many events and may not provide an accurate view of progress, particularly in the early stages of the change initiative.

Clearly, another very important determinant of assessing IT performance is the frame through which organizational operations are assessed. In many organizations, assessment is framed through traditional cost accounting. This perspective is centered on fixed and variable costs, break-even analysis, and a direct labor-centric product costing philosophy. The underlying assumption of this model is that total product or service cost is the sum of the costs of individual operations. The primary audience of such performance assessment is assumed to be government, stockholders, and creditors, while the secondary audience is assumed to be line managers.

In contrast, many organizations that have successfully navigated the challenges of R2 change propositions have centered their performance management on an activity-based view of cost and benefit. This model represents both a different concept of the business process and different ways of measuring. Its basic premise is that manufacturing is an integrated process that spans supply-chain activity. Unlike traditional costing, the technique records the cost of *not* doing tasks such as the cost of machine or network downtime, the cost of waiting for needed information, or the cost of inventory waiting to be shipped. Many of these activities are directly associated to the capabilities and promise of IT. Therefore, activity-based accounting not only yields better cost control and result control but also can be directly related to IT-based initiatives in tangible terms. Working within this framework, it is easier to assess the direct impact of IT-based initiatives and identify new opportunities for deployment of IT.

Table 12.2 illustrates process-based assessment within a progressive firm. As shown, performance is stratified across dimensions of time, quality, and cost. Key process measurements of these three dimensions are benchmarked against the

TABLE 12.2 Process-Based Performance Assessment: Time, Quality, Cost

		Business Unit Score Card					
		Operations Performance vs. Industry					
Key Measurements	Unit	Major Opportunity	Disadvantage	Industry Average	Advantage	Superior	Proposed Target
Time Bid management cycle time							
Standard	Days			11 Days	10 Days	3 Days	4 Days
Nonstandard	Days	NA	17 Days	13 Days		7 Days	5 Days
Network	Days			NA		NA	14 Days
Order fullfillment lead time	Days		119 Days	96 Days		51 Days	90 Days
Upside flexibility	Days			92 Days	82 Days	33 Days	28 Days
Delivery to request date	%	NA		60%		95%	75%
Cash to cash (includes R&D)	Days		156	155 Days		125 Days	135 Days
Quality Forecast accuracy (units)	%			60%	85%	92%	92%
Delivery performance							
Delivery to committed H date	%		52%s	87%		98%	90%
Delivery to committed K date	%		75%	NA		NA	90%
Faultless installs	%		20%	*4%		98%	80%
Cost Inv days of supply (hardware)	Days			115 Days	98 Days	62 Days	80 Days
Inv days of supply (custom R&D)	Days		144 Days	NA		NA	TBD
Total pipeline cost	%		52%s	14.5%	11.6%	8.8%	TBD
Bid mgmt costs (% of prod rev)	%		75%	1.1%	.9%	.28%	TBD

industry average as a means of positioning current performance and identifying new opportunities to leverage IT. In this example, meeting the proposed targets in the final column had a potential benefit to the firm of $25 million. As this and many firms we have studied have discovered, IT-based initiatives typically manifest impact across a process rather than within a functional area. Without cost and control systems that measure such impact, assessing the performance of IT is likely to be conjecture, thereby making the management of IT subjective. In its best form, the firm should understand the costs of the entire supply chain and work actively with other business partners to manage costs and maximize yield. Likewise, the firm must assess its investment and deployment of IT within the context of process within the organization and across the supply chain.

LEARNING

The final key capability for successfully navigating radical change is learning. In general, two broad activities seem to characterize organizations rich with this capability. First, these organizations tend to be very adept at creating, acquiring, and transferring knowledge. Ideas, notions, and experiences are readily known and shared across the organization. This sharing creates a common dialogue and wellspring of information about the motivation and direction of organizational change.

A second activity that characterizes organizational learning is the application of new knowledge in the way that work is accomplished. We distinguish these two activities because some firms may be excellent in the generation of knowledge yet less than adept in its application within the fabric of business process. In short, when both knowledge transfer and application exist, the organization learns. When application is absent, only the potential for learning exists. In the context of radical IT-based change, it is imperative that organizations actively manage the learning process to ensure that it occurs by design rather than by chance.

Similar to firms described in the popular and the academic press (Garvin, 1993; Nevins, DiBella, & Gould, 1995; Leonard, 1998), organizations that are successfully navigating radical IT change seem to build unique skills in four areas: (1) systematic problem solving, (2) experimentation, (3) new understanding based on past experiences, and (4) transferring knowledge quickly and efficiently throughout the organization. We have noticed this effect to be particularly poignant in two areas, strategic planning for information technologies/systems and the development of a system for capturing and disseminating "lessons" learned. In the process for strategic planning, successful firms tend to create a process for planning that is structured, bringing a form of rationality to the activity, yet adaptive, incorporating information from a variety of sources and continuously reconciling it with strategic direction (Segars & Grover, 1999). Strategies tend to emerge as planners, sometimes individually but more often collectively, come to know a competitive context and their organization's capability for response. In other words, the task of strategic planning is viewed as a process of creating, acquiring, and transferring knowledge for the purpose of modifying IT-based initiatives so that they reflect new knowledge and insights. Over time, the organization converges on patterns of agenda and behaviors that are effective and then reconfigures these patterns for new planning challenges. The core belief of IT planners is that strategy emerges as a result of formal and continuous reconciliation of ongoing initiatives throughout the organization and associated opportunities within the competitive context. Importantly, past experiences with traditional forms of planning are not necessarily perceived as ineffective by these organizations; however, the lack of strategic reconciliation and desire to institutionalize the gathering and transfer of knowledge sources throughout the organization seem to create a belief that continuous planning can better identify avenues of innovation and adaptability needed for effective competition. Consistent with this philosophy, no single activity of strategic planning seems readily identifiable. Instead, these organizations seem to resemble a portfolio of strategic-planning initiatives and approaches that are coordinated through cross-functional teams and common project themes. These ongoing strategic-planning processes are reconciled through a formal superstructure of planning activity that is itself ongoing. Hence, the activity of planning is distributed to all levels of the organization and is formally reconciled and coordinated by senior management.

Planning behavior of advanced firms seems best described as an eclectic blend of systematic problem solving, strategic experimentation, formal reconciliation, and efficient knowledge transfer. A key piece of this effort is the codification and dissemination of "lessons learned." Relying on scientific methods for data collection and analysis, teams consisting of IS staff as well as members of other functional areas generate fact-based scenarios of current IT needs and the effectiveness of past planning efforts in meeting organizational needs. The informational products of this exercise are used to continuously refine priorities as well as improve the process for strategic planning. Experimentation also seems to be a notable trait of planning within these firms. In particular, "signature" projects that represent clear breaks from the past and embody principles and approaches that the firm hopes to adopt in the future were used as a means of generating new approaches to strategic planning and implementation. These types of projects tend to provide a useful resource for transforming superficial knowledge about strategic events into deep understanding.

As strongly implied in the previous sections, organizations that successfully manage radical change are able to quickly bring resources to bear on initiatives necessary to compete effectively. Components of knowledge management, innovation, focused decision making, and communication allow such organizations to quickly and accurately assess the competitive context. These unique forms of organizational design are enabled and leveraged with IT to allow these firms to be seamlessly networked within the organizational boundary and across the larger boundary of the supply chain. In the section that follows, we note key implications of this chapter for the research agenda of the IS community.

AN AGENDA FOR RESEARCH AND PRACTICE

Along with managerial challenges, the nexus of IT and radical change presents numerous challenges and opportunities to the community of research. Like modern organizations, the research community of IS will not sustain legitimacy by organizing its research streams into carefully crafted silos. While there is comfort and a sense of rationality that accompanies a bounded research domain, the questions and research agenda of the next decade are inherently cross-disciplinary. Therefore, it seems likely that cutting-edge research in the domain of IT will appear in the leading management, marketing, accounting, and finance journals as well as the leading IS journals. In addition, many scholars who are grounded in these core disciplines will read and contribute to the journals that have been the traditional domain of the "IS community."

For the field of IS and its leading journals, these events will be overwhelmingly positive. A substantial opportunity to create true interdisciplinary research with high scholarly and practitioner impact awaits our community of research and our journals. However, for these promises to be realized, the core field of IS researchers must continue to develop a research agenda that addresses the key issues that confront managers and organizations. If our focus becomes too narrow or if we choose to guard our discipline too vigorously, the research context of the field may be viewed as administrative rather than organizational and strategic. While numerous research agenda can be articulated to meet this objective, we note some very broad themes that we believe will be important foundations for crafting high-impact research over the next decade.

IT LEVERAGE

A key concept for future research is IT leverage. Clearly, the mere investment in, and adoption of, IT is not a recipe for success in the competitive marketplace. In fact, a major underpinning of the "productivity paradox" is the notion that some organizations are more effective than others in leveraging IT. In many organizations, managerial systems as well as beliefs about products and pricing form a foundation of structure and process that inhibits full realization of IT's benefits. In other words, the history of the organization becomes the largest inhibitor in realizing the possibilities of IT that are reality for firms with little or no prior history. Therefore, a key agenda of inquiry for organizations and researchers is to discover how, when, and why IT leverages a business model.

While many perspectives are useful in examining this issue, this chapter's perspective of organizational capabilities seems particularly relevant. It is likely that the capabilities presented here or perhaps another set of entirely different capabilities is behind an organization's success in leveraging IT. Research that articulates and develops a context for understanding points of leverage and their creation provides a prescriptive lens and source of reconciliation for organizations and managers in the midst of escalating IT budgets and radical change. Framing the organization as a portfolio of capabilities underscores the important notion that IT-based change across firms and perhaps across the larger domain of competitive contexts will occur in different magnitudes and at different velocities although the type and amount of IT investment remain constant.

ORGANIZATIONS AS CONFIGURATIONS, CONSORTIUMS, AND SUPPLY CHAINS

In the classic context of competition, one firm competes with another firm for economic advantage within a defined marketplace. As noted in the initial sections of this chapter, the concept of industry is becoming less useful in describing many competitive contexts. Therefore, defining a boundary of competition and the associated influence of IT on an industry is becoming more complex. However, despite this difficulty, a major agenda item for the research community is to look beyond the organization as a means for understanding how IT is changing the competitive landscape. In the world of advanced technologies, competition will be best defined as supply chain versus supply chain rather than firm against firm. Furthermore, the composition and structure of supply chains will likely change instantly in the emerging context of low switching and search costs.

The primary implication of these trends is that organizations should be viewed as configurations or coalitions of firms that together can leverage IT to realize economic efficiency and value. When viewed in the context of strategic groups, these chains may form and reform to achieve the competitive dynamics of consolidation, breakout, redefinition, or transfer illustrated in Figure 12.1. Research that describes how IT enables these dynamics under particular competitive conditions is a much-needed addition to both scholarly understanding and practical knowledge. Furthermore, uncovering the economics and methods of integrating IT within a firm and across a business coalition is a key aspect of building the networked organization illustrated in Figure 12.3.

THE CROSSHAIRS OF KNOWLEDGE AND COMMERCE: E-SERVICE

Within both academic and practitioner literature, the concepts of knowledge management and e-commerce are treated as distinct revolutions in management and organizational design. As illustrated in Figure 12.3, organizations that have embarked on radical transformation have recognized that knowledge and commerce form the crosshairs of a target that enables the firm to deliver both product and service over the IT infrastructure. This new form of service (e-service) will enhance the value proposition of many firms and become an important source of product differentiation. Research that addresses the nature and delivery of service via IT represents a high-impact area for the field. Business models for e-service delivery, the economics of e-service pricing, the identification of dimensions describing e-service effectiveness, and the aspects of e-service marketing represent key issues of such inquiry.

Again, the perspective of organizational capabilities may provide a useful context for understanding the effectiveness of service delivery through IT. It is likely that the set of capabilities and technologies/systems necessary for delivering product content are different or perhaps require enhancement to effectively deliver service. This seems particularly true if organizational or supply-chain expertise/knowledge becomes a key aspect of the value proposition. In these instances, IT and organizational structures that can deliver both knowledge and product content in a customized form will become leverage points of effective competition. Such efforts will be radical transformations for many organizations and their associated supply chains. Research streams that frame service from the perspective of both delivery and receipt in these contexts will be important as both a definitional (what is e-service?) and a prescriptive (how do we deliver e-service?) resource to modern organizations and the scholarly community.

CONCLUSIONS

A key part of managing radical change is determining whether the organization has the energy or capability for the change effort. Assessing organizational readiness is as important as determining the technological feasibility of the change proposition (Leonard, 1998; Benjamin & Levinson, 1993). This chapter frames the notion of radical IT-based change at levels of industry and organization as a basis for developing new thought, practice, and research directions into this compelling set of managerial challenges. While it is tempting to separate concepts such as reengineering, knowledge management, supply chain, and e-commerce into separate silos as a means of facilitating and reconciling research and practice, the implication of this chapter is that each of these movements is an intricate piece of the fully networked organization (Figure 12.3). Perhaps the strongest implication drawn from this finding is that, similar to contemporary organizations, a major research agenda of the scholarly community should be to synthesize and reconcile research to address the broader transformation issues that now confront modern organizations. Our experience suggests that organizations are not equal in terms of effectively leveraging IT. Those that do leverage IT effectively have built key capabilities for navigating change and have also embarked on aggressive programs of reconfiguring their network of suppliers and customers. In other words, their agenda is to create new forms of process and to fully leverage the capabilities of IT. As a community of practitioners and researchers, this nexus of IT and radical change presents a challenging and exciting agenda for invention of new organizations, forms of management, and approaches to research.

ENDNOTES

1. See the chapter by Sampler for additional discussion.
2. A well-organized and complete analysis of these propositions is found in the chapter by Grover and Kettinger.

Business Strategy in Hypercompetitive Environments: Rethinking the Logic of IT Differentiation

V. Sambamurthy

During the last 15 years, strong evidence and managerial belief have accumulated that information technology (IT), when it is effectively deployed, contributes to superior firm performance (Brown, Gatian, & Hicks, 1995; Kettinger et al., 1994; Mason, McKenney, & Copeland, 1997). The early success stories of IT innovation at firms such as American Airlines, American Hospitals Supply/Baxter Travenol, Bank of America, Federal Express, Frito-Lay, and Merrill Lynch fueled awareness about the strategic benefits and competitive advantages feasible through IT. Today, firms such as E-Trade, Charles Schwab, Amazon.com, and Wal-Mart continue to exemplify the strategic value of IT innovation in sustaining superior competitive performance. However, despite the persistence in the strategic value of IT, much of the underlying theory about how and why IT innovation contributes to superior business performance has undergone a paradigm change and needs a fresh examination. Two important reasons underly this need for developing fresh thinking about how IT contributes to business strategy.

First, business environments have become hypercompetitive because of the high magnitude and velocity of interfirm rivalries (D'Aveni, 1994). Innovations in products, services, business processes, and organization designs are shaping dramatic discontinuities in product-market spaces and disrupting the dominant recipes of competition and business conduct in most industries (Christensen, 1997; Byrnes & Judge, 1999;

Venkatraman & Henderson, 1998). A new paradigm of business strategy, "sense and respond," is emerging and taking root in managerial thinking (Bradley & Nolan, 1998; Haeckel & Slywotzky, 1999). This paradigm emphasizes strategic intent as the continuous readiness of a firm to detect "fleeting windows of opportunity" in the marketplace and respond quickly with superior value propositions. The paradigm recognizes the dynamic nature of competition and rewards firms that are agile, flexible, and obsessively attentive to customer value. While information technologies can enable the superior execution of the sense-and-respond paradigm (Brown & Sambamurthy, 1999; Bradley & Nolan, 1998), there is a need to develop frameworks and a deeper understanding of exactly how IT can differentiate business performance in these dynamic and hypercompetitive business environments.

Second, the competitive structure of the IT industry, the nature of IT products and services, and the prevailing wisdom about the management and use of IT in business firms have all undergone dramatic changes (Moschella, 1997). Today, effective IT management and use involve some of the following key principles:

1. Monolithic, mainframe-based IT infrastructures have given way to hybrid IT infrastructures composed of a seamless assemblage of IT products and services from different vendors.
2. The focus of IT activities has shifted away from applications development and toward solutions integration.
3. Firms have evolved from passively buying specific IT products and services toward actively structuring webs of strategic partners and multisourcing networks for acquiring external IT assets, competencies, and knowledge.

Overall, there is a growing realization that firms can sustain strategic IT innovation and differentiate business success only by developing superior capabilities for enterprisewide IT management and use (Feeny & Wilcocks, 1998; Keen, 1991; Sambamurthy & Zmud, 1997; Weill & Broadbent, 1998). There is a need to understand the nature of these competencies and how they enable superior business performance in hypercompetitive business environments.

This chapter intends to articulate the underpinnings of the logic by which managers and academics can understand the linkages among business strategies, IT competencies, and firm performance in dynamic and hypercompetitive business environments. The next section presents a quick overview of the prevailing logic about the strategic role of IT. Subsequently, the chapter describes the underpinnings of the emerging role of IT. Finally, the chapter directs attention toward fresh thinking in the form of issues for future research and practice.

THE TRADITIONAL LOGIC OF IT DIFFERENTIATION: POSITIONING FOR COMPETITIVE ADVANTAGE

IT differentiation is defined as the ability to reap economic rents from a superior execution of business strategy through IT assets, knowledge, and competencies. *IT differentiation* refers to the leverage attained through deployment and management of IT functionalities in business strategies and value-chain activities. The *logic of IT differentiation* refers to the theories, assumptions, and guidelines for directing attention toward how IT can be used to differentiate business strategy.

How can firms reap superior economic rents through IT differentiation? The following sections discuss the theoretical engines underlying the traditional logic of IT differentiation and the implications of this logic for IT strategy.

THEORETICAL ENGINES

The traditional logic of IT differentiation pervaded IT management thinking for much of the 1980s. Two distinct streams of microeconomic theory have served as theoretical engines for the traditional logic. One of these streams is the industrial organization economics (IO), first exemplified by the Bain/Mason paradigms (Bain, 1968; Mason, 1939) and then subsequently articulated as a theory of competitive strategy by Porter (1980).[1] Simply put, the essence of the IO paradigm is that firm performance depends critically on the characteristics of the industry in which it competes. The structure of an industry is described by five competitive forces that influence the ability of firms in that industry to earn abnormal rates of return: the *bargaining power of buyers and of suppliers,* the *threat of new entrants and of substitute products,* and the *pressures of rent dissipation by industry rivals.* Therefore, the goal of competitive strategy is to manipulate these forces and deter the pressure of competition on the ability to earn supernormal profits. Strategists seek to deter competition by raising the switching costs of customers, lowering the switching costs with their suppliers, erecting barriers to entry against prospective rivals, and enhancing mobility barriers that prevent rivals from stealing market share. Guided by these theoretical principles, the traditional logic of IT differentiation directed attention toward the use of IT in manipulating the competitive forces surrounding the firm (Parsons, 1984; McFarlan, 1984). For instance, McFarlan suggests that IT can be used to lower the switching costs of suppliers, raise the switching costs of buyers, or erect barriers to entry.

Although the analysis of the industry forces yields insights into strategic differentiation opportunities for IT, it is not clear how a firm would focus its IT innovation activities to exploit those opportunities. Porter's (1985) analysis of the firm as a sequence of value-chain activities, ranging from logistics and procurement to marketing and sales and service, facilitates a complementary analysis of how IT can be deployed for competitive advantage. Porter and Millar (1985) argue that information pervades every element of the value-chain activities in firms. Therefore, IT can be used to enhance the conduct of value-chain activities in altering the industry forces and gaining a competitive advantage. Furthermore, IT can also be deployed in sustaining the generic strategic thrusts of cost leadership, differentiation, or niche positioning (Rackoff, Wiseman, & Ullrich, 1985). Guided by the frameworks of industry forces, value chain, and competitive strategy thrusts analyses, IS researchers have generated a variety of prescriptive frameworks for the strategic deployment of IT in specific arenas of business conduct. They include the strategic role of IT in competitive pricing strategies (Beath & Ives, 1986), customer relationship management (Ives & Learmonth, 1984; Ives & Mason, 1990; Ives & Vitale, 1988), and business partner relationships (Johnston & Vitale, 1988). The prescriptive power and utility of these frameworks are evident in some of the case studies of IT-based strategic differentiation (Lindsey et al., 1990; Jelassi & Fignon, 1994; Chatfield & Bjorn-Andersen, 1997).

Although frameworks derived from IO theories are valuable in guiding analyses of the opportunities for IT-based differentiation, they are deficient in explaining many important questions related to sustained competitive advantage (Vitale, 1986; Clemons & Row, 1991). For instance, when would IT innovation actions lead to sustained competitive advantage for the pioneering firm? What would deter rivals or entrants from successfully imitating the innovative IT application and thereby dissipating the abnormal returns temporarily enjoyed by the pioneering firm? Would some of the IT differentiation innovations actually place the pioneering firms in a position of significant risk because of competitive retaliation or superior execution of the same innovation by a rival?

IO-based frameworks only direct attention to the IT differentiation opportunities available to all the firms within an industry and to the strategic influence points along the value chain where IT can be gainfully deployed. However, because these theories operate with the assumption that all firms in an industry are homogeneously endowed with resources and capabilities, they cannot provide explanations about when IT innovation might lead to sustained competitive advantage (Porter, 1981).

In this regard, an alternative stream of microeconomic theory, Chamberlinian economics, expands the preceding insights by starting with the assumption that firms are heterogeneously endowed with resources (Chamberlin, 1933; Robinson, 1933). Individual firms are endowed with differential resources, with perhaps some levels of overlaps and resource similarities. When IT innovation is coupled with the unique resource endowments of a firm, it is more difficult for rivals to imitate the strategic innovation because they cannot realize the advantages of the resource endowments possessed by the pioneering firm. Therefore, heterogeneity in asset and resource endowments allows some firms to reap supernormal rents from IT innovation in contrast with other firms. Firm heterogeneity represents an important source of competitive advantage (Barney, 1997; Demsetz, 1973). Examples of key heterogeneous resource endowments include technical "know-how," reputation, brand awareness, and the ability of managers to work together. Thus, while the IO stream permits an analysis of the range of differentiation strategies available to firms in an industry, the Chamberlinian stream allows individual firms to identify which of these strategies they should choose to implement based on an analysis of their own resource, asset, and competency endowments.

Arguments presented by Clemons and Row (1991, p. 289) mirror the theoretical ideas contained in the Chamberlinian economics:

> Benefits resulting from an innovative application of information technology can be more readily defended if the system exploits unique resources of the innovating firm so that competitors do not fully benefit from imitation.

Clemons and Row (1988) illustrate the power of Chamberlinian economics through their case study of the sustained competitive advantage that McKesson gained through its IT innovation actions. Similarly, in an empirical analysis of the competitive advantage accruing due to IT innovation actions at 30 firms that had been acclaimed for their pioneering role in IT-based strategic differentiation in their respective industries, Kettinger et al. (1994) found that "the pre-existence of unique structural characteristics are an important determinant of strategic IT outcomes" (p. 46). The existence of a technological platform (i.e., IT infrastructure) and slack financial resources for investment and research and development characterized firms that were successful in sustaining competitive advantage from IT innovation, years after the introduction of the strategic IT application.

In summary, the traditional logic of IT differentiation suggests that strategists should analyze their industry forces and value-chain activities to identify feasible opportunities for IT innovation. Furthermore, they should examine their firm's asset, resource, and competency endowments and identify those isolating mechanisms that confer a distinctive advantage relative to rivals (Rumelt, 1984). Strategic IT applications that emerge through an analysis of the industry forces, value-chain activities, and distinctive firm competencies are most likely to sustain competitive advantage over time.

IMPLICATIONS FOR IT MANAGEMENT

What are the implications of the traditional logic of IT differentiation for effective IT management practice? This logic directs attention toward specific IT applications that, when appropriately conceptualized and implemented, will yield sustained competitive advantage. Thus, most of the success stories of firms in the 1980s were executed around winning IT applications. Examples include the SABRE airlines reservation application at American Airlines, the Cash Management Account at Merrill Lynch, and the ASAP application at American Hospitals Supply/Baxter Travenol.

Furthermore, the traditional logic of IT differentiation directs attention toward IT alignment. Based on the premise that business strategy and structure drive IT management, the goal of IT management is to ensure that the resources and actions for IT innovation are enabling, not constraining, business strategy. An alignment focus recognizes that IT management and use represent a distinct organizational activity that must be properly managed to stay in synchronization with the business strategy (Henderson & Venkatraman, 1992). Furthermore, the business strategy sets the framework and boundary conditions for the mission, goals, and objectives of IT management and use initiatives. The ultimate measure of success of IT management and use strategies is how well specific IT applications support the differentiation of business strategy and, consequently, the attainment of abnormal profitability.

Figure 13.1 summarizes the ideas in the traditional logic of IT differentiation in the form of a research model that links IT management, business strategy, and firm performance. This model suggests that strategic IT applications and unique firm resources together act as determinants of sustained competitive advantage. Strategic IT applications are specific artifacts created through the application of the analysis frameworks based on the IO and Chamberlinian economics theories. These applications are directed at specific elements of the value-chain activities in the firm, for example, customer relationships, logistics, or manufacturing. Unique firm resources refer to financial assets, reputational assets (brand image), customer loyalty, locational assets, and IT sophistication. The extent to which these resources are distinctive is an index of the firm's ability to exploit them for competitive advantage. When a strategic IT application is appropriately coupled with unique firm resources, the firm will be able to sustain long-term competitive advantage as measured in the form of entry barriers, customer and supplier switching costs, and mobility barriers (Porter, 1980; McFarlan, 1984). Ultimately, these indicators of sustained competitive advantage influence firm performance.

FIGURE 13.1   The Traditional Logic of IT Differentiation

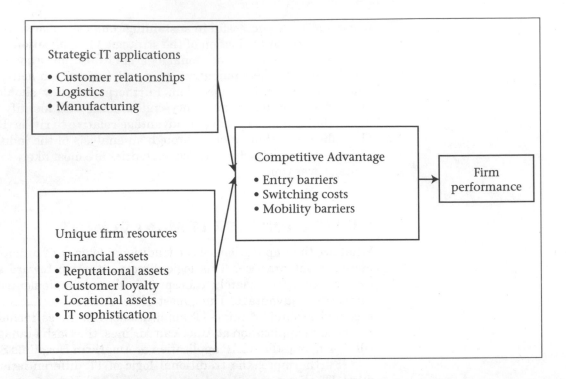

THE EMERGING LOGIC OF IT DIFFERENTIATION: CAPABILITIES FOR COMPETITIVE AGILITY

The IO and Chamberlinian models of business strategy are considered to be inappropriate as frameworks for guiding the strategic actions of business firms in contemporary business environments (Jacobson, 1992; Young, Smith, & Grim, 1996; Thomas, 1996). The traditional frameworks direct attention toward competitive advantage from specific competitive moves. However, in hypercompetitive environments, any advantage from a specific move is short lived. Aggressive innovation actions by other firms either dissipate the initial advantage or disrupt the causal linkage between that specific action and sustained competitive advantage. Therefore, firms must continually recreate competitive advantage through a series of innovation actions. The following sections describe the theoretical engine guiding frameworks for the emerging logic of IT differentiation and the implications of this logic for IT strategy.

THEORETICAL ENGINE

The Austrian school of microeconomic theory, notably the work of Schumpeter (1934, 1950), directs attention toward strategy as a dynamic process of creative destruction and disruption of existing product-market spaces. Whereas the IO and Chamberlinian models focus on a search for positions of static competitive advantage in industry and market structures under equilibrium, the Austrian school directs attention toward the competitive behavior of firms in markets that are in states of disequilibrium.

Firms possess imperfect knowledge and information about their markets and customers because they are in a state of rapid change and complexity (Hayek, 1937). Firms utilize experimentation, discovery, insights, and learning to seek newer knowledge and a better understanding of the causal forces at play in their markets. New knowledge enables firms to sense the imperfections between how the market currently operates and what could be done differently in satisfying their customers' needs. Jacobson (1992) suggests that firms act as arbitrageurs in seeking opportunities presented by market imperfections and launching competitive disruption through innovations in products, services, distribution channels, or organizational processes. In the short run, the entrepreneurial firm reaps supernormal returns as established incumbents and rivals seek to understand the competitive disruptions in their market space and mobilize appropriate response actions (Christensen, 1997). Although the response speed might vary, eventually the incumbents or other imitators will be able to acquire the necessary knowledge and dissipate away the supernormal returns accruing to the pioneer. Alternatively, other pioneers might generate rival knowledge about the markets and launch their own disruption actions to overturn the pioneers' advantages in the marketplace. Thus, competition occurs in the form of a series of market disruption moves by new entrants or entrepreneurial firms and efforts by incumbents or rivals to shape their response actions (Young et al., 1996; Smith, Grimm, & Gannon, 1992). The dynamic of strategy unfolds through these continual competitive moves and action responses. Furthermore, as D'Aveni (1994) suggests, the logic of business strategy is to capture these fleeting positions of competitive advantage through a string of competitive moves and responses. In the long run, superior performance flows not from the success of a specific competitive move but from continual entrepreneurial action.

These theoretical arguments suggest that strategy should be viewed as the process of sensing market imperfections; assembling the requisite assets, knowledge, and competencies to devise innovative competitive moves; and mobilizing the commitment and resources to execute the disruptive moves. Strategy should also be the process of sensing disruptive competitive moves and mobilizing the assets, knowledge, competencies, and commitment to defend against those competitive moves. In a hypercompetitive business environment, what matters most is a firm's *agility* to generate competitive moves with speed and surprise (D'Aveni, 1994; Goldman, Nagel, & Preiss 1995). Traditionally, competitive moves were defined as innovations in products, services, marketing strategies, or distribution channels (Porter, 1980). Here we define *competitive moves* as also including alliance formation, organizational process redesign, and knowledge discovery, capture, and integration. Therefore, the new logic of IT differentiation directs attention toward enhancing the competitive agility of the firm through requisite IT assets, competencies, and innovation actions.

What enhances or constrains the ability of firms to unleash the forces of competitive disruption, defend their established positions, engage in frequent competitive moves, and wrest positions of temporary competitive advantage? The Austrian school of economics does not provide answers to these questions. More appropriately, the theory does not fully explain what senior executives could do to enhance their firms' ability to utilize IT as a strategic resource. For answers to these questions, the resource-based view of the firm (Penrose, 1959) and the dynamic competencies framework (Teece & Pisano, 1994) provide complementary explanations of how firms can position themselves for timely responsiveness and flexible innovation in changing business environments. In hypercompetitive environments when time-to-market, timing of competitive moves, and agility are important, the pace of innovation is dramatic, and it is difficult to anticipate and predict the sources of future rivalry, the dominant strategic challenge is to ready the firm for sense-and-respond entrepreneurship. Firms must develop specific competencies and the ability to renew those competencies in response to shifts in business environments. The dynamic capabilities framework argues that three factors influence firms' ability to engage in competitive disruption: (1) their present position, or their endowments of assets, knowledge, and competencies, (2) their managerial and organizational processes for integrating, renewing, and regenerating their knowledge and competencies, and (3) the available paths of competitive maneuvering (Teece & Pisano, 1994).

The present position of a firm refers to its endowments of knowledge, assets, and competencies. Depending upon the extent to which these endowments are valuable, rare, and inimitable, a firm can create competitive moves that will be more difficult for its rivals to imitate easily or quickly. Thus, the size of the advantage conferred by a competitive move is a function of these resource endowments (Barney, 1991; Reed & DeFillippi, 1990). Furthermore, as argued by Chen (1996), asymmetries in rivals' resource endowments influence the extent to which firms will either initiate a competitive move or choose not to respond to their attackers' actions.

However, in a dynamic business environment, firms cannot expect to be effective only through their present endowments. As Leonard-Barton (1992) notes, an organization's core competencies can easily become core rigidities and barriers to agility. Therefore, the ability to recognize the need to reconfigure existing endowments by either retiring them and acquiring new endowments or by combining existing and new endowments in novel ways to create new assets, knowledge, and competencies is a valuable organizational characteristic (Amit & Schoemaker, 1992). Furthermore, transformations are costly, and not all organizations have the motivation to undertake frequent transformations. Therefore, the capacity for organizational transformation is important (Teece & Pisano, 1994). In addition to their present endowments, the ability of firms to generate new knowledge, assets, and competencies is reflected in the nature of their integration, learning, and renewal processes. *Integration* refers to the ability to locate relevant knowledge and competencies within both the internal and external value streams and facilitate their recombination to create new knowledge and competencies. *Learning* refers to the focus on discovering new knowledge, identification of dysfunctional assets, competencies, and routines, and the creation of new knowledge and competencies. Finally, *renewal* refers to the organizational commitment to anticipate emerging discontinuities, mobilize the organizational readiness to change, and avoid inertia or commitment traps that could impede competitive agility.

Finally, the firms' pools of assets, competencies, knowledge, and dynamic competencies also dictate their range of feasible opportunities for arbitrage, entrepreneurship, and defense against disruption moves. Path dependencies imply that history and the present position of a firm dictate aspects of their learning and intelligence systems. Therefore, every firm has specific growth trajectories or options available to it; other paths are not feasible because of a firm's history and abilities. Therefore, a firm could simply be blindsided by certain strategic changes in its environment or not have the ability to capitalize on those opportunities (Cohen & Levinthal, 1990; Teece & Pisano, 1994). Path dependency implies that a firm is advantageously positioned to exploit some opportunities, but disadvantaged relative to other opportunities. Therefore, firms cannot easily capitalize on all marketplace opportunities.

FIGURE 13.2 The New Logic of IT Differentiaion

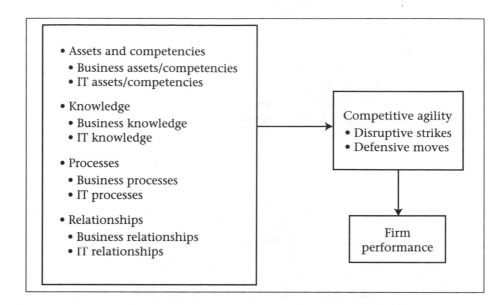

Based on the ideas contained in the Austrian school of economics and the dynamic competencies framework, the emerging logic of IT differentiation directs attention toward the value of IT in enhancing competitive agility. Figure 13.2 depicts the intertwining linkages between IT and business strategy by showing the firm as a configuration of assets and competencies, knowledge, processes, and relationships. *Assets* and *competencies* refer to the physical, locational, reputational, and financial endowments of a firm. *Knowledge* refers to the stocks of intellectual capital accumulated within a firm due to its prior history and ongoing practice. *Processes* and *relationships* embody the dynamic competencies of the firm by facilitating attention to the binding of assets, competencies, and knowledge internal and external to the firm. They also facilitate learning and the generation of new knowledge and competencies. Each one of these four elements can be referred to as a strategic lever of a firm.

Figure 13.2 suggests that IT permeates all of the strategic levers of the firm: Each one of the strategic levers involves a significant IT component. Two important strategic roles of IT become apparent.

1. When appropriately deployed, IT has the power to enhance the efficiency and effectiveness with which each one of the levers can be executed and managed. For instance, collaborative work technologies such as Lotus Notes have significantly enhanced the ability to manage organizations' stocks of knowledge (Alavi, 1997).[2] Firms have made significant investments in ERP technologies in order to build seamless and connected organizational processes (Brown & Sambamurthy, 1999). Similarly, IT enables the creation of a variety of knowledge networks, processes for interactions with customers, and strategies for sourcing of assets and competencies with business partners (Venkatraman & Henderson, 1998).

2. When appropriately deployed, IT enables innovative combinations of the strategic levers and provides a platform for competitive disruption moves. Many of the disruptive competitive moves initiated by Wal-Mart and FDX (formerly FedEx) were significantly shaped by their IT investments and capabilities. New business start-ups, such as Amazon.com and E-Trade, as well as entrepreneurial incumbents

such as Schwab, have been able to redefine their strategy and business scope through novel IT-enabled reconfiguration of the strategic levers in their respective industries. McKenney (1995) analyzed how firms such as American Airlines, Bank of America, USAA, and American Hospital Supply/Baxter Travenol accomplished stellar success in IT-based strategic differentiation. He concluded that these firms had built appropriate IT competencies and then unleashed these competencies in conjunction with their business competencies to create competitive disruption in their respective industries.

In summary, strategists must direct their attention toward harnessing the power of IT for sustaining competitive agility through moves that either enable their firm to launch disruptive strikes against rivals or defend against rival attackers. The emerging logic of IT differentiation points to the value of IT in terms of its ability to sustain competitive agility. The next section discusses the implications of this emerging logic for the practice and theory of IT management.

IMPLICATIONS FOR IT MANAGEMENT

Table 13.1 depicts the implications of the new logic of IT differentiation for IT management. First, the source of IT differentiation shifts from specific applications to enterprisewide IT capabilities. *IT capabilities* refer to the distinctive assets and competencies, knowledge, processes, and relationships that enable firms to effectively acquire, deploy, and manage IT products and services in shaping innovations and business strategies (Feeny & Wilcocks, 1998; Ross, Beath, & Goodhue, 1996; Sambamurthy & Zmud, 1997). IT capabilities are systemic in nature; that is, they describe the ability of the enterprise rather than a business unit or division. Furthermore,

TABLE 13.1 Moving Toward the New Logic of IT Differentiation

	The Traditional Logic	The New Logic
Theoretical engine	Industrial organization • Manipulation of industry forces	Schumpeterian competition • Competitive moves and disruptive strikes
	Chamberlinian theory of heterogeneity of firm resources • Exploitation of unique firm advantages	Dynamic competencies of the firm • Assets and competencies, processes, knowledge, and relationships as sources of value creation
Source of superior firm performance	Strategic IT applications and unique firm resources	IT capabilities coupled with business assets and competencies, processes, knowledge, and relationships
Focus of IT differentiation	Directed at specific elements of the value chain • Customer relationships • Logistics • Manufacturing flow	Transformation of the value constellation, including processes, knowledge, and relationships binding the firm with its customers and external business partners
Objective of IT management	IT alignment with business strategy, structure, and process • Business models drive IT assets and management processes	IT embeddedness in business assets and competencies, processes, knowledge, and relationships • IT assets and management processes shape the business models

IT capabilities refer to the ability of IS managers, business managers, and senior executives to mobilize appropriate behaviors for IT innovation. Examples of valued IT capabilities include a seamless global IT infrastructure (Weill & Broadbent, 1998; Ross et al., 1996; Sambamurthy & Zmud, 1997), technical skills (Ross et al., 1996), partnership networks among the business and IS managers (Ross et al., 1996; Brown & Sambamurthy, 1999), business systems thinking (Feeny & Wilcocks, 1998), and change-readiness (Clark et al., 1997).

Second, the thrust of IT differentiation expands from a search for influence points along the value chain to a search for a reconfiguration of the entire value constellation of the firm (Norman & Ramirez, 1993; Venkatraman, 1994). *Value constellation* refers to the tightly interconnected value chains of the firm and its business partners, including customers, suppliers, vendors, and other key allies. The value constellation is bound together by the strategic levers of the firm. IT differentiation is directed at exploring and exploiting novel combinations of these levers to create and implement superior value constellations that could sustain the ability to launch competitive moves. The shift in focus from value chains to value constellations is consistent with Venkatraman's (1994) framework of IT strategic thrusts, in which he argued that, over time, IT differentiation shifts from localized applications toward reconfiguration of business networks and the expansion of business scope. Thus, Dell's ability to install a reconfigured value constellation through IT enabled it to launch a disruptive move in the form of a business model that is characterized as "build to order." This business model enables Dell to differentiate itself from its rivals (Magretta, 1998). It is particularly noteworthy that its rivals have experienced difficulties in imitating this business model with great success.

Third, the new logic of IT differentiation shifts attention away from alignment as the goal of IT management practice toward IT embeddedness as the motivating force. The rationale for alignment was that the demands of business strategy drove the practice of IT management. Therefore, IT management practice focused on ensuring that the IT capabilities, organization structures, and infrastructures provided appropriate support for the enactment of business strategy. Today, however, a new economics of information is pervading the drivers of business value. Successful firms are deconstructing their physical value chains from their information value chains and reconfiguring their value propositions through information-shaped relationships with their customers and other business partners (Evans & Wurster, 1997). For example, the sense-and-respond paradigm draws attention to the fact that relationships with customers, suppliers, and other business partners can be tightly coupled through interpenetrating information chains, whereby knowledge and information are very rapidly and trustfully shared in order to generate effective solutions to market opportunities (Venkatraman & Henderson, 1998). Many trends point to the embeddedness of IT in the fundamental strategic levers of the firm. They include the success of E-business firms, the transformation of business models in many industries from the traditional physical value chains as the primary drivers of value toward information- and knowledge-based relationships as the primary drivers of value, and the prospects of start-ups in many other industries that intend to leverage information value chains. For IT management practice, IT embeddedness suggests that business and IT strategies must be coevolved, not sequenced as was the case with the alignment logic.

Therefore, as illustrated in Figure 13.2, the new logic of IT differentiation elevates the role of IT from an enabler of business strategy to a valued and embedded element of all the strategic levers of the firm.

DIRECTIONS FOR RESEARCH AND PRACTICE

What are the implications of the emerging logic of IT differentiation for generating fresh thinking about business strategy and IT management? This section discusses some of the salient directions for future research and practice.

DIRECTIONS FOR RESEARCH

What Should Be the Role of IT in the Firm?

Figure 13.2 depicts the role of IT as a strategic lever on par with the other traditionally valued levers: assets and competencies, processes, knowledge, and relationships. As discussed earlier, IT not only enhances the effectiveness of these strategic levers but also facilitates novel combinations of these levers in creating new business models. Contemporary business firms are experimenting with a variety of business models to discover the dominant modes of competing in the next millenium. Particularly, the digital economy has overturned the conventional value logic in many industries and has forced entrenched incumbents to watch upstart rivals seize dramatic market valuations in short bursts of time. The role of IT will emerge at the forefront of experimentation with different business models, particularly as entrenched firms focus their resources and insights on countering the disruptive threats to their businesses. It is clear that the new business models will be designed around combinations of IT and other strategic levers.

Keen (1999, p. 44) articulates this viewpoint when he claims:

> The role of IT is to enable the company to best benefit from technology as a business resource. When your business model is healthy, Web commerce is an opportunity to improve your firm's business performance. When it's fractured, the leadership challenge is one of announcing a new business identity: "What should the company be in five years?" IT must talk to that concern—business model, not technology strategy.

Researchers will need to focus their efforts on tracking the evolving business models, understanding the architecture of these business models and their revenue, cost, and profit drivers, and the conditions under which these models are likely to be sustainable.

Beyond facilitating experimentation with new business models, the role of IT in enhancing strategic flexibility also deserves future attention. Since hypercompetitive environments engender a significant potential for disruption, strategic flexibility has become a vital imperative (Hitt, Keats, & DeMarie, 1998). *Flexibility* refers to the ability of a firm to abandon outmoded business models in favor of profitable new ones, architect new value constellations, and implement change as cost effectively as possible. Flexibility allows firms to act as arbitrageurs in spotting fleeting market opportunities and launching moves to seize the economic benefits of those opportunities. IT enables strategic flexibility because it promises to lower the costs associated with the management and renewal of the strategic levers of the business. Furthermore, IT lowers the commitment costs of executing current strategic postures and enables business firms to pursue new competitive market spaces with speed and surprise (Goldman et al., 1995; Brown & Sambamurthy, 1999). In particular, Keen (1991) argues that IT infrastructures have the potential to significantly expand the degrees of freedom for a firm. Empirical research is needed, however, to examine how IT can contribute to enabling the strategic flexibility of business firms.

What Are the Sources of IT Value in Contemporary Business Firms?

As explained in an earlier section, the new logic of IT differentiation redirects attention away from specific innovative IT applications toward IT capabilities as the source of economic rents. Furthermore, the new logic also directs attention away from the internal value chain toward the use of IT to transform the entire value constellation of a firm and its business partners. Therefore, research is needed to understand the type of IT capabilities that will be the sources of economic value. As illustrated in Table 13.2, IS researchers have begun to identify some of these capabilities (Feeny & Wilcocks, 1998; Sambamurthy & Zmud, 1997; Weill & Broadbent, 1998; Brown & Sambamurthy, 1999). However, research is needed to identify the full range of IT capabilities and how they contribute to the ability to launch competitive moves. Furthermore, studies are needed to examine the dynamics of interactions between IT capabilities and the other strategic levers of the firm in facilitating superior performance. Jarvenpaa and Leidner (1998) conducted a case study of a firm in the information industry in Mexico that competed in a newly opened local market against foreign competitors. They found that strategic foresight and flexibility and the ability to foster intimate learning relationships with lead customers were instrumental to the firm's ability to master its business environment. Similarly, Powell and Dent-Micallef

TABLE 13.2   Illustrative Examples of IT Capabilities

IT Capabilities	Description	Sources of Ideas
Business systems thinking	The ability to envision novel combinations of strategic levers (assets and competencies, processes, relationships, and knowledge) that could be realized through IT and promote IT-based business innovation.	Brown and Sambamurthy, 1999 Feeny and Wilcocks, 1998 McKenney, 1997 Powell and Dent-Micallef, 1997 Sambamurthy and Zmud, 1997
IS/Line partnering	The development of collaborative and harmonious relationships between IT and business managers that enable the sharing of innovation risks, joint ownership of initiatives, and sharing of relevant knowledge.	Brown and Sambamurthy, 1999 Feeny and Wilcocks, 1998 Ross, Beath, and Goodhue, 1996
Seamless IT infrastructure	The ability to architect IT infrastructure technologies to deliver a technical platform that enables and shapes the current and future business needs.	Brown and Sambamurthy, 1999 Ross, Beath and Goodhue, 1996 Sambamurthy and Zmud, 1997 Weill and Broadbent, 1998
Reliable utility provisioning	The ability to deliver cost-effective, reliable, and timely services to the business units.	Sambamurthy and Zmud, 1997 Weill and Broadbent, 1998
Process adaptiveness	The ability to implement flexible business processes that take advantage of IT functionalities and enhance cost efficiencies, cycle time, and effectiveness.	Brown and Sambamurthy, 1999 Sambamurthy and Zmud, 1997
IT management	The ability to manage the IT function with foresight and success in identifying promising infrastructure technologies, technical skills, and IT work procedures, and assimilating them to deliver business value	Clark, Cavanaugh, Brown, and Sambamurthy, 1997 Feeny and Wilcocks, 1998 Ross, Beath, and Goodhue, 1996 Sambamurthy and Zmud, 1997

(1997) found that only when IT capabilities were blended with intangible, complementary human and business assets, such as flexible culture and supplier relationships, did firms in the retail industry obtain superior economic value from IT. There is a need for more studies that investigate economic value from IT capabilities in conjunction with complementary business assets and competencies, knowledge, processes, and relationships.[3]

How Should Firms Develop Their IT Infrastructure Capabilities?

Since IT infrastructures are likely to represent one of the prominent sources of IT value, firms are devoting attention to developing potent IT infrastructures with appropriate reach and range (Keen, 1991; Weill & Broadbent, 1998).[4] Yet answers to some significant managerial challenges are awaited: How should firms devise and implement their IT infrastructures? What strategies are likely to prove effective in convincing senior business executives about the long-range strategic value of IT infrastructure investments because such investments are large, risky, and characterized by ambiguity about the return streams?

Traditionally, IT infrastructures were managed with an attention to the total costs of ownership of physical IT assets, including computing, network, and database technologies. Growing concerns over the costs of ownership led firms to consider outsourcing as an alternative to internal ownership. However, two other criteria have emerged as important in contemporary business and technology environments. First, different elements of the IT infrastructure vary in their strategic importance to the firm. Some of the infrastructure components of the IT infrastructure might be strategic because they are intricately linked with the strategic levers of the firm. Typical examples might be customer databases, human resource databases of people skills, or knowledge bases of best practices. Such assets must invariably be owned and managed inside the firm regardless of the costs of their ownership. Other components might be important to the firm in their consumption but not in their physical ownership. Examples include communication (E-mail) and desktop infrastructures. Therefore, their internal ownership may not be a strategic requisite as long as a seamless and reliable service is available regarding their use in the business. Therefore, IT infrastructures must be managed by identifying core strategic and noncore assets and developing customized governance strategies for managing these assets.[5]

Recently, rapid changes in technology regimes have pointed to another important criterion for managing IT infrastructures: technological flexibility. Even as firms have made enormous investments in computing and network infrastructures, process infrastructures (ERP), and knowledge infrastructures (intranets, Lotus Notes, and groupware), the emergence of the Internet suite of technologies and net-centric computing has posed significant challenges: How should existing IT infrastructures be adapted to assimilate these new infrastructure technologies? More important, should firms continue to assimilate successive generations of technologies through internal ownership? How will the tide of rising investments in prior generations of infrastructure technologies impact the costs of ownership and, more important, strategic flexibility of the firm? On one hand, IT infrastructures might be key to the ability to launch a variety of strategic competitive moves. However, on the other hand, the "legacy" effect of investments in prior generations of infrastructure technologies could limit the ability or willingness to invest in the new infrastructure technologies. The drag effect of prior infrastructure commitments could leave firms vulnerable to more nimble rivals with more current IT infrastructures. Therefore, IT infrastructures must be designed to be technologically flexible so that firms can easily assimilate emerging infrastructure technologies into their existing infrastructure base. In their analysis of IT-based value innovation at Marshall Industries, El Sawy et al. (1999) argue that for some firms, the dynamic pace of their business environment might require technological flexibility; they might be wiser in limiting their robust commitments to specific infrastructure technologies. Technological flexibility might require an IT infrastructure strategy in which firms own specific assets, lease other assets from well-established service providers, and share other assets through collaborative arrangements such as licensing or joint ventures. There is a need to understand the types of governance arrangements that will permit firms to manage the technological flexibility of their IT infrastructures.

Overall, it is clear that the logic for managing IT infrastructures needs significant research attention: How should the criteria of total costs of ownership, strategic value of the assets, and technological flexibility guide decisions about investments in infrastructure technologies? Without significant ex ante commitments to IT infrastructures, firms might not possess the valuable and inimitable resources to outpace their rivals in executing competitive moves with agility. However, if firms do not have adequate foresight about the emerging technology regimes, particularly the disruptive technologies, their massive investments in IT infrastructures could indeed doom them to irrelevant competitive moves. Therefore, how should firms manage IT infrastructures with technological foresight? When is ownership of physical assets important? When should firms consider virtual ownership through claims on physical assets owned by external partners? Growing trends in the economy for leasing telecommunications bandwidth and renting applications suggest that virtual ownership might be emerging as an important IT infrastructure strategy. In this regard, researchers have begun to recognize the value of strategic options theory as an underpinning for examining such questions (Amram & Kulatilaka, 1999).

What Are the Dynamics of IT-Shaped Competitive Moves and Rivalry in Hypercompetitive Business Environments?

Acknowledging the nature of competition in hypercompetitive environments, strategy researchers have evolved theories of dynamic rivalry (for example, Smith et al., 1992; Chen, 1996). These theories argue that rivalry occurs in the form of moves and countermoves between firms and their rivals. Emerging theories of dynamic strategy focus on understanding forces that influence the behavior of firms in launching disruptive strikes as well as in shaping responses to these strikes. For instance, Chen (1996) provides a valuable overview of the accumulated literature and suggests that two factors influence competitive behavior: the extent to which a firm shares common markets with its rivals and the extent to which a firm shares common endowments with its rivals.

As IT capabilities become one of the strategic levers of competitive strategy and market maneuvering, research is needed to advance knowledge about IT-shaped competitive moves and rivalry.[6] Some of the important questions are as follows: What types of IT-shaped moves do firms utilize in competing in the present business environments? What influences the ability of rivals to respond to these moves? Consider the example of Toys-R-Us and its emerging rivalry with E-Toys, a start-up that has threatened the viability of Toys-R-Us business model. The initial competitive moves made by the start-up have yet to be fully countered by the incumbent giant in the toy retailing industry, even as other online rivals position themselves to enter the online market. On the other hand, Schwab appears to have been more successful in responding to the competitive moves initiated by E-Trade in the retail financial services sector, whereas Merrill Lynch has been more cautious in shaping its competitive response behaviors. Researchers should examine the dynamics of these action-response behaviors across firms and industries to generate taxonomies of IT-shaped competitive moves, investigate the effectiveness of alternative moves, and identify conditions influencing the effectiveness of these moves.

DIRECTIONS FOR PRACTICE

The vibrant nature of the IT-shaped conduct of business strategy implies that most of the questions just posed are important not only for research but also for practice. Most business firms are engaged in active experimentation with alternative business models and are interested in learning about IT capabilities, IT-shaped competitive moves, and their effects on performance. Therefore, such research should have valuable lessons for practice.

Additionally, the ideas presented in this chapter point to a significant role for CIOs and senior IT executives: the role of a business strategist.[7] In the 1990s, senior IT executives focused on building valuable IT asset infrastructures (processors, networks, databases, etc.), process infrastructures (ERP, supply chain), knowledge infrastructures (intranets, collaborative work systems), and external electronic integration infrastructures (EDI, extranets, virtual private networks). Many firms have been successful in implementing these infrastructures to squeeze out cost economies and institute seamless connectivity across the corporation. The next significant agenda is likely to be to direct IT's contribution to the top line: Strategize new business models, seek out sources of revenue, generate new alliances, identify alternative distribution channels, and protect the future growth and profitability of the firm. Particularly with the emergence of digital convergence (Moschella, 1997), it will become imperative that senior IT executives actively work with their business executives in shaping and positioning their firms' business strategies. Visionary CIOs and senior IT executives should take the lead in developing partnerships with their business peers and directing conversations about IT-shaped business strategy.

CONCLUSION

Though IT has persisted in its role as a strategic resource of the firm for more than 15 years, significant shifts have occurred in the logic of how IT contributes to superior firm performance. Contemporary hypercompetitive business environments reward firms for agility and the ability to engage in high levels of competitive moves. The new logic of IT differentiation directs attention toward the role of IT in generating new business models and enhancing strategic flexibility. Furthermore, effective management practice should direct attention toward IT capabilities and their role in transforming the value constellations of firms. These ideas should provide a fertile ground for thinking about IT research and practice in the next millennium.

ENDNOTES

1. See the chapter by Sampler on the Internet and strategy for a related discussion of these theories of competitive strategy.
2. The chapter by Alavi on organizational knowledge also discusses the role of IT in facilitating knowledge management.
3. See the chapter by Barua and Mukhopadhyay on IT and business performance for a detailed discussion of the complementarity between IT capabilities and business strategies as a key determinant of business performance.
4. See the chapter by Weill and Broadbent on managing IT infrastructures for a more detailed discussion about the design of IT infrastructure capabilities and their fit with business strategy.
5. See the chapter by Lacity and Willcocks on IT outsourcing for a more detailed discussion about effective governance strategies for outsourcing.
6. See the chapter by Sampler on the Internet and strategy for a richer discussion of how the Internet suite of technologies has impacted the conduct of strategy and demanded a greater attention to the role of IT capabilities in business strategy.
7. See the chapter by Ross and Feeny on the evolving role of the CIO for a more detailed discussion of the role of the CIO as a business strategist.

Chapter 14

The Origins of Software: Acquiring Systems at the End of the Century

Joey F. George

In 1968, the NATO science committee declared a software crisis. More than 30 years later, the \$120+ billion global software industry continues to suffer through this crisis, so-called because software development projects have traditionally gone over budget, and over deadline, and the resulting systems still failed to adequately perform the tasks for which they had been designed. By some estimates, as many as half of systems development projects are canceled before they are finished (Gibbs, 1994), sunk costs notwithstanding.

Despite sustained efforts to migrate software development from an art form to the discipline of engineering, timely, cost-effective, requirements-matching software development remains elusive. Given the state of software development, executives and managers must confront a somewhat risky situation when considering software development and the acquisition of information systems (IS) to support their organizations. Fortunately, managers now have more choices than ever before for acquiring systems or having software developed to meet their business needs.

The purpose of this chapter is to present the issues related to information systems acquisition and software development at the end of the twentieth century from both a practical and an academic perspective. In many ways, the issues related to systems development are at the heart of the IS discipline. The next section provides an overview of these issues, of software acquisition, and of systems development. The following section examines these issues in more detail, focusing on the many choices available to managers for both software acquisition and software development. The chapter closes with some suggestions for future academic research and a summary.

GENERAL OVERVIEW OF SOFTWARE ACQUISITION AND SOFTWARE DEVELOPMENT

In this chapter, we will be using the terms *software acquisition* and *systems acquisition* interchangeably even though there are subtle differences in their meanings. Software consists of instructions written for a computer to perform and is typically only part of a system, although it may be a large part. The system itself also includes computer hardware, procedures, telecommunication components, and the people who interact with the other components to fulfill the system's purpose. There is a similar distinction between *systems development* and *software development,* but we will also use the terms interchangeably.

Software development is the process through which software to perform some specific task is written, tested, and released for general use.[1] It typically involves the activities of analyzing problems and opportunities, including analyzing existing systems, to determine just what it is the software being developed should do. Once the particulars of *what* the software should do to address the problem or opportunity are decided, exactly *how* the software is to accomplish that feat must be determined. Development, then, also typically involves design work because software must be designed the same way any product must be designed. Thus, systems development is often referred to as *systems analysis and design.* Once designed, the software must be written for the computer and then released to those who will use it. In the almost 50 years that software has been produced to support administrative business functions, researchers and practitioners alike have worked to develop better ways to develop software. A key issue, then, is what are the available choices for developing information systems and software. During this time, several different methods and techniques have been created to facilitate and support the development process. We will cover many of the better known methods and techniques later in this chapter.

Software acquisition includes software development because one way to acquire software is to build it yourself. There are, however, many other ways to acquire it. In fact, there are probably more ways for an organization to acquire software now than there have ever been before. A second key issue, then, is what are the available choices for acquiring systems in addition to in-house development. A more detailed discussion of acquisition opportunities immediately follows this section of the chapter.

A third key issue is whether a model can be developed to help both academics and practitioners better understand the systems acquisition and development process. Probably the best known model that represents this process is the systems development life cycle. The life-cycle model and its variants are based on two primary ideas (1) that software and systems development is an ongoing circular process that proceeds from beginning to end and then back to beginning and (2) that the process can be divided into phases that are reasonably distinct from each other. We will present a generic life-cycle model, as well as a spiral variant of the life-cycle model, toward the end of the chapter. Some aspects of the life-cycle model have been the focus of detailed models of their own. We will also review one such model, Lucas's (1997) model of what determines system use once the system has been implemented. Finally, we will review a model of acquisition strategy and implementation based on the work of Iivari and Ervasti (1992).

A FRAME FOR UNDERSTANDING SOFTWARE ACQUISITION AND SOFTWARE DEVELOPMENT

Software Acquisition

While there will always be some debate about when and where the first administrative information system was developed, there is general agreement that the first such system in the United Kingdom was developed at J. Lyons & Sons. In the United States, the first administrative information system was General Electric's payroll system, developed in 1954. At that time, and for many years afterward, acquiring an information system meant one thing only: in-house development. The software industry itself did not even come into existence until a decade after GE's payroll system was implemented.

Since GE's payroll system was brought on-line, in-house development has become a progressively smaller piece of all systems development work that takes place in and for organizations. Internal corporate IS shops now spend a smaller and smaller proportion of their time and effort on developing systems from scratch. In 1998, corporate IS groups reported spending 33% less time and money on traditional software development and maintenance than they did in 1997 (King & Cole-Gomolski, 1999). Instead, they increased work on packaged applications by a factor of 3, and they increased outsourcing by 42%. When in-house development occurred, it was related to Internet technology. This is no doubt due to the limited availability of high-quality packaged Internet applications, given the relative novelty of moving mainstream applications to the Internet. Developers probably also see Internet-related development as being more challenging and more fun.

Managers today have many choices when seeking an information system. The choices we will examine in more detail are packaged applications purchased off the shelf, customized software and systems, outsourced development and operation, enterprisewide systems, and in-house development. These choices, of course, represent points along a continuum of acquisition options. There are many hybrid combinations along the way.

PACKAGED APPLICATIONS

Packaged applications are available in a wide variety of functions, sizes, prices, and platform compatibilities. The Gartner Group projected that the market for packaged applications for the client/server platform alone would reach $44.6 billion for 1999 (Meringer, Deutsch, & Manoussoff, 1997). The market is expected to decline to $37.5 billion by 2002, however, because dollars that would normally go to packaged applications were diverted to Y2K efforts, intranet development services, and component-based applications (discussed later in this chapter).

Packaged applications tend to be complete and somewhat monolithic and resistant to customization. It is rare that a packaged application completely meets the needs of a particular organization, so the temptation to make changes in the application is great. Many vendors ask that their systems not be customized, although many are in practice.

There are many different criteria managers can use to choose the appropriate packaged application. One set is provided, in no particular order of importance, here (Hoffer, George, & Valacich, 1999): cost, functionality, vendor support, viability of vendor, flexibility, documentation, response time, and ease of installation.

Bell Canada follows a series of sequential steps in its software acquisition process (Mayrand & Coallier, 1996). The process begins with the internal identification of a need, followed by the definition of detailed requirements, the issuance of a request for quotation, and vendor preselection. Next, risks are assessed at three levels: development and support capability of the supplier, product, and project. Assessments are followed by vendor selection, negotiation of a contract, and contract management and operation.

Increasingly, software developed for the packaged applications market is being developed with the use of overseas programmers and developers, primarily because of wage rates that are an order of magnitude less than those in the United States. Overseas programmers also have a reputation for being more productive than U.S. programmers and for producing higher-quality software (Yourdon, 1996). The practice of using global software teams, whether internal to a firm or contracted out, is gaining popularity as a way to deal with increased wages and the limited supply of IS professionals in the United States (Carmel, 1997; Boutellier et al., 1998). Using less expensive and more productive labor helps keep down the costs of software development.

Globally based software teams are not beneficial for every software development project. Developing software with globally dispersed teams is motivated by five factors, according to Carmel (1997): (1) employing the best programmers in the world, regardless of where they are located; (2) effectively managing globally dispersed teams through information technology; (3) designing projects so that development work can proceed around the clock, taking advantage of programmers in different time zones; (4) signaling the global presence of a company by locating development activities around the world; and (5) reducing costs through employing programmers in low-wage countries. There are seven primary factors that companies consider in moving programming work to low-wage countries, according to Yourdon (1996). The first factor is programming language familiarity; that is, the development project needs people with expertise in a particular programming language. The second reason is the availability of telecommunications connections, the third is spoken language (typically English), and the fourth factor is large staff. Given the combined costs of information technology infrastructure, travel, and establishing the relationship with a foreign firm, it makes sense to work with a firm with a large staff so that the overhead costs can be distributed over more personnel. The final three factors are low cost, the ability to start on the project quickly, and the experience of the off-shore firm with other projects and other global partners.[2]

CUSTOMIZED SOFTWARE

Customized software as used here does not refer to packaged applications that have been customized to better fit the acquiring organization's needs. Rather, it refers to the development of software that has been commissioned from another firm for the acquiring firm. Typically, when we think of this type of system development, we think of it being provided by large consulting firms, such as Andersen Consulting. But there are hundreds of smaller, regional consulting firms that provide the same services. Rather than have a system designed and developed in-house, an organization can contract with a consulting firm to have the system built. Such an approach works very well when the organization does not have the in-house experience, personnel, or expertise to develop the desired system.

OUTSOURCED OPERATIONS AND DEVELOPMENT

Outsourcing is the process of contracting with a separate business entity to provide some to all information system services. These services can include operations, maintenance, telecommunications, specific application areas, and systems development and support. Outsourcing is a large and growing segment of the IS industry, with a global market of $76 billion in 1995 and a projected global market of over $121 billion in the year 2000 (Lacity & Willcocks, 1998). Outsourcing provides a way for firms to leapfrog their current position in IS and to turn over development and operations to staff with skills not found internally. Outsourcing continues to grow in popularity. According to a 1998 Corbett Group study, 97% of more than 200 executives polled said they increased spending on outsourcing in 1998 over 1997. These executives also expected to increase spending in 1999 over 1998 levels. A total of 60% were satisfied with their outsourcing initiatives (Merrill, 1999).[3]

Enterprisewide Systems

One of the most remarkable trends in systems development in the 1990s is the growth of enterprisewide systems, sometimes called *enterprise resource planning (ERP)* systems. Enterprisewide systems offer the ability to integrate business processes across functional areas so that the focus of the system is the process, not the parochial interests of particular departments or divisions. Although these systems are quite complex, costly to implement, and somewhat inflexible in the way they must be implemented and operated, many organizations have followed the ERP path. The 1998 market for enterprisewide systems is estimated to have been $15 billion, with SAP AG holding 33% of the market. SAP's 1998 revenues of $5 billion represent more than 19,000 installations of its key product, R/3, is in more than 90 countries. The other market leaders in this segment include Baan, PeopleSoft, and Oracle.

Although the general trend with regard to ERP systems has been for a firm to deal exclusively with a single vendor for a single enterprisewide implementation of the vendor's ERP products, some firms have instead followed a best-of-breed strategy. Such strategy typically entails using different products from different ERP vendors as well as specialized products from non-ERP vendors, and developing other software in-house to fill in the gaps and ease cross-product integration. The key advantage of a best-of-breed strategy is that it capitalizes on the strengths of individual vendor products. For example, a firm might use SAP's order entry modules, Oracle's financial systems, and PeopleSoft's human resources products. For the increased system functionality offered in such a scheme, however, the firm gives up the single architecture, single interface, and single vendor connection that come with adopting one ERP vendor's products to support all functions throughout the firm.[4]

IN-HOUSE DEVELOPMENT

Clearly, given the alternative methods of systems development available to managers today, it is no longer as cost effective as it once was (if it ever really was) to completely develop an information system in-house from scratch. One reason is that systems are much more complex and interdependent with other systems now than they have ever been before. Another reason is that in almost 50 years of systems development, many basic administrative systems have been developed so often and in so many different ways that we can say without a doubt that we have mastered these systems. Payroll is certainly an example, as are inventory management and order entry.

Edward Yourdon, the well-known systems development pioneer, says the development of yet another order entry or inventory control system is boring, although it is work that has to be done. Maintaining legacy systems—systems that companies have been using and maintaining for decades due to their mission-critical nature despite their technical obsolescence—falls into the same category. Yourdon (1996, p. 33) says that developing traditional administrative systems (again) and maintaining legacy systems is commodity work and therefore subject to commodity pricing. If true, then it follows that managers would seek low-cost alternatives to in-house development and maintenance.

That software maintenance may account for as much as 50 to 80% of the information systems budget (Nosek & Palvia, 1990) provides additional incentives for finding low-cost alternatives. Obviously, more of the information system budget devoted to maintenance leaves less funding for development. In-house development can lead to a larger maintenance burden than other development methods, such as packaged applications, according to a recent study (Banker, Davis, & Slaughter, 1998). The study found that using a code generator as the basis for in-house development was related to an increase in maintenance hours, while using packaged applications was associated with a decrease in maintenance effort.

CHOOSING AMONG ACQUISITION METHODS

As we have seen, managers have many choices when seeking to acquire software systems. It is useful to compare the choices side by side, even though sometimes the method chosen is determined by political and other organizational factors beyond the manager's control. Table 14.1 compares the five methods introduced here on six different criteria: cost, risk, extent to which the system matches the firm's needs, ease of installation, maintenance, and firmwide impact. As the table shows, there are trade-offs in choosing one acquisition method over others. Determining which criteria are the most crucial will help determine which method is chosen. For example, if meeting the needs of the organization is the most important criterion, then in-house development would be the best method to choose. However, along with the close match between organization needs and system capabilities comes high cost and extensive maintenance needs. There is also some degree of risk involved. Alternatively, if one wants to minimize cost and risk, packaged applications may be the best choice, but packaged applications will never completely match organizational requirements. If an important goal is the integration of business functions and the rationalization of core business processes, then enterprisewide systems are prime candidates because such systems by nature can have far-reaching impacts on the

TABLE 14.1　Comparison of Software Acquisition Choices

Method	Cost	Risk	Meets Needs	Ease of Installation	Maintenance	Firmwide Impact
Packaged applications	Low to Moderate	Low to Moderate	Limited	Moderate	Moderate	Limited
Customized software	Moderate to High	Moderate	Limited to Extensive	Moderate	Moderate to Extensive	Depends on scope
Outsourced operations and development	Moderate to High	Moderate	Limited	Not applicable since systems are installed by someone else	Not applicable since systems are maintained by someone else	Limited to Extensive, depending on amount outsourced
Enterprisewide systems	High	Moderate to High	Limited	Difficult, complex	Moderate to Extensive	Extensive
In-house development	High	Moderate to High	Extensive	Moderate	Extensive	Limited

entire organization. Outsourcing and customized software can also have firmwide impacts if the scope of their design is broad and extensive enough. All three methods can come with high price tags, though. There are, of course, other criteria that could be used to help inform the decision of which method to use; these six are offered as a useful and illustrative set.

SOFTWARE DEVELOPMENT

In the early years, especially in the time before third-generation languages such as COBOL, software development more closely resembled an art form than a production process. Some will argue that software development is still not a regular, repeatable production process, but we are clearly making progress in that direction. Several processes as well as tools and techniques have been developed to make software development more predictable. A number of these are described in the next two sections. We will look first at several tools and techniques, including prototyping, joint application design (JAD), computer-assisted software engineering (CASE) tools, and visual development environments. In the following section we will look at process, and then end with a table that compares the processes discussed.

TOOLS AND TECHNIQUES

Prototyping is a technique, borrowed from engineering, in which a scale model of an object or system is developed, both as a test of concept and as a device to facilitate communication between designer and client. The software tools used for prototyping can be as simple as paint programs or as complex as CASE tools that allow users to enter data and navigate among screens. The main idea behind prototyping as a technique is that it provides a means by which developers can transform user requirements into objects that users can see, touch, and use. Users can then provide feedback to developers about the prototype, about what works and what does not, and about what else they would like to see. The developer can then take that feedback and use it to modify the prototype, beginning another round of iteration between user and developer. At some point, a decision must be made to either keep the prototype as the basis for the production system or to throw it away but use the knowledge gained in the prototyping process to construct the production system. Prototyping marks a huge gain in productivity over earlier means for specifying requirements by which the best that could be done to represent requirements would have been paper-based specifications and diagrams. By its very nature, prototyping encourages meaningful and frequent interaction between user and developer.

Joint application design (JAD) is a technique developed primarily to address the issues involved in determining user requirements for a system. Traditionally, a developer determines requirements by interviewing users, studying existing systems, perusing input form, reports, and other documents, and observing users while working. User interviews are an important source of information for what the system being developed should do and look like. Interviews, however, are difficult to schedule because users must also tend to their regular work while assisting the developer. Contradictions between users must also be reconciled, which requires follow-up interviews. The process can be very time-consuming and frustrating.

JAD was developed to deal with the difficulties in scheduling interviews and reconciling the information collected from them. In JAD, key users meet with management representatives and systems developers, sometimes for a day, sometimes for an entire week, to determine requirements for a system. The process is very structured, typically led by a trained JAD facilitator whose primary role is to keep the process moving. JAD essentially allows for many interviews to be conducted at once and for contradictions to be reconciled on the spot (although that is not always possible). A JAD session is typically held off-site to minimize the distractions that participants experience working at the office. (See Wood & Silver, 1995, for more information on JAD.)

Computer-assisted software engineering (CASE) tools were developed as a way to use the power of information technology to support the software development process. CASE tools are bundles of software tools that make analysis, design, documentation, and coding consistent, complete, and easier to accomplish. They include tools for creating and maintaining data flow diagrams, entity-relationship diagrams, and process flow diagrams, among others. The diagramming tools are linked in that each object created in one of the tools is entered into the central data repository around which the CASE product is built. The repository stores data about all of the different elements that make up the system analysis and design. CASE tools typically also contain facilities that allow for screen and report design, which support prototyping, and that generate database structures and program code. Many CASE tools also allow checking for consistency, completeness, and design errors.

Although CASE tools can be expensive, costing several thousand dollars per copy, including training and support, it is generally believed to increase developer productivity. A case study of the implementation of Texas Instruments' Information Engineering Facility (IEF) at a British firm in 1989–1990 reports productivity improvements of 85% and system delivery rate increases of around 200% (Finlay & Mitchell, 1994). Developers who use CASE are more likely to follow a structured systems development methodology and take part in JAD, prototyping, and rapid application development than their counterparts who do not use CASE (Lending &

Chervany, 1998). However, given the high cost and steep learning curve for using CASE, relatively few firms have adopted CASE tools, and of those that have, relatively few developers have actually used it (Iivari, 1996; Lending & Chervany, 1998). When CASE tools have been adopted, there was strong management support for the approach, the tools were perceived as having relative advantage over non-CASE methods, and use tended to be mandated, not voluntary (Iivari, 1996).

Visual development environments is a term that refers to a new generation of programming tools that make programming more productive. These tools can increase programming productivity through their object-oriented focus (discussed later) and the ability they give developers to easily create screens, reports, and graphical user interface controls. Some of the best known visual development environments include Microsoft's VisualBasic, Powersoft's PowerBuilder, and Inprise's Delphi. Visual development environments are popular, and their use is growing. For example, International Data Corporation forecasts the use of VisualBasic to increase 3.5% per year between 1998 and 2003 to more than 6.8 million users, and 45% of managers surveyed by *Computerworld* identified VisualBasic as one of the two languages they consider most important in their future development efforts (Orenstein, 1999).

COMPARING TOOLS AND TECHNIQUES

The four software development tools and techniques just introduced have two things in common: Each increases the productivity of systems developers, and each can be used to save time in the development process. However, each tool and technique has its own unique advantages and disadvantages, as shown in Table 14.2. Prototyping's primary advantage is speed. Its use can speed the requirements analysis process and the early stages of design and construction. Sometimes, however, the iteration between developers and users can go on indefinitely, potentially prolonging the process. On the other hand, ending the iteration too early can prematurely freeze requirements before they have been fully explored and discovered.

TABLE 14.2   Comparison of Tools and Techniques Used in Software Development

Tool and Technique	Key Advantages	Key Disadvantages
Prototyping	Is speedy Provides tangible model that can become basis for production system	Has iteration that can continue indefinitely Can be too fast—requirements can be frozen too early
JAD	Saves time in interviewing Has very structured process	Is expensive Is low tech
CASE	Enforces structure Acts as repository Facilitates error checking	Enforces structure Has steep learning curve Is expensive
Visual development environments	Has object-oriented focus Is relatively inexpensive Offers ease of window creation	Has a learning curve

JAD helps elicit requirements in a complete and thorough manner, and it saves time in interviewing and data collection time, but it can be expensive in terms of travel and living expenses for participants and in terms of the salary expenses incurred during its course. CASE tools are also expensive, and they have a steep learning curve for developers. Their use, however, engenders structure into the development process, helping make the process more like engineering. (Structure is also a potential disadvantage in IS shops where there was no structure previously or where structure limits creativity and speed.) Perhaps the main advantage for CASE tools is the central repository because it reinforces standards for all members of the development team. The contents of the repository can also potentially be used in other projects. Finally, visual development environments offer the advantages of an object-oriented focus (discussed in the next section under "reuse") and relative low cost. Like CASE tools, though, visual development environments do have a not insubstantial learning curve associated with them.

SOFTWARE DEVELOPMENT PROCESSES

Along with tools and techniques created to increase development productivity, a great deal of attention has also been paid to process. Even the most innovative tools and techniques used to support software development will be less than effective if they are not adequately embedded in a guiding development process. In this section, we briefly cover some of the major processes designed to improve software development: structured analysis and structured design, rapid application design (RAD), reuse, and participatory design.

Structured analysis and structured design were proposed at the end of the 1970s as part of the general push toward moving software development away from an art form toward an engineering discipline. Structured analysis relied on many of the diagrams now standard in CASE tools, such as data flow diagrams and entity relationship diagrams. Structured design focused on tools such as structure charts and concepts such as modularization, coupling, cohesion, and structured programming. But more important than the specific diagrams and tools used in structured analysis and design was the focus on managing the overall process as organized and disciplined (Yourdon, 1989). Despite the intuitive appeal of bringing order to chaos that structured analysis and structured design promise, adoption by software development groups has generally been slow (Fichman & Kemerer, 1993). For many, it was difficult to accept discipline when it had been missing before, and a not insubstantial learning curve was associated with learning how to use the many diagrams and other tools that supported structured analysis and design.

Rapid application development (RAD) is a development methodology generally credited to James Martin, another well-known systems development leader (Martin, 1991). The idea behind RAD is captured in its name: dramatically shorten the time necessary for systems to be developed. Complex business systems can take years to develop using structured analysis and design processes, but with the ever-quickening pace of business in a global economy, firms cannot wait for systems that might no longer be adequate models of the business processes they are supposed to support. According to Martin, following the RAD approach can result in a system in six months, when following the traditional approach would have taken four times as long.

RAD can result in such vast time savings and related savings in other resources such as money because of its design. First RAD makes heavy use of JAD and CASE tools to support prototyping. The first JAD meetings in a rapid application development effort may involve prototyping earlier in the development process than would a traditional JAD. The prototype developed also tends to become the basis for the production system rather than being thrown away, as discussed previously. Second, the prototyping process in a RAD requires more intensive participation from users (in a true partnership with developers). Users may also become involved in the design process itself instead of ending their participation after requirements determination is complete, which is more typically the case. Martin (1991) also argues that for RAD to be successful, developers must be trained in the right skills and methodologies, and management must lend its complete support.

RAD is not without its problems. Sometimes, due to the speed with which systems are developed, some of the basics of software development are overlooked. These include interface consistency across the system, programming standards such as documentation and data-naming standards, upward scalability to larger numbers of more diverse users, and planning for system administration chores such as database maintenance and organization, backup and recovery, and so on (Bourne, 1994).

Reuse is the use of previously written software resources in new applications. Because so many bits and pieces of applications are relatively generic across applications, it seems intuitive that great savings can be achieved in many areas if those generic bits and pieces do not have to be written anew each time they are needed. Reuse should increase programmer productivity because being able to use existing software for some functions means they can perform more work in the same amount of time. Reuse should also decrease development time, minimizing schedule overruns. Because existing pieces of software have already been tested, reusing them should also result in higher-quality software with lower defect rates, which is easier to maintain.

Although reuse can conceivably apply to many different aspects of software, typically it is most commonly applied to two different development technologies, object orientation and component-based development. Object orientation is a marked jump from the traditional approach to programming; it separates the data stored about an entity and the functions the program performs that use those data. In object orientation, both data and function are combined into one item. For example, an employee object would contain both the data about employees and the instructions necessary for calculating payroll for a variety of job types. The object could be used in any application that dealt with employees, but if changes had to be made in calculating payroll for different types of employees, the changes would have to be made only to the object and not to the various applications that used it. By definition, using the employee object in more than one application constitutes reuse. As with CASE tools and structured analysis and design, developers have been slow to adopt object orientation (Fichman & Kemerer, 1993). That has started to change recently, however, with the growing popularity of object-oriented programming languages such as C++ and Java.

Component-based development is similar to object orientation in that the focus is on creating general-purpose pieces of software that can be used interchangeably in many different programs. Components can be as small as objects or as large as pieces of software that handle single business functions, such as currency conversion. The idea behind component-based development is the assembly of an application from many different components at many different levels of complexity and size. Many vendors, such as Sterling Software, are working on developing libraries of components that can be retrieved and assembled as needed into desired applications. While the market for component-based development is small, estimated currently at about 200,000 developers, it is expected to grow at a rate of over 65% per year to a total of 1.5 million developers in 2003 (Orenstein, 1999).

There is some evidence that reuse can be effective, especially from the object-orientation perspective. For example, one laboratory study found reuse of object libraries to result in increased productivity, reduced defect density, and reduced rework (Basili, Briand, & Melo, 1996). However, for reuse to work in an organizational setting, many different issues must be addressed. Technical issues include the current lack of (1) methodologies for creating and clearly defining and labeling reusable components for placement in a library and (2) reusable and reliable software resources. Key organizational issues include the lack of commitment to reuse as well as the lack of proper training and rewards needed to promote it, the lack of organizational support for institutionalizing reuse, and the difficulty in measuring the economic gains from reuse. Critical legal and contractual issues focus on reusing objects and components originally used in other programs and systems (Kim & Stohr, 1998).

Participatory design is an approach to systems development that is very different from anything we have discussed so far. Developed in Northern Europe, participatory design focuses primarily on the system's users and how the system will affect their work lives. In some cases, the entire user community may play an active role in the systems development process; in others, users may select representatives to represent them. Typically, system developers work for the users. Management and outside consultants provide advice but do not control the process. Participatory design efforts include a repertoire of flexible practices and general guidelines. Running through the repertoire are the twin themes of mutual reciprocal learning, in which users and developers teach each other about work and technology respectively, and design by doing, which resembles prototyping but does not necessarily require sophisticated computing to implement (Carmel, Whitaker, & George, 1993). Although well known in Northern Europe, especially in the Nordic countries, participatory design is still in its infancy in North America.

COMPARISON OF SOFTWARE DEVELOPMENT PROCESSES

As with the tools and techniques used to support systems development, each development process promotes improved software development, and each has its own unique advantages and disadvantages, many of which have been discussed. Table 14.3 lists the processes and their key advantages and disadvantages side by side. Although structured analysis and design were introduced more than 20 years ago, structured methodologies have yet to be introduced into all IS shops. Despite the advantage of supporting a more engineeringlike approach to development, IS shops were slow to adopt structured methods due to the learning curves involved in learning the methods and in comprehending how best to use the various diagramming techniques involved. The clear advantage for the rapid application development approach is speed, with heavy user participation also being an advantage. Speed is also the worst enemy of the RAD approach because many of the standards of systems development, such as scalability and planning for systems administration, are sometimes ignored during the accelerated development process. Savings in

TABLE 14.3   Comparison of Software Development Processes

Process	Key Advantages	Key Disadvantages
Structured analysis and structured design	Is a structured method Introduces methodology	Was slow to be adopted by developers Has a learning curve for method Has a learning curve for tools that support method
RAD	Is speedy Offers heavy user participation	Can be too fast—requirements can be frozen too early Can overlook basic standards of systems development
Reuse	Can reduce development time Improves software quality	Was slow to be adopted by developers Requires organizational support
Participatory design	Is user centered	Is not very well known outside Northern Europe May represent radical departure for some North American firms

development time and increased systems quality are advantages of reuse, but as with the structured methods, adoption in IS shops has been slow. For reuse to achieve its maximum benefits, there also needs to be organizational support for encouraging the creation of reusable components and of making those available to other developers. Finally, participatory design has the advantage of being user centered, with the potential to match the systems being developed to the work they support. This approach is not very well known outside Northern Europe, however, and it represents a radical departure from past efforts in many organizations.

MODELS

Unlike many of the other areas of study featured in this book, software acquisition and development has no single universally agreed-upon model that represents all of its key variables and relationships. Perhaps the closest thing there is to a universal model of systems development is the systems development life cycle, although there are as many different versions of the life cycle as there are people who write about it. In the next section, we provide two generic life-cycle models, the waterfall and the spiral models. Following that, we will present a model that attempts to explain system use once a system has been implemented (Lucas, 1977). Finally, we will present a model of software acquisition strategy and implementation based on the work of Iivari and Ervasti (1992).

THE SYSTEMS DEVELOPMENT LIFE CYCLE

The systems development life cycle (SDLC) embodies the key ideas in any product life cycle. At some point, a need is recognized; the need is investigated, and a solution is designed, built, and released. Eventually, the solution reaches its maximum usefulness and begins to decline. It must then be replaced and a new solution must be created. One cycle has ended and a new one begins.

Although no two people in the IS field, either academics or practitioners, seem to agree about the exact form and content of the systems development life cycle, it does constitute a useful model of the systems development process. Figure 14.1 shows a generic SDLC model, typically referred to as a *waterfall model.*

Although different versions of the waterfall SDLC have different numbers of phases, the generic model here has five phases that capture the basic structure of the systems development process. The first phase, *planning,* represents all of the activities that result in the identification of a need for a system. For in-house development, that need comes from a high-level planning process or users and may be the result of a problem or an opportunity. For a software vendor, the need may be identified through market research or other means.

Once the need is recognized, it is important to gain a clear understanding of the problem or opportunity that sparked the need. The existing system should be analyzed, and any additional requirements should be determined in this phase, *analysis.* Useful tools for analysis include JAD and prototyping. Once the existing situation is understood, along with where the system under development needs to be, a solution can be designed, which is what occurs in the *design* phase. Design typically involves both high-level logical design and physical design tied to a particular computing platform and operating environment. Once designed, the solution can be constructed, tested, and installed or released, the primary activities of *implementation.* Once the solution has been installed in an organization, the *maintenance* phase begins. In maintenance, the work centers on keeping the solution viable, including making any changes required due to the changing business environment and changing regulations and legal conditions. In maintenance, programmers also work to correct errors in the system and to optimize system performance. At some point, the solution is no longer viable and a new solution must be sought, ending one cycle and beginning another.

FIGURE 14.1 A Generic Waterfall Systems Development Life Cycle

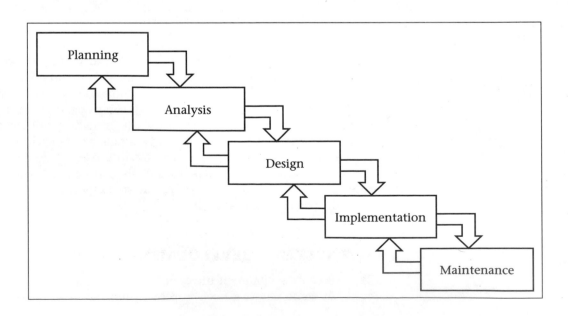

Notice the two sets of arrows connecting the phases in Figure 14.1. One set goes downhill, connecting the phases in the order in which they were just described. Yet the systems development process is rarely this cleanly structured. More typical are returns to earlier phases for one or more iterations before progress can continue. That is the purpose of the set of arrows going backward in the diagram. They allow the work flow to move from one phase to an earlier phase and, in conjunction with the downstream arrows, allow for numerous iterations between phases.

One other point that should be made is that the division of the overall systems development process into distinct phases allows for milestones and concrete deliverables to be specified for the end of each phase. Project management may not allow the next phase to begin until those milestones and deliverables have been met. Distinct phases also allow higher management to review a development project at the end of each phase to determine whether the project should continue or be stopped at that point.

The name *waterfall* refers to the shape of the model in that the work flow cascades from one phase down to the next until the end is reached. Techniques such as RAD use modified versions of the waterfall SDLC. For example, Martin's RAD life cycle combines analysis and logical design into a single phase called *user design* (Martin, 1991).

Another way to visualize the SDLC is the spiral model (see Boehm, 1988), shown in Figure 14.2. The spiral model, also referred to as an evolutionary model,

FIGURE 14.2 A Spiral Systems Development Life Cycle

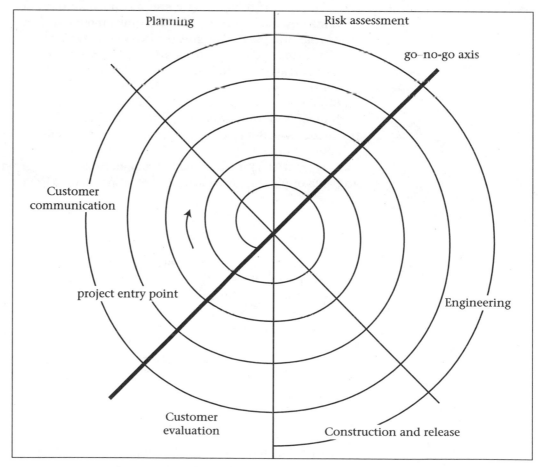

Source: Pressman (1997).

combines the iterative nature of prototyping with the systematic, stepwise approach of the waterfall model. Software is seen as being developed in a series of incremental releases. Early releases might be prototypes, but increasingly the versions of the software developed are more complete. As more complete versions of the software are released, what was conceptualized as maintenance in the waterfall model is conceptualized here as subsequent passes around the spiral.

According to the spiral model, each pass around the spiral, whether for initial iterative development or for later maintenance, moves through six different tasks (Pressman, 1997). The first is *customer communication,* which involves establishing effective communication between the developer and the customer or user. The second task is *planning,* where resources, timelines, and other project information are defined. The third task is *risk assessment.* Here, technical and management risks are assessed, and if they are too high, the project can be ended at the go–no-go axis. The fourth task is *engineering,* which represents the building of the software application. Engineering corresponds to design in the waterfall model. The fifth task is *construction and release,* which contains many of the same activities that were included in the implementation phase of the waterfall life cycle: construction, testing, installation, and providing user support. The sixth task is *customer evaluation.* The evaluation process elicits feedback on the engineering and construction and release tasks.

The waterfall model is a simple and easy-to-understand representation of the systems development process; the spiral model presents a more complex and hence more realistic view. The spiral model adds iteration, risk assessment, and a more sophisticated view of maintenance to the basic waterfall model. Many of the basic tasks central to system development are the same in both models, however, as would be expected. The spiral model has also had great success in practice. Boehm (1988) cites adherence to the model as the cause of productivity improvements as high as 50% in development projects at TRW, where Boehm's particular version of the model was developed and used. The spiral model is not suited to all software development efforts, however. It best fits large-scale development projects. A limitation in practice is its demand for considerable risk-assessment expertise to succeed, an issue of particular concern to both Boehm and Pressman.

A MODEL OF SYSTEM USE

Lucas (1997), who has extensively studied information systems implementation, identified six factors that influence the extent to which a system is used. These factors and their relationships to each other and to system use are shown in Figure 14.3. The variables in the model are defined in Table 14.4.

The six factors that are thought to directly affect use are (1) user's personal stake, (2) user demographics, (3) performance, (4) satisfaction, (5) system characteristics, and 6) organizational support. The first four factors all relate to the user himself or herself. The last two factors are contextual, largely outside the user's control.

The user's personal stake refers to the importance of the system domain for the user, that is, how relevant the system is to the work the user performs. The higher the user's personal stake in the system, the more likely he or she will use it. As the model shows, the user's personal stake is itself influenced by the level of support management provides for implementation and by the urgency of the problem

FIGURE 14.3 Lucas's Model of Factors Affecting Use

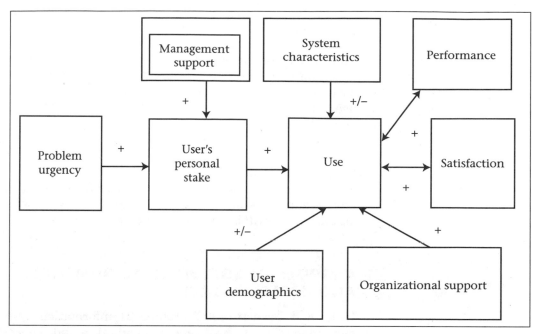

Source: Lucas (1997).

TABLE 14.4   Constructs from Lucas's 1997 Model of Factors Affecting System Use

Construct	Definition
Problem urgency	Extent to which the business problem is pressing
Management support	Extent to which organizational management is in favor of and provides backing for the system and its users
User's personal stake	Important area of the domain of the system for the individual
System characteristics	Aspects of the system's design such as ease of use, reliability, and quality
User demographics	User characteristics, such as personality type, business and social history, and degree of computer experience
Performance	What an individual user can do with a system to support his or her work
Organizational support	Action that makes the system easy to use, such as ease of access
Satisfaction	Extent to which the system fully supplies what is expected, desired, or needed
Use	Extent to which an individual incorporates the system into his or her work life

addressed by the system to the user. The higher the level of management support and the more urgent the problem, the higher the user's personal stake in the system. User demographics are user characteristics, such as personality type, business and social history, and degree of computer experience. The presence of some demographics will lead to higher levels of use; others will be associated with lower levels of use. Performance reflects what an individual user can do with a system to support his or her work. The relationship between performance and use goes both ways. The higher the levels of performance, the more use. The more use, the greater the performance. The relationship between use and satisfaction is also a two-way relationship. The more satisfied the user is with the system, the more he or she will use it. The more he or she uses it, the more satisfied he or she will be.

The two contextual factors are system characteristics and organization support. System characteristics include such aspects of the system's design as ease of use, reliability, quality, and relevance to the tasks that the system supports. As with demographics, some system characteristics will be associated with higher levels of use, and others will be related to lower levels of use. *Organization support* refers to actions that make the system easy to use, such as ease of access. Support often takes the form of a formal support infrastructure in the firm consisting of people and systems that help users with any problems they encounter or questions they have regarding system use. The better the overall level of support, the more likely an individual will be to use a particular system.

A MODEL OF SOFTWARE ACQUISITION AND IMPLEMENTATION

Iivari and Ervasti (1992) studied 21 information systems developed and implemented for the city government of Oulu, Finland. Their study is one of the few that actually took into account software acquisition strategies and the role they play in the systems development process. Iivari and Ervasti focused on three acquisition strategies: (1) packaged applications, (2) joint development between the city government and an external software developer, and (3) in-house development. Using correlational analysis, they found that acquisition strategy was related to job satisfaction, effectiveness of the adopting organizational unit, the structure and process of the adopting unit, and the originality of the system. They found no relationships between acquisition strategy and user participation, management participation, and implementability. (Implementability consists of three different measures: ease of implementation, implementation support, and extent of IS modifications.) A model based on these findings is presented in Figure 14.4, and the variables in the model are defined in Table 14.5. The positive and negative signs in the figure indicate the direction of the statistically significant correlation found to exist between each set of variables in the model.

Even though acquisition strategy is not related to user participation, management participation, or implementability, these constructs were found to be related to other factors. For completeness, these other relationships are shown in the model. Acquisition strategy may not be related to the relative ease of implementation of a system, but user participation is positively related to implementability. Implementability, in turn, is positively related to unit effectiveness and the structure and process of the adopting unit. Acquisition strategy is positively related to both of these factors. Both user and management participation are positively related to the unit effectiveness. Finally, in addition to its direct, positive relationship with the structure and process of the adopting unit, acquisition strategy is indirectly related to structure and process through its positive relationship with originality.

Two findings of note from this research are the lack of relationships between acquisition strategy and user participation, on one hand, and between acquisition strategy and implementability, on the other. It seems intuitive that the role users would play in the development process would depend on the acquisition strategy

FIGURE 14.4   A Model of the Role of Software Acquisition Strategy in Implementation

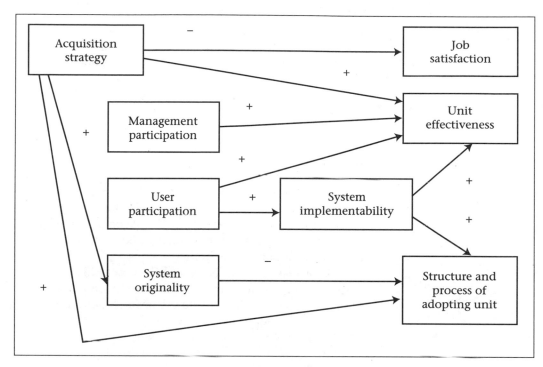

Based on Iivari and Ervasti (1997).

TABLE 14.5   Variables in the Iivari and Ervasti (1992) Model of the Role of Software Acquisition Strategy in Implementation

Acquisition strategy	Strategy used to acquire system: either packaged applications, joint development, or in-house development
Management participation	Extent to which organizational management was involved in the implementation
User participation	Extent to which users were involved in the implementation
System originality	Novelty of the system and the inverse of the number of installations
System implementability	Ease of implementation, extent of training, and extent of modifications required during implementation
Job satisfaction	Extent to which needs, desires, and expectations about the overall job are met
Unit effectiveness	A series of items, including unit rating of quantity of output, quality of output, innovativeness, reputation for excellence, and morale
Structure and process of adopting unit	A series of items, including division of work, unit automation, unit standardization, distribution of unit authority, job dependence among unit personnel, and unit conflict

used. For example, there would be little user participation in the process of acquiring packaged applications beyond the users' role in the analysis process. At the other end of the spectrum, for in-house development, users would have the opportunity for involvement in many aspects of the design and development process in addition to their role in analysis. However, it is generally the case that users have a restricted role in systems development, limited typically to participation in early requirements determination and assessment of completed systems. Such activities would be largely the same, regardless of the acquisition strategy employed, thus helping to explain the lack of a relationship between acquisition strategy and user participation.

It also seems intuitive that there should be a relationship between acquisition strategy and implementability. Again, taking packaged applications as an example, vendors would be expected to provide little implementation support past the somewhat mechanical installation process. The ability to modify the software would also be limited. For in-house implementations, the level of implementation support would be relatively high, given that the designers and developers themselves would be onsite and able to provide assistance. Although modifications during implementation would be discouraged, they could be more easily handled for a system developed in-house than would be the case for packaged applications. The lack of a relationship here is not as easy to explain as the lack of a relationship between acquisition strategy and user participation.

The research by Iivari and Ervasti (1992) is noteworthy because they directly consider acquisition strategy. Given the changing nature of the systems development process in organizations today, acquisition strategy has become an important factor to consider.

FUTURE RESEARCH

As this chapter has shown, there are many choices for managers engaging in systems development and software acquisition. New choices seem to become available on a regular basis as practitioners and academics seek to improve software development methods and make them faster and more effective. Given the continuous introduction of new approaches and techniques, it is difficult to keep up and plan and conduct meaningful research accordingly. Yet much future research can be done to help us understand software development and acquisition, especially since the software crisis identified by NATO in 1968 is still with us. Six different areas for future research—model development, the acquisition process, the trend to enterprisewide systems, the effects of rapid development, reuse, and the effects of the growing pervasiveness of the Internet and corporate intranets—are briefly described.

Four different models were presented in this chapter: the waterfall systems development life cycle, the spiral systems development life cycle, a model of system use, and a model of software acquisition strategy and implementation. Each model captures a piece of the larger software acquisition process, but no model adequately addresses all aspects of the process. A comprehensive model, especially one that takes software acquisition strategy into account, would be useful to both practitioners and academics.

Most research in systems development has focused on in-house development and, more recently, on how software is developed by software vendors. As more and more development work involves acquiring software, assembling applications, and outsourcing development, acquisition strategy becomes an important concept to study. Which strategies are more effective and why? What contextual variables are important to determining the best acquisition strategy?

One acquisition strategy that continues to grow in popularity is the reliance on large-scale enterprisewide systems, such as SAP's R/3. To date, there have been few academic studies of enterprisewide systems, the decision to acquire them, their implementation, and their success or failure. Given the popularity of this acquisition option, rigorous study of them is definitely needed.

As we have seen, for software vendors and in-house development, speed to completion has become more and more important. Rapid development processes have been in place for several years in many organizations, but we know little about how effective they are other than anecdotal evidence that reports faster development. But can faster development be consistent with quality development? How effective and efficient are applications developed at an accelerated rate? Does rapid development lead to what Yourdon (1996) calls "good-enough" software, which can serve its purpose reasonably and then be replaced with something else that is also good enough rather than ideal?

Savings in time to completion is a reason for increased reuse of software components and objects. Although reuse has been a popular topic for decades, there is still much to be done to make it an effective, reliable approach. More research is called for on making reuse viable, both from the perspective of making it easier to prepare objects and components to be used by others and from the perspective of making it easier to find desired objects and components and use them in systems under development.

Finally, software acquisition and development are both going to be affected by increased use of the Internet and of corporate intranets. Intranets will influence the look and functionality of systems developed for internal use. The Internet will facilitate adopting parts of internal systems for shared use with external constituencies, such as customers and suppliers. But the Internet itself also has the potential to affect the software acquisition and development process. Already, the Internet is a prime vehicle for acquiring software specifications and demos. Being able to find existing software by easily searching the Net may expedite the early stages of acquisition and development. It will also become more common for application assemblers to use the Internet to find, download, and pay for existing objects and components they can use. Indeed, as competition continues to increase and as business cycles become increasingly shorter, it will become vital for firms to acquire and develop some systems in very short time frames. This "living in Internet time," where things seem to change on a daily basis, has the potential to dramatically affect the speed and process of systems development. The overall impact of the Internet on systems acquisition and development is an area ripe for more research.

SUMMARY

The software crisis identified more than 30 years ago continues, in large part because advances in computing hardware outstrip advances in software development. It is difficult for information systems personnel to keep up with the demand for effective, quality software to support business administrative processes. Increasingly, IS shops are focusing more on software acquisition and application assembly than on outright software development to develop and implement applications more quickly. Given the continuing software crisis, we asked three key questions at the beginning of the chapter.

1. *What are the available choices for developing information systems and software?* We answered this question in two ways: by looking at tools and techniques and by reviewing different processes. Under tools and techniques, we discussed prototyping, JAD, CASE tools, and visual development environments. Under process, we reviewed structured analysis and structured design, RAD, reuse, and participatory design. The most promising approaches in coming years appear to be prototyping, visual development environments, RAD, and reuse.

2. *What are the available choices for acquiring systems?* The primary options now available to managers that we discussed were (1) packaged applications, (2) customized software, (3) outsourcing, (4) enterprisewide systems, and (5) in-house development. Each option has its own advantages and disadvantages, but given forecasts regarding each option, it appears that outsourcing and enterprisewide systems will become the predominant modes for software acquisition in the next few years.

3. *Can a model can be developed that helps both academics and practitioners better understand the systems acquisition and development process?* We presented three models, one of the systems development life cycle, one of the factors influencing system use after implementation, and one that related acquisition strategy and aspects of the implementation process. None of these models captures the entire systems development and acquisition process. Creating such a model was one of the six areas of future research we suggested.

Clearly, much research is left to be done in the area of systems development and software acquisition. This is a dynamic field. Although some members of the development community are sometimes slow to embrace new approaches, other members are quick to invent new and better ways of doing things. When new approaches are finally adopted, they become part of established standards that are in turn difficult to dislodge. Yet new ways of doing things are continually being developed and made available to those responsible for acquiring and developing software. If a follow-up for this chapter were written 10 years from now, many of the methodologies and tools discussed here would not be included, and new, as-yet-undeveloped approaches would take their place. In the meantime, we can do our best to understand the choices that are available now and that best suit our immediate and long-term goals.

ENDNOTES

1. Software project management is a crucial part of software development. For insight into this important activity, see the chapter by Kirsch on software project management.
2. See the chapter by Saunders on virtual teams for insight into the issues related to organizing and managing distributed teams, such as the global virtual teams used to develop software.
3. See the chapter by Lacity and Willcocks on outsourcing for a more complete view of stakeholder relationships in outsourcing, as well as an analysis of outsourcing phases and activities.
4. See the chapter by Markus and Tanis on enterprise systems for a more complete treatment of the special characteristics of enterprise systems and the reasons that these systems are adopted.

Chapter 15

Software Project Management: An Integrated Perspective for an Emerging Paradigm

Laurie J. Kirsch

Practically since the birth of computing in organizations in the 1950s, individuals have struggled to successfully manage software projects to deliver the "right" software solutions on time and within budget. Early reports of project management difficulties and outright failures are numerous. For example, in his landmark writings, Brooks (1974, 1987, 1995) describes in vivid detail the many challenges and problems associated with managing large and complex efforts during the 1960s. The reporting of problems continued into the 1970s, the 1980s, and even more recently into the 1990s with the recounting of spectacular failures such as the Denver airport baggage system (O'Brien, 1994; Kaufman-Rosen & Glick, 1995) and the Confirm project, a joint effort among AMR, Marriott, Hilton, and Budget Rent-A-Car to develop a hotel and car rental reservations system (McPartlin, 1992; Oz, 1994). The failures are not unique to the United States: Sauer (1999) describes failed systems efforts in Europe, Australia, and New Zealand as well.

Software project management is the application of formal and informal techniques, tools, methods, and heuristics (collectively called "project management practices"), which are used by the project manager to motivate and guide a team to carry out a software project within a given set of constraints. Project management encompasses both hard skills, such as estimating and scheduling tasks, and soft skills, which include motivating and managing team members.

Formal project management techniques came into consciousness during World War II, when the U.S. government was undertaking massive projects, such as the Manhattan Project, but lacked a means of systematically tracking progress (Frame, 1994, 1995). The U.S. Navy, along with Booz-Allen Hamilton and the Lockheed Corporation, developed PERT (Program Evaluation and Review Techniques) to help manage the Polaris missile and submarine project in 1958 (Meredith & Mantel, 1995). During that same time period, DuPont Inc. developed the Critical Path Method (Meredith & Mantel, 1995). Techniques to manage software projects, including walk-throughs, code inspections, and sign-offs, evolved somewhat independently of general project management tools. While these techniques are still very much in use, software project managers are increasingly applying general project management techniques as well.

There has been extensive research in the area of project management. Much of this research emphasizes hard skills and examines the application and effectiveness of specific project management practices, focusing on how to use a tool or technique to improve the project process (Might & Fischer, 1985; Keil, 1995). In contrast, there is less research on topics related to the management of people, including topics such as project politics, motivation or control, and building and nurturing relationships among project stakeholders (Morris, 1996; Rodrigues & Williams, 1997). These topics represent the soft skills of project management.

Much of the extant empirical research on software project management was done in the context of the "traditional" computing paradigm of centralized mainframe processing, in which the majority of software projects involved the custom development of large applications using a procedural programming language (Rockart, Earl, & Ross, 1996). Many of these applications were "back office" or tactical in focus. Overall, the computing environment in firms was relatively homogeneous, as was the type of project, and project management practices were fairly similar across projects. Over time, this environment evolved to accommodate end-user computing (Gerrity & Rockart, 1986). The deployment of user-developed applications increased dramatically when access to relatively inexpensive but powerful computers become commonplace (Leitheiser & Wetherbe, 1986).

Today the computing environment in firms is undergoing another transition.[1] The dynamic and global business environment means that many firms require flexible, cross-functional, global software solutions that can be deployed quickly (Wetherbe, Vitalari, & Milner, 1994; Rockart et al., 1996; Collins & Kirsch, 1999). These systems are increasingly strategic in nature. Moreover, many firms recognize that the data processed and stored by existing legacy systems are extremely valuable, especially if they can be leveraged via data warehousing and mining techniques (Brachman et al., 1996; Watson & Haley, 1998). Increasingly, firms are undertaking fewer projects to build large custom-designed stand-alone applications and are instead implementing packaged software, such as data warehousing and enterprisewide resource planning (ERP) packages (Yourdon, 1996; Bancroft, Seip, & Sprengel, 1998).[2] Though fewer large applications are being developed, firms are building and deploying a wide range of relatively small applications. Some of these are Web-based applications intended to support strategic initiatives; others are stand-alone systems designed for a single functional area or business unit. Still others are designed to access and leverage the data captured and stored by legacy or ERP systems. In addition, firms are often buffering their legacy systems by building graphical user interfaces or Web-based front ends to make them more accessible and user friendly. This diversity of software applications, both large and small, tactical and strategic, is made possible, in part, by the availability of hardware that is extremely powerful and affordable and that facilitates the distribution of technology solutions across geographical locations and platforms.

The changing business environment, coupled with technological trends such as sophisticated packaged software solutions, the World Wide Web, and distributed hardware platforms, is pushing the transition from a traditional computing paradigm to an "emerging" one in which software applications and hardware platforms are increasingly more diverse. Firms now have a much more varied portfolio of new and existing applications to develop or enhance for both centralized and distributed hardware platforms (Wetherbe et al., 1994).[3] With this diversity, project management practices may vary considerably across projects. For example, the business unit may take a more active role in initiating, sponsoring, and managing strategic IT projects (Rockart et al., 1996; Bashein et al., 1997). Project team members may be scattered around the globe, adding challenges to the project manager's effort to control and coordinate their activities (Carmel, 1999), or the project itself may be outsourced (McFarlan & Nolan, 1995; Lacity & Willcocks, 1998). Therefore, the relevance of existing project management research, which reflects a fairly homogeneous computing environment, for this emerging paradigm is unclear.

This chapter is organized as follows. In the next section, empirical research related to the hard skills of project management is reviewed and is followed by a review of the evidence related to soft skills. The next part of the chapter integrates the reviewed literature by extracting core theoretical constructs underlying it and examining the relationships among the constructs. In the following section, project management practices as they relate to the emerging computing paradigm are discussed. Needed areas of future research are identified throughout these sections. The chapter concludes with some final comments on software project management.

PROJECT MANAGEMENT: THE HARD SKILLS

This section examines research related to the hard skills of project management and includes research on planning and monitoring projects, on risk and uncertainty, and on uncertainty and coordination.

PLANNING AND MONITORING PROJECTS

Project planning involves articulating tasks to accomplish a project; estimating the time, effort, and costs required to accomplish the tasks and the project; and allocating resources to the tasks. Empirical studies have demonstrated a positive relationship between effective planning and satisfactory project outcomes (Deephouse et al., 1995–96; Guinan, Cooprider, & Faraj, 1998). Reliable estimates are critical for effective project planning and monitoring (Boehm, 1984), yet estimating time, effort, and costs is one of the most difficult and challenging aspects of project management (Abdel-Hamid & Madnick, 1986; Lederer et al., 1990; Kemerer, 1997; Lind & Sulek, 1998).

Estimates can be derived from *historical data, algorithmic models* such as CO-COMO (COnstructive COst MOdel), or *expert opinion* (Linkman & Walker, 1991). To this list, Boehm (1984) adds four approaches: *Parkinson,* where the cost of a project is equal to the resources available; *price to win,* where the project cost is a price necessary to win a bid; *top down,* where the overall cost is derived from the global properties of the product; and *bottom up,* where each component is separately estimated and then the costs are aggregated. While some suggest that estimation by expert opinion is the most common approach (Linkman & Walker, 1991), others note the growing use of algorithmic models (Jones, 1991; Kemerer, 1993).

Much of the empirical research on estimating has examined the efficacy of algorithmic models. These models determine cost and effort estimates from a set of variables that are believed to be major cost drivers (Boehm, 1984). Some models, such as COCOMO, use source lines of code as a key input variable. However, this presents a number of difficulties. Chief among them are the inaccuracy of the lines of code estimate and the inability to compare these metrics across programs written in different languages (Boehm, 1984; Kemerer, 1993). To respond to these and other issues, researchers have developed alternative models. One of the most influential is function points (Albrecht & Gaffney, 1983). This approach focuses on the function that a program performs rather than its size.

In a set of field studies, Kemerer (1987, 1993) found that (1) algorithmic models must be calibrated to adjust for particular organizational environments; (2) models based on source lines of code estimates performed more poorly than models such as function points; (3) across individuals using the function points approach, interrater reliability is high; and (4) intermethod reliability is high when variations of the function point approach are used. Although most research on estimating has taken a rational view of the process, Lederer et al. (1990) point out that estimating can also be charged politically. Because there are many stakeholders involved in a typical software project, individual goals may not be aligned, and estimates can be inflated or deflated accordingly. Lederer et al. argue that estimating can therefore be viewed as both rational and political in nature.

Abdel-Hamid (1988a, 1988b) has proposed a systems dynamic model that integrates managerial aspects of software project management, such as planning and monitoring, with the technical aspects of software production. Running simulations to predict project behaviors and outcomes has produced insights into Brooks law (which states that adding people to a late project makes it later) (Abdel-Hamid & Madnick, 1989; Abdel-Hamid, 1990), as well as the relationship between different estimates for a particular project and project behavior (Abdel-Hamid & Madnick, 1986).

This work on the systems dynamic model also speaks to the issue of project monitoring: comparing actual progress to planned progress (Boehm & Papaccio, 1988). Monitoring projects involves collecting information about costs, schedules, and technical output such as code, designs, documentation, test plans, training materials, and procedures (Weinberg & Freedman, 1983). Information can be gathered via meetings, interviews, walk-throughs, and formal technical reviews. Examining the cost-benefit trade-offs of techniques such as structured walk-throughs and reviews revealed the significant cost of using such techniques (Abdel-Hamid, 1988b), although few would deny the benefits of monitoring. Some researchers have reported on the "90% syndrome," which refers to individuals' tendency to continue to report that steady progress has been made on the project until a level of about 90% has been reached, at which point estimates of completion increase very slowly (Boehm, 1981; Abdel-Hamid, 1988a). Reasons for the 90% syndrome include poor estimating and monitoring techniques, largely due to the intangible nature of the software product itself (Abdel-Hamid, 1988a).

RISK AND UNCERTAINTY

Another hard skill related to managing projects is risk management. Researchers generally define risk exposure in terms of the potential loss due to an unsatisfactory outcome multiplied by the probability of the unsatisfactory outcome (Boehm, 1991). Unsatisfactory outcomes can be schedule slippages, budget overruns, wrong functionality, and poor-quality software (Boehm, 1991). Sources of risk include project size, the level of experience with technologies being used, developer and user expertise, application complexity and structure, lack of top management and user commitment, and misunderstood requirements (McFarlan, 1981; Barki, Rivard, & Talbot, 1993; Keil et al., 1998).

Several researchers have proposed frameworks for managing risk. In general, these frameworks involve identifying and prioritizing risks; determining the likelihood of the risks; and developing strategies for mitigating and addressing the risks (Boehm, 1991; Fairley, 1994; Keil et al., 1998). Boehm (1991) argues that risk management strategies must be integrated into the software life cycle and has proposed the spiral model (Boehm, 1988) as an explicit means of doing so. Baskerville and Stage (1996) make a similar argument and propose that risk analysis be integrated into an evolutionary prototyping development framework. Because no single risk management framework is all-encompassing, scholars encourage a broad view that incorporates multiple perspectives of risk (Willcocks & Margetts, 1994; Keil et al., 1998; Lyytinen, Mathiassen, & Ropponen, 1998).

Uncertainty, the lack of information, is believed to drive risk (McFarlan, 1981; Barki et al., 1993). In software projects, the primary source of uncertainty comes from lack of information about requirements and about technology (Zmud, 1980; Davis, 1982; Nidumolu, 1995). In a survey of 64 projects, Nidumolu (1995) examined the relationships among uncertainty, residual performance risk (extent of difficulty in estimating outcomes such as cost, completion time, and system benefits), and project performance. Results suggest that project uncertainty increases residual performance risk and that project uncertainty and residual performance risk have strong negative effects on overall performance. Findings from a follow-up study (Nidumolu, 1996) suggest that requirements uncertainty is positively related to risk and negatively related to control of the development process. Moreover, software performance risk appears to mediate the relationship between requirements uncertainty and process control.

UNCERTAINTY AND COORDINATION

Researchers have long argued that coordination is one means of addressing uncertainty (Van de Ven, Delbecq, & Koenig, 1976; Zmud, 1980). Coordination mechanisms integrate and link different parts of an organization to accomplish some tasks (Van de Ven et al., 1976):

> In software development, it means that different people working on a common project agree to a common definition of what they are building, share information, and mesh their activities . . . they must coordinate their work so that it gets done and fits together, so that it isn't done redundantly, and so that components of the work are handed off expeditiously (Kraut & Streeter, 1995, p. 69).

Zmud (1980) suggests that different modes of coordination should be used for different levels of project uncertainty. In particular, he advocates a group mode of coordination in which there is considerable communication and interaction among members of a group for high levels of uncertainty. If uncertainty is low, Zmud suggests an impersonal coordination mode using policies, standards, rules, and procedures. Finally, for a moderate level of project uncertainty, Zmud argues that the most appropriate coordination mode is personal; that is, a person assumes a liaison or boundary-spanning role. In their study of 65 projects in one large firm, Kraut and Streeter (1995) found that both formal and informal mechanisms of coordination were necessary and effective over the course of systems development efforts. Other researchers have come to similar conclusions (Curtis, Krasner, & Iscoe, 1988; Kirsch & Beath, 1996).

In the studies discussed previously, Nidumolu (1995, 1996) also investigated the effect of coordination modes and project uncertainty on project performance. Focusing on clients and IS staff, Nidumolu distinguishes between vertical and horizontal coordination. The former is achieved through a strong project manger and the use of steering committees, whereas horizontal coordination is based on mutual adjustments and lateral communication. The results suggest that high levels of both vertical and horizontal coordination lead to higher project performance and that vertical coordination reduces project uncertainty and risk. Moreover, vertical coordination was positively linked to process control while horizontal coordination was positively associated with the quality of interactions between analysts and users, and with software flexibility.

SUMMARY

A significant body of research is devoted to the hard skills of project management. Numerous empirical studies have investigated issues related to project planning and estimating, monitoring, risk, uncertainty, and coordination. Some overall conclusions are that algorithmic estimating models that do not rely on source lines of code for input are more robust than those that do; uncertainty contributes to project risk; coordination can be exercised using formal and informal mechanisms; different levels and types of coordination seem more effective for different levels of risk; and risk management strategies should be explicitly incorporated into project management methodologies.

Underlying much of this work on the hard skills are two themes. First is the importance of measurement or metrics. Metrics are standard measures of some aspects of the software development process or product, such as size, effort, or defects (Grady & Caswell, 1987). Planning, estimating, risk management, and dealing with uncertainty all depend on accurate, timely, and useful information. Without precise information and clear and measurable targets, managing software projects effectively and efficiently is extremely difficult, if not impossible (Linkman & Walker, 1991; Jones, 1991; Yourdon, 1996).

The importance of measurement to software project management can be seen by the emphasis it is given in the capability maturity model (CMM), which provides a framework for understanding and improving software practices. The CMM describes five steps of software development process maturity (Humphrey, 1988): *initial,* in which software deployment processes are nonexistent or ad hoc at best; *repeatable,* when stable processes have been achieved by closely managing project costs, schedules, and changes; *defined,* when the deployment process is consistent across projects; *management,* in which process measurements are in place and the organization initiates software process improvements; and *optimizing,* in which the organization has laid the foundation for continuous process improvement.

While researchers and practitioners seem to understand the importance of metrics and measurement for improving software projects and progressing along the CMM's maturity levels, many organizations find it difficult to implement metrics (Ray, 1993; Hetzel, 1995), and, indeed, most organizations are at the initial or repeatable level (Kemerer, 1997). The introduction of measurement programs is difficult for many reasons, including resistance of the IS staff; expense; inadequate incentives; and lack of training (Grady & Caswell, 1987; Humphrey, 1988; Jones, 1991; Yourdon, 1992). Despite the implementation difficulties, most academics and practitioners acknowledge the importance of improved measurement to improve the software project process. Consequently, research in this area continues.

A second theme underlying much of this research on the hard skills is the importance of formal tools and techniques—formal algorithmic models, formal documented rules and standards, and formal risk management procedures.[4] While tools and techniques can obviously improve the project process, it is clear that they alone will not cure what ails software project management. One of the most significant impacts on project costs is related to "the selection, motivation, and management of the people involved in the software process" (Boehm & Papaccio, 1988, p. 1465). Moreover

> Software development tools and practices had disappointingly small effects in earlier studies, probably because they did not improve the most troublesome processes in software development. Understanding the behavioral processes of software development allows us to evaluate the claims for software tools and practices. (Curtis et al., 1988, p. 1283).

PROJECT MANAGEMENT: THE SOFT SKILLS

Soft skills are primarily concerned with managing and working with people. This section of the chapter reviews three areas of research: control; power and politics, conflict, and negotiation; and team composition and leadership.

CONTROL

Control is a means of motivating individuals to achieve desired objectives (Jaworski, 1988; Kirsch, 1996). It is exercised with mechanisms such as incentives, norms, values, and commendations to motivate and guide individuals. There are both formal and informal modes of control (Ouchi, 1979, 1980). Formal modes of control are generally viewed as performance evaluation strategies (Eisenhardt, 1985). Exercising formal modes of control involves specifying appropriate behaviors for individuals to follow (behavior control) or outcomes to achieve (outcome control), and evaluating them on whether they followed the behaviors or produced the outcomes. Several studies have found that outcome measurability, which refers to the ability to measure achieved results, has a positive relationship with outcome control (Eisenhardt, 1985; Snell, 1992; Kirsch, 1996). Two antecedents of behavior control are knowledge of the transformation process and behavior observability, or the extent to which the controller can observe individual behaviors (Ouchi & Maguire, 1975; Eisenhardt, 1985, 1988; Snell, 1992). Moreover, there is evidence that for software projects, behavior observability and knowledge of the transformation process (i.e., knowledge of the systems development process) positively interact to determine the level of behavior control (Kirsch, 1996).

Informal control is based on personal and social relationships (Jaworski, 1988; Abernethy & Stoelwinder, 1994). Two modes of informal control are self (Manz, Mossholder, & Luthans, 1987) and clan (Ouchi, 1980). An individual exercises self-control when he sets goals for himself, monitors whether he meets those goals, and rewards or sanctions himself accordingly. Some research has found a negative relationship between self-control and task predictability (Hrebiniak, 1974) and between work oversight and self-control (Manz & Angle, 1986; Alavi, Phillips, & Freedman, 1986). In the context of systems development projects, there is also evidence that the exercise of self-control increases as organizational tenure increases, project size decreases, and formalization increases (Kirsch & Cummings, 1996).

Unlike the focus on the individual in self-control, clan control is instituted by a clan, a group of individuals whose goals are aligned and who are dependent on each other to accomplish specific objectives (Ouchi, 1980). When team members' behaviors are governed by clan control, the individuals share a commitment to the same goals, and they adopt compatible decision-making and problem-solving approaches (Ouchi, 1979; Jaworski, 1988). Results from a qualitative study suggest that clan control is exercised when it is difficult to observe behaviors or measure outcomes, when the controller wants to build trusting and collegial relationships, and when the exercise of clan control is consistent with organizational norms (Kirsch, 1997).

POWER AND POLITICS, CONFLICT, AND NEGOTIATION

A number of researchers recognize the role that power and politics play in projects. Power is the potential ability to influence events and behaviors; politics concerns the act of developing and using power in organizations (Pfeffer, 1981, 1992). Markus and Pfeffer (1983) argue that accounting and control systems can be viewed from a power perspective because they imply a distribution of power among designers and users. Furthermore, people may resist the implementation of a system because of the interaction of specific design features with aspects of the organizational context in which the system will be used: Those losing control and power will resist the implementation while those gaining power will support it (Markus, 1983).

Differences in power can lead to conflict (Markus & Bjorn-Andersen, 1987; Levine & Rossmore, 1994–95). Conflicts occur when there is interdependence among parties and a divergence of interests, opinions, or goals among participants; moreover, the differences are incompatible (Barki & Hartwick, 1994). As many researchers have noted, these conditions are likely in the software project context. Beath and Orlikowski (1994), for instance, provide a detailed look at the differences and interdependencies between clients and analysts.

Conflict can have negative repercussions (Markus 1983; Robey & Markus, 1984). For example, excessive conflict between IS and functional units can lead to withdrawal of support of and commitment to a project (Newman & Sabherwal, 1996) or escalating commitment to a failing project (Keil, 1995); both conditions can result in poor project performance. However, conflict is not always destructive and, in fact, can play a constructive role in projects. In a survey of 84 project stakeholders, Robey, Smith, and Vijayasarathy (1993) found that conflicts, when successfully resolved, contribute to project success, but that unresolved conflict is negatively correlated with success. Influence was positively associated with both conflict and conflict resolution, consistent with findings from an earlier study (Robey, Farrow, & Franz, 1989).

Other researchers have reached similar conclusions about the role of conflict on projects. In their field study, for example, Walz, Elam, and Curtis (1993) examined how group members acquire, share, and integrate project-relevant knowledge. Among other results, they found that conflict can be a mechanism for facilitating learning rather than a debilitating factor that needs to be suppressed. Barki and Hartwick (1994) extended the earlier work of Robey and his colleagues (e.g., Robey et al., 1989, 1993) and found a direct and positive relationship between user participation and conflict and both positive and negative effects of influence on conflict. Researchers generally agree that it is by participating that users influence a project, and that it is through influence that conflicts are resolved (Robey, 1994; Hartwick & Barki, 1994b).

Whether conflict is constructive or destructive depends considerably on how individuals handle it (Robey et al., 1989; Barki & Hartwick, 1994). Individuals bring not only technical skills to a project but also their abilities to raise and resolve conflicts, negotiate, and communicate (Curtis et al., 1988). Researchers argue that effective individuals know how to resolve conflicts and negotiate with key stakeholders (Curtis et al., 1988; Boehm & Ross, 1989). Newman and Noble (1990) suggest a two-stage model to managing conflict. The first stage involves the structuring of conflict between client and analyst, in which contextual issues influence whether the conflict leads to mutual learning, a negotiated solution, or an escalation of conflict with a win/lose outcome. In the second stage, the conflict is resolved one way or another.

A number of practitioners and researchers argue that project managers should facilitate conflict management, yet few methodologies explicitly incorporate conflict management techniques (Robey et al., 1989; Beath & Orlikowski, 1994; Kirsch & Beath, 1996). Two examples of formal techniques for managing conflict are the devil's advocate decision program and the dialectic method (Walz et al., 1993). Boehm and Ross (1989) have proposed a software project management theory that is called Theory-W: Make everyone a winner. This theory espouses the importance of recognizing all key stakeholders in the software project process, and it views the role of the project manager as a negotiator among the various stakeholders. Applying Theory-W means that project managers must identify the stakeholders, understand their different goals and objectives, resolve conflicts as they arise, and negotiate mutually acceptable solutions. In short, the project manager must create win-win situations.[5]

TEAM COMPOSITION AND LEADERSHIP

A third soft skill revolves around the structuring of the team. Researchers and practitioners alike have argued that the composition of the project team, in terms of attributes such as experience with the technology or the business domain, can impact the effectiveness of the team (Boehm, 1981; Brooks, 1995). Some studies have found that teams with broad technical and functional expertise are more effective (White & Leifer, 1986; Rasch & Tosi, 1992; Deephouse et al., 1995–96). Guinan et al. (1998) surveyed approximately 500 project team members and project stakeholders associated with 66 midsized projects. Among other insights, Guinan et al. found that team skill (the breadth of abilities provided by team members) is positively related to team performance. Moreover, they found a direct relationship between experience spread—or the relative diversity of the team's work experience—and performance.

In a study of 17 large systems projects, Curtis et al. (1988) found that individual talent and experience can result in a productivity boost for the project. But it is not just experience and talent that matter. Curtis et al. argue that sharing and integrating knowledge across project team members is crucial for effective project management, and therefore the recruitment of individual talent must be combined with team-building efforts. Similarly, Walz et al. (1993), after observing a design team in depth, found that the most influential team members were those with the most knowledge *and* with the skills to share and integrate knowledge.

Team leadership in the context of software projects refers to the question of who should assume the project manager role. The traditional answer to this question has been "an IS specialist," and much of the relevant empirical research seems to assume that an IS specialist is the project manager. Consonant with that assumption, there is evidence that methodologies ascribe passive roles to users. For example, a deconstruction of the information engineering methodology (Martin, 1989, 1990) revealed that though the methodology espouses user involvement, users are engaged only marginally and passively (Beath & Orlikowski, 1994).

However, there is now more uncertainty about team leadership (Morris, 1996). Some researchers (Doll & Torkzadeh, 1989; Lawrence & Low, 1993) have argued that users may assume additional responsibilities, for example, assuming team leadership when projects are highly uncertain (Hartwick & Barki, 1994a; McKeen & Guimaraes, 1997) or when projects call for managers who possess rich understanding of business processes. In line with this suggestion, practitioner books devoted to ERP implementations—projects that are likely to be high in uncertainty and to require in-depth knowledge of current and future business activities—advise that a functional specialist assume the project manager role (e.g., Bancroft et al., 1998). Other researchers suggest there may be times when it is appropriate for IT specialists and users to share project management responsibilities (Zmud, 1980; Bashein et al., 1997). For example, if a user lacks sufficient technical knowledge to understand the nuances of a software project, she might co-manage the project with an IT specialist (Kirsch, 1997).

SUMMARY

Research on the soft skills has produced numerous insights into the management of people associated with software projects. This body of research suggests that control is a powerful means of motivating individuals and fostering relationships across stakeholders, that projects can change the distribution of power in firms, that conflicts and conflict resolution influence project processes, and that team composition and leadership are critical to success.

Several themes underly this research. First is the key role that knowledge plays in managing projects. In particular, the exercise of formal behavior control is partially dependent on knowledge of the systems development process, and the lack of knowledge may lead to reliance on informal modes of control. Effective project team members are those who are knowledgeable about the technology and the business and those with the ability to integrate their knowledge with that of others. Thus, the knowledge of the project participants impacts the viability and effectiveness of specific project management practices.

Relationship management is a second theme underlying this research. Software projects involve stakeholders from the IS and client communities and may involve others as well. To be successful, project managers and team members must understand the need to manage conflicts and negotiate and communicate with a variety of stakeholders. Moreover, clan control, an informal mode of control, is built on trusting, collegial relationships; the implication is that successful use of clan control presumes strong relationships. The overarching message from this stream of work is that effective project management depends on effective relationship management.

The third theme found in this work is that sole responsibility for the success of software projects does not rest with IS professionals alone. Users play critical roles: from furnishing knowledge to the project, to exercising control, to providing full or partial leadership of projects. Ignoring or minimizing the role of the user is likely to impede project progress and have negative repercussions for project outcomes.

PROJECT MANAGEMENT: AN INTEGRATED PERSPECTIVE

In the project management literature, these two streams—the hard and the soft skills—tend to be distinct. Though there are exceptions (e.g., Abdel-Hamid, 1988a, 1988b; Rodrigues & Williams, 1997), much of the research focuses on one area or the other. One example of an integrated perspective is McFarlan's (1981) contingency model in which variations in project structure, size, and experience with the technology are related to differences in planning, control (i.e., monitoring), external integration (linkages with the customer), and internal integration (cohesiveness of the project team). In this model, McFarlan integrates hard skills (planning and monitoring) with the soft skills of attending to relationships with clients and team members.

In this section of the chapter, key underlying constructs are extracted from the literature reviewed earlier to build a contingency model of software project management. These constructs are related to characteristics of the project and attributes of the individuals involved. Prior research suggests that project characteristics directly affect project management practices while individual attributes may have both direct and moderating effects on such practices.

Three project management practices of relevance are the degree of formalization of the practices, the project leadership, and the nature of the relationship between IS and clients. Project management practices that are formal tend to be written, documented rules, procedures, and techniques, whereas informal practices are much more implicit and tacit. Project leadership refers to whether the project manager is an IS or business specialist or whether there is joint IS-client leadership. The IS-client relationship is also considered a project management practice in that project stakeholders can actively structure this relationship to determine its form. For example, research suggests that clients participate in projects if they need (Doll & Torkzadeh, 1989) or want (Kirsch & Beath, 1996) to participate. This need or desire to participate affects the resulting IS-client relationship, which can be characterized at the extremes as arm's length or as a partnership. These three project management practices—formalization, project leadership, and IS-client relationship—are, in turn, believed to affect project performance. Performance can be conceptualized in a variety of ways. It is typically thought of in terms of meeting schedules and budgets and in delivering quality systems. Performance might also refer to a stakeholder's satisfaction with the project team or the value of the resulting system to the business.

The model is shown in Figure 15.1. The relationships among the constructs are elaborated next.

FIGURE 15.1   A Contingency Model of Project Management

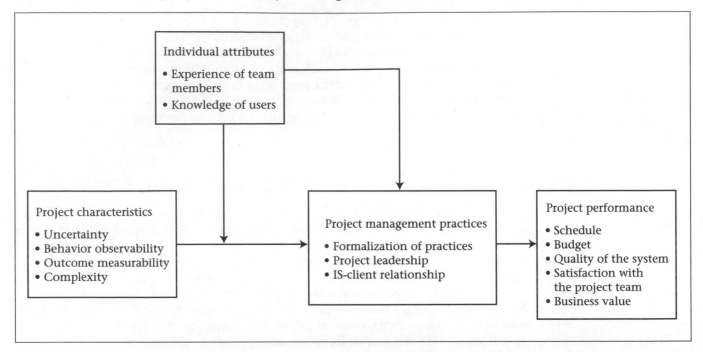

PROJECT MANAGEMENT PRACTICES AND PROJECT PERFORMANCE

Formalization

A recent survey of European project management practices revealed that a large percentage of firms rely on formal tools, techniques, and approaches (Dutta, Van Wassenhove, & Kulandaiswamy, 1998). In particular, 74% of the firms surveyed have formal procedures to assess project benefits, risks, and viability while 81% conduct formal periodic reviews of progress. In addition, the majority of firms (66%) apply coding standards, and 51% use formal procedures to estimate effort, schedule, and cost.

Several studies have investigated the relationship between formal tools and techniques, on the one hand, and performance, on the other. One effort found a positive correlation between "production processes" (clear goals, plans, procedures, and milestones) and project team effectiveness (Guinan et al., 1998). In another study of 87 senior IS practitioners, Deephouse et al. (1995–96) found a strong positive correlation between planning and meeting project schedule and budget targets. They also found that planning, as well as functional and technical expertise in the team, was positively related to project performance in terms of meeting user needs.

Some project management practices, such as control and coordination, are typically exercised with both formal and informal mechanisms (Kraut & Streeter, 1995; Kirsch, 1997). The relationship between formal versus informal practices and performance can therefore be difficult to tease out. For example, in their empirical study of eight software development projects, Kirsch and Beath (1996) found mixed results related to the effect of coordination, which was exercised with both formal and informal mechanisms, on schedule and budget outcomes (which they termed "efficiencies"). In particular

> Overall, the data . . . suggests that when the coordination process is poorly enacted . . . there seems to be a negative effect on efficiencies despite considerable use of plans and schedules. However, even when the coordination process is enacted more effectively, the impact on efficiencies is far from certain. (p. 245)

Similarly, control can be exercised formally and informally, and various control choices have been found to correlate with project performance. There is some evidence that the exercise of formal control is positively associated with effectiveness and efficiency performance measures (Henderson & Lee, 1992). Studies have also demonstrated a positive relationship between self-control and project performance (Henderson & Lee, 1992; Kirsch & Cummings, 1996).

In general, this line of research suggests that formal and informal project management practices can impact project performance. The exact nature of this relationship, however, is not clear. For example, under what conditions can informal practices effectively substitute for formal ones? What mix of formal and informal practices is most effective? How and why does the mix vary for different types of projects (e.g., strategic versus tactical, packaged solution versus custom development)? Additional empirical studies are needed to investigate the effect of formalization on project performance.

Project Leadership

Although many acknowledge the importance of strong project leadership in the form of project champions, executive sponsors, and steering committees (e.g., Beath, 1991; Morris, 1996), few studies have empirically examined the association between project team leadership and project performance. One study found that project performance was positively associated with project managers who had been granted high levels of authority by senior management (Might & Fischer, 1985). The results of Guinan et al.'s (1998) survey of midsized projects suggest that the "active involvement" of project managers is positively associated with high team performance. The authors argue that an involved manager is one who is more "directive" and "hands on" in the daily activities of the project. This study therefore implies that managers who take a "hands-off" approach may be less effective.

The issue of project leadership seems increasingly important as projects become more complex, integrated, and global in scope, and as projects (both large and small) become more strategic in focus (e.g., developing applications to support e-commerce initiatives). Additional research is needed to help clarify the circumstances that call for IS project leadership, business manager project leadership, or joint project leadership. For example, must a business project manager lead ERP implementations, and, if so, why? The rapid deployment of small Web-based applications would seem to require close and intense interaction between technical and functional specialists, which raises the question of whether project management responsibilities ought to be divided between IS and client staff, and, if so, how to do it.

The IS-Client Relationship

The relationship between client and IS staff is critically important, yet it can also be problematic (Beath, 1987; Newman & Robey, 1992; Robey & Newman, 1996). This relationship can take on several forms and, depending on the form, the consequences can vary. Kirsch and Beath (1996) argue that the IS-client relationship, as characterized by the user's participation, can be token, shared, or compliant. *Token* participation describes an ineffective working relationship between IS and client staff in which conflicts go unresolved; however, it may still be possible to achieve task-system fit. A second relationship, called *shared,* exists when clients and IS staff work effectively as a team, sharing responsibilities and providing needed expertise. Conflicts are successfully managed and resolved, and project outcomes tend to be positive. The third form is termed *compliant,* in which clients and IS staff take on distinct roles and there are few conflicts. Clients are persuaded by the IS staff to accept design compromises so that the resulting system can be used by other functional areas in the firm. This type of relationship tends to result in mixed project outcomes.

Another study found that trusting and open communication between team members and stakeholders is positively correlated with project performance (Guinan et al., 1998). In particular, "external visionary activities," those activities that the team uses to manage upward and to attend to external stakeholders, are positively related to performance. In contrast, "guard activities" that restrict interaction with the external environment are negatively related to performance.

Although there is evidence that the nature of the relationship between IS and clients has an effect on performance, much is not known about this relationship. For example, under what situations will different forms of the IS-client relationship be most effective? Do partnership or "shared" relations always contribute to successful projects, or is this close relationship required only when the project is highly uncertain or involves the delivery of strategic applications? Future research is needed to shed light on these and other questions.

CHARACTERISTICS OF THE PROJECT AND PROJECT MANAGEMENT PRACTICES

Uncertainty

The level of uncertainty seems to impact various project management practices. As discussed earlier, when uncertainty is low, formal modes of coordination may be appropriate, but as uncertainty increases, more informal and flexible modes of coordination may be called for (Zmud, 1980). McFarlan's (1981) contingency model of project management suggests that if a primary source of uncertainty is the technology, then a high degree of internal integration is required, which means that a cohesive team with open and strong communications is appropriate. On the other hand, if the uncertainty stems from lack of knowledge about the business domain, his model suggests maintaining a strong link with the clients. However, these assertions are largely untested and need empirical validation. Future research might examine the relationship between uncertainty and project leadership. If, for example, the primary source of project risk and uncertainty stems from lack of knowledge of the business domain, it seems reasonable to propose a business manager as project manager. If the uncertainty and risk come from the technology, an IS specialist ought to assume project leadership.

There is some evidence about the association between uncertainty and the IS-client relationship. IS-client relationships based on classical contracting (checkpoints and reviews) may be effective for projects low in uncertainty, but projects high in uncertainty require a relationship based on implicit or social contracting (Beath, 1987, 1988). This research suggests that in the presence of uncertainty, "shared" (Kirsch & Beath, 1996) or partnering (Henderson, 1990) relationships are needed between IS and their clients to successfully navigate the project. When uncertainty is low, however, a relationship that can be described as arm's length, token, or compliant might be appropriate. Future research is needed to tease out these relationships.

OBSERVABILITY OF BEHAVIORS/ MEASURABILITY OF OUTCOMES

Research in this area suggests relationships between behavior observability and outcome measurability, on the one hand, and formal project management practices, project leadership, and IS-client relationships, on the other hand. As noted earlier, the use of formal control modes is dependent on the observability of behaviors and the measurability of outcomes (Eisenhardt, 1985; Snell, 1992). Research has also demonstrated that if behavior observability is high but knowledge of the systems development process is low, formal behavior control will not be exercised (Kirsch, 1996). This finding suggests that, in this case, project leadership ought to reside with an IT specialist or, alternatively, jointly—the user who lacks knowledge about software projects can be paired with an IT specialist.

When behaviors cannot be observed or outcomes cannot be measured, project managers cannot rely on formal modes of control, but instead can exercise clan control (Ouchi, 1980). Because clan control is based on common values, norms, and trust among team members, it suggests that the IS-client relationship must be more like a partnership. This again seems to be a situation in which joint project management might be appropriate since the client and the IS specialist must work together collaboratively and must establish a trusting relationship in which goals and values are shared.

Although there is a body of research examining the relationships among behavior observability, outcome measurability, and the exercise of formal and informal controls, there is little research investigating the impact of these contingencies on project leadership and IS-client relationships. Future research might explore how a person's ability to observe behaviors or measure outcomes influences the nature of the IS-client relationship and project leadership. In addition, it would be useful to identify potential moderators of these relationships.

Complexity

Complexity is often thought of in terms of project size (e.g., lines of code, number of modules). A large software project consists of many interrelated parts, and it is critical that all of the parts are completed in a timely manner so that they can all be integrated into the final product. Therefore, projects that are high in complexity demand formal and detailed planning and control in order to track and integrate all of the separate pieces.

There is little discussion in the literature about the impact of project size on project leadership and IS-client relationships. Much of the literature, in fact, does not make allowances for different types of projects, although project characteristics ought to impact type of management practice (Powers & Dickson, 1973; Abdel-Hamid & Madnick, 1989). For example, managing a small, in-house development effort differs considerably from managing the installation of an ERP package, which differs considerably from managing the rapid deployment of small but strategic Web-based applications. Specific tools and techniques will vary, as will the roles and responsibilities of various parties involved. However, exactly how project management practices will vary as a function of project complexity is a question for empirical work to examine.

ATTRIBUTES OF THE INDIVIDUALS AND PROJECT MANAGEMENT PRACTICES

Experience of the Project Team Members

Some research has examined the relationships between experience and project management practices. For example, more experienced team members seem to understand the need for effective communication and coordination during a project and thus combine formal and informal techniques (Kirsch, 1997). Different types of experience (e.g., experience with a certain technology or a functional area, or experience with conflict resolution or negotiation) might affect the choice of a project management practice. An experienced IS negotiator, for example, may choose to structure a partnership with a client or to keep the client at arm's length, depending on the nature of the project. Few studies have systematically examined the relationship between experience levels and project management practices. Research is needed to examine this relationship, as well as how experience may moderate the relationship between project characteristics and project management practices.

Knowledge of Users

There is some evidence that users with relevant knowledge of systems projects will choose to implement formal control modes, provided that behaviors are observable, whereas users without this knowledge will not (Kirsch, 1996). Common wisdom suggests that managing software projects requires at least some relevant technical knowledge, but how much knowledge do users need to be effective? What kind of knowledge is necessary for what types of projects? The level of understanding that users possess about systems projects may also affect their relationship with IS. For those users lacking relevant knowledge, the IS staff may assume the role of educators, instructing the users about the role of technology in the firm, the specific system itself, and the systems development process (Kirsch & Beath, 1996). As was the case with team member experience, there is relatively little research examining the impact of client knowledge on the use of specific project management practices or its possible role as a moderator. This would seem to be an important area of research, however, as users increasingly are being asked to manage technology-based projects.

PROJECT MANAGEMENT: THE TRADITIONAL AND EMERGING PARADIGMS

As noted at the beginning of the chapter, the computing paradigm is changing. No longer is the dominant paradigm the traditional and relatively homogeneous environment of stand-alone, back-office, custom-developed applications running on a mainframe. Instead, the paradigm is shifting to a heterogeneous environment that includes the rapid deployment of cross-functional software solutions running on distributed platforms, Web-based applications, sophisticated front ends to legacy systems, packaged solutions, and small custom-developed applications (Wetherbe et al., 1994; Rockart et al., 1996). In addition, many of these technology-based solutions are strategic in nature and tightly linked with organizational goals and objectives. In this emerging paradigm, project teams may be distributed around the globe,[6] and the leadership is just as likely to come from the business unit as from the IS community (Bashein et al., 1997; Carmel, 1999).

There are fundamental questions about projects in this emerging paradigm that are unanswered. How are project teams structured, and what are the consequences of different structures? Are there additional sources of uncertainty when working in a global or virtual context? How does the management of small Web-based applications differ from the management of packaged software or large custom-developed systems? How are distributed teams controlled and managed, and how is the work of distributed team members coordinated? To what extent are existing planning and estimation tools valuable in a distributed computing environment or in an environment that emphasizes rapid deployment? These and other questions need focused research efforts.

There is some evidence related to project management in this new paradigm. Tractinsky and Jarvenpaa (1995), for example, investigated the way in which decisions were made about the distribution of hardware, software, and data in a global context. From their study, they identified three contingency factors influencing those decisions: variability in the context of the countries involved, the project manager's unfamiliarity with working in a global environment, and complexity in terms of the number of relevant factors that must be addressed in a decision.

Some researchers have focused on issues related to project team composition and leadership. Comparing global teams to domestic teams, three unique aspects stand out: distance between developers and between developers and their clients, differences in time zones, and differences in culture (Carmel, 1999). One study found that global project managers are more cosmopolitan and tend to have a broader understanding of contextual issues such as power distribution between headquarters and local units and local government regulations (Tractinsky & Jarvenpaa, 1995). Other researchers have explored control and coordination in a global or distributed environment. This research suggests that formal modes of control and coordination become more difficult as the team is distributed, in part because it is more difficult to observe and guide behaviors of individuals; moreover, few effective mechanisms seem to be available for coordinating action on a global scale (Carmel, 1999; Collins & Kirsch, 1999).

While there has been some research on project management issues in this emerging paradigm, there is a need for sustained research programs. Two issues in particular stand out. First, many of the systems being deployed are distributed in nature. The applications consist of many interrelated components running on

FIGURE 15.2 A Revised Contingency Model of Project Management

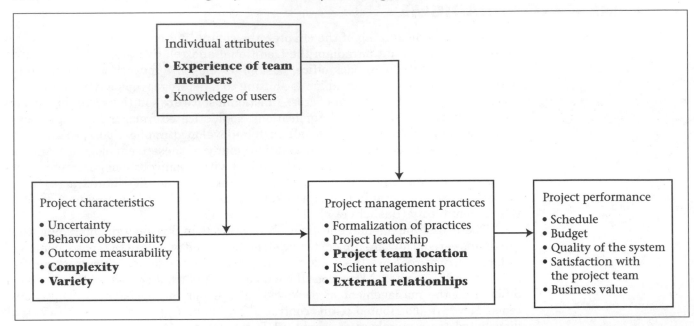

different platforms in different locations; these pieces must eventually be integrated into a cohesive unit. Second, the trend toward dispersing project team members around the globe coupled with an increased reliance on vendors, consultants, and outsourcers suggests that a project manager will spend more time and effort managing a variety of relationships. These issues have implications for the model proposed in Figure 15.1. A revised model in which changes are in bold type will be discussed and is shown in Figure 15.2

Two additional project management practices are relevant in this emerging paradigm. First is the location of the project team members. In today's environment, team members may be co-located or distributed around the globe (Bashein et al., 1997; Carmel, 1999). If they are distributed, questions arise as to what project functions are assigned to which locations. Some firms choose to assign the development of "core" or "common" pieces of a solution to a headquarters team and the development of "local" pieces to local units, while other firms choose to assign all functionality to one location (Collins & Kirsch, 1999). A second project management practice is the nature of the relationship with external constituents. While systems projects have often involved external constituents, it is likely that there are many more to worry about in today's environment: There may be more vendors, more internal stakeholders, more consultants. Rockart et al. (1996) note that IT units may interface with as many as 100 suppliers, up considerably from the 5 to 10 suppliers typically used in the past. Moreover, just as the IS-client relationship might assume various forms, so might the relationships between the project team and external constituents.

Two constructs identified in Figure 15.1—experience of team members and complexity—take on broader meanings in the emerging paradigm. For global projects, team members need global experience to be effective (Tractinsky & Jarvenpaa, 1995; Collins & Kirsch, 1999). Technical and business experience is still critical, but sensitivity to different cultures, norms, and ways of working will greatly aid a team's ability to successfully complete a project.[7] In addition, the type of expertise needed on a project is dependent on the type of project. For example, using a rapid development approach to deploy small strategic applications requires expertise in prototyping as well as considerable skill in working and negotiating with clients. These skills may be less important when installing a back-office package. The notion of complexity also takes on an expanded meaning. Because projects may include distributed hardware and software, system complexity is a function of the number of components and interfaces to build and manage. In general, the more distributed the solution, the greater the complexity.

As Figure 15.2 indicates, there is one additional project characteristic: variety. This characteristic reflects variation in terms of cultures, languages, and regulations. Some projects will deploy a software solution in many countries, and local regulations and laws may impact the functionality of the solution. Similarly, some projects involve working with business and technical professionals from many countries. The more contextual variation there is in terms of culture, language, time zones, and so on, the more challenging it will be to manage the project (Tractinsky & Jarvenpaa, 1995; Carmel, 1999). Variety can also be viewed in terms of the number of options facing a development team. When a firm has standards in place, such as the use of common Web interfaces and infrastructure, variety decreases since the technology choices are constrained. Any one of these three characteristics—experience, complexity, and variety—can influence the choice and efficacy of various project management practices. But the exact nature of the relationships depicted in Figure 15.2 is unknown, and empirical research is needed to understand project management in today's world.

CONCLUSIONS

This chapter has reviewed the research related to the hard and soft skills of software project management. Using this research as a springboard, a contingency model of software project management was developed and elaborated upon. This model was then revised to suggest additional relationships of importance in the emerging paradigm of computing in organizations.

There is a great need for additional empirical research on software project management. Many of the contingencies proposed in Figures 15.1 and 15.2 have not been empirically tested or the evidence is scant, especially as these relationships relate to the emerging computing paradigm. A number of theoretical lenses could be applied to such studies, including theories of change, organizational control, goal setting, coordination, organizational learning, and knowledge transfer. In addition to testing single contingencies, empirical studies examining the joint effects of multiple contingencies would be of considerable value. Project managers do not implement one technique at a time but instead put together portfolios of practices. There is little evidence about the effect that bundles of practices have on various performance indicators.

Finally, the model presented in Figure 15.2 is a static model. Increasingly, researchers have called for studies that explore the dynamics of project management (Keil, 1995). Such studies might examine how the exercise of control changes over a project's life cycle, for example, or when and how effective knowledge transfer occurs from various external constituents to project teams. Some research has examined project dynamics. Bashein et al. (1997) found that because risks cannot be fully anticipated, project managers must periodically reassess their risk management strategies as their projects progress. Keil and Robey (1999) point out that commitment to a failing project can escalate over time and that changes in project management practices (e.g., changes in leadership or meeting frequency) may be needed to bring a troubled project under control. Additional research that takes a temporal view would shed valuable insight on how the process of project management unfolds over time and how different patterns of events affect project outcomes (Newman & Robey, 1992).

ENDNOTES

1. For a more in-depth discussion of how computing in organizations has evolved over time, see the chapter on the CIO's role by Ross and Feeny.
2. The chapters on software origins (by George) and on ERP (by Markus and Tanis) provide additional perspective on the use of packaged software.
3. For a rich description of these types of applications, see the case studies described in Bashein, Markus, and Finley (1997).
4. An exception is the work investigating informal mechanisms of coordination. However, even this research tends to be coupled with research on the formal mechanisms of coordination.
5. For more discussion on the role of users in the deployment of systems, see the chapter on software origins by George.
6. More on virtual teams can be found in the chapter by Saunders.
7. For a discussion on skills and expertise needed for today's environment, see the chapter on information technology personnel by Ang and Slaughter.

The Missing Context of Information Technology Personnel: A Review and Future Directions for Research

Soon Ang and Sandra A. Slaughter

In an era of global competition, turbulent markets, and demand for high-quality products at low cost and short cycle times, organizations depend more than ever on information technology (IT). The irony is that effectively designing and deploying IT depends not only on the technology per se but also on the *people* who develop and work directly with it. In this environment, a highly skilled, adaptable IT staff becomes an important asset in the successful exploitation of IT (Clark et al., 1997; Feeny & Wilcocks, 1998). Attracting, developing, and retaining highly competent and motivated IT personnel are thus critical managerial imperatives for the success of any organization that wants to leverage IT. It is no surprise that effectively managing IT human resources has consistently been rated as one of the most important issues in the management of the IT function (Brancheau, Janz, & Wetherbe, 1996).

Since the introduction of IT into the workplace in the 1960s, the world of work for an IT professional has changed dramatically. In the past, developers and maintainers could base a career on their knowledge of COBOL, IMS, and other IBM mainframe tools and systems. Today, however, the primary role of IT professionals in organizations is to solve business problems and address business opportunities through IT (Ross, Beath, & Goodhue, 1996). IT personnel must be knowledgeable in a range of hardware and software technologies, from mainframe to client-server to Web-based technologies. In addition, the software development process has changed dramatically from customized development of information systems to commercial off-the-shelf assembly and integration of software packages and components. Increasingly, software development is outsourced to consulting firms, independent contractors, vendors, and offshore companies. Thus, the critical skills and competencies of IT personnel as well as human resource management practices are constantly evolving. As a result, the study of IT personnel offers new and exciting opportunities and challenges for research.

In this chapter, we review the major themes of research on IT personnel to date and identify new dynamics and features that are emerging as important issues. Specifically, we find that IT personnel research has focused exclusively on the individual. We describe the disadvantages of this paradigm and assert the importance of anchoring research on IT personnel in the context in which the work is being done. We identify the different aspects of the domain of managing IT personnel in context, drawing upon relevant theoretical perspectives based in economics, management, sociology, and psychology, and conclude by providing an integrative model for IT personnel research.

PRIOR RESEARCH IN IT PERSONNEL

Prior research in IT personnel can be classified into three broad themes: (1) knowledge and skills taxonomies for IT professionals, (2) IT jobs and roles, and (3) IT professionals' career orientations and career pathing (Table 16.1).

Prior work has focused on motivation and quality of work life for IT professionals, in particular IT development professionals such as programmers and analysts. Very little research has focused on IT professionals in IT infrastructure jobs such as computer operators and technical specialists (database administrators, network specialists, etc.). Furthermore, prior work has focused on job satisfaction and turnover as primary outcome variables. Other key personnel-related variables such as individual performance and compensation are sorely missing. Although there have been studies that offer taxonomies of knowledge and skills of IT professionals, relatively little research has been done to systematically link knowledge and skills to topics such as attitudes, behaviors, performance, and IT careers.

As we accumulate more knowledge about internal IT careers, empirical research on external careers is needed. With the exception of Kaiser's study on data processing career paths in the early 1980s (Kaiser, 1983), we have not found recent studies of external careers in IT. Given the myriad and evolving roles and jobs in IT, it is unclear whether there are prototypical career paths in IT, and, if so, what these career paths may be. Thus far, the focus of prior research has been on careers of IT professionals who primarily reside in the IT user organization because that is the context in which many IT professionals are hired. However, with the rapid emergence of a vibrant IT industry in numerous parts of the world, many IT professionals are employed by new IT firms. Whether the knowledge and skill sets, motivations,

TABLE 16.1 Themes in Prior Research of IT Personnel

	Research Objective(s)	Representative Studies	Theory Base(s)	Methodology	Key Findings
Theme 1 Knowledge and skills for IT professionals	Identifying skills and knowledge requirements of IT professionals			Varied	Trend toward broadening of skill sets for IT professionals (technical, business, and managerial skills required)
		Benbasat et al., 1980 Cheney and Lyons, 1980 Green, 1989 Nelson, 1991 Leitheiser, 1992 Lee et al., 1995		Large-scale surveys	
		Feeny and Wilcocks, 1998 Rockart et al., 1996		Intensive case studies based on interviews and observation	
		Todd et al., 1995		Analysis of Secondary data (job ads)	
Theme 2 Jobs and roles of IT professionals	Ascertaining the motivating and demotivating aspects of IT jobs Linking perceptions of IT jobs to behaviors		Varied	Surveys	Varied
		Couger et al., 1979 Khalil et al., 1997 Burn et al., 1994	Job characteristics model (Hackman and Oldham, 1979)		IT professionals have high growth need strength, high need for achievement, low social needs
		Goldstein and Rockart, 1984 Baroudi, 1985 Igbaria and Greenhaus, 1992 Igbaria et al., 1994 Guimaraes and Igbaria, 1993 Igbaria, 1993	Role theory (Rizzo et al., 1970)		IT professionals intend to turn over when there are high role stressors (conflict and ambiguity) in a job
		McLean et al., 1991 Smits et al., 1993	Needs-based theories of motivation (McClelland, 1961)		IT professionals prefer jobs with high creativity, challenge, autonomy, and feedback
		Ferratt and Short, 1988 Ferratt and Short, 1986 Bartol and Martin, 1982			IT professionals do not appear to be significantly different than other professionals

(continued on the next page)

TABLE 16.1 (continued)

	Research Objective(s)	Representative Studies	Theory Base(s)	Methodology	Key Findings
Theme 3 Careers of IT professionals	Understanding the internal careers (cognitive and affective attitudes toward job experiences within an organization) of IT professionals		Varied	Large-scale surveys	Varied
	Understanding the external careers (career pathing and advancement) in the IT profession				
		Ginzberg and Baroudi, 1988 Igbaria et al., 1991 Crepeau et al., 1992	Career anchors and orientations (Schein, 1985)		Dominant career orientations for IT professionals include managerial content and technical content; IT professionals with mismatch between job type and career orientation are less satisfied
		Ginzberg and Baroudi, 1988 Loh et al., 1995	Career development (Van Manaan and Schein, 1977)		IT professionals with mismatch between career advancement prospects and career orientation are less satisfied
		Smits et al., 1993 Baroudi and Igbaria, 1995 Igbaria and Wormley, 1995			Race and gender impact the career progression of IT professionals

and career paths of IT professionals in IT firms are similar to those in IT user organizations is an open research question.

A final pattern we have detected in prior research on IT personnel is that it has almost exclusively focused on the individual as the unit of analysis. That is, research has examined the influence of individual factors such as demographic differences in gender, race, and age, drawing upon theories from cognitive, organizational, and social psychology to explain the attitudes, behaviors, and performance of IT professionals. Very little research on IT professionals examines the effects of team, organization, industry, and labor market factors.

By ignoring the external environment and the broader context in which individuals function, research in IT personnel encounters a series of dilemmas. One problem is that the focus on individual factors could mistakenly lead to the conclusion that the variance in the behaviors and performance of IT personnel is due primarily to unique individual differences while environmental factors or an interaction between environmental and individual factors may actually explain much of the variance. Furthermore, individual factors are often unpredictable, idiosyncratic, or outside of the influence of organizations, which makes it difficult to link findings to human resource practices. Finally, neglecting the external environment in explaining the responses of individuals is problematic because employees have attachments and relationships not only to their employer's organization but also to the labor market outside those organizations. In fact, labor market developments and organizational practices that buffer labor market pressures may influence a wide range of employee behaviors within organizations.

To embrace the context in IT personnel research, the field must expand its disciplinary roots beyond psychology. Specifically, a focus should be on developing theories that identify relationships between organizational characteristics and individual responses (Jackson & Schuler, 1995). These relationships constitute a *mesoscopic* (Cappelli & Sherer, 1991) or intermediate level of analysis between traditional macro- and micro-level research. We propose in this chapter that understanding the role(s) an IT professional plays in his or her context is the key to a meso-level analysis of IT personnel research. Thus, while prior research has revealed many important, valuable, and intriguing findings about individual characteristics of IT personnel, our understanding of the behaviors and performance of IT personnel will be greatly enhanced with an explicit focus on the varied roles IT personnel play in different contexts.

UNDERSTANDING IT PERSONNEL IN CONTEXT

The term *context* refers to the environmental or situational surroundings associated with a particular phenomenon that help to illuminate it. These surroundings are typically factors associated with units of analysis above those expressly under investigation. For IT personnel research, the contexts in which IT professionals are embedded can be viewed as layers (Figure 16.1), with each layer representing a higher level of analysis including the organization and the external environment. In the following parts of this section, we identify important factors in the external and internal contexts that impact IT personnel research.

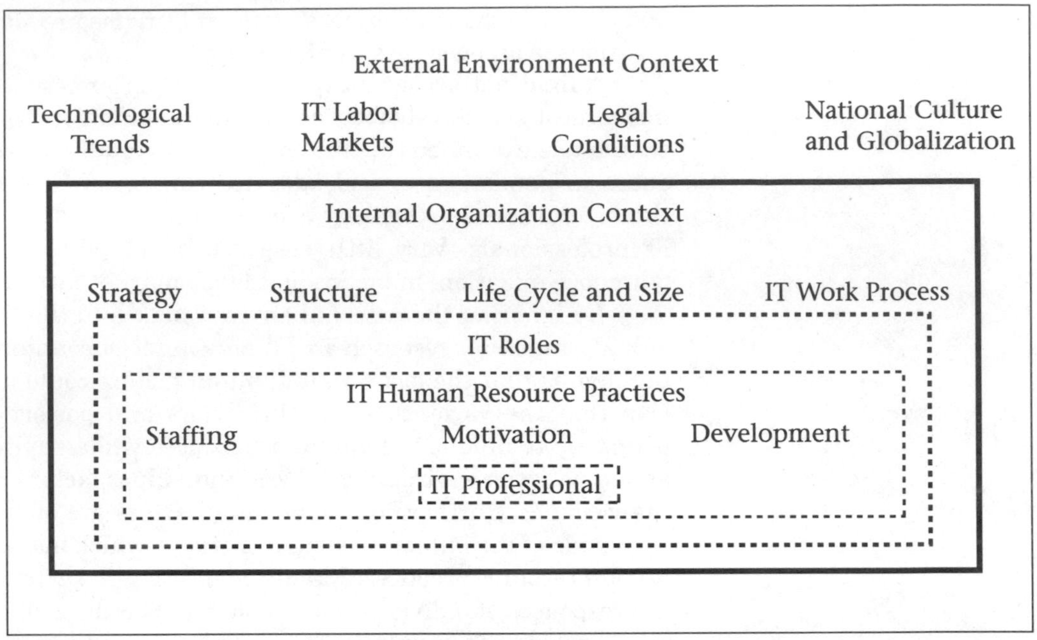

FIGURE 16.1   A
Contextual Perspective
of IT Professionals

External Environment Context

| Technological Trends | IT Labor Markets | Legal Conditions | National Culture and Globalization |

Internal Organization Context

| Strategy | Structure | Life Cycle and Size | IT Work Process |

IT Roles

IT Human Resource Practices

| Staffing | Motivation | Development |

IT Professional

IMPORTANT ELEMENTS OF THE EXTERNAL CONTEXT

As depicted in Figure 16.1, relevant dimensions of the external context for IT professionals include technological trends, labor market conditions, laws and regulations, and national culture and globalization.

Technological Trends

A critical aspect of the external environment that is unique in its impact on IT professionals is the rapid evolution of information technology. New competence-destroying information technologies constantly emerge, and these technologies often have an extremely limited shelf life (sometimes less than a year). This means that, in contrast to other professions in which individuals' competence increases over time with experience, the technical competencies and skills of IT professionals erode quickly in terms of relevance and value.

Furthermore, the relevant skill sets for IT professionals have changed dramatically in ways that are often discontinuous with the past. To illustrate, the software development paradigm and relevant skills have shifted from custom in-house development of mainframe-centric information systems in the 1960s and 1970s to assembly of reusable software objects and packages that are purchased from IT vendors and integrated into complex, distributed IT architectures.[1]

Labor Market Conditions

Employment levels (the demand for labor relative to the supply) impact firms' abilities to attract and retain workers. The widespread infiltration of IT within organizations and the transformation to a knowledge-based economy have created unprecedented and robust demand for workers highly skilled in the use of IT. According to the Information Technology Association of America (ITAA), the labor shortage for IT workers has become a crisis. A report by the ITAA (1998) estimated the shortage of software development professionals in the United States at 346,000 jobs, representing a 10% gap between supply and demand. Rubin further estimated that the U.S. gap alone will grow to about 1 million by 2002 (see www.hrubin.com). The severe supply-demand imbalance in the IT labor market is likely to have a strong influence on IT compensation, turnover patterns, career paths, and other human issues. For example, innovative recruiting and retention strategies may be needed to attract new IT personnel and retain incumbents, given the dramatic IT labor shortages.

In addition to severe worker shortages, the nature of the IT labor market itself varies in different contexts and geographical regions. This suggests that human resource strategies may need to be customized to fit the characteristics of IT labor markets in different regions. In addition, more and more IT professionals are employed by IT firms rather than by IT user organizations. Labor markets for IT firms may be very different from more traditional employment markets. For example, Saxenian (1996) showed that Silicon Valley represents the epitome of an open labor market, and the corresponding career paths in this market are the antithesis of traditional corporate job ladders.

Legal Environments

Almost all aspects of IT personnel are affected by the legal and regulatory environment. Two legal aspects in particular are likely to affect the management of IT professionals: professional liability for defects in the technology as IT becomes more pervasive and the definition of "employee" with the greater adoption of IT outsourcing by firms.

As IT becomes an integral part of organizations and society, defects in information systems can have serious and wide-ranging consequences. IT professionals and their employing firms can be sued not only for breach of contract in system delivery but also for torts of strict product liability and negligence that can arise from poor testing of systems, inadequate warning, or failure to use state-of-the-art technology. For example, see Brannigan and Dayhoff (1981) regarding liability for personal injuries caused by defective medical computer programs and Hagendorf (1990) for errors in computer advisory programs. The fallout from Y2K may yet trigger lawsuits against IT professionals and companies who are responsible for creating and maintaining the systems (Kappelman, 1999).

As outsourcing becomes a common practice in organizations, a number of legal issues that impact the management of IT professionals surface. The legal literature identifies several problems relating to defining the employment status of the professional as either employee or independent contractor (Nimmer, 1985; Reed, 1990). The most common type of IT employment disputes concern restraint of trade (Ang & Endeshaw, 1997). *Restraint of trade* relates to the degree of permitted use of information and skills acquired during the engagement with the employer both during the terms of employment and afterward. Developing software is a highly tacit endeavor. Knowledge about the software developed resides in the heads of software developers and is seldom explicitly codified. Often, the distinction between skills and knowledge acquired on the job, which professionals are allowed to use for their own purposes, and the proprietary information that they will have to leave behind for the employer is blurred.

Consequently, employers are keen to protect the information generated with the resources they provide the employee or independent contractor by prohibiting any kind of leakage to competitors, including situations in which employees set themselves up independently in the line of activity of the employer. Whether the employers get their way in prohibiting competition and for how long or to what extent has been contested repeatedly. Courts have had to settle these issues by reference to law and public policy. The need to allow skills acquired while under contractual engagements with employers to be transferred to other settings has constantly pushed back the employer's urge to prohibit and constrain contracting parties.

Another IT employment dispute concerns the status of the employee. With increases in the number of contingent IT workers in firms, the importance of effective human resource practices for managing contingent workers as well as permanent workers is highlighted. Of particular concern are the status of hired contract IT professionals and the corresponding rights and obligations they have vis-à-vis the employer and the obligations of the employer by law such as in paying benefits to the professional. The traditional legal test concerning the existence of control or supervision by the employer over the contracting party has increasingly become irrelevant since technology has made the test redundant or irrelevant. The compensation that employers have to pay to permanent workers versus contingent workers, particularly in the form of stock options in the case of IT, has also become a bone of contention, linked as it is with the status of the professional.

National Culture and Globalization

According to Carmel (1999), two important trends increase the importance of national culture and globalization in the external context for managing IT professionals. First is the transition of software development away from the traditional co-located form to global software teams working on the same IT project that collaborate across national borders. Second is the spread of software development activities to newly industrialized and developing nations (Apte & Mason, 1995; Jones, 1994). Part of the motivation for the move across national boundaries is that as IT labor shortages intensify, companies want to scout for the best IT talent regardless of geographic location.

The challenge of managing global software teams or hiring IT professionals from different cultures is that cultural differences affect the work behaviors and performance of individuals in culturally diverse teams and organizations (Kumar & Bjorn-Andersen, 1990). Depending on the diversity of the nationalities and cultures of IT professionals, individuals can differ on dimensions of power distance (attitudes toward hierarchy); individualism versus collectivism (concepts of independent versus interdependent self); risk or uncertainty avoidance; long- versus short-term orientation or Confucian dynamism; and high versus low communication contexts (Hall, 1976; Hampden-Turnver & Trompenaars, 1993; Hofstede, 1991). Such cultural differences may present unusual or unforeseen difficulties in managing IT professionals.

IMPORTANT ELEMENTS OF THE INTERNAL CONTEXT

As shown in Figure 16.1, several factors in the internal environment are salient for IT professionals: organization strategy, structure, life cycle and size, and the IT work process.

Organization Strategy

Strategy is a plan of action for investing resources to develop core competences to achieve long-term goals and objectives. Organizations develop strategies to increase the value they can create for their stakeholders. Both business strategy and IT strategy have implications for the management of IT professionals.

There are many ways of characterizing business strategies. One of the most popular typologies for business strategy is that proposed by Miles and Snow (1978, 1984). They classified organizations as defenders, prospectors, or analyzers. *Defenders* strive to retain market share and position in a stable environment in which firm-specific and deep functional knowledge is required to be competitive. *Prospectors* actively seek to grow by searching for new products and markets. *Analyzers* seek to grow by developing new products internally rather than creating new markets. The business strategy followed by the organization has implications for the flow of its IT human resources. For example, for defenders, deep functional expertise is required to be competitive. Thus, organizations following this strategy focus more on development than recruitment of human resources. In contrast, prospectors focus more on recruitment than development of human resources as they seek to expand into new products and markets.

The objective of IT strategy is to define a plan for the use of IT to achieve or sustain competitive advantage.[2] Specifically, firms create strategies for their IT infrastructure: their portfolio of hardware, software, electronically stored data, and telecommunications. In their groundbreaking research IT infrastructure strategy across 75 firms in nine different countries, Weill and Broadbent (1998) identify four IT strategy types: none, utility, dependent, and enabling. The *none* approach is characterized by firms that have no firmwide IT infrastructure. In the *utility* view, there is a firmwide IT infrastructure; however, IT is not a strategic resource but a utility service run at the lowest cost. In the *dependent* strategy, IT strategy is derived from the current business strategy. In the *enabling* strategy, IT *defines* the business strategy: IT is a core competence and creates strategic options for the firm. The IT strategy impacts the IT human resource strategy. For example, IT professionals in firms with a utility IT strategy are likely to find limited opportunities for promotion and career development because the focus is on cost containment through consolidating data centers and standardizing systems. These firms may find it difficult to attract and retain qualified IT professionals.

Organization Structure

Organization structure describes the allocation of tasks and responsibilities and the linkages and interdependencies between individuals and departments. It designates the nature and means of formal reporting relationships as well as the groupings of individuals within the organization. The impact of organizational structures on the management of IT personnel is particularly salient with the advent of innovative organizational forms.

An ongoing debate ever since the introduction of IT into organizations is where to locate the IT function. In the 1960s and 1970s, organizations achieved economies of scale by centralizing computing resources. In the 1980s, computing resources were decentralized and distributed within organizations in an effort to improve the relevance of IT for end users. Both centralization and decentralization approaches have advantages and disadvantages (Tavakolian, 1991); in the 1990s and beyond, the focus in the organizational design for IT is how to balance achieving economies of scale from centralization while also achieving relevance from a distributed approach. Where the IT function is located in organizations has implications for the management of IT personnel. For example, IT jobs in firms pursuing a centralized approach are likely to require very different skill sets than IT jobs in firms pursuing a decentralized approach.

Innovative organizational forms (such as cross-functional teams, matrix organizations, virtual organizations, and divisionalizing IT) impact the allocation of decision rights, roles, and responsibilities for IT professionals. This can affect motivation, incentives, and performance appraisal. For example, divisionalized firms (the IT subsidiary form) are more likely to emphasize results over process than those structured around functional departments, reflecting greater integration across units and a more externally oriented focus.

Organization Life Cycle and Size

Organizations vary in size and traverse through a number of developmental stages. As firms change, their managerial priorities are likely to change and will in turn have implications for IT human resource management. Similar to other entities, organizations progress through various development stages such as start-up, growth, maturity, and decline (Baird & Meshoulam, 1988). The kind of IT human resources needed in each stage may be quite different. For example, CIO positions in IT start-up firms may require very different skill sets and managerial styles than CIO positions in mature IT firms. Performance assessment criteria may also be quite different for IT professionals in firms that are in different stages of the life cycle. From a human resource strategy perspective, start-up firms may emphasize recruitment and selection while mature firms may emphasize development and retention strategies.

Firm size is also likely to have a significant impact on IT personnel. Larger organizations have the resources and can achieve economies of scale from implementing more sophisticated human resource practices. Thus, the scale and scope of IT human resource practices are likely to vary with organization size. IT professionals in large firms are likely to be compensated more and have greater opportunities for training and development due to more highly developed internal labor markets in large firms. On the other hand, smaller organizations may need to adopt more innovative practices to attract and retain IT professionals to compete against the larger firms for scarce IT human resources. The relevant roles for IT professionals could also differ in large and small firms: IT professionals in small firms may need to play broader roles because the jobs may be less specialized.

IT Work Process

The IT work process refers to the activities required to transform user (customer) specifications into information technologies and systems. These activities can vary along several dimensions, including the degree to which tasks are routinized and predictable, and the types and levels of knowledge required to effectively perform different tasks. Each of these dimensions can impact the management and research of IT personnel.

User specifications for information systems are by their very nature quite unpredictable and uncertain. This uncertainty leads to unpredictability in IT project tasks and instability in project scope. IT development tools, methodologies, and process improvement programs (such as ISO9000-3 and the capability maturity model) attempt to standardize project tasks and to reduce the variance in project outcomes (Paulk, 1995). Such standardization could improve the IT professional's ability to estimate reasonable project deadlines and to deliver on schedule and within budget. Thus, it is possible that the adoption of development tools and methodologies as well as process improvement programs could significantly improve the morale of IT professionals. On the other hand, IT professionals may believe that these methodologies are restrictive and inhibit their creativity.

A second dimension of the IT work process that is relevant for the management of IT personnel includes the different types and levels of knowledge required to effectively perform different activities. In contrast to other professionals, IT professionals need cross-functional business knowledge as well as specialized technical, managerial, and interpersonal skills. Furthermore, the development, maintenance, and infrastructure tasks are quite distinct in nature and require different capabilities. The widespread adoption of outsourcing is also likely to dramatically impact the activities, competencies, motivation, and performance of IT personnel. With outsourcing, IT personnel shift from internal development work to performing tasks involved with the selection, contracting, and monitoring of vendors.[3]

FUTURE RESEARCH DIRECTIONS: IT PERSONNEL IN CONTEXT

In the preceding sections, we examined prior research on IT personnel. We found that it has generally anchored on the individual, exploring many of the human resource issues solely from the perspective of the individual. We then identified the importance of context (both external and internal) and delineated important dimensions of these contexts in terms of their consequences for IT human resource practices.

In this section, we build an integrative model (Figure 16.2) and outline a future research agenda for the management of IT professionals. We begin by considering IT roles in context. Roles are the basic building blocks of organizations and must be both internally consistent and congruent with contextual factors such as business strategies and labor market conditions. As indicated in Figure 16.2, roles can fully or partially mediate the effects of external and internal contextual factors on IT human resource practices. We propose new directions and strategies for research on IT personnel that consider the direct effects of contextual factors as well as the indirect effects mediated through roles in terms of the stages within the natural progression of the human resource life cycle of staffing, motivating, and developing IT personnel. Finally, we consider the individual-, organizational-, and macro-level outcomes associated with the management of IT personnel in context.

FIGURE 16.2 An Integrated Model for IT Personnel Research in Context

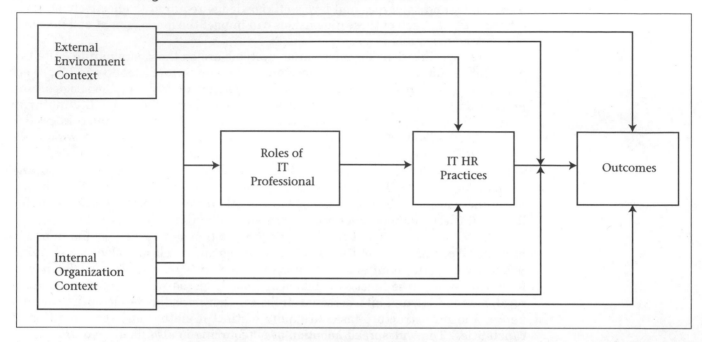

IT ROLES IN CONTEXT

A *role* is an interdependent component in an organizational system (Katz & Kahn, 1978). It is a comprehensive pattern for behavior and attitudes: Roles in organizations are those designed explicitly to accomplish some function and are often formalized by means of a job or position description (Robey, 1982). To be effective, roles must be clearly defined and communicated in the organization so that the expectations and evaluation of the behaviors required of the role are unambiguous. We first consider the impact of the external and internal contexts on IT roles; then we outline research strategies for examining IT roles in context.

Effect of Context on IT Roles

As new technologies emerge, current roles change or become obsolete and new roles appear. For example, the emergence of electronic commerce has resulted in a new senior executive role: chief e-commerce officer. Existing technical roles (such as programmer) may expand and become more complex as the IT professional of the twenty-first century must be conversant in multiple (old and new) technologies and platforms. The severe supply-demand imbalance in the IT labor market is also likely to have a strong influence on IT roles. For example, roles may need to be redesigned or new roles created to attract new IT personnel and to retain incumbents. Furthermore, with the development of a vibrant IT industry, new roles emerge for IT professionals in IT firms.

As IT becomes a critical component of the business strategy for firms, roles of IT professionals can change. For example, CIOs must develop *leadership* abilities and take the initiative to set business goals and directions as well as technology strategy. Thus, it is important to reanalyze the role of CIOs as leaders using concepts of transformational leadership (visionary and charismatic) and to examine how CIOs contribute to the value of the organization. Because of the unique position of the CIO, the role of the CIO as a leader is a challenging one. Unlike leaders from other functional areas, a CIO must juxtapose between technical leadership as well as business leadership.[4]

Alternative sourcing strategies for performing IT work impact roles. For example, a recent study by Ang, Wong, and Soh (1999) suggested that when an IT organization undergoes outsourcing, the survivors of the outsourcing suddenly experience an upsurge in role stressors—including role overload, ambiguity, and conflict. In outsourcing, previous subordinates of project leaders—analysts and programmers—are transplanted to the outsourcing vendor. Suddenly, the project leaders, the survivors of organizational change, have lost their subordinates, must undertake responsibilities that previously belonged to their subordinates, and must learn to manage their previous subordinates as vendors. Supervisory skills may not necessarily translate smoothly to vendor management skills.

Research Strategies for Studying IT Roles in Context

Roles can be studied either at a micro level, using the methodologies from cognitive psychology or industrial organization (IO) psychology, or at a more macro level, using methodologies from sociology.

From a cognitive psychology perspective, studies could examine the knowledge structures, cognitive strategies, and processes of high performers in emerging roles. The primary aim of such studies can be to facilitate the progression of a novice IT professional to an expert by understanding how novices and experts function and by evolving strategies to close the gap between the two. Studies of this nature can rely on protocol analysis as a way of producing an account of the latent problem-solving processes embedded within the minds of the professionals (Ericsson & Simon, 1984).

Because of the micro orientation, methodologies from cognitive and IO psychology tend to focus on the individual and to ignore the context within which the individual is embedded. Accordingly, researchers must consciously design and take into account the various contexts in which IT professionals work. For example, researchers could analyze the similarities and differences in the roles of programmers working in different technological environments (e.g., mainframe-based systems versus client server versus multitiered architectures; Web-based, object-oriented environments versus COBOL environments). Or researchers could examine systems analysts working in different labor markets (e.g., IT user organizations versus IT vendor firms) or in different industry sectors (e.g., public- versus private-sector firms).

Unlike methodologies from psychology, methodologies from sociology are more macro-oriented and are therefore more context embedded. Future research from a sociological perspective could undertake ethnographic studies of new roles. Exemplars of ethnographic studies of roles have been conducted by Barley and his associates (Barley & Bechky, 1994; Barley & Orr, 1997; Orr, 1996). Ethnographies portray work life in the social setting and examine in detail the activities of professionals at the workplace. Failing to understand the roles of IT professionals may lead not only to an unrealistic picture of the IT development process but also to a misrepresentation and stereotyping of IT work. Without detailed (and accurate) information on IT work, it is difficult to attract people to the profession given stereotypical images of what IT professionals know and do.

STAFFING IN CONTEXT

Staffing involves bringing new IT professionals into the organization and making sure they serve as valuable additions to the workforce. The goal of staffing is to match, or align, the abilities of the job candidate with the roles defined by the firm. After defining the roles required and identifying the competencies required to fill the roles, individuals are recruited and selected to match those roles. In the following sections, we examine the impact of the contextual environment for the staffing of IT professionals. We consider the impact on job analysis first and then on selection activities. We conclude with a discussion of strategies for research on staffing in context.

Job Analysis

Once IT roles have been defined by an organization, they are formalized by means of a job description, which includes a summary of the basic tasks making up a job. These tasks are identified using a systematic job analysis. The dynamic external and internal environments for IT professionals serve to create new roles and alter existing roles by expanding, changing, or reducing their content. As such, systematically analyzing and reanalyzing the content for new and changing IT roles is an imperative.

Selection

Once roles and jobs are understood, the next task is to find people to *fit* the roles. Personality is a complex set of inherent dispositional and emotional characteristics that can be used to uniquely identify a person. Although prior research on the usefulness of personality measures has been pessimistic (e.g., Mischel, 1968; Weiss & Adler, 1984), recent research in IO psychology has seen a resurgence of the importance of personality in predicting job fit and job performance. The inherent belief is that people do, in fact, have long-term dispositional traits that make them particularly suited for certain jobs and influence their behavior in work settings. Specifically, research has been extremely productive when thousands of potential traits are reduced to a small number of factors, particularly the "Big Five" dimensions of extraversion, emotional stability, agreeableness, conscientiousness, and openness to experience (see Mount & Barrick, 1995) for a meta-analysis of studies linking personality to performance).

Research Strategies for Studying Staffing in Context

Researchers could undertake a systematic job analysis of new and existing roles in IT across different external and internal contexts (e.g., chief e-commerce officers in public- and private-sector firms). Thus far, skills inventory studies have been conducted based on inductive, free-recall, and focus group discussions on the possible skill sets of IT professionals. Recent job analysis methodologies from IO psychology offer deductive methods to systematically reduce each role to a logically coherent set of tasks and job clusters (see Peterson & Jeanneret, 1997). The methodologies are especially suited for assessing role changes, role overload, or role underload. For example, one could study IT project leaders' roles before and after IT outsourcing to assess whether their roles have expanded or contracted in scope.

Selection research could continue from the IO discipline by examining personality and dispositional characteristics and their relationship to job fit and performance. For example, tolerance for ambiguity is a desirable trait for programmers since by nature programming has requirements that are incomplete, conflicting or contradictory requirements (Hohmann, 1997). Given the complexity and variety of work environments facing IT professionals, additional research must be done to understand the appropriate personality profiles fitting the various kinds of IT roles found in different external and internal contexts.

IT staffing can also be studied from a more macro-level perspective. To understand the antecedents predicting the choice of different IT staffing strategies or when different staffing practices are more or less effective, it is also necessary to consider the direct influence of the external and internal contexts. For example, investment in IT recruitment is likely to vary with employment levels. When the IT labor supply is tight, organizations may adopt more expensive, innovative, and intensive recruiting strategies for their IT professionals. Alternatively, firms could relax their hiring standards as a means to fill vacant positions. Recruiting effectiveness may be lower under conditions of tight IT labor supply. Macroeconomic studies using econometric analysis of firm-level data on IT professionals would be useful to tease out the effects of the external context on staffing activities.

MOTIVATION IN CONTEXT

Individual performance in organizations is a function of motivation as well as skills and abilities. Individuals can choose to vary their behaviors in response to conditions at the workplace, including incentives and disincentives that are built into the organization's reward system. The goals of motivation are to define and provide mechanisms in the workplace to evaluate employee performance and to design reward systems to motivate desired behaviors. In the following sections, we examine the impact of the contextual environment for the motivation of IT professionals. We consider the impact first on the motivating aspects of roles, then on performance appraisal, and finally on compensation. We conclude with a discussion of strategies for research on motivation in context.

Beyond JCM

Job design characteristics provide opportunities and constraints for work activity. In a recent review of the area (Kelly, 1992), the job characteristics model (JCM) (Hackman & Oldham, 1979) still stimulates a considerable amount of research. However, the most frequently noted limitation of the JCM is that it does not include relevant dimensions of the work context. This becomes particularly evident in the context of advanced manufacturing technology (Wall et al., 1990). For example, Jackson et al. (1993) showed that additional measures must be developed within the JCM to assess constructs that reflect contextual work aspects such as control over time and methods, monitoring and problem-solving demand, and production responsibility. Analogously, in IT, the work context has changed significantly in terms of increasing automation and outsourcing of the development process. While prior applications of JCM to IT professionals have suggested that IT work is motivating, it is not clear whether IT developers would perceive these new dimensions of the IT work context to be as motivating.

Performance Appraisal

Performance appraisal refers to the assessment and measurement of employee behaviors relative to the behaviors required by the employee's role in the organization. The dynamic external and internal environments for IT professionals serve to create new roles and alter existing roles. Performance appraisal approaches must be designed and redesigned to fit these new and changing IT roles. For example, the study of Bell Atlantic by Clark et al. (1997) illustrates how performance appraisal must change to fit new IT roles. Bell Atlantic adopted the "centers of excellence" organizational design to foster "change-ready" capabilities in the IT organization. The roles of IT professionals in this new organizational design were very different from traditional IT roles, and Bell Atlantic adjusted its performance appraisal approach to fit these new roles. Specifically, a 360-degree performance appraisal behavioral approach was implemented so that performance in IT roles was assessed by peers, IT managers, and clients.

Compensation/Rewards

The salary paid to IT employees, as well as other job benefits, depends in part on how well these professionals perform in their roles. Other factors influencing compensation are contextual and include the relative worth of each role within the firm (in the internal labor market), external labor market conditions and prevailing wage rates, and the type of pay system used.

Labor supply and demand cause the wages for some jobs to be higher than for others, even though the jobs may be of similar difficulty, responsibility, and so on. In IT this is particularly the case when there are labor shortages for certain technical skills. For example, programmers experienced in COBOL may be compensated less than programmers experienced in XML because the supply of qualified workers in Web technologies is low relative to demand. The level of wages is also influenced by the competitive wage in the local area. Even after the value of a job has been determined and the local and regional wage differences are taken into consideration, one person may be paid more for the same job than another person, depending on seniority in the company, level of individual performance, the level of group performance (if the individual is part of a work group), and the level of organization performance (if the firm uses profit-sharing systems).

Research Strategies for Studying Motivation in Context

There are a number of strategies for studying motivation in context. For applications of JCM, it is evident that relevant dimensions of the IT work context must be operationalized and included in the model. Given the increasing automation, teamwork, and level of outsourcing in IT development, it is necessary to add constructs to the JCM to assess the motivating potential of these contextual work characteristics. Longitudinal studies of IT roles (such as developers and project leaders) using an expanded JCM would be interesting in determining whether IT jobs today are as motivating as in the past and predicting the motivating potential of new IT roles. In addition, a meta-analysis of studies (Kelly, 1992) examined the relationship between JCM and job satisfaction and job performance and has questioned the accepted proposition from job design theory that job redesign will affect both satisfaction and performance. Instead, Kelly suggests that there is a twin-track model in which satisfaction and performance are influenced by different determinants, the former by changing dimensions of job content and the latter by other organizational context variables not adequately taken into account by the job characteristics model. Thus, the twin-track model suggests a further extension of the job characteristics model in IT to include different contextual factors, depending on whether job performance or job satisfaction is studied.

Performance appraisal can be studied from the IO psychology paradigm. Basic research questions concern how the performance of IT professionals can be appraised and what types of performance appraisal approaches are best suited to different kinds of IT roles. Appraisal can focus on traits, behaviors, or accomplishments. Under trait approaches, a performance appraiser rates an employee on traits such as friendliness, efficiency, and reliability. Behavioral approaches such as the critical incidents method involve recording specific employee actions. Outcome approaches such as management by objectives rate what the employee is supposed to accomplish on the job. Another research question concerns who is best suited to appraise performance (superiors, subordinates, clients, peers) for new and changing IT roles.

Because compensation is directly influenced by contextual factors as well as role factors, research must take into account the multilevel determinants of compensation. That is, to understand the antecedents of compensation, it is important to analyze factors at multiple levels of analysis, including the effects of different labor markets, regions, and organizational pay systems as well as the performance of the individual in the IT role. A fundamental research question could address the relative impact of the external context and organizational context versus individual factors in determining compensation. For example, are similar IT roles (such as systems analysts compensated differently in IT firms and IT user firms? In public and private companies? These questions could also be examined longitudinally by studying compensation patterns for a particular IT role (such as a programmer) in different settings over time. Other important areas for research concern the efficacy of different incentive systems. For example, under what conditions is a broad-banding approach more effective than other approaches such as individual performance-based, seniority-based, or profit-sharing incentive schemes?

DEVELOPMENT IN CONTEXT

Because many of the skills required of IT roles are acquired or improved with on-the-job training and experience, it is important in developing talent in IT professionals to consciously structure the roles and the progression of roles an individual undertakes in an IT career. The goal of development is to help the firm meet its immediate human resource needs based upon the roles defined in the organization and to ensure that the firm's employees are ready to meet future needs for new and changed roles. In the following sections, we examine the impact of the contextual environment for the development of IT professionals. We consider the impact first on training and then on career paths and planning. We conclude with a discussion of strategies for research on development in context.

Training

As IT roles emerge and change, training can be used to help existing employees to acquire the skills needed to fill these roles. The constant pace of technological change has impacted the technical skills required for existing roles and for new roles. A primary question that arises is how training approaches can best be designed to teach incumbents the technical skills required for new and changing IT roles. For example, for which technical skills are different methods (such as classroom training, role playing, programmed instruction, simulation, or behavior modeling) most effective?

To facilitate the advancement of IT professionals to higher-level roles (such as systems analyst, project leader, senior executive), it is also important to consider how the "soft" skills of IT professionals can be developed. Although the soft (i.e., nontechnical) skills of IT professionals are recognized as important for job performance, there are few guidelines on how to conceptualize, measure, and develop soft skills. The irony is that organizations often select and recruit IT professionals based solely on technical skills, yet soft skills are needed to advance to higher level job positions. Although IT professionals with good technical skills may perform competently in their roles as programmers in the early stages of their careers, they may not perform as well when they become systems analysts or project leaders.

Paradoxically, although soft skills are rated as important, there is still a widely held perception among organizations that soft skills among IT professionals are "nice to have," not "must have." It appears that organizations are more concerned with sourcing for and retaining IT personnel with hard technical skills. Nevertheless, if companies begin to pay greater attention to soft skills, there is a strong possibility that IT professionals with the requisite soft skills may contribute more effectively in their deployment of technical skills. One of the impediments in incorporating soft skills in the training of IT professionals is that soft skills remain a nebulous concept. Unlike technical skills, for which one can become certified through pencil-and-paper tests, soft skills are more difficult to assess and calibrate.

Career Pathing and Planning

Career paths trace the training outcomes and job transitions of individuals over their work lives. The professional career path represents the observable history of how individuals have been socialized into roles. The typical professional career path is likely to change if the diversity of organizational settings leads to diversity of interests and demographic diversity among professional workers (Kunda, 1992). In IT, the variety of organizational settings and the emergence of new professional roles have increased dramatically in recent years. The growing use of outsourcing and the emergence of IT firms have opened mobility alternatives to in-house salaried careers within IT user organizations. New technologies have created new IT roles (such as Webmaster, knowledge officer, e-commerce officer) that provide new career opportunities for IT professionals.

Research Strategies for Studying Development in Context

Research on the training of IT professionals in technical and soft skills could be conducted from the paradigms of cognitive and IO psychology. An essential task is first to develop assessments of skill sets required for IT roles so that it is clear what skills are required. These assessments can also be used to evaluate the efficacy of different training approaches. For example, the Guttman approach to behavioral rating scales can be used to identify and rank the major dimensions of job behaviors and skill sets that are used to evaluate IT professionals (Arvey & Hoyle, 1974). Recent research by Joseph, Ang, and colleagues (Joseph & Ang, 1999; Joseph, Ang, & Tan, 1997) illustrates how work on the measurement of practical intelligence and tacit knowledge at work by cognitive psychologists (Wagner & Sternberg, 1985) can be leveraged to develop and validate a computer-based psychological instrument that diagnoses and assesses soft skills of IT professionals. Using the knowledge-based approach of eliciting behaviors in critical work situations, they find that soft skills of IT professionals can be categorized into three areas of management and self-regulation: managing self, managing careers, and managing others. The findings also suggest that significantly high levels and a mix of soft skills are required of IT professionals when they face complex work situations that involve managing multiple stakeholders: superiors, subordinates, peers, users, clients, and vendors in a myriad of intraorganizational versus interorganizational contexts. Future work must continue to explore both the assessment and development of soft skills required of IT professionals.

As we have noted, research on external career paths for IT professionals is limited. The new mobility opportunities created by diverse organizational settings and new IT roles suggest a number of interesting and important research questions to study. One question raised by research on diverse professional settings is whether the labor market for professionals is segmented by function into elites and practitioners. Elites represent a small percentage of knowledge producers for the professions, whereas the nonelite practitioners consume and apply the knowledge produced and disseminated by elites (Friedson, 1984). In IT, the elite is represented by firms such as Microsoft and start-up firms that offer new IT products and services; nonelite practitioners are those who use the IT tools to serve the needs of IT user organizations.

Another question one could ask as organizational settings diversify is whether there are systematic differences in career paths for those recruited in different professional roles in different settings. A key question to be addressed by future research is whether professionals with different characteristics are more likely to spend their careers in some specific organizational contexts rather than in others and what motivates such choices. Another related question is whether there is significant and typical career mobility across diverse work settings, and, if so, what the consequences are for those who move between settings. Such movement may be a highly significant indicator of fragmentation and segmentation in professional work. Alternatively, if the boundaries between organizational settings are relatively permeable and show no consistent pattern of career movements, this would suggest that professionals have been able to maintain a relatively coherent occupational (Saxenian, 1996) labor market tied to generalist knowledge.

A further extension of this question is whether mobility across organizational contexts is more valuable for a professional career than mobility within specific contexts. Sometimes a specific organizational context may constrain a professional's individual movement. For example, Ang and Slaughter (1998) found that consulting firms are open to job mobility at all levels. Individuals can enter the consulting firm as either an apprentice or a guru. However, in many IT user organizations, the entry to more senior managerial positions is often closed to external parties, thereby restricting the inflow of external talent. Mobility also is constrained by the age or number of years of experience of the IT professional.

A key to understanding the impact of contextual factors on IT careers is to engage in systematic comparisons of the career mobility of IT professionals and others who work in the same organizational settings. In situations in which organizations establish the agenda for the context of professional work, there should be divergent mobility patterns in different organizational settings. However, this is only part of the comparison that is needed. Researchers should also examine the question of whether the career patterns of professionals are distinctive. If there is considerable isomorphic pressure from employing organizations, IT professional career mobility will look like the career mobility of other white-collar employees, implying that IT professional norms are not well established or have been subordinated.

IT PERSONNEL OUTCOMES IN CONTEXT

As reflected in our integrative model in Figure 16.2, a number of outcomes are relevant to the study of IT personnel in context. In this section, we identify outcomes at the individual-, organization-, and macro-levels of analysis and discuss research strategies for studying IT personnel outcomes in context.

Outcomes at Different Levels of Analysis

At the individual level, attitudes and behaviors represent an individual's responses to various human resource practices as well as contextual contingencies. Relevant attitudinal outcomes include constructs such as job satisfaction, organizational commitment, and job stress. Behavioral outcomes include job performance, extra-role behaviors, and turnover. At the organizational level, there are human resource management outcomes as well as business outcomes. Examples of human resource outcomes include retention rates, hiring rates, grievance rates, absenteeism, and employee morale. Business outcomes include firm performance, market share, return on investment, and return on assets. At the macro level, outcomes include such aspects as productivity in different industry sectors or countries, quality of life, and human capital development.

Research Strategies for Studying Outcomes in Context

In studying the outcomes of IT personnel in context, research must be explicitly designed to consider the effects of factors at multiple levels of analysis. For example, research examining the turnover behavior of IT personnel should consider labor market contextual factors (such as availability of jobs in a region or relative supply/demand imbalance for a particular skill set), organization contextual factors (such as whether the individual works in a public or private firm), and human resource strategies (such as staffing and training policies), and individual factors (such as job satisfaction). Data must be collected at multiple levels of analysis, and strategies to conceptualize models and analyze data at multiple levels of analysis are needed to determine the multilevel effects of contextual factors on outcomes. It may be useful to design studies of IT personnel based on the research strategies used in educational psychology. For example, hierarchical linear modeling research designs have been developed by Bryk and Raudenbush (1992) to study the impact of regional factors, public/private school, and teaching practices on student achievement. Such approaches may be usefully adapted to the study of IT professionals.

It is also important to examine the relationship between IT human resource outcomes and business outcomes, particularly as IT grows in strategic importance to firms; that is, how do IT employee turnover rates, morale, work attendance, and grievance rates relate to net profit, return on investment, and market share? However, establishing and measuring the relationships between human resource management outcomes and business outcomes is a tricky endeavor because one must control for the many other factors (such as industry, capital/labor ratio, and company size and age) that can influence business performance. It may be useful to design studies based on the approaches used to investigate the effects on business organizations of employee unionism and collective bargaining. For example, using a standard microeconomic framework of analysis, researchers have statistically measured the effects of unionism on wages and fringe benefits, productivity, capital investment, research and development expenditures, firm profitability, and market value (measured by stock prices); for example, see studies by Becker and Olson (1986), Clark (1984), Hirsch (1992), and Voos and Mishel (1986).

CONCLUSIONS

In this chapter, we have examined the research on IT professionals. We have seen that many studies of IT professionals thus far suffer from percept-percept bias. That is, researchers tend to apply existing theories (in particular, micro-level theories) to IT personnel. The challenge is to move beyond studies that apply only theories from other fields and instead to use the IT context to revise, modify, and develop theories. It is our contention that the area of IT personnel can progress significantly if research moves away from questions about individual differences and focuses instead on the organizational, environmental, and situational contexts that differentiate the reactions of IT professionals to their workplaces. Shifting the focus from the individual to the context has a number of implications for IT personnel research. In the following sections, we elaborate the theoretical implications and methodological issues suggested by a contextual perspective of IT personnel.

IMPLICATIONS FOR RESEARCH

To examine *context* in research of IT personnel requires consideration of additional theoretical perspectives beyond those from cognitive psychology or IO psychology. In the economics literature, human capital theory, transaction costs theory, and agency theory may be useful theory bases. For example, human capital theory refers to the productive capabilities of workers (Becker, 1964). The skills, experience, and knowledge of workers are valuable to organizations because workers constitute the organization's human capital and, thereby, its productivity and flexibility. The human resource costs related to securing human capital assets from the market and motivating, monitoring, and retaining them can be considered human capital investments made in anticipation of future returns (Lewin & Mitchell, 1995). In human capital theory, contextual elements such as labor market conditions, business strategy, and technology are important because they can impact human resource costs or the value of the anticipated returns from investment in human capital.

Macro-level theories such as institutional theory and resource dependence theory focus on the relationship between an organization and its external constituencies. These theories may be useful in helping to understand why organizations adopt similar IT human resource strategies. For example, institutional theory (Zucker, 1977, 1987) asserts that organizations in institutionalized environments are pressured to become similar. This suggests that organizations may adopt certain IT human resource practices because they are imitating the practices of leading organizations in their environment.

To fully understand IT personnel in context requires consideration of multiple theoretical perspectives as well as theories that can cross levels of analysis. Future research needs to recognize that the internal and external contexts can moderate the effects of IT human resource practices on outcomes. Furthermore, theories from economics, sociology, psychology, and organizational behavior must be adapted to fit the unique contexts of IT personnel. To illustrate, human capital theory presumes that the value of human capital increases with job experience, ceteris paribus. However, in IT we have seen that the rapid change of IT leads to obsolescence of technical skills absent constant training in the newest technologies. This suggests that the value of IT human capital (at least technical IT human capital) erodes with experience, contrary to what human capital theory would predict. Thus, the boundary conditions within which human capital theory holds for IT personnel must be specified; for example, the predictions of human capital theory may be valid only for managerially oriented IT roles or for IT roles in IT user organizations or for IT roles in public sector firms.

Methodologically, there are significant measurement and analytical challenges to studying contextual factors. A major difficulty is defining and measuring the relevant constructs and dimensions in the external and internal contexts. That is, methodologies must switch from treating context as sources of error variance to explicitly incorporating relevant dimensions in models. For example, as we noted earlier, the job characteristics model must be expanded to include characteristics that are relevant for the work and organizational contexts. However, it may be difficult to identify the relevant dimensions of these contexts and the relationships between them. Analytical challenges and opportunities abound as well. First is the need to consider outcomes and factors at multiple levels of analysis. For example, models predicting individual compensation need to assess the effects of determinants at multiple levels of analysis (such as the organization, industry, labor market, and geographical region). Analytical techniques such as multilevel modeling are useful for this kind of analysis; however, it can be challenging to collect sufficient data at multiple levels of analysis to assess the effects of different contextual factors.

CONCLUDING REMARKS

Researchers interested in the changing contexts of IT professional work face an exciting, new, and complicated empirical world for their research. We hope our review will stimulate new generations of researchers to enter an area of study that represents a unique interface between organizational theory, social stratification, and historical analysis of institutional change in IT professional work.

ENDNOTES

1. See the chapter on software origins by George for a description of how software development has changed.
2. See the chapters by Sambamurthy on business strategy and by Weill and Broadbent on managing IT infrastructure that describe the strategic role of IT.
3. The chapter by Kirsch on project management identifies software skills needed in IT projects. The chapter by Lacity and Willcocks on IT outsourcing describes the relationship between the vendor and client in IT outsourcing.
4. See the chapter by Ross and Feeny on the CIO for an analysis of the role of the CIO and how it has evolved.

Chapter 17

Managing IT Infrastructure: A Strategic Choice

Peter Weill and Marianne Broadbent

Business has embarked on a new era of competition that is faster, more global, and increasingly volatile, simultaneously requiring a relentless reduction of costs as well as the agility to find new ways to differentiate and create value. The merging of the computing, telephony, telecommunications, publishing, and entertainment industries and the pervasiveness of the Internet and other vehicles for electronic commerce present strategic opportunities and threats for every firm. Business and technology managers are anxious to make smart use of this powerful combination of business unit, firm, industry, and public infrastructures. However, many firms struggle with their information technology infrastructure investments, grappling with a multitude of technical and business choices and working on the optimal balance of capabilities at corporate and business unit levels. Concurrently, managers need to consider how their firm's technology infrastructure intersects with emerging industry and public infrastructures.

In the past there were fewer options and limited infrastructures providing channels to customers. Today there are multiple options. As we move into the

This chapter draws heavily on material published by Weill and Broadbent in several sources, including *Leveraging the New Infrastructure: How Market Leaders Capitalize on Information Technology* (Boston, MA: Harvard Business School Press, 1998).

twenty-first century and more and more of a firm's cash flow is on-line, the longer-term decisions about information technology infrastructure investments will differentiate competitive capabilities. The opportunities of the new electronic infrastructures will test many business and organizational decision-making processes. Making the best technology infrastructure decisions for the firm will be as critical for creating long-term shareholder value as the previous waves of infrastructure decisions were for the physical infrastructure of location, buildings, and plant. People will still be the core asset of a firm, but the infrastructures they operate will be electronic. We will see the growing importance of the new electronic infrastructure and a declining importance of physical location. Identifying how to benefit from the new infrastructures is a challenge for senior management, who must now take responsibility for these critical longer-term information technology decisions. These decisions of IT infrastructure capability are strategic choices requiring trade-offs (Porter, 1996).

Firms make different strategic choices about information technology infrastructure capability. Consider the examples of these market leaders:

- The Hong Kong–based conglomerates Jardine Matheson and Hutchison Whampoa decided to make no firmwide investments in information technology infrastructure services (Whitman, Farhoomand, & Tricker, 1995).
- Honda Motor Corporation developed a highly sophisticated communications network linking designers in Tokyo and Los Angeles to reduce cycle time in new car production (Broadbent, 1995).
- The international paper and packaging manufacturer Amcor Ltd provided no information technology infrastructure services among its paper, packaging, and containers businesses (Butler, Broadbent, & Niemann, 1995).
- Monsanto restructured from autonomous divisions to a series of strategic business units to achieve greater business agility while concurrently placing greater emphasis on shared business services, including selected information technology infrastructure services (Monsanto, 1995).
- Citibank Asia is centralizing and standardizing all back-office information technology processes into one location for all of its Asian country operations, while its parent company, Citicorp, is forging ahead with higher levels of centralized and standardized infrastructure services throughout its world operations (Neo & Soh, 1995).

Can each of these firms have made the correct strategic choices? How did these firms make these decisions?

From our research it was evident that executive management in each of these firms made deliberate decisions about infrastructure capability based on their strategic context. For example, the Hong Kong conglomerates regularly buy and sell businesses and may be constrained by information technology infrastructures integrating businesses units. At the other end of the strategic choice spectrum, some firms view information technology infrastructure as enabling centrally coordinated strategic flexibility. The aim is to facilitate international agility and fast responses to changes in their global marketplace. At Honda, the ability for designers in different locations to communicate and exchange designs is critical for reducing cycle time in new car production.

This chapter explores the issue of managing IT infrastructure and draws heavily on a research program we have conducted with colleagues[1] from several universities around the world. A number of citations to this work and to many other researchers are provided as pointers to sources of more information. The research program investigated the role and value of information technology infrastructure, including conceptual work on definitions and the analogy with public infrastructure (Weill, 1993), empirical work on measuring infrastructure and investigating the relationship to firm context (Broadbent et al., 1996), investigating how firms link information technology infrastructure capability to business strategy (Broadbent & Weill, 1997), and empirical evidence for the business value of infrastructure (Weill & Broadbent, 1998).

The following questions are addressed in this chapter: What is IT infrastructure? How can we describe and compare infrastructure capabilities? Why do firms choose different infrastructure capabilities? What is the evidence for payoff for different levels of infrastructure capability? What have we learned about strategic choices in managing IT infrastructure?

WHAT IS IT INFRASTRUCTURE: A FRAMEWORK

The definition and the concept of information technology infrastructure have slowly evolved as technology has become more ubiquitous and standardized over time. A conceptual and physical separation between infrastructure and applications has occurred. There are many similarities between information technology infrastructure within a firm and the public infrastructure of roads, railways, schools, hospitals, and bridges (Keen, 1991).

There have been a number of careful economic studies on the value of public infrastructure. At the international level, a strong indicator is the relationship between public infrastructure investment (as a percentage of gross domestic product) and the annual growth of labor productivity. Countries with higher public infrastructure investment had higher productivity (Aschauer, 1989).

At the national level, Aschauer (1989) also shows a significant statistical relationship between the stock of U.S. public infrastructure and output per unit of private capital. A similar relationship was demonstrated between the stock of public infrastructure and productivity growth. Munnell (1990a) found a strong positive relationship between the U.S. stock of public infrastructure and labor productivity. Infrastructure investment increases the return on private capital and thus will stimulate new private investment (Aschauer, 1989). The rationale for public infrastructure investment is that these services will not be produced by the private market (Munnell, 1990a).

At the state and regional levels, the evidence is equally strong. Munnell (1990b) studied the differences between regions in the United States and found overwhelming evidence that public capital has a positive impact on private sector output, investment, and employment. Public infrastructure investment also appears to come before a pickup in economic activity (Munnell, 1990b). The analogy between public infrastructure and IT infrastructure is compelling because there are striking similarities, including these:

1. Both IT and public infrastructure are provided by a central agency funded by some form of taxation.
2. Both types of infrastructure require large investments and are long term in nature.
3. The central agency in both cases provides an essential service that users would generally not be motivated or able to provide.

4. The right amount of investment is a delicate balance for both types of infrastructure. Too little will lead to duplication, incompatibility, and nonoptimal use of resources. Too much will discourage user investment and involvement and may result in unused capacity.

The strength of the analogy and the demonstrated value of public infrastructure provide significant insights and encouragement for modeling and measuring the value of information technology infrastructure.

IT INFRASTRUCTURE REVIEWED

IT infrastructure is the enabling base of shared IT capabilities, which provide the foundation for other business systems (McKay & Brockway, 1989). This capability includes both the internal technical (equipment, software, and cabling) and managerial expertise required to provide reliable services (McKay & Brockway, 1989; Weill, 1993). This complex set of technological and managerial resources is developed over time, and its precise description and value are difficult to define (Duncan, 1995).

IT infrastructure differs from applications in its purpose as a base for future applications rather than current business functionality and in the way in which it must cope with the uncertainty of future needs (Grossman & Packer, 1989). IT infrastructure is usually justified and financed differently from applications, its benefits are often difficult to quantify (Parker & Benson, 1988; CSC Index, 1993) and such investments often require board-level or executive management approval (Weill, 1993; P.E. International, 1995).

The technical components of IT infrastructure are hardware platforms, base software platforms, communications technology, client-server technology, and other software (or embedded) components that provide common services to a range of applications, common handling mechanisms for different data types, and methods, standards, and tools (Turnbull, 1991; Darnton & Giacoletto, 1992). IT infrastructure capability is often provided by the corporate information systems (IS) group (Weill & Broadbent, 1994) but often encompasses public or outsourced facilities used by the firm (P.E. International, 1995).

A purpose of building IT infrastructures is to support the commonality between different applications or uses (CSC Index, 1992) facilitating information sharing across the enterprise and cross-functional integration (Darnton & Giacoletto, 1992), and to obtain economies of scale. IT infrastructure flexibility refers to the degree to which its resources are shareable and reusable (Duncan, 1995). Building in flexibility adds cost and complexity but provides a business option that may be exercised in the future (Kambil, Henderson, & Mohsenzadeh, 1993), widening the variety of customer needs a firm can handle without increased costs (Weill, 1993). Firms take different approaches to IT infrastructure investments, depending on strategic objectives for costs savings through economies of scale, current strategy needs, or longer-term requirements for flexibility (Venkatraman, 1991; Weill, 1993).

IT infrastructure is a major business resource and a potential source for attaining sustainable competitive advantage (Keen, 1991; McKenney, 1995). Greater IT infrastructure capability is required when firms need to respond more rapidly to changes in the marketplace (Quinn, 1992) and when there is higher interdependence between business units. The increasing importance of relationship-based services and cross selling raises the stakes for information sharing across the business to capitalize on opportunities for cross selling and synergy. This business flexibility requires IT capability (Duncan, 1995) to share information across products, services, locations, companies, and countries, and thus a common IT infrastructure rather than separate IT platforms and services for separate business activities is required (Keen, 1991).

The mortar that binds all technical IT components into robust and functional services includes a specific body of knowledge, skill sets, and experience embodied in the human infrastructure (McKay & Brockway, 1989; Davenport & Linder, 1994). This human component provides the policies, architectures (Keen, 1995), planning, design, construction, and operations capability necessary for a viable IT infrastructure and usually resides in the corporate IS group.

IT INFRASTRUCTURE DEFINED

From a study of the literature and empirical data analysis, we propose the following definition (Weill & Broadbent, 1998):

> *IT Infrastructure is the base foundation of information technology capability, delivered as reliable services shared throughout the firm and coordinated centrally, usually by the information systems group.*

The various elements of information technology infrastructure are presented in Figure 17.1. At the base of this framework are the technology components such as computers, printers, database software packages, operating systems, and scanners. These devices are commodities readily available in the marketplace.

FIGURE 17.1   The Structure of Information Technology Infrastructure

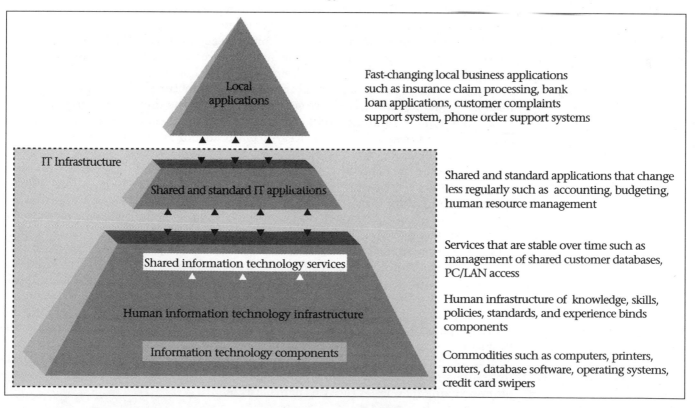

The second layer comprises a set of shared information technology services. The technology components are converted into useful shared services by a human information technology infrastructure composed of knowledge, skills, standards, and experience. This human infrastructure binds the technology components into reliable services that form the firm's information technology infrastructure.

The infrastructure services in a firm often include telecommunications network services, management, and provision of large-scale computing (such as mainframes); the management of shared customer databases; and research and development expertise aimed at identifying the usefulness of emerging technologies to the business. An increasing number of firms have an additional layer of shared and standard infrastructure applications used by all business units. These often include firmwide applications that support shared services in functional and support areas such as accounting, human resources management, and budgeting.

The infrastructure set of services required by a firm has usually been relatively stable over time. Similar services are often required from year to year (e.g., PC/LAN service for desktops) with gradual improvements occurring over time to take advantage of new technologies and efficiencies. New services are required often as a result of significant changes in business need (e.g., electronic commerce, knowledge management) or a major enabling technology change (e.g., TCP/IP). Infrastructure services regularly have lives of three to five or even seven years. However, as uncertainty of business need increases, very short infrastructure services lives are more likely. For example, with the uncertainty surrounding electronic commerce and which business models will be viable, some firms are conducting strategic experiments often requiring new infrastructure services, which may quickly either disappear or grow exponentially.[2]

In contrast, the information technology required for business processes—applications—changes more frequently, often on an annual basis as business processes are altered to better suit customer needs or in response to competitor activity. The information technology for business processes utilizes the infrastructure services necessary for the particular application. For example, in building a new order-processing system, a particular process manufacturing firm will use the information technology infrastructure services of mainframe processing, customer databases, personal computers, and local area and national communications networks. Having those infrastructure services in place should reduce the time and cost to build the order-processing system.

Infrastructure capability is a firm resource (Barney, 1991) that is difficult to imitate because it is created through the fusion of technology and human assets. These types of capabilities have long lead times to emulate (i.e., five to seven years), which can provide a source of competitive advantage. Building an infrastructure tailored to a firm's strategic context takes considerable time and expertise. While the components are commodities, the management processes to implement the best mix of infrastructure capabilities to suit a specific firm are a much more scarce resource.

Shared infrastructure applications have traditionally accounted for a small proportion of a firm's IT portfolio but are rapidly increasing. Implementation of a particular shared infrastructure application requires agreement on and the standardization of that process across the firm. In recent years, shared infrastructure applications have become increasingly popular with the advent of enterprise resource planning (ERP) systems such as Baan, PeopleSoft, and SAP. Some of the difficulties firms experience in implementing ERPs stem from the challenges in standardizing business processes across firms.

The nature of infrastructure capability can be described from a business perspective combining two useful concepts: information technology infrastructure services and the infrastructure reach and range. *Services* describes the business functionality provided by the infrastructure, and *reach and range* describes its business dimensions.

BUSINESS FUNCTIONALITY OF THE INFRASTRUCTURE: SERVICES

Based on empirical work in 54 businesses, 25 infrastructure services were identified that were typically provided on a firmwide basis. The services are presented in Table 17.1[3] (Weill & Broadbent, 1998). All of the firms studied that had any

TABLE 17.1   Firmwide Information Technology Infrastructure Services

Five Core IT Infrastructure Services in Firms	Percentage of Firms Offering Services
1. Manage firmwide communication network services	100
2. Manage groupwide or firmwide messaging services	100
3. Recommend standards for at least one component of IT architecture (e.g., hardware, operating systems, data communications)	100
4. Provide security, disaster planning, and business recovery services for firmwide installations and applications	100
5. Provide technology advice and support services	100
Twenty Additional IT Infrastructure Services	
6. Manage, maintain, support large-scale data processing facilities (e.g., mainframe operations)	96
7. Manage firmwide or business unit applications and databases	96
8. Perform IS project management	88
9. Provide data management advice and consultancy services	84
10. Perform IS planning for business units	80
11. Enforce IT architecture and standards	76
12. Manage firmwide or business-unit workstation networks (e.g., LANS, POS)	76
13. Manage and negotiate with suppliers and outsourcers	76
14. Identify and test new technologies for business purposes	72
15. Develop business-unit–specific applications (usually on a chargeback or contractual basis)	68
16. Implement security, disaster planning, and recovery for business units	60
17. Provide electronic management information (e.g., EIS)	56
18. Manage business-unit–specific applications	56
19. Provide firmwide or business-unit data management, including standards	52
20. Develop and manage electronic linkages to suppliers or customers	52
21. Develop a common systems development environment	52
22. Provide technology education services (e.g., training)	36
23. Provide multimedia operations and development (e.g., video-conferencing)	16
24. Provide firmwide intranet capability (e.g., information access, multiple system access)	↑
25. Provide firmwide electronic support for groups (e.g., Lotus Notes)	↑

TABLE 17.2   Examples of Selective and Extensive Services

Service 1: Manage Firmwide Communication Network Services	Service 3: Recommend Standards for at Least One Component of IT Architecture	Service 23: Multimedia Operations and Development
Selective:	**Selective:**	**Selective:**
A Wide Area Network (WAN) links most of Southcorp's domestic and international operations, with day-to-day management of the WAN undertaken by the Wines Business Group for which it receives a management fee	Selected IT standards to support the implementation of enterprisewide information architectures that include data and voice telecommunications, electronic mail, document interchange format, and video conferencing	Provision of video-conferencing facilities
Extensive:	**Extensive:**	**Extensive:**
The management of all communication networks within the firm, including headquarters and the 226 branches throughout Malaysia	The development of an integrated set of information, applications, and technology architectures to ensure timely and usable business data, protect IT investments, minimize costs, and deliver solutions more quickly	The development and management of multimedia applications to support high-bandwidth technical information and human communication across countries
Development and management of the corporate communication network for all Australian, New Zealand, and international operations		

firmwide information technology infrastructure services had the first five of the core services. The remaining services were provided to varying levels, depending on the strategic context of each firm. For example, one of the banks provided the 5 core and 12 additional services, while a manufacturer provided the 5 core and 3 others centrally. The right-hand column in Table 17.1 indicates the percentage of firms that provided each of the services.

Each service can be offered at different levels from selective to extensive. A selective level of service implies selectivity in one of three ways:

1. Only a basic level of this service is provided in terms of functionality.
2. The service is not available across all international locations.
3. The service is not mandatory across the firm.

An extensive level of service indicates that this service has extensive functionality and is offered across all business units and/or that its use is mandatory. Table 17.2 presents examples of three of the services, indicating different depths of each.

The number of infrastructure services and their depth offered by a firm indicate different degrees of business functionality offered via the firm or business unit infrastructures. Together, the services and the reach and range describe an infrastructure's capability.

BUSINESS SCOPE OF THE INFRASTRUCTURE: REACH AND RANGE

The concept of reach and range, first proposed by Peter Keen (1991), describes the business scope of the firm's infrastructure: what types of messages can be sent and transactions processed among employees, suppliers, and customers (see Figure 17.2).

Reach refers to the locations and people the infrastructure is capable of connecting. Reach can extend from within a single business unit to the ultimate level of connecting to anyone, anywhere. *Range* refers to functionality in terms of the business activities that can be completed and shared automatically and seamlessly across each level of reach.

DESCRIBING REACH AND RANGE

A large reach and range means a firm is able to simultaneously perform transactions on multiple applications updating all databases across different business units, be they located in the home country, such as the United States, or in other countries (see Figure 17.2, Point A). In a Chicago-based firm with the A level of reach and range, a business unit located in Madrid could take an order; process it through inventory, production, scheduling, and eventually accounts receivable; and automatically update the centralized executive information system back in Chicago. A small reach and range, indicated by Point B in Figure 17.2, supports sending standard messages within a single business unit location.

The Internet has added another dimension to the reach and range of many firms by significantly increasing their reach, particularly for the first two levels of range. ERPs and browsers are significantly increasing the reach for the higher levels of range.

FIGURE 17.2   Infrastructure Reach and Range

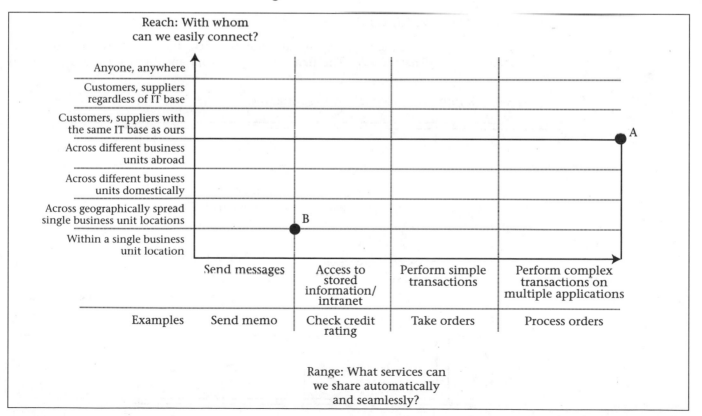

THE CAPABILITIES OF IT INFRASTRUCTURE

During our research, we conceptually posited and statistically confirmed[4] four approaches to information technology infrastructure investments.[5] We call these approaches to infrastructure investment *views* of information technology infrastructure. One of four views of information technology infrastructure predominated in each firm:

1. *None:* No firmwide information technology infrastructure in place.
2. *Utility:* Firmwide infrastructure employed to achieve clear cost savings.
3. *Dependent:* Infrastructure capability driven by a current business strategy such as "leading with customer care."
4. *Enabling:* Infrastructure a core competence and extensive capability provided to increase strategic options.

The four views involve different levels of up-front infrastructure investment, with different approaches to cost justification and different benefit profiles. Figure 17.3 describes the characteristics of the four views of infrastructure. The lower boxes identify the benefit expectations of each view.

In moving from none to utility to dependent to enabling, the extent and level of top management attention that need to be focused on information technology infrastructure increase, as do the investment and capability in the form of extent of infrastructure services provided and the reach and range.

Information technology infrastructure investments are large and often occur in bursts. Changing the firm's view of infrastructure is typically a deliberate process that takes time to implement.

NO INFRASTRUCTURE VIEW

A *none* view of infrastructure implies that the firm has no firmwide information technology infrastructure. The firm usually has independent business units with

FIGURE 17.3 Different Views of Information Technology Infrastructure

View	None	Utility	Dependent	Enabling
	• Independent business units • No synergies	• Often not a strategic resource • Utility service at lowest cost • Administrative expense	• Response to particular current strategy • Derived from business plans • Business expense	• Integrated with strategic process • Enables new strategies • Influenced by strategies • Business investment to achieve agility
Management objective	Independence forgoing any economies of scale	Cost savings via economies of scale	Life of strategy business benefits	Current and future flexibility

few synergies. This type of firm usually operates with a minimum of mandates from the headquarters or the corporate center. Each business unit is encouraged to invest independently in information technology as in other assets. In taking this view, the firm forgoes any potential economies of scale or business synergies from sharing information technology infrastructure.

UTILITY VIEW

A *utility* view of infrastructure implies that expenditure on IT infrastructure is primarily undertaken to achieve cost savings through economics of scale (Venkataraman, 1991). Infrastructure is not regarded as a strategic resource but as an IT utility of the business that incurs administrative expense while providing a necessary and unavoidable service (P.E. International, 1995). The aim of this view is to minimize the expense for a desired level of utility service. As a result, services may be fragmented and exhibit incompatibility.

The common drivers for utility IT infrastructure investment are as follows:

- The need to consolidate multiple sites—perhaps in different states or regions or from two firms that have merged.
- Decreases in the cost of technology that allow replacement and modernization of existing services at significant cost savings.

Utility view firms focus on achieving costs savings, such as through standardization of systems and consolidating data centers. Nolan Norton and Co. has studied the economics of data center consolidation and report an average per annum savings of 26 to 48% (McKay & Connolly, 1991), depending on the firm's cost base. The potential for this type of savings is likely to occur in large firms at regular intervals of five to seven years as mergers occur and technology prices drop. Capturing these potential savings requires senior management attention to focus the firm's information technology infrastructure investment on relentlessly pursuing cost savings.

DEPENDENT VIEW

A *dependent* view of infrastructure implies that investments are primarily intended and tailored toward a particular business strategy (e.g., leading with customer care). Dependent infrastructure investments are usually reactive and undertaken after current business strategies have been established. This strategy-driven investment approach relies heavily on the firm's ability to accurately determine its planned business applications and shared infrastructure requirements (P.E. International, 1995).

A dependent view of infrastructure implies that the infrastructure investments are primarily for and in response to articulated business strategies. Dependent infrastructure investments are derived from business plans that specify strategic objectives including strategic intent, current strategies, and business goals. These objectives lead to or imply information technology needs. Thus, planning for infrastructure is undertaken after current business strategies have been shaped and articulated (Venkataraman, 1991). For example, a bank might invest heavily by consolidating previously independent databases into an integrated customer relationship database. This infrastructure investment depends on a current strategy of differentiating customer service through relationship banking with top levels of customer care. Previously, the bank could not determine its full relationship with a customer because the different account information was spread over a series of data files that were developed at different times and linked to different account types.

ENABLING VIEW

An *enabling* view of infrastructure implies that infrastructure capability is a core competence strongly integrated with the strategic context. Enabling infrastructure provides extensive infrastructure capability, thus increasing strategic options and agility. Enabling infrastructures are often created by expanding the reach and/or range of dependent infrastructure and increasing services beyond the current requirements of the business. In this way, the infrastructure provides future options (Kambil, Henderson, & Mohsenzadeh, 1993) for implementing current strategies consistent with the strategic intent (Venkataraman, 1991). The flexibility of the infrastructure enables a number of as yet unspecified business strategies to be implemented more rapidly than firms with a dependent or utility view of infrastructure. To take an enabling view, senior managers must perceive a flexible infrastructure as an asset of the firm that provides a competitive advantage and thus overinvest in infrastructure based on current needs. This view also implies that the firm values this future flexibility during the project justification process.

INFRASTRUCTURE CAPABILITY: A STRATEGIC CHOICE

Infrastructure capability is a strategic choice, and no one view of infrastructure suits all firms. However, we posit that a particular view is best suited to a particular firm at any point in time. When greater flexibility and agility to utilize firmwide resources are part of the firm's strategic intent, an enabling rather than a utility view of the role of infrastructure provides a higher level of alignment between information technology and business strategy. When cost competition and cost savings dominate a firm's strategic intent, a utility view is usually appropriate. Thus, a strategic choice is required (Porter, 1996). Firms may focus on executing a single strategy, but they must also build and maintain a portfolio of strategic options for future investing in new capabilities (Williamson, 1999). Adopting Williamson's strategic options approach would lead firms to an enabling view of information technology infrastructure.

In any one firm over a period of several years, different projects that will cover the full range of views likely will be undertaken. For example, an enabling telecommunications network may be installed and then a utility approach to data center location may occur in the same firm. However, as we observed, one view tends to underpin the firm's approach to IT infrastructure.

MEASURING AND BENCHMARKING IT INFRASTRUCTURE CAPABILITY

To provide a basis for comparison, we present a series of benchmarks of information technology investment and infrastructure capability by industry (Table 17.3). The first two lines of the table indicate how extensively the firms invest in information

TABLE 17.3   Benchmarks of Information Technology Investments

	Number of Firms				
	Finance 12	Manuf. 10	Retail 5	All 27	All 27
	5-Yr. Av.	5-Yr. Av.	5-Yr. Av.	5-Yr. Av.	Av. Percent Change per Year
1. IT as percentage of revenues	7.0	1.7	1.0	4.1	2.6
2. IT as percentage of expenses	14.2	2.0	1.1	7.7	3.0
3. Centrally coordinated IT as a percentage of total IT	73.0	52.0	66.0	64.0	4.4
4. Percentage of infrastructure of centrally coordinated IT	69.0	64.0	82.0	70.0	8.0
5. Percentage of centrally coordinated infrastructure of total IT	49.0	34.0	52.0	45.0	11.0
6. Number of services (0–23)	17.0	14.0	18.0	16	
7. Reach and range (0–100)	38.0	32.0	32.0	35	

technology. The third line describes the level of information technology resources coordinated at the corporate level. Line 4 is the percentage of the centrally coordinated information technology investment that is infrastructure. Line 5 describes the percentage of the firm's total information technology investment in firmwide shared infrastructure. Line 6 identifies, on average, how many of the 23 services were coordinated and provided centrally. Line 7 presents the scope of the typical infrastructure, on a scale from 0 to 100, using the reach and range framework in the appendix to this chapter. The far right-hand column is the average percentage change in the figure per year over five years.

Lines 4 and 5 indicate how much of the firm's information technology resources are used to provide the infrastructure; lines 6 and 7 indicate the capability of the infrastructure the firm has achieved for its investment.

We combined five items to create a measure of view for information technology infrastructure. (The Appendix provides details of the measures.)

1. Firmwide information technology infrastructure investment as a proportion of the firm's total information technology investment (measured as a percentage averaged over five years).
2. Firmwide information technology infrastructure investment as a proportion of revenue (average over five years).
3. Approach to the justification (average of seven items) for firmwide information technology infrastructure investment ranging from a focus only on cost savings (score of 1) to only providing flexibility (score of 5).
4. The reach and range of the firmwide information technology infrastructure (from a minimum of 0 to a maximum of 100).
5. The number of firmwide infrastructure services (from 0–23).

Table 17.4 presents the views and their information technology benchmarks.[6] In moving from a none to an enabling view, the relative level of infrastructure

TABLE 17.4 View and Information Technology Benchmarks

	Number of Firms				
	None **1**	**Utility** **8**	**Dependent** **10**	**Enabling** **8**	**All** **27**
Percentage of centrally coordinated infrastructure of total IT	0.0	29.0	50.0	59.0	45.0
Percentage of centrally coordinated infrastructure of revenue	0.0	0.4	1.9	3.1	1.8
Justification; 1 = cost, 5 = flexibility	n/a	3.2	3.5	3.6	3.4
Reach and range (0–100)	9.0	27.0	33.0	48.0	35.0
Number of services (0–23)	0.0	14.0	16.0	20.0	16.0
View of Infrastructure*	**16.7**	**43.0**	**51.0**	**59.0**	**50.0**

*None = 0 – <25   Utility = 25 – <45   Dependent = 45 – <55   Enabling = 55+

investment increases as a percentage of the entire IT portfolio, as does the percentage of resources dedicated to infrastructure (i.e., as a percentage of revenues). As investment increases, so does infrastructure capability in the form of reach and range and the number of services. Firms that take a none view of infrastructure have no firmwide investment or justification and, thus, provide no services. Firms taking a none view typically have a small reach and range that supports doing business electronically only within a business unit.

The first three measures identify what funds are invested and how they are invested, and the last two measures identify the capability achieved. For the majority of firms studied, the characteristics of investment and capability lined up consistently to one view. However, the quality of management can have an impact on value for money in infrastructure investment, that is, in the level of capability for a given level of investment. One very well managed firm achieved the level of capability of an enabling infrastructure with 21 services and a reach and range of 78 but spent the amount typical of a dependent firm. The characteristics of each view are summarized in Table 17.5.

In our research, senior corporate executives (e.g., CEO, COO) provided input on the strategic objectives of the firm. This was correlated with the measure of view and resulted in the findings about each view listed here. Data for the components of view were collected independently from the CIO and the IT managers in business units.

Firms are more likely to take a utility[7] view if they

1. Operate in less information-intense industries such as manufacturing.
2. Focus on the cost savings that shared infrastructure can provide.
3. Do not require or seek an electronic platform to enable cross selling or synergies between business units.
4. Are larger firms with more business units.

Firms are more likely to take an enabling view if they

1. Operate in a more information-intense industry such as finance or retailing.
2. Desire the firmwide strategic flexibility and agility that an extensive infrastructure can provide.

TABLE 17.5   Characteristics of the Four Views of Infrastructure

	View of Infrastructure			
	None	**Utility**	**Dependent**	**Enabling**
Investment in IT relative to competitors	Lowest	Low	Average	Highest
Investment in firmwide infrastructure	None	Lower than average (37% of total IT)	Just above average (45% of total IT)	Well above average (50% of total IT)
Approach to justification	No attempt	Cost focus	Balance cost and flexibility	Flexibility focus
Reach and range	Within business units	Within and between business units for data and simple transactions	Within and between business units; some complex transactions; some customers	Within and between business units; complex transactions; any customer
Extent of infrastructure services	None	Basic (13 of the 23 services in Table 17.1)	Basic plus a few strategic services (16)	Extensive (20)

3. Wish to exploit increased synergies and cross selling between business units.
4. Are smaller firms with fewer business units. It is organizationally and politically easier to integrate electronically via a firmwide infrastructure in smaller firms.
5. Have integrated the process for determining the information and information technology needs more fully into business planning processes.

EVIDENCE FOR PAYOFF FROM IT INFRASTRUCTURE

By their very nature, information technology infrastructure investments are large and long term and have no real value on their own. Infrastructure's value is in the ability to quickly and economically enable the implementation of new applications, often across business units or the firm, which in turn generate business value.

We developed and applied a four-level hierarchy of business value measures to help track the relationships between information technology infrastructure investments and different types of business value.[8] This hierarchy of business value measures is depicted in Figure 17.4. At the top level are the financial outcomes the firm desires. Second are business operational measures, such as time to market and low-cost provider. These vary greatly across firms and often between business units in one firm.

The third and fourth levels are values that relate to IT investments, for example, value delivered by implementing applications on time and on budget and the value of very high availability of infrastructure. We posit an increasing dilution of impact of IT infrastructure capability as measures of performance are assessed moving up the hierarchy of business value. Measures of business value at the top of the hierarchy are influenced by many other factors (e.g., pricing decisions, competitor strategies) apart

FIGURE 17.4   Hierarchy of Impact of Information Technology Investments

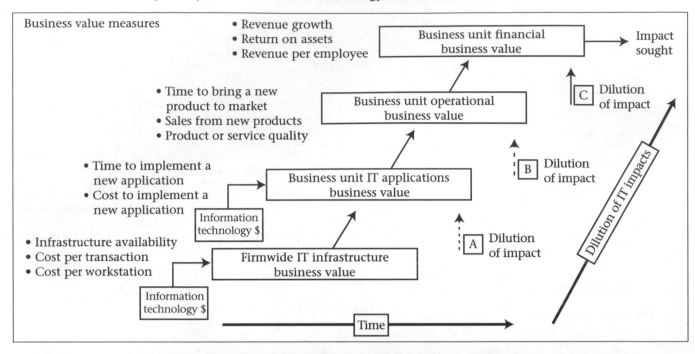

from infrastructure capability. The objective is to identify a pattern of value creation associated with infrastructure capability moving up the hierarchy of performance.

We statistically compared five measures of business value at each of the four levels in Figure 17.4 with IT infrastructure investment.

An intricate set of relationships unfolds, revealing a delicate balance between the costs and benefits of extensive infrastructure capability. The relationships to the hierarchy of performance measures for having more or increasing infrastructure are summarized in Table 17.6. These statistically significant relationships were identified using hierarchical regression controlling for previous performance (using five years of data) and correlational analysis.

Firms with increasing infrastructure had a faster growth in revenue per employee while firms with more infrastructure had higher revenues per employee. Firms with increasing infrastructure also had stronger overall revenue growths. The effect on overall revenue growths was found in industries with a strong reliance on information flows, such as banking and insurance. Firms with more infrastructure also had significantly more sales from new products and a faster time to market for new products. Firms with more infrastructure had more integrated firmwide infrastructures, allowing easier cross selling of products between business units and faster introduction of new products. The faster delivery of new products appears to increase sales from new products, which increases revenue growth.

The time to market was particularly sensitive to the extent of infrastructure. Firms with more extensive infrastructures linked business units and integrated different business processes as well as reached beyond the firm electronically to customers and suppliers. These firms had faster times to market. Firms with extensive, tailored business unit infrastructure were also more agile in bringing new products to market faster. A more extensive infrastructure enabled business integration and

TABLE 17.6   Evidence for Business Value of Information Technology Infrastructure

	Less or Decreasing Infrastructure	More or Increasing Infrastructure
Business unit (BU) financial performance	• Lower growth in revenue per employee • Higher return on assets (ROA) • Lower revenue growth* • Lower revenue per employee	• Higher growth in revenue per employee • Lower ROA • Higher revenue growth* • Lower revenue per employee
BU operational performance	• Less sales from new products • Slower time to market	• More sales from new products • Faster time to market
BU IT performance	• Shorter time to build new applications • No difference in cost to build new applications	• Longer time to build new applications • No difference in cost to build new applications
Firmwide infrastructure performance	• Less processing power per $ • No difference in $ per workstation • Less system availability	• More processing power per $ • No difference in $ per workstation • More system availability

Note: These relationships are statistically significant after controlling for industry differences.

* In the finance sector.

communications across business units for products and processes with a firmwide focus, such as cross selling.

Contrary to our expectation, firms with more extensive infrastructures require a significantly longer time to build new applications. These firmwide infrastructures are complex, and any new application must interface with existing infrastructure services and applications. This level of integration and testing takes longer to build than new applications on stand-alone infrastructures not requiring such extensive integration. In addition, extensive infrastructures inevitably contain a combination of technologies from different eras of computing and different architectures. These differences combine to contribute to the longer time to integrate. Costs to build new applications were also higher when more infrastructure was at the business level rather than firmwide.

The positive impacts on business value of more infrastructure also appear to come at a cost in financial terms. Although firms with less infrastructure have lower revenue per employee or revenue growths, they also have significantly higher profitabilities (as measured by return on assets), particularly in the short term. The firms with less infrastructure also have lower sales from new products and take longer to bring new products to market.

Empirically, firms with less integrated infrastructures can build new applications more quickly and at lower cost because less effort is required for integration. It is interesting that, although the applications are built faster and for less money, they appear to generate less sales from new products. Therefore, these new applications are unlikely to be strategic applications or those associated with new products.

In terms of firmwide information technology costs and performance, there was no difference in response times to screen commands and recovery times from failures for firms with more or less firmwide infrastructure. However, firms with increasing firmwide infrastructure have significant economies of scale in terms of the ability to provide more processing power (i.e., MIPS) at a significantly cheaper cost. It is interesting that these economies do not extend to the cost per workstation. There was no significant difference in cost per workstation between firms with less or more firmwide information technology infrastructure.

In summary, firms with less extensive infrastructures have fewer resources tied up in infrastructure and are more profitable. However, these firms have lower sales from new products and take more time to reach the market with those new products. This means that although firms with less infrastructure may be currently performing profitably, they are not as well positioned to react to shifts in market needs effecting the whole firm as firms with a more extensive firmwide infrastructure capability. Firms with less infrastructure have lower revenues per employee, with a lower rate of increase as well as lower revenue growths. This less extensive approach to infrastructure is well suited to firms that compete predominantly on cost.

Firms with more extensive infrastructures have more resources tied up in infrastructure but have more sales from new products with a faster time to market. These firms also have faster increasing revenues per employee and stronger revenue growths but lower profits.

Thus, a delicate balance exists between short-term profitability and revenue growth. Less extensive infrastructures require less investment, but these firms are slower to produce new products, and they get less sales from them. These firms also increase revenue per employee at a slower rate and have lower overall revenue growth. This delicate balance reinforces the need to make strategic choices.

IDENTIFYING IT INFRASTRUCTURE CAPABILITIES: A STRATEGIC CHOICE

Although there is no single universally accepted definition of business strategy (Mintzberg & Quinn, 1991), a number of scholars emphasize the importance of choice. Porter (1996) argues that competitive strategy is the creation of a unique and valuable position that requires the choice of a different set of activities and capabilities from competitors to deliver a unique mix of value. Markides (1999) identifies three dimensions in which firms must make tough choices: whom to target as customers, what products to offer, and how to undertake the related activities efficiently. Core competencies are at the center of strategic choice (Kay, 1993; Hamel & Prahalad, 1989) to create and sustain advantage and implement effectively. Infrastructure capability is a firm resource (Barney, 1991) and a potential core competence that is difficult to imitate, requiring a fusion of human and technical assets.

Information technology (IT) infrastructure is increasingly seen as a fundamental differentiator in the competitive performance of firms (McKenney, 1995). New competitive strategies (Boynton, Victor, & Pine, 1993) and progression through higher levels of organizational transformation (Davidson & Movizzo, 1996) require major IT infrastructure investments. IT infrastructure capabilities underpin the emergence of new organisational forms (Davidow & Malone, 1992), such as global virtual corporations (Miller, Clemons, & Row, 1993), and facilitate the development of virtual value chains (Rayport & Sviokla, 1995). IT infrastructure capability is critical to globally competing firms (IS Analyzer, 1991; Clemons, Row & Venkateswaran, 1989; Neo, 1991) to provide connectivity and integration.

IT infrastructure can be a significant barrier or enabler in the practical options available to planning and changing business processes (Keen, 1991; Grover, Teng, & Fiedler, 1993; Wastell, White, & Kawalek, 1994). The support of enabling technologies and platforms is an important contributor to successful business process change (Furey & Diorio, 1994; Ramcharamdas, 1994; Caron, Jarvenpaa, & Stoddard, 1994). Cross-functional process changes require a shift in the role of the IT function from being guardians of information systems to providing infrastructure support, particularly in the form of data management expertise (Dixon et al., 1994; Earl & Kuan, 1994) and connectivity across areas and computer platforms.

The decision of how much infrastructure capability to put in place depends heavily on the strategic choices of the firm and the measures of performance that are the highest priority. Firms with goals including revenue growth and fast response to market shifts are better served by more infrastructure, particularly firmwide infrastructure if cross selling is desired. Firms with a focus on shorter-term profitability are better served with less infrastructure both in terms of investment dollars and as a proportion of the information technology portfolio. A prudent strategy to maximize short-term profit is to minimize infrastructure investments and focus on transactional uses of information technology.

WHAT WE DON'T KNOW: FUTURE RESEARCH ON IT INFRASTRUCTURE

Research on information technology infrastructure is in its infancy. Knowledge of the value of IT infrastructure remains largely "in the realms of conjecture and anecdote" (Duncan, 1995). Many intriguing issues need to be investigated both conceptually and empirically; they provide a rich source of research questions for future work. We have compiled a series of research questions that we believe are sources of significant potential insights as well as practical value for firms struggling to make the strategic choices around IT infrastructure investments and capability.

- Will the definition of infrastructure used in this chapter remain viable given the fast-changing technology componentry? For example, will the capability and definition of the infrastructure change with the ability to deliver IT application functionality (e.g., SAP modules, spreadsheets, electronic commerce agents) via the Internet on a demand basis, perhaps via Java code?
- What are the new infrastructure services required by emergent strategic initiatives in firms? For example, what will be the infrastructure services needed for a major knowledge management initiative or a push to globalization? Establishing information technology infrastructures in developing markets, such as Vietnam or Bangladesh, for firms with strong infrastructures in their domestic markets has proved to be a significant challenge.
- How will new technologies influence the costs and ability to increase reach and range? The Internet and the TCP/IP standard have significantly increased a firm's reach, particularly for the first two levels of range. Will browsers (or some other technology) significantly reduce the cost for firms to integrate multiple-legacy applications across different computing platforms, thus increasing reach for the higher levels of range?
- Do start-up firms have a significant cost and agility advantage over existing firms in being able to invest in new IT infrastructures rather than migrate from existing infrastructures? For example, does this explain why some banks (e.g., Bank of Montreal) have chosen to create separate Internet banks?

- As ERPs become more standard in a particular industry, how do firms create a competitive advantage enabled by IT? Will firms build or acquire add-on applications to achieve this advantage? How will the IT infrastructures evolve to support these developments?
- Many of the concepts and empirical results described in this chapter stimulate the need for detailed case-based research to understand how and why they occur. For example, what are the detailed differences in the approach to managing and investing in infrastructure in firms that take radically different views? Firms that take an enabling view of infrastructure must find ways to value the flexibility they seek in the investment justification process. By contrast, firms with a utility view of infrastructure will probably use more traditional cost savings approaches to justification. Understanding the process these firms followed would add significantly to our understanding of the role, value, and management of IT infrastructure.
- Will the emerging IT trends (e.g., open systems, outsourcing, client server, network computing, reducing costs of processing, Internet) so change the underlying economics that the distinction between the views of infrastructure will disappear because it will be no more costly to take one view or the other? To date, firms generally have had to trade off cost savings with flexibility, and an enabling view was far more costly up front than a utility view. Will the emerging trends allow the simultaneous achievement of cost savings and flexibility?

CONCLUSION

As firms face the new reality of competition that is faster, more global, and increasingly electronic and volatile, simultaneously requiring a relentless reduction of costs as well as agility, information technology infrastructure capability will become even more important. The decision of how much and what type of IT infrastructure capability a firm needs is a critical strategic choice.

The key learning from this chapter is that a careful strategic choice about infrastructure capability is necessary for several reasons:

- Different infrastructure capabilities are observed in firms requiring significantly different levels of investment, expertise, and integration.
- Higher levels of infrastructure capability are associated with stronger firm performance on some metrics while less infrastructure capability is associated with stronger performance on different metrics.
- Information technology infrastructure capabilities are difficult to emulate and take many years to achieve.
- The increase in use of ERPs, the Internet technologies (e.g., browsers and TCP/IP), and electronic commerce raises the stakes for strategic choice of infrastructure capability.

Senior management responsibility is integral in making this strategic choice and achieving business value from the IT infrastructure. Decision making on infrastructure capability should be the joint responsibility of executive and information technology management. An organizational process that engages both business and information technology management in a focused and sustained dialogue to determine and deliver the needed infrastructure capabilities is necessary. The quality of executive leadership for IT infrastructure rather than the technology is the likely source of any competitive differentiation.

APPENDIX: CALCULATING THE COMPONENTS OF INFRASTRUCTURE VIEW

Firms can calculate the components of their infrastructure view using the five items listed in this chapter. Three of the items are self-explanatory, but items 3 and 4 require further explanation. This appendix contains details of (1) how to calculate motivation for information technology infrastructure (item 3) and (2) how to calculate reach and range (item 4).

CALCULATING MOTIVATION FOR INFORMATION TECHNOLOGY INFRASTRUCTURE

A series of questions in Figure 17.5 identifies the view of infrastructure adopted by the board and investments committees. In your answers, consider the two years of information technology infrastructure investment cases put to senior management and discussions between business and information technology managers.

We have found that the answers to these questions are good indicators of the approach to information technology justification by firms taking different views. Ask as many business and information technology managers as you can to complete the questions. Then calculate the average scores for the odd and even question numbers. High scores on the odd-numbered questions indicate a utility view; high scores on the even-numbered questions indicate an enabling view.

The justification benchmark = $\dfrac{(Q2 + Q4 + Q6)}{3} + \left(6 - \dfrac{(Q1 + Q3 + Q5 + Q7)}{4}\right)$

where $Q1$, $Q2$, and so on are the answers to the questions 1, 2, and so on on a scale from 1 to 5. It is often instructive to compare the answers from the information technology professionals in the firm to those of the business managers. Significant differences are a strong indicator of a poor partnership between the two groups, which often leads to poor alignment of strategy and the information technology portfolio.

CALCULATING REACH AND RANGE

In the following example, the reach and range score is calculated for Company X. Figure 17.6 shows a plot of Company X's reach and range.

When calculating the reach and range score, each level of range (i.e., each column) should be considered in isolation. For a given range, there are seven levels of reach (i.e., seven groups to which the company can extend that range capability). The first four levels of reach are groups *internal* to the company. The final three levels of reach are groups *external* to the company.

FIGURE 17.5   Information Technology Infrastructure Motivation

1. IT infrastructure is primarily viewed as a utility providing the base IT services at minimum cost.

1	2	3	4	5
Strongly Disagree	Disagree	Neutral	Agree	Strongly

2. In forming business strategies, the BUSINESS UNITS (BU) consider the capabilities of the IT infrastructure.

1	2	3	4	5
Strongly Disagree	Disagree	Neutral	Agree	Strongly

3. The main reason for investing in IT infrastructure is to reduce the total IT costs of the FIRM.

1	2	3	4	5
Strongly Disagree	Disagree	Neutral	Agree	Strongly

4. Senior managers of the FIRM perceive a flexible IT infrastructure as providing a competitive advantage.

1	2	3	4	5
Strongly Disagree	Disagree	Neutral	Agree	Strongly

5. In justifying IT infrastructure investment, each project must show clear cost savings.

1	2	3	4	5
Strongly Disagree	Disagree	Neutral	Agree	Strongly

6. Meetings between senior IT managers and senior BUSINESS UNIT managers, the most important topic is the capabilities of IT to enable new business strategies.

1	2	3	4	5
Never	Rarely	Sometimes	Usually	Always

7. Meetings between senior IT managers and senior BUSINESS UNIT managers, the most important topic is the cost and quality of IT services.

1	2	3	4	5
Never	Rarely	Sometimes	Usually	Always

FIGURE 17.6   Company X's Reach and Range

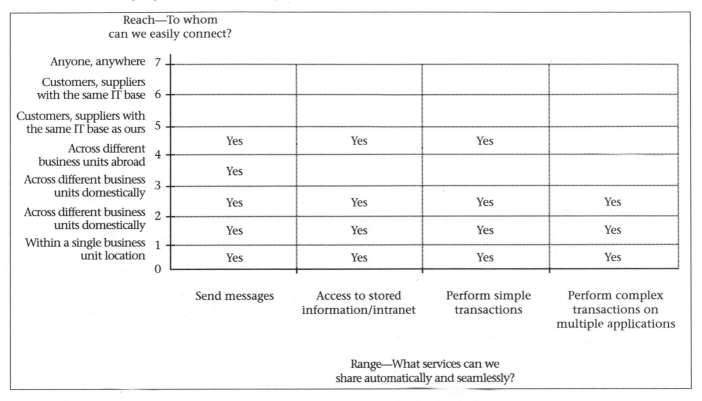

To facilitate comparison, a formula was developed to convert the plot into a score ranging from 0 to 100 using the grid in Figure 17.6 and a simple point-counting procedure. As a company extends its reach for a particular range capability, it accumulates "points." In providing the most basic range capability, "Send Messages," a company accumulates 1 point for each of the internal groups to which it can send messages and 2 points for each of the external groups to which it can send messages (see Figure 17.7).

Hence, each cell in the reach and range grid represents a value that may contribute to the reach and range score. The cell values are shown in Figure 17.6. Simply add the points for each level of reach and range provided. If a company were able to provide complete reach and range, it would score the *maximum 100 points*. Calculation of Company X's points (43) is shown in Figure 17.7.

Because it is more difficult to extend a service to external groups than to internal groups as a result issues such as security, standardization, and connectivity, an external connection is weighted twice an internal connection.

Because it is more difficult to extend reach as the range capability moves from left to right in Figure 17.6 as a result issues such as incompatible systems, politics, security, and data incompatibilities, the four levels of range are weighted 1, 2, 3, and 4, respectively.

To calculate a firm's reach and range, first circle the cells in Figure 17.6 that represent the current reach and range. Then count the points for each cell to obtain a score between 0 to 100. To put a score in context, compare the mean reach and range scores for firms in Tables 17.3 and 17.4. Of the firms covered by the study, the highest reach and range score was 80, and the lowest was 9.

FIGURE 17.7 Calculating Reach and Range

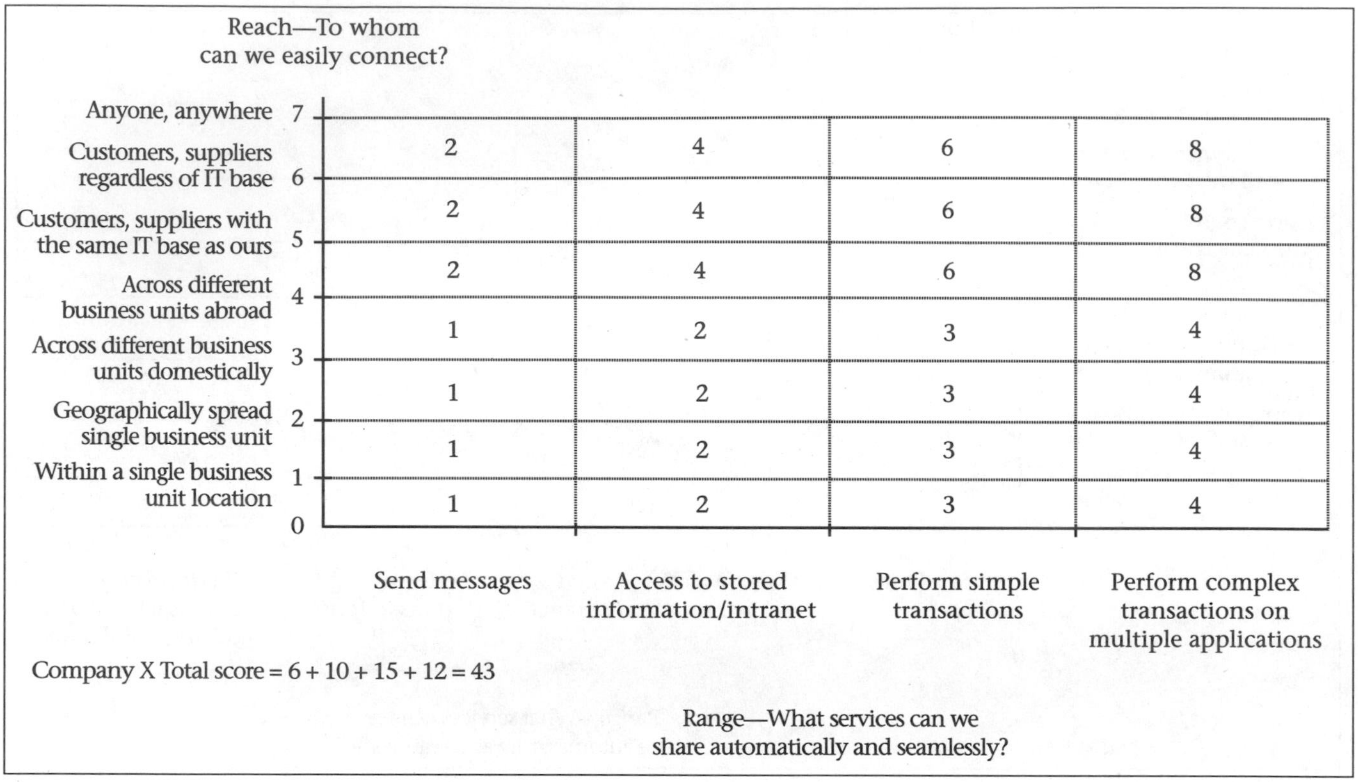

Reach—To whom can we easily connect?	Send messages	Access to stored information/intranet	Perform simple transactions	Perform complex transactions on multiple applications
Anyone, anywhere — 7				
Customers, suppliers regardless of IT base — 6	2	4	6	8
Customers, suppliers with the same IT base as ours — 5	2	4	6	8
Across different business units abroad — 4	2	4	6	8
Across different business units domestically — 3	1	2	3	4
Geographically spread single business unit — 2	1	2	3	4
Within a single business unit location — 1	1	2	3	4
0	1	2	3	4

Company X Total score = 6 + 10 + 15 + 12 = 43

Range—What services can we share automatically and seamlessly?

ENDNOTES

1. Carey Butler and Tim O'Brien, Melbourne Business School, University of Melbourne; John Henderson and Christine Lentz, Boston University; Jim Short and Jeff Sampler, London Business School; Bob Tricker, John Whitman, and Ali Farhoomand, Hong Kong University; Peter Keen, International Centre for Information Technology; Jack Rockart, Jeanne Ross, and Judith Quillard, Massachusetts Institute of Technology; Boon Siong Neo and Christina Soh, Nanyang Technological University, Singapore.
2. For an in-depth discussion of the impact of the Internet and electronic commerce on strategic context, see the chapter by Sampler.
3. Services 24 and 25 emerged as important during the process of the study, and very few firms had these services in place. Both services are being implemented in many firms today. To facilitate comparison, we have used the number 23 rather than 25, dropping the last two.
4. The process of statistical confirmation involved collecting data from 27 firms on their information technology infrastructure investments and capabilities across five different dimensions. The firms were categorized into the four views and then were tested to see whether the seven dimensions all increased when comparing none to utility to dependent to enabling views. The dimensions all increase together, verifying that the four types of view were internally consistent.

5. For a detailed description of how the views were identified during the research process see the following articles listed in chronological order to show the development process: Weill (1993, pp. 547–572); Weill and Broadbent (1994, pp. 35–39), and Weill, Broadbent, and St.Clair (1996, pp. 361–384).

6. The measures for each of these items are converted statistically into a score from 0 to 100 with an average of 50. As different units of measure were involved, each component was converted into a set of standard (or z) scores. With the exception of component 3 (firmwide IT infrastructure investment as a proportion of revenue), the set of z scores was based on the entire sample of firms in the study. To remove the industry effects for component 3, the z scores were calculated using only the firms within industry groupings. To generate a score out of 100 to represent the view, the set of z scores for each component was converted linearly to a set of numbers between 0 and 100 with a mean of 50 and a standard deviation of 50/3. The view of IT infrastructure was calculated as the mean of five components and had a mean of approximately 50. To fit the measure of view into our theoretical classification, ranges were arbitrarily defined with the objective of having a similar number of firms classified as both utility and enabling, and the majority classified as dependent. See also note 1 and the acknowledgment on page 329.

7. These relationships were demonstrated statistically using hierarchical regression controlling for previous performance and correlational analysis. For more details, see Weill et al. (1995) and Weill, Broadbent, and Butler (1996).

8. For a detailed discussion on the challenges of measuring the business value of IT, see the chapter in this book by Barua and Mukhopadhyay.

Chapter 18

Relationships in IT Outsourcing: A Stakeholder Perspective

Mary C. Lacity and Leslie P. Willcocks

Since 1990, global IT outsourcing revenues have increased from $US 9 billion to a projected $US 121 billion by year 2001. The underlying compound annual growth rate has been 15–20% in the period 1992–1998, with the leading markets in the United States and United Kingdom. Other countries are also showing market increases. The Australian market, for example, is estimated to grow 24% annually from $AUS 2.2 billion in 1998 to $AUS 3.87 billion in 2002. A recent conference with Japanese CIOs also indicates that Japan is interested in IT outsourcing as a turnaround practice in response to the Asian monetary crisis (Lacity & Willcocks, 2000). Clearly, IT outsourcing has outlived the five-year period typical of a management fad.

IT outsourcing success rates have improved as the practice has matured. We studied 61 sourcing decisions and found that deals signed before 1989 had success rates of only 40%. Deals signed between 1989 and 1991 had success rates of 85%, and those signed after 1991 had success rates of 90% (Lacity & Willcocks, 1998.) Thus, a significant amount of organizational learning has occurred, and proven practices of success have emerged, including selective outsourcing (rather than total outsourcing), extensive evaluation of multiple suppliers against in-house bids, short-term contracts of less than four years in duration, and detailed contracts. But despite the healthy report card of IT outsourcing as indicated by the continued growth in demand and increasing success rates, a central issue still plagues this practice. How should customer–supplier relationships be managed? Are customers and suppliers strategic partners? Are they merely agents in a transactional exchange? In other words, to what degrees, and in what contexts, can customers and suppliers be allies or adversaries?

Customer–supplier relationships in the context of IT outsourcing are a challenge globally. The largest IT outsourcing customers have even formed a user's group, called the International Information Technology Users Group (IITUG; see the Web site at http://www.iitug.org), whose central purpose is to develop value-added aspects to their relationships with major suppliers such as EDS, IBM, and CSC. A survey of 162 smaller IT outsourcing customers in the United States, United Kingdom, and Scandinavia surfaced other customer–supplier relationship challenges (Lacity, Willcocks, & Feeny, 1999):

- 43% of respondents indicate that the supplier does not properly staff the contract.
- 41% of respondents indicate serious or difficult problems attributable to service-level definitions.
- 38% of respondents indicate severe/difficult problems with services beyond the contract.

We note that these problems exist, even though the majority of respondents followed "best" practices. Most pursue selective outsourcing, 79% use multiple rather than single suppliers, 89% have service-level agreements, and the average contract was only 3.8 years in duration. Overall, the customers gave suppliers a good performance rating of 6.22 on a 10-point Likert scale (with 0 indicating poor performance and 10 indicating excellent performance). Thus, although the survey indicates a generally successful report card, significant customer/supplier management issues still exist.

To improve customer–supplier relationships, we must first understand the underlying nature of the relationship. We have just completed the analysis of in-depth case studies of 116 sourcing decisions in 75 organizations in the United States, United Kingdom, Australia, and Europe (Lacity & Willcocks, 2000). We conducted 271 in-depth interviews during the past eight years with senior executives, CIOs, suppliers, IT staff, IT users, and IT outsourcing consultants. We found that the customer–supplier dichotomy fails to appreciate the complexity of all stakeholder relationships involved in IT outsourcing. Thus "customers" include senior business managers who pay for IT, senior IT managers who manage IT, IT staff who deliver IT, and, finally, the users who actually receive the service. "Suppliers" include senior management who negotiate deals, account managers responsible for earning a profit on the deal, and supplier IT staff charged with delivery. If IT unions, external consultants, lawyers, subcontractors, or multisourcing are involved, additional sets of stakeholders are added to the party. By attending to these multiple stakeholders, we have a better understanding of the complex relationships among stakeholders and operate from a more informed base for improving these relationships.

This chapter summarizes previous research on IT outsourcing, pointing out, as do Kern and Willcocks (2000), a surprising shortage of specific research on the relationship dimension despite widespread recognition of its importance. It then presents an overall framework for understanding relationships among stakeholders before, during, and after IT outsourcing contracts are signed. The primary contribution of the chapter is an IT outsourcing relationship framework, derived from research, that focuses on three key elements: (1) relationship stakeholders, (2) relationship types, and (3) six relationship phases and their related activities. We found that IT outsourcing stakeholders behave antagonistically, cooperatively, and collaboratively, depending on the alignment of goals for the issue at hand. Relationships turn out to be dynamic, and organizations that face up to the complex realities of shared, complementary, and conflicting goals are much more likely to develop productive outsourcing arrangements over time. Thus, our research indicates that the "allies or adversaries" question has to be reframed and that relationships are dependent on the particular task facing the stakeholders involved and the particular phase reached in the outsourcing arrangement.

THE RESEARCH LITERATURE ON IT OUTSOURCING

As organizations accumulated IT outsourcing experiences in the 1990s, academic research increasingly described and analyzed the phenomenon. Table 18.1 lists major IT outsourcing research, including descriptive case studies, surveys of current outsourcing practices, surveys of practitioners' perceptions of risks and benefits of outsourcing, studies of determinants of outsourcing, and identification of best practices that distinguish success from failure.

There is still considerable debate among the body of research on best practices that distinguish successes from failures, and our primary contribution has been to address this debate by relating actual sourcing outcomes to various managerial practices (Lacity & Willcocks, 1998, 1999, 2000). Most of the empirical research agrees that a detailed formal evaluation process is required and that shorter-term contracts, outsourcing commodity IT on a selective basis, and retention of requisite management capabilities contribute to success (Grover et al., 1996; Klepper, 1995; Lacity & Hirschheim, 1993,1995; Willcocks & Fitzgerald, 1994; DeLooff, 1995). Controversy, however, still surrounds the appropriate governance structure. Some research has found that "strategic alliances" are the best governance structure (McFarlan & Nolan, 1995; Klepper, 1995; and McLellan, Malcolm, & Beamish, 1995), while other research has found that detailed contracts and performance measures remain central to any outsourcing arrangement (for example, Douglass, 1993; Lacity & Hirschheim, 1993; Lacity & Willcocks, 1998; Willcocks & Fitzgerald, 1994). All of these studies also recognize the importance of relationships in determining success or failure, but as Kern (1999) points out in a foundational study on the topic, none really study the complexities of the relationship dimension. Instead, most research either accepts customer–supplier assumptions of shared goals or focuses on the dichotomous relationship between them (Kern & Willcocks, 2000). Thus, the trading partners are the only relevant stakeholders, the only winners or losers—in short, the only unit of analysis.

In the context of IT outsourcing relationships, we found that the dyadic customer–supplier relationship perspective sheds only limited understanding. Instead, we found that a more microanalysis of multiple stakeholders within the trading partners is required for in-depth understanding. Our own research study also showed that the general notion of phases of relationship development over time could be transferred across from the interorganizational research literature, but that a particular model, with its own stakeholders, relationships, phases, and activities, grew out of our specific analyses of IT outsourcing arrangements.

TABLE 18.1 Empirical Research on IT Outsourcing

Author(s)	Research Method	Scope of the Research	Findings
Ang and Straub (1998)	Survey of 243 U.S. banks	Influence of production, transaction economies, and financial slack on outsourcing decisions	Banks were strongly influenced by production cost advantages in their decisions to outsource. Transaction economies was much less of a determinant while financial slack was not a significant explanator.
Applegate and Montealagre (1991)	Case study	Kodak's IS outsourcing decision	Documented the immediate impact on processes and services of Kodak's decision.
Arnett and Jones (1994)	Survey of 40 CIOs	Description of sourcing practices in U.S. companies	The most commonly outsourced IT functions were contract programming (67%), software support training (56%), workstation/PC maintenance (39%), and systems integration (28%).
Auwers and Deschoolmeester (1993)	Case study	Belgium Chocolate company's outsourcing decision	Found that outsourcing helped leverage resources during a mainframe conversion to SAP.
Clark, Zmud, and McCray (1995)	Interviews with 63 executives	Analyzed the forces driving IS outsourcing and developed a sourcing decision framework	The perceived benefits identified: • Reducing costs and/or infusing cash. • Developing IT applications more rapidly. • Improving service quality and productivity. • Gaining access to leading-edge technologies. • Reducing technological risk and increasing technological flexibility. • Implementing change more rapidly. • Assessing current information management capabilities. • Enhancing the status of senior IS executive. • Easing the IS management task of senior management. The perceived risks identified: • Increased costs. • Increased risk. • Loss of internal technical knowledge. • Loss of flexibility. • Increased IS management complexity.
Collins and Millen (1995)	Survey of 110 U.S. companies	Description of U.S. outsourcing practices	Outsourcing as follows: 50%, education and training; 49%, PC support; 33%, network services; 33%, applications development; 33%, application maintenance; and 24%, data centers.
Cullen (1997)	120-plus surveys of Australian organizations	Type, rationale, gains, and problems in outsourcing	Findings indicate 80% of organizations outsourcing, mainly on a selective basis, and mainly hardware support, education, and applications support/development. Skills, technology, then costs savings were the main reasons. Substantial cost savings were not achieved, but technological and some service improvements were noted. Cost was the main item benchmarked, and fixed fees were the dominant cost structure.
Currie and Willcocks (1998)	53 case studies and a 150-organization survey	Study of success factors in total, selective, in-house, and single and multiple supplier sourcing	Selective IT outsourcing was the most successful set of practices, but delineate effective and ineffective practices in all forms of sourcing, and note generic capabilities required to run any IT sourcing arrangement.

TABLE 18.1 *(continued)*

Author(s)	Research Method	Scope of the Research	Findings
De Looff (1995)	30 interviews with individuals in Dutch organizations	Identified critical factors associated with successful IS outsourcing	Few decisions were formally evaluated.
Earl (1996)	Unspecified methodology, based on discussions with senior executives and IT managers	Limits to IT outsourcing	Identifies 11 risks in outsourcing.
Griese (1993)	Survey of 65 Swiss companies	Perceived benefits and risks of outsourcing	The perceived benefits of outsourcing in rank order: • Cost reductions. • Concentration on core business. • Smaller lead times. • Less overcapacity. • More flexibility. • Higher innovation. The perceived risks: • Special requirements. • Sensitive data. • Partnership risk. • Contract risk. • Opposition of the IS department.
Grover et al. (1994, 1996)	Survey of 63 U.S. companies; survey of 188 companies	Described the sourcing practices in U.S. companies; correlated perceived success with type of function outsourced	36% outsource systems operations, 30% outsource applications development and maintenance, 17% outsource telecommunications management, and 16% outsource end-user support. (They did not ask respondents about other IT activities such as data entry, training); IS managers perceive a high success with outsourcing systems operations and telecommunications, but not with outsourcing applications development, end-user support, or management.
Heinzl (1993)	Survey of 359 companies in Germany, Europe, and the United States	Looked at linkages between company characteristics and outsourcing behavior; analyzed motives and effects of outsourcing.	The main motives for outsourcing are: • Achieve cost improvements. • Increase the poor service mentality. • Ameliorate management and control problems. • Improve rate of innovation. German companies are likely to outsource their IS services within the company more often than other European or U.S. corporations.
Hu, Gebelt, and Saunders (1997) Hu, Saunders, and Gebelt (1997)	Study of 175 firms outsourcing between 1985 and 1995	Assessed the determinants of outsourcing	The main sources of influence on IT outsourcing adoptions were a mix of external media, vendor pressure, and internal communications at a personal level.

(continued on next page)

TABLE 18.1 (*continued*)

Author(s)	Research Method	Scope of the Research	Findings
Huber (1993)	Case study	Continental Bank	The bank used outsourcing of many services, including IT, to help turn around poor financial performance due to bad loans.
Klepper (1995)	Two case studies	Proposes that marketing theories can be used to understand IS outsourcing relationships	Found that the most important aspects of good relationships are determined prior to forming the partnership, including vendor screening and prepartnering exchanges.
Lacity and Hirschheim (1993, 1995)	63 interviews in 21 organizations	Studied total outsourcing and total insourcing decisions, identified myths of IS outsourcing propagated in the trade literature	Total outsourcing decisions were fraught with problems due to poor contracts. High excess fees for services beyond the base contract and degrading service levels were the main problems. Insourcing may lead to lower costs if internal IT managers replicate cost-reduction tactics.
Lacity, Willcocks, and Feeny 1996; 1999; Lacity and Willcocks (1998)	145 interviews in 40 US and UK organizations	Managerial frameworks for making sourcing decisions	The authors developed frameworks to assist practitioners with s sourcing decisions based on strategic, economic, and technical factors. The paper distills the learning points for managers. The 1998 paper reanalyzes the data and delineates six success/failure factors in outsourcing. Also analyzes 1995–1998 outsourcing developments.
Lacity and Willcocks (1999, 2000); Willcocks and Lacity (1999); Lacity, Willcocks, and Olsen (1999)	101 organization U.K./U.S. survey, and 114 case histories 1991–1998; also Scandinavian survey	Documents current (1998/99) practices and outcomes; issues revealed by longitudinal analysis	Dominant form is selective outsourcing (U.S., 83%; U.S., 75%) with multiple suppliers (79% of organizations outsourcing). Good satisfaction rates but array of problems still identified. Cases show a 38% success rate for total outsourcing, and a 76% and 77% success rate for in-house sourcing and selective outsourcing, respectively. Identifies reasons for these outcomes.
Loh and Venkatraman (1991 and 1992a, b)	Secondary sources, including stock market data and annual reports	Determinants of information technology outsourcing	Identified Kodak's IS outsourcing decision as a critical event in the diffusion of innovation; identified the determinants of IS outsourcing, including high IS costs and poor IS performance; demonstrated positive stock market reaction to IS outsourcing announcements.
McFarlan and Nolan (1995)	Case studies of over a dozen outsourcing situations	Applied strategic grid model to IS outsourcing decision	Found that strategic alliances were the key to successful outsourcing.
McLellan et al. (1995)	Case studies of North American banks	Studied the motives of IS outsourcing as well as the relationships	IT was outsourced even though it was considered a core competency.
Pantane and Jurison (1994)	Survey of U.S. companies	Trends in offshore outsourcing	Strategic applications are not typically outsourced and will not likely be in the future.
Reponen (1993)	Study of six Finnish companies	Looked at the main reasons, difficulties, and consequences of outsourcing	The structure of outsourcing was primarily the setting up of new companies.
Saarinen and Saaksjarvi (1993)	Case studies of two Finnish woodworking companies	Studied the differences in the sourcing strategies of two companies	The heavily insourced IS function performed much better than the heavily outsourced IS function.

TABLE 18.1 (continued)

Author(s)	Research Method	Scope of the Research	Findings
Sobel and Apte (1995); Apte et al. (1997)	Survey of 48 U.S., 86 Japanese, and 141 Finnish companies	Description of sourcing practices in the U.S.	The most commonly outsourced functions in the U.S. were support operations (47.9%), training and education (47.9%), disaster recovery (39.6%), and data entry (22.9%). The perceived benefits in the U.S.: • Allows cost containment. • Reduces need to hire IS professionals. • Improves cost predictability. • Leaves more time to focus on strategic IS use. • Makes more vendors available. • Gives access to leading-edge technologies. • Reduces need for capital investment in new technology. The perceived disadvantages in the United States: • Difficulty in monitoring outsourcing vendors. • Loss of quality and time control. • Difficulty in explaining business needs to vendors. • Potential loss of secrets and intellectual property. • Limit of long-term career prospects of IS staff. • High cost of outsourcing controls. • IS department size decreased.
Strassmann (1995)	Analysis of financial statements of Fortune 1000 companies	Determinants of outsourcing	Found that companies with poor financial performance are the most likely to outsource.
Valor et al. (1993)	Survey of 63 Spanish CEOs	Perceptions of benefits and risks of outsourcing	The top perceived benefits: • Focus on own business. • Reduction of IT staff. • Access to experts. • Access to the latest technology. The top perceived risks: • Leakage of confidential information. • Breach of contract by vendors. • Dependence on specific vendors.
Willcocks and Fitzgerald (1994), Willcocks et al. (1995, 1999).	In-depth interviews with 75 individuals in 30 UK firms	Studied selective sourcing decisions; identified best practices for sourcing evaluations, contract negotiations, and vendor management	Identified the need for a thorough evaluation process, including accounting for the full costs of internal services. They found that technically mature activities are easiest to outsource, but success still depends on a sound contract.
Willcocks and Kern (1998)	Longitudinal case study of relationships in a total outsourcing single-supplier deal	Focused on the development of issues and relationships over time	Even in a well-prepared outsourcing arrangement, the relationship dimension was neglected at first, but relationships, processes, and trust can develop over time if managed proactively.

INFORMATION TECHNOLOGY OUTSOURCING STAKEHOLDERS

An IT stakeholder group consists of people tending to have the same expectations, perceptions, and goals for IT and outsourcing. Rather than merely categorizing people as either "customers" or "suppliers," our research identified eight types of IT stakeholders (See Table 18.2). However, while our stakeholder analysis is richer than previous dichotomous analyses, we still note that stereotypes ignore individual personalities. In the conclusion, we address how personal charisma (or abrasiveness) can sometimes supercede stakeholder stereotypes.

In general, we found four distinct customer IT stakeholders and three distinct supplier stakeholders. In cases of multisourcing (such as the sourcing options pursued from 1993 to 1998 by British Petroleum Exploration with three suppliers and DuPont in 1996/1997 with two suppliers), the number of supplier stakeholders and interactions among stakeholders increase. The additional complexity of multisourcing is often deemed worthwhile because of the benefits of best sourcing and eliminating the monopoly power of a sole supplier. In addition, it is quite common for suppliers on large IT outsourcing contracts to hire subcontractors.

CUSTOMER SENIOR BUSINESS MANAGERS

Although responsible for achieving business results from IT expenditures, in many of our cases, senior business managers did not have the tools to assess whether the IT function was adding value. They often asked senior IT managers for evidence of business value. When senior managers could not assess the value of IT, they focused primarily on the

TABLE 18.2 Stakeholder Expectations and Goals

Stakeholder	IT Expectations/Goals
Customer senior business managers	Customer senior business managers expected demonstrated business value for IT expenditures. Inability to assess the benefits of IT often caused senior business managers to focus on IT costs.
Customer senior IT managers	Customer senior IT managers balanced service excellence expectations from users with cost-containment expectations from senior business managers.
Customer IT staff	As technical enthusiasts, customer IT staff focused primarily on service excellence but within budget and time constraints.
Customer IT users	IT users expected service excellence. Cost implications were often not apparent due to centralized accounting and contracting for IT.
Supplier senior managers	Supplier senior managers negotiated deals that would satisfy the customer while maximizing profits.
Supplier account managers	Supplier senior managers balanced customer service and profitability.
Supplier IT staff	As technical enthusiasts, supplier IT staff primarily focused on service excellence but within budget and time constraints.
Subcontractors	Delivering on their contracts.

financing and costs of IT. The questions naturally arose: Can IT be delivered more efficiently? Can IT assets (which may represent up to 20% of all capital assets) be removed from the balance sheet? Can large fixed annual IT budgets be transformed into a "pay-for-use" model? And, ultimately, "Can an IT outsourcer save us money?"

CUSTOMER SENIOR IT MANAGERS

Typically customer senior IT managers are centralized and responsible for balancing the costs of IT with the services provided to ensure value for money. In general, senior IT managers were often frustrated by their charge. Users often demanded service excellence while their bosses often demanded cost containment. One senior IT manager, the former director of IS for a U.S. petroleum company, explains:

> I cannot get any support in how to allocate these resources. And we cannot be the traffic cop in this whole process because it is not right. I'm trying to satisfy everybody and it's not working.

In most of our cases, senior IT managers maintained their focus on balancing IT costs and services throughout an outsourcing process. Senior IT managers are rarely threatened by IT outsourcing, which means that their roles are being redefined rather than lost. Indeed, most senior IT managers became valuable contributors to outsourcing evaluations, contract negotiations, and postcontract management. Although we discussed the political behavior of a few IT managers biased against outsourcing in Lacity and Willcocks (1998), by far the preponderance of IT managers expressed a goal to balance costs and service delivery.[1]

CUSTOMER IT STAFF

Customer IT staff are responsible for IT service delivery. Although they are expected to meet budgets and deadlines, we found that IT professionals are generally technology enthusiasts who also seek to please users.[2] The internal IT staff were often the stakeholder groups most profoundly affected by outsourcing evaluations. They felt their senior managers were making life choices for them about transition and retention, often without their input on careers, salaries, and benefits. When IT staff are unionized, the unions were often very vocally against outsourcing. For example, unions initially opposed the decisions at British Aerospace, Inland Revenue, and Westchester County. Ultimately, we found customer IT employees almost always agreeing to transfer to the supplier. Acceptance rates were above 95% in all our cases except at a U.S. public sector organization and at a U.S. metal company.

IT USERS

IT users typically focused throughout all phases on IT *service excellence,* expecting systems to be up and running, to provide business functionality, and to facilitate the execution of their business responsibilities. IT users rarely resisted outsourcing, although they frequently had questions about confidentiality and integrity of data.

In most instances, IT users were supportive of outsourcing because they perceived that the supplier would radically improve IT service.[3] But IT users' expectations for service excellence were often unrealistic; they believed that an infusion of new IT and better service would be provided by the supplier virtually free of charge. The gap between expectations and reality often dampened their initial enthusiasm.

SUPPLIER SENIOR MANAGERS

Supplier senior managers are responsible for sales and negotiations. They must balance the need to satisfy their customers with the need to generate a profit for their organization. A tremendous amount of judgment, typically based on years of experience, is often needed to assess what can be delivered at what price while still generating a profit.

According to one supplier senior manager, suppliers "never knowingly sell a deal by reducing IT cost" because the margins are too small. For his company, IT cost-reduction deals typically require 50% overhead (25% for supplier corporate headquarters, 25% for profit on the account) while still being able to reduce customers' costs by 10 to 20%. Few IT cost-reduction deals qualify. Instead, supplier senior managers typically focus on the value they can add to a customer in terms of improving service, redesigning business processes, providing scarce IT skills, helping customers refinance IT, and developing new added-value systems.

SUPPLIER ACCOUNT MANAGERS

Supplier account managers are responsible for profitability and customer satisfaction on a given IT contract. They also must strike a delicate balance between the often conflicting goals of service excellence and cost containment. Because the supplier account manager is so critical to the success of an outsourcing relationship, many customers include approval clauses in the contract for this role.

SUPPLIER IT STAFF

A primary concern of supplier IT staff is providing good customer service. Like customer IT staff, supplier IT staff are generally technology enthusiasts who are anxious to please users. Sometimes their enthusiasm for customer service has to be harnessed by their management to protect profit margins. Most IT staff, however, are well aware of budget and time requirements. Although they aim to please their customers, their organizations must earn a profit as noted by the quality manager of an IT supplier:

> We are an IT company, so we can transfuse current IT, state of the art IT, future IT, conceptual IT. But of course that transfusion as far as we are concerned is not free. The big problem is these people think that transfusion is free.

SUBCONTRACTORS

Subcontractors are hired by prime suppliers to deliver part of the service to customers. According to International Data Corporation (IDC), 36% of IT outsourcing contracts involve subcontractors. An *InformationWeek* (Caldwell, Violino, & McGee, 1997) survey found an even higher frequency of subcontractors: 50% of IT suppliers hire contractors.

Customers often have limited or no interaction with subcontractors. More than 15% of 55 IT managers surveyed by IDC stated that their IT suppliers do not notify them when they hire subcontractors. Half of the suppliers in the *InformationWeek* survey admitted that subcontractors sometimes cause problems, including service quality (67%), costs (30%), viruses (17%), and security (10%).

According to surveys, prime contractors hire subcontractors to access scarce technical skills. Ironically, customers often outsourced for the same reason: to gain access to scarce IT skills of the prime contractor. But prime contractors face the same global shortage of IT skills as everyone else (Caldwell et al., 1997). Clearly, the widespread usage of subcontracting brings additional dimensions and issues to outsourcing; our research experience is that these are all too often overlooked by client organizations (Lacity & Willcocks, 2000).

In summary, the eight types of stakeholders generally held different IT expectations and goals. Some stakeholders primarily focus on IT costs because they are the ones paying for IT. Other stakeholders focus on service excellence because they are the ones using the IT service. Other stakeholders must strike a delicate balance between service excellence and cost containment. Clearly, such diverse goals and orientations among typical stakeholders can have a profound impact on the types of relationships that can develop.

TYPES OF STAKEHOLDER RELATIONSHIPS

As previously noted, stakeholder relationships are quite dynamic. The same two people can fight one minute and collaborate the next, and we found stakeholders regularly operating at different points along the relationship continuum. In general, at least four types of relationships were evident (see Figure 18.1).

FIGURE 18.1   Types of Relationship in IT Outsourcing

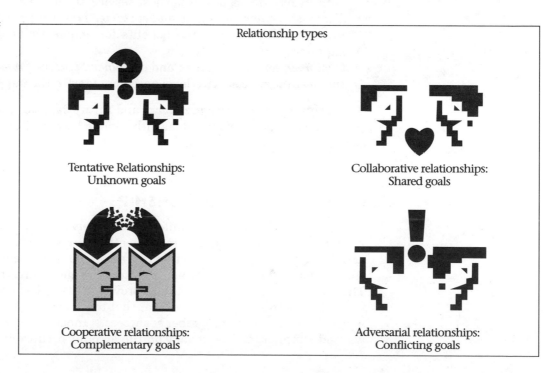

TENTATIVE RELATIONSHIPS

These relationships were quite common when stakeholders had no shared history. Thus, stakeholders were unsure whether goals were shared, complementary, or conflicting. Most of the time behavior manifested itself in polite caution, but sometimes a predisposition toward enthusiasm was evident. For example, *customer* and *supplier senior managers* were often quite enthusiastic—albeit tentative—when exploring the possibility of a "partnership." At this stage, there was no commitment and thus no motivation to behave aggressively or antagonistically. One informant described senior management talks as a "peacock dance" because each party was anxious to impress the other with its organization's assets and capabilities.

The first few meetings between *supplier stakeholders* and *customer IT staff* identified for transfer represent another common example of tentative relationships. The tentativeness mostly occurred on the part of the IT staff, who were quite naturally concerned about their new careers, salaries, and benefits. Most supplier stakeholders immediately began to build confidence by guaranteeing equivalent salaries and benefits and by allowing potential transfers to speak with previously transferred employees.

COLLABORATIVE RELATIONSHIPS

Collaborative relationships occurred when stakeholders' goals were shared. In many cases, shared goals were fostered by being part of the same organization. Customer stakeholder goals were often aligned for a number of negotiation activities:

- *Customer senior business* managers and *customer senior IT managers* typically both wanted to negotiate the best service at the lowest cost.
- *Customer senior managers* and *customer IT staff* typically both wanted to negotiate the best salaries and benefits for employees targeted for transfer to the supplier.
- *Customer senior managers* and *customer IT users* typically wanted to negotiate the best possible service-level agreements with the supplier.

Similarly, *supplier senior managers* and future *supplier account managers* had the shared goal of negotiating a deal with enough leeway to ensure profit margins, even assuming unforeseen events.

COOPERATIVE RELATIONSHIPS

Cooperative relationships manifested themselves when goals were complementary. Each party needs something from the other party to succeed. Many IT outsourcing activities are based on the notion of an exchange—a customer pays a fee in exchange for a service. Customer and supplier goals are therefore complementary: The customer needs the supplier to provide the service; the supplier needs the customer to pay the fee. While it is clear that these goals are not shared, each party has a vested interest in the other's success.[4] Indeed, customer stakeholders never wanted suppliers to lose money on the account because if the supplier suffers, the customer suffers, as the contract administrator of a South Australian government office noted:

> Suppliers have to make a reasonable margin to stay in business. You don't want them to lose money because the worse their business gets, the worse your business gets. At the same time you don't want them to make outrageous profits at your expense.

ADVERSARIAL RELATIONSHIPS

Adversarial relationships occurred when stakeholder goals were in *conflict*. Stakeholders were adversarial when the conflict entailed millions of dollars, such as a conflict over an interpretation of financial responsibility in a contract clause. In particular, three activities are inherently adversarial:

- Negotiating the original contract.
- Establishing precedents for contract interpretation during the transition phase.
- Renegotiating or realigning the contract midway through the contract.

The key here was for the customer and supplier to have equal power to achieve an equitable outcome. When one party had more power than the other, the stronger party clearly dominated the weaker. In the early mega-deals, suppliers clearly had more power due to information impactedness. Oliver Williamson (1975, p. 4) defines information impactedness as follows:

> It exists in circumstances in which one of the parties to an exchange is much better informed than is the other regarding underlying conditions germane to the trade, and the second party cannot achieve information parity except at great cost—because he cannot rely on the first party to disclose the information in a fully candid manner.

Customers were often inexperienced with negotiating IT outsourcing contracts. To balance the power during contract negotiations, customers are hiring more outside experts to represent their interests. In fact, few new IT outsourcing deals were signed without the customer's extensive reliance on outside technical and legal consultants. Customers employed a number of other strategies to balance the power:

- Established nonexclusivity clauses that enabled the customer to competitively bid beyond baseline services.
- Multisourced rather than gave monopoly power to a sole supplier.
- Used selective sourcing to limit the power of a supplier to a targeted subset of IT activities.

The objective of these strategies, again, is not necessarily to dominate the other party but to have enough power to favorably and fairly resolve adversarial tasks. Indeed, customer empowerment contributes to our understanding of why newer contracts have had higher success rates than older contracts (Lacity & Willcocks, 1998).

In summary, the dynamic nature of stakeholder relationships was clearly evident in case-study organizations. The same stakeholders can have tentative, collaborative, cooperative, and adversarial relationships, depending on the task at hand. By understanding relationship complexities, customers and suppliers can abandon the naive quest for continual harmony. Instead, stakeholders should accept the ebbs and flows of the evolution of relationships. Stakeholders can occasionally fight yet can still have an effective relationship overall.

RELATIONSHIP PHASES AND ACTIVITIES

We identified six outsourcing phases, each composed of multiple activities. (See Table 18.3). Stakeholder relationships vary during activities within phases, depending on goal alignment. For each of the phases, we describe the major stakeholder goals, interactions, and outcomes witnessed in our cases.

PHASE 1: SCOPING—CUSTOMER GOAL: "CREATE A STRATEGIC VISION OF IT SOURCING"

The two main activities in this phase were identifying core IT capabilities and identifying IT activities for potential outsourcing.[5] Typically, the *customer senior business managers* and *customer senior IT managers* were the primary stakeholders involved during this initial phase. Senior business managers had agendas prompted by financial pressures. Such pressures often led to a "core competency" strategy by which the organization focused on the "core" and downsized or outsourced the rest. Because senior business managers viewed much of IT as a noncore competency, they regularly questioned whether some or all of the IT function could be potentially outsourced.

Senior IT managers had typically coped with a legacy of trying to balance service excellence demands from the user population with IT cost-containment pressures from their senior managers. In the past, there was often tension between CEOs and senior IT managers because the latter often struggled to demonstrate value for IT expenditures to their bosses. (See Feeny, Edwards, & Simpson, 1992; Willcocks, Feeny, & Isle, 1997 and the chapter by Ross and Feeny for detailed research on CEO/CIO relationships).

A full-blown investigation of IT sourcing options, however, often served to align goals between senior business and IT managers. As previously noted, because senior IT managers rarely lose their jobs as a consequence of outsourcing, they usually welcomed a reasoned approach to sourcing the IT function. With the support of their bosses, senior IT managers could overcome user resistance and implement cost-reduction and outsourcing strategies (see Lacity and Hirschheim [1995] for case studies on IT empowerment as a consequence of outsourcing evaluations).

Supplier stakeholders were not typically involved until the evaluation phase. However, in a few cases, *supplier senior managers* actually prompted the decision to consider outsourcing by wooing customer senior executives in this phase. For example, the vice-president of IS at one U.S. petroleum company told us that EDS prompted a sourcing decision by offering cash during a major court battle at his company:

> The Chairman of the Board of EDS wrote a letter to our chief executive officer saying that they would be most interested in paying substantial cash for our whole IS organization. That includes all the people, and they would be very happy to meet him and discuss that with him.

Customer and supplier senior executive interactions were typically characterized by tentative enthusiasm and optimism during the scoping phase. But one lesson that clearly emerged from our body of research is that customer and supplier senior executives should not make outsourcing decisions without IT managements' input. The "CEO handshake deals" typically failed because of inattention to detail. Two CEOs can get very excited about an alliance, but the success of IT outsourcing deals relies on the details of the cost and service to be delivered.

TABLE 18.3 IT Outsourcing Phases and Activities

	Scoping Phase	Evaluation Phase	Negotiation Phase	Transition Phase	Middle Phase	Mature Phase
Activities:	• Identify core IT capabilities • Identify IT activities for potential outsourcing using business, economic, and technical criteria	• Measure baseline services • Measure baseline costs • Create RFP • Develop evaluation criteria • Invite external and internal bids	• Conduct due diligence to verify RFP baseline claims • Negotiate service-level agreements • Create responsibility matrixes • Price work units • Negotiate terms for employee transfer • Negotiate mechanisms for contractual change, including benchmarking, book accounting, non-exclusivity clauses, and pricing schedules	• Distribute contract to IT users • Interpret the contract • Establish post-contract management infrastructure and processes • Implement consolidation, rationalization, and standardization • Validate service scope, costs, levels, and responsibilities for baseline services • Manage additional service requests • Foster realistic expectations of supplier performance • Publicly promote the contract	• Benchmark performance to (theoretically) reset prices • Realign the contract to reflect changes in technology and business • Involve the supplier in more value-added areas	• Recalibrate investment criteria to reflect shorter time horizon for recouping investments • Determine if the relationship will be terminated or extended
Objective:	Identify flexible IT organization, including IT activities for potential outsourcing	Select best and final offer	Sign contract(s)	Establish operational performance	Achieve value-added above operational performance	No lapses in operational performance during final transition

PHASE 2: EVALUATION—CUSTOMER GOAL: "IDENTIFY THE BEST SOURCE FOR IT ACTIVITIES"

The major activities during this phase follow:

- Measuring baseline services and costs.
- Creating an RFP (request for proposal).
- Developing evaluation criteria.
- Inviting internal and external bids.

Lacity and Willcocks (1998) discussed the need for joint senior management and IT management participation in sourcing evaluations. We also discussed the evaluation process that most frequently led to success: create an RFP and invite both external and internal bids. We showed how this practice ensures that a supplier's bid is not merely compared with current IT performance but with IT performance that could be achieved if internal managers were empowered to behave like suppliers.[6]

Supplier stakeholders became much more active during this phase. In addition to the *supplier senior management* team, a host of supplier experts attended bid presentations. In some cases, such as British Aerospace (BAe), suppliers helped to win the bid by talking to many customer stakeholders. While CSC obviously talked to senior business managers about finances, they also talked to BAe users about service, to the IT staff about career paths/benefits, and to IT managers about baseline service-level agreements. Several BAe and CSC informants indicated that CSC was successful in winning the bid, in large part because of its expertise in aerospace and its ability to talk business language, as reported by a CSC quality manager transferred from BAe:

> The senior managers within BAe and even more the managers within the business wanted to hear people talking their language, the language of making airplanes. And we were able to do that, we were able to produce these people who talked their language.

As with the previous phase, the customer/supplier interactions—although tentative—were typically characterized by enthusiasm and optimism at the senior management level during the evaluation phase.

The *customer IT users* were primarily concerned with service excellence during the entire outsourcing evaluation. As previously noted, IT users sometimes questioned confidentiality and privacy of data with IT outsourcing. But in general, IT users typically supported outsourcing because they perceived that suppliers—with their IT expertise—would increase service and provide new IT to the user community.

At the *customer IT staff level,* however, IT professionals were frequently threatened by the impending decision. Some organizations, particularly those with an IT labor union, experienced significant resistance from this stakeholder group. Indeed, both British Aerospace's and Inland Revenue's unionized IT staff held strikes in opposition to outsourcing.

In cases in which IT staff were invited to submit an alternative bid, the internal bid process often served as a galvanizing force. In some cases, senior management granted a request for an internal bid more as a "morale preserver" than as a serious contender against external bidders. Once given free rein to compete based on cost efficiency, internal IT managers from eight of our cases surprised senior management by submitting the winning bid. Sourcing evaluations, which led to continued insourcing of the IT function, proceeded to a transition phase. The primary activity of the insourcing transition phase is the implementation of consolidation, rationalization, and standardization of the internal bid proposal (see Lacity and Hirschheim [1995] for details of implementing insourcing proposals).

Sourcing evaluations that result in outsourcing were found to proceed through the four additional phases whose descriptions follow later in this section. Unlike insourcing, IT outsourcing requires significant changes in duties and responsibilities of IT management, staff, and users (Currie & Willcocks, 1998; Feeny & Willcocks, 1998). Also, more stakeholders must adapt and learn to interact with each other to deliver a cost-effective IT service.

PHASE 3: NEGOTIATION—CUSTOMER GOAL: "NEGOTIATE A CONTRACT TO ENSURE SOURCING EXPECTATIONS ARE REALIZED"

Lacity and Willcocks (1998) discussed some of the principles of negotiating deals, including the proven practices of negotiating short-term contracts and detailed contracts. The government of South Australia as well as DuPont, British Aerospace, and Inland Revenue spent more than a year negotiating contract details. These contract details included the following:

- Conducting due diligence to verify RFP baseline claims.
- Negotiating service-level agreements for 500 or more IT services.
- Creating customer/supplier responsibility matrixes for more than 700 responsibilities.
- Pricing 20 to 30 units of work, such as CPU minutes, number of UNIX boxes, and manhours of analyst time.
- Negotiating terms for transfer of employees at equivalent or better benefits.
- Agreeing on mechanisms for contractual change, including benchmarking, open-book accounting, nonexclusivity clauses, and pricing schedules.

It is quite clear that contract negotiations are antagonistic because the customer stakeholders and supplier stakeholders are both accountable to protecting the interests of their respective organizations. Participants have used the nouns *war, bloodbath,* and *battle* to describe negotiations. No parties, however, seemed to expect a different type of relationship during contract negotiations. Each side expected the other to be a tough negotiator. Indeed, one CSC account executive even complimented BAe on its negotiating skills:

> BAe, say for Military Aircraft, 70% of the cost of that Eurofighter is brought in from somewhere else. So they are used to, and their whole culture is around one of deal-making and negotiating and hard-bargaining. And they are brought up in that and they play hard ball extremely well.

During outsourcing negotiations, *customer IT managers* were typically tough negotiators. They fought very hard to represent the interests of their organizations. At a U.S. bank, for example, the VP of IS was adamant that she was not going to pay a $500,000 software license transfer fee. The supplier threatened to shut down the data center (and thus the bank) unless the bill was paid. Here is how she and the financial manager responded:

> We called our attorneys. Our attorneys called their attorneys. Ours said, "How dare you threaten to shut down a national bank? You think you can shut down a national bank?" But that was a very difficult period, after they sent us that shut down letter. Finally,

> they said, 'I think we better go see these people.' Thursday morning they came in and it was a shouting match back and forth. And they said, 'We don't have to put up with this.' And they got up and left. Their attorneys called me the next day and apologized for their marketers. The next week we negotiated from $500,000 down to $110,000."

Despite tough negotiations, the bank's deal ended up being a success. We found similar situations in many organizations: Tough battles during contract negotiations between customer and supplier constituents often led to successful arrangements. After a contract is signed, however, the customers and suppliers sought a more harmonious relationship. The South Australian (SA) government even hosted a session between SA IT managers and EDS managers to transition quickly from the adversarial posturing of contract negotiations to the more cooperative delivery of the contract.

IT users are another stakeholder group involved in contract negotiations. Because IT outsourcing contracts typically rely on a baseline measure of services, users became involved in documenting current service levels and volumes. IT users were generally motivated actually to inflate current service levels. In essence, this would enable them to get the supplier to increase service levels under a fixed-fee baseline price. But suppliers were keenly aware of the motivation and therefore required a documented and detailed due diligence process to verify baseline claims.

During the negotiation phase, potential *supplier account managers* are often interviewed by the customer stakeholders. Initial meetings were often characterized by tentativeness as each party explored the other's motivations and values. Customer stakeholders were motivated to select a person who would primarily focus on customer service. Supplier stakeholders—who are accountable to their shareholders—needed a person who would protect their profit margins. In many of our cases, customers did not select a person who was part of the supplier negotiating team. When customers experienced a supplier's tough negotiating skills firsthand, they naturally retreated from the individual. Instead, a fresh face often helped the transition from antagonism during the negotiation phase to cooperation during the transition phase.

In general, all parties agree that even though contract negotiations are antagonistic, the process is worthwhile for both sides. Detailed contracts document expectations and are therefore a prerequisite for a successful relationship, as a CSC vice president noted:

> It is important to have a sound base contract. It is important because that's how operating trust is built.

A CSC account manager on the BAe contract commented:

> There should be no ambiguity in the contract as to what is baseline or fixed price or essentially free, in scope. What is actually there to be done and who is paying for it. It should be totally crystal-clear.

PHASE 4: TRANSITION—CUSTOMER GOAL: "ESTABLISH PRECEDENTS FOR OPERATIONAL PERFORMANCE"

On large contracts, transition activities may last from 18 months to more than 2 years. Our research shows eight main areas of activity here, as we now detail.

Distributing the Contract

Many actual IT outsourcing contracts are impossible to execute because they are typically massive documents written in obscure legal terminology. Megacontracts may contain 30,000 lines and require several legal-sized boxes for a single copy. In the early days of megacontracts, one of the major tasks of the centralized contract management team was to develop user guides to the contract, which are designed to describe what the supplier is obligated to provide under the fixed-fee structure in user terms.

The major stakeholders involved in this activity are the *customer IT managers* and the *IT users*. Often the stakeholders' goals were in conflict. IT users, particularly division managers, wanted to see the entire contract. IT managers wanted to distribute only summaries of the contract because they felt every IT user would interpret the contract differently. A global alliance manager at DuPont stated:

> We find anything you write down and distribute to a group of people, those people interpret it differently and they try to execute against their interpretation.

Indeed, on many contracts, *IT users* fought with *supplier IT staff* over the contract. At DuPont, for example, work on 150 major projects was halted because of a lack of project pricing. Lower-level employees were not sure how to behave—they questioned how they could do this work when it had not been properly priced and approved. Once the DuPont IT managers and CSC account managers were aware of the problem, they sent clear messages to lower-level employees: Do the work and we'll worry about the price. A dual BAe/CSC account executive explained:

> But just last week, they had a client that was doing design work for them on the network connection. CSC quoted a price they felt too high. And I looked at it and said, 'We'll just do it, we'll worry about the quote later.'

Interpreting the Contract

No matter how well the negotiating teams believed they had nailed down the details, the contract was always open for interpretation. Typically, the *customer IT managers* and *supplier account managers* were in charge of resolving contract interpretation issues. Clearly, stakeholder goals are conflicting because each side is charged with protecting the interests of its own organization. Each side sought a fair resolution, but financial pressures fueled the tension; a precedent resolved during the transition phase could have millions of dollars worth of consequences during the remainder of the contract, as an IT services manager at BAe noted:

> What may be only £6000 today might set a precedent worth £10 million.

Some examples serve to illustrate the ambiguity typically found in contracts:

- If the customer needs system maintenance that requires the supplier to bring the data center down over the weekend, who pays supplier overtime?
- What is included in the fixed price of a standard hardware upgrade? Is analyst time spent identifying requirements billable or included in the fixed price? Are installation, wiring, and shipping and handling costs included or billable?

DuPont, like other customers, realized that more staff should have been retained to address these issues, as its global alliance manager noted:

> Had we known that was coming, we would have saved more resources, or kept more resources to help with both the continuing negotiation, definition of the deal, as well as I would say it has taken more resources than anticipated to put in place all these managing processes that are required as part of the transition or start-up of the deal.

Establishing Postcontract Management Infrastructure and Processes

Customers typically established centralized teams to facilitate the contract monitoring and vendor development roles. Centralized teams focused on financial and strategic management of the contract. Contract facilitation roles were typically decentralized (see Feeny and Willcocks [1998] and Willcocks et al. [1997] for details on these roles). Decentralized teams focused on daily operations.

For problem resolution, many customers and suppliers sought cooperative processes rather than unproductive adversarial processes. At DuPont and Inland Revenue in 1999, joint customer–supplier teams were delegated responsibility for solving operational problems. The teams are typically composed of *customer IT users, customer IT staff,* and *supplier IT staff.* The goal is for the joint teams to resolve the problem before escalating the issue to their superiors, as an Inland Revenue account manager explained:

> If we think that there are any stand-offs that are occurring, any differences of opinion we can't get to the bottom of, we attempt to try and sort it as joint teams . . . we apply it at the contract level and the two contract management teams . . . have active discussions about particular issues and they consider positions from both sides. And . . . where they can't come to some agreement, it comes up the management hierarchy and will come to myself and an equivalent within EDS to see if we can mediate on these things.

Although customers are expected to represent customer interests, and suppliers are expected to represent supplier interests, the joint teams create an environment of compromise. The operating principle of joint teams is to be fair and not to exploit any contract inefficiencies. At Dupont, by late 1998, 120 operational problems had been successfully resolved in this manner.

Implementing Consolidation, Rationalization, and Standardization

Customer stakeholders were well aware that suppliers' bids were based, in part, on projected savings from implementing cost-reduction practices after the contract was signed. Cost-reduction tactics included consolidating data centers, standardizing software and hardware platforms, creating stringent service request approval processes, centralizing IT staff, implementing chargeback systems, and so on. These practices were often unpopular with IT users because they perceived that such practices would reduce service levels. In fact, insourcing proposals were often rejected because senior executives perceived that internal IT managers lacked the political clout to overcome user resistance to cost-reduction tactics. Once a supplier takes over a customer's assets, however, it clearly has the power to manage resources in a more efficient manner.

Customer IT managers supported *supplier account managers* in their cost-reduction practices. They realized that the supplier needed the savings to earn a profit on the account. Indeed, many customers complimented suppliers on their ability to consolidate, rationalize, and standardize. A contract administrator for the government of South Australia noted:

> EDS did in 12 months what we couldn't do in four years.

A manager of IS for a U.S. metal company commented:

> I was so impressed with the preparation activities and the actual execution of the migration to their data center. Their [sic] were few interruptions in service to the users. [The vendor] made this very detailed, complex move look like it wasn't difficult at all.

Validating Baseline Service Scope, Costs, Levels, and Responsibilities

A major transition challenge for all relationships was validating the baseline. Supplier bids were based on the RFP and discoveries made during due diligence. Any undiscovered items were typically subject to excess fees. After the Inland Revenue/EDS contract went into effect, for example, IR had to pay for the following items that surfaced:

- £100,000 for software license fees.
- £5 million per year caused by inaccuracies in the original tender offers.
- £15 million per year for hardware maintenance.

As far as validating baseline service levels, typically *customer IT staff* and *supplier IT staff* are charged with the task. At DuPont, for example, baseline service levels are verified by joint teams distributed around the globe. Because failure to meet service levels can result in financial penalties, the stakeholder goals were typically in conflict. Each is motivated to blame the other for service lapses. To avoid disputes during the transition phase, DuPont agreed to suspend cash penalties for nonperformance for the first year of the contract. As one DuPont employee noted, "90% of the service lapses were inherited from us." Because the financial consequence was removed, parties at DuPont are working together to improve service lapses, rather than merely trying to blame one another.

Managing Additional Service Requests Beyond Baseline

Services beyond baseline—and thus subject to excess fees—can be triggered by

1. Exceeding projected volumes on existing services.
2. Changing the composition of baseline services.
3. Demanding entirely new services.

Nearly every outsourcing customer we studied experienced all three sources of change. Indeed, a common lament among *customer IT managers* and *supplier account managers* was "we completely underestimated user demand." During an outsourcing decision process that often took two years, many organizations instituted a buying freeze. Once the contract went into effect, user demands were no longer constrained. A vendor VP of operations in a major central government deal described what happened:

> The whole process until we had a contract in place was about two and a half years. During that period of time, the government pretty much put a freeze on buying equipment, things like that. So there was a pent-up demand that we all underestimated. The

number of change requests overwhelmed us. The number of change requests so far has been something like 2,000. And this is new servers, new LANs, those kind of things. We went for example, and these are approximate numbers, at the time of taking over the baseline, they had about 1,000 LAN servers out there. And there are now about 1,800. So that's an example.

Supplier account managers typically have the resources and financial motivation to meet any volume of demand. *Customer IT managers* were typically charged with keeping excess fees to a minimum. Thus, stakeholder goals were often in conflict during this task. At the very least, customer IT managers tried to ensure that users requested beyond-baseline items only if the benefits generated covered the excess costs. For example, one business unit manager at BAe requested a shop control system that would save him £250,000. But the BAe contract manager pointed out that it would cost £500,000 to build!

Fostering Realistic Expectations of Supplier Performance

We have noted several times that *IT users* often have misperceptions about what the supplier is obligated to provide the customer. Although contract summaries are distributed to IT users, the user community can include thousands of individuals.

IT users often expected a step-change in service, but contracts typically required maintenance of current service levels at a reduced cost. Both *customer IT managers* and *supplier account managers* shared the goal of communicating contractual obligations to the IT user community. Customer IT managers wanted users to have realistic expectations for several reasons:

- Not wanting IT users to demand a higher level of service that could trigger excess fees.
- Not wanting IT users to be disappointed in their management of the contract.
- Not wanting IT users to complain unfairly to the supplier because this causes tension and requires management intervention.

Suppliers also wanted users to understand the contractual obligations because customer satisfaction is obviously a goal of all suppliers—and customer satisfaction requires realistic expectations of supplier performance.

Because goals are shared, customer IT managers were generally very supportive of the supplier for this activity. Internal IT managers have historically been in the same position of trying to balance user expectations for service excellence with cost constraints. The contract administrator at the South Australian government, for example, expressed his support of the supplier in achieving realistic IT user expectations:

> I've actually been an outsourcer before . . . . There is generally an expectation of management on the user side that here is this knight in shining armor, I'll get three times better service at half the price. And also what happens, that expectation grows as you get closer to contract, so you have this large gap in expectations from the start.

Publicly Promoting the IT Contract

Another common activity in which customer and supplier stakeholders had shared goals was promoting the IT contract to the general public. Particularly in public sector outsourcing, taxpayers and opposing elected officials were often critical of outsourcing and thus the *customer senior managers* and *supplier senior managers* would often jointly hold press conferences to explain the benefits of the relationship to the public. Although both sides admit that relationships are not always easy, customers and suppliers stress the overall value to taxpayers.

At U.K.'s Inland Revenue, the status of the contract is actually reported to Parliament. Both Inland Revenue contract managers and EDS supplier account managers collaborate on parliamentary and strategic planning committees, as an Inland Revenue account manager described:

> It's a Committee chaired by the Deputy Chairman, and actually we have representation from EDS on that committee. So we have joint representation on that committee and of course when we are providing estimates of what certain policy changes would cost, estimates are coming from the EDS camp. We've got [EDS and IR] people collaborating with our feasibility appraisal team in what those estimates would be and what the costs would be.

PHASE 5: MIDDLE PHASE: GOAL: "CUSTOMERS ACHIEVE VALUE-ADDED ABOVE AND BEYOND OPERATIONAL PERFORMANCE"

Customers seek to adapt and to improve the contract beyond the baseline. Cost reduction, service improvement, and more strategic views of IT service delivery are sought. The major activities in this phase included benchmarking performance, realigning the contract, and involving the supplier in value-added areas. Because of the history of working with the supplier, parties during the middle phase were typically comfortable changing hats from adversaries to cooperators to collaborators, depending on the task at hand. By the middle phase, the complexity of relationships had become second nature, although the relational climate depended on how the overall outsourcing arrangement was turning out.

Benchmarking Performance

Benchmarking is the practice of comparing a customer's IT performance against a reference group of similar organizations. In this phase, benchmarking is used as a tool to ensure that the supplier's cost and services are among the best of breed. Customers view benchmarking as a powerful tool to leverage their bargaining position with the supplier.

The major stakeholders involved in this activity were the *customer IT managers* and the *supplier account managers*. Customers wanted to use benchmarking to reduce prices or increase service levels under the fixed-fee umbrella. Suppliers wanted to use benchmarking to demonstrate that their performance was already superior and therefore prices need not be reduced. Thus, it is quite clear that stakeholder goals conflict. In addition, because benchmarks could result in resetting prices, the financial consequences of this activity could again result in millions of dollars, serving to add to the tension.

In general, benchmarking firms competently measure the cost and service of technical platforms, such as IBM mainframe data centers, UNIX midrange computing, or LAN performance. Customer and supplier participants both agree, however, that the benchmarking industry is immature in a number of areas, particularly desktop computing and applications development and support. A few customers, for example, used function points to measure application productivity and quality. But benchmarking results were contested by the supplier. Application productivity depends not only on the supplier's performance but also on the quality of the systems inherited from the customer. Overcustomized and jury-rigged legacy systems required a significant amount of supplier support. Is it fair to compare their performance against the productivity of application packages? A BAe contract manager noted:

> Our experience being honest is that I haven't been terribly happy with the benchmarking process. This is not happy for CSC nor BAe. It's just the process seems to be a little bit naive.

Despite the limitations of benchmarking, customers believe it is still a valuable tool because it provides at least some rational data on performance (see Lacity and Hirschheim [1995] for a detailed analysis).

Realigning the Contract

Customers frequently found that the original contract became obsolete as technology advanced, business requirements changed, and false assumptions became illuminated. Technology changes included a shift from mainframe computing to client/server, deregulation of the telecommunications industry, and the emergence of new technologies such as the Internet and enterprisewide systems (such as SAP). Business requirement changes were prompted by government regulations (such as the self-assessment project at Inland Revenue), acquisitions, mergers, and divestitures. Illuminated false assumptions included poor estimates of baseline services, volumes, and costs. In addition, original contract mechanisms designed for one purpose may be operationalized in unintended ways. Some customers capped supplier margins, such as awarding the supplier a set markup on new capital IT investments, which actually motivated supplier underperformance in practice: The more the technology cost, the more the supplier earned.

A number of participants claimed that contracts could not be valid for a period of more than three years. After that, contracts had to be renegotiated. A director of IS planning for an energy company explained:

> The nature of this technology is volatile, that it was extremely difficult to predict for even two or three years, much less ten, with any degree of confidence. . . . And whether it's two years, three years, five years, you're increasingly going to see involvement in renegotiating to cover the kinds of technology situations that were unforeseeable when you struck the deal.

During a contract realignment, *customer IT managers* and *supplier account managers* were the most active stakeholders. Stakeholder goals were in conflict because each side is motivated to protect the interests of its own organizations. By this stage in the relationship, however, relationships have progressed beyond the tentativeness of original contract negotiations. The customer and supplier constituents had a history of working together, and both were committed to perpetuating the relationship. At BAe and Inland Revenue, both sides wanted to realign the contract to help set realistic expectations. Indeed, parties expect to go through a realignment exercise every few years, as a BAe general contract manager described:

> We've come to the conclusion that actually what we have is, and what we need to do intellectually, is come to terms with the contract itself. [It] has to be a much more dynamic, moving, changing thing, rather than a set-in-stone thing. And without wishing

to change the past, we've jointly been working to realign the mechanisms so that they produce results which are more in keeping with what we went after. But the important factor is that we anticipate to do the same thing again in two to three years time. And then two to three years after that, we will do the same thing again. Not because we got it wrong, but because the change in technologies and changing user requirements.

Involving the Supplier in Value-Added Areas

The primary focus of the transition phase was to establish operational performance. From the number of transition activities discussed in the previous phase, it was quite apparent that customers and suppliers devote all their time and resources to making the IT service work. Once transition tasks have been accomplished, customer and supplier stakeholders alike sought ways to extend the relationship into more value-added areas. Indeed, one of the nine core IT capabilities discussed in Willcocks et al. (1997) is this "vendor development" role in which the "value added" may include cooperative relationships or collaborative relationships, depending on whether goals are complementary or shared. Value-added areas included the following:

- Supplier participation on steering committees. The idea was to include an IT perspective on business initiatives and strategies.
- Selling customer IT assets and jointly sharing profits. We only have a few limited examples of this activity, such as a supplier selling a customer's data models at a U.K. retailer.
- Supplier participation on business processing reengineering projects. Again, we only have a few examples of this value added, such as reengineering the invoicing process at U.K. Inland Revenue.

The search for value added continues to be a goal—albeit an elusive one—among participants. While everyone was talking about "value added," few had actually achieved it. The following quotations express these sentiments:

> Value-added, it's one of the goals. It's value adding but has to be done on both sides. CSC has to turn a profit and has to allow BAe to turn a profit. If you were signing up a partner, you wouldn't want your partner to lose money. You want your partner to be successful. So I think the value-added term is used with the implicit understanding that that implies that CSC is also prospering to some level.—CSC account executive

> One of the things that the customers seem most disappointed in is that they looked at these kind of suppliers as "you understand the future of IT and what its capabilities are and harnessing IT for the business value." And from that perspective, they seem to be disappointed that now everything is very technical—how many LANs, WANs, desktops, etc.... They complain that the contract is getting in the way. And I think the contract is getting in the way of that kind of vision. We took IT strategy right out of the contract.—Consultant, South Australia government

PHASE 6: THE MATURE PHASE—CUSTOMER GOAL: "DETERMINE AND PLAN FOR THE FATE OF CURRENT SOURCING OPTIONS"

During the mature phase, the customer's goal is first to ensure continued operational performance if the relationship is not to be renewed. When relationships are extended, the mature phase provides an opportunity to learn from past experiences as well as to explore creative options when constructing a new deal. Assessment of these options depends as much on business strategic concerns and the nature of the current and future competitive climate as on the strength of relationships and past value of the outsourcing arrangement. Although only a few of our long-term deals have reached this stage, two activities were apparent.

Recalibrate Investment Criteria

When suppliers make IT investments on behalf of a customer, the supplier needs time to recoup the investment. As the contract reaches the expiration date, reinvestment becomes a major issue. The suppliers will not want to invest in new capital assets if the customer decides not to extend the relationship. At Inland Revenue, for example, both sides must make sure that EDS has an opportunity to gain a return on investment as the contract matures. An IR account manager commented:

> Unless we can some way manage a revenue stream for them beyond the contract, that's going to be increasingly difficult if we are asking them for investment. We are both jointly aware that that's a real difficulty for us. We've got to re-explore how we are going to cope with that. Otherwise we are going to stultify entirely as we get closer and closer to the end of the contract.

Determine Whether Relationship Will Be Extended or Terminated

Some participants were so concerned about what happens at the end of contracts that they avoided outsourcing altogether. The corporate manager of planning and administration for a petroleum company explained:

> Another concern that we had was that if we did a five year deal say, what happens at the end of the five years? If we don't get along well, or we want it back and we had transferred the people, then we are in a real bad situation.

But are customers in a bad position? In general, three options are possible: (1) extend the contract with current supplier(s), (2) switch supplier(s), or (3) bring the IT activity back in-house. Our CIO survey data also show that all three options are commonly practiced in the U.S. and U.K. markets: 51% switched supplier, 34% brought the activity back in-house, and 11% renewed the original contract (according to other 1999 surveys, mainland European organizations show much less propensity to change supplier or bring IT back in-house at the end of contracts). On termination of agreements in 1998, BP Exploration successfully renewed some contracts, reduced others, and brought in a new supplier. We have examples of all three options from our case studies. In no situation were the consequences devastating—indeed, all three options can be executed without serious disruption in service as long as customers plan for events well in advance.

DIRECTIONS FOR RESEARCH

This chapter has provided an overview of research findings within an organizing framework of relationships and their management across six phases of any IT outsourcing arrangement. It is clear that we already know a great deal about certain aspects of the outsourcing phenomenon. Research has been particularly strong in applying and assessing the usefulness of transaction cost analyses to various IT sourcing options (see, for example, Ang and Straub [1998] and Lacity and Willcocks [1996]). Less work has been done on the applicability of other theoretical frameworks, such as contingency theories, game theory, investment option theory, and the role of knowledge sourcing, whose importance is implied by the chapter in this volume by Alavi, and is discussed in detail by Scarbrough (1998). The need for further theoretical development and testing it empirically remain as significant academic tasks, especially in the light of our findings on the limited usefulness of transaction cost economics to understanding and explaining IT sourcing phenomena.

The urgency of this agenda for theory building is underlined by the fact that IT outsourcing has outlived the five-year lifetime of a management fad. Many organizations are working through into permanent changes in the ways in which they are organized and managed. We estimate that by 2003 in the developed economies, on average 30 to 35% of most organizations' IT budgets will be under third-party management. In light of these developments, continued empirical analyses and longitudinal case study research remain imperative. Much research has already been conducted on making IT sourcing decisions: What can be outsourced and what cannot; how vendor bids are assessed, contracts constructed, assessment regimes operated and needed before and after contracts are signed; and what practices make for success and failure. However, in changing circumstances, ongoing research on a case and survey basis needs to continue to be conducted in different sectors and economies on these already-established themes, not the least because cultural factors in different countries and organizations have been underrated as influencing factors.

Past research has neglected several other themes that we see emerging as critical. One theme is more exploration of suppliers, their strategies and capabilities, and the changing nature of the vendor marketplace. An early paper by Michell and Fitzgerald (1997) leads the way, but much more needs to be understood as the IT service marketplace and its players dynamically evolve. A second, strangely neglected area has been in-depth theorizing and analysis of relationship dimensions in IT outsourcing, despite the fact that students and stakeholders of outsourcing invariably assign key importance to relationship characteristics and issues, and despite the existence of extensive work on these themes in marketing, organizational theory, strategy, and economics. Kern (1999) has done the lead research so far in this area in developing and convincingly applying a relationship framework to illuminate issues in total and selective IT outsourcing arrangements. The work is further developed in Kern and Willcocks (2000), but much more still needs to be done in this area.

Since about 1995 there has been an ongoing debate, fed by many emerging practices, that focuses on effective ways of utilizing external IT services. Some, like McFarlan and Nolan (1995), have argued for strategic alliances through long-term deals, usually with single suppliers while recognizing the risks of such an approach, and the need for devices such as equity shares in each other, selling jointly developed products/services on the external market, and/or payment on business results, to secure the relationship. In 1995 many such deals and emerging practices were in their early phases. Additional longitudinal research can now be carried out to find out whether such arrangements, or indeed more selective approaches, did prove effective and how they could be improved on. As one example, Davis (1996) found the Xerox–EDS deal to be almost an exemplar of how strategic partnering can be achieved. However, the deal was signed only in 1994. Kern (1999) revisited the deal and found that it had been radically restructured subsequently on the basis of some significant issues and disappointments and that there was much less certainty, in retrospect, that a single supplier, long-term total outsourcing arrangement was the most effective option. The use of our six-phase model, or a variant thereon, may well prove a useful tool for pursuing such longitudinal research.

In IT outsourcing, a perennial judgment to be made, and revisited, as to which IT assets, activities, and skills are core, critical, and differentiating, and which are commodity (Lacity, Willcocks, & Feeny, 1995, 1996). We have found organizations running regularly into a number of difficulties in making such assessments, not least because much depends on circumstances, the business an organization is in, the technologies being used and newly adopted, and how dynamic these factors reveal themselves to be. In our view, the continuing study of these circumstances and decisions will produce dividends for academics and practitioners alike. The additional study of what might be called "backsourcing" will add another intriguing dimension to and illumination of such a judgment area. Why would organizations backsource, that is take back in-house assets, activities, and skills previously outsourced? And should backsourcing be total or selective? What criteria could be used for making such judgments? Our own studies have already provided examples of both total backsourcing, for example, the cancellation in late 1997 by U.K.-based retailer Sears of a 1996, £344 million 10-year deal with a single supplier. More frequent has been incremental backsourcing. For example, when Australian-based financial services giant MLC renegotiated its outsourcing deal with a single supplier in 1998, it also arranged to bring back in-house the management of its application development and maintenance. In such examples, organizations reveal that circumstances have changed and that what was previously commodity is now differentiating in character or that the outsourcing experience has shown that the original assessment was flawed in some ways and that some degree of corrective backsourcing needs to take place. Feeny and Willcocks (1998) found this phenomenon particularly prevalent in the IS human resource capabilities and skills area where organizations in practice have found it difficult to make accurate assessments of the requisite in-house capabilities needed to identify and deliver on business requirements and to retain control of IT destiny while managing external supply. In our estimation, future research needs to be conducted in these important and neglected areas.

At the same time, the degree to which changes in technology and the speed of such changes impact choices in, and the conduct of, IT sourcing has emerged as both significant and underestimated. John Cross, IT director of BP in 1998, said that in the course of the 1993–1998 deals with three suppliers, the organization went through two generations of technology. How organizations can source for such dynamic technological trajectories and how they can contract effectively with the IT services market are increasingly important academic and practitioner questions deserving in-depth research distinctive to the IT field.

Changes in technology can also be tied to a number of emerging practices that are increasingly worth studying. According to some estimates, business process outsourcing, with IT embodied in the process—already current in areas such as billing, accounting, and check processing—will be the leading growth market, set to reach US$16 billion in 2002. Increasingly, application service providers such as Oracle, SAP, and Baan are offering Web-based remotely hosted enterprise software services that can stretch from provision to software management, while companies such as Compaq offer "future sourcing"—installing and running new systems while not straying into the strategy and policy areas of the client. Other suppliers, such as

IBM and EDS, have picked up on the staff shortages and rapid speed needed to build e-business capability and to offer to source e-business projects, both in technology and sometimes business planning areas. For similar reasons, some organizations have also moved into technology partnering with suppliers in order to source IT development and provision. One example is the joint venture by Bank of Scotland and the FI Group in the United Kingdom. Here a separate entity, First Banking Systems, has 310 bank staff and 120 FI staff; with a $US220 million budget over five years, it will provide commercial software development and IT systems planning and architecture for the bank. Conversely, in some cases IT services have become, over time, such a standardized commodity in a specific sector that, for example, a company such as Andersen Consulting can provide accounting services on a shared service basis to seven oil companies—an example of client companies cooperating over aspects of IT supply to compete more effectively in other, less-commodified areas. Such new developments or in some cases reapplications of old practices are innovative ways of attempting to leverage the uses of the external services market for business advantage in the face of changes in technology or in their business value. In our view, as such developments and their accompanying practices grow, they too will increasingly require further study.

CONCLUSIONS

Many interorganizational relationship perspectives consider the customer and supplier as the only relevant stakeholders. Our research has found this duality to be very oversimplified. To fill the gap in the literature, this chapter focused on the dynamic relationships among at least eight distinct types of stakeholder. Furthermore, while much prior research has focused on making sourcing decisions, little academic work has addressed in detail postcontract management transition as well as middle and mature phases—in our opinion, still a potentially highly productive research area. By understanding the common postcontract management activities and the inherent stakeholder goals and relationships during these activities, customers and suppliers can better plan and manage their contracts.

By attending to the expectations and goals of many IT outsourcing stakeholders, apparent anomalies in relationships are understood. Why, for example, do customer contract managers and supplier account managers *collaborate* to mediate IT user expectations and then feel perfectly comfortable *fighting over* a monthly bill? Quite simply, *the dynamics of stakeholder relationships vary with the task*. We do note, however, one caveat about stereotyping stakeholders. Our stakeholder analysis described the general goals and perceptions of stakeholder members. Although generalizations are an effective tool for summarizing common experiences, they ignore the role of individual personalities in the success of customer/supplier relationships. In several instances, stakeholder relationships improved when the person was replaced. Customer and supplier account managers, in particular, had a high turnover rate in several of the mega-deals studied. The following participant quotes testify to the effectiveness of new faces:

> I think the major thing that's driven change in the relationship is the fact that there has been a change in the head of IT and there's been a change of CSC account executive. It just so happened that [the CSC Account Executive] and myself worked in another British Aerospace industry together which was much smaller with less problems

so that we were able to develop a good working relationship and we've brought that relationship to MAD.—BAe contract manager, MAD Division

At the beginning of this contract, we actually had to change both of the contract managers three months into the contract to get a more reasonable basis for the relationship because the two of them over the opening three months had continued the negotiations. They were locking horns day-in-day-out. We had to take both of those individuals out and try to recover that relationship. I think that's been successful.—account manager, public sector organization

I think it's unhealthy in any case to perpetuate the same relationships for too long, because you then know each other so well that you very rarely bring a new perspective onto things, a fresh pair of eyes with a new set of ideas.—BAe general contract manager

Thus, management relationship requires not only an understanding of stakeholder goals and expectations but also a human resource sensitivity as to the individuals who fill these roles.

ENDNOTES

1. See the chapter by Ross and Feeny in this volume for further insight into business and IT managerial perceptions and roles.
2. A more detailed analysis appears in the chapter by Ang and Slaughter.
3. Of course, much will still depend on the extent of IT user training, following the logic set up by Olfman and Pitsatorn in their chapter.
4. Cooperative relationships become particularly significant where external suppliers are involved, as is frequently the case, in new software projects (see the Kirsch and George chapters) and in major change projects as exemplified by business process reengineering (see the chapter by Grover and Kettinger) and by ERP implementations (see the chapter by Markus and Tanis).
5. Such work must, of course, occur in the context of strategic business and IT considerations detailed in the chapter by Sabamurthy in this volume.
6. A detailed discussion of evaluation issues appears in the chapter by Barua and Mukhopadhyay. For a comprehensive review, including evaluation in IT outsourcing arrangements, see Willcocks and Lester, 1999.

Chapter 19

The Evolving Role of the CIO

Jeanne W. Ross and David F. Feeny

From humble beginnings in the back rooms of most large companies, information technology has emerged as a topic of considerable interest in many, if not most, corporate boardrooms. In 1999 executive teams were reviewing their companies' progress toward Y2K compliance; directing often massive IT infrastructure investments, such as ERP systems and pervasive intranets; and speculating about potential impacts of their own Internet and e-commerce initiatives as well as those of new information age competitors. Over the years executive teams have experienced a high degree of discomfort in these discussions of IT-related topics. Consequently, the functional IT head has often been on the "hot seat" to address persistent concerns about the firm's ability to identify opportunities presented by new technologies, respond to those opportunities in a timely fashion, and achieve demonstrable benefits from IT investments.

As business dependence on IT—both operationally and strategically—has grown, the IT leader has increasingly gained acceptance as a member of the executive team. Since the mid-1980s, this individual has typically been labeled the chief information officer or CIO (Bock, Carpenter, & Ellen, 1986). But soon after this terminology came into use, the signs of distress began to appear. CIOs have struggled with noticeably short tenures (e.g., Rothfeder & Driscoll, 1990), a lack of credibility within the executive team, and problematic relationships with their CEOs (Feeny, Edward, & Simpson, 1992).

More recently, CIOs have felt the impact of the dramatic development of the IT services industry and increasingly computer-literate line managers. If all or most of IT activities are outsourced, what then is the role of the CIO (McFarlan & Nolan, 1995)? As line managers become comfortable assuming responsibility for their computing needs, do many of the CIO's responsibilities become redundant? Does the role of the CIO have a future or merely a problematic past? In this chapter we review the role of the CIO, taking a historical perspective on its evolution to better understand the potential sources of CIO value and its continuing relevance, and leading to further research questions that may help to illuminate the future of the role.

PROJECTING THE FUTURE THROUGH THE PAST: A MODEL OF THE CIO'S ROLE

Clearly, dramatic technological changes have transformed computing from a back-room utility to a strategic organizational resource. This transformation has led to many changes in the use and management of information technology, including the reach and range of the technologies (Keen, 1991), the requisite skills and qualifications of the users of information technologies,[1] the requisite skills and qualifications of IS professionals,[2] the impacts—real and intended—of the technologies,[3] and the amount of organizational spending on IT.

Changing technologies have also led to major changes in the responsibilities of the CIO. We would argue, however, that the effects of technology on the role of the CIO are not direct. Rather, the CIO's role has evolved through its interaction with three intermediate forces. Figure 19.1 depicts these forces in a model that we shall use to examine the evolution over time of the role of the CIO. It suggests that changes in the role are related to wider changes in (1) existing and planned applications of technology in the host organization, (2) attitudes of senior executives toward

FIGURE 19.1 Forces Influencing the CIO Role

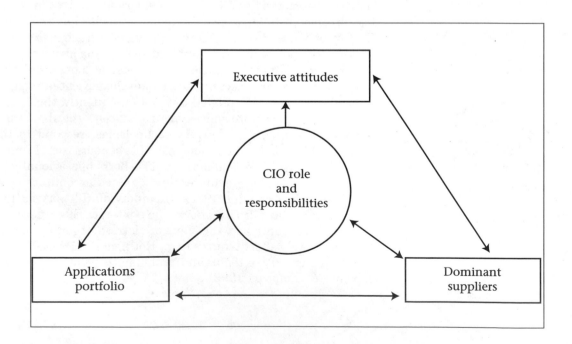

technology and its potential impacts and role, and (3) characteristics of the principal vendors who deliver and service the technologies.

First, an organization's actual and planned *applications portfolio* influences the role of the CIO by establishing the extent to which the organization's operations and strategy are dependent upon IT and the range of people within the business who are impacted by IT. Second, *business executives' attitudes* toward IT influence the role of the CIO by defining the level of investment available for IT and the organization's predisposition to apply IT strategically. Third, *dominant IT suppliers* influence the role of the CIO by determining the range of technological architectures and solutions that are perceived to be reliably available, as well as the quality and extent of external resources and services that can be acquired to substitute for or complement internal resources.

We also note that these three forces interact with one another. Business executive attitudes toward IT help to shape the existing and anticipated applications portfolio while the success (or otherwise) of that portfolio in action strongly influences the ongoing attitudes of the executives. The dominant suppliers of the day, because of their prominence, often gain access to senior business executives and use that access to further influence executive attitudes. Meanwhile, dominant suppliers become dominant by proactively influencing the applications portfolio of early-adopter businesses, generating a momentum that convinces additional businesses of the importance of investments in their products and services.

Clearly, the CIO is not a passive pawn at the mercy of three surrounding forces. On the contrary, successful CIOs influence their own roles in the organization and create further interactions among the elements of the model. We argue that CIOs influence their roles by addressing the forces we have identified: through relationship building and education, they influence the attitudes of key executives toward IT; by identifying and working with (both existing and emergent) dominant suppliers, they shape their vendors' offerings and thus the services and technologies available to their firms; by successfully managing and extending the applications portfolio, they directly influence the strategic impact of IT in their organizations.

Finally, we note that the model makes no specific mention of corporate strategy. We would argue that corporate strategy does have a pervasive impact on the role of the CIO but, like the technology itself, its impact is felt through the three intermediate forces. In particular, a firm's applications portfolio is a reflection of organizational strategic priorities. Similarly, executive attitudes toward IT investment and the status and role of the CIO define how the firm has decided to position itself to shape and enact strategy through IT. Finally, the offerings of dominant suppliers reflect vendors' perceptions of the aggregate strategic imperatives of their existing and potential customers.

We will use the model to examine the changing role of the CIO across three technological eras:

1. The *mainframe* era covering roughly the 1960s into the early 1980s, during which time IT was largely synonymous with mainframe computers.
2. The *distributed* era, starting at the end of the 1970s, during which corporate IT became characterized by integrated networks of workstation PCs, minicomputers, and mainframes connected through local and wide-area networks.
3. The *Web-based* era, starting for most in the mid-1990s, with a rapidly growing emphasis on the use of Internet and Web protocols to drive both internally and externally oriented applications of IT.

FIGURE 19.2   Major
Technical Eras

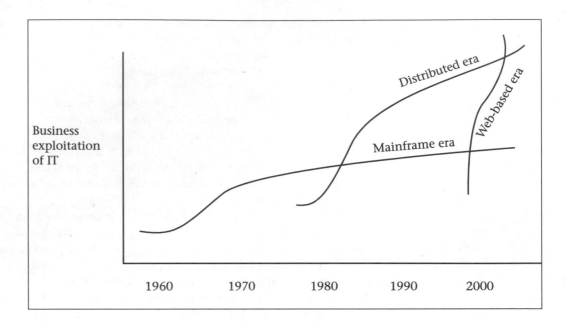

We distinguish between these eras because, as we shall demonstrate, there are clear discontinuities in the elements of our model as each new era becomes established. We can also chart more evolutionary change in the elements of the model as each era follows the *S*-shaped adoption curve first identified for the mainframe era by Gibson and Nolan (1974) and graphically illustrated in Figure 19.2. The eras are defined by major technological innovations, which provide vastly more powerful opportunities for business applications of IT than did earlier technologies. The impacts of the innovations are realized gradually as the technologies mature and organizations learn how to apply them. Taken together, Figures 19.1 and 19.2 provide the platform for analysis of the changing role of the CIO.

FORCES INFLUENCING THE ROLE OF THE CIO—THE MAINFRAME ERA

The introduction of mainframe computers into the back offices of business organizations in the late 1950s and 1960s represented the first application of computing to business. At the start of the mainframe era, firms recognized the potential of systems to cut time, cost, and human error from repetitive business tasks. Years later, computing had penetrated most functional areas, and the typical business had moved from pure cost-reduction objectives to recognizing the value of on-line data for organizational decision making (Gibson & Nolan, 1974). Along the way, the data processing department evolved into an information systems function (Rockart, Ball, & Bullen, 1982). Although "distributed" has long since supplanted "mainframe" as the dominant paradigm, mainframe computers still retain an important role in many large organizations' computing environments. Indeed, migrating from or managing the legacy systems created during the mainframe era still challenges many CIOs (and their host organizations).

MAINFRAME ERA—APPLICATIONS PORTFOLIO

The applications of the mainframe era started with the automation of clerical tasks. Over time, companies developed large-scale and highly efficient transaction-processing capabilities. In most cases, electronic data processing (EDP) started in the accounting function, simplifying general ledger entries and account reconciliation. Shortly thereafter, firms took on production planning and control tasks and began to make available on-line the data captured through their systems until ultimately mainframe computing touched most organizational activities in the order-to-delivery value chain of large organizations.

MAINFRAME ERA—EXECUTIVE ATTITUDES

Business executives experienced a common pattern of attitudes toward, and expectations for, information systems as the mainframe era evolved (Gibson & Nolan, 1974). Initially, they viewed EDP as an accounting tool. Then they became enthusiastic about the range of tasks that systems could support. Later they became concerned about the cost of ongoing operations and runaway systems projects. Because business executives during the mainframe era viewed electronic data processing as a cost-cutting tool, they typically based IS investment decisions on the expected ROI of new information systems. As they established information systems functions, business executives agonized over the gap between the information utopia they were promised and the reality of data labyrinths that they experienced (Ackoff, 1967; Zani, 1970; Rockart, 1979). Most often executives looked for an IS leader who could successfully manage large projects, contain IS costs, and respond effectively to their personal needs for information.

MAINFRAME ERA—DOMINANT SUPPLIERS

IBM was unquestionably the dominant supplier of computing products and services during the mainframe era. It sold and serviced the computers and accompanying operating systems. If the internal staff could not solve a technical problem, IBM could usually handle it for them. Through its System 360 series, IBM provided an evolutionary route for its customers to increase capacity and move to new technology while protecting their existing systems investment. It was easy for customers to grow with IBM and very difficult and expensive to move away from them. IBM became the safe choice. "Nobody gets fired for buying from IBM" became a familiar mantra. User emphasis on the need for high reliability in increasingly pervasive transaction-processing systems further reinforced a conservative approach to procurement. As a result, the DP managers of the day rarely engaged in appraising technology innovations from new entrants, preferring to wait for IBM to market more reliable industrial-strength versions. IBM was also perceived to be adept at using its high profile to gain access to corporate business executives, further enhancing its ability to set expectations and influence the pace of evolution.

MAINFRAME ERA—CIO ROLE AND RESPONSIBILITIES

From this discussion, we can see that, during the mainframe era, the *role* of the DP/IS manager—precursor of the CIO—was predominantly that of an operational manager (i.e., a delivery orientation). With the dominant supplier nearly dictating the pace and direction of applications portfolio development and procurement strategy, the key *tasks* demanded of the IS leader were to develop new systems to time and budget and to operate existing ones to a high level of reliability.

As the era evolved (Gibson & Nolan, 1974; Nolan, 1976), the IS leader became more visible and frequently more controversial, paralleling the evolution of systems development, implementation, and use in the organization. IS departments took on large projects with big budgets and high expectations. Accordingly, applications backlogs increased, high-profile projects often experienced runaway costs, and firms felt the impacts of operational service failures. Those experiences led to rapidly growing IS staffs, introducing issues of internal organization and personnel management. Negative systems experiences also resulted in increased scrutiny of IS departments using the types of service and financial management measures applied elsewhere in the firms. Increasingly, the IS leader and IS department were expected to understand and be responsive to the context and needs of the business.

But while the level of challenge was increasing throughout the era, the nature of the role remained essentially that of operational manager in a specialist domain. Not surprisingly, therefore, the *status* of the IS leader was that of senior or middle manager reporting to an established functional head—often the first applications champion—typically the chief financial officer or perhaps the director/vice president of operations.

Arguably the biggest evolutionary change during this era was in the skills and abilities sought in the IS leader (Ives & Olson, 1981). Increasingly, the emphasis moved from personal technical aptitude to effective management and communication abilities. Toward the end of the era, some companies had begun to appoint as IS leaders proven managers from elsewhere in the business. Their mandate was to instill in the IS function the necessary performance orientation, processes, and disciplines.

ROLE OF THE CIO—THE DISTRIBUTED ERA

By the early 1980s, the distributed era was becoming well established (Withington, 1980). Departmental minicomputers (often installed as a reaction to a lack of responsiveness in the IS function) had liberated the computer from the back room and invited more decentralized control over organizational computing (King, 1983). Personal computers began to proliferate rapidly on the desks of corporate staff, also commonly representing acts of independence from central IS control. However, as the era progressed, its evolution was influenced by three further developments:

1. Rapid developments in telecommunications technologies brought the potential to link the distributed pieces together in local and wide-area networks.
2. The client/server concept argued convincingly that the various elements of computing should be seen to have complementary rather than competing roles in a distributed network.
3. Business managers at all levels learned that direct business ownership and operation of computing did not result in cost-efficient or effective computing; IS professional skills—from either a coherent corporate IS organization or the rapidly growing external market for IS services—were required to manage an effective distributed network that supported organizationwide goals.

By the time the Web era had started to emerge, most firms had recentralized responsibility for a standardized and enterprisewide IT infrastructure.

DISTRIBUTED ERA—APPLICATIONS PORTFOLIO

At the start of the distributed era, business applications developed for minicomputers and personal computers were typically targeted at the needs of local knowledge workers. Consequently, distributed technologies initially resulted in "islands" of computing in organizations, and corporate needs were subjugated to the demands of local users (McKenney & McFarlan, 1982). Desktop computers exacerbated the tension between corporate and local needs as users experienced the responsiveness and flexibility provided by personal productivity software. However, the emergence of networking technologies and the reworking of applications and database software to operate in distributed environments led to a new emphasis on integration. Indeed, IT increasingly began to be perceived as a tool for enabling new levels of integration and collaboration across the functions of the business (Rockart & Short, 1989).

In the mid-1980s a series of influential articles (e.g., McFarlan, 1984; Porter & Millar, 1985) took the argument further. IT, it was suggested, was now a competitive weapon: By using technology to link activity across firm boundaries, companies such as American Airlines, American Hospital Supply/Baxter Travenol, and Merrill Lynch had changed the basis of competition to their own advantage. Other companies then strove to innovate with applications that linked to customers, distribution channels, or suppliers. Although few were seen to emulate the business success of the referenced exemplars, many had established systems that reached out along the supply chain by the end of the distributed era.

The theme of using IT as an agent of integration became evident in two other contexts. The first was globalization. As large corporations sought to coordinate more closely their international operations they made major investments in data networks to support EDI and electronic mail traffic, often subsuming the corporate voice communications network as well. The second, quite different, development was triggered by the idea of business process reengineering (Davenport & Short, 1990; Hammer & Champy, 1993). Rather than automate existing business processes that had been evolved within a functionally driven business structure, the firm should, it was argued, redesign its processes to take advantage of the capability of new technology.

Finally the applications portfolio of the distributed era was influenced by the emergence of packaged enterprise resource planning (ERP) systems. ERP offered the ultimate in systems integration: the seamless operation of all required transaction-processing systems across a distributed network. Frequently encouraged by the additional need to have systems that were Y2K (millennium) compliant, firms committed huge sums to ERP rollout in the later stages of the distributed era.[4]

DISTRIBUTED ERA—EXECUTIVE ATTITUDES

The espousal of IT as a new competitive weapon was a high-profile wake-up call for business executives. Not only did Porter—the most prominent business strategy guru of the day—add his imprimatur to the ideas of McFarlan and other information management academics, but also the practitioner press took up the call (e.g., *Business Week,* 1985). Increasingly, business executives began to demand the development of an IT strategy that was aligned to the strategy of the business. Globalization and business process reengineering were further boardroom-level topics that clearly had significant IT content. Later, the millennium bug issue served to highlight to executives the extent to which their businesses had become dependent on IT.

The mad rush to develop competitive advantage through IT led to burgeoning IT costs and tumbling systems reliability. The increasing importance to the business of a robust and coherent IT infrastructure often contrasted with the situation on the ground, where multiple technical architectures had come into use. Recessionary pressures reinforced the urgent need, in the minds of executives, for IT activities to be rationalized and IT costs to be brought under control and significantly reduced.

At the same time, executives were becoming aware of a seductively attractive new option—the outsourcing of IT activity. IT is not a core activity of this business, the argument ran; we should look to outsource it to a world-class supplier whose core business is IT. Leading IT outsourcing companies were happy to reinforce the argument with claims of substantial potential cost savings, typically on the order of 20 percent. The promise of ERP systems struck a further chord with many executives. Surely it made obvious economic sense to standardize on packaged software, millennium compliant and maintained for the future by the vendor, rather than allow further in-house reinvention of the necessary wheels. By the late 1990s, IT outsourcing and ERP systems were industry sectors worth tens of billions of dollars each (Lacity, Willcocks, & Feeney, 1996; Kirkpatrick, 1998).[5]

But as IT in various forms became a frequent topic for the boardroom, executives found that pursuing the new ideas was not straightforward. The idea that IT was a new competitive weapon—rather than a competitive necessity—was widely questioned (Warner, 1987; Kettinger et al., 1994; Mata, Fuerst, & Barney, 1995). Hammer and Champy's (1993) warning that the failure rate of business process reengineering might be as high as 70 percent was echoed elsewhere (Moad, 1993). Various authors challenged whether wholesale and simplistic IT outsourcing contracts were viable (Lacity & Hirschheim, 1993; Lacity et al., 1996; Earl, 1996). The real business benefits of massive ERP projects began to come into question (Feeny & McMullen, 1999). By the mid-1990s, it was suggested (Earl & Feeny, 1994) that executive attitudes toward IT had become polarized in the distributed era. While some senior management teams viewed IT as an asset that could transform the organization, others viewed it as a liability with uncertain benefits and high costs. Consequently, some firms invested in the development of highly competent IT organizations (Clark et al., 1997; Earl & Sampler, 1998), while others slashed IT investment spending or outsourced the entire function to save money (Huber, 1993).

DISTRIBUTED ERA—DOMINANT SUPPLIERS

As individuals in organizations gained computing power through distributed technologies, organizations lost IBM as the guardian of their computing environments. The dominance of IBM was dispersed across a wide variety of suppliers. Microsoft and Intel emerged as the first influential suppliers of the era as they created a demand for desktop computing products by addressing the demands of individuals, who learned to expect powerful, flexible technologies on their desktops. Concurrently, individual users learned to live with the idiosyncrasies of new technologies. They substituted a demand for "bulletproof" systems upon implementation with a demand for responsive support organizations and continuous improvement in the postimplementation stage. As firms developed corporate IT architectures, they almost invariably featured products of the so-called Wintel alliance.

Another important group of suppliers built the IT outsourcing industry. Firms such as EDS, Andersen Consulting, CSC, and IBM sold economies of scale and service expertise to firms that viewed their IT functions as commodities rather than unique business competencies. The major outsourcers were particularly aggressive in approaching the business executive team directly with offers that were hard to refuse. As a result, a number of multibillion-dollar deals involved the outsourcing of the entire IT function. Over time, however, most firms elected to selectively outsource specific IT activities (Lacity et al., 1996).

The final rise to prominence featured the software development firms—such as SAP, PeopleSoft, and Oracle—that built enterprise resource planning packages. While these software package providers allowed firms to outsource primary responsibility for transaction-processing systems development and maintenance, major consulting firms assumed a major role in systems implementation. Most noticeably the so-called Big 5 firms, who had long had access to the boardroom through their accounting activities, became involved first in BPR initiatives and then ERP projects. External providers were substituting their services for more and more of the in-house unit's traditional activities.

DISTRIBUTED ERA—CIO ROLE AND RESPONSIBILITIES

With all of these changes in the elements of our model, it is not surprising that CIOs experienced difficult and turbulent times in the distributed era. After the relative stability of the mainframe era, CIOs had to learn and master multiple *roles* to survive and prosper. Earl and Feeny (1994), Ross, Beath, and Goodhue (1996), and Rockart, Earl, and Ross (1996) provide examples of the pressures and imperatives that CIOs faced. We can capture the essence of their findings by identifying and discussing in turn four CIO roles for the distributed era: organizational designer, strategic partner, technology architect, and informed buyer.

In the *role* of organizational designer, the CIO had to devise and continuously adapt an IT organization that responded to the business-side realities of the distributed era. Generally, this meant the creation of a "federal" IT structure (Rockart et al., 1996; Sambamurthy & Zmud, 1999) in which a central IT unit shared responsibilities for IT with IT units that were located within business units and commonly had a dotted-line relationship with the CIO. The *tasks* required to fulfill this role included clearly delineating responsibilities between central and distributed units. This involved the management of a broad and dynamic array of coordinating mechanisms (Brown & Sambamurthy, 1998). At the same time, the CIO was responsible for recruiting and developing a professional staff that was both technically proficient and business oriented. Even as the selective use of IT outsourcing grew, the CIO had to ensure that the firm retained the capability to exploit the changing technology (Ross et al., 1996; Feeny & Willcocks, 1998).

The objective of the CIO's *role* as strategic partner was to achieve strategic alignment between business and technology (Rockart et al., 1996). Key *tasks* within this role were twofold. On the one hand, CIOs engaged in persistent efforts to educate business management about the opportunities presented by information technologies. On the other hand, CIOs focused IT resources on solving business problems and identifying business opportunities (Earl & Feeny, 1994). These tasks demanded a continuous investment in relationship building with business executives (Henderson, 1990). In fact, studies of the activities of CIOs (Stephens et al., 1992; Applegate & Elam, 1992) indicated that they spent much more of their time outside the IT function compared to their mainframe era predecessors (Ives & Olson, 1981).

Shorn of the mainframe era's IBM security blanket, the CIO had to support corporatewide computing requirements even as much development and operations activity became dispersed. Accordingly, the CIO's operational responsibilities expanded beyond those of the previous era and evolved into a technology architect *role* (Ross et al., 1996; Rockart et al., 1996). *Tasks* included first scanning emerging technologies to identify existing and future capabilities. The technical architect was also responsible for designing a corporate IT architecture that satisfied firmwide computing needs and then persuading IT and business management of the necessity to adopt consequent technical standards. Finally, in the role of technology architect, the CIO was responsible for achieving high service levels across what were invariably highly complex platforms involving multiple vendors. Whether or not they used external service providers to resource some or all of these *tasks,* the CIOs' personal credibility was critically affected by the track record established in this role (Earl & Feeny, 1994).

Finally, a shrewd CIO mastered the *role* of informed buyer to strategically deploy external resources in a manner that maximized the effectiveness of internal resources and lowered organizational costs. The *tasks* involved proactively scanning the developing IT services market; analyzing how IT activity could be successfully disaggregated and appropriately contracted; building relationships with chosen suppliers; and monitoring service provided against both the contractual requirements and the developing capability of the marketplace (Lacity et al., 1996; Feeny & Willcocks, 1998). CIOs such as BP's Cross deliberately made intensive use of the service marketplace to reorient remaining in-house IT resources in support of the strategic partner role (Earl & Sampler, 1998).

CIOs who mastered all four of these roles came to enjoy the status of executive team member during the distributed era. Whether or not they reported directly, they enjoyed excellent relationships with their CEO and indeed often achieved a special relationship (Feeny et al., 1992; McKenney, 1995). In achieving such status (many did not), the single most important role seemed to be that of strategic partner, the person who could successfully provide the CEO and other executives with an understanding of the role of IT within a future business vision. CIOs who convincingly fulfilled this role were forgiven relative weaknesses in other roles (Feeny et al., 1992), provided they built a strong team of subordinates. Rockart et al. (1996) suggested that it would become increasingly common for CIOs to create the position of chief network officer (CNO) to focus on the roles we have labeled *technology architect* and *informed buyer.*

Consequently, the most important personal *skills* for CIOs in the distributed era can be seen as those required for relationship building and for strategic and organizational development. Earl and Feeny (1994) stressed the importance of consultative/facilitation/communication skills together with an orientation toward goals, ideas, and systems thinking. In their experience, the most successful practitioners had emerged from predominantly IT backgrounds, like the "maestros" chronicled by McKenney (1995). But Applegate and Elam (1992) noted that new CIO appointees commonly had mainly business or hybrid (business and IT) experience. And one large-scale empirical study (Armstrong & Sambamurthy, 1996) concluded that the extent of the firm's IT deployment was positively associated with CIOs who had both IT and business knowledge, as perceived by other members of the business executive team. Whatever their career record, it seemed clear that successful CIOs had to demonstrate a strong business orientation and understanding as well as a mastery of the fundamentals and directions of IT.

THE WEB-BASED ERA

The Web-based era began with the commercial introduction of the public Internet in the early 1990s. The evolution of the Internet introduced concepts such as e-commerce and e-business and a flurry of activity within existing organizations to try to understand the implications of the Internet for their business.[6] Because the Internet was fundamentally an information technology with enormous strategic implications, its importance firmly cemented the link between IT and business strategy. As CEOs proclaimed that their businesses had embraced e-commerce, IT could be seen to be influencing corporate strategy (or at least the discussions of it) to an unprecedented degree.

Technologically, the distinction between the distributed era and the Web-based era is that networks in the distributed era were centrally designed around a vendor's protocols to link internal machines. Networks in the Web-based era use the public Internet protocol standard (TCP/IP), which allows rapid growth in internal and external links and at much lower costs. But the felt difference between the distributed and Web-based eras is that senior management's earlier concern for aligning IT with business strategy shifted to a concern for aligning business strategy with the opportunities presented by new technologies better or faster than their competitors.[7] As we write this, the Web-based era is very young, and it is not clear how it will evolve, but some early developments allow us to speculate on how the Web-based era may affect the role of the CIO.

WEB-BASED ERA—APPLICATIONS PORTFOLIO

The development of Internet, extranet, and intranet applications has implications for the customer interface, for the supply chain, and for intraorganizational communications. While the longer-term expectations are that the Internet will drive new organizational models (Venkatraman & Henderson, 1998),[8] the early impacts are dramatic for just a handful of organizations. New Internet firms—the darlings of investors—that substitute electronic exchange for brick-and-mortar facilities have emerged. Meanwhile, existing firms have more often extended existing business models to incorporate an electronic customer interface, but they are increasingly recognizing the opportunity to offer value-added services to customers at low cost across the Web.

Initial intranet applications have focused on general organizational communications. These could have useful implications for strengthening individuals' sense of belonging and their general awareness of organizational policies and services, but they are hard to view as strategic developments. Over time, intranet applications are expected to allow significant changes in the infrastructures used to share data across business units and to standardize business processes. The communications they foster will facilitate new, more virtual organizational designs (Venkatraman & Henderson, 1998). In addition, intranets have the potential to support the knowledge management initiatives that are already at the core of corporate strategies in companies such as BP (Prokesch, 1997).[9]

Extranet applications have, in many cases, represented marginally revised electronic data interchange (EDI) applications. These, too, however, offer the potential for new and more sophisticated linkages with larger numbers of suppliers, designers, customers, and alliance partners. At GE, a purchasing extranet has allowed the firm to relax its policy of working with a limited number of suppliers in order to minimize procurement management costs. Now GE uses the extranet to display its needs to an expanded supplier base in perpetual competition with one another (Meyer, 1999). Web-based technology is also being used to support the alternate procurement philosophy of ever-closer collaboration with supplier-partners to achieve reduced time to market for new products or the build-to-the-customer-order approach of companies such as Dell.

WEB-BASED ERA—EXECUTIVE ATTITUDES

While many executives were cynical about the "competitive advantage" applications of the 1980s, the idea of new Web-based opportunities has attracted universal attention in boardrooms. The hype around Internet start-up firms and the publicity given to Web applications of existing firms suggest that executives who do not move quickly may be putting their firms at risk (Hamel & Sampler, 1998). At the very least, CIOs are the individuals to whom executives look to ensure they have the necessary IT infrastructure in place to support e-commerce initiatives. Most often CIOs are also expected to help senior executives understand the opportunities and the business implications of competitors' e-commerce initiatives.

A second important factor for CIOs is that executives seem to have changed, at least temporarily, their attitudes toward investment appraisal. Given the rhetoric of Internet time, more emphasis is being placed on urgent pursuit of promising application ideas than on the traditional and lengthy development of detailed cost-benefit cases. Furthermore, the investment required to pilot new ideas and the time required for application development are seen to be dramatically lower than in previous eras. In the minds of executives, IT-based initiatives are at last demonstrating the favorable characteristics of low cost, short time scales, and potentially high rewards.

WEB-BASED ERA—DOMINANT SUPPLIERS

The fortunes of vendors in the Web-based era seem likely to rise and fall as readily as Internet start-up firms. Network systems and equipment providers such as Sun, Cisco, and 3Com seem to have secure commercial positions as providers of critical components, but there is little evidence that they are influencing the strategic thinking of their corporate customers. Companies that provide technologies such as browsers, portals, and search engines offer important support to firms that are forging ahead in Web-based applications, but it is unclear whether they are establishing positions of lasting influence and bargaining power. Most likely, the important dominance will belong to whichever of the many large suppliers now "betting their future on e-business" proves the most effective. The list includes what traditionally were hardware or software companies such as IBM, Hewlett Packard, Microsoft, Oracle; the big service companies such as EDS and CSC; and the major consulting companies, including PricewaterhouseCooper and Andersen. Uncertainty currently abounds.

WEB-BASED ERA—CIO ROLE AND RESPONSIBILITIES

We saw in the distributed era how three elements of our model each presented considerable difficulties for CIOs, and their fortunes varied as a result. Earl and Feeny (1994) argued that the CIO was personally instrumental in determining whether the host organization positioned IT as a liability or a strategic asset. In the early years of the Web-based era, we see these same three model elements in a much more favorable light: Executives are in listening mode, looking for ideas; there is almost unlimited scope for new applications, and it is relatively straightforward to build them quickly and securely; and suppliers are desperately keen to help, and hence secure their own position in the new era. How then will the *role* of the CIO evolve? A number of scenarios seem possible.

One clear possibility is that the CIO will take increasing responsibility for defining an organization's strategic future—as the networker, who has an unrivaled understanding of the ideas that are being deployed throughout the organization and even outside its boundaries; as the strategic thinker, who leads the executive team in developing a business vision that captures the opportunities presented by IT; and perhaps even as the entrepreneur who line manages the market introduction of new business initiatives. The CIO surely has a better opportunity than ever before to influence the organization at the highest level.

If CIOs are not able to step up to these roles, the roles presumably will be distributed among other executives. There will still be a need for someone to play the roles of technology architect and informed buyer. But this scenario implies that the CIO essentially becomes the CNO described earlier, a valued member of the organization but a senior operating manager rather than a member of the top executive team. Alternatively, the CIO might migrate to another specialist role such as chief knowledge officer, or CKO (Earl & Scott, 1999), as the various strands of the full CIO role unravel.

In a third scenario, greater interest in IT-related issues across the organization, greater availability of external expertise, and minimal enthusiasm for centrally managed IT lead to the rebirth of decentralized IT. In this scenario, communications, networking, data, information, and knowledge initiatives spring up throughout the organization, and responsibility for managing both the initiative and the underlying technology rests with the interested business. This arrangement is likely to result in pockets of innovation and excellence. Experience from the distributed era, however, has taught that this governance arrangement typically results in a high-cost, unreliable infrastructure, as well as difficulty responding to strategic imperatives. Thus, we anticipate that a lack of strong corporate IT leadership during the Web-based era will invariably lead to disillusionment with IT.

To avoid the third scenario and to maximize the chances of the first, we see CIOs having to pay particular attention to a number of tasks. First, the CIO needs to persuade all concerned that the Web-based era is more about fundamental business change than about technology. Technology is now the easy bit, relatively speaking (especially if the CIO has built a competent IT management team). The challenge is to think through new business models that address concerns about cost structures, pricing, and channel conflict and to introduce new management processes that leverage the intranet. Vision and holistic thinking rather than technology rollout are the key requirements.

Second, the CIO will need to argue for a greater measure of central coordination. In the Web-based era, the corporation will be more directly visible to stakeholders of all varieties. As they access Web sites, these stakeholders should experience a consistent and coherent picture of a purposeful company, but they may instead view a smorgasbord resulting from a myriad of individual initiatives.

Third, the CIO must work with executive colleagues to define and implement approval processes appropriate to the Web-based era. There has always been a temptation to do the many things that technology allows. Now it allows many more things than ever before. A financial analysis filter is unlikely to sort the wheat from the chaff. More likely, all proposals must be ruthlessly assessed for their relevance to a small number of corporate strategic directions.

Through particular attention to these tasks, we would expect the CIO to emerge with the *status* of leading member of the executive team—increasingly an obvious candidate for a future CEO position. The *skills* CIOs will need most seem to be those we have already rehearsed in the discussion of the distributed era: the skills of relationship building across an even wider base of stakeholders and of strategic and organizational development in now more innovative and far-reaching directions. Although the Web-based era represents a revolution in technology, for the ambitious CIO it may feel more like an evolution—with the benefit of a trailing wind!

SYNTHESIS OF THE EVOLUTION OF THE CIO ROLE

Table 19.1 brings together the highlights of our discussion of each of the three eras and positions us to overview the evolution of the CIO role. As the table shows, we see the CIO role changing from functional manager to (potentially) business visionary as the firm evolves from the mainframe to the Web-based era. However, this should be seen as a growth process. Clearly, the CIO who has become successfully established as an executive team member in the distributed era is far more likely to become a business visionary than one who has not. To illustrate this idea, we can adapt a model first proposed by Hirschheim et al. (1988) and subsequently developed by Feeny (1997) as a result of a longitudinal study of 10 leading CIOs. Figure 19.3 shows our adapted version. It depicts growth in CIO credibility and status through three stages as a function of organizational learning.

In the first of the three stages, the CIO is a functional head with responsibility to deliver on promises. The promises involve developing new systems to time and budget; achieving the ROI expected when the investment was approved; and operating the portfolio of developed systems to the agreed service levels and satisfaction of the user community. The success (or otherwise) of the CIO's track record for delivering on these promises determines the initial credibility of the CIO and the CIO's ability to convince executive management of the appropriateness of further investment in IT. At the same time, successful organizational experience with each new system supports the organizational learning of both how to apply technology and how to recognize its value.

The credibility generated in the first stage is a prerequisite for progressing to the second stage. In this stage, we have emphasized the CIO's position as strategic partner, recognizing the suggestion of Henderson (1990) that CIOs should view their roles as being akin to a strategic partnership with the business. The key task is to align, and be seen to align, investments in IT with strategic business priorities. This involves designing and developing a complex IT organization that can address immediate business needs while building an infrastructure that supports ongoing needs as well. Success in this stage further promotes CIO credibility and organizational learning about IT. In particular, it brings the realization that IT can be integral to new ways of organizing and doing business. The approach to evaluating IT investment also begins to change as it becomes obvious that the contribution of IT cannot be meaningfully separated from the wider impacts of the strategic initiatives in which that investment is embedded.

TABLE 19.1   The CIO Role and Its Driving Forces

	Mainframe Era	Distributed Era	Web-Based Era
Applications portfolio	Transaction processing from order through delivery	Knowledge worker support; interorganizational systems; process reengineering; ERP systems	Electronic commerce; knowledge management; virtual organization and supply chain reengineering
Executive attitudes	IT for cost displacement and automation; from enthusiasm to cost consciousness	Increased involvement in IT issues and governance; polarization of attitudes: IT as strategic asset or cost to be minimized	IT, particularly the Internet, viewed as transformational, a driver of strategy; IT investments now more attractive in terms of costs and time scales
Dominant suppliers	IBM	Desktop providers—Microsoft, Intel; ERP software providers—SAP, Oracle; outsourcing companies—EDS, Andersen, CSC, IBM	Network product firms—Sun, Cisco, 3Com; browser/portal/search engine providers? E-business consulting and service companies
CIO role and responsibilities	*Role:* Operational manager of specialist function *Tasks:* On-time delivery; reliable operations	*Role:* Executive team member; organizational designer; strategic partner; technology architect; informed buyer *Tasks:* Manage federal IT organization; recruit and develop staff; educate line management; align IT with business; design corporate architecture; scan technologies; stabilize and standardize infrastructure; scan services market; develop alliances with key vendors	*Role:* Business visionary? *Tasks:* Develop new business models for the Internet; introduce management processes that leverage the intranet

FIGURE 19.3   The Evolution of the CIO Role

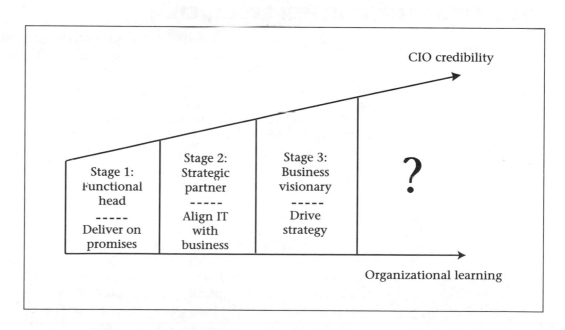

This paves the way for the third stage, in which the CIO potentially becomes a more proactive business visionary. In this stage, the CIO begins to be one of the main drivers of strategy by recognizing the emerging capabilities and applications of information technology and arguing their significance to the business.

For some organizations, the three stages of the model will align with the three technological eras. However, the model's potential power is to highlight two crucial points. Firstly, organizations and their CIOs do not automatically progress through the three stages as technology changes. In any of the technological eras, it is possible to identify organizations and CIOs in each stage of the model. The eras determine the forces with which the CIO has to contend, not the organizational learning achieved in any specific company.

Secondly, the stages of the model define growth, not substitution in the CIO's role. A CIO in stage 3 is still held responsible for delivering on promises and for aligning IT with business strategy as well as developing the business vision.[10] The means of achieving the imperatives of stages 1 and 2 may have now changed, but imperatives they remain. It is therefore possible for CIOs to regress rather than progress through the stages of the model. Earl (1996) and Feeny (1997) provide instances of such regression in which CIOs were fired or pitched back from stage 2 to stage 1 due to high-profile systems delivery failures or the arrival of new CEOs with different attitudes.

We suggest that the variability in CIO roles, CIO credibility, and organizational learning about IT are far greater than the variability in the positioning of firms within each of the technological eras. This is so because firms are generally pushed into subsequent technological eras, whereas changes in the role and attitudes of management can evolve more slowly. Clearly, however, the model suggests that firms that are attempting to function in the Web-based era with a CIO who is positioned as a stage 1 functional manager risk a troublesome mismatch.

QUESTIONS FOR FURTHER RESEARCH

Research questions associated with the role and responsibilities of the CIO can first be reviewed by reference to debates arising in each of the technological eras. For example, in the mainframe era, questions arose about the background, skills, and characteristics of the effective IT manager; in particular, executives wrestled with the question of whether a business or IT background provided the best preparation for the new CIO role, and arguments continued over the appropriate reporting line and level for the CIO. As a few firms started to unveil strategic applications of IT, organizations became interested in understanding the role of line management in systems implementation. In addition, business executives and IT management alike searched for insights into whether the IT unit should be centralized or decentralized as the applications portfolio grew to the point where multiple mainframes were a corporate commonplace.

These questions have, for the most part, been researched and understood to the point that we believe they no longer prove interesting. For example, it is clear that CIOs should have both IT and business understanding, but there are plenty of examples of successful CIOs acquiring missing experience in one or another area after accepting the CIO position (Applegate & Elam, 1992; Earl, 1996; Feeny, 1997). Similarly, it is clear that the optimal reporting level of the CIO depends on the firm's sophistication and expectations for the strategic use of IT—and the extent senior management expects the CIO to fulfill the role of strategic partner or business visionary. The centralization-decentralization debate is another one that depends on organizational demands for IT, although the federal model has become a dominant model that allows firms the benefits of both alternative structures (Rockart et al., 1996; Von Simson, 1990). Finally, line management's role in systems implementation includes both clarifying needs for the system and ensuring the organizational change that must accompany systems implementation (Davenport, 1993; Rockart, 1988).

A second set of research questions addresses issues that arose during the distributed era. This includes questions about how firms should govern IT and assess its value; how firms can move IT from a cost to be minimized to a strategic asset; and how firms make successful IT outsourcing decisions. All of these questions have been researched, and some general parameters have been provided. However, these issues still trouble IT management. The success rate in handling these distributed era concerns is still remarkably low. Researchers can provide useful insights by identifying how to elevate current practice, perhaps by doing large-scale, multidisciplinary research or by applying important learnings from other disciplines.

Finally, a whole set of questions is just starting to emerge that will help us better understand IT management in the Web-based era. The questions will address issues such as management responsibilities for IT, business models for firms in the Web-based era, the role definition of the CNOs and CKOs versus CIOs, and the development of core IT skills in organizations. Because firms are just entering into the Web-based era, these questions are not, we suggest, well suited for large-scale studies. Instead, a few leading-edge organizations can provide insights through case studies into how firms might address the opportunities and challenges that IT continues to present.

Focusing specifically on the future of the CIO, we make two suggestions. First, it seems the right time now to be studying the activities and time usage of CIOs in firms that are demonstrably living in the Web-based era. Some of these firms may be long-established corporations in sectors that are particularly impacted by Web technology (e.g., publishing, financial services); others might be Internet start-up companies. For example, what is the role of a CIO at Amazon.com? At E-bay? Such studies can contrast with their equivalents in earlier eras (Ives & Olson, 1981; Stephens et al., 1992; Applegate & Elam, 1992). Second, it may be a good time to research IT leadership by considering the future of the IT function through comparison with the evolution of other functions. Will the evolution of the IT function parallel that of finance and accounting, with retention of a strong professional community? Will it become more like HRM, where typically the HR executive takes a primarily policy role with business line managers directly responsible for execution? Does marketing provide a better analog? Or R&D? Or will IT evolve a distinctive model of its own? More than 20 years have passed since Dearden (1987) predicted "the withering away of the IS organization." Whither now the CIO?

ENDNOTES

1. In this book, the chapter by Todd and Benbast on decision making provides insights into changes in the skills and qualifications of users.
2. See the chapter by Ang and Slaughter on IT personnel for background on changing skills and qualifications of IS professionals.

3. The chapter by Robey and Boudreau on organizational consequences discusses organizational impacts; the chapter by Barua and Mukhopadhyay on information technology and business performance analyzes financial impacts.

4. The chapter by Markus and Tanis on enterprise resource planning systems discusses success and failure in the implementation of ERPs.

5. See the chapter by Lacity and Willcocks on IT outsourcing for a discussion of the issues associated with IT outsourcing.

6. The chapter by Sampler on the Internet describes the extent to which it will impact businesses.

7. See the chapter by Sambamurthy on business strategy.

8. See also the chapter by Segars and Dean on information technology and radical change.

9. See the chapter by Alavi on organizational knowledge for an overview of knowledge management issues.

10. See the chapter by George on the origins of software and by Kirsch on software project management as examples of how CIO responsibilities have evolved.

References

CHAPTER 1, PETER TODD AND IZAK BENBASAT

Beach, L.R., and T.R. Mitchell (1978). A contingency model for the selection of decision strategies. *Academy of Management Review,* **3,** 439–449.

Benbasat, I., G. DeSanctis, and B.R. Nault (1993). Empirical Research in Managerial Support Systems: A Review and Assessment. In *Recent Developments in Decision Support Systems,* C. Holsapple and A.H. Whinston (eds.). NATO ASI Series F: Computer and Systems Sciences, Vol. 101. Springer-Verlag Publishers, 383-437.

Benbasat, I. and A.S. Dexter (1982, Spring). Individual Differences in the Use of Decision Support Aids. *Journal of Accounting Research,* Vol. 20, No. 1, pp. 1–11.

Benbasat, I., and A.S. Dexter (1985, November). An Experimental Evaluation of Graphical and Color-Enhanced Information Presentation. *Management Science,* Vol. 31, pp. 1348–1363.

Benbasat, I., A.S. Dexter, and P. Todd (1986). An Experimental Program Investigating Color-Enhanced and Graphical Information Presentation: An Integration of the Findings. *Communications of the ACM,* **29, 11,** 1094–1105.

Benbasat, I., and R.N. Taylor (1982, July/August). Behavioral Aspects of Information Processing for the Design of Management Information Systems. *IEEE Transactions on Systems, Man, and Cybernetics,* Vol. SMC–12, No. 4, pp. 439–450.

Bennett, John L. (1983). *Building Decision Support Systems.* Reading, MA: Addison-Wesley.

Bettman, J.R., and P. Kakkar (1977). Effects of information presentation format on consumer information acquisition. In *Advances in Consumer Research,* B. Anderson (ed.), **3,** 316–320.

Bettman, J.R., E.J. Johnson, and J. W. Payne (1990). A componential analysis of cognitive effort in choice. *Organizational Behavior and Human Decision Processes,* **45,** 111–139.

Chase, W.G. (1978). Elementary Information Processes. In *Handbook of Learning and Cognition,* **5,** W.K. Estes (ed.) Hillsdale, IL: Laurence Earlbaum, 19–90.

Christensen-Szalanski, J.J.J. (1980). Problem solving strategies: A selection mechanism, some implications and some data. *Organizational Behavior and Human Performance,* **25,** 307–323.

Dhaliwal, J.S., and I. Benbasat (1996, September) The Use and Effects of Knowledge-Based System Explanations: Theoretical Foundations and a Framework for Empirical Evaluation. *Information Systems Research,* Vol. 7, No. 3, 342–362.

Dickson, G.W., J.A. Senn, and N.L. Chervany (1977, May). Research in Management Information Systems: The Minnesota Experiments. *Management Science.*

Eierman, M.A., F. Niederman, and C. Adams (1995). DSS Theory: A Model of Constructs and Relationships. *Decision Support Systems,* **14,** 1–26.

Einhorn, H., and R. Hogarth (1978). Confidence in judgement: Persistance of the illusion of validity. *Psychological Review,* **85,** 395–416.

Eom, S.B. (1996). Mapping the Intellectual Structure of Research in Decision Support Systems Through Author Cocitation Analysis (1971–1993). *Decision Support Systems,* **16,** 315–338.

Goodhue, Dale (1995). Understanding User Evaluations of Information Systems. *Management Science,* **41, 12,** 1827–1995.

Gorry, G.A., and M.S. Scott Morton (1971, Fall). A Framework for Management Information Systems. *Sloan Management Review,* **13** (1), 55–70.

Gregor, S. and I. Benbasat (1999). Explanations from knowledge-based systems: A review of theoretical, foundations and empirical work. *Management Information Systems Quarterly,* **23,** 4

Huber, G. (1983, May). Cognitive Style as a Basis for MIS & DSS Design: Much Ado About Nothing. *Management Science,* **29** (5), 567–579.

Jarvenpaa, S. (1989). The effect of task and graphical format congruence on information processing strategies and decision making performance. *Management Science,* **35,** 285–303.

Johnson, E., and J. Payne (1985). Effort and Accuracy in Choice. *Management Science,* **31,** 395–415.

Johnson, E., J. Payne, and J. Bettman (1988). Information Displays and Preference Reversals. *Orgainzational Behavior and Human Decision Performance,* **42,** 1–21.

Jungerman, H. (1985). The two camps on rationality. In *Decision making under uncertainty,* R. W. Scholtz (ed.). Elsevier Science Publishers.

Kahneman, D., P. Slovic, and A. Tversky (1982). *Judgement Under Uncertainty: Heuristics and Biases.* Cambridge: Cambridge University Press.

Keen, P., and Michael Scott Morton. *Decision Support Systems.* Reading MA: Addison-Wesley, 1978.

Kleinmuntz, D.N., and D.A. Schkade (1993). Information displays and decision processes. *Psychological Science,* **4,** 221–227.

Mao, J., and I. Benbasat (1999). The Effects of Contextualized Access to Explanatory Knowledge on Judgments. Working paper, Faculty of Commerce & Business Administration, University of British Columbia, Canada.

March, J.G. (1978). Bounded rationality, ambiguity and the engineering of choice. *The Bell Journal of Economics,* **19,** 587–608.

Nah, F.H., J. Mao, and I. Benbasat (1999). Effectiveness of using expert support technology for individual and small group decision making. *Journal of Information Technology,* Vol. 14, 137–147.

Newell, A., and H.A. Simon (1972). *Human Problem Solving.* New York: Prentice-Hall.

Payne, J.W., J. Bettman, and E.J. Johnson (1990). Adaptive strategy selection in decision making. *Journal of Experimental Psychology: Human Learning, Memory and Cognition,* **14,** 534–552.

Payne, J.W., J. Bettman, and E. J. Johnson (1993). *The Adaptive Decision-Maker.* New York: Cambridge University Press.

Russo, J., and B. Dosher (1983). Strategies for multiattribute binary choice. *Journal of Experimental Psychology: Learning, Memory and Cognition,* **9,** 676–696.

Scott Morton, M.S. (1971). *Management Decision Systems: Computer Based Support for Decision Making.* Cambridge MA: Division of Research, Harvard University.

Sharda, R., Steve H. Barr, and James C McDonnell (1988). Decision Support System Effectiveness: A Review and an Empirical Test. *Management Science,* **34, 2** 139–159.

Shugan, S. (1979). The cost of thinking. *Journal of Consumer Research,* **7,** 99–111.

Silver, M.S. (1988). Descriptive analysis for computer-based decision support. *Operations Research,* **36, 6,** 904–916.

Silver, M.S. (1990). Decision support systems: Directed and non-directed change. *Information Systems Research,* **1, 1,** 47–70. 22.

Silver, M.S. (1991). *Systems That Support Decision Makers: Description and Analysis.* New York: John Wiley.

Simon, H.A. (1957). *Administrative Behavior.* New York: Macmillian.

Thorngate, W. (1980). Efficient decision heuristics. *Behavioral Science,* **25,** 219–225.

Todd, P., and I. Benbasat (1987, December). Process Training in Decision Support Systems Research: Exploring the Black Box. *MIS Quarterly,* **11, 4,** 493–514.

Todd, P., and I. Benbasat (1991). An experimental investigation the impact of computer based decision aids on the decision making process. *Information Systems Research,* **2, 2,** 87–115.

Todd, P., and I. Benbasat (1992). An experimental investigation of the impact of computer based DSS on processing effort. *MIS Quarterly,* **16, 3,** 373–393.

Todd, P., and I. Benbasat (1993). Decision-makers, DSS and Decision Making Effort: An Experimental Investigation, *INFOR,* **31, 2,** 1–21.

Todd, P., and I. Benbasat (1994a). The Influence of DSS on Choice Strategies: An Experimental Analysis of the Role of Cognitive Effort. *Organizational Behavior and Human Decision Processes,* **60,** 36–74.

Todd, P., and I. Benbasat (1994b). The Influence of DSS on Choice Strategies Under Conditions of High Cognitive Load. *IEEE Transactions on Systems, Man and Cybernetics,* **24, 4,** 537–547.

Todd, P., and I. Benbasat (1999). Evaluating the impact of DSS, cognitive effort & incentives on strategy selection. *Information Systems Research.* **10, 4,** 356–374.

Todd, P, and I. Benbasat (2000). Inducing Compensatory Information Processing Through Decision Aids That Facilitate Effort Reduction: An Experimental Assessment. *Journal of Behavioral Decision Making,* **13, 1,** 91–106.

Vessey, I. (1991). Cognitive fit: A theory-based analysis of the graphs versus tables literature. *Decision Sciences,* **22,** 219–241.

Vessey, I., and D. Galetta (1991). Cognitive fit: An empirical study of information acquisition. *Information Systems Research,* **2, 1,** 63–84.

Zachary, W.W. (1988). Decision support systems: Designing to extend the cognitive limits. In *Handbook of Human-Computer Interaction,* M. Helander (ed.). Elsevier Science Publishers.

CHAPTER 2, MARYAM ALAVI

Alavi, M., and D. Leidner. " Knowledge Management Systems: Issues, Challenges, and Benefits." *Communications of the Association for Information Systems,* an electronic journal (1: 2), 1999a.

Alavi, M., and D. Leidner. "Conceptual Foundations of Knowledge Management and Knowledge Management Systems." Working Paper, Robert H. Smith School of Business, University of Maryland at College Park, College Park, MD 20742, 1999b.

Argote, L., S. Beckman, and D. Epple. "The Persistence and Transfer of Learning in Industrial Settings." *Management Science* (36), 1990, pp. 140–154.

Argyris, C., and D. A. Schon. *Organizational Learning: A Theory of Action Perspective.* Reading, MA: Addison-Wesley, 1978.

Berger, P., and T. Luckmann. *The Social Construction of Reality.* Garden City, NY: Doubleday, 1967.

Brown, J., C., and P. Duguit. "Organizing Knowledge." *California Management Review* (40:3), 1998, pp. 90–111.

Cross, R. " Knowledge and Knowledge Management in Organizations: A Literature Review." Working Paper, Systems Research Center, Boston University School of Management, Boston, MA, 1997.

Darr, E. D., L. Argote, and D. Epple. "The Acquisition, Transfer and Depreciation of Knowledge in Service Organizations: Productivity Franchises." *Management Science* (41:11), 1995, 1750–1762.

Davenport, T. H., and P. Klahr. "Managing Customer Support Knowledge." *California Management Review* (40:3), 1998, pp. 195–208.

Davenport, T. H., and L. Prusak. *Working Knowledge.* Boston, MA: Harvard Business School Press, 1997.

Davis, S., and C. Meyer. *Blur.* Reading, MA: Addison-Wesley, 1998.

Demsetz, H. "The Theory of the Firm Revisited." In *The Nature of the Firm,* J. Willimason and S. Winter (eds.). NY: Oxford University Press, 1991, pp. 159–178.

Denison, D., and A. Mishra. "Toward a Theory of Organizational Culture and Effectiveness." *Organization Science* (6: 2), 1995, pp. 204–223.

Dierick, I., and K. Cool. "Asset Stock Accumulation and Sustainability of Competitive Advantage." *Management Science* (35), 1989, pp. 1504–1514.

Fahey, L., and L. Prusak. "The Eleven Deadliest Sins of Knowledge Management." *California Management Review* (40: 3), 1998, pp. 265–280.

Gill, T. G. "High-Tech Hidebound: Case Studies of Information Technologies that Inhibited Organizational Learning." *Accounting, Management and Information Technologies* (5:1), 1995, pp. 41–60.

Gioia, D. A., and P. P. Pool. "Scripts in Organizational Behavior." *Academy of Management Review* (9: 3), 1984, pp. 449–459.

Grant, R. M. "Prospering in Dynamically Competitive Environments: Organizational Capability as Knowledge Integration." *Organizational Science* (7, 4), 1996, pp. 375–389.

Gurvitch, G. *The Social Frameworks of Knowledge.* Oxford, England: Basil Blackwell, 1971.

Hansen, M. T., N. Nohira, and T. Tierney. "What's Your Strategy for Managing Knowledge?" *Harvard Business Review,* March–April 1999, pp. 106–116.

Hayek, F. A. "The Pretense of Knowledge." *The American Economic Review* (79), 1989, pp. 3–7.

Holzner, B. and J. Marx. *The Knowledge Application: The Knowledge System in Society.* Boston, MA: Allyn & Bacon, 1979.

Huber, G. "Organizational Learning: The Contributing Processes and the Literatures" *Organizational Science* (2:1), 1991, pp. 88–115.

Kantrow, A. M. The Constraints of Corporate Tradition. New York: Harper & Row, NY, 1987.

Larwood, L., and W Whitaker.. "Managerial Myopia: Self-Serving Biases in Organizational Planning. *Journal of Applied Psychology,* Vol. 62, 1997, pp. 194–198.

Leonard, D., and S. Sensiper. "The Role of Tacit Knowledge in Group Innovation." *California Management Review* (40:3), 1998, pp. 112–132.

Lippman, S. A., and R. P. Rumelt. "Uncertain Imitability: An Analysis of Interfirm Differences in Efficiency Under Competition." *Bell Journal of Economics* (13), 1982, pp. 418–438.

Malhotra, Y. "Role of Organizational Control in IT Enabled Knowledge Creation: From Knowledge Restraint to Knowledge Enabler." Working Paper, Katz Graduate School of Business, University of Pittsburgh, PA, 1996.

Moss, E. *The Grammar of Consciousness.* Houndmills, U.K.: St. Martin's Press, 1995.

Nonaka, I. "A Dynamic Theory of Organizational Knowledge Creation." *Organizational Science* (5: 1), February 1994, pp. 14–37.

O'Dell, C., and C. J. Grayson. "If Only We Knew What We Know: Identification and Transfer of Internal Best Practices." *California Management Review* (40: 3), 1998, pp. 154–174.

Penrose, E. T. *The Theory of the Growth of the Firm.* New York: John Wiley, 1959.

Pentland, B. T. "Information Systems and Organizational Learning: The Social Epistemology of Organizational Knowledge Systems." *Accounting, Management and Information Technologies* (5:1), 1995, pp. 1–21.

Polanyi, M. "Personal Knowledge." In *Meaning,* M. Polanyi and H. Prosch (eds.). Chicago: University of Chicago Press, 1975, pp. 22–45.

Polanyi, M. *The Tacit Dimension.* London: Routledge and Kegan Paul, 1967.

Polanyi, M. *Personal Knowledge: Toward a Post-Critical Philosophy.* New York: Harper Torchbooks, 1962.

Prusak, L. *Knowledge in Organizations.* Boston, MA: Butterworth-Heiemann, 1997.

Quinn, J. B. The Intelligent Enterprise: A Knowledge and Service Based Paradigm for Industry. New York: Maxwell Macmillan International, 1992.

Ruggles, R. "The State of the Notion: Knowledge Management in Practice." *California Management Review* (40:3), 1998, pp. 80–89.

Sanderland, L. E., and R. E. Stablein. "The Concept of Organizational Mind." In *Research in the Sociology of Organization* (5), S. Bachrach, and N. DiTomaso (eds.). Greenwich, CT: JAI Press, 1987, pp. 135–162.

Schutz, A. *Collected Papers,* Vol. 1. The Hague: Nighoff, 1962.

Spender, J. C. "Making Knowledge the Basis of a Dynamic Theory of the Firm." *Strategic Management Journal* (17), Winter 1996, pp. 45–62.

Starbuck, W., and B. Hedberg. "Saving an Organization from a Stagnating Environment." In *Strategy + Performance,* H. Thorelli. (ed.). Bloomington, IN: University Press, 1977, pp. 249–258.

Szulanski, G. "Exploring Internal Stickiness: Impediments to the Transfer of Best Practice Within the Firm." *Strategic Management Journal,* 1996, pp. 29–43.

Teece, D. "Capturing Value From Knowledge Assets: The New Economy, Markets for Know-How, and Intangible Assets." *California Management Review* (40: 3), 1998, pp. 55–79.

Tsoukas, H. "The Firm as a Distributed Knowledge System: A Constructions Approach." *Strategic Management Journal,* 1996, pp. 11–25.

Walsh, J. P., and G. R. Ungson. "Organizational Memory." *Academy of Management Review,* Vol. 16, no. 1, 1991, pp. 57–91.

Wilkins, A. L., and N. J. Brestow. "For Successful Organization Culture, Honor Your Past." *Academy of Management Executive* (1), 1987, pp. 221–229.

Winter, S. G. "Four Rs of Profitability: Rents, Resources, Routines, and Replications." In *Resource-Based and Evolutionary Theories of the Firm: Towards a Synthesis,* C. A. Montgomery (ed.). Norwell, MA: Kluwer, 1995, pp. 147–178.

Zack, M. "Managing Codified Knowledge." *Sloan Management Review* (40:6), 1999a, 45–58.

Zack, M. "Developing a Knowledge Strategy." *California Management Review* (41: 3), Spring 1999b, pp. 25–45.

CHAPTER 3, CAROL STOAK SAUNDERS

Ahuja, M., Galletta, D., and Carley, K.M. (1998) "Individual Centrality and Performacne in Virtual Design Groups: An Empirical Study." Working paper, Florida State University.

Belanger, F., and Collins, R. (1998) "Distributed Work Arrangements: A Research Framework." In *The Information Society,* 14, 137–152.

Benbasat, I., and Lim, L. (1993) "The Effects of Group, Task, Context, and Technology Variables on Usefulness of Group Support Systems: A Meta-Analysis of Experimental Studies." *Small Group Research,* 24, No. 4, 430–462.

Boudreau, Marie-Claude, Loch, Karen, Robey, Daniel, and Straub, Detmar (1998) "Going global: Using information technology to advance the competitiveeness of the virtual transnational organization." *Academy of Management Executive,* 12, No. 4, 120–128.

Brandon, D.P., and Pratt, M.G. (1999) "Managing Identity in On-line Virtual Teams: A SIT/SCT Perspective." Paper presented at the 1999 Academy of Management Meeting, Chicago, IL.

Brooks, Frederick P. (1975) *The Mythical Man Month: Essays on Software Engineering.* Reading, MA: Addison-Wesley.

Carlson, John R., and Zmud, Robert W. (1999) "Channel Expansion Theory and the Experiential Nature of Media Richness Perceptions." *Academy of Management Journal,* 42, No. 2, 153–170.

Chidambaram, L. (1996) "Relational Development in Computer-Supported Groups." *MIS Quarterly,* 18, No. 2, 143–165.

Citurs, A.B., and Yoo, Y. (1999) "Development of Expertise Coordination Patterns in Electronic Teams." Paper presented at the 1999 Academy of Management Meeting, Chicago, IL.

Clapper, D.L., Mclean, E.R., and Watson, R.T. (1991) "An Experimental Investigation of the Effect of a Group Decision Support System on Normative Influence in Small Groups." In *Proceedings of the Twelfth International Conference on Information Systems,* 273-282.

Coutu, D.L. (1998) "Trust in virtual teams." *Harvard Business Review,* 76, No. 3, May–June, 20–21.

Daft, R.L., and Lengel, R.H. (1984) "Information Richness: A new approach to managerial behavior and organizational design." In *Research in organizational behavior,* 6, L.L. Cummings and B.M. Staw (eds.). Greenwich, CT: JAI, 233.

Davis, J.H. (1969) *Group Performance.* Reading, MA: Addison-Wesley.

DeSanctis, G., and Gallupe, R. B. (1987) "A Foundation for the Study of Group Decision Support Systems." *Management Science,* 33, 589–609.

DeSanctis, G., and Poole, M.S. (1994) "Capturing the complexity in advanced technology use: Adaptive structuration theory." *Organization Science,* 5, No. 2, 121–147.

Duarte, D., and Snyder, N. (1999) *Mastering Virtual Teams: Strategies, Tools and Techniques That Succeed.* San Francisco, CA: Jossey-Bass.

Easton, G., George, J., Nunamaker, J, and Pendergast, M. (1990) "Using Two Different Electronic-Meeting System Tools for the Same Task: An Experimental Comparison." *Journal of Management Information Systems,* 7, No. 1, 85–100.

Finholt, T., and Sproull, L. (1990) "Electronic Groups at Work." *Organization Science,* 1, 41–61.

Finholt, T., Sproull, L., and Kiesler, S. (1990) "Communcaiton and Performace in Ad Hoc Groups." In *Intellectual Teamwork: Social and Technological Foundations of Cooperative Work,* J. Galegher, R. Kraut, and C. Egido (eds.). Hillsdale, NJ: Erlbaum.

Fritz, M.B.W., Narashimhan, S, and Rhee, H.S. (1998) "Communication and coordination in the virtual office." *Journal of Management Information Systems,* 14, No. 4, 7–28.

Fulk, J., and Boyd, B. (1991) "Emerging theories of communication in organizations." *Journal of Management,* 17, No. 2, 407–446.

Furst, S., Blackburn, R., and Rosen, B. (1999) "Virtual Teams: A Proposed Research Agenda." Paper presented at the 1999 Academy of Management meeting, Chicago, IL.

Galup, S., Saunders, C., Nelson, R., and Cerveny, R. (1997) "The Use of Temporary Staff and Managers in a Local Government Environment." *Communication Research,* 24, No. 6, 698–730.

George, J., Easton, G., Nunamaker, J., and Northcraft, G. (1990) "A Study of Collaborative Group Work with and without Computer-based Support." *Information Systems Research,* 1, No. 4, 394–415.

Gersick, C.J. (1988) "Time and transition in work teams: Toward a new model of group development." *Academy of Management Journal,* 31, 9–41.

Gersick, C.J. (1989) "Marking time: Predictable transitions in task groups." *Academy of Management,* 32, 274–309.

Hackman, J.R. (1983) *A Normative Model of Work Team Effectiveness.* New Haven, CT: Yale School of Organization and Management, Research Program on Group Effectiveness.

Hackman, J.R., Brousseau, K.R, and Wiess, J.A. (1977) "The interaction of task design and group performance strategies in determining group effectiveness." *Organizational Behavior and Human Performance,* 16, 350–365.

Hackman, J.R., and Morris, C.G. (1972) "Group tasks, group interaction process, and group performance effectiveness: A review and proposed integration." In *Advances in Experimental Social Psychology,* Vol. 8, L. Berkowitz (ed.). New York: Academic Press.

Hightower, R., and Sayeed, L. (1996) "Effects of communication mode and prediscussion information distribution characteristics on information exchange in groups." *Information Systems Research,* 7, No. 4, 451–465.

Hiltz, S.R., Johnson, K, and Turoff, M. (1986) "Experiments in Group Decision Making: Communcation Process and Outcome in Face-to-face versus Computerized Conferences." *Human Communication Research,* 13, No. 2, 225–252.

Hiltz, S.R., Johnson, K, and Turoff, M. (1991) "Group Decision Support: The Effects of Designated Human Leaders and Statistical Feedback in Computerized Conferences." *Journal of Management Information Systems,* 8, 81–108.

Hollingshead, A.B. (1996) "The rank-order effect in group decision making." *Organizational Behavior and Human Decision Processes,* 68, No. 3, 181–193.

Hollingshead, A.B, and McGrath, J.E. (1995) "Computer-Assisted Groups: A Critical Review of the Empirical Research." In *Team Effectiveness and Decision Making in Organizations,* R. Guzzo and E. Salas, and Associates (eds). San Francisco, CA: Jossey-Bass, 46–78.

Hollingshead, A.B., McGrath, J.E., and O'Connor, K.M. (1993) "Group Task Performance and Communication Technology: A Longitudinal Study of Computer Mediated versus Face-to-face Groups." *Small Group Research,* 24, No. 3, 307–333.

Horvath, L., and Tobin, T.J. (1999) "Twenty-First Century Teamwork: Defining Competencies for Virtual Teams." Paper presented at the 1999 Academy of Management meeting, Chicago, IL.

Huang, W., Raman, K.S., and Wei, K.K. (1993) "A Process Study of Effects of GSS and Task Type on Informational and Normative Influence in Small Groups." In *Proceedings of the Fourteenth International Conference on Information Systems,* J. DeGross, R.P. Bostrom, and D. Robey (eds.), 91–101.

Jarvenpaa, S.L., Knoll, K., and Leidner, D.E. (1998) "Is anybody out there? Antecedents of trust in global virtual teams." *Journal of Management Information Systems,* 14, No. 4, 29–64.

Kavan, B., and Saunders, C. (1988) "Managers: A Key Ingredient to Alternative Work Arrangements Program Success." *Journal of End User Computing.* 10, No. 4, 23–32.

Kelly, H.H., and Thibaut, J.W. (1978) *Interpersonal relations: A theory of interdependence.* New York: Wiley.

Kiser, Kim (1999) "Working on world time." *Training,* 36, No. 3, 28–34.

Klimoski, R., and Jones, R. (1995) "Staffing for effective group decision making: Key issues in matching people and teams." In *Team Effectiveness and Decision Making in Organizations,* R. Guzzo and E. Salas, and Associates. San Francisco: Jossey-Bass, 291–332.

Lee, A.S. (1994) "Electronic mail as a medium for rich communication: An empirical investigation using hermeneutic interpretation." *MIS Quarterly,* 18, 143–157.

Lim, L.H., and Benbasat, I. (1996–97) "Framework for Addressing Group Judgement Biases with Group Technology." *Journal of Management Information Systems,* 13, No. 3, 7–24.

Lipnack, J., and Stamps, J. (1994) *The Age of the Network: Organizing Principles for the 21ˢᵗ Century.* New York: John Wiley.

Lipnack, J., and Stamps, J. (1999) "Virtual teams: The new way to work." *Strategy & Leadership,* 27, 4–9.

Locke, E., Shaw, K., Saari, L., and Latham, G. (1981) "Goal-setting and task performance." *Psychological Bulletin,* 90, 125–152

Markus, M.L. (1994) "Electronic mail as the medium of managerial choice." *Organization Science,* 5, No. 4, 502–527.

McLeod, P.L., and Liker, J.K. (1992) " Electronic meeting systems: Evidence from a low structure environment." *Information Systems Research,* 3, No. 3, 524–572.

McGrath, J.E. (1984) *Groups: Interaction and Performance.* Englewood Cliffs, NJ: Prentice Hall.

McGrath, J.E. (1991) "Time, interaction, and performance (TIP): A theory of groups." *Small Group Research,* 22, No. 2, 147–174.

McGrath, J.E., Arrow, H., Gruenfeld, D.H., Hollingsehad, A.B., and O'Connor, K.M. (1993) "Groups, tasks, and technology: The effects of experience and change. " *Small Group Research,* 24, No. 3, 406–420.

McLeod, P.L. (1997, August) "Group support systems and the discovery of hidden profiles." Paper presented at the Academy of Management, Boston, MA.

Melymuka, K. (1997, April 28) "Virtual realities." *Computerworld,* 31, No. 7, 70–72.

Meyerson, D., Weick, K.E., and Kramer, R.M. (1996) "Swift trust and temporary groups." In *Trust in Organizations: Frontiers of Theory and Research,* R.M. Kramer and T.R. Tyler (eds.). Thousand Oaks, CA:Sage Publications, 166–195.

Miranda, S. M. (1991) *Cohesiveness and Conflict Management in Group Decision Support Systems.* Unpublished doctoral dissertation, University of Georgia, Athens, GA.

Nilles, J. (1994) *Making telecommuting happen.* New York: Van Nostrand Reinhold.

Orlikowski, W. (1992) "Learning from Notes: Organizational Issues in Groupware Implementation. *CSCW96 Proceedings,* 219–228.

Pape, W. (1997) "Group Insurance." *Inc. Tech,* 2, 29–31.

Pearce, J.L. (1993) "Toward an organizational behavior of contract laborers: Their psychological involvement and effects on employee co-workers." *Academy of Management Journal,* 36, 1082–1096.

Ramsower, R. (1985) *Telecommuting: The organizational and behavioral effects of working at home.* Ann Arbor, MI: UMI Research Press.

Saunders, C., and Miranda, S. (1998) "Information Acquisition in Group Decision Making." *Information and Management,* 34, 55–74.

Saunders, C., Robey, D., and Vaverek, K. (1994) "The Persistence of Status Differentials in Computer Conferencing." *Human Communication Research,* 20, No. 4, 443–472.

Siegel, J., Dubrovsky, V., Kiesler, S., and McGuire, T.W. (1986) "Group Processes in Computer-Mediated Communication." *Organizational Behavior and Human Decision Processes,* 37, 157–187.

Smith, R.W. (1994, March–April) "Bell Atlantic's Virtual Work Force." *Futurist.*

Snow, C.C., Snell, S.A. and Davison, S.C. (1996) "Use transnational teams to globalize your company." *Organizational Dynamics,* 24, No. 4, 50–67.

Stevens, M.J., and Campion, M.A. (1994) "The knowledge, skill, and ability requirements for teamwork: Implications for human resource management." *Journal of Management,* 20, 503–530.

Strauss, S.G., and McGrath, J.E. (1994) "Does the Medium Really Matter? The Interaction of Task Type and Technology on Group Performance and Member Reactions." *Journal of Applied Psychology,* 79, 87–97.

Tan, B.C.Y., Raman, K.S., and Wei, K.K. (1994) "An Empirical Study of Task Dimension of Group Support Systems." *IEEE Transactions on Systems, Man and Cybernetics,* 24, No. 7, 1056–1060.

Tan, B.C.Y., Wei, K.K., and Watson, R.T. (1993) "Dampening Status Influence Using a Group Support System: An Empirical Study." In *Proceedings of the Fourteenth International Conference on Information Systems,* J. DeGross, R.P. Bostrom, and D. Robey (eds.), 77–89.

Tan, B.C.Y., Wei, K.K., Watson, R.T., Clapper, D.L., and McLean, E. (1998) "Computer-Mediated Communication and Majority Influence: Assessing the Impact in an Individualtistic and a Collectivistic Culture." *Management Science,* 44, No. 9, 1263–1278.

Townsend, A.M., DeMarie, S., and Hendrickson, A.R. (1998) "Virtual Teams: Technology and the Workplace of the Future." *Academy of Management Executive,* 12, No. 3, 17–28.

Tuckman, B. (1965) "Developmental Sequence in Small Groups." *Psychological Bulletin,* 63, 419–427.

Walther, J.B. (1992) "Interpersonal Effects in Computer-Mediated Interaction: A Relational Perspective." *Communication Research,* 19, 52–90.

Walther, J.B. (1995) "Relational Aspects of Computer-Mediated Communication: Experimental Observations over Time." *Organization Science,* 6, No. 2, 186–203.

Warkentin, M.E., Sayeed, L., and Hightower, R. (1997) "Virtual Teams versus Face-to-Face Teams: An Exporatory Study of a Web-based Conference System." *Decision Sciences Journal,* 28, No. 4, 975–996.

Weisband, S.P., Schneider, S.K., and Connolly, T. (1995) "Computer-Mediated Communication and Social Information: Status Salience and Status Differences." *Academy of Management Journal,* 38, No. 4, 1124–1151.

Zigurs, I., and Buckland, B.K. (1998) "A Theory of Task/Technology Fit and Group Support Systems Effectiveness." *MIS Quarterly,* 22, No. 3, 313–334.

Zigurs, I., Poole, M.S., and DeSanctis, G. (1988) "A Study of Influence in Computer-Mediated Group Decision Making." *MIS Quarterly,* 12, No. 4, 625–644.

CHAPTER 4, DANIEL ROBEY AND MARIE-CLAUDE BOUDREAU

Alavi, M., and E. A. Joachimsthaler. "Revisiting DSS Implementation Research: A Meta-Analysis of the Literature and Suggestions for Researchers." *MIS Quarterly* (16), 1992, pp. 95–116.

Ang, J. and F. Pavri. "A Survey and Critique of the Impacts of Information Technology." *International Journal of Information Management* (14), 1994, pp. 122–133.

Attewell, P., and J. Rule. "Computing and Organizations: What We Know and What We Don't Know." *Communications of the ACM* (27), 1984, pp. 1184–1192.

Bacharach, S. B., P. Bamberger, and W. J. Sonnenstuhl. "The Organizational Transformation Process: The Micropolitics of Dissonance Reduction and the Alignment of Logics of Action." *Administrative Science Quarterly* (41), 1996, pp. 477–506.

Barley, S.R. "Technology as an Occasion for Structuring: Evidence from Observation of CT Scanners and the Social Order of Radiology Departments. " *Administrative Science Quarterly* (31), 1986, pp. 78–108.

Barley, S.R. "The Alignment of Technology and Structure through Roles and Networks." *Administrative Science Quarterly* (35), 1990, pp. 61–103.

Baroudi, J.J., and W.J. Orlikowski. "The Problem of Statistical Power in MIS Research." *MIS Quarterly* (13), 1989, pp. 87–106.

Baskerville, R., and S. Smithson. "Information Technology and New Organizational Forms: Choosing Chaos over Panaceas." *European Journal of Information Systems* (4:2), 1995, pp. 66–73.

Bjørn-Andersen, N., K. Eason, and D. Robey. *Managing Computer Impact: An International Study of Management and Organizations.* Norwood, NJ: Ablex, 1986.

Bjørn-Andersen, N., and J. Turner. "The Metamorphosis of Oticon." In *Information Technology and Organizational Transformation*, R. D. Galliers and W. R. J. Baets (eds). Chichester, UK: Wiley, 1998, pp. 65–83.

Blau, P. M., C. M. Falbe, W. McKinley, and P. K. Tracy, "Technology and Organization in Manufacturing." *Administrative Science Quarterly* (21), 1976, pp. 20–81.

Boudreau, M-C., and D. Robey. "Organizational Transition to Enterprise Resource Planning Systems: Theoretical Choices for Process Research." *Proceedings of the International Conference on Information Systems,* Charlotte, 1999, pp. 291–299.

Brynjolfsson, E., T. W. Malone, V. Gurbaxani, and A. Kambil. "Does Information Technology Lead to Smaller Firms?" *Management Science* (40:12), 1994, pp. 1628–1644.

Burkhardt, M.E., and D.J. Brass. "Changing Patterns or Patterns of Change: The Effects of a Change in Technology on Social Network Structure and Power." *Administrative Science Quarterly* (35), 1990, pp. 104–127.

Carlson, P.J., B.K. Kahn, and F. Rowe. "Organizational Impacts of New Communication Technology: A Comparison of Cellular Phone Adoption in France and the United States." *Journal of Global Information Management* (7:3), 1999, pp. 19–29.

Crowston, K., T.W. Malone, and F. Lin. "Cognitive Science and Organization Design: A Case Study in Computer Conferencing." *Human Computer Interaction* (3), 1987, pp. 59–85.

Culnan, M. J. "The Intellectual Development of Management Information Systems, 1972–1982: A Co-Citation Analysis." *Management Science* (32:2), 1986, pp. 156–172.

DeSanctis, G., and M.S. Poole. "Capturing the Complexity in Advanced Technology Use: Adaptive Structuration Theory." *Organization Science* (5:2), 1994, pp. 121–147.

Dickson, G.W., G. DeSanctis, M.S. Poole, and B.M. Jackson. "Help or Hindrance? The Role of Communication Technologies in Changing Organizational Form." *Academy of Management Best Paper Proceedings.* Fifty-Seventh Annual Meeting of the Academy of Management, Boston, MA, 1997, pp. 303–307.

Drummond, H. "The Politics of Risk: Trials and Tribulations of the Taurus Project." *Journal of Information Technology* (11), 1996, pp. 347–357.

Ewusi-Mensah, K. "Critical Issues in Abandoned Information Systems Development Projects." *Communications of the ACM* (40:9), 1997, pp. 74–80.

Foster, L.W., and D.M. Flynn. "Management Information Technology: Its Effects on Organizational Form and Function." *MIS Quarterly* (8), 1984, pp. 229–235.

Fox-Wolfgramm, S.J., K.B. Boal, and J.G. Hunt. "Organizational Adaptation to Institutional Change: A Comparative Study of First-Order Change in Prospector and Defender Banks." *Administrative Science Quarterly* (43), 1998, pp. 87–126.

Franz, C.R., D. Robey, and R.R. Koeblitz. "User Response to an Online Information System: A Field Experiment." *MIS Quarterly* (10), 1986, pp. 29–42.

Fulk, J., and G. DeSanctis. "Electronic Communication and Changing Organizational Forms." *Organization Science* (6:4), 1995, pp. 337–349.

Gibson, C., and R. L. Nolan. "Managing the Four Stages of EDP Growth." *Harvard Business Review* (52:1), 1974, pp. 76–88.

Hirschheim, R.A. *Office Automation: A Social and Organizational Perspective.* Chichester, UK: Wiley, 1985.

Huber, G. "A Theory of the Effects of Advanced Information Technologies on Organizational Design, Intelligence, and Decision Making." *Academy of Management Review* (15:1), 1990, pp. 47–71.

Jarvenpaa, S.L., G.W. Dickson, and G. DeSanctis. "Methodological Issues in Experimental Research: Experiences and Recommendations." *MIS Quarterly* (9), 1985, pp. 141–156.

Johnson, J. "Chaos: The Dollar Drain of IT Project Failures." *Application Development Trends* (2:1), 1995, pp. 41–47.

Kaplan, B. "Models of Change and Information Systems Research." In *Information Systems Research: Contemporary Approaches and Emergent Traditions,* H.-E. Nissen, H.K. Klein, and R. Hirschheim (ed.). North-Holland: Elsevier 1991, pp. 593–611.

Karsten, H. " 'It's Like Everyone Working Around the Same Desk': Organisational Readings of Lotus Notes." *Scandinavian Journal of Information Systems* (7:1), 1995, pp. 3–32.

Klatzky, S.R. "Automation, Size and the Locus of Decision-Making: The Cascade Effect." *Journal of Business* (43), 1970, pp. 141–151.

Klein, K.J., F. Dansereau, and R.J. Hall. "Levels Issues in Theory Development, Data Collection, and Analysis." *Academy of Management Review* (19:2), 1994, pp. 195–229.

Kling, R. "Social Analyses of Computing: Theoretical Perspectives in Recent Empirical Research." *Computing Surveys* (12), 1980, pp. 61–110.

Kraut, R., S. Dumais, and S. Koch. "Computerization, Productivity, and Quality of Work-life." *Communications of the ACM* (32), 1989, pp. 220–238.

Larsen, M.A., and M.D. Myers. "BPR Success or Failure? A Business Process Reengineering Project in the Financial Services Industry." *Proceedings of the Eighteenth International Conference on Information Systems,* Atlanta, Georgia, 1997, pp. 367–382.

Leavitt, H.J., and T.L. Whisler. "Management in the 1980s." *Harvard Business Review,* November–December 1958 pp. 41–48.

Leidner, D. E., and J.J. Elam. "The Impact of Executive Information Systems on Organizational Design, Intelligence, and Decision Making." *Information Systems Research* (6), 1995, pp. 645–664.

Manning, P.D. "Information Technology in the Police Context: The 'Sailor' Phone." *Information Systems Research* (7:1), 1996, pp. 52–62.

Markus, M.L. "Finding a Happy Medium: Explaining the Negative Effects of Electronic Communication on Social Life at Work." *ACM Transactions on Information Systems* (12), 1994a, pp. 119–149.

Markus, M.L. "Electronic Mail as the Medium of Managerial Choice." *Organization Science* (5:4), 1994b, pp. 502–527.

Markus, M.L., and D. Robey. "Information Technology and Organizational Change: Causal Structure in Theory and Research." *Management Science* (34), 1988, pp. 583–598.

Mitev, N.N. "More Than a Failure? The Computerized Reservation Systems at French Railways." *Information Technology & People* (9:4), 1996, pp. 8–19.

Mohr, L.B. *Explaining Organizational Behavior.* San Francisco, CA: Jossey-Bass, 1982.

Mowshowitz, A. "On Approaches to the Study of Social Issues in Computing." *Communications of the ACM* (24), 1981, pp. 146–155.

Myers, M.D. "A Disaster for Everyone to See: An Interpretive Analysis of a Failed IS Project." *Accounting, Management and Information Technologies* (4:4), 1994, pp. 185–201.

Nelson, D.L. "Individual Adjustment to Information-Driven Technologies: A Critical Review." *MIS Quarterly* (14), 1990, pp. 79–98.

Nolan, R. L. "Managing the Crises in Data Processing." *Harvard Business Review* (57: 2), 1979, pp. 115–126.

Orlikowski, W.J. "Integrated Information Environment or Matrix of Control? The Contradictory Implications of Information Technology." *Accounting, Management and Information Technologies* (1), 1991, pp. 9–42.

Orlikowski, W.J. "CASE Tools as Organizational Change: Investigating Incremental and Radical Changes in Systems Development." *MIS Quarterly* (17), 1993, pp. 309–340.

Orlikowski, W.J. "Improvising Organizational Transformation over Time: A Situated Change Perspective." *Information Systems Research* (7:1), 1996, pp. 63–92.

Orlikowski, W.J., and D.C. Gash. "Technological Frames: Making Sense of Information Technology in Organizations." *ACM Transactions on Information Systems* (12), 1994, pp. 174–207.

Orlikowski, W.J., and D. Robey. "Information Technology and the Structuring of Organizations." *Information Systems Research* (2), 1991, pp. 143–169.

Orlikowski, W.J., and J. Yates. "Genre Repertoire: The Structuring of Communicative Practices in Organizations." *Administrative Science Quarterly* (39), 1994, pp. 541–574.

Orlikowski, W.J., J. Yates, K. Okamura, and M. Fujimoto. "Shaping Electronic Communication: The Metastructuring of Technology in the Context of Use." *Organization Science* (6:4), 1995, pp. 423–444.

Paré, G., and J. Elam. "Using Case Study Research to Build Theories of IT Implementation." *Information Systems and Qualitative Research: Proceedings of the IFIP TC8 WG8.2 International Conference on Information Systems and Qualitative Research,* Philadelphia, 1997, pp. 542–568.

Pinsonneault, A., and K.L. Kraemer. "Middle Management Downsizing: An Empirical Investigation of the Impact of Information Technology." *Management Science* (43), 1997, pp. 659–679.

Rashford, N.S., and D. Coghlan. *The Dynamics of Organizational Levels.* Reading, MA: Addison-Wesley, 1994.

Robey, D. "Task Design, Work Values, and Worker Response—An Experimental Test." *Organizational Behavior & Human Performance* (12:2), 1974, pp. 264–273.

Robey, D. "The Impact of Alternate Decision Techniques on User Behavior." *Decision Sciences* (7:1), 1976, pp. 93–105.

Robey, D. "Computers and Management Structure: Some Empirical Findings Re-examined." *Human Relations* (30), 1977, pp. 963–976.

Robey, D., and M.-C. Boudreau. "Accounting for the Contradictory Organizational Consequences of Information Technology: Theoretical Directions and Methodological Implications." *Information Systems Research* (10:2), 1999, pp. 167–185.

Robey, D., and M. Newman. "Sequential Patterns in Information Systems Development: An Application of a Social Process Model." *ACM Transactions on Information Systems* (14:1), 1996, pp. 30–63.

Robey, D., and S. Sahay. "Transforming Work Through Information Technology: A Comparative Case Study of Geographic Information Systems in County Government." *Information Systems Research* (7:1), 1996, pp. 93–110.

Rousseau, D. "Issues of Level in Organizational Research: Multilevel and Cross-level Perspectives." In *Research in Organizational Behavior,* L.L. Cummings and B.M. Staw (eds.), Vol. 7. Greenwich, CT: JAI, 1985, pp. 1–37.

Sabherwal, R., and D. Robey. "An Empirical Taxonomy of Implementation Processes Based on Sequences of Events in Information System Development." *Organizational Science* (4:4), 1993, pp. 548–576.

Sabherwal, R., and D. Robey. "Reconciling Variance and Process Strategies for Studying Information Systems Development." *Information Systems Research* (6:4), 1995, pp. 303–327.

Sahay, S., and D. Robey. "Organizational Context, Social Interpretation, and the Implementation and Consequences of Geographic Information Systems." *Accounting, Management and Information Technologies* (6:4), 1996, pp. 255–282.

Schaubroeck, J., and K. Muralidhar. "A Meta-Analysis of the Relative Effects of Tabular and Graphical Display Formats on Decision Making Performance." *Human Performance* (4), 1991, pp. 127–145.

Segars, A. H., and V. Grover. "The Industry-Level Impact of Information Technology: An Empirical Analysis of Three Industries." *Decision Sciences* (26:3), 1995, pp. 337–368.

Star, S.L., and K. Ruhleder. "Steps Toward an Ecology of Infrastructure: Design and Access for Large Information Spaces." *Information Systems Research* (7), 1996, pp. 111–134.

Straub, D.W. "Validating Instruments in MIS Research." *MIS Quarterly* (13), 1989, pp. 147–169.

Vandenbosch, B., and M.J. Ginzberg. "Lotus Notes and Collaboration: Plus ça change...." *Journal of Management Information Systems* (13:3), 1996–97, pp. 65–81.

Van de Ven, A.H. "Suggestions for Studying Strategy Process: A Research Note." *Strategic Management Journal* (13), 1992, pp. 169–188.

Van de Ven, A.H., and G.P. Huber. "Longitudinal Field Research Methods for Studying Processes of Organizational Change." *Organization Science* (1:3), 1990, pp. 213–219.

Van de Ven, A.H., and M.S. Poole. "Explaining Development and Change in Organizations." *Academy of Management Review* (20), 1995, pp. 510–540.

Walsham, G. *Interpreting Information Systems in Organizations.* Chichester, UK: Wiley, 1993.

Whisler, T.L. *Information Technology and Organizational Change.* Wadsworth, 1970.

Wilson, F. "The Socio-Cybernetic Paradox of the Networked Firm" *Information Technology and People* (9), 1996, pp. 3–23.

Zack, M. H., and J.L. McKenney. "Social Context and Interaction in Ongoing Computer-Supported Management Groups." *Organization Science* (6:4), 1995, pp. 394–422.

CHAPTER 5, ANITESH BARUA AND TRIDAS MUKHOPADHYAY

Ahituv, N. "Assessing the value of information: Problems and approaches." Proceedings of the Tenth International Conference on Information Systems, pp. 315–325, Boston, MA, 1989.

Alpar, P., and Kim, M. "A microeconomic approach to the measurement of information technology value." *Journal of Management Information Systems,* 7, 2, pp. 55–69, Fall 1990.

Attewell, P. "Information technology and the productivity paradox." Paper presented to the Markle Foundation/Social Science Research Council Conference on Social Aspects of Computing, Washington, DC, September 1991.

Baily, M.N., and Chakrabarti, A.K. *Innovation and the productivity crisis.* The Brookings Institution, Washington, DC, 1988.

Baily, M.N., and Gordon, R.J. "The productivity slowdown, measurement issues and the explosion of computer power." In *Brookings Paper on Economic Activity,* 19, 2, 1988.

Banker, R.D., and Kauffman, R.J. "Strategic contributions of information technology: An empirical study of ATM networks." Proceedings of the Ninth International Conference on Information Systems, pp. 141–150, 1988.

Banker, R.D., Kauffman, R.J., and Mahmood, M.A. "Information technology, strategy and firm performance evaluation." In *Strategic Information Technology Management: Perspectives on Organizational Growth and Competitive Advantage,* R.D. Banker, R.J. Kauffman, and M.A. Mahmood (eds.). Harrisburg, PA: Idea Group Publishing, 1993.

Barua, A. "The elusive value: Measuring return on IT investment." *Exec: The Unisys Online Journal for Senior Managers,* January 1998. http://www.unisys.com/execmag/1998-01/viewpoints1.htm

Barua, A., Fang, Y., and Whinston, A.B. "Not all dot coms are created equal." Working paper, The University of Texas at Austin, 1999.

Barua, A., Kriebel, C.H., and Mukhopadhyay, T. "MIS and information economics: Augmenting rich descriptions with analytical rigor in information systems design." *Proceedings of the Tenth International Conference on Information Systems,* Boston, MA, pp. 327–339, 1989.

Barua, A., Kriebel, C.H., and Mukhopadhyay, T. "Information technologies and business value: An analytical and empirical investigation." *Information Systems Research,* 6, 1, pp. 3–23, 1995.

Barua, A., and Lee, B. "The IT productivity paradox revisited: A theoretical and empirical investigation in the manufacturing sector." *The International Journal of Flexible Manufacturing Systems,* Vol. 9, pp. 145–166, 1997.

Barua, A., Lee, S., and Whinston, A.B. "The calculus of reengineering." *Information Systems Research,* Vol. 7, No. 4, December 1996.

Barua, A., and Whinston, A.B. "An information economics approach to analyzing information systems for cooperative decision making." *Proceedings of the Twelfth International Conference on Information Systems,* New York, pp. 15–27, 1991.

Barua, A., and Whinston, A.B. "Complementarity based decision support for managing organizational design dynamics." *Decision Support Systems,* 22, pp. 45–58, 1998.

Bender, D.H. "Financial impact of information processing." Journal of Management Information Systems, 3, 2, pp. 22–32, 1986.

Berndt, E.R., and Morrsion, C.J. "High-tech capital, economic performance and labor composition in the U.S. manufacturing industries: An exploratory analysis." Working paper, Massachusetts Institute of Technology, 1991.

Bharadwaj, A.S., Bharadwaj, S.G., and Konsynski, B.R. "Information technology effects on firm performance as measured by Tobin's q." *Management Science,* 45 (6), pp. 1008–1024, June 1999.

Bresnahan, T.F. "Measuring the spillovers from technical advance: Mainframe computers in financial services." *American Economic Review,* 76, 34, pp. 742–755, 1986.

Brynjolfsson, E. "The productivity paradox of information technology." *Communications of the ACM,* 36, 12, pp. 66–77, 1993.

Brynjolfsson, E. "The contribution of information technology to consumer welfare." *Information Systems Research,* 7, 3, pp. 281–300, 1996.

Brynjolfsson, E., and Hitt, L. "Is information systems spending productive? New evidence and new results." *Proceedings of the Fourteenth International Conference on Information Systems,* Orlando, FL, 1993.

Brynjolfsson, E., and Hitt, L. "Paradox lost? Firm-level evidence of the returns to information systems spending." *Management Science,* 42, pp. 541–558, April 1996.

Brynjolfsson, E., and Hitt, L.M. "Information technology and organizational design: Evidence from micro data." Working paper, Massachusetts Institute of Technology, January 1998.

Brynjolfsson, E., Renshaw, A., and Van Alstyne, M. "The matrix of change." *Sloan Management Review,* Winter 1997.

Christensen, L.R., and Greene, W.H. "Economies of scale in U.S. electric power generation." *Journal of Political Economy,* 84, 4, pp. 654–676, August 1976.

Cron, W.L., and Sobol, M.G. "The relationship between computerization and performance: A strategy for maximizing the economic benefits of computerization." *Information and Management,* 6, pp. 171–181, 1983.

Crowston, K., and Treacy, M.E. "Assessing the impact of information technology on enterprise level performance." *Proceedings of the Seventh International Conference on Information Systems,* San Diego, CA, December 1986.

Davamanirajan, P., Mukhopadhyay, T., and Kriebel, C.H. "Assessing the business value of information technologies in global wholesale banking: The case of trade services." *Journal of Organizational Computing,* 1998.

Davamanirajan, P., Mukhopadhyay, T., and Kriebel, C.H. "Systems design, process performance and economic outcome." Working Paper, GSIA, Carnegie Mellon University, 2000.

Dewan, S., and Min, C.K. "Substitution of information technology for other factors of production: A firm level analysis." *Management Science,* 43, 12, pp. 1660–1675, 1997.

Dos Santos, B.L., Peffers, G.K., and Mauer, D.C. "The impact of information technology investment announcements on the market value of the firm." *Information Systems Research,* 4 (1), pp. 1–23, 1993.

Gordon, R.J. "What are computers doing in the service sector? Are they unproductive, and if so, why?" Notes from presentation at panel discussion on Information Technology and the Productivity Paradox. Tenth International Conference on Information Systems, Boston, MA, 1989.

Grenci, R., Barua, A., and Whinston, A.B. "A theory of the impact of technology-enabled customization." Working paper, University of Texas at Austin, 1998.

Harris, S.E., and Katz, J.L. "Predicting organizational performance using information technology managerial control ratios." *Proceedings of the Twenty-Second Hawaii International Conference on System Sciences,* 4, pp. 197–204, 1989.

Harris, S.E., and Katz, J.L. "Organizational performance and information technology investment in the insurance industry." *Organization Science,* 2, pp. 263–296, 1991.

Henry, D., Buckley, P., Gill, G., Cooke, S., Dumagan, J., Pastore, D., and LaPorte, S. "The emerging digital economy II." Economics and Statistics Administration, Office of Policy Development, http://www.doc.gov, June 1999.

Hilton, R. "The determinants of information value: Synthesizing some general results." *Management Science,* 27(1), 1981 pp. 57–64.

Hitt, L.M., and Brynjolfsson, E. "Information technology and internal firm organization: An exploratory analysis." *Journal of Management Information Systems,* Fall 1997.

Hitt, L.M., and Brynjolfsson, E. "Beyond computation: Information technology, organizational transformation and business performance." Working Paper, Massachusetts Institute of Technology, September 1998.

Kauffman, R.J., and Kriebel, C.H. "Modeling and measuring the business value of information technologies." In *Measuring the Business Value of Information Technologies*, P.A. Strassman, P. Berger, E.B. Swanson, C.H. Kriebel, and R.J. Kauffman (eds.). Washington, DC: ICIT Press, 1988a.

Kauffman, R.J. and Kriebel, C.H. "Identifying business value linkages for information technology: An exploratory application to treasury workstations." Working paper CRIS #182, New York University, New York, NY, April 1988b.

Kauffman, R.J., and Kriebel, C.H. "Identifying business value linkages for production processes involving information technology." In *Advances in Working Capital Management*, Y. Kim and V. Srinivasan (eds.), Vol. 2. Greenwich, CT: JAI, 1991.

Kauffman, R.J., and Weill, P. "An evaluative framework for research on the performance effects of information technology investment." *Proceedings of the Ninth International Conference on Information Systems*, Boston, MA, pp. 377–388, 1989.

Kauffman, R.J., Kriebel, C.H., and Zajonc, P.C. "Measuring business value for investments in point-of-sale technology." Working paper, New York University, New York, NY, 1989.

Kekre, S., and Mukhopadhyay, T. "Impact of electronic data interchange on quality improvement and inventory reduction programs: A field study." *International Journal of Production Economics*, 28, pp. 265–282, 1992.

Krafcik, J. "High performance manufacturing: An international study of auto assembly practice." Working paper, Massachusetts Institute of Technology, Cambridge, MA, 1988.

Kreps, D. "A course in microeconomic theory." Princeton, NJ: Princeton University Press, 1990.

Kumbhakar, S.C. "The specification of technical and allocative inefficiency in stochastic production and profit frontiers." *Journal of Econometrics*, 34, pp. 335–348, 1987.

Kumbhakar, S.C., Biswas, B., and Bailey, D. Von. "A study of economic efficiency of Utah dairy farmers: A systems approach." *The Review of Economics and Statistics*, pp. 595–604, 1989.

Lee, B., and Barua, A. "Assessing productivity and efficiency impacts of information technologies: Old data, new analysis and evidence." *Journal of Productivity Analysis*, 12(1), 1999, pp. 21–43.

Lichtenberg, F.R. "The output contributions of computer equipment and personnel: A firm-level analysis." *Economics of Innovation and New Technology*, 3, pp. 201–217, 1995 (previously Working Paper, 1993).

Lohr, S. "Computer Age Gains Respect of Economists." *New York Times*, p. A1, April 14, 1999.

Loveman, G.W. "An assessment of the productivity impact of information technologies." In *Information Technology and the Corporation of the 1990s: Research Studies*, T.J. Allen and M.S. Scott-Morton (eds.), Cambridge, MA: MIT Press, 1994 (previously MIT Working Paper, 1988).

McKeen, J.D., and Smith, H.A. "The relationship between information technology and organizational performance." In *Strategic Information Technology Management: Perspectives on Organizational Growth and Competitive Advantage*, R.D. Banker, R.J. Kauffman, and M.A. Mahmood (eds.). Harrisburg, PA: Idea Group Publishing, 1993.

Markus, M.L. and Soh, C. "Banking on information technology: Converting IT spending into firm performance." In *Strategic Information Technology Management: Perspectives on Organizational Growth and Competitive Advantage*, R.D. Banker, R.J. Kauffman, and M.A. Mahmood (eds.). Harrisburg, PA: Idea Group Publishing, 1993.

Marschak, J. "The payoff relevant description of states and acts." *Econometrica*, Vol. 31, No. 4, pp. 719–725, 1963.

Marschak, J. "Efficient choice of information services." In *Management Information Systems: Progress and Perspectives,* C.H. Kriebel et al. (eds.). Pittsburgh, PA: Carnegie Press, 1971.

Marschak, J., and Radner, R. *Economic Theory of Teams.* New Haven, CT: Yale University Press, 1972.

Menon, N., Lee, B., and Eldenburg, L. "Productivity of information systems in the health-care industry." forthcoming *Information Systems Research,* 2000.

Milgrom, P., and Roberts, J. "The economics of modern manufacturing: Technology, strategy and organization." *American Economic Review,* pp. 511–528, June 1990.

Moore, J.C., and Whinston, A.B. "A model of decision making with sequential information acquisition (Part 1)." *Decision Support Systems,* Vol. 2, pp. 285–307, 1986.

Moore, J.C., and Whinston, A.B. "A model of decision making with sequential information acquisition (Part 2)." *Decision Support Systems,* Vol. 3, pp. 47–72, 1987.

Morrison, C.J., and Berndt, E.R. "Assessing the productivity of information technology equipment in U.S. manufacturing industries." Paper presented at the 1990 Annual Meeting of the American Economic Association, Washington, DC, December 1990.

Mukhopadhyay, T. "Assessing the economic impacts of electronic data interchange technology." In *Strategic Information Technology Management: Perspectives on Organizational Growth and Competitive Advantage,* R.D. Banker, R.J. Kauffman, and M.A. Mahmood (eds.). Harrisburg, PA: Idea Group Publishing, 1993.

Mukhopadhyay, T., and Cooper, R.B. "Impact of management information systems on decisions." *Omega,* Vol. 20 (1), pp. 37–49, 1992a.

Mukhopadhyay, T., and Cooper, R.B. "Impact of management information systems on firm productivity." Pittsburgh, PA: Carnegie Mellon University, 1992b.

Mukhopadhyay, T., Kekre, S., and Kalathur, S. "Business value of information technology: A study of electronic data interchange." *MIS Quarterly,* 19 (2), pp. 137–156, 1995.

Mukhopadhyay, T., Lerch, F.J., and Mangal, V. "Assessing the impact of information technology on labor productivity—A field study." *Decision Support Systems,* 19, 2, pp. 109–122, 1997.

Mukhopadhyay, T., and Mangal, V. "Direct and indirect impacts of information technology applications on productivity: A field study." *International Journal of Electronic Commerce,* 1 (3), pp. 85–100, 1997.

Mukhopadhyay, T., Rajiv, S., and Srinivasan, K. "Information technology impact on process output and quality." *Management Science,* 43, 12, pp. 1645–1659, 1997.

Oman, R.C., and Ayers, T. "Productivity and cost-benefit analysis for information technology decisions." *Information Management Review,* 3, 3, pp. 31–41, 1988.

Panko, R. "Is office productivity stagnant?" *MIS Quarterly,* 15, pp. 191–203, 1991.

Pentland, B.T. "Use and productivity in personal computing." *Proceedings of the Tenth International Conference on Information Systems,* Boston, MA, pp. 211–222, 1989.

Roach, S.S. "America's technology dilemma: A profile of the information economy." Special Economic Study, Morgan Stanley and Co., April 1987.

Roach, S.S. "Stop rolling the dice on technology spending." Interview with G. Harrar, editor, *Computerworld Extra,* June 20, 1988.

Roach, S.S. "The case of the missing technology payback." Paper presented at the Tenth International Conference on Information Systems, Boston, MA, 1989.

Roach, S.S. "Services under siege: The restructuring imperative." *Harvard Business Review,* 69, 5, pp. 82–91, September–October 1991.

Rockart, J.F. "Chief executives define their own data needs." *Harvard Business Review,* 57, 2, pp. 81–93, 1979.

Rogawoski, A., and Adams, D.A. "Assessing IT value through organizational activities." Working paper, Wayne State University, 1998.

Schmidt, P., and Lovell, C.A.K. "Estimating technical and allocative efficiency relative to stochastic production and cost frontiers." *Journal of Econometrics,* 9, pp. 343–366, 1979.

Solow, R.M. "We'd better watch out." *New York Times,* p. 36, July 12, 1987.

Srinivasan, K., Kekre, S., and Mukhopadhyay, T. "Impact of electronic data interchange technology on JIT shipments." *Management Science,* 40 (10), pp. 1291–1304, 1994.

Strassman, P.A. *Information payoff.* New York: The Free Press, 1985.

Turner, J. "Organizational performance, size and the use of data processing resources." Working paper 58, Center for Research in Information Systems, New York University, 1988.

Venkatraman, N., and Zaheer, A. "Electronic integration and strategic advantage: A quasi-experimental study in the insurance industry." *Information Systems Research,* 1, 4, pp. 377–393, 1990.

Weill, P. "Do computers pay off?" Washington, DC: ICIT Press, 1990.

Weill, P. "The relationship between investment in information technology and firm performance: A study of the valve manufacturing sector." *Information Systems Research,* 3, 4, pp. 307–333, 1992.

Wilson, D.D. "Assessing the impact of information technology on organizational performance." In *Strategic Information Technology Management: Perspectives on Organizational Growth and Competitive Advantage,* R.D. Banker, R.J. Kauffman, and M.A. Mahmood (eds.). Harrisburg, PA: Idea Group Publishing, 1993.

CHAPTER 6, RITU AGARWAL

Adams, D., Nelson R.R., and Todd, P. "Perceived Usefulness, Ease of Use, and Usage of Information Technology: A Replication." *MIS Quarterly* (16:2), 1992, 227–248.

Agarwal, R., and Prasad, J. "The Role of Innovation Characteristics and Perceived Voluntariness in the Acceptance of Information Technologies." *Decision Sciences* (28:3), 1997, 557–582.

Agarwal, R., and Prasad, J. "A Conceptual and Operational Definition of Personal Innovativeness in the Domain of Information Technology." *Information Systems Research* (9:2), 1998a, 204–215.

Agarwal, R., and Prasad, J. "The Antecedents and Consequents of User Perceptions in Information Technology Acceptance." *Decision Support Systems* (22), 1998b, 15–29.

Agarwal, R., and Prasad, J. "Are Individual Differences Germane to the Acceptance of Information Technologies?" *Decision Sciences* (30:2), 1999, 361–391.

Agarwal, R., Prasad, J., and Zanino, M. "Training Experiences and Usage Intentions: A Field-Study of a Graphical User Interface." *International Journal of Human-Computer Studies* (45), 1996, 215–241.

Agarwal, R., Sambamurthy, V., and Stair, R. "Cognitive Absorption and the Adoption of New Information Technologies." *Proceedings of the Academy of Management Best Papers,* Boston, 1997.

Ajzen, I. "The Theory of Planned Behavior." *Organizational Behavior and Human Decision Processes* (50), 1991, 179–211.

Ajzen, I., and Fishbein, M. *Understanding Attitudes and Predicting Social Behavior,* Englewood Cliffs, NJ: Prentice-Hall, 1980.

Ajzen, I., and Madden, T.J. "Prediction of Goal-Directed Behavior: Attitudes, Intentions and Perceived Behavioral Control." *Journal of Experimental Social Psychology* (22:5), 1986, 453–474.

Bagozzi, R.P. "Expectancy Value Attitude Models: An Analysis of Critical Measurement Issues." *International Journal of Research in Marketing* (1), 1984, 295–310.

Bandura, A. "Self-Efficacy: Toward a Unifying Theory of Behavioral Change." *Psychological Review* (84:2), 1977, 191–215.

Bandura, A. *Social Foundations of Thought and Action: A Social Cognitive Theory.* Englewood Cliffs, NJ: Prentice-Hall, 1986.

Bandura, A. *Self-Efficacy: The Exercise of Control.* New York: W.H. Freeman, 1997.

Barki, H., and Hartwick, J. "Rethinking the Concept of User Involvement." *MIS Quarterly* (13:1), 1989, 53–63.

Barki, H., and Hartwick, J. "Measuring User Participation, User Involvement, and User Attitude." *MIS Quarterly* (18:1), 1994.

Beath, C.M. "Supporting the Information Technology Champion." *MIS Quarterly* (15:3), 1991, 355–371.

Benbasat, I., and Taylor, R.N. "The Impact of Cognitive Styles on Information Systems Design." *MIS Quarterly* (2:2), 1978, 43–54.

Bostrom, R.P., Olfman, L., and Sein, M.K. "End-User Computing: A Research Framework for Investigating the Training/Learning Process." In *Human Factors in Management Information Systems,* ed. J.M. Carey. Norwood, NJ: Ablex, 1988, 221–250.

Bostrom, R.P., Olfman, L., and Sein, M.K. "The Importance of Learning Style in End-User Training." *MIS Quarterly* (14:1), 1990, 101–119.

Boynton, A.C., Zmud, R.W., and Jacobs, G.C. "The Influence of IT Management Practice on IT Use in Large Organizations." *MIS Quarterly* (18:3), 1994, 299–318.

Brancheau, J.C., and Wetherbe, J.C. "The Adoption of Spreadsheet Software: Testing Innovation Diffusion Theory in the Context of End-User Computing." *Information Systems Research* (1:2), 1990, 115–143.

Burns, T., and Stalker, G. *The Management of Innovation.* London: Tavistock, 1961.

Carlson, J.R., and Zmud, R.W. "Channel Expansion Theory and the Experiential Nature of Media Richness Perceptions." *Academy of Management Journal* (42:2), 1999, 153–170.

Compeau, D.R., and Higgins, C.A. "Computer Self-Efficacy: Development of a Measure and Initial Test." *MIS Quarterly* (19:2), 1995a, 189–211.

Compeau, D.R.. and Higgins, C.A. "Application of Social Cognitive Theory to Training for Computer Skills." *Information Systems Research* (6:2), 1995b, 118–143.

Cooper, R.B., and Zmud, R.W. "Information Technology Implementation Research: A Technological Diffusion Approach." *Management Science* (36:2), 1990, 123–139.

Davis, F.D. "Perceived Usefulness, Perceived Ease of Use, and User Acceptance of Information Technology." *MIS Quarterly* (13:3), December 1989, 319–340.

Davis, F.D. "User Acceptance of Information Technology: System Characteristics, User Perceptions and Behavioral Impacts." *International Journal of Man-Machine Studies* (38), 1993, 475–487.

Davis, F.D., Bagozzi, R., and Warshaw, P.R. "User Acceptance of Computer Technology." *Management Science* (35:8), August 1989, 982–1003.

Davis, F.D., Bagozzi, R.P., and Warshaw, P.R. "Extrinsic and Intrinsic Motivation to Use Computers in the Workplace." *Journal of Applied Social Psychology* (22:14), 1992, 1111–1132.

Davis, S.A., and Bostrom, R.P. "Training End Users: An Experimental Investigation of the Roles of the Computer Interface and Training Methods." *MIS Quarterly* (17:1), 1993, 61–85.

Delone, W.H. "Determinants of Success for Computer Usage in Small Business." *MIS Quarterly* (12:1), 1988, 51–61.

DeSanctis, G. "An Examination of an Expectancy Theory Model of Decision Support System Use." *Proceedings of the Third International Conference on Information Systems.* Ann Arbor, MI, 1982, 121–135.

Ellen, P.S., Bearden, W.O., and Sharma, S. "Resistance to Technological Innovations: An Examination of the Role of Self-Efficacy and Performance Satisfaction." *Journal of the Academy of Marketing Science* (19:4), 1991, 297–307.

Fishbein, M., and Ajzen, I. *Belief, Attitude, Intention and Behavior: An Introduction to Theory and Research.* Reading, MA: Addison-Wesley, 1975.

Fuerst, W.L., and Cheney, P.H. "Factors Affecting the Perceived Utilization of Computer-Based Decision Support Systems in the Oil Industry." *Decision Sciences* (13), 1982, 554–569.

Fulk, J. "Social Construction of Communication Technology." *Academy of Management Journal* (36:5), 1993, 921–950.

Gist, M., Schwoerer, C., and Rosen, B. "Effects of Alternative Training Methods on Self-Efficacy and Performance in Computer Software Training." *Journal of Applied Psychology* (74:6), 1989, 884–891.

Goodhue, D.L. "Development and Measurement Validity of a Task-Technology Fit Instrument for User Evaluations of Information Systems." *Decision Sciences* (29:1), 1998, 105–138.

Goodhue, D.L., and Thompson, R.L. "Task-Technology Fit and Individual Performance." *MIS Quarterly* (19:2), 1995, 213–236.

Hage, J., and Aiken, M. *Social Change in Complex Organizations.* New York: Random House, 1970.

Hartwick, J., and Barki, H. "Explaining the Role of User Participation in Information Systems Use." *Management Science* (40:4), 1994, 440–465.

Harrison, A.W., and Rainer, R.K., Jr. "The Influence of Individual Differences on Skill in End-User Computing." *Journal of Management Information Systems* (9:1), 1992, 93–111.

Igbaria, M., Gamers, T., and Davis, G.B. "Testing the Determinants of Microcomputer Usage via a Structural Equation Model." *Journal of Management Information Systems* (11:4), 1995, 87–114.

Karahanna, E., and Straub, D.W. "The Psychological Origins of Perceived Usefulness and Ease of Use." *Information and Management* (35), 1999, 237–250.

Karahanna, E., Straub, D.W., and Chervany, N.L. "Information Technology Adoption Across Time: A Cross-Sectional Comparison of Pre-Adoption and Post-Adoption Beliefs." *MIS Quarterly* (23:2), 1999.

King, J. "Shipping Firms Exploit IT to Deliver E-Commerce Goods." *Computerworld Online,* August 2, 1999.

Kraut, R.E., Rice, R.E., Cool, C., and Fish, R.S. "Varieties of Social Influence: The Role of Utility and Norms in the Success of a New Communication Medium." *Organization Science* (9:4), 1998, 437–453.

Kwon, T.H., and Zmud, R.W. "Unifying the Fragmented Models of Information Systems Implementation." In *Critical Issues in Information Systems Research,* ed. R. Boland and R. Hirscheim. Chichester, UK: Wiley, 1987, 88–97.

Leonard-Barton, D. "Implementation Structured Software Methodologies: A Case of Innovation in Process Technology." *Interfaces* (17:3), 1987, 6–17.

Leonard-Barton, D., and Deschamps, I. "Managerial Influence in the Implementation of New Technology." *Management Science* (34:10), 1988, 1252–1265.

Lutz, R.J. "The Role of Attitude Theory in Marketing." In *Perspectives in Consumer Behavior,* ed. H.H. Kassarjian and T.S. Robertson. Glenview, IL: Scott Foresman, 1976, 233–250.

Majchrzak, A., and Cotton, J. "A Longitudinal Study of Adjustment to Technological Change: From Mass to Computer-Automated Batch Production." *Journal of Occupational Psychology* (61), 1988, 43–66.

Marakas, G., Yi, M., and Johnson, R. "The Multilevel and Multifaceted Character of Computer Self-Efficacy: Toward Clarification of the Construct and an Integrative Framework for Research." *Information Systems Research* (9:2), 1998, 126–163.

Martocchio, J.J. "Effects of Conceptions of Ability on Anxiety, Self-Efficacy, and Learning in Training." *Journal of Applied Psychology* (79:6), 1994, 819–825.

Mathieson, K. "Predicting User Intentions: Comparing the Technology Acceptance Model with the Theory of Planned Behavior." *Information Systems Research* (2:3), September 1991, 173–191.

Monge, P.R., Cozzens, M.D., and Contractor, N.S. "Communication and Motivational Predictors of the Dynamics of Organizational Innovation." *Organization Science* (3:2), 1992, 250–274.

Moore, G.C., and Benbasat, I. "Development of an Instrument to Measure the Perceptions of Adopting an Information Technology Innovation." *Information Systems Research* (2:3), September 1991, 192–222.

Nambisan, S., Agarwal, R., and Tanniru, M. "Organizational Mechanisms for Enhancing User Innovation in Information Technology." *MIS Quarterly* (23:3), 1999.

Nonaka, I., and Takeuchi, H. *The Knowledge Creating Company.* New York: Oxford University Press, 1995.

Orlikowski, W.J., Yates, J., Okamura, K., and Fujimoto, M. "Shaping Electronic Communication: The Metastructuring of Technology in the Context of Use." *Organization Science* (6:4), 1995, 423–444.

Pennings, J.M., and Harianto, F. "The Diffusion of Technological Innovation in the Commercial Banking Industry." *Strategic Management Journal* (13:1), 1992, 29–46.

Ram, S., and Jung, H.-S. "'Forced' Adoption of Innovation in Organizations: Consequences and Implications." *Journal of Production and Innovation Management* (8:2), 1991, 117–126.

Raymond, L. "The Impact of Computer Training on the Attitudes and Usage Behavior of Small Business Managers." *Journal of Small Business Management* (26), 1988, 8–13.

Ritti, R., and Silver, J. "Early Processes of Institutionalization: The Dramaturgy of Exchange in Interorganizational Relationships." *Administrative Science Quarterly* (31:1), 1986, 25–42.

Rogers, E.M. *The Diffusion of Innovations.* 3d ed. New York: Free Press, 1983.

Rogers, E.M. *The Diffusion of Innovations.* 4th ed. New York: Free Press, 1995.

Saga, V., and Zmud, R.W. "The Nature and Determinants of IT Acceptance, Routinization, and Infusion." In *Diffusion, Transfer, and Implementation of Information Technology,* ed. L. Levine. New York: North-Holland, 1994, 67–86.

Sanders, L., and Courtney, J. "A Field Study of Organizational Factors Influencing DSS Success." *MIS Quarterly* (9:1), 1985, 77–93.

Schmidt, F.L. "Implications of a Measurement Problem for Expectancy Theory Research." *Organizational Behavior and Human Performance* (10), 1973, 243–251.

Schmitz, J., and Fulk, J. "Organizational Colleagues, Media Richness, and Electronic Mail: A Test of the Social Influence Model of Technology Use." *Communication Research* (18:4), 1991, 487–523.

Scott, S.G., and Bruce, R.A. "Determinants of Innovative Behavior: A Path Model of Individual Innovation in the Workplace." *Academy of Management Journal* (37:3), 1994, 580–607.

Scott, W.R. *Institutions and Organizations.* Thousand Oaks, CA: Sage, 1995.

Sheppard, B.H., Hartwick, J., and Warshaw, P.R. "The Theory of Reasoned Action: A Meta-Analysis of Past Research with Recommendations for Modifications and Future Research." *Journal of Consumer Research* (15), December 1988, 325–343.

Szajna, B. "Empirical Evaluation of the Revised Technology Acceptance Model." *Management Science* (42:1), January 1996, 85–92.

Taylor, S., and Todd, P. "Understanding Information Technology Usage: A Test of Competing Models." *Information Systems Research* (6:2), 1995a, 144–176.

Taylor, S., and Todd, P. "Assessing IT Usage: The Role of Prior Experience." *MIS Quarterly* (19:4), 1995b, 561–570.

Thompson, R.L., Higgins, C., and Howell, J.M. "Personal Computing: Towards a Conceptual Model of Utilization." *MIS Quarterly* (15:1), 1991, 125–143.

Thompson, R.L., Higgins, C., and Howell, J.M. "Influence of Experience on Personal Computer Utilization: Testing a Conceptual Model." *Journal of Management Information Systems* (11:1), 1994, 167–187.

Tornatzky, L.G., Eveland, J.D., and Fleischer, M. "Technological Innovation: Definitions and Perspectives." In *The Processes of Technological Innovation,* ed. L.G. Tornatzky and M. Fleischer. Lexington, MA: Lexington Books, 1990, 9–25.

Tornatzky, L.G., and Klein, K.J. "Innovation Characteristics and Innovation Adoption-Implementation: A Meta-Analysis of Findings." *IEEE Transactions on Engineering Management* (EM29:1), February 1982.

Walsh, J.P., and Ungson, G.R. "Organizational Memory." *Academy of Management Review* (16:1), 1991, 57–91.

Webster, J., and Ho, H. "Audience Engagement in Multi-Media Presentations." *The DATA-BASE for Advances in Information Systems* (28:2), 1997, 63–77.

Webster, J., and Martocchio, J.J. "Microcomputer Playfulness: Development of a Measure with Workplace Implications." *MIS Quarterly* (16:2), 1992, 201–226.

Webster, J., Trevino, L.K., and Ryan, L. "The Dimensionality and Correlates of Flow in Human-Computer Interactions." *Computers in Human Behavior* (9), 1993, 411–426.

Weick, K.E. *Sensemaking in Organizations.* Thousand Oaks, CA: Sage, 1995.

Wynekoop, J.L., Senn, J.A., and Conger, S.A. "The Implementation of CASE Tools: An Innovation Diffusion Approach." In *The Impact of Computer Supported Technologies on Information Systems Development,* ed. K.E. Kendall et al. Amsterdam: Elsevier, 1992, 25–41.

Yin, R.K. "Life Histories of Innovations: How New Practices Become Routinized." *Public Administration Review* (41:1), 1981, 21–28.

Zaltman G., Duncan, R., and Holbek, J. *Innovations and Organizations.* New York: Wiley, 1973.

Zinkhan, G.M., Joachimsthaler, E.A., and Kinnear, T.C. "Individual Differences and Marketing Decision Support System Usage and Satisfaction." *Journal of Marketing Research* (24:2), 1987, 208–214.

Zmud, R.W. "Individual Differences and MIS Success: A Review of the Empirical Literature." *Management Science* (25:10), 1979, 966–979.

Zmud, R.W. "Diffusion of Modern Software Practices: Influence of Centralization and Formalization." *Management Science* (28), 1982, 1421–1431.

Zmud, R.W. "An Examination of 'Push-Pull' Theory Applied to Process Innovation in Knowledge Work." *Management Science* (30:6), 1984, 727–738.

CHAPTER 7, ROBERT G. FICHMAN

Abrahamson, E. "Managerial Fads and Fashions: The Diffusion and Rejection of Innovations." *Academy of Management Review* (16:3), 1991, pp. 586–612.

Abrahamson, E. "Management Fashion." *Academy of Management Review* (21:1), 1996, pp. 254–285.

Abrahamson, E., and Rosenkopf, L. "Social Network Effects on the Extent of Innovation Diffusion: A Computer Simulation." *Organization Science* (8:3), 1997, pp. 289–309.

Afuah, A. *Innovation Management: Strategies, Implementation, and Profits.* New York: Oxford University Press, 1998.

Arthur, W.B. "Competing Technologies: An Overview." In *Technical Change and Economic Theory*, ed. G. Dosi, C. Freeman, R. Nelson, G. Silverberg, and L. Soete. London: Pinter Publishers, 1988, pp. 590–607.

Arthur, W.B. "Increasing Returns and the New World of Business." *Harvard Business Review* (74:4), 1996, pp. 101–109.

Attewell, P. "Technology Diffusion and Organizational Learning: The Case of Business Computing." *Organization Science* (3:1), 1992, pp. 1–19.

Ball, L.D., Dambolena, I.G., and Hennessey, H.D. "Identifying Early Adopters of Large Software Systems." *Database* (Fall/Winter 1987/88), 1987, pp. 21–27.

Boynton, A.C., Zmud, R.W. and Jacobs, G.C. "The Influence of IT Management Practice on IT Use in Large Organizations." *MIS Quarterly* (18:3), 1994, pp. 299–318.

Brancheau, J.C., and Wetherbe, J.C. "The Adoption of Spreadsheet Software: Testing Innovation Diffusion Theory in the Context of End-User Computing." *Information Systems Research* (1:2), 1990, pp. 115–143.

Bretschneider, S., and Wittmer, D. "Organizational Adoption of Microcomputer Technology: The Role of Sector." *Information Systems Research* (4:1), 1993, pp. 88–109.

Brynjolfsson, E., and Kemerer, C.F. "Network Externalities in Microcomputer Software: An Econometric Analysis of the Spreadsheet Market." *Management Science* (42:12), 1997, pp. 1627–1647.

Brynjolfsson, E., Renshaw, A.A., and Van Alstyne, M. "The Matrix of Change." *Sloan Management Review* (38:2), 1997, pp. 22–40.

Carlson, J.R., and Zmud, R.W. "Channel Expansion Theory and the Experiential Nature of Media Richness Perceptions." *Academy of Management Journal* (42:2), 1999, pp. 153–170.

Cats-Baril, W.L., and Jelassi, T. "The French Videotex System Minitel: A Successful Implementation of a National Information Technology Infrastructure." *MIS Quarterly* (18:1), 1994, pp. 1–20.

Chew, B.W., Leonard-Barton, D., and Bohn, R.E. "Beating Murphy's Law." *Sloan Management Review* (32:3), 1991, pp. 5–16.

Chin, W.W., Gopal, A., and Salisbury, W.D. "Advancing the Theory of Adaptive Structuration: The Development of a Scale to Measure Faithfulness of Appropriation." *Information Systems Research* (8:4), 1997, pp. 342–367.

Cohen, W.M., and Levinthal, D.A. "Absorptive Capacity: A New Perspective on Learning and Innovation." *Administrative Science Quarterly* (35:1), 1990, pp. 128–152.

Cool, K.O., Diericks, I., and Szulanski, G. "Diffusion of Innovations Within Organizations: Electronic Switching in the Bell System, 1971–1982." *Organization Science* (8:5), 1997, pp. 543–559.

Cooper, R.B., and Zmud, R.W. "Information Technology Implementation Research: A Technological Diffusion Approach." *Management Science* (36:2), 1990, pp. 123–139.

Cusumano, M.A., Mylonadis, Y., and Rosenbloom, R. "Strategic Maneuvering and Mass-Market Dynamics: The Triumph of VHS over Beta." *Business History Review* (6:1), 1992, pp. 51–94.

Damanpour, F. "Organizational Innovation: A Meta-Analysis of Effects of Determinants and Moderators." *Academy of Management Journal* (34:3), 1991, pp. 555–590.

David, P.A. "Clio and the Economics of QWERTY." *American Economic Review, Proceedings* (75), 1985, pp. 332–337.

Davis, F. "Perceived Usefulness, Perceived Ease of Use, and User Acceptance of Information Technology." *MIS Quarterly* (13:3), 1989, pp. 319–340.

Davis, F., Bagozzi, R., and Warshaw, R. "User Acceptance of Computer Technology: A Comparison of Two Theoretical Models." *Management Science* (35:8), 1989, pp. 982–1003.

DeSanctis, G., and Poole, M.S. "Capturing the Complexity in Advanced Technology Use: Adaptive Structuration Theory." *Organization Science* (5:2), 1994, pp. 121–147.

Downs, G.W., and Mohr, L.B. "Conceptual Issues in the Study of Innovation." *Administrative Science Quarterly* (21:December), 1976, pp. 700–714.

Eveland, J.D., and Tornatzky, L.G. "The Deployment of Technology." In *The Processes of Technological Innovation,* ed. L.G. Tornatzky and M. Fleischer. Lexington, MA: Lexington Books, 1990, pp. 117–148.

Farrell, J., and Saloner, G. "Competition, Compatibility and Standards: The Economics of Horses, Penguins and Lemmings." In *Product Standardization and Competitive Strategy,* ed. H.L. Gabel. North-Holland: Elsevier Science, 1987, pp. 940–955.

Fichman, R.G. "Information Technology Diffusion: A Review of Empirical Research." *Proceedings of the Thirteenth International Conference on Information Systems.* Dallas, 1992, pp. 195–206.

Fichman, R.G. "The Measurement of Adopter Innovativeness." Working paper. Available from the author, 1999.

Fichman, R.G., and Kemerer, C.F. "Adoption of Software Engineering Process Innovations: The Case of Object Orientation." *Sloan Management Review* (34:2), 1993, pp. 7–22.

Fichman, R.G., and Kemerer, C.F. "The Assimilation of Software Process Innovations: An Organizational Learning Perspective." *Management Science* (43:10), 1997a, pp. 1345–1363.

Fichman, R.G., and Kemerer, C.F. "Object Technology and Reuse: Lessons from Early Adopters." *IEEE Computer* (30:10), 1997b, pp. 47–59.

Fichman, R.G., and Kemerer, C.F. "The Illusory Diffusion of Innovation: An Examination of Assimilation Gaps." *Information Systems Research* (10:3), 1999.

Fichman, R.G., and Moses, S.A. "An Incremental Process for Software Implementation." *Sloan Management Review* (40:2), 1999, pp. 39–52.

Frank, R.H., and Cook, P.J. *The Winner-Take-All Society.* New York: Free Press, 1995.

Fulk, J. "Social Construction of Communication Technology." *Academy of Management Journal* (36:5), 1993, pp. 921–950.

Gallivan, M.J., Hofman, J.D., and Orlikowski, W.J. "Implementing Radical Change: Gradual Versus Rapid Pace." *Proceedings of the Fifteenth International Conference on Information Systems.* Vancouver, British Columbia, Canada, 1994, pp. 325–339.

Gatignon, H., and Robertson, T.S. "Technology Diffusion: An Empirical Test of Competitive Effects." *Journal of Marketing* (53:1), 1989, pp. 35–49.

Gefen, D., and Straub, D.W. "Gender Differences in the Perception and Use of E-Mail: An Extension to the Technology Acceptance Model." *MIS Quarterly* (21:4), 1997, pp. 389–400.

Gill, T.G. "Early expert systems: Where Are They Now?" *MIS Quarterly* (19:1), 1995, pp. 51–81.

Granovetter, M., and Soong, R. "Threshold Models of Diffusion and Collective Behavior." *The Journal of Mathematical Sociology* (9), 1983, pp. 165–179.

Grover, V., Fiedler, K., and Teng, J. "Empirical Evidence on Swanson's Tri-Core Model of Information Systems Innovation." *Information Systems Research* (8:3), 1997, pp. 273–287.

Grover, V., and Goslar, M.D. "The Initiation, Adoption and Implementation of Telecommunications Technologies in U.S. Organizations." *Journal of Management Information Systems* (10:1), 1993, pp. 141–163.

Gurbaxani, V. "Diffusion in Computing Networks: The Case of BITNET." *Communications of the ACM* (33:12), 1990, pp. 65–75.

Gurbaxani, V., and Mendelson, H. "An Integrative Model of Information Systems Spending Growth." *Information Systems Research* (1:1), 1990, pp. 23–47.

Hamel, G. "The Challenge Today: Changing the Rules of the Game." *Business Strategy Review* (9:2), 1998, pp. 19–26.

Hart, P., and Saunders, C. "Power and Trust: Critical Factors in the Adoption and Use of Electronic Data Interchange." *Organization Science* (8:1), 1997, pp. 23–42.

Hart, P.J., and Saunders, C.S. "Emerging Electronic Partnerships: Antecedents and Dimensions of EDI Use from the Supplier's Perspective." *Journal of Management Information Systems* (14:4), 1998, pp. 87–111.

Hoffer, J.A., and Alexander, M.B. "The Diffusion of Database Machines." *Data Base* (23), 1992, pp. 13–19.

Hoffman, C.C. "Innovations in Research-Based Practice—Applying Range Restriction Corrections Using Published Norms: Three Case Studies." *Personnel Psychology* (48:4), 1995, pp. 913–923.

Howard, G.S., and Rai, A. "Promise and Problems: CASE Usage in the U.S." *Journal of Information Technology* (8:2), 1993, pp. 65–73.

Howell, J.M., and Higgens, C.A. "Champions of Technological Innovation." *Administrative Science Quarterly* (35:2), 1990, pp. 317–341.

Hu, Q., Saunders, C., and Gebelt, M. "Research Report: Diffusion of Information Systems Outsourcing: A Reevaluation of Influence Sources." *Information Systems Research* (8:3), 1997, pp. 288–301.

Huff, S.L., and Munro, M.C. "Managing Micro Proliferation." *Journal of Information Systems Management* (6:4), 1989, pp. 72–75.

Iacovou, C.L., Benbasat, I., and Dexter, A.S. "Electronic Data Interchange and Small Organizations: Adoption and Impact of Technology." *MIS Quarterly* (19:4), 1995, pp. 465–485.

Karahanna, E., and Straub, D.W. "The Psychological Origins of Perceived Usefulness and Ease-of-Use." *Information Management* (35:4), 1999, pp. 237–250.

Katz, M.L., and Shapiro, C. "Technology Adoption in the Presence of Network Externalities." *Journal of Political Economy* (94:4), 1986, pp. 822–841.

Kelly, P., and Kranzberg, M. "Technological Innovation: A Critical Review of Current Knowledge." San Francisco: San Francisco Press, 1978.

Kimberley, J.R., and Evanisko, M.J. "Organizational Innovation: The Influence of Individual, Organizational, and Contextual Factors on Hospital Adoption of Technical and Administrative Innovations." *Academy of Management Journal* (24:4), 1981, pp. 689–713.

King, J.L., Gurbaxani, V., Kraemer, K.L., McFarlan, F.W., Raman, K.S., and Yap, C.S. "Institutional Factors in Information Technology Innovation." *Information Systems Research* (5:2), 1994, pp. 139–169.

Kogut, B. "Joint Ventures: Theoretical and Empirical Perspectives." *Strategic Management Journal* (9:4), 1988, pp. 319–332.

Kraut, R.E., Rice, R.E., Cool, C., and Fish, R.S. "Varieties of Social Influence: The Role of Utility and Norms in the Success of a New Communication Medium." *Organization Science* (9:4), 1998, pp. 437–453.

Kwon, T.H., and Zmud, R.W. "Unifying the Fragmented Models of Information Systems Implementation." In *Critical Issues in Information Systems Research*, ed. J.R. Boland and R. Hirshheim. New York: John Wiley, 1987, pp. 227–251.

Lai, V.S. "Critical Factors of ISDN Implementation: An Exploratory Study." *Information Management* (33:2), 1997, pp. 87–97.

Lai, V.S., Guynes, J.L., and Bordoloi, B. "ISDN: Adoption and Diffusion Issues." *Information Systems Management* (10:4), 1993, pp. 46–54.

Leonard-Barton, D. "Experts as Negative Opinion Leaders in the Diffusion of a Technological Innovation." *Journal of Consumer Research* (11:4), 1985, pp. 914–926.

Leonard-Barton, D. "Implementation Characteristics of Organizational Innovations." *Communication Research* (15:5), 1988a, pp. 603–631.

Leonard-Barton, D. "Implementation as Mutual Adaptation of Technology and Organization." *Research Policy* (17:5), 1988b, pp. 251–267.

Leonard-Barton, D., and Deschamps, I. "Managerial Influence in the Implementation of New Technology." *Management Science* (34:10), 1988, pp. 1252–1265.

Levitt, T. *The Marketing Imagination*. New York: Free Press, 1986.

Liker, J.K., Fleischer, M., and Arnsdorf, D. "Fulfilling the Promises of CAD." *Sloan Management Review* (33:3), 1992, pp. 74–86.

Lind, M.R., Zmud, R.W., and Fischer, W.A. "Microcomputer Adoption—The Impact of Organizational Size and Structure." *Information & Management* (16:3), 1989, pp. 157–162.

Loh, L., and Venkatraman, N. "Determinants of Information Technology Outsourcing: A Cross-Sectional Analysis." *Journal of Management Information Systems* (9:1), 1992, pp. 7–24.

McGraith, R.G. "A Real Options Logic for Initiating Technology Positioning Investments." *Academy of Management Review* (22:4), 1997, pp. 974–996.

Mahajan, V., Muller, E., and Bass, F.M. "New Product Diffusion Models in Marketing: A Review and Directions for Research." *Journal of Marketing* (54:January), 1990, pp. 1–26.

Mahajan, V., and Peterson, R. *Models for Innovation Diffusion*. Beverly Hills, CA: Sage Publications, 1985.

Mansfield, E.D. "The Diffusion of Flexible Manufacturing Systems in Japan, Europe and the United States." *Management Science* (39:2), 1993, pp. 149–159.

Markus, M.L. "Toward a 'Critical Mass' Theory of Interactive Media: Universal Access, Interdependence and Diffusion." *Communications Research* (14:5), 1987, pp. 491–511.

Markus, M.L., and Keil, M. "If We Build It, They Will Come: Designing Information Systems That People Want to Use." *Sloan Management Review* (35:4), 1994, pp. 11–25.

Massetti, B., and Zmud, R.W. "Measuring the Extent of EDI Usage in Complex Organizations: Strategies and Illustrative Examples." *MIS Quarterly* (20:3), 1996, pp. 331–345.

Meyer, A.D., and Goes, J.B. "Organizational Assimilation of Innovations: A Multilevel Contextual Analysis." *Academy of Management Journal* (31:4), 1988, pp. 897–923.

Moore, G.A. *Crossing the Chasm.* New York: HarperBusiness, 1992.

Moore, G.C., and Benbasat, I. "Development of an Instrument to Measure the Perceptions of Adopting an Information Technology Innovation." *Information Systems Research* (2:3), 1991, pp. 192–222.

Nilakanta, S., and Scamell, R.W. "The Effect of Information Sources and Communication Channels on the Diffusion of an Innovation in a Data Base Environment." *Management Science* (36:1), 1990, pp. 24–40.

Oliver, P., Marwell, G., and Teixeira, R. "A Theory of the Critical Mass. I. Interdependence, Group Heterogeneity, and the Production of Collective Action." *American Journal of Sociology* (91:3), 1985, pp. 522–556.

Orlikowski, W.J. "CASE Tools as Organizational Change: Investigating Incremental and Radical Changes in Systems Development." *MIS Quarterly* (17:3), 1993, pp. 309–340.

Orlikowski, W.J., and Hofman, J.D. "An Improvisational Model for Change Management: The Case of Groupware Technologies." *Sloan Management Review* (38:2), 1997, pp. 11–21.

Parker, P.M. "Aggregate Diffusion Forecasting Models in Marketing: A Critical Review." *International Journal of Forecasting* (10:2), 1994, pp. 353 380.

Pennings, J.M., and Harianto, F. "Technological Networking and Innovation Implementation." *Organization Science* (3:3), 1992, pp. 356–382.

Premkumar, G., Ramamurthy, K., and Nilakanta, S. "Implementation of Electronic Data Interchange: An Innovation Diffusion Perspective." *Journal of Management Information Systems* (11:2), 1994, pp. 157–186.

Prescott, M.B. "Diffusion of Innovation Theory: Borrowings, Extensions, and Modifications from IT Researchers." *Database* (26:2&3), 1995, pp. 16–19.

Raho, L.E., Belohlav, J.A., and Fiedler, K.D. "Assimilating New Technology into the Organization: An Assessment of McFarlan and McKenney's Model." *MIS Quarterly* (11:1), 1987, pp. 43–56.

Rai, A. "External Information Source and Channel Effectiveness and the Diffusion of CASE Innovations: An Empirical Study." *European Journal of Information Systems* (4:2), 1995, pp. 93–102.

Rai, A., and Bajwa, D.S. "An Empirical Investigation into Factors Relating to the Adoption of Executive Information Systems: An Analysis of EIS for Collaboration and Decision Support." *Decision Sciences* (28:4), 1997, pp. 939–974.

Rai, A., Ravichandran, T., and Samaddar, S. "How to Anticipate the Internet's Global Diffusion," *Communications of the ACM* (41:10), 1998, pp. 97–106.

Ramiller, N.C. "Perceived Compatibility of Information Technology Innovations among Secondary Adopters: Toward a Reassessment." *Journal of Engineering Technology Management* (11:1), 1994, pp. 1–23.

Reddy, N.M., Aram, J.D., and Lynn, L.H. "The Institutional Domain of Technology Diffusion." *Journal of Product Innovation Management* (8:4), 1991, pp. 295–304.

Robertson, T.S., and Gatignon, H. "Competitive Effects on Technology Diffusion." *Journal of Marketing* (50:3), 1986, pp. 1–12.

Rogers, E.M. "The 'Critical Mass' in the Diffusion of Interactive Technologies in Organizations." In *The Information Systems Research Challenge: Survey Research Methods*, Vol. 3, ed. K.L. Kraemer, J.I. Cash, and J.F. Nunamaker. Boston: Harvard Business School Research Colloquium, 1991.

Rogers, E.M. *Diffusion of Innovations.* New York: Free Press, 1995.

Rosenberg, N. "On Technological Expectations." *The Economic Journal* (86:September), 1976, pp. 523–535.

Rosenberg, N. *Exploring the Black Box: Technology, Economics and History.* Cambridge, UK: Cambridge University Press, 1994.

Russo, M.V. "The Multidivisional Structure as an Enabling Device: A Longitudinal Study of Discretionary Cash as a Strategic Resource." *Academy of Management Journal* (34:3), 1991, pp. 718–733.

Sambamurthy, V., and Chin, W.W. "The Effects of Group Attitudes Toward Alternative GDSS Designs on the Decision-Making Performance of Computer-Supported Groups." *Decision Sciences* (25:2), 1994, pp. 215–241.

Schilling, M.A. "Technological Lockout: An Integrative Model of the Economic and Strategic Factors Driving Technology Success and Failure." *Academy of Management Review* (23:2), 1998, pp. 267–284.

Shapiro, C., and Varian, H.R. *Information Rules: A Strategic Guide to the Network Economy.* Boston: Harvard Business School Press, 1998.

Singer, J.D., and Willett, J.B. "Modeling the Days of Our Lives: Using Survival Analysis When Designing and Analyzing Longitudinal Studies of Duration and Timing of Events." *Psychological Bulletin* (110:2), 1991, pp. 268–290.

Swanson, E.B. "Information Systems Innovations among Organizations." *Management Science* (40:9), 1994, pp. 1069–1092.

Swanson, E.B., and Ramiller, N.C. "The Organizing Vision in Information Systems Innovation." *Organization Science* (8:5), 1997, pp. 458–474.

Szajna, B. "Empirical Evaluation of the Revised Technology Acceptance Model." *Management Science* (42:1), 1996, pp. 85–92.

Tornatzky, L.G., and Fleischer, M. *The Processes of Technological Innovation.* Lexington, MA: Lexington Books, 1990.

Tornatzky, L.G., and Klein, K.J. "Innovation Characteristics and Innovation Adoption-Implementation: A Meta-Analysis of Findings." *IEEE Transactions on Engineering Management* (EM–29:1), 1982, pp. 28–45.

Venkatraman, N., Loh, L., and Koh, J. "The Adoption of Corporate Governance Mechanisms: A Test of Competing Diffusion Models." *Management Science* (40:4), 1994, pp. 496–507.

Webster, J., and Trevino, L.K. "Rational and Social Theories as Complementary Explanations of Communication Media Choices: Two Policy-Capturing Studies." *Academy of Management Journal* (38:6), 1995, pp. 1544–1572.

Wheeler, B.C., and Valacich, J.S. "Facilitation, GSS, and Training as Sources of Process Restrictiveness and Guidance for Structured Group Decision Making: An Empirical Assessment." *Information Systems Research* (7:4), 1996, pp. 429–450.

Williams, L.R. "Understanding Distribution Channels: An Interorganizational Study of EDI Adoption." *Journal of Business Logistics* (15:2), 1994, pp. 173–203.

Yin, R.K. *Changing Urban Bureaucracies.* Lexington, MA: Lexington Books, 1979.

Zaltman, G., Duncan, R., and Nolbeck, J. *Innovations and Organizations.* New York: John Wiley, 1973.

Zmud, R.W. "Diffusion of Modern Software Practices: Influence of Centralization and Formalization." *Management Science* (28:12), 1982, pp. 1421–1431.

Zmud, R.W. "The Effectiveness of External Information Channels in Facilitating Innovation Within Software Groups." *MIS Quarterly* (June 1983), 1983, pp. 43–56.

Zmud, R.W., and Apple, L.E. "Measuring Technology Incorporation/Infusion." *Journal of Product Innovation Management* (9:2), 1992, pp. 148–155.

Zmud, R.W., Lind, M.R., and Young, F.W. "An Attribute Space for Organizational Communication Channels." *Information Systems Research* (1:4), 1990, pp. 440–457.

CHAPTER 8, LORNE OLFMAN AND PROADPRAN PITSATORN

Anonymous. 1996. 1996 Industry report: Technology and training. *Training,* 73–79.

Atlas, Robert, Larry Cornett, David M. Lane, and H. Albert Napier. 1997. The use of animation in software training: Pitfalls and benefits. In *Training for a rapidly changing workplace: Applications of psychological research,* ed. M. A. Quinones and A. Ehrenstein. Washington, DC: American Psychological Association.

Benko, Shelia. 1997. Preparing for EPSS projects. *Communications of the ACM* 40 (7):60–63.

Bohlen, George A., and Thomas W. Ferratt. 1997. End user training: An experimental comparison of lecture versus computer-based training. *Journal of End User Computing* 9 (3):14–27.

Bostrom, Robert P., Lorne Olfman, and Maung K. Sein. 1990. The importance of learning style in end-user training. *MIS Quarterly* (March 1990):101–119.

Bowman, Brent J., Fritz H. Grupe, and Mark G. Simkin. 1995. Teaching end-user applications with computer-based training: Theory and an empirical investigation. *Journal of End User Computing* 7 (2):12–18.

Carroll, John M. 1997. Toward minimalist training: Supporting the sense-making activities of computer users. In *Training for a rapidly changing workplace,* ed. M. A. Quinones and A. Ehrenstein. Washington, DC: American Psychological Association.

Carroll, J. M., J. R. Olson, and N. Anderson. 1987. *Mental models in human-computer interaction: Research issues about what the user of software knows.* Ann Arbor, MI: Cognitive Science and Machine Intelligence Laboratory, University of Michigan.

Carroll, John M., and Mary Beth Rosson. 1995. Managing evaluation goals for training. *Communications of the ACM* 38 (7):40–48.

Compeau, Deborah R., and Christopher A. Higgins. 1995. Application of social cognitive theory to training for computer skills. *Information Systems Research* 6 (2):118–143.

Compeau, Deborah, Lorne Olfman, Maung Sein, and Jane Webster. 1995. End-user training and learning. *Communications of the ACM* 39 (7):24–26.

Davis, S. A., and R. P. Bostrom. 1993. Training end-users: An experimental investigation of the roles of computer interface and training methods. *MIS Quarterly* 17 (1):61–85.

Desmarais, Michel C., Richard Leclair, Jean-Yves Fiset, and Hichem Talbi. 1997. Cost-justifying electronic performance support systems. *Communications of the ACM* 40 (7):39–48.

Fitzgerald, Edmond P., and Aileen Cater-Steel. 1995. Champagne training on a beer budget. *Communications of the ACM* 38 (7):49–60.

Ford, Nelson F., William N. Ledbetter, and Tom L. Roberts. 1996. The impact of decision support training on computer use: The effect of prior training, age, and gender. *Journal of End User Computing* 8:15–23.

Galletta, Dennis F., Manju K. Ahuja, Amir Hartman, Thompson Teo, and A. Graham Peace. 1995. Social influence and end-user training. *Communications of the ACM* 38 (7):70–79.

Gist, Marilyn E., Chatherine Schwoerer, and Benson Rosen. 1989. Effects of alternative training methods on self-efficacy and performance in computer software training. *Journal of Applied Psychology* 74 (6):884–891.

Hayen, Roger L., Wells F. Cook, and Gregory H. Jecker. 1990. End user training in office automation: Matching expectations. *Journal of Systems Management* 4 (3):7–12.

Kappelman, Leon A., and Carl Stephen Guynes. 1995. End-user training and empowerment. *Journal of Systems Management* 46 (5):36–41.

Karten, Naomi. 1991. Integrating IS disciplines into end-user training. *Journal of Information Systems Management* 8 (1):75–78.

Kay, Judy, and Rochard C. Thomas. 1995. Studying long-term system use. *Communications of the ACM* 38 (7):61–69.

Kraiger, Kurt, J. Kevin Ford, and Eduardo Salas. 1993. Application of cognitive, skill-based, and effective theories of learning outcomes to new methods of training evaluation. *Journal of Applied Psychology* 78 (2):311–328.

Kraiger, Kurt, and Katharine M. Jung. 1997. Linking training objectives to evaluation criteria. In *Training for a rapidly changing workplace: Applications of psychological research*, ed. M. A. Quinones and A. Ehrenstein. Washington, DC: American Psychological Association.

Lee, Sang M., Yeong R. Kim, and Jaejung Lee. 1995. An empirical study of the relationships among end-user information systems acceptance, training, and effectiveness. *Journal of Management Information Systems* 12 (2):189–202.

Mackay, Jane M., and Charles W. Lamb Jr. 1991. Training needs of novices and experts with referent experience and task domain knowledge. *Information Management* 20 (3):183–189.

Martocchio, Joseph J., and Timothy A. Judge. 1997. Relationship between conscientiousness and learning in employee training: Mediating influences of self-deception and self-efficacy. *Journal of Applied Psychology* 82 (5):764–773.

Martocchio, Joseph J., and Jane Webster. 1992. Effects of feedback and cognitive playfulness on performance in microcomputer software training. *Personnel Psychology* 45 (3):553–578.

Nelson, Ryan R., Ellen M. Whitener, and Henry H. Philcox. 1995. The assessment of end-user training needs. *Communications of the ACM* 38 (7):27–39.

Olfman, L., and R. P. Bostrom. 1991. End-user software training: An experimental comparison of methods to enhance motivation. *Journal of Information Systems* (1):249–266.

Olfman, L., and M. Mandviwalla. 1994. Conceptual versus procedural software training for graphical user interfaces: A longitudinal field experiment. *MIS Quarterly* 18 (4):405–426.

Olfman, L., and M. K. Sein. 1997. Ten lessons from research for end-user trainers. In *End User Computing Management*. Boston: Auerbach Publishers.

Robey, D., and W. Taggart. 1982. Human information processing in information and decision support systems. *MIS Quarterly* 6 (1):61–73.

Santhanam, Radhika, and Maung K. Sein. 1994. Improving end-user proficiency: Effects of conceptual training and nature of interaction. *Information Systems Research* 5 (4):378–399.

Sein, M. K., and R. P. Bostrom. 1989. Individual differences and conceptual models in training novice users. *Human-Computer Interaction* 4:197–229.

Sein, Maung K., Robert Bostrom, and Lorne Olfman. 1987. Training end-users to computer: Cognitive, motivational and social issues. *INFOR* 25:236–255.

Sein, Maung K., Robert P. Bostrom, and Lorne Olfman. 1999. Rethinking end-user training strategy: Applying a hierarchical knowledge-level model. *Journal of End User Computing* 11 (1):32–39.

Sein, Maung K., Lorne Olfman, Robert P. Bostrom, and Sidney A. Davis. 1993. Visualization ability as a predictor of user learning success. *International Journal of Man-Machine Studies* 39 (4):559–620.

Shayo, Conrad, and Lorne Olfman. 2000. The role of training in preparing end users to learn related software. *Journal of End User Computing* (12):3–14.

Shayo, Conrad, Lorne Olfman, and Ricardo Teitelroit. 1999. An exploratory study of the value of pretraining end-user participation. *Information Systems Journal* (9):55–79.

Simon, Steven J., Varun Grover, James T. C. Teng, and Kathleen Whitcomb. 1996. The relationship of information system training methods and cognitive ability to end-user satisfaction, comprehension, and skill transfer: A longitudinal field study. *Information Systems Research* 7 (4):466–490.

Snell, N. 1997. Why can't Johnny do client/server? *Inside Technology Training* (July/August):21–26.

Szajna, Bernadette, and Jane M. Mackay. 1995. Predictors of learning performance in a computer-user training environment: A path-analytic study. *International Journal of Human-Computer Interaction* 7 (2):167–185.

Webster, Jane, and Joseph J. Martocchio. 1993. Turning work into play: Implications for microcomputer software training. *Journal of Management* 19 (1):127–146.

Webster, Jane, and Joseph J. Martocchio. 1995. The differential effects of software training previews on training outcomes. *Journal of Management* 21 (4):757–787.

CHAPTER 9, VARUN GROVER AND WILLIAM J. KETTINGER

Cooper, R., and Markus, M.L. (1995). Human reengineering. *Sloan Management Review* 36(4), 39–50.

Davenport, T. H. (1993) *Process Innovation: Reengineering Work Through Information Technology*. Boston: Harvard Business School Press.

Davenport, T.H. (1995) Business process reengineering: Where it's been, where it's going. In *Business Process Change: Concepts, Methods & Technologies,* ed. V. Grover and W.J. Kettinger. Harrisburg, PA: Idea Publishing.

DeLone, W., and McLean, E.R. (1992) Information systems success: The quest for the dependent variable. *Information Systems Research* 3(1), 60–95.

Earl, M.J. (1994) The old and new of business process design. *Journal of Strategic Information Systems* 3 (1), 5–22.

French, W L., and Bell, C.H. (1978) *Organization Development*. Englewood Cliffs, NJ: Prentice Hall.

Ginzberg, M.J. (1981) Early diagnosis of MIS implementation failure: Promising results and unanswered questions. *Management Science* 27(4), 459–478.

Grover, V. (1993) An empirically derived model for the adoption of customer-based interorganizational systems. *Decision Sciences* 24(3), 603–640.

Grover, V. (1999) From business reengineering to business process change management: A longitudinal study of trends and practices. *IEEE Transactions on Engineering Management* 46(1), 36–46.

Grover, V., Fiedler, K.D., and Teng, J.T.C. (1994) Exploring the success of information technology enabled business process reengineering. *IEEE Transactions on Engineering Management* 41(3), 1–8.

Grover, V., Jeong, S.Y., Kettinger, W.J., and Teng, J.T.C. (1995) The implementation of business process reengineering. *Journal of Management Information Systems* 12(1), 109–144.

Grover, V., Teng, J.T.C., and Fiedler, K.D. (1993) Information technology enabled business process redesign: An integrated planning framework. *OMEGA* 21(4), 433–447.

Guha, S., Grover, V., Kettinger W.J., and Teng, J.T.C. (1997) Business process change and organizational performance: exploring an antecedent model. *Journal of Management Information Systems* 14(1), 119–154.

Hall, G., Rosenthal, J., and Wade, J. (1993) How reengineering really works. *Harvard Business Review* 71(6), 119–131.

Hamilton, S., and Chervany, N.L. (1981) Evaluating information system effectiveness—part I: Comparing evaluation approaches. *MIS Quarterly* 5(3), 55–69.

Hammer, M. (1990) Reengineering works: Don't automate, obliterate. *Harvard Business Review* 68(4), 104–112.

Huber, G.P., and Power, D.J. (1985) Research notes and communications retrospective reports of strategic-level managers: Guidelines for increasing their accuracy. *Strategic Management Journal* 6, 171–180.

Ives, B., and Mason, R.O. (1990) Can information technology revitalize your customer service? *Academy of Management Executives* 4(4), 52–69.

Keen, P.G.W. (1981) Information systems and organizational change. *Communications of the ACM* 24(1), 24–33.

Kettinger, W.S., and Grover, V. (1995). Toward a theory of business process change management. *Journal of Management Information Systems* 12(1), 1–30.

Kettinger, W.J., and Teng, J.T.C. (1998) Aligning BPC to strategy: A framework for analysis. *Long Range Planning* 31(1), 93–107.

Kettinger, W.J., Guha, S., and Teng, J.T.C. (1995) The process reengineering life cycle methodology: A case study. In *Business Process Change: Reengineering Concepts, Methods and Technologies,* ed. V. Grover and W.J. Kettinger. Harrisburg, PA: Idea Publishing, 210–244.

Kettinger, W.J., Teng J.T.C., and Guha, S. (1997) Business process change: A study of methodologies, techniques and tools. *MIS Quarterly* 21(1), 55–80.

Lewin, K. (1951) *Field Theory in Social Science.* New York: Harper and Row.

Liker, J., Roitman, D.B., and Roskies, E. (1987–Summer) Changing everything all at once: Work life and technological change. *Sloan Management Review,* 29–47.

Lucas, H.C. (1978) Empirical evidence for a descriptive model of implementation. *MIS Quarterly* 2(2), 27–41.

Lucas H.C. Jr. (1984) Organizational power and the information services department. *Communications of the ACM* 27(1), 58–65.

Markus, M.L. (1983) Power, politics and MIS implementation. *Communications of the ACM,* 26(6), 583–598.

Markus, M.L., and Robey, D. (1995) Business process reengineering and the role of information systems professionals. In *Business Process Change: Concepts, Methods and Technologies,* ed. V. Grover and W.J. Kettinger. Harrisburg, PA: Idea Publishing.

Melone, N.P. (1995) When people work scared: Understanding attitudes and gaining compliance in business process re-engineering. In *Business Process Change: Concepts, Methods, and Technologies,* ed. V.B. Grover and W.J. Kettinger. Harrisburg, PA: Idea Publishing.

Miller, W. (1987) *The Creative Edge.* Reading, MA: Addison-Wesley.

Morris, D., and Brandon, J. (1993) *Re-engineering your business.* New York: McGraw-Hill.

Mumford, E. (1994) New treatment or old remedies: Is BPC really socio-technical design? *Journal of Strategic Information Systems* 3(4), 313–326.

Mumford, E., and Weir, M. (1979) *Computer Systems in Work Designs: The ETHICS Method.* New York: Wiley.

Nadler, D., and Tushman, M. (1980, Spring) A model for diagnosing organizational behavior. *Organizational Dynamics,* 143–163.

Nutt, P.C. (1986–June) Tactics of implementation. *Academy of Management Journal,* 230–261.

O'Hara, M.T., and Watson, R.T. (1995) Automation, business process reengineering and client server computing. In *Business Process Change: Reengineering Concepts, Methods and Technology,* ed. V. Grover and W.J. Kettinger. Harrisburg, PA: Idea Publishing, 143–164.

Pierce J.L., and Delbecq, A.L. (1977) Organizational structure, individual attributes and innovation. *Academy of Management Review* 2, 27–37.

Premkumar, G., and King, W.R. (1992) An empirical assessment of information systems planning and the role of information systems in organizations. *Journal of Management Information Systems* (2), 94–125.

Ramamurthy, K. (1990) *Role of Environmental, Organizational and Technological Factors in Information Technology Implementation in Advanced Manufacturing: An Innovation-Adoption-Diffusion Perspective.* Unpublished doctoral dissertation, University of Pittsburgh.

Saunders, C.S., and Scamell, R.W. (1986) Organizational power and the information services department: A reexamination. *Communications of the ACM* 29(2), 142–147.

Schriven, M. (1972) The methodology of evaluation: Formative and summative evaluation. In *Evaluating Action Programs,* ed. C.H. Weiss. Boston, MA: Allyn and Bacon.

Scott Morton, M.S. (ed.) (1991) *The Corporation of the 1990s: Information Technology and Organizational Transformation.* New York: Oxford University Press.

Smith, G., and Willcocks, L. (1995) Business process reengineering, politics management: From methodologies to processes. In *Business Process Change: Reengineering Concepts, Methods and Technologies,* ed. V. Grover and W.J. Kettinger. Harrisburg, PA: Idea Publishing.

Stoddard, D., and Jarvenpaa, S. (1995) Business process reengineering: Tactics for managing radical change. *Journal of Management Information Systems* 12(1), 81–108.

Teng, J.T.C., Fiedler, K.D., and Grover V. (1998) An exploratory study of the influence of the IS function and organizational context on business process reengineering project initiatives. *OMEGA* 26(6), 679–698.

Teng, J.T.C., Grover, V., and Fiedler, K.D. (1994) Re-engineering business processes using information technology. *Long Range Planning* 27(1), 95–106.

Teng, J.T.C., Grover, V., and Fiedler, K.D. (1996) Developing strategic perspectives on business process reengineering: From process reconfiguration to organizational change. *OMEGA* 24(3), 271–294.

Teng, J.T.C., Jeong, S.R., and Grover V. (1998) Profiling successful reengineering projects. *Communications of the ACM* 41(6), 96–102.

Teng, J.T.C., and Kettinger, W.J. (1995) Business process redesign and information architecture: Exploring the relationships. *Data Base* 26(1), 30–42.

Zmud, R. (1982) Diffusion of modern software practices: Impact of centralization and formalization. *Management Science* 28(12), 420–430.

CHAPTER 10, M. LYNNE MARKUS AND CORNELIS TANIS

Alter, S. "A General, Yet Useful Theory of Information Systems." *Communications of the Association for Information Systems,* Volume 1, Number 13, 1999.

AMR Research. "AMR Research Predicts ERP Market Will Reach $66.6 Billion by 2003." May 28, 1999.

Aragon, L. "Backup in the Expresso Lane: Starbucks Finds Fixes to Its Supply Chain Come Slowly with the Company's Best-of-Breed Approach." *PC Week*, November 10, 1997.

Bailey, J. "Trash Haulers Are Taking Fancy Software to the Dump: Allied Waste, Following Waste Management, to Shed SAP's Costly R/3." *The Wall Street Journal,* June 9, 1999, p. B4.

Bancroft, N. H.; Seip, H.; and Sprengel, A. *Implementing SAP R/3: How to Introduce a Large System into a Large Organization.* Greenwich, CT: Manning, 1997.

Bashein, B. J., and Markus, M. L. *Data Warehousing: More Than Just Mining.* Morristown, NJ: Financial Executives Research Foundation, 2000.

Bashein, B. J.; Markus, M. L.; and Finley, J. B. *Safety Nets: Secrets of Effective Information Technology Controls.* Morristown, NJ: Financial Executives Research Foundation, 1997.

Brown, D. Personal communication, May 27, 1999.

Bulkeley, W. M. "A Cautionary Network Tale: Fox-Meyer's High-Tech Gamble." *The Wall Street Journal* Interactive Edition, November 18, 1996.

Caldwell, B., and Stein, T. "New IT Agenda." *InformationWeek,* November 30, 1998, pp. 30–38.

Cole-Gomolski, B. "ERP! Excuse Us As We Digest Our New System—Ripple Effect Can Hurt Customer Service." *Computerworld,* September 21, 1998, pp. 1, 100.

Connolly, J. "ERP: Corporate Cleanup. The Appeal of ERP May Come Less from Any Cash Benefits and More from Its Ability to Untangle Snarled Business Practices and Systems." *Computerworld,* March 1, 1999, pp. 74, 78.

Davenport, T. H. "Putting the Enterprise into the Enterprise System." *Harvard Business Review,* July–August 1998, pp. 121–131.

Davis, F. D.; Bagozzi, R. P.; and Warshaw, P. R. "User Acceptance of Computer Technology: A Comparison of Two Theoretical Models." *Management Science,* Volume 35, Number 8, 1989, pp. 982–1003.

Dearden, J. "MIS Is a Mirage." *Harvard Business Review,* January–February 1972, pp. 101–110.

DeSanctis, G., and Poole, M. S. "Capturing the Complexity in Advanced Technology Use: Adaptive Structuration Theory." *Organization Science,* Volume 5, Number 2, 1994, pp. 121–147.

Ferranti, M. "Debunking ERP Misconceptions." *Infoworld,* September 17, 1998.

Fichman, R. G., and Kemerer, C. F. "The Assimilation of Software Process Innovations: An Organizational Learning Perspective." *Management Science,* Volume 43, Number 10, 1997, pp. 135–1363.

Hammer, M. "Reengineering Works: Don't Automate, Obliterate." *Harvard Business Review,* Volume 68, Number 4, 1990, pp. 104–112.

Hirt, S. G., and Swanson, E. B. "Adopting SAP at Siemens Power Corporation." *Journal of Information Technology,* Volume 14, Number 3, 1999, pp. 243–252.

King, J. L. "Informal Remarks on Information Systems Research at WISRD '99, Lake Arrowhead, CA." April 17, 1999.

Kling, R. "Social Analyses of Computing: Theoretical Perspectives in Recent Empirical Research." *Computing Surveys,* Volume 12, 1980, pp. 61–110.

Koch, C. "The Big Uneasy." *CIO Magazine,* October 15, 1997.

KPMG. "Exploiting Packaged Software: A Business Guide to Package-Focused Business Solutions." http:/www.kpmg.co.uk/uk/services/manage/pubs/siipsap.html. 1998.

Larsen, M. A., and Myers, M. D. "BPR Success or Failure? A Business Process Reengineering Model in the Financial Services Industry." *Proceedings of the International Conference on Information Systems, Atlanta, GA,* 1997, pp. 367–382.

Lientz, B. P., and Swanson, E. B. *Software Maintenance Management: A Study of the Maintenance of Computer Application Software in 487 Data Processing Organizations.* Reading, MA: Addison-Wesley, 1980.

McKenney, J. L.; Copeland, D. C.; and Mason, R. O. *Waves of Change: Business Evolution Through Information Technology.* Boston, MA: Harvard Business School Press, 1995.

McKenney, J. L., and McFarlan, F. W. "Information Archipelago—Maps and Bridges." *Harvard Business Review,* September–October 1982.

Markus, M. L., and Robey, D. "Information Technology and Organizational Change: Causal Structure in Theory and Research." *Management Science,* Volume 34, Number 5, 1988, pp. 583–598.

Nidumolu, S. "The Effect of Coordination and Uncertainty on Software Project Performance: Residual Performance Risk as an Intervening Variable." *Information Systems Research,* Volume 6, Number 3, 1995, pp. 191–219.

Orlikowski, W. J. "Improvising Organizational Transformation over Time: A Situated Change Perspective." *Information Systems Research,* Volume 7, Number 1, 1996, pp. 63–92.

Orlikowski, W. J., and Robey, D. "Information Technology and the Structuring of Organizations." *Information Systems Research,* Volume 2, Number 2, 1991, pp. 143–169.

Perrow, C. *Complex Organizations: A Critical Essay.* Glenview, IL: Scott Foresman, 1972.

Pfeffer, J. *Organizations and Organization Theory.* Marshfield, MA: Pitman, 1982.

Radosevich, L. "Quantum's Leap: One Computer Manufacturer's Risky Decision to Overhaul Its Worldwide Business Systems in a Single Bound Paid Off." *CIO,* February 15, 1997.

Ross, J. "The ERP Revolution: Surviving Versus Thriving." Working Paper #307, Center for Information Systems Research, MIT, August 1999.

Schneider, P. "Wanted: ERPeople Skills." *CIO Magazine,* March 1, 1999.

Silver, M. S.; Markus, M. L.; and Beath, C. M. "The Information Technology Interaction Model: A Foundation for the MBA Core Course." *MIS Quarterly,* Volume 19, Number 3, 1995, pp. 361–390.

Slater, D. "An ERP Package for You . . . and You . . . and You . . . and Even You." *CIO Magazine,* February 15, 1999.

Soh, C., and Markus, M. L. "How IT Creates Business Value: A Process Theory Synthesis." *Proceedings of the Sixteenth International Conference on Information Systems,* Amsterdam, The Netherlands, 1995, pp. 29–41.

Stedman, C. "ERP Can Magnify Errors." *Computerworld,* October 19, 1998a, pp. 1, 14.

Stedman, C. "Grocer Trips over SAP: Early-Release R/3 Stymies System Performance." *Computerworld,* December 7, 1998b, pp. 1, 89.

Stedman, C. "Shoemakers Wrestle with SAP Projects." *Computerworld,* December 14 1998c, p. 4.

Stedman, C., "ERP Projects Cost More Than Their 'Measurable' Payback, Study Says." *Computerworld,* March 29, 1999a, http://www.computerworld.com/home/news.nsf/all/9903291meterp, access date 1/18/2000.

Stedman, C. "Supply-Chain Plans Pay Off: After Clearing Early ERP Hurdles, Benefits Start to Flow." *Computerworld,* March 1, 1999b, http://www.computerworld.com/home/print.nsf/all/99030193SE, access date 1/18/2000

Stein, T. "Midmarket ERP." *InformationWeek,* December 14, 1998, p. 62.

Taylor, J. C. *Performance by Design: Sociotechnical Systems in North America.* Englewood Cliffs, NJ: Prentice Hall, 1993.

Tyre, M. J., and Orlikowski, W. J. "Windows of Opportunity: Temporal Patterns of Technological Adaptation in Organizations." *Organization Science,* Volume 5, Number 1, 1994, pp. 98–118.

CHAPTER 11, JEFFREY L. SAMPLER

Alchian, A. (1969) "Information Costs, Pricing, and Resource Unemployment." *Western Economic Journal*, Vol. 7, pp. 109–128.

Anshen, M. (1960) "The Manager and the Black Box." *Harvard Business Review,* Vol. 38, No. 6, pp. 85–92.

Applegate, L.M., Cash, J.I., and Miles, D.Q. (1988) "Information Technology and Tomorrow's Manager." *Harvard Business Review,* Vol. 66, No. 6, pp. 128–136.

Arrow, K. (1962) *Economic Welfare and the Allocation of Resources for Invention, in the Rate and Direction of Inventive Activity.* Princeton, NJ: Princeton University Press, pp. 609–625.

Arrow, K. (1971) *Essays in the Theory of Risk Bearing.* Chicago: Markham.

Arrow, K. (1974) *The Limits of Organization.* New York: Norton.

Bain, J.S. (1956) *Barriers to New Competition.* Cambridge, MA: Harvard University Press.

Bakos, J.Y., and Brynjolfsson, E. (1993) "Information Technology, Incentives and the Optimal Number of Suppliers." *Journal of Management Information Systems,* Vol. 10, No. 2, pp. 37–53.

Barney, J.B. (1986) "Strategic Factor Markets: Expectations, Luck, and Business Strategy." *Management Science,* Vol. 32, pp. 1231–1241.

Barney, J.B. (1991) "Firm Resources and Sustained Competitive Advantage." *Journal of Management,* Vol. 17, pp. 99–120.

Bartlett, C.A., and Ghoshal, S. (1998) *Managing Across Borders: The Transnational Solution* (2d ed.). Boston: Harvard Business School Press.

Barua, A., Ravindran, S., and Whinston, A.B. (1997) "Efficient Selection of Suppliers over the Internet." *Journal of Management Information Systems,* Vol. 13, No. 4, pp. 117–137.

Bell, D. (1981) *The Crisis in Economic Theory.* New York: Basic Books.

Bettis, R.A., and Hitt, M.A. (1995) "The New Competitive Landscape." *Strategic Management Journal,* Special Issue, Vol. 16, pp. 7–19.

Blau, P.M., Falbe, C.M., McKinley, W., and Tracy, P.K. (1976) "Technology and Organizing in Manufacturing." *Administrative Science Quarterly,* Vol. 21, No. 1, pp. 20–40.

Brown, S.L., and Eisenhardt, K.M. (1998) *Competing on the Edge.* Boston: Harvard Business School Press.

Brynjolfsson, E. (1993) "The Productivity Paradox of Information Technology." *Communications of the ACM,* Vol. 16, No. 12, pp. 66–77.

Caves, R.E., and Porter, M.E. (1977) "From Entry Barriers to Mobility Barriers: Conjectural Decisions and Contrived Deterrence to New Competition." *Quarterly Journal of Economics,* Vol. 91, pp. 241–261.

Chandler, A.D. (1994) *Scale and Scope: The Dynamics of Industrial Capitalism.* New York: Belknap Press.

Chesbrough, H.W., and Teece, D.J. (1996) "When Is Virtual Virtuous? Organizing for Innovation." *Harvard Business Review,* Vol. 74, No. 1, pp. 65–73.

Child, J. (1973) "Predicting and Understanding Organization Structure." *Administrative Science Quarterly,* Vol. 18, pp. 168–185.

Choudhury, V., and Sampler, J.L. (1997) "Information Specificity and Environmental Scanning: An Economic Perspective." *MIS Quarterly,* Vol. 21, No. 1, pp. 25–53.

Christensen, C.M. (1997) *The Innovator's Dilemma.* Boston: Harvard Business School Press.

D'Aveni, R. (1994) *Hypercompetition: Managing the Dynamics of Strategic Manoeuvring.* New York: Free Press.

Davidse, J. (1983) "Characteristics of Growth and Limitations in Electronics." *Technological Forecasting and Social Change,* Vol. 24, pp. 125–135.

Financial Times. (1999) "E-Commerce Could Reduce VAT Revenues." August 30, p. 5.

Fukuyama, F. (1999) *The Great Disruption: Human Nature and the Reconstruction of Social Order.* New York: Free Press.

Gilder, G. (1989) *Microcosm: The Quantum Revolution in Economics and Technology.* New York: Simon and Schuster.

Grant, R.M. (1996) "Prospering in Dynamically-Competitive Environments: Organizational Capability as Knowledge Integration." *Organization Science,* Vol. 7, No. 4, pp. 375–387.

Hamel, G. (1996) "Strategy as Revolution." *Harvard Business Review,* Vol. 74, No. 4, pp. 69–82.

Hamel, G., and Prahalad, C.K. (1994) *Competing for the Future.* Boston: Harvard Business School Press.

Hamel, G., and Sampler, J.L. (1998) "The E-Corporation." *Fortune,* December 7, pp. 80–92.

Hart, S., and Banbury, C. (1994) "How Strategy-Making Processes Can Make a Difference." *Strategic Management Journal,* Vol. 15, No. 4, pp. 251–269.

Hawken, P. (1983) *The Next Economy.* New York: Holt, Rinehart, and Winston.

Itami, H. (1987) *Mobilizing Invisible Assets.* Cambridge, MA: Harvard Business School Press.

Johnston, H.R. and Vitale, M.R. (1988) "Creating Competitive Advantage with Interorganizational Information Systems." *MIS Quarterly,* Vol. 12, No. 2, pp. 153–165.

Kogut, B., and Zander, U. (1992) "Knowledge of the Firm, Combinative Capabilities, and the Replication of Technology." *Organization Science,* Vol. 3, No. 3, pp. 383–397.

Leavitt, H.J. and. Whisler, T.L. (1958) "Management in the 1980s." *Harvard Business Review,* Vol. 36, No. 6, pp. 41–48.

Lippman, S.A., and Rumelt, R. (1982) "Uncertain Imitability: An Analysis of Interfirm Differences in Efficiency Under Competition." *Bell Journal of Economics,* Vol. 13, pp. 418–438.

McGahan, A.M., and Porter, M.E. (1997) "How Much Does Industry Matter, Really?" *Strategic Management Journal,* Vol. 18, Special Issue, pp. 15–30.

McKenney, J.L. (1995) *Waves of Change.* Boston, MA: Harvard Business School Press.

Mason, E. (1939) "Price and Production Policies of Large-Scale Enterprises." *American Economic Review,* 29, pp. 61–74.

Nelson, R.R. (1994) "Why Do Firms Differ, and How Much Does It Matter? In *Fundamental Issues in Strategy Research,* ed. Rumelt, Schendel, and Teece. Boston, MA: Harvard Business School Press, pp. 247–269.

Nonaka, I. (1994) "A Dynamic Theory of Organizational Knowledge Creation." *Organization Science,* Vol. 5, No. 1, pp. 14–37.

Ohmae, K. (1995) *The End of the Nation State: The Rise of Regional Economies.* New York: Free Press.

Ohmae, K. (1999) *The Borderless World: Power and Strategy in the Interlinked Economy.* New York: Harper Business.

Pascale, R.T. (1999) "Surfing the Edge of Chaos." *Sloan Management Review,* Vol. 40, No. 3, pp. 83–94.

Perrow, C. (1967) "A Framework for the Comparative Analysis of Organizations." *American Sociological Review,* Vol. 32, pp. 194–208.

Perrow, C. (1970) *Organizational Analysis: A Sociological Review.* Belmont, CA: Wadsworth.

Peteraf, M. (1993) "The Cornerstones of Competitive Advantage: A Resource-Based View." *Strategic Management Journal,* Vol. 14, No. 3, pp. 179–192.

Porter, M.E. (1980) *Competitive Strategy.* New York: Free Press.

Powell, T.C. (1996) "How Much Does Industry Really Matter? An Alternative Empirical Test." *Strategic Management Journal,* Vol. 17, No. 4, pp. 323–334.

Prahalad, C.K., and Hamel, G. (1990) "The Core Competence of the Corporation." *Harvard Business Review,* May–June, pp. 79–91.

Quinn, J.B. (1992) *Intelligent Enterprise: A New Paradigm for a New Era.* New York: The Free Press.

Robey, D. (1977) "Computers and Management Structure: Some Empirical Findings Re-Examined." *Human Relations,* Vol. 30, pp. 963–976.

Robey, D. (1981) "Computer Information Systems and Organizational Structure." *Communications of the ACM,* Vol. 24, No. 10, pp. 679–687.

Rosenberg, N. (1982) *Inside the Black Box: Technology and Economics.* Cambridge, UK: Cambridge University Press.

Rothschild, M. (1973) "Models of Market Organization with Imperfect Information: A Survey." *Journal of Political Economy,* Vol. 81, pp. 1283–1308.

Rumelt, R.P. (1991) "How Much Does Industry Matter?" *Strategic Management Journal,* Vol. 12, No. 3, pp. 167–185.

Sampler, J.L. (1998) "Redefining Industry Structure for the Information Age." *Strategic Management Journal,* Vol. 19, No. 4, pp. 343–355.

Schmalensee, R. (1985) "Do Markets Differ Much?" *American Economic Review,* Vol. 75, No. 3, pp. 341–351.

Senge, P.M. (1990) *The Fifth Discipline.* New York: Doubleday.

Spence, A. (1973) *Market Signalling.* Cambridge, MA: Harvard University Press.

Stalk, G., and Hout, T.M. (1990) *Competing Against Time.* New York: Free Press.

Stigler, G. (1961) "The Economics of Information." *Journal of Political Economy,* Vol. 69, pp. 213–225.

Trigeorgis, L. (1996) *Real Options: Managerial Flexibility and Strategic Resource Allocation.* Boston, MA: MIT Press.

Turkle, S. (1997) *Life on the Screen: Identity in the Age of the Internet.* New York: Touchstone Books.

Venkatraman, N., and Henderson, J.C. (1998) "Real Strategies for Virtual Organizing." *Sloan Management Review,* Fall, pp. 33–48.

Volberda, H.W. (1996) "Toward the Flexible Form: How to Remain Vital in Hypercompetitive Environments." *Organization Science,* Vol. 7, No. 4, pp. 359–374.

Wernerfelt, B. (1984) "A Resource-Based View of the Firm." *Strategic Management Journal,* Vol. 5, No. 3, pp. 171–180.

Wernerfelt, B., and Montgomery, C.A. (1988) "Tobin's q and the Importance of Focus in Firm Performance." *American Economic Review*, Vol. 78, No. 1, pp. 246–250.

Winter, S.G. (1987) "Knowledge and Competence as Strategic Assets." In *The Competitive Challenge,* ed. D. Teece. Cambridge, MA: Ballinger, pp. 159–184.

Woodward, J. (1965) *Industrial Organization: Theory and Practice.* London: Oxford University Press.

CHAPTER 12, ALBERT H. SEGARS AND JAMES W. DEAN

Bakos, J.Y., and Treacy, M.E. "Information Technology and Corporate Strategy: A Research Perspective." *MIS Quarterly* (10:2), 1986, pp. 107–119.

Benjamin, R.I., and Levinson, E. "A Framework for Managing IT-Enabled Change." *Sloan Management Review,* Summer 1993, pp. 23–33.

Cash, J.I., and Konsynski, B. "IS Redraws Competitive Boundaries." *Harvard Business Review,* March–April 1985, pp. 134–142.

Clemons, E.K. "Information Systems for Sustainable Competitive Advantage." *Information and Management* (9:3), 1986, pp. 131–136.

Clemons, E.K., and McFarlan, W.F. "Telecom: Hook Up or Lose Out." *Harvard Business Review,* July–August 1986, pp. 91–97.

Davenport, T. *Process Innovation: Reengineering Work Through Information Technology.* Boston: Harvard Business School Press, 1994.

Davenport, T., and Short, J. "The New Industrial Engineering: Information Technology and Business Process Redesign." *Sloan Management Review,* Summer 1990, pp. 11–27.

Dean, J.W. Jr., and Snell, S.A. "The Strategic Use of Integrated Manufacturing: An Empirical Investigation." *Strategic Management Journal* (17:6), 1996, pp. 459–480.

Dewar, R.D., and Dutton, J.E. "The Adoption of Radical and Incremental Innovations: An Empirical Analysis." *Management Science* (32:11), 1986, pp. 1422–1433.

Downes, L., and Mui, C. *Unleasing the Killer App.* Boston: Harvard Business School Press, 1998.

Eisenhardt, K.M. "Making Fast Strategic Decisions in High-Velocity Environments." *Academy of Management Journal* (32:3), 1989, pp. 543–576.

El Sawy, O., Malhotra, A., Gosain, S., and Young, K. "IT-Intensive Value Innovation in the Electronic Economy: Insights from Marshall Industries." *MIS Quarterly* (23:3), 1999.

Euske, K.J., and Player, R.S. "Leveraging Management Improvement Techniques." *Sloan Management Review,* Fall 1996, pp. 69–79.

Feeny, D.F., and Ives, B. "In Search of Sustainability: Reaping Long-Term Advantage from Investments in Information Technology. *Journal of Management Information Systems* (7:1), 1990, pp. 27–42.

Garvin, D.A. "Building a Learning Organization." *Harvard Business Review,* July–August 1993, pp. 78–91.

Grover, V. "An Empirically Derived Model for the Adoption of Customer-Based Interorganizational Systems." *Decision Sciences* (24:3), 1993, pp. 603–641.

Gurbaxani, V., and Whang, S. "The Impact of Information Systems on Organizations and Markets." *Communications of the ACM,* January 1991, pp. 59–73.

Hamel, G., and Sampler, J. "The E Corporation." *Fortune* (138:11), 1998, pp. 80–91.

Hammer, M., and Champy, J. *Reengineering the Corporation.* New York: Free Press, 1993.

Hammer, M., and Mangurian, G.E. "The Changing Value of Communications Technology." *Sloan Management Review,* Winter 1987, pp. 65–71.

Johnston, H.R., and Vitale, M.R. "Creating Competitive Advantage with Interorganizational Systems." *MIS Quarterly,* (10:2), 1988, pp. 153-165.

Kettinger, W.J., Grover, V., Guha, S., and Segars, A.H. "Strategic Information Systems Revisited: A Study in Performance and Sustainability." *MIS Quarterly* (18:1), 1994, pp. 63–85.

Kettinger, W.J., Teng, J.T.C., and Guha, S. "Business Process Change: A Study of Methodologies, Techniques, and Tools." *MIS Quarterly* (21:1), 1997, pp. 55–80.

Kettinger, W.J., Harkness, W., and Segars, A. "The Road to Process Management at Bose Corporation: Lessons Learned in Sustaining Process Change and Innovation." *MIS Quarterly* (25:3), 1996, pp. 349–368.

Leonard, D. *Wellsprings of Knowledge: Building and Sustaining the Sources of Innovation.* Boston: Harvard Business School Press, 1998.

McGee, J., and Thomas, H. "Strategic Groups: Theory, Research and Taxonomy." *Strategic Management Journal* (7:2), 1986, pp. 141–160.

Malone, T., Yates, J., and Benjamin, R.I. "Electronic Markets and Hierarchies: Effects of Information Technology on Market Structure and Corporate Strategies." *Communications of the ACM,* January 1987, pp. 59–73.

Markus, M.L., and Benjamin, R.I. "Change Agentry—the Next IS Frontier." *MIS Quarterly* (20:4), 1996, pp. 385–407.

Markus, M.L., and Benjamin, R.I. "The Magic Bullet Theory in IT-Enabled Transformation." *Sloan Management Review,* Winter 1997, pp. 55–68.

Markus, M.L., and Robey, D. "Information Technology and Organizational Change: Causal Structure in Theory and Research." *Management Science,* 1988, pp. 583–598.

Nevis, E.C., DiBella, A.J., and Gould, J. "Understanding Organizations as Learning Systems." *Sloan Management Review,* Winter 1995, pp. 73–85.

Raymond, E. The Cathedral and Bazzaar. http://www.tuxedo.org/~esr/writings/cathedral-bazaar/cathedral-bazaar.html, 1999.

Segars, A.H., and Grover, V. "The Industry-Level Impact of Information Technology: An Empirical Analysis of Three Industries." *Decision Sciences* (26:3), 1995, pp. 337–368.

Segars, A.H., and Grover, V. "Profiles of Strategic Information Systems Planning." *Information Systems Research* (10:3), 1999.

Short, J.E., and Venkatraman, N. "Beyond Business Process Redesign: Redefining Baxter's Business Network. *Sloan Management Review,* Fall 1992, pp. 7–12.

Venkatraman, N. "IT-Enabled Transformation: From Automation to Business Scope Redefinition." *Sloan Management Review,* Winter 1994, pp. 73–87.

Venkatraman, N., and Henderson, J.C. "Real Strategies for Virtual Organizing." *Sloan Management Review,* Fall 1998, pp. 33–48.

Venkatramen, N., and Zaheer, A. "Electronic Integration and Strategic Advantage: A Quasi-Experimental Study in the Insurance Industry." *Information Systems Research,* 1990, pp. 377–393.

Vitale, M.R. "The Growing Risks of Information Systems Success." *MIS Quarterly* (10:4), 1986, pp. 327–334.

CHAPTER 13, V. SAMBAMURTHY

Alavi, M. "KPMG Peat Marwick US: One Giant Brain." Harvard Business School, Case 9-397-108, 1997.

Amit, R., and Schoemaker, P.J.H. "Strategic asscts and organizational rent," *Strategic Management Journal,* 14, 1993, pp. 33–46.

Amram, M., and Kulatilaka, N. *Real Options: Managing Strategic Investment in an Uncertain World.* Boston, MA: Harvard Business School Press, 1999.

Bain, J.S. *Industrial Organization,* 2d ed. New York: Wiley, 1968.

Barney, J.B. "Firm resources and sustained competitive advantage," *Journal of Management,* 17, 1991, pp. 99–120.

Barney, J.B. *Gaining and Sustaining Competitive Advantage.* Reading, MA: Addison-Wesley, 1997.

Bcath, C.M., and Ives, B. "Competitive information systems in support of pricing." *MIS Quarterly,* 10(1), 1986, pp. 85–96.

Bradley, S.P., and Nolan, R.L. (eds.). *Sense and Respond: Capturing Value in the Network Era.* Boston, MA: Harvard Business School Press, 1998.

Brown, C.V., and Sambamurthy, V. *Repositioning the IT Organization to Enable Business Transformation.* Cincinnati, OH: Pinnaflex Press, 1999.

Brown, R.M., Gatian, A.W., and Hicks, J.O. "Strategic information systems and financial performance." *Journal of Management Information Systems,* 11 (4), 1995, pp. 215–248.

Byrnes, N., and Judge, P.C. "Intcrnet anxiety." *Business Week,* June 28, 1999, pp. 79–88.

Chamberlin, R.H. *The Theory of Monopolistic Competition,* Cambridge, MA: Harvard University Press, 1933.

Chatfield, A.T., and Bjorn-Andersen, N. "The impact of IOS-enabled business process change on business outcomes: Transformation of the value chain of Japan Airlines." *Journal of Management Information Systems,* 14(1), 1997, pp. 13–40.

Chen, M. "Competitor analysis and inter-firm rivalry: Toward a theoretical integration." *Academy of Management Review,* 21(1), 1996, pp. 100–134.

Christensen, C.M., *The Innovator's Dilemma: When New Technologies Cause Great Firms to Fail.* Boston, MA: Harvard Business School Press, 1997.

Clark, C., Cavanaugh, N., Brown, C., and Sambamurthy, V. "Building change-readiness IT capabilities: Insights from the Bell Atlantic experience." *MIS Quarterly,* December 1997.

Clemons, E.K., and Row, M.C. "Case study: A strategic information system: McKesson Drug Company's Economost." *Planning Review,* 16(5), 1988, pp. 14–19.

Clemons, E.K., and Row, M.C. "Sustaining IT advantage: The role of structural differences." *MIS Quarterly* 15(3), 1991, pp. 275–292.

Cohen, W., and Levinthal, D. "Absorptive capacity: A new perspective on learning and innovation." *Administrative Sciences Quarterly,* 35(1), 1990, pp. 128–152.

D'Aveni, R.A. *Hypercompetition: Managing the Dynamics of Strategic Maneuvering.* New York: The Free Press, 1994.

Demsetz, H. "Industry structure, market rivalry, and public policy." *Journal of Law and Economics,* 16, 1973, pp. 1–9.

El Sawy, O., Malhotra, A., Gosain, S., and Young, K. "IT-intensive value innovation in the electronic economy: Insights from Marshall Industries." *MIS Quarterly,* 23(3), 1999.

Evans, P.B., and Wurster, T.S. "Strategy and the new economics of information." *Harvard Business Review,* 75(5), 1997, pp. 70–82.

Feeny, D.F., and Wilcocks, L.P. "Core IS capabilities for exploiting information technology." *Sloan Management Review,* 39(3), 1998, pp. 9–21.

Goldman, S.L., Nagel, R.N., and Preiss, K. *Agile Competitors and Virtual Organizations: Strategies for Enriching the Customer.* New York: Van Nostrand Reinhold, 1995.

Haeckel, S.H., and Slywotzky, A.J. *Adaptive Enterprise: Creating and Leading Sense-and-Respond Organizations.* Boston, MA: Harvard Business School Press, 1999.

Hayek, F.A. "Economics and knowledge." *Economica,* 3, 1937, pp. 33–54.

Henderson, J., and Venkatraman, N. "Strategic alignment: A framework for strategic information technology management," In T. Kochan and M. Useem (eds.), *Transforming Organizations.* New York: Oxford Press, 1992, pp. 97–117.

Hitt, M.A., Keats, B.W., and DeMarie, S.M. "Navigating in the new competitive landscape: Building strategic flexibility and competitive advantage in the 21st century." *The Academy of Management Executive,* 12(4), 1998, pp. 22–42.

Ives, B., and Learmonth, G.P. "The information system as a competitive weapon." *Communications of the ACM,* 27(12), 1984, pp. 1193–1201.

Ives, B., and Mason, R.O. "Can information technology revitalize your customer service?" *The Academy of Management Executive,* 4(4), 1990, pp. 52–69.

Ives, B., and Vitale, M.R. "After the sale: Leveraging maintenance with information technology." *MIS Quarterly,* 12(1), 1988, pp. 7–21.

Jacobson, R. "The 'Austrian' school of strategy." *Academy of Management Review,* 17(4), 1992, pp. 782–807.

Jarvenpaa, S.L., and Leidner, D.E. "An information company in Mexico: Extending the resource-based view of the firm to a developing country." *Information Systems Research,* 9(4), 1998, pp. 342–362.

Jelassi, T., and Fignon, O. "Competing through EDI at Brun Passot: Achievements in France and ambitions for the single European market," *MIS Quarterly,* 18(4), 1994, pp. 337–352.

Johnston, R.H., and Vitale, M.R. "Creating competitive advantage with interorganizational information systems." *MIS Quarterly,* 12(2), 1988, pp. 153–165.

Keen, P.G.W. *Shaping the Future: Business Design Through Information Technology,* Boston, MA: Harvard Business School Press, 1991.

Keen, P.G.W. "Business re-model." *Computerworld,* July 12, 1999, p. 44.

Kettinger, W.J., Grover, V., Guha, S., and Segars, A.H. "Strategic information systems revisited: A study in sustainability and performance." *MIS Quarterly,* 18(1), 1994, pp. 31–58.

Leonard-Barton, D. "Core capabilities and core rigidities: A paradox in managing new product development." *Strategic Management Journal,* 13, 1992, pp. 111–125.

Lindsey, D., Cheney, P.H., Kasper, G.M., and Ives, B. "TELCOT: An application of information technology for competitive advantage in the cotton industry." *MIS Quarterly,* 14(4), 1990, pp. 347–357.

McKenney, J.L. *Waves of Change: Business Evolution Through Information Technology.* Boston, MA: Harvard Business School Press, 1995.

McFarlan, F.W. "Information technology changes the way you compete." *Harvard Business Review,* 62(3), 1984, pp. 98–103.

Magrettta, J. "The power of virtual integration: An interview with Dell Computer's Michael Dell." *Harvard Business Review,* 76(2), 1998, pp. 72–85.

Mason, E.S. "Price and production policies of large-scale enterprises." *American Economic Review,* 29, 1939, pp. 61–74.

Mason, R.O., McKenney, J.L., and Copeland, D.G. "Developing an historical tradition in MIS research." *MIS Quarterly,* 21(3), 1997, pp. 257–277.

Moschella, D.C. *Waves of Power: The Dynamics of Global Technology Leadership, 1964–2010.* New York: Amacom, 1997.

Norman, R., and Ramirez, R. "From value chain to value constellation." *Harvard Business Review,* 71(4), 1993, pp. 65–77.

Parsons, G.L. "Information technology: A new competitive weapon." *Sloan Management Review,* 25(1), 1984, pp. 3–14.

Penrose, E.T. *The Theory of the Growth of the Firm.* New York: Wiley, 1959.

Porter, M.E. *Competitive Strategy: Techniques for Analyzing Industries and Competitors.* New York: The Free Press, 1980.

Porter, M.E. "The contributions of industrial organization to strategic management." *Academy of Management Review,* 6, 1981, pp. 609–620.

Porter, M.E., *Competitive Advantage.* New York: The Free Press, 1985.

Porter, M.E., and Millar, V. "How information technology gives you competitive advantage." *Harvard Business Review,* 63(4), 1985, pp. 149–160.

Powell, T.C., and Dent-Micallef, A. "Information technology as competitive advantage: The role of human, business, and technology resources." *Strategic Management Journal,* 18(5), 1997, pp. 375–405.

Rackoff, N., Wiseman, C., and Ullrich, W.A. "Information systems for competitive advantage: Implementation of a planning process." *MIS Quarterly,* 9(4), 1985, pp. 112–124.

Reed, R., and DeFillippi, R.J. "Causal ambiguity, barriers to imitation, and sustainable competitive advantage." *Academy of Management Review,* 15(1), 1990, pp. 88–102.

Robinson, J. *Economics of Imperfect Competition.* London: MacMillan, 1933.

Ross, J.W., Beath, C.M., and Goodhue, D.L. "Develop long-term competitiveness through IT assets." *Sloan Management Review,* Fall 1996, pp. 31–42.

Rumelt, R.P. "Towards a strategic theory of the firm." In R.B. Lamb (ed.), *Competitive Strategic Management.* Englewood Cliffs, NJ: Prentice Hall, 1984, pp. 556–570.

Sambamurthy, V., and Zmud, R.W. "At the heart of success: Organizationwide management competencies." In P. Yetton and C. Sauer (eds.), *The Dynamics of IT-Based Organizational Transformation.* San Francisco: Jossey-Bass, 1997, pp. 143–164.

Schumpeter, J.A. *The Theory of Economic Development.* Boston, MA: Harvard University Press, 1934.

Schumpeter, J.A. *Capitalism, Socialism, and Democracy,* 3d ed. New York: Harper & Row, 1950.

Smith, K.G., Grimm, C.M., and Gannon, M.J. *Dynamics of Competitive Strategy.* Sage Publications, 1992.

Teece, D., and Pisano, G. "The dynamic capabilities of firms: An introduction." *Industrial and Corporate Change,* 3(3), 1994, pp. 537–556.

Thomas, L.G. III. "The two faces of competition: Dynamic resourcefulness and the hypercompetitive shift." *Organization Science,* 7(3), 1996, pp. 221–242.

Venkatraman, N. "IT–Enabled business transformation: From automation to business scope redefinition." *Sloan Management Review,* 35(2), 1994, pp. 73–87.

Venkatraman, N., and Henderson, J.C. "Real strategies for virtual organizing." *Sloan Management Review,* 40(1), 1998, pp. 33–48

Vitale, M.R. "The growing risks of information systems success." *MIS Quarterly,* 19(4), 1986, pp. 327–334.

Weill, P., and Broadbent, M. *Leveraging the New Infrastructure: How Market Leaders Capitalize on Information Technology.* Boston, MA: Harvard Business School Press, 1998.

Young, G., Smith, K.G., and Grim, C.M. "'Austrian' and industrial organization perspectives on firm-level competitive activity and performance." *Organization Science,* 7(3), 1996, pp. 243–254.

CHAPTER 14, JOEY F. GEORGE

Banker, R.D., Davis, G.B., and Slaughter, S.A. 1998. "Software Development Practices, Software Complexity, and Software Maintenance Performance: A Field Study." *Management Science* 44(4), 433–450.

Basili, V.R., Briand, L.C., and Melo, W.L. 1996. "How Reuse Influences Productivity in Object-Oriented Systems." *Communications of the ACM* 39(10), 104–116.

Boehm, B.W. 1988. "A Spiral Model of Software Development and Enhancement." *Computer* 21(5), 61–72.

Bourne, K.C. 1994. "Putting Rigor Back in RAD." *Database Programming and Design* 7(8), 25–30.

Boutellier, R., Gassmann, O., Macho, H., and Roux, M. 1998. "Management of Dispersed Product Teams: The Role of Information Technologies." *R&D Management* 28(1), 13–25.

Carmel, E. 1997. "The Explosion of Global Software Teams." *Computerworld* 31(49), December 8, C6+.

Carmel, E., Whitaker, R., and George, J.F. 1993. "PD and Joint Application Design: A Transatlantic Comparison." *Communications of the ACM* 36(6), 40–48.

Fichman, R.G., and Kemerer, C.F. "Adoption of Software Engineering Process Innovations: An Organizational Learning Perspective." *Sloan Management Review* 34(2), 1983, 7–22.

Finlay, P.N., and Mitchell, A.C. 1994. "Perceptions of the Benefits from the Introduction of CASE: An Empirical Study." *MIS Quarterly* 18(4), 353–370.

Gibbs, W.W. 1994. "Software's Chronic Crisis" *Scientific American,* September, 86–95.

Hoffer, J.A., George, J.F., and Valacich, J.S. 1999. *Modern Systems Analysis and Design,* 2d ed. Reading, MA: Addison Wesley.

Iivari, J. 1996. "Why Are CASE Tools Not Used?" *Communications of the ACM* 39(10), 94–103.

Iivari, J., and Ervasti, I. 1992. "The Impact of Alternative IS Acquisition Options Upon the IS Implementation and Success." *Proceedings of the 1992 ACM SIGCPR Conference on Computer Personnel Research,* 338–349.

Kim, Y., and Stohr, E.A. 1998. "Software Reuse: Survey and Research Directions." *Journal of MIS* 14(4), 113–147.

King, J., and Cole–Gomolski, B. 1999. "IT Doing Less Development, More Installation, Outsourcing." *Computerworld,* January 25, 4+.

Lacity, M.C., and Willcocks, L.P. 1998. "An Empirical Investigation of Information Technology Sourcing Practices: Lessons from Experience." *MIS Quarterly* 22(3), 363–408.

Lending, D., and Chervany, N. 1998. "The Use of CASE Tools." *Computer Personnel Research 98.* Boston, MA: 49–58.

Lucas, H.C. 1997. *Information Technology for Management.* New York: McGraw-Hill.

Martin, J. *Rapid Application Development.* New York: Macmillan, 1991.

Mayrand, J., and Coallier, F. 1996. "System Acquisition Based on Software Product Assessment." *Proceedings of ICSE-18,* 210–219.

Meringer, J., Deutsch, W., and Manoussoff, L. 1997. "Sizing Technology Services." *The Forrester Report,* 14(8). www.forrester.com/

Mcrrill, Kevin. 1999. "Poll: IT Outsourcing Shows No Signs of Slowing." *TechWeb,* March 3. www.techweb.com.

Nosek, J.T., and Palvia, P. 1990. "Software Maintenance Management: Changes in the Past Decade." *Journal of Software Maintenance* 2(3), 157–174.

Orenstein, D. 1999. "Java, VisualBasic Seen as Languages of the Future." *Computerworld,* March 29, 1999.

Pressman, R.S. 1997. "Software Engineering." In M. Dorfman and R.H.Thayer (eds.), *Software Engineering.* Los Alamitos, CA: IEEE Computer Society Press, 57–74.

SAP. 1998. *1998 Annual Report.*

Wood, J., and Silver, D. 1995. *Joint Application Design,* 2d ed. New York: John Wiley.

Yourdon, E. 1989. *Managing the Structured Techniques,* 4th ed. Englewood Cliffs, NJ: Prentice Hall.

Yourdon, E. 1996. *Rise and Resurrection of the American Programmer.* Upper Saddle River, NJ: Prentice Hall.

CHAPTER 15, LAURIE J. KIRSCH

Abdel-Hamid, T.K. "Understanding the '90% Syndrome' in Software Project Management: A Simulation-Based Case Study." *The Journal of Systems and Software* (8), 1988a, pp. 319–330.

Abdel-Hamid, T.K. "The Economics of Software Quality Assurance: A Simulation-Based Case Study." *MIS Quarterly* (12:3), 1988b, pp. 395–411.

Abdel-Hamid, T.K. "Investigating Cost/Schedule Trade-Off in Software Development." *IEEE Software,* January 1990, pp. 97–105.

Abdel-Hamid, T.K. and S. Madnick. "Impact of Estimation on Software Project Behavior." *IEEE Software,* 1986, pp. 70–75.

Abdel-Hamid, T.K., and S.E. Madnick. "Lessons Learned from Modeling the Dynamics of Software Development." *Communications of the ACM* (32:12), 1989, pp. 1426–1438.

Abernethy, M.A., and J.U. Stoelwinder. "The Role of Professional Control in the Management of Complex Organizations." *Accounting, Organizations and Society* (20:1), 1994, pp. 1–17.

Alavi, M., J.S. Phillips, and S.M. Freedman. "Strategies for Control of End-User Computing: Impact on End Users." In L. Maggi, R. Zmud, and J. Wetherbe (eds.), *Proceedings of the Seventh International Conference on Information Systems,* San Diego, CA, 1986, pp. 57–66.

Albrecht, A.J., and J.E. Gaffney Jr. "Software Function, Source Lines of Code, and Development Effort Prediction: A Software Science Validation." *IEEE Transactions on Software Engineering* (SE-9:6), 1983, pp. 639–648.

Bancroft, N.H., H. Seip, and A. Sprengel. *Implementing SAP R/3* (2d ed.). Greenwich, CT: Manning Publications, 1998.

Barki, H., and J. Hartwick. "User Participation, Conflict, and Conflict Resolution: The Mediating Roles of Influence." *Information Systems Research* (5:4), 1994, pp. 422–438.

Barki, H., S. Rivard, and J. Talbot. "Toward an Assessment of Software Development Risk." *Journal of Management Information Systems* (10:2), Fall 1993, pp. 203–225.

Bashein, B.J., M.L. Markus, and J.B. Finley. *Safety Nets: Secrets of Effective Information Technology Controls*. Morristown, NJ: Financial Executives Research Foundation, 1997.

Baskerville, R.L., and J. Stage. "Controlling Prototype Development Through Risk Analysis." *MIS Quarterly* (20:4), 1996, pp. 481–504.

Beath, C.M. "Managing the User Relationship in Information Systems Development Projects: A Transaction Governance Approach." In *Proceedings of the Eighth International Conference on Information Systems,* Pittsburgh, PA, 1987, pp. 415–427.

Beath, C.M. "User Roles and Responsibilities." *Journal of Information Systems Management* (5:4), 1988, pp. 54–61.

Beath, C.M. "Supporting the Information Technology Champion." *MIS Quarterly* (15:3), September 1991, pp. 355–377.

Beath, C.M., and W.J. Orlikowski. "The Contradictory Structure of Systems Development Methodologies: Deconstructing the IS-User Relationship in Information Engineering." *Information Systems Research* (5:4), 1994, pp. 350–377.

Boehm, B.W. *Software Engineering Economics*. Englewood Cliffs, NJ: Prentice Hall, 1981.

Boehm, B.W. "Software Engineering Economics." *IEEE Transactions on Software Engineering* (SE-10:1), 1984, pp. 4–21.

Boehm, B.W. "A Spiral Model of Software Development and Enhancement." *IEEE Computer* (5), 1988, pp. 61–72.

Boehm, B.W. "Software Risk Management: Principles and Practices." *IEEE Software* (1), 1991, pp. 32–41.

Boehm, B.W., and P.N. Papaccio, "Understanding and Controlling Software Costs." *IEEE Transactions on Software Engineering* (14:10), 1988, p. 1462–1477.

Boehm, B.W., and R. Ross. "Theory-W Software Project Management: Principles and Examples." *IEEE Transactions on Software Engineering* (15:7), 1989, pp. 902–916.

Brachman, R.J., T. Khabaza, W. Kloesgen, G. Piatetsky-Shapiro, and E. Simoudis. "Mining Business Databases." *Communications of the ACM* (39:11), 1996, pp. 43–48.

Brooks, F.P. Jr. "The Mythical Man-Month." *Datamation* (20:12), 1974, pp. 45–52.

Brooks, F.P. Jr. "No Silver Bullet: Essence and Accidents of Software Engineering." *IEEE Computer* (20:4), 1987, pp. 10–19.

Brooks, F.P. Jr. *The Mythical Man-Month: Essays on Software Engineering* (anniversary ed.). Reading, MA: Addison-Wesley, 1995.

Carmel, E. *Global Software Teams: Collaborating Across Borders and Time Zones*. Upper Saddle River, NJ: Prentice Hall, 1999.

Collins, R.W., and L.J. Kirsch. *Crossing Boundaries: The Deployment of Global IT Solutions*. Cincinnati, OH: Pinnaflex Educational Resources, 1999.

Curtis, B., H. Krasner, and N. Iscoe. "A Field Study of the Software Design Process for Large Systems." *Communications of the ACM* (31:11), 1988, pp. 1268–1287.

Davis, G.B. "Strategies for Information Requirements Determination." *IBM Systems Journal* (21:1), 1982, pp. 4–30.

Deephouse, C., T. Mukhopadhyay, D.R Goldenson, and M.I. Keller. "Software Processes and Project Performance." *Journal of Management Information Systems* (12:3), 1995–96, pp. 187–205.

Doll, W.J., and G. Torkzadeh. "Discrepancy Model of End-User Computing Involvement." *Management Science* (35:10), 1989, pp. 1151–1171.

Dutta, S., L.N. Van Wassenhove, and S. Kulandaiswamy. "Benchmarking European Software Management Practices." *Communications of the ACM* (41:6), 1998, pp. 77–86.

Eisenhardt, K.M. "Control: Organizational and Economic Approaches." *Management Science* (31:2), 1985, pp. 134–149.

Eisenhardt, K.M. "Agency- and Institutional-Theory Explanations: The Case of Retail Sales Compensation." *Academy of Management Journal* (31:3), 1988, pp. 488–511.

Fairley, R. "Risk Management for Software Projects." *IEEE Software* (11:3), 1994, pp. 57–67.

Frame, J.D. *The New Project Management: Corporate Reengineering & Other Business Realities.* San Francisco: CA: Jossey-Bass, 1994.

Frame, J.D. *Managing Projects in Organizations: How to Make the Best Use of Time, Techniques, and People* (rev. ed.). San Francisco, CA: Jossey-Bass, 1995.

Gerrity, T.P., and J.F. Rockart. "End-User Computing: Are You a Leader or a Laggard?" *Sloan Management Review* (27:4), 1986, pp. 25–34.

Grady, R.B., and D.L. Caswell. *Software Metrics: Establishing a Company-Wide Program.* Englewood Cliffs, NJ: Prentice Hall, 1987.

Guinan, P.J., J.G. Cooprider, and S. Faraj. "Enabling Software Development Team Performance During Requirements Definition: A Behavioral Versus Technical Approach." *Information Systems Research* (9:2), 1998, pp. 101–125.

Hartwick, J., and H. Barki. "Explaining the Role of User Participation in Information System Use." *Management Science* (40:4), 1994a, pp. 440–465.

Hartwick, J., and H. Barki. "Hypothesis Testing and Hypothesis Generating Research: An Example from the User Participation Literature." *Information Systems Research* (5:4), 1994b, pp. 446–449.

Henderson, J.C. "Plugging into Strategic Partnerships: The Critical IS Connection." *Sloan Management Review* (31:3), 1990, pp. 7–18.

Henderson, J.C., and S. Lee. "Managing I/S Design Teams: A Control Theories Perspective." *Management Science* (38:6), 1992, pp. 757–777.

Hetzel, W.C. "The Sorry State of Software Practice Measurement and Evaluation." *Journal of Systems and Software* (31), 1995, pp. 171–179.

Hrebiniak, L.G. "Job Technology, Supervision, and Work-Group Structure." *Administrative Science Quarterly* (19), 1974, pp. 395–410.

Humphrey, W.S. "Characterizing the Software Process: A Maturity Framework." *IEEE Software* (5:3), 1988, pp. 73–79.

Jaworski, B.J. "Toward a Theory of Marketing Control: Environmental Context, Control Types, and Consequences." *Journal of Marketing* (52), 1988, pp. 23–39.

Jones, C. *Applied Software Measurement: Assuring Productivity and Quality.* New York: McGraw-Hill, 1991.

Kaufman-Rosen, L., and D. Glick. "Finally! It's Here!" *Newsweek,* March 6, 1995, pp. 45–56.

Keil, M. "Pulling the Plug: Software Project Management and the Problem of Project Escalation." *MIS Quarterly* (19:4), 1995, pp. 421–447.

Keil, M., P.E. Cule, K. Lyytinen, and R.C. Schmidt. "A Framework for Identifying Software Project Risks." *Communications of the ACM* (41:11), 1998, pp. 76–83.

Keil, M., and D. Robey. "Turning Around Troubled Software Projects: An Exploratory Study of the Deescalation of Commitment to Failing Courses of Action." *Journal of Management Information Systems* (15:4), 1999, pp. 63–87.

Kemerer, C.F. "An Empirical Validation of Software Cost Estimation Models." *Communications of the ACM* (30:5), 1987, pp. 416–429.

Kemerer, C.F. "Reliability of Function Points Measurement: A Field Experiment." *Communications of the ACM* (36:2), 1993, pp. 85–97.

Kemerer, C.F. *Software Project Management: Readings and Cases*. Chicago: Irwin/McGraw Hill, 1997.

Kirsch, L.J. "The Management of Complex Tasks in Organizations: Controlling the Systems Development Process." *Organization Science* (7), 1996, pp. 1–21.

Kirsch, L.J. "Portfolios of Control Modes and IS Project Management." *Information Systems Research* (8:3), 1997, pp. 215–239.

Kirsch, L.J., and C.M. Beath. "The Enactments and Consequences of Token, Shared, and Compliant Participation in Information Systems Development." *Accounting, Management and Information Technologies* (6:4), 1996, pp. 221–254.

Kirsch, L.J., and L.L. Cummings. "Contextual Influences on Self-Control of IS Professionals Engaged in Systems Development." *Accounting, Management and Information Technologies* (6:3), 1996, pp. 191–219.

Kraut, R.E., and L.A. Streeter. "Coordination in Software Development." *Communications of the ACM* (38:3), March 1995, pp. 69–81.

Lacity, M.C., and L.P. Willcocks. "An Empirical Investigation of Information Technology Sourcing Practices: Lessons from Experience." *MIS Quarterly* (22:3), 1998, pp. 363–408.

Lederer, A.L., R. Mirani, B.S. Neo, C. Pollard, and K. Ramamurthy. "Information System Cost Estimating: A Management Perspective." *MIS Quarterly* (14:2), 1990, pp. 159–176.

Lawrence, M., and G. Low. "Exploring Individual User Satisfaction Within User-Led Development." *MIS Quarterly* (17:2), 1993, pp. 195–208.

Leitheiser, R.L., and J.C. Wetherbe. "Service Support Levels: An Organized Approach to End-User Computing." *MIS Quarterly* (10:4), 1986, pp. 337–349.

Levine, H.G., and D. Rossmore. "Politics and the Function of Power in a Case Study of IT Implementation." *Journal of Management Information Systems* (11:3), 1994–95, pp. 115–133.

Lind, M.R., and J.M. Sulek. "Undersizing Software Systems: Third versus Fourth Generation Software Development." *European Journal of Information Systems* (7:4), 1998, pp. 261–268.

Linkman, S.G., and J.G. Walker. "Controlling Programmes Through Measurement." *Information and Software Technology* (33:1), 1991, pp. 93–102.

Lyytinen, K., L. Mathiassen, and J. Ropponen. "Attention Shaping and Software Risk—A Categorical Analysis of Four Classical Risk Management Approaches." *Information Systems Research* (9:3), 1998, pp. 233–255.

McFarlan, F.W. "Portfolio Approach to Information Systems." *Harvard Business Review* (59:5), 1981, pp. 142–150.

McFarlan, W., and R. Nolan. "How to Manage an IT Outsourcing Alliance." *Sloan Management Review* (36:2), 1995, pp. 9–23.

McKeen, J.D., and T. Guimaraes. "Successful Strategies for User Participation in Systems Development." *Journal of Management Information Systems* (14:2), 1997, pp. 133–150.

McPartlin, J.P. "The Collapse of CONFIRM." *Informationweek,* October 19, 1992, pp. 12–14.

Manz, C.C., and H. Angle. "Can Group Self-Management Mean a Loss of Personal Control: Triangulating a Paradox." *Group & Organization Studies* (14), 1986, pp. 309–334.

Manz, C.C., K.W. Mossholder, and F. Luthans. "An Integrated Perspective of Self-Control in Organizations." *Administration & Society* (19:1), 1987, pp. 3–24.

Markus, M.L. "Power, Politics, and MIS Implementation." *Communications of the ACM* (26:6), 1983, pp. 430–444.

Markus, M.L., and N. Bjorn-Andersen. "Power Over Users: Its Exercise by System Professionals." *Communications of the ACM* (30:6), 1987, pp. 498–504.

Markus, M.L., and J. Pfeffer. "Power and the Design and Implementation of Accounting and Control Systems." *Accounting, Organizations and Society* (8:2/3), 1983, pp. 205–218.

Martin, J.L. *Information Engineering: Book I*. Englewood Cliffs, NJ: Prentice Hall,1989.

Martin, J.L. *Information Engineering: Books II and III*. Englewood Cliffs, NJ: Prentice Hall, 1990.

Meredith, J.R., and S.J. Mantel Jr. *Project Management: A Managerial Approach* (3d ed.). New York: John Wiley, 1995.

Might, R.J., and W.A. Fischer. "The Role of Structural Factors in Determining Project Management Success." *IEEE Transactions on Engineering Management* (EM-32:2), 1985, pp. 71–77.

Morris, P.W.G. "Project Management: Lessons from IT and Non-IT Projects." In M.J. Earl (ed.), *Information Management: The Organizational Dimension*. Oxford: Oxford University Press, 1996, pp. 321–336.

Newman, M., and F. Noble. "User Involvement as an Interaction Process: A Case Study." *Information Systems Research* (1:1), 1990, pp. 89–113.

Newman, M., and D. Robey. "A Social Process Model of User-Analyst Relationships." *MIS Quarterly* (16:2), 1992, pp. 249–266.

Newman, M., and R. Sabherwal. "Determinants of Commitment to Information Systems Development: A Longitudinal Investigation." *MIS Quarterly* (20:1), 1996, pp. 23–54.

Nidumolu, S.R. "Structural Contingency and Risk-Based Perspectives on Coordination in Software-Development Projects." *Journal of Management Information Systems* (13:2), Fall 1996, pp. 77–113.

Nidumolu, S.R. "The Effect of Coordination and Uncertainty on Software Project Performance: Residual Performance Risk as an Intervening Variable." *Information Systems Research* (6:3), 1995, pp. 191–219.

O'Brien, L. "Bad Software, Meet Your Party at Luggage Carousel Three." *Software Development*, November 1994, pp. 7–8.

Ouchi, W.G. "A Conceptual Framework for the Design of Organizational Control Mechanisms." *Management Science* (25:9), 1979, pp. 833–848.

Ouchi, W.G. "Markets, Bureaucracies, and Clans." *Administrative Science Quarterly* (25), March 1980, pp. 129–141.

Ouchi, W.G., and M.A. Maguire. "Organizational Control: Two Functions." *Administrative Science Quarterly* (20:4), 1975, pp. 559–569.

Oz, E. "When Professional Standards Are Lax: The CONFIRM Failure and Its Lessons." *Communications of the ACM* (37:10), 1994, pp. 29–36.

Pfeffer, J. *Power in Organizations*. Marshfield, MA: Pitman, 1981.

Pfeffer, J. *Managing with Power: Politics and Influence in Organizations*. Boston, MA: Harvard Business School Press, 1992.

Powers, R.F., and G.W. Dickson. "MisProject Management: Myths, Opinions, and Reality." *California Management Review* (XV:3), 1973, pp. 127–156.

Rasch, R.H., and H.L. Tosi. "Factors Affecting Software Developers' Performance: An Integrated Approach." *MIS Quarterly* (16:3), 1992, pp. 395–413.

Ray, G. "Measurement Programs Need Vision." *Computerworld,* 1993, p. 99.

Robey, D. "Modeling Interpersonal Processes During Systems Developing: Further Thoughts and Suggestions." *Information Systems Research* (5:4), 1994, pp. 439–445.

Robey, D., D.L. Farrow, and C.R. Franz. "Group Process and Conflict in System Development." *Management Science* (35:10), 1989, pp. 1172–1191.

Robey, D., and M.L. Markus. "Rituals in Information Systems Design." *MIS Quarterly* (8:1), 1984, pp. 5–15.

Robey, D., and M. Newman. "Sequential Patterns in Information Systems Development: An Application of a Social Process Model." *ACM Transactions on Information Systems* (14:1), 1996, pp. 30–63.

Robey, D., L.A. Smith, and L.R. Vijayasarathy. "Perceptions of Conflict and Success in Information Systems Development Projects." *Journal of Management Information Systems* (27:4), 1993, pp. 459–478.

Rockart, J.F., M.J. Earl, and J.W. Ross. "Eight Imperatives for the New IT Organization." *Sloan Management Review*, Fall 1996, pp. 43–55.

Rodrigues, A.G., and T.M. Williams. "System Dynamics in Software Project Management: Towards the Development of a Formal Integrated Framework." *European Journal of Information Systems* (6:1), 1997, pp. 51–66.

Sauer, C. "Deciding the Future for IS Failures." In W. Currie and B. Galliers (eds.), *Rethinking Management Information Systems: An Interdisciplinary Perspective*. Oxford: Oxford University Press, 1999, pp. 279–309.

Snell, S.A. "Control Theory in Strategic Human Resource Management: The Mediating Effect of Administrative Information." *Academy of Management Journal* (35:2), 1992, pp. 292–327.

Tractinsky, N., and S.L. Jarvenpaa. "Information Systems Design Decisions in a Global Versus Domestic Context." *MIS Quarterly* (19:4), 1995, pp. 507–534.

Van de Ven, A.H., A.L. Delbecq, and R. Koenig. "Determinants of Coordination Modes Within Organizations." *American Sociological Review* (41), 1976, pp. 322–338.

Walz, D.B., J.J. Elam, and B. Curtis. "Inside a Software Design Team: Knowledge Acquisition, Sharing, and Integration." *Communications of the ACM* (36:10), 1993, pp. 63–77.

Watson, H.J., and B.J. Haley. "Managerial Considerations." *Communications of the ACM* (41:9), 1998, pp. 32–37.

Weinberg, G.M., and D.P. Freedman. "Reviews, Walkthroughs, and Inspections." *IEEE Transactions on Software Engineering* (SE10:1), 1983, pp. 68–72.

Wetherbe, J.C., N.P. Vitalari, and A. Milner. "Key Trends in Systems Development in Europe and North America." *Journal of Global Information Management* (2:2), 1994, pp. 5–20.

White, K.B., and R. Leifer. "Information Systems Development Success: Perspectives from Project Team Participants." *MIS Quarterly* (10:3), 1986, pp. 215–223.

Willcocks, L., and H. Margetts. "Risk Assessment and Information Systems." *European Journal of Information Systems* (3:2), 1994, pp. 127–138.

Yourdon, E. *Decline and Fall of the American Programmer.* Englewood Cliffs, NJ: Yourdon Press, PTR Prentice Hall, 1992.

Yourdon, E. *Rise & Resurrection of the American Programmer.* Englewood Cliffs, NJ: Yourdon Press, PTR Prentice Hall, 1996.

Zmud, R.W. "Management of Large Software Development Efforts." *MIS Quarterly* (4:2), 1980, pp. 45–55.

CHAPTER 16, SOON ANG AND SANDRA A. SLAUGHTER

Ang, S., and Endeshaw, A. "Legal case analysis in IS research: Failures in employing and outsourcing for IT professionals." In *Information Systems and Qualitative Research,* ed. A.S. Lee, J. Liebenau, and J.I. DeGross, London, U.K.: Chapman & Hall, 1997, pp. 497–523.

Ang, S., and Slaughter, S. "Internal labor market structures and information systems turnover." GSIA Working Paper 1998–02, Carnegie Mellon University, 1998.

Ang, S., Wong, S.S., and Soh, C. "Survivors of outsourcing." *Technical Report, Information Management Research Center.* Nanyang Business School, 1999.

Apte, U.M., and Mason, R.O. "Global disaggregation of information-intensive services." *Management Science* (41:7), 1995, pp. 1250–1262.

Arvey, R.D., and Hoyle, J.C. "A Guttman approach to the development of behaviorally based rating scales for systems analysts and programmer analysts." *Journal of Applied Psychology* (59:1), 1974, pp. 61–68.

Baird, L., and Meshoulam, I. "Managing the two fits of strategic human resource management." *Academy of Management Review* (13), 1988, pp. 116–128.

Barley, S.R., and Bechky, B.A. "In the backroom of science: The work of technicians in science labs." *Work and Occupations* (21:1), 1994, pp. 85–126.

Barley, S.R., and Orr, J.E. *Beyond Craft and Science: Technical Work in U.S. Settings.* Ithaca, NY: IRL Press, 1997.

Baroudi, J.J. "Impact of role variables on IS personnel work attitudes and intentions." *MIS Quarterly* (9:4), 1985, pp. 341–356.

Baroudi, J., and Igbaria, M. "An examination of gender effects on career success of information systems employees." *Journal of Management Information Systems* (11:3), 1995, pp. 181–202.

Bartol, K.M., and Martin, D.C. "Managing information systems personnel: A review of the literature and managerial implications." *MIS Quarterly* (8:Special Issue), 1982, pp. 49–70.

Becker, B., and Olson, C. "The impact of strikes on shareholder equity." *Industrial and Labor Relations Review* (39), 1986, pp. 425–438.

Becker, G. *Human Capital.* New York: National Bureau of Economic Research, 1964.

Benbasat, I., Dexter, A.S., and Mantha, R.W. "Impact of organizational maturity on information system skill needs." *MIS Quarterly* (4:1), 1980, pp. 21–34.

Brancheau, J., Janz, B., and Wetherbe, J. "Key issues in information systems management: 1994–95 SIM Delphi results." *MIS Quarterly* (20:2), 1996, pp. 225–243.

Brannigan, A., and Dayhoff, J. "Liability for personal injuries caused by defective medical computer programs." *American Journal of Law and Medicine* (7), 1981, pp. 123–132.

Bryk, A., and Raudenbush, S. *Hierarchical Linear Models: Applications and Data Analysis Methods.* Newbury Park, CA: Sage Publications, 1992.

Burn, J.M., W., N.-T.E.M., Ma, L.C.J. and Poon, R.S.K. "Job expectations of IS professionals in Hong Kong." *Proceedings of the 1994 ACM SIGCPR Conference,* 1994, pp. 231–241.

Cappelli, P, and Sherer, P.D. "The missing role of context in OB." In *Research in Organizational Behavior,* L.L. Cummings and B.M. Staw, Volume 13. Greenwich, CT: JAI Press, 1991, pp. 55–110.

Carmel, E. *Global Software Teams.* Upper Saddle River, NJ: Prentice Hall, 1999.

Cheney, P.H., and Lyons, N.R. "Information systems skill requirements: A survey." *MIS Quarterly* (4:1), 1980, pp. 35–43.

Clark, C., Cavanaugh, N., Brown, C., and Sambamurthy, V. "Building change-readiness capabilities in the IS organization: Insights from the Bell Atlantic experience." *MIS Quarterly* (21:4), 1997, pp. 425–455.

Clark, K. "Unionization and firm performance: The impact on profits, growth and productivity." *American Economic Review* (74), 1984, pp. 893–919.

Couger, J.D., Zawacki, R.A., and Oppermann, E.B. "Motivation levels of MIS managers versus those of their employees." *MIS Quarterly* (3:3), 1979, pp. 47–56.

Crepeau, R.G., Crook, C.W., Goslar, M.D., and McMurtrey, M.E. "Career anchors of information systems personnel." *Journal of MIS* (9:2), 1992, pp. 145–161.

Ericsson, K.A. and Simon, H.A. *Protocol Analysis: Verbal Reports as Data*. Cambridge, MA: MIT Press, 1984.

Feeny, D.F., and Wilcocks, L.P. "Core IS capabilities for exploiting information technology." *Sloan Management Review* (Spring), 1998, pp. 9–21.

Ferratt, T.W., and Short, L.E. "Are information systems people different? An investigation of motivational differences." *MIS Quarterly* (10:4), 1986, pp. 377–387.

Ferratt, T.W., and Short, L.E. "Are information systems people different? An investigation of how they are managed and should be managed." *MIS Quarterly* (12:3), 1988, pp. 427–433.

Friedson, E. "The changing nature of professional control." *Annual Review of Sociology* (10), 1984, pp. 1–20.

Ginzberg, M.J., and Baroudi, J.J. "MIS careers—A theoretical perspective." *Communications of the ACM* (31), 1988, pp. 586–594.

Goldstein, D.K., and Rockart, J.F. "An examination of work-related correlates of job satisfaction in programmer/analysts." *MIS Quarterly* (8:2), 1984, pp. 103–115.

Green, G.I. "Perceived importance of systems analysts' job skills, roles, and non-salary incentives." *MIS Quarterly* (13:2), 1989, pp. 115–133.

Guimaraes, T., and Igbaria, M. "Determinants of turnover intentions: comparing IC and IS personnel." *Information Systems Research* (3:3), 1993, pp. 273–303.

Hackman, J.R., and Oldham, G.R. "Development of the job diagnostic survey." *Journal of Applied Psychology* (60), 1979, pp. 159–170.

Hagendorf, W. "Bulls & bears: Computer investment advisory programs that go awry." *Computer/Law Journal* (10), 1990, pp. 47–69.

Hall, E.T. *The Silent Language*. New York: Doubleday, 1976.

Hampden-Turnver, C., and Trompenaars, A. *The Seven Cultures of Capitalism*. New York: Currency Doubleday, 1993.

Hirsch, B. "Firm investment behavior and collective bargaining strategy." *Industrial Relations* (31), 1992, pp. 95–121.

Hofstede, G. *Cultures and Organizations: Software of the Mind*. London, U.K.: McGraw-Hill, 1991.

Hohmann, L. *Journey of the Software Professional*. Upper Saddle River, NJ: Prentice Hall, 1997.

Igbaria, M., and Greenhaus, J.H. "Determinants of MIS employees' turnover intentions: A structural equation model." *Communications of the ACM* (35:2), 1992, pp. 35–49.

Igbaria, M., Greenhaus, J.H., and Parasuraman, S. "Career orientations of MIS employees: An empirical analysis." *MIS Quarterly* (15:2), 1991, pp. 151–168.

Igbaria, M., Parasuraman, S., and Badawy, M.K. "Work experiences, job involvement, and quality of work life among information systems personnel." *MIS Quarterly* (18:2), 1994, pp. 175–201.

Igbaria, M., and Wormley, W. "Race differences in job performance and career success." *Communications of the ACM* (38:3), 1995, pp. 82–92.

ITAA. "Help wanted: The IT workforce gap at the dawn of a new century." Information Technology Association of America, 1998. (www.itaa.org/workforce/studies/hw98-htm)

Jackson, P., Wall, T., Martin, R., and Davids, K. "New measures of job control, cognitive demand, and production responsibility." *Journal of Applied Psychology* (78:5), 1993, pp. 753–763.

Jackson, S., and Schuler, R. "Understanding human resource management in the context of organizations and their environments." *Annual Review of Psychology* (46), 1995, pp. 237–264.

Jones, C. "Globalization of software supply and demand." *IEEE Software* (11:6), 1994, pp. 17–24.

Joseph, D., and Ang, S. *SOFTKIT: Software for Assessing Soft Skills of IT Professionals—A Technical Manual.* Singapore: Information Management Research Center, Nanyang Business School, 1999.

Joseph, D., Ang, S., and Tan, H.T. "Beyond technical thinking: Practical knowledge of information systems professionals." *Proceedings of the Seventh International Conference on Thinking,* Singapore, 1997.

Kaiser, K.M. "DP career paths." *Datamation* (29:12), 1983, pp. 178–188.

Kappelman, L.A. "Saving our sacred honor." *Communications of the ACM* (42:5), 1999, pp. 23–25.

Katz, D., and Kahn, R.L. *The Social Psychology of Organizations.* New York: John Wiley, 1978.

Kelly, J. "Does job redesign theory explain job redesign outcomes?" *Human Relations* (45:8), 1992, p. 753.

Khalil, O.E.M., Zawacki, R.A., Zawacki, P.A., and Selim, A. "What motivates Egyptian IS managers and personnel: Some preliminary results." *Proceedings of the 1997 ACM SIGCPR Conference,* San Francisco, 1997, pp. 187–196.

Kumar, K., and Bjorn-Andersen, N. "A cross-cultural comparison of IS designer values." *Communications of the ACM* (33:5), 1990, pp. 528–538.

Kunda, G. *Engineering Culture: Control and Commitment in a High-Tech Corporation.* Philadelphia: Temple University Press, 1992.

Lee, D.M.S., Trauth, E.M., and Farwell, D. "Critical skills and knowledge requirements of IS professionals: A joint academic/industry investigation." *MIS Quarterly* (19:3), 1995, pp. 311–340.

Leitheiser, R.L. "MIS skills for the 1990s: A survey of MIS managers' perceptions." *Journal of MIS* (9:1), 1992, pp. 69–92.

Lewin, D., and Mitchell, D. *Human Resource Management: An Economic Approach.* Cincinnati, OH: South-Western College Publishing, 1995.

Loh, L., Sankar, C., and Yeong, W. "Job orientation, perceptions, and satisfaction—A study of information technology professionals in Singapore." *Information & Management* (29:5), 1995, pp. 240–251.

McClelland, D.C. *The Achieving Society.* Princeton, NJ: Van Nostrand, 1961.

McLean, E.R., Smits, S.J., and Tanner, J.R. "Managing new MIS professionals." *Information & Management* (20:4), 1991, pp. 257–269.

Miles, R., and Snow, C. *Organization Strategy, Structure and Process.* New York: McGraw-Hill, 1978.

Miles, R., and Snow, C. "Designing strategic human resource systems." *Organization Dynamics* (16), 1984, pp. 36–52.

Mischel, W. *Personality and Assessment*. New York: John Wiley, 1968.

Mount, M.K., and Barrick, M.R. "The Big Five personality dimensions: Implications for research and practice in human resource management." *Research in Personnel and Human Resources Management*. Greenwich, CT: JAI Press, Volume 13, 1995, pp. 153–200.

Nelson, R.R. "Educational needs as perceived by IS and end-user personnel: A survey of knowledge and skill requirements." *MIS Quarterly* (15:4), 1991, pp. 503–525.

Nimmer, R.T. *Law of Computer Technology*. Boston, MA: Warren, Gorham & Lamont, 1985.

Orr, J.E. *Talking About Machines: An Ethnography of a Modern Job*. Ithaca, NY: ILR Press, 1996.

Paulk, M. *The Capability Maturity Model: Guidelines for Improving the Software Process*. Reading, MA: Addison-Wesley, 1995.

Peterson, N., and Jeanneret, P. "Job analysis: Overview and description of deductive methods." In *Applied Measurement Methods in Industrial Psychology,* ed. D. Whetzel and G. Wheaton. Palo Alto, CA: Davies-Black, 1997, pp. 13–50.

Reed, C. *Computer Law*. London, U.K.: Blackstone Press Limited, 1990.

Rizzo, J.R., House, R.J., and Lirtzman, S.J. "Role conflict and ambiguity in complex organizations." *Administrative Science Quarterly* (15:2), 1970, pp. 150–163.

Robey, D. *Designing Organizations: A Macro Perspective*. Homewood, IL: Irwin, 1982.

Rockart, J.F., Earl, M.J., and Ross, J.W. "Eight imperatives for the New IT organization." *Sloan Management Review* (Fall), 1996, pp. 43–55.

Ross, J.W., Beath, C.M., and Goodhue, D.L. "Develop long-term competitiveness through IT assets." *Sloan Management Review* (Fall), 1996, pp. 31–42.

Saxenian, A. "Beyond boundaries: Open labor markets and learning in Silicon Valley." In *Boundaryless Careers*, ed. M.A. Arthur and D.M. Rousseau. New York: Oxford University Press, 1996, pp. 23–39.

Schein, E.H. *Career Anchors: Discovering Your Real Values*. San Diego, CA: University Associates, 1985.

Smits, S.J., McLean, E.R., and Tanner, J.R. "Managing high-achieving information system professionals." *Journal of Management Information Systems* (9:4), 1993, pp. 103–120.

Tavakolian, H. "The organization of IT functions in the 1990s: A managerial perspective." *The Journal of Management Development* (10:2), 1991, pp. 31–38.

Todd, P.A., McKeen, J.D., and Gallupe, R.B. "The evolution of IS job skills: A content analysis of IS job advertisements from 1970 to 1990." *MIS Quarterly* (19:1), 1995, pp. 1–27.

Van Manaan, J., and Schein, E. "Improving the quality of worklife: Career development." In *Improving Life at Work*, ed. J.R. Hackman and J.L. Suttle. Santa Monica, CA: Goodyear, 1977, pp. 30–95.

Voos, P., and Mishel, L. "The union impact on profits: Evidence from industry price-cost margin data." *Journal of Labor Economics* (4), 1986, pp. 105–133.

Wagner, R.K., and Sternberg, R.J. " Practical intelligence in real-world pursuits: The role of tacit knowledge." *Journal of Personality and Social Psychology* (49:2), 1985, pp. 436–458.

Wall, T., Corbett, J., Clegg, C., Jackson, P., and Martin, R. "Advanced manufacturing technology and work design: Towards a theoretical framework." *Journal of Organizational Behavior* (11:3), 1990, pp. 201–220.

Weill, P., and Broadbent, M. *Leveraging the New Infrastructure: How Market Leaders Capitalize on Information Technology*. Boston, MA: Harvard Business School Press, 1998.

Weiss, H.M., and Adler, S. "Personality and organizational behavior." In *Research in Organizational Behavior,* ed. B.M. Staw and L.L. Cummings. Greenwich, CT: JAI Press, Volume 6, 1984, pp. 1–50.

Zucker, L. "The role of institutionalization in cultural persistence." *American Sociological Review* (42), 1977, pp. 726–743.

Zucker, L. "Institutional theories of organization." *Annual Review of Sociology* (13), 1987, pp. 443–464.

CHAPTER 17, PETER WEILL AND MARIANNE BROADBENT

Aschauer, D. A. (1989). "Is Public Expenditure Productive?" *Journal of Monetary Economics,* 23, 177–200.

Barney, J. (1991). "Firm Resources and Sustained Competitive Advantage." *Journal of Management,* 17(1), 99–120.

Boynton, A., B. Victor, and J. Pine (1993). "New Competitive Strategies: Challenges to Organizations and Information Technology." *IBM Systems Journal,* 32(1), 40–64.

Broadbent, M. (1995). *The Role of Information Technology in International Business Operations: The Case of Honda Motor Co., Ltd.* Melbourne: Melbourne Business School, The University of Melbourne.

Broadbent, M., P. Weill, T. O'Brien, and B. Neo (1996). *Firm Context and Patterns of Infrastructure Capability.* Proceedings of the Seventeenth International Conference on Information Systems (ICIS), Cleveland, Ohio, December 1996.

Broadbent, M., and P. Weill (1997). "Management by Maxim: How Business and IT Managers Can Create IT Infrastructures." *Sloan Management Review,* 38(3), 77–92.

Butler, C., M. Broadbent, and S. Niemann (1995). *Management of Information Technology at Amcor Ltd.* CL334, Melbourne Case Study Services, Melbourne Business School, The University of Melbourne.

Caron, J., S. Jarvenpaa, and D. Stoddard (1994). "Business Reengineering at CIGNA Corporation: Experiences and Lessons from the First Five Years." *MIS Quarterly,* 18(3), 233–250.

Clemons, E., M. Row, and R. Venkateswaran (1989). "The Bell Canada CRISP Project: A Case Study of Migration of Information Systems Infrastructure for Strategic Positioning." *Office: Technology and People,* 5(4), 299–315.

CSC Index (1992). "Building a New Information Infrastructure." *CSC Index,* November 1992.

CSC Index (1993). *Relating Strategic Positioning to Information Needs: Building the New Information Infrastructure.* London, CSC Index.

Darnton, G., and S. Giacoletto (1992). Information and IT Infastructures. In *Information in the Enterprise: It's More Than Technology.* Salem, MA: Digital Press: 273–294.

Davenport, R., and J. Linder (1994). *Information Management Infrastructure: The New Competitive Weapon.* Proceedings of the Twenty-seventh Annual Hawai International Conference on Systems Science, IEEE.

Davidow, W., and M. Malone. (1992). *The Virtual Corporation.* New York, Harper Business.

Davidson, W., and J. Movizzo (1996). "Managing the Transformation Process: Planning for a Perilous Journey." In *Competing in the Information Age: Strategic Alignment in Practice,* ed. J. Luftman. New York: Oxford University Press.

Dixon, J., P. Arnold, J. Heineke, J. S. Kim, and P. Mulligan. (1994). "Business Process Reengineering: Improving in New Strategic Directions." *California Management Review,* 36(4), 93–108.

Duncan, N. B. (1995). "Capturing Flexibility of Information Technology Infrastructure: A Study of Resource Characteristics and Their Measure." *Journal of Management Information Systems,* 12(2), Fall 1995.

Earl, M. J., and B. Kuan (1994). "How New Is Business Process Redesign?" *European Management Journal,* 12(1), 20–30.

Furey, T. R., and S. G. Diorio (1994). "Making Reengineering Strategic." *Planning Review,* 22(2), 7–11, 43.

Grossman, R. B., and M. B. Packer (1989). "Betting the Business: Strategic Programs to Rebuild Core Information Systems." *Office: Technology and People,* 5(4), 235–243.

Grover, T., J. Teng, and K. Fiedler (1993). "Information Technology Enabled Business Process Redesign: An Integrated Planning Framework." *OMEGA, International Journal of Management Science,* 21(4), 433–447.

Hamel, G., and C. K. Prahalad (1989). "Strategic Intent." *Harvard Business Review,* 67(3), 63–76.

I/S Analyzer (1991). "Building a Global IT Infrastructure." *I/S Analyzer,* 29 June 1991, 1–16.

Kambil, A., J. C. Henderson, and H. Mohsenzadeh (1993). "Strategic Management of Information Technology Investments: An Options Perspective." In *Perspectives on the Strategic and Economic Value of Information Technology,* ed. R. D. Banker. Middletown, PA: Idea Group Publishing.

Kay, J. (1993). *Foundations of Corporate Success: How Business Strategies Add Value.* Oxford, Oxford University Press.

Keen, P. G. W. (1991). *Shaping the Future: Business Design Through Information Technology.* Cambridge, MA:

Keen, P. G. W. (1995). *Every Manager's Guide to Information Technology* (2d ed.). Boston, MA: Harvard Business School Press.

McKay, D. T. and D. W. Brockway (1989). "Building I/T Infrastructure for the 1990s." *Stage by Stage,* 9(3), 1–11.

McKay, D. T. and M. J. Connolly (1991). "It's Not Business as Usual in the Data Center." *Journal of Information Systems,* Spring (1991), 80–83.

McKenney, J. L. (1995). *Waves of Change: Business Evolution Through Information Technology.* Boston, MA: Harvard Business School.

Markides, C. (1999). "A Dynamic View of Strategy." *Sloan Management Review* (Spring 1999), 55–64.

Miller, D. B., E. K. Clemons, and M. Row (1993). "Information Technology and the Global Virtual Corporation." In *Globalisation, Technology and Competition: The Fusion of Computers and Telecommunications in the 1990s,* ed. S. P. Bradley, R. L. Nolan, and J. A. Hausman. Boston, MA: Harvard Business School Press, 283–308.

Mintzberg, H., and J. Quinn (1991). *The Strategy Process.* New York: Prentice Hall.

Monsanto Magazine, No. 2, 1995.

Munnell, A. H. (1990a). "Why Has Productivity Growth Declined? Productivity and Public Investment." *New England Economic Review,* January/February, 3–22.

Munnell, A. H. (1990b). "How Does Public Infrastructure Affect Regional Economic Performance?" *New England Economic Review,* September/October, 3–22.

Neo, B. S. (1991). "Information Technology and Global Competition: A Framework for Analysis." *Information and Management,* 20(3), 151–160.

Neo. B. S. and C. Soh (1995). *Case Vignette of Citibank Asia Pacific: Information Technology Infrastructure Study.* Melbourne: Melbourne Business School, The University of Melbourne.

Parker, M., and R. J. Benson (1988). *Information Economics: Linking Business Performance to Information Technology.* Englewood Cliffs, NJ: Prentice Hall.

P.E. International (1995). *IT Management Programme Report.* Egham, U.K.: Centre for Management Research, P.E.

Porter, M. (1996). "What Is Strategy?" *HBR,* November–December, Reprint 96608.

Quinn, J. B. (1992). *Intelligent Enterprise: A Knowledge and Service Based Paradigm for Industry.* New York: The Free Press.

Ramcharamdas, E. (1994). "Xerox Creates a Continuous Learning Environment for Business Transformation." *Planning Review,* 22(2), 34–38.

Rayport, J. F., and J. J. Sviokla (1995). "Exploiting the Virtual Value Chain." *Harvard Business Review,* 73(6), November–December, 75–85.

Turnbull, P. D. (1991). "Effective Investments in Information Infrastructures." *Information and Software Technology,* 33(3), 191–199.

Venkatraman, N. (1991). "IT-Induced Business Reconfiguration." In *The Corporation of the 1990s: Information Technology and Organizational Transformation,* ed. M. S. Scott Morton. New York: Oxford University Press.

Wastell, D. G., P. White, and P. Kawalek (1994). "A Methodology for Business Process Redesign: Experiences and Issues." *Journal of Strategic Information Systems,* 3(1), 23–40.

Weill, P. (1993). "The Role and Value of Information Technology Infrastructure: Some Empirical Observations." In *Strategic Information Technology Management: Perspectives on Organizational Growth and Competitive Advantage,* ed. R. D. Banker. Middleton, PA: Idea Group Publishing.

Weill, P., and M. Broadbent (1998). *Leveraging the New Infrastructure: How Market Leaders Capitalize on Information Technology.* Boston, MA: Harvard Business School Press.

Weill, P., M. Broadbent, and D. St.Clair (1996). "IT Value and the Role of IT Infrastructure Investments." In *Competing in the Information Age: Strategic Alignment in Practice,* ed. J. Luftman. New York: Oxford University Press, 1996, 361–384.

Whitman, J., A. Farhoomand, and B. Tricker (1995). *How Hong Kong Firms View Information Technology: Information Technology Infrastructure Study.* Melbourne: Melbourne Business School, The University of Melbourne.

Williamson, P. (1999). "Strategy as Options on the Future." *Sloan Management Review,* Spring 1999, 117–126.

CHAPTER 18, MARY C. LACITY AND LESLIE P. WILLCOCKS

Ang, S., and Straub, D. "Production and Transaction Economies and Information Systems Outsourcing—A Study of the US Banking Industry." *MIS Quarterly,* 22, 4, 535–552, 1998.

Applegate, L., and Montealegre, R. "Eastman Kodak Organization: Managing Information Systems Through Strategic Alliances." Boston, MA: Harvard Business School Case 9-192-030, 1991.

Apte, U., Sobol, M., Hanaoka, S., Shimada, T., Saarinen, T., Salmela, T., and Vepsalainen, A. "IS Outsourcing Practices in the USA, Japan, and Finland: A Comparative Study." *Journal of Information Technology,* Vol. 12, 4, 289–304, 1997.

Arnett, K., and Jones, M. "Firms That Choose Outsourcing: A Profile." *Information & Management,* Vol. 26, 179–188, 1994.

Auwers, T., and Deschoolmeester, D. "The Dynamics of an Outsourcing Relationship: A Case in the Belgium Food Industry." Paper presented at The International Conference of Outsourcing of Information Services, University of Twente, The Netherlands, May 20–22, 1993.

Caldwell, B., Violino, B., and McGee, M. "Hidden Partners, Hidden Dangers: Security and Service Quality May Be at Risk When Your Outsourcing Vendors Use Subcontractors." *InformationWeek*, January 20, 1997.

Clark, T., Zmud, R., and McCray, G. "The Outsourcing of Information Services: Transforming the Nature of the Business in the Information Industry." *Journal of Information Technology,* Vol. 10, 4, 221–237, 1995.

Collins, J., and Millen, R. "Information Systems Outsourcing by Large American Industrial Firms: Choices and Impacts." *Information Resources Management Journal,* Vol. 8, 1, 5–13, 1995.

Cullen, S. *Information Technology Survey: A Comprehensive Analysis of IT Outsourcing in Australia.* Melbourne: Deloitte & Touche, 1997.

Currie, W., and Willcocks, L. *New Strategies in IT Outsourcing.* London: Business Intelligence, 1998.

Davis, K. "IT Outsourcing Relationships: An Exploratory Study of Interorganizational Control Mechanisms." Unpublished DBA thesis, Harvard University, Boston, 1996.

De Looff, L. "Information Systems Outsourcing Decision-Making: A Framework, Organizational Theories, and Case Studies." The *Journal of Information Technology,* Vol. 10, 281–297, 1995.

Douglass, D. "New Wrinkles in IS Outsourcing." *I/S Analyzer,* Vol. 31, 9, 1993.

Earl, M. "Limits to IT Outsourcing." *Sloan Management Review,* Vol. 37, 3, 1996.

Feeny, D., Edwards, B., and Simpson, K. "Understanding the CEO/CIO Relationship." *MIS Quarterly,* Vol. 16, 4, 435–448, 1992.

Feeny, D., and Willcocks, L. "Core IS Capabilities for Exploiting Information Technology." *Sloan Management Review,* 39, 3, 9–21, 1998.

Griese, J., "Outsourcing of Information Systems in Switzerland: A Status Report." Paper presented at The International Conference of Outsourcing of Information Services, University of Twente, The Netherlands, May 20–22, 1993.

Grover, V., Cheon, M., and Teng, J. "A Descriptive Study on the Outsourcing of Information Systems Functions." *Information & Management,* Vol. 27, 33–44, 1994.

Grover, V., Cheon, M., and Teng, J. "The Effect of Service Quality and Partnership on the Outsourcing of Information Systems Functions." *Journal of Management Information Systems,* Vol. 12, 4, 89–116, 1996.

Heinzl, A. "Outsourcing the Information Systems Function Within the Company: An Empirical Survey." Paper presented at The International Conference of Outsourcing of Information Services, University of Twente, The Netherlands, May 20–22, 1993.

Huber, R. "How Continental Bank Outsourced Its 'Crown Jewels.'" *Harvard Business Review,* January–February, 121–129, 1993.

Hu, Q., Gebelt, M., and Saunders, C. "Achieving Success in Information Systems Outsourcing." *California Management Review,* Vol. 39, 2, 63–79, 1997.

Hu, Q., Saunders, C., and Gebelt, M. "Research Report: Diffusion of IS Outsourcing: A Reevaluation of Diffusion Sources." *Information Systems Research,* Vol. 8, 3, 288–301, 1997.

Kern, T. "A Framework for Analyzing IT Outsourcing Relationships." Unpublished DPhil thesis, Oxford University, Oxford, 1999.

Kern, T., and Willcocks, L. *The Relationship Advantage: IT, Outsourcing and Management.* Oxford, UK: Oxford University Press, 2000.

Klepper, R. "The Management of Partnering Development in I/S Outsourcing." *The Journal of Information Technology,* Vol. 10, 4, 249–258, 1995.

Lacity, M., and Hirschheim, R. *Information Systems Outsourcing: Metaphors, Myths and Realities.* Chichester: Wiley, 1993.

Lacity, M., and Hirschheim, R. *Beyond the Information Systems Outsourcing Bandwagon: The Insourcing Response.* Chicester: Wiley, 1995.

Lacity, M., and Willcocks, L. "Interpreting Information Technology Sourcing Decisions from a Transaction Cost Perspective: Findings and Critique." *Accounting, Management and Information Technologies,* Vol. 5, 3, 203–244, 1996.

Lacity, M., and Willcocks, L. "An Empirical Investigation of Information Technology Sourcing Practices: Lessons from Experience." *MIS Quarterly,* September, 363–408, 1998.

Lacity, M., and Willcocks, L. "A Survey of IT Outsourcing Experiences in US and UK Organizations." *Journal of Global Information Management,* Vol. 8, 2, 2000.

Lacity, M., and Willcocks, L. *Global Information Technology Outsourcing: In Search of Business Advantage.* Chichester: Wiley, 2000.

Lacity, M., Willcocks, L., and Feeny, D. "The Value of Selective IT Sourcing." *Sloan Management Review,* 37, 3, 13–25, 1996.

Lacity, M., Willcocks, L., and Feeny, D. "IT Outsourcing: Maximize Flexibility and Control." Harvard Business Review (1995), reprinted in *Business Value from IT.* Vol. 73, May–June, 84–93. Boston, MA: Harvard Business Press, 1999.

Lacity, M., Willcocks, L., and Olsen, T. "Information Technology Outsourcing Experiences in Scandinavia, United Kingdom and United States." Oxford Institute of Information Management Working Paper, Templeton College, Oxford, 1999.

Loh, L., and Venkatraman, N. "Joint Venture Formations and Stock Market Reactions: An Assessment in the Information Technology Sector." *Academy of Management Journal,* Vol. 34, 869–892, 1991.

Loh, L., and Venkatraman, N. "Diffusion of Information Technology Outsourcing: Influence Sources and the Kodak Effect." *Information Systems Research,* 334–358, 1992a.

Loh, L., and Venkatraman, N. "Stock Market Reaction to Information Technology Outsourcing: An Event Study." Working Paper 3499-92BPS, Alfred P. Sloan School of Management, MIT, 1992b.

McFarlan, F.W., and Nolan, R. "How to Manage an IT Outsourcing Alliance." *Sloan Management Review,* Winter, 9–23, 1995.

McLellan, K., Marcolin, B., and Beamish, P. "Financial and Strategic Motivations Behind IS Outsourcing." *Journal of Information Technology,* Vol. 10, 4, 299–321, 1995.

Michell, V., and Fitzgerald, G. "The IT Outsourcing Marketplace: Vendors and Their Selection." *Journal of Information Technology,* Vol. 12, 3, 130–148, 1997.

Pantane, J., and Jurison, J. "Is Global Outsourcing Diminishing the Prospects for American Programmers?" *Journal of Systems Management,* Vol. 45, 6, 6–10, 1994.

Reponen, T. "Outsourcing or Insourcing." *Proceedings of the Fourteenth International Conference on Information Systems.* Orlando, FL, 103–116, 1993.

Saarinen, T., and Saaksjarvi, M. "Empirical Evaluation of Two Different I.S. Outsourcing Strategies in Finnish Wood Working Industry." Paper presented at The International Conference of Outsourcing of Information Services, University of Twente, The Netherlands, May 20–22, 1993.

Scarbrough, H. "The External Acquisition of Information Systems Knowledge." In *Strategic Sourcing of Information Systems,* ed. L. Willcocks and M. Lacity. Chichester: Wiley, 1998.

Sobel, M., and Apte, U. "Domestic and Global Outsourcing Practices of America's Most Effective IS users." The *Journal of Information Technology,* Vol. 10, 4, 269–280, 1995.

Strassmann, P. "Outsourcing, A Game for Losers." *ComputerWorld,* Vol. 29, 34, 75, 1995.

Valor, J., Fonstad, D., and Andreu, R. "Outsourcing in Spain: An Empirical Study of Top Management's Perspective." Paper presented at The International Conference of Outsourcing of Information Services, University of Twente, The Netherlands, May 20–22, 1993.

Willcocks, L., Feeny, D., and Islei, G. (eds.). *Managing IT As a Strategic Resource.* Maidenhead, UK: McGraw-Hill, 1997.

Willcocks, L., and Fitzgerald, G. *A Business Guide to IT Outsourcing.* London: Business Intelligence, 1994.

Willcocks, L., Fitzgerald, G., and Lacity, M. "IT Outsourcing in Europe and the USA: Assessment Issues." *International Journal of Information Management,* Vol. 15, 5, 333–351, 1995.

Willcocks, L., and Kern, T. "IT Outsourcing as Strategic Partnering: The Case of the UK Inland Revenue." *European Journal of Information Systems,* Vol. 7, 29–45, 1998.

Willcocks, L., and Lacity, M. "Information Technology Outsourcing: Practices, Lessons and Prospects." *ASX Perspective,* April, 44–49, 1999.

Willcocks, L., Lacity, M., and Fitzgerald, G. "To Outsource IT or Not? Research on Economics and Evaluation Practices." In *Beyond the IT Productivity Paradox,* ed. L. Willcocks and S. Lester. Chichester: Wiley, 1999.

Willcocks, L., and Lester, S. (eds.) *Beyond the IT Productivity Paradox.* Chichester: Wiley, 1999.

Williamson, O. *Markets and Hierarchies: Analysis and Antitrust Implications. A Study in the Economics of Internal Organization.* New York: The Free Press, 1995.

Chapter 19, JEANNE W. ROSS AND DAVID F. FEENY

Ackoff, R.L. "Management Misinformation Systems." *Management Science* (14:4), 1967, pp. B147–156.

Applegate, L.J., and J.J. Elam. "New Information Systems Leaders: A Changing Role in a Changing World." *MIS Quarterly* (16:4), December 1992, pp. 469–490.

Armstrong, C.P., and V. Sambamurthy. "Creating Business Value through Information Technology: The Effects of Chief Information Officer and Top Management Team Characteristics." *Proceedings of the Seventeenth International Conference on Information Systems,* Cleveland, Ohio, December 1996, pp. 195–208.

Bock, G., K. Carpenter, and J. Ellen. "Management's Newest Star: Meet the Chief Information Officer." *Business Week,* 13 October 1986, pp. 84–92.

Brown, C.V., and V. Sambamurthy. "Linking Intra-Organizational Stakeholders: CIO Perspectives on the Use of Coordination Mechanisms." MIT Sloan School of Management, CISR Working Paper No. 304, November 1998.

Business Week. "Information Power." 14 October 1985.

Clark, C.E., N.C. Cavanaugh, C.V. Brown, and V. Sambamurthy. "Building Change-Readiness Capabilities in the IS Organization: Insights from the Bell Atlantic Experience." *MIS Quarterly* (21:4), December 1997, pp. 425–455.

Davenport, T.H. *Process Innovation: Reengineering Work Through Information Technology.* Boston, MA: Harvard Business School Press, 1993.

Davenport, T.H., and J.E. Short. "The New Industrial Engineering: Information Technology and Business Process Redesign." *Sloan Management Review* (31:4), 1990, pp. 11–27.

Dearden, J. "The Withering Away of the IS Organization." *Sloan Management Review* (28:4), Summer 1987, pp. 87–91.

Earl, M.J. "The Chief Information Officer: Past, Present and Future." in M.J. Earl (ed.), *Information Management: The Organizational Dimension,* Oxford: Oxford University Press, 1996.

Earl, M.J. "The Risks of Outsourcing IT." *Sloan Management Review* (37:3), Spring 1996, pp. 26–32.

Earl, M.J., and D.F. Feeny. "Is Your CIO Adding Value?" *Sloan Management Review* (35:3), Spring 1994, pp. 11–20.

Earl, M.J., and J.L. Sampler. "Market Management to Transform the IT Organization." *Sloan Management Review* (39:4), Summer 1998, pp. 9–18.

Earl, M.J., and I.A. Scott. "What Is a Chief Knowledge Officer?" *Sloan Management Review* (40:2), Winter 1999, pp. 29–38.

Feeny, D.F. "The Five-Year Learning of Ten IT Directors." In L. Willcocks, D. Feeny, and G. Islei (eds.), *Managing IT as a Strategic Resource.* London: McGraw-Hill, 1997.

Feeny, D.F., B.R. Edwards, and K.M. Simpson. "Understanding the CEO/CIO Relationship." *MIS Quarterly* (16:4), December 1992, pp. 435–446.

Feeny, D.F., and G. McMullen. "Is Standardised Global IS Worth the Bother?" *Financial Times,* 1 March 1999.

Feeny, D.F., and L.P. Willcocks. "Core IS Capabilities for Exploiting Information Technology." *Sloan Management Review* (39:3), Spring 1998, pp. 9–21.

Gibson, C.F., and R.L. Nolan. "Managing the Four Stages of EDP Growth." *Harvard Business Review,* January–February 1974, pp. 76–88.

Hamel, G., and J. Sampler. "The E-Corporation." *Fortune,* 7 December 1998, pp. 80–92.

Hammer, M., and J. Champy, *Re-engineering the Corporation.* New York: Harper Business, 1993.

Henderson, J.C. "Plugging into Strategic Partnerships: The Critical IS Connection." *Sloan Management Review* (31:3), Spring 1990, pp. 7–18.

Hirschheim, R., M. Earl, D. Feeny, and M. Lockett. "An Exploration into the Management of the Information Systems Function: Key Issues and an Evolutionary Model." *Information Technology Management for Productivity and Competitive Advantage,* IFIP TC–8 Open Conference, Singapore, March 1988.

Huber, R.L. "How Continental Bank Outsourced Its 'Crown Jewels.'" *Harvard Business Review,* January–February 1993, pp. 121–129.

Ives, B., and M. Olson. "Manager or Technician? The Nature of the Information Systems Manager's Job." *MIS Quarterly* (5:4), December 1981, 49–63.

Keen, P.G.W. *Competing in Time.* Cambridge, MA: Ballinger Press, 1988.

Keen, P.G.W. *Shaping the Future: Business Design Through Information Technology.* Boston, MA: Harvard Business School Press, 1991.

Kettinger, W.J., V. Grover, S. Guhar, and A.H. Segars. "Strategic Information Systems Revisited: A Study in Sustainability and Performance." *MIS Quarterly* (18:1), March 1994.

King, J.L. "Centralized versus Decentralized Computing: Organizational Considerations and Management Options." *Computing Surveys* (15:4), December 1983, pp. 319–349.

Kirkpatrick, D., "The E-Ware War: Competition Comes to Enterprise Software." *Fortune,* 7 December 1998, pp. 62–68.

Lacity, M.C., and R. Hirschheim. *Information Systems Outsourcing: Myths, Metaphors, and Realities.* Chichester, England: Wiley, 1993.

Lacity, M.C., L.P. Willcocks, and D.F. Feeny. "The Value of Selective IT Sourcing." *Sloan Management Review* (37:3), Spring 1996, pp. 13–25.

McFarlan, F.W. "Information Technology Changes the Way You Compete." *Harvard Business Review,* May–June 1984, pp. 98–103.

McFarlan, F.W., and R.L. Nolan. "How to Manage an IT Outsourcing Alliance." *Sloan Management Review* (36), Winter 1995, pp. 9–23.

McKenney, J.L. *Waves of Change: Business Evolution Through Information Technology,* Boston, MA: Harvard Business School Press, 1995.

McKenney, J.L., and F.W. McFarlan. "The Information Archipelago—Maps and Bridges." *Harvard Business Review,* September–October 1982, pp. 109–119.

Mata, F.J., W.L. Fuerst, and J.B. Barney. "Information Technology and Sustained Competitive Advantage: A Resource-Based Analysis." *MIS Quarterly* (19:4), December 1995.

Meyer, A. "GE's Trading Process Network: Business Buying and Selling via the Web." Unpublished case study, Sloan School of Management, MIT, 1999.

Moad, J. "Does Reengineering Really Work?" *Datamation,* August 1, 1993, pp. 22–28.

Nolan, R.L. "Business Needs a New Breed of EDP Manager." *Harvard Business Review,* March–April 1976, pp. 123–133.

Porter, M.E., and V.E. Millar. "How Information Gives You Competitive Advantage." *Harvard Business Review,* July–August 1985, pp. 149–160.

Prokesch, S.E. "Unleashing the Power of Learning: An Interview with British Petroleum's John Browne." *Harvard Business Review,* September–October 1997, pp. 5–19.

Raghunathan, B., and T.S. Raghunathan. "Relationship of the Rank of Information Systems Executive to the Organizational Role and Planning Dimensions of Information Systems." *Journal of Management Information Systems* (6:1), Summer 1989, pp. 111–126.

Rockart, J.F. "Chief Executives Define Their Own Data Needs." *Harvard Business Review,* March–April, 1979, pp. 81–92.

Rockart, J.F. "The Line Takes the Leadership—IS Management in a Wired Society." *Sloan Management Review* (29:4), Summer 1988, pp. 57–64.

Rockart, J.F., L. Ball, and C.V. Bullen. "Future Role of the Information Systems Executive." *MIS Quarterly,* Special Issue, 1982, pp. 1–14.

Rockart, J.F., M.J. Earl, and J.W. Ross. "Eight Imperatives for the New IT Organization." *Sloan Management Review* (38:1), Fall 1996, pp. 43–55.

Rockart, J.F., and J.E. Short. "IT in the 1990s: Managing Organizational Interdependence." *Sloan Management Review* (30:2), Winter 1989, pp. 7–17.

Ross, J.W., C.M. Beath, and D.L. Goodhue. "Develop Long-Term Competitiveness Through IT Assets." *Sloan Management Review* (38:1), Fall 1996, pp. 31–42.

Rothfeder, J., and L. Driscoll. "CIO Is Starting to Stand for Career Is Over." *Business Week,* February 26, 1990, pp. 47–48.

Sambamurthy, V., and R.W. Zmud. "Arrangements for Information Technology Governance: A Theory of Multiple Contingencies." *MIS Quarterly* (23:2), June 1999, pp. 261–288.

Stephens, C.S., W.N. Ledbetter, A. Mitra, and F.N. Ford. "Executive or Functional Manager? The Nature of the CIO's Job." *MIS Quarterly* (16:4), December 1992, pp. 449–468.

Venkatraman, N., and J.C. Henderson. "Real Strategies for Virtual Organizing." *Sloan Management Review* (40:1), Fall 1998, pp. 33–48.

Von Simson, E.M. "The 'Centrally Decentralized' IS Organization." *Harvard Business Review,* July–August 1990, pp. 158–162.

Warner, T. "Information Technology as Competitive Burden." *Sloan Management Review* (29:1), Fall 1987, pp. 55–61.

Withington, F.G. "Coping with Computer Proliferation." *Harvard Business Review,* May–June 1980, pp. 151–164.

Zani, W.M. "Blueprint for MIS." *Harvard Business Review,* November–December 1970, pp. 95–100.